Great British Commanders

Great British Commanders

Leadership, Strategy and Luck

Michael Clarke

Pen & Sword
MILITARY

First published in Great Britain in 2024 by
Pen & Sword Military
An imprint of Pen & Sword Books Limited
Yorkshire – Philadelphia

Copyright © Michael Clarke 2024

ISBN 978 1 52678 899 3

The right of Michael Clarke to be identified as
Author of this Work has been asserted by him in accordance
with the Copyright, Designs and Patents Act 1988.

A CIP catalogue record for this book is
available from the British Library

All rights reserved. No part of this book may be reproduced,
transmitted, downloaded, decompiled or reverse engineered in any
form or by any means, electronic or mechanical including
photocopying, recording or by any information storage and retrieval
system, without permission from the Publisher in writing. No part of
this book may be used or reproduced in any manner for the purpose
of training artificial intelligence technologies or systems.

Typeset by Mac Style
Printed in the UK by CPI Group (UK) Ltd, Croydon, CR0 4YY.

The Publisher's authorised representative in the EU for product safety
is
Authorised Rep Compliance Ltd., Ground Floor, 71 Lower Baggot
Street, Dublin D02 P593, Ireland.

www.arccompliance.com

For a complete list of Pen & Sword titles please contact

PEN & SWORD BOOKS LIMITED
47 Church Street, Barnsley, South Yorkshire, S70 2AS, England
E-mail: enquiries@pen-and-sword.co.uk
Website: www.pen-and-sword.co.uk
or
PEN AND SWORD BOOKS
1950 Lawrence Road, Havertown, PA 19083, USA
E-mail: uspen-and-sword@casematepublishers.com
Website: www.penandswordbooks.com

For Harriet and Alex

Contents

Author		ix
Acknowledgements		x
Introduction		xi
1	Boudica – Queen of the Iceni	1
2	Alfred the Great	10
3	Lady Aethelflaed of Mercia	18
4	Harold II – the Last Saxon King	26
5	William I – The Conqueror	39
6	The Empress Matilda	47
7	William Marshal – the 'greatest knight'	55
8	Edward I – 'hammer of the Scots'	64
9	Edward III – warrior King	75
10	Edward, The Black Prince	86
11	Henry V	94
12	Sir Francis Drake	103
13	Sir Walter Raleigh	115
14	Oliver Cromwell, Lord Protector	124
15	John Churchill, Duke of Marlborough	136
16	John Jervis, Earl of St Vincent	146
17	Admiral Cuthbert Collingwood	155
18	Admiral Horatio Nelson	166
19	Thomas Cochrane – the Sea Wolf	180

20	General Sir John Moore	189
21	The Duke of Wellington	197
22	FitzRoy Somerset, Lord Raglan	211
23	Field Marshal Lord Kitchener	220
24	Field Marshal Douglas Haig	230
25	Admiral John Jellicoe	243
26	Admiral David Beatty	253
27	Field Marshal John Gort	264
28	Air Chief Marshal Hugh Dowding	274
29	Field Marshal Harold Alexander	285
30	Admiral Dudley Pound	297
31	Field Marshal Bernard Montgomery	309
32	Field Marshal William Slim	323
33	Marshal of the Royal Air Force, Arthur Harris	334
34	Success in Command	347
35	Contemporary Command and Modern Commanders	361

Chronological Table   373
Select Bibliography for Further Reading   382
Index   387

Author

Professor Michael Clarke is a defence and security analyst. He taught international relations and defence studies at the Universities of Manchester and Newcastle-upon-Tyne. He was the founding Director of the Centre for Defence Studies at King's College London in 1990 and went on to establish the International Policy Institute at KCL. From 2007 to 2015 he was the Director General of the Royal United Services Institute. Since 2015 he has held visiting Professorships at KCL and the University of Exeter. He is a Fellow of the University of Aberystwyth, King's College London, and the Royal College of Defence Studies. He remains a Distinguished Fellow at the Royal United Services Institute.

Acknowledgements

I acknowledge with gratitude the valuable presentational and historical advice I received from Helen Ramscar – my friend and co-author in other books – as this collection of essays was being compiled. In particular, I am deeply indebted to Patricia Arnold for her painstaking work in textual editing and in making several valuable suggestions in the text. I am also grateful to Nicholas Ramscar for a very careful reading of the draft, though of course, all these people are blameless for any of my grammatical or factual errors still lurking in the text. I owe a debt to Lester Crook and Harriet Fielding at Pen & Sword; to Lester for all his wise encouragement at the writing stage, and to Harriet for her invaluable help in the production process. I would also like to thank the many British military figures who spoke to me about their own experiences of command, in particular for the ideas contained in chapter 35, but also for their (never less than illuminating) views on many of the characters sketched in these essays.

A Note on the Text

The units of measurement for size, distance, weight, and so on, are forever changing, the more so over the historical eras spanned in this book. For the sake of clarity and the flow of the text, imperial units of measurement are generally used throughout, since they still represent the nearest to a common currency of expression when writing about British history.

Introduction

'I am not afraid of an army of lions led by sheep; I am afraid of an army of sheep led by lions.' So said Alexander the Great. Or perhaps it was Niccolo Machiavelli, or Daniel Defoe, or Prince Talleyrand. Among many others, they have all claimed this thought. No one actually knows who first said it. Maybe no one did, though Alexander gets most of the credit, thanks largely to historians of the historian Polybius. But the fact that this particular pearl of wisdom is ascribed to so many across the centuries suggests it encapsulates something important. The business of command, it is saying, is not just a vital element of military action; it is *the* most vital element. It makes the difference between success or failure in campaigns, victory or defeat in battle.

It is fashionable these days for writers to pay a lot more attention than was traditionally the case to the ordinary people involved in wars; the foot soldiers, the conscripts, the civilian population, those that served who only stood and waited – all swept into the maelstrom of violence and disruption that warfare brings with it. This modern change in emphasis is as it should be. It is all too easy to fall into a 'great man (yes, man) theory of history' which almost always leads to a series of sterile explanations of the causes and courses of warfare. Our Victorian ancestors, and many in the twentieth century, entered gleefully into such myopic landscapes. Mercifully, modern studies in military history have viewed the landscape with far more acute and multi-focus vision. As a result, military history seems to be in robust good health; never more well-researched, never more popular.

And yet, Alexander's thought – if it was his – persists. However more nuanced our appreciation of warfare becomes, there is no getting away from the critical importance of command and its role in determining the outcome. In his magnificent *War and Peace*, Tolstoy mischievously presents Napoleon and General Kutuzov 'with all the foresight and genius of the generals' who nevertheless, among 'the blind instruments of history were the most enslaved and involuntary'. They had no personal power to affect the tides of history of which they were a part. Not true. It's just a tease in favour of what Tolstoy would have preferred to be true. 'Command' matters; and the people who become commanders – the way they function as people, as individuals – will never be less than important, if not critical, to the outcome of wars and the flows of at least some of the tides of history. Command and commanders are naturally fascinating to those of us seeking to understand.

In this collection of short pen portraits, I wanted to present a number of 'Great British Commanders' as individuals; not because I am a devotee of the 'great man, or woman, school of history' but simply because the task is interesting. And I am not aware of other recent studies that are reckless enough to present too many – and at the same time too few – portraits across the long history of one country.

Readers may wonder immediately how the commanders included in this list have been selected. My title is deliberately ambiguous. Some of these characters are indeed regarded as 'great' commanders. Some are not so great – I am interested in elements of failure as well as success – but they have been commanders at some time in British history. Boudica was queen of one of the British tribes; she was an ancient Brit. William the Conqueror and King Harold of Wessex fought over an England that was the political centre of Great Britain, geographically defined within the British Isles. And the Duke of Marlborough fought for a country that, during his own lifetime, transformed itself into the political entity of Great Britain. From 1801 it was officially called the United Kingdom of Great Britain and Ireland – England, Wales, Scotland and Ireland – as served by the Duke of Wellington and subsequently defended by Douglas Haig. After 1922, that political union became the United Kingdom of Great Britain and Northern Ireland, in recognition of the foundation of the Irish Free State. But for most people, the inelegance of the term 'United Kingdom' – even worse, 'UK' – can be mitigated by referring to it still as 'Great Britain', albeit using that geographical term in a politically inaccurate way. The national Olympic team is branded as 'Team GB' and we all know which parts of the – rather extensive – British Isles that does, and does not, include. Not being a slave to pedantry, I have therefore taken liberties with both the political and geographical constructions of 'Great Britain' to offer pen portraits of thirty-three 'Great British Commanders' across a dizzying span of 2,000 years.

This is not, in any sense, a priority list of thirty or so people whom I judge to have been the best commanders in British history. Some readers might be indignant with my selection. Where is King Aethelstan, King Richard 'the lionheart', Robert 'the Bruce' of Scotland, General Allenby, Winston Churchill? I have tried to restrict the list to some of those individuals whom I judge to have directly commanded significant military forces in ways that have made an impact on British history. I have not usually concentrated on their political contributions as commanders, or on the political careers that might have preceded, or followed, their lives in the military. But as commanders, I am essentially interested in them as people – what shaped their command experience, their historical context and the various legacies they left in military-political terms.

I am a storyteller, not a professional historian, and I wanted to tell some of the stories of these characters covering the military parts of their lives. For that reason, and because I would not presume to pose as a proper historian, I have tried wherever possible to avoid the sifting of conflicting or contradictory evidence about particular events. That is the stuff of real historical research. Where there are important inconsistencies of evidence, I have tried instead, to offer the most plausible explanation as relevant to these characters in their guise as military commanders. In the case of our more historically distant subjects, readers will see that I am sometimes making an educated guess, but I hope they will forgive me in light of my mission to describe some essential characteristics of these people.

Ultimately, this book is a personal indulgence. If space permitted, there are many more individuals I would have liked to include – and I apologise to King Aethelstan; less so to Richard the Lionheart. But if I have to pick over thirty individuals across two millennia of British history, then these are the people whose stories I wanted briefly to tell. They are short stories, told in headline terms. Even headlines offer important personal vignettes and I hope that readers who may be very familiar with some of these commanders will nevertheless enjoy reading a brief account of others with whom they may be less well acquainted.

I also wanted to use these stories to reflect on something on which I *can* claim some professional expertise, as a long-time military analyst. There is a fascination in looking at how commanders reacted to their circumstances in different situations. There is also an urge to compare the styles of commanders who make up natural historical pairings – Harold II and William the Conqueror; Edward III and the Black Prince; Drake and Raleigh; Nelson and Collingwood; Beatty and Jellicoe, even Marlborough and Wellington.

Always nagging in the shadows of these comparisons is the question of what makes for successful command. Is success or failure wholly determined by the contingent circumstances each commander faces – little more than the lottery of history? Or are there some eternal verities of command that are somehow fundamental to the business of conflict and war, leadership and followership, something intrinsic in human nature which makes the difference between failure and success?

Many eminent writers have considered such questions in exquisite detail. In a short book I will certainly not attempt that. But at the end, I try to draw together some of the threads that glisten in the tapestries of these stories, to comment in a more generic way on the business of being a commander. The notion of 'command' – particularly military command where life and death is the currency of conflict – is too fascinating an abstract noun to be left alone. I have interviewed a number of living British commanders – those who have taken responsibility for campaigns and for battle itself – asking them to reflect on the experience and their own sense of what success and failure looks, and feels like, to the individual.

As a military and security analyst, I cannot tell personal stories without wanting to draw some wider conclusions from them. It is the besetting vice of a policy wonk; it all has to *mean* something. Perhaps it doesn't. Stories should be worth telling for their own sake. But in a book that is already self-indulgent, I have also succumbed to the dangerous temptation of trying to compare the past with the present. I would like to hope that it offers a richer, or at least a different, understanding of military command itself.

1

Boudica – Queen of the Iceni

Even her name is uncertain. Boadicea, as the Victorians liked to think. Or Buddug, as the Welsh have it. Boudicca, in the ancient Roman histories of Tacitus. Or Boudica, as a more correct modern spelling maintains, based on the etymology that her name was always intended to mean 'victory'.

Boudica's famous Victorian statue on Westminster Bridge, just opposite Parliament, depicts the general image of her that has come down to us in popular history.[1] She stands precipitously upright in a small, Roman-style chariot, sporting scythe blades on its wheel-hubs. The chariot's two horses are rearing fiercely. The rushing wind pins her gown to highlight Boudica's body contours, and if that didn't titillate her Victorian admirers enough, her two teenage daughters, bare-breasted and dishevelled, cling onto their mother as the chariot careers along. Boudica brandishes a spear in her right hand and holds her left hand aloft in a gesture of regal defiance. No one is controlling the horses.

In a way, it does encapsulate Boudica's story. She was Queen of the Iceni, her two daughters were violated by the Romans, she took on her oppressors on their own terms, and she briefly reigned triumphant before her metaphorical horses, unstoppable, plunged her to bitter defeat and an eternity of romantic re-invention.

No wonder that she stands now in one of the most prominent spots of the city she burnt to the ground; or that she was adopted on suffragette banners by the sort of young metropolitan women her forces massacred; or that, as it says (probably inaccurately) on the plinth of her statue, she was 'Queen of the Iceni, Who died in AD 61, After leading her people, Against the Roman invader'.[2] She became an enduring Victorian symbol of ancient British opposition to any invasion of these islands.

Revolts against Roman rule were common enough throughout the Empire, and much bigger revolts were to begin in Batavia and Judea within twenty years of the Boudican uprising. But this one shocked Imperial Rome, and the way it unfolded and the woman who led it, gripped the imagination of Romans and ancient Britons alike to make it a landmark in the history of Roman Britain. It didn't last long, but the brutal tactics of Boudica's revolt were not unthinking, and the strategy behind it

---

1. The statue, by Thomas Thorneycroft, was commissioned by Prince Albert and designed between 1856 and 1885. It was not cast, however, and erected on Westminster Bridge until 1902. Its heroic inscription, picked out in large gold lettering, is these days completely obscured by having hard up against it a wooden kiosk selling open-top bus tours of the capital.
2. The Boudican revolt stretched into AD 61, but Boudica herself was very likely dead before the end of the previous year.

– deliberate or not – came closer to success than is popularly assumed. Boudica isn't just a historical curiosity; she earns her place as a British commander whose story is compelling.

Of course, we have only fragmentary evidence about Boudica and the revolt she led. But Agricola, the father-in-law of the historian Tacitus, served three times in Britain as military tribune and witnessed the revolt at first hand as a young officer. He was there at the final battle; so his account of events to his son-in-law may be authentic and is generally borne out by other fragmentary sources.

The British revolt of 60–61 AD had multiple roots. But some of them were cruelly personal to Boudica. Almost a century before, Julius Caesar had conducted two reconnaissance expeditions from Gaul to Britannia in 55 and 54 BC, mostly out of curiosity about what lay across the Oceanus Britannicus. This began a Roman connection to the territory and piqued Rome's interest in the life of Belgic tribes who were crossing regularly from Flanders to trade and settle at the edge of the world in south-east England. Then in 43 AD the Emperor Claudius, taking advantage of deep tribal in-fighting, ordered a full invasion to incorporate Britannia into the Empire. The British tribes of the south-east were quickly brought to accept Roman overlordship. The prosperous Trinovantes of modern-day Suffolk and the Iceni in the lands now largely bounded by Norfolk made advantageous peace with the invaders.

The Iceni, known to the Romans as the 'horse people', may have been the most prosperous of all British tribes, noted for hunting with their prized dogs, as well as for their chariots and chariot racing. The Iceni seem originally to have been divided into greater and lesser Iceni peoples. A revolt in 49 AD, apparently led by one or other of the Iceni, was swiftly put down by the Romans and it appears that Iceni King Prasutagus may have emerged as the intra-tribal winner of the uprising. Certainly, he had been compliant with Roman rule from their invasion in 43 AD until his death in 59 or 60 AD. He was evidently rich and was said to have ruled a long time, though we have no precise dates. Prasutagus even named the Emperor Nero as his co-heir, alongside his two young daughters, which bequeathed some Iceni tribal lands to Rome. This was not unusual in the Roman world and was a way for rich citizens to ingratiate themselves with the Emperor and fend off other potential claims on their wealth. Prasutagus presumably hoped for the same.

Sometime before 49 AD Prasutagus had taken a younger wife, Boudica. She was of 'royal birth', born perhaps in 26 or 27 AD, probably as an Iceni, though she might possibly have been of another tribe, married to Prasutagus to cement relations. She would have been a young woman when she witnessed the easy suppression of the Iceni revolt of 49 AD. Queen Boudica's appearance was distinctive enough to be described by Roman contemporaries; tall, apparently strong, with long, waist-length auburn hair. In fact, Romans tended to characterise most Celtic women in such ways and always claimed to be impressed by the ferocity of Celtic wives. Boudica was evidently regarded as a classic Celtic woman. The later Roman historian, Lucius Cassius Dio also commented on Boudica's evident 'intelligence'. Her voice and countenance – both unusually strong – were also apparently notable. We don't know if she was a queen in her own right or only by marriage to Prasutagus, but such snippets suggest she commanded some personal admiration as well as the respect due to her royal status. Indeed, it is likely she was – or became – a priestess among her own people. Celtic mythology is full of warrior queens and her actions as she took control of the Iceni after her husband's death were punctuated at every stage, it was reported, by heavy mystical symbolism.

Resentment against the Romans was brewing strongly before the death of Prasutagus. The more distant tribes were never reconciled to Roman conquest, but even the client Iceni and Trinovantes were increasingly disillusioned. As the *Colonia* of Camulodunum (Colchester) developed, its colonists seemed ever more insensitive to the native Britons as they displaced them in tribal lands. During the early days of the new colony powerful men in Rome had invested in Britannia with loans, or grants, to tribal leaders. But five years of increasing extravagance by the Emperor Nero in the late-50s had created an acute cash crisis for many of them and loans and gifts to the British tribes were peremptorily reversed or called in, with due interest. The new provincial governor in Britain, Gaius Suetonius Paulinus, was anxious for military glory and wanted to take on recalcitrant elements in the colony – particularly the Druids who seemed to exercise a malign influence over British tribes. And both Paulinus and his Procurator, Catus Decianus, were greedy men who used the Procurator's role as official tax gatherer and his *publicani* – the franchised tax collectors – to enrich themselves at the expense of native British estates.

In these circumstances, Prasutagus's naming of Nero as co-heir to his inheritance proved disastrous for the Iceni and sparked the atrocity in March 60 AD that Tacitus cites as the beginning of the revolt.

It appears that Catus Decianus had decided to expropriate all Iceni territory on the basis of Prasutagus's will. There was, presumably, growing resistance to this high-handed land grab as the Procurator and his *publicani* swept through Iceni territory. When he arrived at Boudica's capital, possibly around present-day Caister St Edmund, tempers were probably running very high. Some sort of incident must have occurred, though we can only guess what. But in response Catus Decianus had Boudica, Queen of the Iceni, flogged and her two teenage daughters gang-raped.

Throughout the history of empires, this was just the sort of casual atrocity local imperial officials, out of control, all too often perpetrated. Catus Decianus might have arrested the Queen and her two daughters – the royal co-heirs. They might even have faced execution. But he presumably felt a better lesson could be administered by violating and humiliating all three women. For that reason we can assume the flogging was public, perhaps also the gang rape. Apart from his *publicani*, the Procurator was accompanied by slaves and soldiers on his journeys. Any of them could have been involved.

Neither Catus Decianus nor governor Paulinus, had he known about this event, could have imagined how deeply the atrocity focused Iceni resentment against Roman rule. The Queen, and priestess among the Iceni, and the royal family – heirs to the lands of great King Prasutagus, not long deceased – had been viciously humiliated by administrators with whom they had previously cooperated. For them, Roman rule had turned greedy and arbitrarily brutal.

The revolt that had been brewing now became a reality. Iceni and Trinovante communities had long been officially disarmed by the Romans, but they re-armed and organised themselves discreetly as word spread of Boudica's humiliation. Governor Paulinus was pursuing his military ambitions 270 miles away in Wales, campaigning for three years with the XIV and XX Legions against the remnants of the Silures and Ordovices tribes who had earlier supported King Caratacus's resistance, and taken refuge at the spiritual home of the Druids on the island of Mona (Anglesey). More Roman troops were drawn into the northwest campaign. Paulinus eventually crossed the Menai Straits to suppress the Druids completely, destroying everything on Mona. Druid leaders must have been using their extensive religious networks for some time to call for a general uprising.

Preoccupied in Mona, Paulinus only heard about the revolt in late June and by then the Britons were on the march with Boudica at their head.[3] She and her daughters would have needed some time to recover from their ordeal, while weapons, horses and chariots were collected and tribal warriors converged during June towards a vast assembly, probably at Thetford, in readiness for the campaign.

Though there was no question that Queen Boudica, now in her early thirties, was the commander of a confederation of British tribes, it did not include all. The Iceni and Trinovantes were united behind her, large elements of the Catuvellauni, and perhaps some of the Coritani and Cornovii; perhaps, too, some of the Cantiaci and the Atrebates from south of the Thames, swept into it as the revolt gathered pace. But the extensive Brigante tribe, straddling the Pennines over much of Yorkshire and Lancashire, and ruled by the equally colourful Queen Cartimandua, sat the whole event out. Nevertheless, several tens of thousands of Britons – warriors and communities, followers and families – flocked to Boudica. She drew together a temporary confederation that included, interestingly, Trinovantes and Catuvellauni who were traditionally hostile to each other. That in itself says much for her natural charisma and political skill. She addressed them all in terms that were at once fierce, visionary and mystical. And then, in late June and early July, they turned their anger against the most significant Roman target of all – Camulodunum.

In modern-day Colchester, the base of the Temple of Claudius where the climax of the subsequent massacre happened, still exists in the foundations of the Norman castle. As a *colonia*, and now capital of the province of Britannia, Camulodunum was a good distance from the frontier of the military zone far to the northwest and it lacked any defensive walls. Its early fortifications had long been overbuilt with houses and shops. The authorities in Camulodunum must have been aware of the tribal gatherings forty-five miles to the north – two to three days march away. At some point the authorities appealed to Catus Decianus in Londonium, sixty-five miles south-west, for military help. In a gesture either of stupid complacency or deep

---

3. There is uncertainty among historians as to whether the revolt happened, in fact, during the year 60 or in 61 AD, since Roman sources confuse the cross-referencing dates. Some historians conclude that Boudica's phase of the revolt spanned both years. But this is improbable because of its helter-skelter nature and it is very hard to imagine Roman forces being so tardy when confronting such a major threat as she posed.

cynicism, he sent two hundred poorly equipped legionaries to Camulodunum (three days march) to join the ageing veterans and residual troops based there. They could make no difference to anything. The population of Camulodunum was between ten and twenty thousand. Boudica's multitudes could hardly have been the 120,000 cited by Dio, but must still have outnumbered the citizens of the *colonia* several times over. If the rebels chose to attack it, Camulodunum was doomed.

From the beginning, Boudica's strategy was very ambitious. Perhaps she felt that neither she nor the British tribes had anything left to lose. Quite possibly, she felt divinely inspired under the personal influence of Andraste, warrior goddess and protector of the Iceni. And perhaps the undefended *colonia* – deep in Trinovante territory – was a temptation that simply created an irresistible momentum among her followers.

She nevertheless seems to have maintained discipline and clarity of purpose among her forces, structured carefully within their own tribal contingents. Over a decade before, King Caratacus of the Catuvellauni had conducted an extended campaign of guerrilla war against the Romans along the fringes of their expanding military zone. His elusiveness and sheer nuisance to them made him legendary until his defeat in open battle in 50 AD.[4] But he never posed a strategic challenge to them. He was pushed out of his own Catuvellauni homeland – these days the home counties and part of the midlands – and had to make common cause with distant rebels. He could only nibble away at Roman forces operating mainly from Silures tribal territories across south and central Wales.

In contrast, and for whatever mix of personal and political motives, Boudica was going for broke against the Romans. The move against Camulodunum was not especially hasty. Archaeological evidence shows that at least one villa at Foxton in Cambridgeshire, a long way west of the route between Thetford and Colchester, was suddenly and brutally destroyed. Local forts were taken. And the citizens of the *colonia* had quite a few days, maybe more, to anticipate what was about to occur. There is no indication that they tried to flee ahead of Boudica's arrival. Perhaps they did not believe such an outrage could ever really happen; or perhaps they assumed Camulodunum's meagre forces would somehow repel any barbarian hoard, regardless of numbers.

The Britons moved first to surround the *colonia*, probably as far as Fingringhoe four miles to the south, which was a supply port for the settlement. Then they moved in quickly, first aristocrats in fighting chariots, then warriors on horse and foot, burning everything as they converged on the centre. Despite later Roman accounts assuming days of desperate siege, the wooden structures of the city must have been aflame within a few hours. The desperate day, or days, occurred inside the stone-built Temple of Claudius where the women, children, and the vulnerable had taken shelter with a few troops, evidently trying to re-use some obsolete weapons and armour. But there would be no dramatic Roman cavalry rescue for them. The Britons smashed through the roof and the great iron door and slaughtered those inside as they incinerated the

---

4. Which he escaped, fleeing to Brigante territory to place himself under the protection of Queen Cartimandua; who duly handed him over in chains to the Romans.

temple. There is abundant evidence of sudden destruction everywhere, burned hard into the clay as a result of ferocious fires – though little evidence of looting within the extravagant wealth the city offered. The Britons destroyed all symbols of Rome as they came across them. They took the trouble to desecrate the Roman cemetery outside the western entrance.

Boudica and her (unknown) tribal advisers almost certainly knew, via Druid networks if nothing else, that Suetonius Paulinus and most of the XIV and XX legions were still far away in north Wales. They would also have realised that he would react immediately. Paulinus appears to have sent urgent messengers to Quintus Cerialis, commander of the IX Legion at Lindum (Lincoln) to engage the rebels without delay. Even if he had already heard about the attack on Camulodunum, Quintus Cerialis seems not to have appreciated the size of the uprising he was facing. His forces were more than 100 miles north of the rebels and he deployed only a vexillation of the legion – three cohorts and 500 cavalry, perhaps 2,000 men – to march quickly to Durovigutum (Godmanchester) and then begin sweeping southwards searching for Boudica's main force.[5] He may have had thoughts of relieving Cumulodunum, but that had been destroyed over a week before.

Instead, some of Boudica's forces had moved north again to lie in wait for the soldiers of the IX Legion, probably no more than twenty miles from Camulodunum among the dense forests of Essex. There they evidently executed a near-perfect ambush which cost the lives of 'all' (according to Tacitus) the infantry – certainly more than 1,000 legionaries. Cerialis himself narrowly escaped with some of his cavalry to the nearest camp at Longthorpe, near Peterborough, and thence back to Lindum.

No matter that Cerialis had deployed only a vexillation of perhaps half the depleted strength of the IX Legion available to him at Lindum. Never mind that Camulodunum was simply indefensible. Boudica and her forces had completely erased Rome's capital in Britannia, and now they had beaten and effectively massacred the IX Legion sent to destroy them. It astonished Rome when the news reached the imperial city, even as the revolt was ongoing.

There was, of course, no going back for Boudica. The next target was self-evident – Londinium, the wealthy settlement that also sported a bridge over the sacred Thames itself.

At this time, Roman London was not a *colonia*, nor even a *municipum* or a more vaguely-defined *civitas*. It was a trading post and though Catus Decianus, as Procurator, was based in the settlement, there is no evidence it then contained any civil or governmental buildings. Its streets were completely ad hoc and had not been set in Roman fashion. Its centre was at present-day Cornhill and Leadenhall Market but spreading rapidly outwards so that by 60 AD it occupied twice the land area of Camulodunum. The importance of Londinium was based on its Thames crossing point around the tidal limit of the river running from the East. Londinium then became

---

5. A vexillation was a temporary task force brought together from different units. A cohort was normally 480 men, roughly equivalent to a modern battalion. In the first century AD a full legion would have been 5–6,000 men, including cavalry – roughly equivalent to a modern brigade.

the natural confluence of vital roads running north, west and south from that crossing point. This first London was a boom town, a commercial centre of more than ten thousand people, run by a highly cosmopolitan community of trading entrepreneurs.

Paulinus had already set the XIV and XX legions on their way south from Mona to deal with the revolt. He himself came hotfoot to Londinium with his cavalry force to assess the situation. Catus Decianus, ever mindful of his responsibilities, had already fled to Gaul. Paulinus immediately decided there was nothing to be done for the settlement and abandoned it, calling for the II Legion in Isca Dumnoniorum (Exeter) to march north-east and join up with his XIV and XX legions coming south.[6] He would pick his ground for the reckoning.

The population of Londinium fled. Though in a foretaste of subsequent centuries, a number of Londiniumers, it was reported, and for their own cussed reasons, refused to go. Boudica's forces swept through the settlement and burned it to the ground, killing and ritually torturing in the Walbrook stream, anyone they found there. In present-day terms the destruction centred around Lombard, Fenchurch and Gracechurch Streets, the Guildhall and the areas around St Paul's and as far west as Oxford Street. Some of Boudica's forces crossed into Southwark (presumably using the bridge) to burn shops and foundries before destroying the bridge as well. It was all over very quickly, though the Romans subsequently made much of the gruesome tortures they ascribed to Boudica's savages.

Boudica was already turning north towards the last of the three most significant targets in the province; the *municipum* of Verulamium (St Albans). Whatever her thinking at this point, the strategy remained consistent. She may already have lost a number of Trinovante warriors who had achieved their immediate objective at Camulodunum. But she was now in solid Catuvellauni territory. If she followed the Caratacus model of resistance she might have tried to raise rebellion further afield and attack Roman settlements piecemeal in a spreading guerrilla campaign. With only four legions and some auxiliary units, Paulinus could never hope to secure Britannia against a truly national revolt.

Boudica may or may not have known that other revolts were springing up around Lindum, and in the east midlands, even in Somerset, which may have been tying the II Legion down. But Boudica's tribal confederation was as much a vast host of peoples as an army of warriors; with families, horses, wagons, and an ever-growing baggage train of ox-carts. By mid-summer, feeding her itinerant hoard was becoming a problem. And there was always the possibility of Roman reinforcements from Gaul arriving at Richborough to her rear. Rather than embark on a prolonged, indirect campaign, everything in her own situation and the fact that she must have known the legions were coming south, led her to understand that this was a now-or-never moment. She accepted the inevitability of – probably wanted – a decisive showdown against Rome's military centre of gravity. If she could triumph directly against Paulinus, the Britons would then have an excellent chance of destroying the remnants of the IX

---

6. Though for reasons only to be guessed at, the II Legion did not march. Afterwards, its acting commander, the Camp Prefect, Poenius Postumus, fell on his sword in disgrace.

Legion at Lindum and the II Legion in the south-west. Other tribes would by then surely have joined them.

Boudica led her army steadily northwest on the heels of Paulinus. They appear to have ignored easy targets – Roman villas and settlements – en route to Verulamium. When they arrived at the municipium it was, unsurprisingly, deserted. Verulamium's population had probably followed Paulinus's cavalry north up Watling Street to reach the safety of his combined legions coming south. Boudica burned it and quickly followed them up the line of Watling Street towards the major engagement that was now inevitable.

It came later in the summer at Manduessedum, meaning 'place of the chariots' (modern-day Mancetter, near Nuneaton). Generally styled the 'Battle of Watling Street', it took place where the route crosses the river Anker and where the present London to Manchester inter-city rail line bisects the likely Roman dispositions.[7]

Paulinus had chosen his spot well; a defile on higher ground, with forest at his back and either side, boggy ground and the river Anker lower down. His 10–15,000 troops, facing Watling Street down the slope, could not be outflanked by the British hoards. Boudica's force, by this time very large, (probably more than 50,000[8]) straddled Watling Street lengthwise, as they turned to face the Romans on the higher ground to their left, with a shallow river to negotiate before they could get within range of their enemy. Their carts and baggage, families and children were all assembled on the northeastern side of Watling Street while in front of them their warriors were looking south-west across the famous route to face the Romans in their tight defile. It was an unfavourable position for a massed attack.

The Britons may have felt this hardly mattered. In one sense, they would win or lose this battle before any fighting began. Their numbers, the fearsome noise, woad-painted bodies, their lime-washed spiked hair making them tall and gruesome, was all designed to turn the stoutest hearts to water. We can assume that quite some time might have been spent confronting the legionaries with their noise and ferocity before Boudica was ready to launch her main attack.

When it came, it consisted first of war chariots and mounted warriors charging the Roman lines to launch spears and missiles. It was completely ineffective. The legionaries' javelins were devastating in response and Roman lines remained unmoved. Chariots had, in fact, long been obsolete in battle-fighting. They were easily countered by disciplined infantry deploying long spears and were more a hazard to their occupants than a mechanised threat to any organised enemy. The massed attack followed. This must have been much more testing for Roman troops. But it was restricted by the bottle neck created by the narrowness of the defile and it still made no impression in splitting the Roman line or pushing it back. This phase of the battle evidently lasted quite a while. Paulinus relied on the discipline and steadiness of his troops to let the

---

7. Many sites have been canvassed for this final battle, but common sense and most modern scholarship suggests Hartshill Ridge at Mancetter as the most probable.
8. Tacitus suggests 100,000; Dio 250,000. Neither are likely to be accurate on this point.

Britons expend their energy against his front ranks with their shields, armour and stabbing swords.

At some point, Paulinus gave the signal for his lines to move forward and they drove in a wedge formation relentlessly down the slope, on and on, straight into the baggage train in the Britons' rear – splitting them into groups which Roman cavalry and auxiliaries attacked, driving the bulk of the Britons against their own barrier of ox-carts. It was carnage, in the true sense that the killing was merciless. Warriors, mixed now with their women and children, all fought in vain against units of legionaries. Roman losses in the battle were estimated in the hundreds; Britons in the many tens of thousands. A reckoning, indeed, after Camulodunum, Londinium and Verulamium.

Boudica survived the battle and was spirited away, apparently back to Iceni territory where, (according to Tacitus) she subsequently took poison, and (according to Dio) was buried secretly with many Iceni treasures. That grave is lost forever, even if something that might fit the description were ever unearthed. But romantics have insisted on speculating. For many years stories circulated that Boudica could be found in a number of places, including under Stonehenge, at Hampstead Heath, or somewhere under platforms 8–10 at King's Cross station – all charming ideas for which there is not a scrap of evidence either in archaeology or sense.

Gaius Suetonius Paulinus reorganised his province and moved with reinforcements from Gaul to suppress more outbreaks of tribal resistance until the spring of 61 AD. Boudica's 'tribal confederacy' had been broken, but the revolt persisted elsewhere. Eastern England north of the Thames became a famine-ravaged wasteland. Paulinus took due revenge on all the tribal lands from Lincoln to Colchester, with an unrelenting harshness that reflected both the cruelties of the revolt and the fact that though he had restored Roman rule in Britannia, he had also come close to losing it.

There were future battles of conquest in Caledonia but no further revolts, and for the next fifteen generations Britannia was part of the Empire. That is Boudica's legacy in history. Hers was the last and most important revolt against the Romans in Britain. They were deeply shocked by it. Tacitus described the revolt as the Empire's worst moment in Britannia. Nero commissioned an official enquiry into the revolt and sent investigators to the province. Voices in the imperial capital wondered whether Britannia was worth the effort. Fifty years before, Roman expansion had faltered in Germania and retrenched along the Rhine frontier after Varus famously lost his three legions in the Teutoburg Forest. It is impossible to imagine Rome giving up provinces as vital as Germania, Gaul or Palestine if they rebelled in the way Boudica did. But Britannia – a backward province at the edge of the world? Why sacrifice legions for it?

Boudica did not lead a national revolt, but it was the nearest thing to one that the Romans ever faced in Britannia. A victory for the Britons at the Battle of Watling Street, or a battle in more favourable circumstances somewhere else, might have expelled Roman administration for a century or more and changed the trajectory of early British history. For that thought alone, Boudica is worth more subtle consideration than is implied by her frankly comical statue on Westminster Bridge.

Alfred the Great

Alfred is the only king to whom British history has accorded the epithet 'great'. That, in itself, should be a warning that his memory is surrounded by legend and romance as much as historical fact. Of course, there are some strong documentary sources for ninth century Britain – including the *Anglo-Saxon Chronicle* which he probably commissioned. He almost certainly oversaw some of its writing. Alfred's contribution to English history also left many indelible marks on government, law and the landscape itself to have established a reliable basis of knowledge about his reign and his wars. And yet, the urge to romanticise a 'great' king who achieved so much was irresistible to later Anglo-Saxons, medieval English and Victorian British alike, and it has coloured most popular views of Alfred both as king and military commander.

Legend and historical truth, however, do seem to have come together at the battle of Edington in Wiltshire one morning sometime between 6th and 12th May in the year 878. Here was a turning point both for Alfred and for British history that rolled Alfred's past and England's future up into a ball of desperate fighting that began just after dawn, high on the western escarpment of Salisbury Plain, and ended later that night in front of the palisades of Chippenham twelve miles away.

For by the winter of 877 the twenty-eight-year-old King Alfred of Wessex had already been fighting Viking invaders for twelve years. Three of the four Anglo-Saxon Kingdoms – East Anglia, Northumbria and Mercia – had already been decisively conquered or reduced to vassalage and all political organisation within Anglo-Saxon society was being effectively dismantled. Only Wessex had not been conquered. The 'Great Heathen Army', as the *Chronicle* referred to it, that had landed in 865 had come to settle in Anglo-Saxon territory, rather than merely plunder it. And when the 'Great Summer Army' joined it in 871 a new Viking leader, Guthrum, led those parts of the heathen army still with a taste for conquest to launch a series of determined campaigns against Wessex.

Guthrum had beaten Alfred at Wilton in 871 but then been bought off with *danegeld*. In turn, Alfred had thwarted a major invasion campaign by Guthrum in 876, but again bought him off in the hope of a respite. Wessex faced constant Viking threats during that decade, but alone among the Anglo-Saxon kingdoms, was still precariously functioning.

Then on 6th January 878 – Twelfth Night in the Christmas festivities – Alfred had been suddenly attacked in his own palace at Chippenham by Guthrum's men. Alfred managed to escape with his family and a few followers to find concealment and refuge at Athelney, deep in the Somerset marshes. That winter Anglo-Saxon Britain faced political extinction, and Wessex would surely succumb once its young king, hiding out like a rebel in Somerset, had been dealt with. But the defeated king built a small fort in the marshes at Athelney and survived long enough to devise a plan to fight back. If he was scolded by a formidable woman for 'burning the cakes' while he sat, anonymous and distracted, then this is where it happened. In fact, the famous story was first written down within a century of his death, based presumably on an oft-repeated anecdote. Perhaps it was true. Or perhaps it reflected the romance of defeat-into-victory that later historians preferred to believe.

And in May 878, Alfred emerged from the marshes, as he knew he must, gathering the troops of the fyrd – his farmer and peasant army – to confront Guthrum at Edington, on the road back to Chippenham. For Guthrum and the Viking warriors of East Anglia who had followed him, and many others who joined him from as far afield as Ireland and France, it was clear that the riches of Wessex were now there for the taking. This would be the last throw both for Alfred and for Anglo-Saxon Wessex. At dawn, Guthrum arranged his warriors using the contours of the old iron age hill fort at Bratton Castle, just above Edington. It was a good defensive layout. Alfred's forces were coming at him along the narrow, high ridge that was their only way into Guthrum's position. So it was to be a pitched battle of shieldwalls.

Both Saxons and Vikings used large round shields. Like ancient Greek and Roman troops before them, they overlapped shields for battle into a wall, with spears protruding from it and swords and seaxes (at least among the warrior classes) held ready.[1] Opposing shieldwalls would get close to each other before they formed – close enough for shouted insults, then for launching missiles – arrows, javelins, throwing axes, even stones – until the decisive move was made.

And then it was forward, one side-step at a time, shield held by the left arm, weapons in the right, always maintaining the overlapping wall of shields and the phalanx of spears. Well-trained troops might stagger a shieldwall into an arrowhead formation, or an envelopment, to create the best pressure points on an enemy line. But ultimately it was a clash of massed shields and a contest of pushing and shoving, stabbing, and hand to hand scuffling until one wall broke somewhere and a deadly mêlée would ensue, quite possibly punctuated by the rapid creation of new, reduced shieldwalls, until one side was overwhelmed and warriors had to choose between flight, surrender or death.

The battle on the ridge above Edington was reportedly fierce and lasted well into the afternoon before Viking defences broke. Guthrum and his survivors fell back on Chippenham in some confusion before nightfall, the stragglers being shown no quarter by Saxon warriors. Guthrum was briefly besieged, before he had to surrender. The battle on the ridge above Edington and the merciless pursuit to Chippenham was a stunning victory for Alfred. It completely shifted the momentum of events. The 'marsh king' had saved Wessex and he went on to create the conditions for the emergence of a united Anglo-Saxon England during the reign of his grandson, Aethelstan. No

---

1. The seax was a large knife, shorter than a full sword, and so commonly worn by most Saxon men that it gave its name to their race in vernacular speech.

wonder so much romance and legend surrounds a figure who, in only twenty-one years, went from marsh king to father of a country after that hard-fought day in May 878.

The romance would prefer not to dwell on the fact that 'the fugitive' Alfred conducted some sort of steady fighting retreat from Chippenham after the Christmas attack and actually spent only a few weeks in the marshes of Athelney, launching guerrilla raids on Viking patrols from there. Or that the fyrd and his fighting troops from parts of Somerset, Wiltshire and Hampshire flocked quickly to his standard once the call came – so he evidently maintained good planning and communication with other Saxon communities; or that another large Viking warband sailing from South Wales who would have joined Guthrum in a classic pincer movement of conquest, were annihilated at Countisbury Hill in Devon by local Saxon forces. Nor would the romance look too closely at Guthrum's numbers. His Danes had already made two unsuccessful attempts to overrun Wessex, after which many had then turned away to occupy eastern Mercia. And Guthrum appears to have dispersed his forces to patrol Wessex and had been forced to march out of Chippenham before they could all be recalled when the Saxons approached. Alfred's forces probably outnumbered him. They were based on the fyrd of locally raised troops from the land, stiffened by thegns who would command their own professional fighters and were generally led by an ealdormen who would be close to, or members of, the royal family. Alfred probably had around 4,000 troops in total that day.

The professionals on both sides were fit and practiced fighting men – warriors who possessed more than the common spear as weapons, and who would also have helmets and probably some chainmail. They could cut through swathes of non-professional troops with little risk to themselves. A small number of them, a few hundred, could turn a large battle – one reason why Viking warbands were so successful. At Edington, Guthrum had taken up a good position that forced Alfred's troops onto a narrow front across the ridge, which would have negated any superior numbers. The battle was probably so hard-fought precisely because, for a while, it was a struggle between roughly equal numbers of professional warriors, before the mass of Alfred's fyrd eventually broke through, sometime later in the afternoon, and created the rout.

But if the Battle of Edington was not quite so miraculous as the poets would prefer to believe, it was nevertheless strategically decisive and ranks with Heavenfield in 633[2] and Hastings in 1066 as one of the three critical battles on which the early history of Britain turned. If Wessex had fallen to Guthrum's Vikings at Edington, there would have been no base from which Anglo-Saxon England would emerge. Instead, a Pagan, Scandinavian confederation was the almost inevitable outcome. And that would likely have been prosperous and strong enough to have deterred or defeated the Norsemen who later settled in Normandy from coveting the riches of southern Britain in 1066.

---

2. The battle of Heavenfield near Hexham, in 633 or possibly 634, where King Oswald of Northumberland defeated King Cadwallon ap Cadfan of Gwynedd, determined that Anglo-Saxon, rather than Brythonic, peoples would dominate the territories that would become England. Whereas mainland Britain was destined to contain kingdoms of Scots, Welsh and English, the boundaries of those kingdoms were by no means predictable in the early seventh century.

Alfred could not have won his Anglo-Saxon kingdom at Edington; but he could certainly have lost it there. And the simple, dramatic truth was that the 'Great Heathen Army' of 865, augmented by the 'Great Summer Army' of 871, had come not to raid Britain but to conquer and colonise it. But thanks to Alfred – the Great – it failed.

Yet Alfred was a commander who either lost, or did not decisively win, many fights in the four separate Viking wars he fought; at least twenty-one pitched battles and sieges that we know of, and innumerable skirmishes, running fights and several engagements at sea or on the rivers. But after Edington, if he did not win all his battles, he certainly won his campaigns. At the end of his reign Alfred's Wessex was little bigger than before, but immeasurably stronger, and his successors immediately went onto the offensive beyond Wessex against the Viking settlers in the *Danelaw* of eastern England.

In truth, Alfred was never born to kingship, or even to military command. But he emerges from the romances of history as a man who learned and adapted, and who became a superb strategist, over and above his abilities to lead in battle. For this, he would have been judged an excellent leader in any age, but in the early medieval period, he was remarkable.

Alfred was born into the royal household of Wessex, in or around 849, the youngest of six children; his three eldest brothers and a sister were evidently of an older generation. Only his immediately elder brother, Ethelred, was close to him in age. As the youngest of the family, both his father, King Ethelwulf, and his mother Osburh, seem to have held him in real affection. As a very small boy he was sent on a pilgrimage to Rome in 853 to be received by Pope Leo IV who became his godfather; then personally taken there a second time by his father to meet (what turned out to be) a new Pope in 855. He was a conscientious and thoughtful boy, with neither the build nor the outlook of a natural warrior. He was plagued throughout his life with what these days might be diagnosed as Crohn's disease, affecting the bowel. But he was imbued with the power of the Christian god from the very beginning. For Alfred, Christianity grafted seamlessly onto his royal Wessex pedigree, which claimed – however dubiously – an unbroken link to Cerdic, supposedly the first Saxon king of Wessex who had arrived in Britain in 495. The several sons of Ethelwulf, of the ancient House of Cerdic, linked themselves in a direct line of descent to Sceaf, a (previously unknown) son of the biblical Noah, and thence to Adam.[3] This divine, royal legitimacy would become a vital part both of Alfred's strategic thinking, and his military success.

But this was a time of great personal turbulence for the young boy. When he and his father returned from Rome in 856 they were confronted effectively by a palace coup engineered by Ethelwulf's eldest son, which split the kingdom into eastern and western territories, and restricted Ethelwulf's court to the eastern portion. Alfred's natural mother was already dead, as now was his papal godfather. Ethelwulf had taken a much younger wife who became Alfred's stepmother. But in 858, when Alfred was nine years old, his father died; and he lost his fifteen-year-old stepmother too, when she remarried Ethelwulf's eldest son. If there was one fixed companion in his early

---

3. The Anglo-Saxon Chronicle for the year 855 traces that precise line of descent to Adam.

life it was probably his brother Ethelred, perhaps eleven at this time, with whom he was to share some of the most traumatic battle experiences in the years ahead.

Ethelwulf's second and third sons both ruled Wessex after 858, but when the third son, Ethelberht, died in 865 – the very year the Great Heathen Army arrived in Kent – the kingship of Wessex moved down a generation and devolved on the eighteen or nineteen-year-old Ethelred, supported by his sixteen-year-old brother, Alfred. Together, the two young brothers were plunged into the first general war against Viking invaders, fought for five years across Northumbria and Mercia. The brothers led Wessex forces to join the Mercians in besieging Vikings at Nottingham, though the result was inconclusive. During this campaign, or just after it, in 868, Alfred married Ealhswith of the Mercian royal family, strengthening the bond between the two kingdoms. All the evidence suggests that Alfred and Ealhswith were content in a strongly Christian marriage, but it was also a good political move. Between 868 and 870 the Great Heathen Army turned its attention from York to Peterborough. It swept into East Anglia and killed the Saxon King Edmund, and then established a base at Reading in preparation for the conquest of Wessex.

So began Alfred's second Viking war – another five-year affair starting in 870 – this time in direct defence of his homeland against the Great Heathen Army, now led by Halfden, one of the famous 'sons of Ragnar'. The Wessex brothers led their forces in no fewer than nine pitched battles against Halfden in that year – five of them inside three months. They fought at Englefield, Reading, Basing and Meretun. There was a major victory for the brothers at Ashdown, where they split their forces and Alfred led 'like a wild boar', said his contemporary biographer, in a risky uphill charge, to draw the Vikings onto Ethelred's other troops. And there were innumerable engagements and skirmishes. If the twenty-two-year-old Alfred learned battlefield leadership anywhere, it was surely in these dangerous and exhausting months fighting Halfden.

But in 871 the wheel turned again. In April that year, Ethelred died, perhaps of wounds sustained a few weeks earlier at the battle of Meretun. Now Alfred became the fourth of Ethelwulf's five sons to assume the kingship, as agreed by the Witan – the 'council' – of royal Wessex ealdormen. Yet at that very moment the Great Summer Army of Vikings arrived in Britain to add their weight to the Great Heathen Army, and Guthrum, whose fate was to be bound up with Alfred's for the rest of his life, was leading them in a bid to conquer this richest of Britain's Anglo-Saxon kingdoms.

Within a month of becoming king, clearly outnumbered, Alfred fought and lost his first battle in sole charge of Wessex when Guthrum heavily defeated him at Wilton, followed immediately by other unnamed engagements. But after being bought off, Guthrum repaired to London, and within the year 873 Viking forces launched a further attack on Northumbria and then reduced Mercia to client status with a puppet king. Alfred fought Viking raiders at sea – vicious hand to hand battles across ships locked together. He personally led several such naval engagements during his reign. Alfred's third Viking war began in 876 when he was extremely lucky to prevent Guthrum achieving a devastating land and sea link up of forces across the south coast of Wessex. Guthrum lost his fleet in a huge storm off Swanage as Alfred besieged, negotiated and screened Viking ground forces in Wareham and Poole and thence to Exeter, finally doing yet another expensive *danegeld* deal with Guthrum in late 877 that left Viking forces wintering in Gloucester, just inside the Mercian border. Now Guthrum was sitting merely twenty-nine miles from Alfred's Christmas court at Chippenham.

Which is where the defining moment of Alfred's life occurred on Twelfth Night in 878. There is every reason to suppose that Alfred was not attacked out of the blue by Viking forces that night. He was betrayed; certainly by Wulfhere, his ealdorman of Wiltshire (whose territory Guthrum raced through) and by whoever opened the gates into what was a very defensible site at Chippenham. He probably faced a palace coup of possibly six other ealdormen and clerics who wanted to remove him in favour of a Viking client king who might do less expensive deals with Guthrum. His Saxon betrayers, and Guthrum's men awaiting the signal to sweep into Chippenham, probably assumed he would flee abroad exactly as King Burgred of Mercia had done in a remarkably similar situation four years earlier. But he didn't. He carried on the fight from the Somerset marshes as the legitimate king of Wessex; son of the ancient House of Cerdic, sanctified by God.

More importantly, he reflected deeply and learned all the hard lessons of his situation. He may have reproached himself for being so reactive to Viking strategy, even complacent, in the seven years of his rule that had made him seem to his betrayers like a hard-fighting but ineffective protector of Wessex who also cost them ruinous amounts of *danegeld*. He understood why small numbers of professional Viking warriors were so destructive when they could ride quickly overland and link up with their ships moving up the rivers. He had come to understand all the limitations of the slow-moving and unwieldy fyrd, and the problem of maintaining sieges when peasant soldiers needed to get back to their fields. He also now understood Viking weaknesses, if only he could keep them wrong-footed and deny them their secure forward bases on his territory.

Above all, he thought he understood what Wessex, Mercia, East Anglia and even Northumbria should be fighting for – the triumph of Christian Saxon kingdoms over the Pagan hordes. Like many pious Christians in the ninth century, he was convinced that the heathen invaders and their psychotic violence was not an accident of history; it was divine punishment for his people's lack of true Christianity, of learning and of moral strength. The 'marsh king' that emerged to fight at Edington would prove to be a very different person from the one who faced the Twelfth Night coup. He had devised a new, ruthless, and revolutionary strategy that engaged the whole of Wessex society and from which a united Anglo-Saxon England would eventually emerge.

For the next twenty years, Alfred was a dynamo of military and social activity. His famous creation of the *Burhs* – the fortified settlements that became the towns of England – in Chichester, Wallingford, Malmesbury, Worcester, Bath, Hastings, Cricklade, Southampton – were far more than just fortresses. True, the thirty-three he created were designed so that no one was more than twenty miles away from a *Burh*; a single day's march. But far more important, the *Burhs* were intended, for the first time since Roman occupation, to become self-sustaining urban centres. They could feed themselves, trade, support a growing merchant class who could be taxed, and they could raise independent local forces and fight for themselves. They were the foundation stones of a very evident 'defence in depth' strategy; which also laid the basis for the Anglo-Saxon state that followed. Not least, Alfred re-occupied London and fortified it to restore the settlement to the major trading status its geographic location offered.

Alfred made heavy demands on his people in providing for their protection. Military service was compulsory but the fyrd was divided into two rotating halves; one to serve while the other stayed on the land. He created a large force of mounted infantry to move swiftly across the kingdom, confronting invaders before they could settle. He built fighting ships and organised a navy. His drive for literacy among his illiterate people was grounded in a deep commitment to recreate the seventh century 'golden age of scholarship' that had been largely destroyed by Viking invasions. But the court school, where his grumbling ealdormen and thegns were compelled to become literate in their own English language, also gave him a great advantage in command and control over his opponents – he could write down instructions that his commanders could then read for themselves. Taxes were high, but at least they were being spent on defence and social building rather than protection-racket *danegeld*.

Alfred's diplomacy also showed a ruthless maturity in these years. He preserved all of Wessex's territory, and sacrificed half of Mercia's, by officially settling the boundaries of the *Danelaw* in 886. The agreement with the Danes split England from the Thames to the Trent into a Danish East and a Saxon West. It was a *realpolitik* accommodation with the inevitable. He manoeuvred Wessex's Witan to ensure that the problematical line of succession would flow inevitably from him to his eldest son when the time came.[4] And after the puppet king of Mercia died in 879, Mercian territory west of the *Danelaw* fell progressively under his direct control – which also gave him influence in the fractious politics of the eight separate Welsh kingdoms.

What would nowadays be called Alfred's 'strategic communications' were also masterly. He committed himself to deep cultural renewal within Anglo-Saxon society; to promoting, and even himself writing, vernacular versions of religious and ethical Latin texts. He rapidly became a true philosopher king and a living symbol – albeit pernickety and highly strung – of the moral and military power of Christianity. This took some surprising forms. We know from the *Chronicle* that he hanged pirates out of hand and had at least one group of criminals tortured to death. Yet when he had at his mercy, Guthrum – the greatest pirate and criminal of his reign – Alfred had him convert to Christianity, became his godfather, and set him up in 878 as Aethelstan the (Danish) king of East Anglia. And he surrounded the whole bizarre arrangement with symbols of Christian mystique, alongside showy demonstrations of his political power, grandeur and personal generosity. It worked. Though in 885 when it slipped and the East Anglian Vikings could not resist a little raiding at Rochester, Alfred sent a naval force directly into their territories around the river Stour to exact revenge. Just

---

4. Though in the event it was not straightforward. Ethelwold, son of Alfred's elder brother Ethelred, tried to foment a coup when Alfred died, then allowed himself to become a puppet king among the Northumbrian Vikings. He was trying to lead yet another Viking invasion of Wessex in 902, when his forces fought at the Battle of Holme in East Anglia, which cost him his life and that of some of his Viking sponsors.

as he proved to be a ruthless diplomat, he was a ruthless Christian where the security of Wessex was concerned.

These elements were coming together, though not completed, in 892 when Alfred faced a fourth war against a new Viking host – the biggest single Viking force ever to descend on Britain. It was led in part by the fearsome Haesten, who had tried to lead a Viking army to sack Rome itself. Some 330 ships in two fleets landed in Kent. They split into two armies, either of which might tempt the old warriors living in the *Danelaw* to join them. Indeed, an opportunist Viking fleet of another 100 ships arrived from Northumbria and East Anglia and sailed to Devon, landing two more armies. Alfred faced a multi-front war. For the next four years his strategy was severely tested, but it was working. His son, Edward 'the Elder' took an equal part in command, alongside ealdormen Ethelhelm of Wiltshire and the ever-faithful Ethelnoth of Somerset. Together, Alfred's men of Wessex and Mercian forces led by Aethelred, Lord of Mercia, besieged and contained the Viking forces in Devon, and harried the two bigger Viking armies around their kingdoms; from Benfleet and Appledore across Kent and Essex, from Farnham to London, into Welshpool and towards Chester and then Gwynedd in North Wales, back to Hertford and London between forts on the river Lea, and finally to Bridgnorth in Shropshire; always keeping them moving, denying them any secure bases. Eventually, in 896 the exhausted survivors of those Viking armies decided to give up. Most drifted away deep into *Danelaw* territory while others opted to try their luck back on the Continent. They left the shores of southern England, it was said, in just five ships.

And Alfred had three years left to him to enjoy the peace he had created, before he died on 26th October 899, aged fifty or perhaps fifty-one.

Alfred had inherited the Wessex troops his father and elder brothers had fashioned. They were tough to beat, as Viking warbands – accustomed to easy victories elsewhere – repeatedly found to their cost. But eventually they would almost certainly have been overwhelmed were it not for Alfred's remarkable strategic instincts. Battles, glory and warriorhood were essential to leaders like Halfden, Guthrum and Haesten. But Alfred positively eschewed these virtues; his politico-military aspirations were on a higher plane altogether. In creating a new Wessex, he was creating a society that was militarily and socially resilient against the existential Pagan threat of the age. Alfred was building Wessex as the well-spring of renewal for a powerful, Christian Anglo-Saxon society. He saw at least some of that come to fruition in his lifetime.

If there was a single moment when a unified Anglo-Saxon England unquestionably existed, it was during the great court at Easter 928, when Alfred's grandson, Aethelstan, was unanimously recognised by lesser kings and magnates from all over Britain as the powerful – and only – King of 'Englaland', as it was first styled. That was exactly fifty years to the week since Alfred had built his makeshift fort in the marshes at Athelney.

3

Lady Aethelflaed of Mercia

Aethelflaed was born into the royal household of Wessex, the eldest child of Alfred the Great. Though evidently admired and respected in her lifetime as Lady Aethelflaed of Mercia, she receives short shrift in most surviving historical records. First, because her greatest deeds were in the service of Mercia, not Wessex, where history was written for the glorification of Alfred's kingdom. And second, because Aethelflaed was a woman. Anglo-Saxon society accorded women many important legal and property rights, but leading military forces was neither expected or much remembered. In 500 years of Anglo-Saxon history, she is among only four recorded examples of female leaders who might have had some involvement with armies.[1] Aethelflaed received more attention in some of the regional variations of the *Anglo-Saxon Chronicle* – a group of which became known as the *Mercian Register* – and in Irish sources like the *Fragmentary Annals of Ireland*, along with some Welsh fragments, and in William of Malmesbury's twelfth century writings. Some of these sources were so taken with the novelty of her situation that they gave credence to a good deal of romantic invention around her story.

The urge to portray her, like Boudica as a 'warrior queen' has proved irresistible to many writers, even to the present day. But in truth, she was neither a warrior nor a queen, but something much more important. Aethelflaed was a commander in a very modern sense. She commanded in battles and campaigns, while also being a political leader of Mercian society, which underpinned military success. She never wielded a sword, but was never beaten on the battlefield. As a true commander in an age of warriors, she not only had the respect and loyalty of her own forces, but also the respect, and finally the acquiescence, of some of her adversaries.

The relative paucity of the historical evidence about Aethelflaed means that more of her story has to be inferred than is the case for most royal figures of this era. But the inferences nevertheless point to a woman of great intellect, willpower, guile and strength. She lived and died in indefatigable service to Christian Anglo-Saxon society and to Mercia.

She was born, around 869, probably in Chippenham, as the first child of Alfred and Ealhswith, his Mercian wife. Aethelflaed was born into the wars that would define her. She lived her early life during the height of the first two Viking wars her father fought. She was perhaps two-years old when Alfred fought nine battles within the year 871 – lost his elder brother, the King of Wessex, became King in his place, lost

---

1. Queen Cynethryth of Mercia, wife of King Offa, has a claim to this status, as does the ill-fated Queen Seaxburgh of Wessex. Queen Aethelburh, however, wife of King Ine of Wessex is the only woman recorded as having led warriors of Wessex to retake Taunton from a usurper in 722.

another major battle to Guthrum the Viking, and was lucky himself to escape on that occasion. After that tumultuous year Aethelflaed's father settled into a long attritional struggle to maintain Wessex against constant Viking pressure. She was a young girl at her father's Christmas court in Chippenham in the winter of 877–8 when Guthrum's Vikings famously mounted their surprise Twelfth Night attack, and Alfred and his family had to flee for their lives. At that age she would certainly have understood what was happening – as Alfred, his family, and his handful of supporters hid away in the Somerset marshes at Athelney while they tried to devise a realistic strategy for recovery. As a highly intelligent young woman she personally witnessed the humiliation of betrayal and defeat that had brought her father to this.

She seems, too, to have been imbued from the beginning with his unshakeable Christian piety, his belief in the destiny of the ancient House of Cerdic into which they had both been born, as well as the belief that Cerdic's Anglo-Saxons were, like the biblical Israelites, a chosen people with a God-given mission. Perhaps as she grew up, she never doubted. Or perhaps, like Alfred, she subsumed her doubts in a ferocious energy to embrace that divinely-inspired destiny wherever it would take her.

She will have seen the fight-back almost at first hand as Alfred turned the tide at the battle of Edington in May 878. Equally astonishing, she will have witnessed Alfred's successful imposition of Christian conversion on the Pagan Guthrum after his Edington defeat. The re-naming and baptism of Guthrum and thirty of his closest lieutenants at Aller in Somerset; the taking of godparents, the anointing of their hands and binding in white linen, only unbound eight days later at Wedmore; the twelve days of feasting that followed with entertainment, vows, oaths and munificent gift-giving. The nine-year-old Aethelflaed was witnessing the biggest demonstration of military domination and Christian ritual that Alfred was able to conjure up.

In the less fraught years that followed, Aethelflaed would have had an easier path pursuing the education her father regarded as essential. She was not fostered elsewhere – though fostering was a fairly common practice in Saxon royal courts – and she never went abroad. Indeed, her whole life was apparently spent south of the Mersey and Humber rivers and she only ever spoke old English. She was almost certainly educated in the Wessex court, alongside her brother Edward, younger by five years, and perhaps sister Aethelgifu who was born sometime in the 870s. Her education was intensely religious, since her father favoured biblical studies and particularly *Proverbs* and *Psalms*, that were often learned for recitation. She would probably have been instructed in the writings of St Gregory and Boethius, in works such as *Beowulf* and in the ancestry of her own legendary House of Cerdic. The writings of the Venerable Bede must have featured prominently. She might have learned from Bede that the world was not flat but 'a sphere in the middle of the whole universe', in which the moon affected the tides. She would certainly have been strongly acquainted with Bede's *Ecclesiastical History of the English People* with its stories of St Augustine, King Oswald, St Cuthbert, and all the tragic beauty of what ninth century Saxons held up as the lost 'golden age' of seventh century Britain. The evidence from Alfred's own writings suggests that he would have been an austere but loving, if frequently absent, father who had a strong relationship with Aethelflaed's mother and all five of their children.

Her marriage to Lord Aethelred of Mercia, probably in 886 when she was seventeen, was a natural extension of her upbringing. She was in any case half-Mercian through her mother (and thereby a descendant of the ancient Gaini tribe of Mercia; Angles rather than Saxons).[2] She would already be well acquainted with members of the Mercian nobility who were very prevalent at Alfred's new court as he sought to re-build a European centre of power and learning. Lord Aethelred was evidently somewhat older than Aethelflaed, though we don't know by how much; but it seems very likely that she would have known him prior to their marriage. It is certainly unlikely that when she travelled to Mercia to begin her married life, it would have been a strange kingdom to her.

As with all royal marriages, it was, of course, politically significant. The Viking puppet king of Mercia had died around 879, not long after Edington, and Aethelflaed's new husband had assumed control only of the western half of Mercia, since the eastern half now lay in the *Danelaw* under Viking control. Lord Aethelred had little choice but to accept Alfred as King, while he, exercising monarchical powers in half of Mercia, accepted the title 'Aethelred, Lord of Mercia'. The young Aethelflaed, who would have become a queen in previous years, was eventually to adopt – indeed insisted only on using – the title 'Lady of the Mercians'. In the year of their marriage King Alfred 'gave' his reconquered and rapidly developing London (previously within Mercia) back to Aethelred's kingdom – quite possibly as a dowry or a wedding present, but certainly as part of the dynastic fusion this marriage was intended to promote.

Alfred had set himself at the centre of a family network that would serve his military and political purposes well. His son, Edward ('the Elder') and younger brother of Aethelflaed, was being groomed as Alfred's successor in Wessex, both on the battlefield and at court. In what was now the dependent kingdom of Mercia, Alfred outranked his ageing son-in-law; whose new young wife was nothing if not Alfred's daughter. Between them, Edward, Lord Aethelred and the Lady Aethelflaed appeared to be in complete harmony with King Alfred's strategic vision. That was the unifying effect on Anglo-Saxon society of years of Viking campaigns that had turned from opportunistic raiding to the undisguised ambition of national conquest.

That dynastic network became even tighter when Aethelstan, Edward the Elder's son – Alfred's grandson – was sent to Mercia to be fostered by Aethelflaed, who would oversee his growth to manhood. Though doubt was subsequently cast on Aethelstan's claim to the throne, he nevertheless emerged to become the king who would definitively unite Anglo-Saxon England.[3] So, the young bride Aethelflaed,

---

2. Aethelflaed was thereby also the great grand-daughter of King Offa of Mercia – an impeccable pedigree for a royal princess.
3. Edward the Elder subsequently took a second, and then a third wife, though we do not know why – whether as a widower or simply as a king who discarded wives. But he had four more sons (two of whom would become Kings of England) and seven or eight more daughters in addition to Athelstan and his sister Edith by his first marriage to Ecgwynn. It was a situation made for intrigue, and unfounded rumours that Athelstan was actually illegitimate, or had murdered his rivals, were in constant circulation. Athelstan did very well to ride his luck – or his destiny – in 924 when his father died to have himself ostentatiously crowned, anointed and consecrated at Kingston on Thames in 925.

daughter of Alfred, elder sister to his successor, wife to his close ally and neighbour, and eventually mentoring aunt to his grandson, not to mention mother to her own female successor in Mercia, grew into all these roles as she assumed progressively the mantle of 'Lady of the Mercians'.

And that mantle, one might suspect, was interpreted by her in an extremely proactive way. For a decade she evidently accompanied Aethelred around the kingdom and put her name jointly with her husband's (not uncommon among Saxon royalty) to charters that granted land for the founding of new towns, or as gifts to monasteries and Orders, or favoured causes. Over a thousand Anglo-Saxon charters still exist, and the names appended are a strong indication of who was present on these occasions and of their status. They make it clear that the principles of King Alfred's grand strategic vision for Wessex were also given full expression in Mercia by Aethelred acting jointly with his wife.

Burhs were created or strengthened; the fortified towns that could be self-sustaining and which provided defence in depth against roving Viking armies. London and Gloucester were re-fortified, new *burhs* were created in Worcester, Shrewsbury, Hereford and Winchcombe. After Aethelred's death in 911 Aethelflaed carried on the programme with, it appears, the utmost vigour. More work was done at Hereford, the old defences of Chester and Tamworth were greatly strengthened; more new *burhs* were founded at Bridgnorth, Stafford, Eddisbury Hill, Warwick, Chirbury, Runcorn, and at locations, still impossible to pin down, but named as Scergeat, Bremesbyrig and Weardbyrig. Alfred's instincts as a town planner were followed in Mercia, based on the much-admired principles of Roman urban planning, and where possible, as in London or Chester, rebuilding from the extant Roman ruins.

Learning and literacy were promoted with a corresponding energy. Anglo-Saxon history and culture were seen as a vital defence against Paganism, as, of course, was Christian piety – the ultimate weapon against Viking privations. Aethelflaed actively promoted cults of St Alkmund who, along with another Northumbrian, St Oswald, both came to be revered in Mercia as the embodiment of that seventh century 'golden age' before the Vikings arrived. Both saints were honoured directly, amid their own remains, in Shrewsbury and at Gloucester – which was also adopted by Aethelred and Aethelflaed as the political and spiritual centre of their kingdom.

Court matters took up due time throughout all these years. The management of Mercia's Witan of ealdormen, rewards for faithful retainers, taxation and the new principles of Alfredian law that now extended across all King Alfred's territories, were on the Mercian lord and lady's agenda. We can only guess at the involvement the young Aethelflaed might have had in these affairs of state, though her wifely role must have affected her early priorities. Sometime between 887 and 890 Aethelflaed gave birth to a daughter, Aelfwynn – Alfred's eldest grandchild and Aethelflaed's only child. By around 897 she was acting as foster mother to Alfred's eldest grandson, the young Aethelstan, for whom destiny had so much in store. During that first decade of Aethelflaed's marriage there is no indication of any domestic unrest in Mercia. Aethelred's political and military instincts seem to have been sound and his young wife's toughness and industry probably impressed the ealdormen of Mercia's Witan. As a young princess of Wessex, she must have learned a lot from Alfred, and during this decade of her twenties she seems also to have risen to the challenges of high politics.

This was just as well, as Aethelflaed's life was changing dramatically. She was deep into the restoration of London in 898 and 899. But in 899 her father, King Alfred, died. In 902 her mother, Ealhswith, also died. And from 902 it became apparent that her husband was suffering from some form of progressive illness, which implies that it was developing in the years before. Lord Aethelred more or less disappears from the records from 902 until his death in 911. Aethelflaed emerges increasingly in charge of Mercian affairs. And in 902 one of Alfred's rebellious young nephews was campaigning with the Vikings of Northumbria and East Anglia against Alfred's kingdom now that his uncle was dead. Simultaneously, Aethelflaed was facing, apparently on her own, another Viking invasion; this time across the Wirral peninsula in the northwest of the kingdom.

Which brings us to Aethelflaed's unique and genuinely astonishing role as a military commander. The programme of founding *burhs* and building more immediate fortifications was proceeding apace. Lord Aethelred had evidently been effective in reforming the Mercian army after the years of Viking puppet government. He organised it along Alfredian lines. He had commanded very successfully in defending Mercia and helping Wessex deal with Haesten's Viking armies during the 890s. He backed up prince Edward of Wessex[4] after the great victory at Farnham and helped pursue Haesten's Vikings the length and breadth of Wessex and Mercia in the fourth of Alfred's Viking wars. The Mercians had led a large joint force including Wessex and Welsh contingents to besiege Haesten's army at Welshpool and beaten his forces in a fierce battle in 894 when they tried to break out and cross the Severn. Mercians had besieged them again at Bridgnorth until most of the raiders simply gave up and slipped away into the safety of the *Danelaw*.

But now, in the crisis of 902, the attempt to unseat King Alfred's chosen successor – King Edward as he had now become – was a moment of decision for the dynasty. It ended in fiasco that December at Holme near Peterborough where the Vikings won a pyrrhic victory over the undisciplined army of Kent that left the pretender and a number of Viking chiefs dead on the battlefield. Their deaths marked the last throw of the Vikings to conquer all the territories west of the *Danelaw*.

Mercia's role in these campaigns were greatly to Lord Aethelred's credit, progressively ill though he may have been. The strategy – to defend in depth and reinvigorate the social and religious fabric of Mercian society, all in lockstep with the various armies of Wessex – was very clear. In modern parlance one would say that the operational plan, the essential moral component of war-fighting, and the coalition/alliance structure, were all well in hand, even if they had not reached a mature stage. We have no idea how closely Aethelflaed may have been involved in these campaigns. Given the military skills she subsequently displayed, she must have been learning from them somehow. For in 902 Aethelflaed herself took on the defence of the kingdom as commander of Mercian forces.

---

4. Generally referred to as 'atheling'; roughly equivalent to the modern concept of a prince.

Whatever was happening around Holme in that year, the Norse Vikings who had colonised Ireland had been ejected from Dublin in 901 and duly arrived during 902 along the western coast of Britain, looking for new settlements. A group of Norse Vikings led by Ingimund sailed up the Dee Estuary to camp near Chester, requesting talks, specifically it seems, with the 'Queen of Mercia'. Aethelflaed, assessing her options both in northwest and south-east Mercia, decided to grant Ingimund's people the territory of the Wirral peninsula, on condition that they would defend that gateway into Mercia from any other Viking warbands. The arrangement was successful – for both sides – for about four years, during which time Aethelflaed was rebuilding and fortifying Chester to make it a prosperous, and defensible, *Burh*.

The ageing Ingimund might have foresworn any more plundering but he simply couldn't resist the new Chester emerging nearby. He began to plot a joint attack on it with Northumbrian Vikings. In 906 Aethelflaed seems to have been in the vicinity and either got intelligence of the plot, or perhaps just guessed from what she could observe. She ordered local forces to rush into the *Burh*, just in time to defend it from Ingimund's attack. Chester's defences were up to the siege, but the Vikings got inside the outer walls and occupied parts of the settlement. The struggle was prolonged and ended with fighting in the tunnels that Ingimund's men had dug under the Mercian defences, when the invaders were finally beaten back beyond the original walls and put to bloody flight. Aethelflaed was not inside Chester during this time, but evidently directed her forces from outside – conspiring to divide Ingimund's mixed troops and prevent any new Northumbrian arrivals from joining him.

She immediately set about re-fortifying Chester, around a new church dedicated to the Mercian Saint Werburgh. It became her biggest building project. And her experience of the Norse Vikings led Aethelflaed to initiate important defensive works along the kingdom's River Mersey frontier. One such was at Eddisbury, and as part of a new, large *Burh* at Runcorn there was a powerful river fort, the last remains of which stand under the existing Victorian railway bridge.

Aethelflaed's taxation for Mercia's renewal – like Alfred's in Wessex – continued to be high. But ever solicitous to keep the clergy onside, Lord Aethelred and Lady Aethelflaed had always made a habit of pledging half of some very profitable taxes to the church. More than this, Aethelflaed herself staged something of a religious coup in 909 when she managed (alas we don't know how) to retrieve St Oswald's bones from Bardney in Lincolnshire – deep in the *Danelaw* – and bring them back to safe interment in Gloucester. It was a powerful omen for the future. It symbolised the underlying shift in Anglo-Saxon strategy from defending against the Vikings to pushing them back and re-taking the *Danelaw* territories.

In 909 King Edward of Wessex, and his elder sister, launched their forces jointly on a lightening invasion of Northumbria, withdrawing five weeks later after dictating a truce. In 910 the Vikings retaliated with a massive invasion of Mercia, but were caught at Tettenhall on 5 August – the very anniversary of St Oswald's martyrdom – in a crushing and bitter defeat that proved pivotal to Viking fortunes across Britain. We know that King Edward was not present at Tettenhall. Mercian forces took the lead in a battle that was in the centre of their own territory, near present-day Wolverhampton.

And Lord Aethelred died only a few months later in 911. So perhaps Aethelflaed was in sole command at Tettenhall.

Credit for this victory would certainly be consistent with the extraordinary fact that immediately on Lord Aethelred's death, his wife appears to have been the swift and unanimous choice of the Witan as his successor. King Edward of Wessex obviously did not object. Saxons and Danes were again at war and Mercia was open to Viking reprisals, so the Witan must have had real confidence in the military acumen of their chosen leader. No woman had ever before been elected to rule an Anglo-Saxon kingdom in her own right.[5] Aethelflaed was perhaps forty-two at this time.

She did not disappoint her noble backers – working with King Edward to recolonise lands inside the *Danelaw* – and launching pre-emptive strikes against any potential Norse warbands around the northern and Welsh fringes of Mercia. Her fortress-building was prolific. She pushed Danish settlements out of *Danelaw* frontierlands building Tamworth – almost a new Mercian capital – and then Stafford.

In 914 her Mercian army fought off an invasion of Vikings from Brittany who tried to plunder west of the Severn, around Hereford. These were also years of constant tension between Mercia and its Welsh neighbours, and in 916, when Abbot Ecgberht under her protection was murdered in Wales, Aethelflaed, at the head of her troops, led an immediate raid from Hereford into Llangorse, Powys, to take royal Welsh hostages in reprisal. At least three Welsh kings, whose territories extended from north to south, eventually bowed to her authority over them.

She must have displayed great confidence during these years of sole command. Traditional king warriors would stand in the centre of a battle line, surrounded by their greatest thegns with all their individual standards; a statement of personal bravery and intent. Aethelflaed, we know, rode in battle. She would have been in the danger zone, vulnerable to arrows and spears or sudden enemy breakthroughs. But she was mobile around the battlespace, able to assess and redeploy her forces; to use her evident tactical skills to best effect – fighting like a modern commander in an age of male warriorhood. Perhaps that's why there's no record of her losing any battles.

The climax came in the next three years. And the great Viking armies of the past were splitting into smaller, uncoordinated, forces – defenders of their own *Danelaw* settlements and Norse warbands expelled from Ireland. In what seems to have been a coordinated pincer movement in July 917, King Edward's Wessex army moved north into the *Danelaw* from Towcester (in Northamptonshire), while Aethelflaed led her Mercians south in a direct attack against the strong Viking settlement of Derby. There was evidently a desperate struggle at the fortress gates, which the Mercians set on fire before they were through, losing four of Aethelflaed's 'most beloved thegns' in the process.[6]

---

5. We have no evidence that a formal 'election' took place in this case. But Anglo-Saxon succession was not generally based on the principles of primogeniture, and the Witan's approval for one among a number of athelings was essential for legitimacy.
6. They were described as 'Besorge', old English for 'beloved', as used in the *Chronicle* (C) for 917.

The capture of Derby and its surrounding Danish 'borough' was Aethelflaed's greatest victory. Over the winter of 917 she then prepared her forces to advance on the borough and fortress of Leicester. But the news of her fierce Derby attack persuaded the Danes of Leicester to submit and place themselves under Mercian protection. In 918, as King Edward pushed into Stamford and East Anglia, Aethelflaed's next objectives were almost certainly Nottingham and then maybe Lincoln. But in that summer the Northumbrians – the Anglo-Danish kingdom centred on York – approached Aethelflaed and offered to submit to her authority. Threatened from Strathclyde and Bamburgh and by Norse warbands from Ireland, the pagan Northumbrians of York now preferred to put themselves under Aethelflaed's Christian protection. It marked a real turnaround in Britain's political landscape.

But at that very moment, on 12 June 918, Aethelflaed died at Tamworth, apparently of natural causes. The Northumbrians withdrew their request – they would submit to the Lady of the Mercians but not to King Edward, who was then obliged to continue campaigning against York into the 920s. Aethelflaed's body was swiftly conveyed to Gloucester where she was interred, next to Lord Aethelred, in a church that is today marked by the remains of St Oswald's Priory.

Aethelflaed's daughter, Aelfwynn then in her late twenties, succeeded to her mother's title; the next Lady of the Mercians. This was another astonishing development; the only example in Britain's early medieval history of one woman succeeding another. It is strongly suspected that the unmarried Aelfwynn had been groomed for this role by her mother. She must have had many of Aethelflaed's characteristics to be so smoothly adopted by the Witan. But it was not to last more than six months. King Edward initially seemed to accept the idea, then in December swept in to absorb Mercia completely into his kingdom, bringing his niece Aelfwynn – against her will – into Wessex and then, we assume, packing her off to a nunnery.

That was the footnote to the epic tale of one of the most remarkable, and overlooked, military figures in the story of England's creation. Aethelflaed was born at the top of Anglo-Saxon aristocracy, and witnessed their warfare against the Pagans, from near extinction in 878 to the verge – but not quite – of their ultimate triumph by the time of her death at about the age of fifty. We might speculate that by then she may have become tired, cynical and perhaps very hard-hearted. We can be more certain from the records that as she grew older, she put Mercia's interests ahead of those of her younger brother in Wessex. But most fundamental to her driving ambition – that sense of destiny she absorbed from the mystical side of her father – was to prevail in the existential battle against Paganism; that plague of extreme violence and conquest that God had visited on her Anglo-Saxons as punishment for their Christian weakness.

Lady Aethelflaed stood as the female hub of a network of kings and warriors – King Alfred, Lord Aethelred, King Edward, King Aethelstan, and those hardy ealdormen of Mercia, and, yes, of Wessex, who took military orders from her. Anglo Saxon England was united as one kingdom, indisputably so, by the time of King Aethelstan's Easter court in 928 – not quite ten years after her death.

4

Harold II – the Last Saxon King

King Harold II of England, defeated at Hastings on 14th October 1066, is popularly known for two things; that he was the last Saxon king of England before Norman rule, and that he died after an arrow hit him in the eye. The first of these facts is only true in a manner of speaking, and the second is probably not true at all. Even if he was struck in the eye by an arrow, which is very debatable, it was not that which killed him. Though it is possible, if that particular arrow *did* exist, while it did not kill Harold, it may have been the one missile among many thousands launched that day which finally turned the battle for Duke William of Normandy and changed English history.

And why was he only 'in a manner of speaking', the last Saxon king of England? To understand the dynastic significance of Harold II, it is important to appreciate the way Saxon royal lineage had evolved in the hundred and fifty years since Alfred the Great. The English royal line went back to Alfred, and through him to the ancient Saxon House of Cerdic. But Saxon England in the mid-eleventh century was in the midst of rapid evolution, influenced both by the political pull of Scandinavia and by new rising powers on the Continent. The English succession from Alfred had become Anglo-Danish in many significant respects. Harold himself was Anglo-Danish, but not of royal blood. His accession to the throne in 1066 actually broke the direct dynastic link to Alfred.

King Alfred and his immediate successors had successfully fought the Danes and finally united the disparate kingdoms in a single, Saxon England under King Aethelstan. But the later, outrageous mismanagement of King Aethelred ('the Unready'[1]) had created openings for more Viking invasions led first by Sweyn Forkbeard and then his son, Cnut; fighting initially against poor Saxon resistance, led by Aethelred and then eventually, and much more effectively, by *his* son, Edmund 'Ironside'. A military stalemate between Edmund Ironside and Cnut was resolved with an agreement to divide the monarchy and the country between them. But when Edmund died suddenly only a few months later, Cnut was able to rule as King of all England and make it briefly part of a large Scandinavian confederation, albeit with England as a united Saxon and

---

1. Aethelred's nickname emerged almost two centuries later, but seems to have been based on a contemporary pun. 'Aethel' meant 'noble' and 'raed' meant 'counsel' or 'judgement'. So, Aethelred the 'Unready' referred not to the fact that he was unprepared to fight the Danes – though that was certainly true – but to his 'un-raedness'; his unfitness of judgement and counsel, even to his evilness.

Christian kingdom.[2] Though Saxon society was never seriously compromised – as it would have been had Alfred lost his wars with the Danes – the result of the Cnut reign, where for a few years he was simultaneously King of Denmark, Norway and England, had lasting effects on the Saxon ruling elites. Cnut's rule, and then in brief succession, that of his two sons, Harold I and then Harthacnut, was to last twenty-six years from 1016 to 1042. It created an Anglo-Danish nobility who had family roots in Scandinavia but who could still trace their ancestry, at least on the Saxon side, back to the founding house of Cerdic.

Edward ('the Confessor') ruled after Harthacnut. The natural, and seventh, son of Aethelred the Unready and a pious Christian, Edward's kingship restored the throne to its full legitimacy in direct line again from Alfred the Great. True, King Cnut had married Emma of Normandy as his second, and Christian, wife and taken some trouble to observe Christian customs and adopt Saxon law to help integrate Danish and Saxon cultures. But Edward was not Anglo-Danish. He had no need of any artifice. He came from the ancient line and was a legitimate Saxon king.

Except that he was half Norman on his mother's side, he became the stepson of Cnut when his mother remarried, and he was effectively placed on the English throne by the Anglo-Danish nobility – in particular by Harold's own Godwin family. Brought up in Normandy, Edward then surrounded himself with French courtiers, French language in official documents, and began to centralise government administration, French-style, through the King's shire reeves (sheriffs) who paralleled the authority of the traditional Saxon ealdormen. Edward was not, as some contrarian historians have contended, the 'first Norman ruler of England'. His penchant for French fashion and administration was not especially 'Norman', just French. Nor was he the weak and pliant King that his sobriquet 'the Confessor' implies.

Harold II's defence of his kingdom in 1066, therefore, was more a clash of multi-ethnic dynasties than of countries or societies. It featured Anglo-Saxons, Anglo-Danes, Scandinavians and Normans, with plentiful Papal dabbling. It has been compared to the wars between mafia families, all competing for control of 'lands' rather than the societies that inhabited them. It was surprisingly common, for example, for a noble who had been officially exiled from England to take his treasure to the Continent, or to Denmark or Ireland, recruit a foreign mercenary army and then return to England, 'ravaging', 'killing many' or 'burning', as the *Anglo-Saxon Chronicle* frequently puts it, the lands of the country in which he claimed a legitimate place. The magnates of eleventh century England thought it normal to 'ravage' each other's lands, and even on occasion their own former lands, as part of their rightful ambitions. If an exile could become enough of a threat, or just a persistent nuisance, there was a reasonable chance

---

2. Cnut became King of England in 1016, King of Denmark in 1019 and King of Norway in 1028. He ruled in Pomerania and Schleswig, he claimed parts of Sweden, received the submission of King Malcolm II of Scotland, and had political influence with the Norse of Ireland. This confederation was not easy to hold together and did not last long after his death in 1035, but for a few years Cnut's English-Danish kingdom was the core of a power network that dominated northwest Europe.

he could negotiate a restoration of his former position and privilege. It happened on a number of occasions in the life of the Godwin dynasty; indeed, they did it themselves.

But the popular conception that 1066 was a turning point in English *national* history is not entirely misplaced. The *Anglo-Saxon Chronicle* for the early years of the eleventh century certainly displays a growing sense of real national identity. More telling, the English regions showed their staunch loyalty by raising no fewer than four separate armies to defend Harold's kingdom during 1066 – a reign of only nine months and nine days (almost the shortest in English history). This suggests some significant national consciousness to support their chosen Anglo-Danish dynasty – the Godwin family – even if Harold's kingship had broken the dynastic link to Alfred's House of Cerdic. Those four armies may have been fighting for a particular family, but they were also fighting to defend the lands of England from three different groups of foreign invaders during a pivotal year.

The Godwin family had arisen from obscure roots, but when Harold was born, around 1020, he was destined to be part of an ever-growing network of personal power around England's kings. His father, Earl Godwin, seems to have been descended from a thegn of Sussex, who was subsequently exiled. But young Godwin, born around 1001, was the epitome of a self-made man. His outlawed father did not prevent him getting close to the 'Unready' King Aethelred's retinue and particularly to Edmund Ironside for whom he fought ferociously as a teenager in the campaigns against Cnut in 1016. And when Cnut became king of all England, Godwin was one of the few English nobility who were not purged by the new Danish ruler. He was retained for his sterling warrior loyalty which he transferred willingly to Cnut; so much so that when Cnut campaigned in Denmark to shore up his troubled empire, he either took Godwin with him, or, more likely, left the newly created, young Earl of Wessex effectively to act as regent. Cnut's own base in England was shored up by the three great earls of the day – Leofric in Mercia, Siward in Northumbria and Godwin in Wessex. They were the power-brokers around the Danish king. And over the years they wielded their influence through four different reigns; first Cnut, then during the succession crisis where his two sons ruled briefly, and then when they effectively placed Edward 'the Confessor' on the throne. By that time, in 1041, Earl Godwin was first and greatest among them. He got his eldest daughter married to King Edward and proceeded to influence, then dominate, his royal son-in-law right up to the great crisis of 1051 where his overweening ambition seemed finally to have ruined him.

In the years before that crisis Godwin's second son, Harold – destined to become Harold II of England – was navigating his own way as a young man through the tangled web of England's dynastic politics. He was, it seems, a physically impressive figure and, like his father, had a natural warrior temperament, though less prone than his father to vain impetuosity. Harold seems to have possessed a cooler head both in politics and battle. Around 1044 he was made Earl of East Anglia when King Edward became worried about renewed Scandinavian coastal attacks in the post-Cnut era – a tribute to Harold's competence during years when, it appears, he also commanded ships in service to the King.

At this time, and probably in connection with his new earldom, Harold married Edith Swanneshals – Edith Swan-neck as she is known to history – Edith 'the fair', the 'beautiful', or in one source, Edith 'the rich'. She was noted for her beautiful white skin, presumably also for her posture, and the fact that she was a young heiress to extensive lands in Hertfordshire, Buckinghamshire, Cambridgeshire, Suffolk and Essex. Harold was then a twenty-four-year-old Earl and the lands that Edith would eventually inherit were a perfect match for his own in East Anglia. And Harold's own status would, in turn, provide protection for Edith's wealth and unite her with the most eligible man in the kingdom.

The marriage was *more Danico* – a Danish 'hand-fast' marriage – effectively a common law ceremony, not consecrated and therefore not recognised by the Christian church. Harold was half-Danish through his mother, Gytha, and such arrangements were not uncommon among Danish nobility in England. They allowed for the political convenience of a Christian marriage to a second wife if that became desirable. King Cnut had done exactly that, taking first a Danish wife (who was confined to living in the north) and then later, an official, Christian wife (who was confined to living in the south, at Exeter). Such traditional arrangements were not recognised or accepted across most of the Continent, and both contemporary and later Norman writers would habitually refer to Edith Swan-neck as Harold's 'mistress' or his 'concubine', even as they were titillated by the thought of her evident beauty.

This was deliberately insulting and manifestly unfair. Harold and Edith must have become the most glamorous couple in England; he, the second son of all-powerful Earl Godwin, tall and impressive, with long fair or auburn hair, and the drooping moustaches of the Saxon warrior; she, the noted society beauty who would inherit so much land. At least one near-contemporary source reported that in her relationship with Harold, she had 'known him well and loved him much'.[3] They did, at any rate, have seven children together, beginning in 1045 or 1046 – four boys and two girls and one who died in infancy and was buried with some solemnity in Canterbury cathedral. And the evidence from Edith's benefactions to Christian abbeys, and the way in which she educated her female children, indicate that she behaved with aristocratic grace and style. It also suggests that she was literate, whereas Harold may or may not have been. Either way, Harold Godwinson and Edith Swan-neck pursued a high-status and fashionable life, raising a significant family over the next twenty years.

Harold had to negotiate his way through choppy political waters. His father's relations with King Edward were deteriorating fast, primarily over the outrageous behaviour of Swein, his eldest son and Harold's older brother. Earl Godwin indulged his eldest, who was exiled three times but kept returning with ever-greater outrages and demands. But Harold opposed any restoration for his brother, acting against his father's wishes and aligning himself with King Edward. In 1048 he was at sea with an English fleet from Sandwich to chase German pirates away, and immediately again

---

3. This phrase is used in the *Vita Haroldi*, which is otherwise a very fanciful story about Edith and Harold together *after* the battle of Hastings. But there is reason to assume that this phrase may have accorded to a common image of the couple during their lives.

in a large fleet to see off Swein's second attempt at an armed comeback. The damage between the King and Earl Godwin had become irrevocable by then. In the great crisis of 1051, following a minor incident in Dover and then a full-scale military standoff, the Godwin family were exiled, and Queen Edith – a Godwin, Harold's sister and, more importantly, childless – was turfed out of the King's bed. It was a power struggle in which King Edward attempted to destroy, once and for all, the influence of his father-in-law and the troublesome Godwins.

A difficult moment for Harold, but the family reacted in time-honoured fashion. Godwin went to Bruges and Harold went to Dublin where they each recruited mercenaries and returned to England the following year in a military pincer movement, raiding the coasts as they went. Their forces converged and sailed up the Thames to London, after which the customary restoration of rank and lands was negotiated with King Edward. It was Harold's good fortune that elder brother Swein had died abroad in 1052 and Earl Godwin died in 1053, just seven months after his restoration. That left Harold near to King Edward, who showed no particular animosity toward the thirty-three-year-old warrior whom he now promoted to become the new Earl of Wessex. Harold became a loyal, and increasingly powerful, voice beside the fifty-year-old monarch who remained without an heir, whichever part of his household Queen Edith henceforth inhabited.

In one of the more mischievous threads of history, the contemporary story of Scotland's Macbeth was to play into Harold's own ultimate tragedy. Macbeth, the Mormaer of Moray with a plausible claim to the throne of a united Scotland, defended his own territory from a largely gratuitous attack by Scotland's King Duncan I in 1040. Near Elgin, King Duncan's forces were defeated by Macbeth's and Duncan himself was killed, making Macbeth King of Scotland.

In contrast to his Shakespearean alter ego, Macbeth ruled largely peacefully for seventeen years. In the wake of the great English crisis of 1051–2, he received Norman exiles from Edward the Confessor's court, who then served him. Perhaps it was a mistake to receive them. Certainly, though Macbeth was preoccupied with Scotland and showed no designs against northern England, the English nobility feared him and wanted to install Malcolm, son of Duncan I, on the Scottish throne. Since Malcolm had fled to Edward the Confessor's court as a small boy after his father's defeat and lived there most of his life, it was assumed that Malcolm would be a pliant Scottish king. Malcolm's family had already tried and failed to unseat Macbeth in 1045, but in 1057 Earl Siward of Northumbria led a large force into Scotland largely on Malcolm's behalf. It included some of King Edward's own housecarls and other contingents from Cumberland. The whole operation must have been approved by Harold who by then was King Edward's de facto commander in chief.

The strategy, if deeply cynical, appeared sound enough at the time. But it was to go completely wrong when it became apparent that having put a puppet prince on the throne of Scotland, Malcolm III became an independent and powerful king who also had major designs on Northumbria and Cumberland. He became a continual nuisance to English rulers over his long, thirty-five-year reign. Yet that particular historical thread was not to prove the most important to Harold or the English.

Instead, it was Macbeth's famous defeat at the battle of Dunsinane in 1054, alongside his Norman warriors, that played most strongly into Harold's personal tragedy. The real Macbeth, unlike Shakespeare's Macbeth, wasn't killed at Dunsinane – he died three years later at Lumphanan fighting Malcolm again. But the eldest son of Earl Siward *was* killed that day at Dunsinane, in what by all accounts was a fierce battle. And only months after Earl Siward returned in triumph to Northumbria, he himself died, leaving only a young son as successor to his earldom. Harold and the English court quickly decided that a strong successor to Siward was required as Earl of Northumbria. With Siward's natural heir slain at Dunsinane, and now with only a youngster to step into his shoes, they skipped the family and appointed Harold's younger brother, Tostig.

And that decision, to give Northumbria to Tostig, was to play out a decade later in the tumultuous twelve months up to October 1066, in ways that made Harold's defence of his kingdom all but impossible. Of course, Harold's defeat at Hastings did not begin at Dunsinane. But the weavers of history started a thread there that became stronger as it wove in and out of the picture over the next eleven years, until it emerged as a prominent skein in the fateful tapestry that described Harold's rise to kingship and his fall in battle.

Tostig spent most of his time at the English court, or in Wessex. Meanwhile, Harold conducted a campaign into Wales in 1056 to defeat the troublesome Gruffydd ap Llewelyn, King of North Wales, though he subsequently opted for negotiation with Gruffydd. Harold then seems to have undertaken a long diplomatic mission to Hungary to settle the vexing question of King Edward's succession by getting the exiled atheling Edward ('the exile')[4] and his family back to England to assume the throne in succession to childless King Edward (the Confessor) when that moment eventually arrived. In 1063 Harold again tried, and failed, to capture Gruffydd in a swift mounted raid into Wales. Then, that summer Harold and Tostig together led a much bigger, and devastating, land and sea invasion of Wales, this time delivering the head of Gruffydd personally to King Edward. It was Harold's triumph, if not of mercy, at least of strategic and tactical skill.

But the events that were to tumble towards October 1066 were moving on apace. In 1064 Harold was on another (unknown) foreign mission when his ship was blown onto the French coast and he was briefly imprisoned by Count Guy of Ponthieu, but then released into the custody of Duke William of Normandy as his guest; though a guest who could only leave Rouen when Duke William allowed it. During the weeks he was royally hosted by William, Harold campaigned with him against the Bretons and apparently demonstrated his strength and valour by rescuing two of William's men from quicksand.

William believed – or claimed to believe – that he had a legitimate right to be King Edward's successor. This was nonsense, and even post-Conquest Norman writers had some trouble making the idea stick. King Edward, with Harold's help, had already provided for an orderly succession by bringing atheling Edward the Exile to the English court. And though Edward the Exile had died soon after his arrival,

---

4. Son of the (briefly) King Edmund Ironside, who was a popular memory in England.

his young son, Edgar, was now the atheling and in line when he grew up to be the legitimate, Alfredian, successor to King Edward. Nevertheless, before William allowed his guest to leave Normandy, he made Harold swear an oath. There are no details of its content, but it was undoubtedly an oath that somehow supported William's claim to the English throne. Early medieval society took oaths very seriously, but this was made under duress and Harold evidently ignored it.

More important for Harold was that by the summer of 1065 there was a major armed rebellion in Northumbria against Tostig's wayward and unjust rule. Rebellious forces marched south and Harold met them at Northampton, where he tried to mediate. But the Northumbrians were adamant they would not have Tostig back. To Tostig's fury, and against King Edward's pale advice, Harold found in their favour and Tostig was exiled. True to form, Tostig went to Flanders to raise forces for a return to England as soon as possible. It was October 1065.

Even in late 1065, despite rumours that King Edward had suffered some strokes, there is no indication that he was ailing fatally. In that autumn he went hunting. The young atheling Edgar would be a rightful successor when the time eventually came. But the time came precipitously. The king seems to have fallen seriously ill only around Christmas, and on 5th January 1066, at the age of sixty-three, King Edward 'the Confessor' died. A succession crisis had sprung from nowhere. In Normandy, William was blindsided by events, so evidently had no idea that King Edward was likely to die just then. England was facing new threats from Flanders and Normandy, old threats from Scandinavia, Malcolm III of Scotland had already launched raids into Northumbria and would certainly exploit any weakness, and the atheling Edgar, aged fourteen or fifteen in 1066, was still too young for the Witan to put him on the throne at such a moment.

Edward was buried in his new Abbey at Westminster on 6th January. On the same day, in the same place, his successor was crowned and anointed as King Harold II of England. It was a swift and decisive move by Harold and the Witan, negotiated during the Christmas court even as the King was declining. It broke the natural Alfredian line of succession, but there is no dispute that as he slipped away, King Edward had named Harold as his chosen successor. The outcome was certainly consistent with Saxon tradition that with or without a dying King's wishes, the Witan had the right to choose.

Harold began his reign by contracting a Christian marriage to Alditha, sister of the two brothers – the 'northern earls' – of Mercia and now also of Northumbria, who thus became his brothers-in-law.[5] He travelled to the north to reinforce their loyalty and was back from York in April for the Easter festival at Westminster. A week later Halley's comet was clearly visible for several days over England, provoking both prophesy and fear.

Then in May, the first of three invasions began when Tostig led ships from Flanders to raid the south coast. Harold summoned ships and soldiers of the fyrd and easily

---

5. Alditha's first husband had been Gruffydd ap Llewelyn, whose head Harold had delivered to King Edward three years earlier.

forced him to retreat. Tostig sailed round to Norfolk, then the Humber, raiding as he went, and was sent packing by the northern earls, thence to take shelter with Malcolm III in Scotland.

Harold was far more concerned about the second threat of invasion he knew was now developing in Normandy. He assembled a uniquely large land and naval force to screen most of the south coast, basing himself on the Isle of Wight. Harold's spies in Normandy would have told him that by July Duke William had created a fleet and was ready to make his move. But the invasion didn't come. On 8th September Harold had to disband his forces. They could not be supplied and held at readiness indefinitely; and he must have assumed that by then, Duke William had missed his chance of a successful crossing before the autumn storms and the winter.

Having failed miserably with his first invasion, Tostig, however, now initiated the third threat of the year, seeking support first from Denmark, but then from Norway where he was able to interest the legendary King Harald Hardrada[6] in an opportunistic adventure to invade England, using Tostig as his handy puppet. Hardrada duly arrived with 300 ships and 8,000 men and joined Tostig's small force from Scotland, sacking Scarborough and then sailing up the Humber and the Ouse to Riccall, landing there in precisely the week that Harold had stood down his army in the south. The two northern earls gathered their forces again and on 20th September blocked the road to York at Fulford. The brother earls were no match in tactical skill for Hardrada and his Norse warriors, though in the event, it was a close and long struggle around the marshes at Fulford before the earls were defeated.

Of course, they should have waited – King Harold was already on his way. But they could not have realised the speed with which he was joining them. Harold had reached Tadcaster by nightfall on 24th September, probably having left London no earlier than 16th. It was one of the great feats of eleventh century military history for Harold and his troops – riding hard, sending messengers ahead to gather the fyrd from distant shires, assembling them at points en route, moving an army two hundred miles in no more than eight days and then going into battle with it on the ninth. It's an indelible testament both to his ability and their loyalty.

When he arrived at Tadcaster Harold realised that Hardrada and Tostig had been foolish. Assuming they had time to spare, they split their forces, leaving some at Riccall with the ships – and most of their armour – and taking the rest to Stamford Bridge where they were awaiting the arrival of local hostages. Harold immediately appreciated his advantage and marched straight through York and onto Stamford Bridge seven miles to the east. He caught them dead, camped either side of the bridge over the Derwent. The Norsemen tried to defend the bridge while they escaped over it to assemble on the eastern side of the river, but the English forced the bridge and were

---

6. Harald Hardrada, known even in his lifetime as 'thunderbolt of the North' had been forced to flee Norway as a teenager, lived in Russia, served successive Byzantine emperors in Constantinople, returned with great wealth to inveigle himself into the Danish/Norwegian war, became an iron-fisted King of Norway in 1045 and opened a new war with Denmark in 1047. By 1064 he had to accept a permanent peace with Denmark. In 1066 he was ready for a new conquest. When he sailed to England, he was accompanied by his wife and their household.

immediately in among the lightly armed enemy in another ferocious engagement. At one point, the Norsemen's defensive shieldwall was reportedly close to a complete circle. Hardrada died with an arrow through the throat and Tostig was killed later on, as the Vikings fled back towards their ships at Riccall, pursued at intervals by mounted English housecarls. At Riccall, presumably on the following day, Harold negotiated with the survivors, offering them quarter if they left immediately. It was said that he was displaying mercy. It is more likely he was displaying sheer exhaustion, and didn't want to take on even a small force of fresh Viking warriors if he could chase them away for good. Indeed he could, and Harold's Stamford Bridge victory over the fearsome Hardrada was so overwhelming that it finally ended the 'Viking age' in Britain. Harold rested in York, at the very peak of his career.

But by then the weavers of history were working ever shorter threads for Harold. The prevailing northerly wind switched round abruptly and Duke William took a great gamble with the weather and landed safely at Pevensey on 28th September – unopposed – with what turned out to be seventeen clear days to consolidate his position. He would have known that Harold had already stood his forces down, but probably not that Hardrada had invaded and that Harold and his army were now far away in the north. His audacity had been rewarded with extraordinary good luck. Across the twenty-one weeks of the 1066 invasions, William had hit the three-week window in which England's south coast could not be defended nor any counter-attack mounted. By 1st October King Harold knew that William had landed. This, Harold knew, was the real threat.

He set off from York immediately with his housecarls, retracing his steps southwards down the roman Ermine Street, calling now for fresh fyrd soldiers to join him or assemble at London and await his arrival. Just outside London Harold visited Waltham Holy Cross, his personal church and college foundation, where he prayed alone for a while before re-joining the column. His fyrd was composed of contingents spanning shires from the south-west to the south-east of England, with Mercian and Northumbrian troops following up as they reorganised themselves after Fulford and Stamford Bridge. Monks of the English abbeys, including some of the famous warrior Abbots (who would die at Hastings), joined the force, from abbeys in Bury St Edmunds, Holme, Abingdon, Peterborough and Canterbury. Harold entered London on the 8th or 9th October. By 11th October, at the very latest, he was marching his soldiers to confront William at Hastings sixty miles away. And late in the afternoon on 13th his forces emerged through the Sussex Weald, within striking distance of the Normans. They were just coming towards Senlac Ridge, about seven miles northwest of William's camp at Hastings.

Harold's luck was deserting him, but so too was his military judgement. Perhaps he was overconfident after Stamford Bridge, or perhaps he was just too exhausted to reason clearly. He seems to have hoped to repeat his trick and catch William by surprise. But on 13th William was expecting him and he had his Norman army stand-to during that night in case of a sudden attack. Nevertheless, Harold had William bottled up on the Sussex coast without access to further supplies. English ships were already dispatched from the Thames to block William's fleet. Duke William's forces were the size they were; but Harold's army could be reinforced almost indefinitely. More troops were arriving from London and the northern earls were on their way with the Mercians and the Northumbrians. At some point Harold would have to fight and destroy William; but not today, not on Saturday 14th October. Harold's biggest tactical advantage was time. But he spurned it, and it was the Normans who sprung the surprise, moving up at dawn that morning for an imminent attack, albeit in very unfavourable conditions, and forcing Harold to move half a mile forward onto Senlac Ridge. There, he took up a defensive position, doubtless hoping to break the Norman army on it, or else maul it enough to allow him to re-focus his own tactics.

After Harold's naval commands, his mobile campaigns in Wales, his fast manoeuvre battles against the Norsemen – all on the offensive – it had come down to this; a traditional Saxon shieldwall, backing itself to hold out against William's mix of infantry, archers and his feared heavy cavalry. Their numbers were roughly equal, upwards of around 8,000 on either side[7], though Harold's forces were still arriving and being deployed around the ridge as the battle went on. Their armies were differently structured. The English sometimes used horses in running battles but never developed cavalry horses, or cavalry tactics. They fought predominantly on foot and did not use Norman crossbows – still a novel weapon in 1066. The famous English longbow was still at least a century away. But they used 'short bows', an array of throwing missiles, spears, swords, maces and the ferocious long-handled, double-bladed, Danish axe – wielded with great skill by the housecarls. Harold's housecarls were arguably the most powerful foot soldiers in Christendom and continental armies were right to fear them. Harold's defensive position was a good one. The ridge, about eight hundred yards wide, was also narrow enough that he could not be outflanked. Norman forces would have to attack from the front, uphill, over rough ground crossed by streams and following weeks of wet weather. Harold's position, in itself, did much to negate the advantage of Norman cavalry, and made archery – firing uphill – less lethal.

William launched his first attack at about nine o'clock, using his thousand or so archers with their mix of crossbows and short-bows, and followed up with some of his 4,000 or more light and heavy infantry. But the storm of arrows and missiles from the English shieldwall broke these assaults almost immediately. Norman cavalry then attacked the line, lumbering up the soggy hill to throw spears and try lance charges against parts of the shieldwall. But disciplined shieldwalls knew how to ground their long spears at an angle to create a porcupine against oncoming horses, and as the cavalry attacks broke up the Danish axes proved deadly against both horse and rider. Harold's forces inside the middle of the shieldwall were all steady; well organised into local subdivisions within each shire's contingent. The troops of Kent and Essex were believed to make up the front ranks, men from Wiltshire, Devon and Cornwall the second line, light infantry from Hertfordshire were in support, while Londoners comprised the King's bodyguard standing beneath his royal banners in the centre.

---

7. Traditional accounts assumed a conservative 6–8,000 troops on each side, though more recent research suggest Norman numbers were as high as 12,000 or perhaps more. Whatever they were, English numbers must have been roughly comparable or the battle would have been much briefer.

Around three or four more cavalry attacks were made during the morning, always with infantry and archers harassing the English shieldwall. But Norman writers observed that the English seemed 'rooted to the ground'. The first breakthrough occurred around midday. William's Breton forces on his left fled from the ridge with part of Harold's right flank in deadly pursuit. His cavalry in the centre wavered and there were cries that William had been killed. For a while it seemed that William's whole position might collapse if the English followed up vigorously. But Harold was not prepared to give up his good position for a broken fight in open ground against Norman cavalry. William had time. He rallied his forces, turned against the pursuing English on his left and cut them down even as they tried to regain their position on the ridge.

There was a lull, as Normans and English recovered from what was a near defeat for them both. In the afternoon the pattern was repeated; no recorded massed infantry assaults, but more cavalry attacks against the 'close formation' that Harold was maintaining. But on his right, Harold was steadily losing the integrity of the deep shieldwall. Whether or not the Normans were now feigning attacks against the flanks to persuade the English once again to pursue them and then be cut down by cavalry, or whether they were simply being worn down, has been a matter of hot debate ever since. Either way, the forces on Harold's right flank, in particular, were suffering a lack of cohesion and probably of discipline. Duke William, with his demonic energy, was everywhere on the battlefield that day – like a commander. King Harold, apparently, remained brave and defiant all day at the centre of his line – like a warrior. He may have dispatched his brother, Earl Gyrth, to the right flank to sort out the problem, but we know that Gyrth was back under the royal standards at the end of the day and nothing much changed on the right. By late afternoon Harold's line was becoming ragged as one flank began to collapse.

Around this time, was Harold struck in the eye by an arrow? Possible but uncertain. The Bayeux Tapestry is ambiguous in that the figure always presented as depicting this moment was liberally restored in the mid-nineteenth century. It is just as likely that the 'arrow' was originally a spear or javelin the figure was throwing, or a piece of unresolved background. The restorers appear to have shifted the position of the top of the shaft which now bends towards the figure's eye, and helpfully added flights to the other end of the bare shaft so we could all see it was an arrow.[8] The inscription above seems to have been tampered with and there are other inconsistencies in the various Harold figures in this part of the Tapestry. If he *was* hit in the face by an arrow – unless it was a crossbow bolt – there is every chance he was injured but not killed. Henry V was hit full in the face by an arrow at the Battle of Shrewsbury and carried on fighting. In fact, almost all the best sources agree that Harold died in more mundane ways.

Dusk arrived about five o'clock on 14th October; complete darkness by six-thirty. William was out of time. Harold, however, could move on to victory tomorrow, or in

---

8. Extensive eighteenth century French drawings of the whole tapestry do not include this feature as an arrow at all, and no mention is made of 'Harold's arrow' by any earlier observers of the tapestry.

the days after that, if he personally just survived today. Perhaps it was a serious injury, or sheer befuddlement. Or perhaps it was his warrior pride that made him stay at the centre of his army until it was too late. If he was down injured and thought to be dead, the diminishing shieldwall must have started to collapse quickly. Sometime around five o'clock or five-thirty Norman cavalry finally broke through and William's knights cut down those around the standards; slashing, mutilating and beheading Harold. The bodies of his brothers, Leofwine and Gyrth, lay close by, along with his most prominent housecarls and three of Edward the Confessor's nephews. Abbot Aelfwig of New Minster, and at least twelve of his Winchester monks, Eadric the Deacon and Abbot Aelfric of Yelling all lay near the standards in the centre. Others were cut down as they slipped and slithered in the failing light down the escarpment behind the ridge. At least one hopeless last stand was mounted there which accounted for a number of exuberant Norman knights. The housecarls, it has been observed many times, were magnificent in defeat. And that defeat hinged on less than an hour of daylight.

In the aftermath of the battle there are wildly conflicting accounts over what happened to Harold's body. In the circumstances, a plausible account is that Edith Swan-neck, who, alongside Harold's mother, Gytha, were perhaps not far away from the battle site, were either summoned or gained an audience with Duke William to arrange an identification of Harold's body to have it given over to two Canons (both named in many sources) of Waltham Holy Cross for burial. William would certainly have wanted Harold's body identified, to be assured that his adversary had not escaped, and so that he could control the story of what happened to it. As a seasoned warrior he would also have realised that within an hour or so of a battle, the corpses of any dead nobles would have been stripped naked – by the victors, by soldiers following up, by local battlefield scavengers. Several of Harold's personal effects had already been delivered to William in triumph. But he must have known that neither he, nor any of his senior officers, could have identified Harold's corpse from the remains he knew would be headless, naked and mutilated. William seems to have agreed that Edith could identify Harold's remains and have them taken to Waltham Holy Cross, on condition that the Canons did not promote a religious cult around them – something subsequent clerics at Waltham, doubtless with William's shadow hovering over them, seem to have honoured.

So, sometime in the early dawn that followed, or at most the day after, Edith Swan-neck, love of his life, mother to seven of Harold's children, probably picked her way through the tangle of mutilated corpses around Senlac Ridge. The Canons and clerks from Waltham must have accompanied her, presumably along with a detachment of Norman troops. She must have found his severed head and, we are told, was able to identify other mutilated remains, have them taken back to Waltham and there, one imagines, tried to restore some dignity to Harold's body, before both wife and mother interred it without public ceremony within the church. Edith was in her late thirties or early-forties. After that she disappears from the historical record altogether.

But the rest of Harold's family were more prominent, and were the focus of early resistance to Duke William's conquest. One of them is of some dynastic interest. Harold's eldest daughter, another Gytha, escaped from an attempt at rebellion in

Exeter in 1068 travelling to Flanders and thence to the court of her cousin, King Sweyn Estridsen of Denmark in the early 1070s. In 1074 she married the very rich, and very Christian, Prince Vladimir Monomakh of Smolensk. As he moved up the Russian hierarchy, she became progressively Princess of Chernigov and then of Pereyaslavl. She proved as fertile as Edith Swan-neck, her mother, and had eight sons and three daughters with Vladimir. She died in 1107 and never saw her husband become the Grand Prince of Kyiv in 1113. But her eldest son, Msistislav – Harold II's grandson, and known in the Norse world as Harold – succeeded as Grand Prince of Kyiv. He married a Swedish princess and their eldest daughter, Ingeborg, married Cnut Lavard of Denmark. Their son became Valdemar I ('the Great') of Denmark in 1154, from whom the current royal families in Denmark and Great Britain are both descended. A tiny thread of Harold II's line with Edith Swan-neck still persists in Britain's own royal tapestry.

Though he left a small trace in the royal linage, Harold II was not, from a genealogical point of view, the last truly Saxon King of England. But from a political point of view, and given the national loyalty he inspired in 1066, he probably was.

5

William I – The Conqueror

Duke William of Normandy elevated himself to a national throne when he successfully invaded the Anglo-Saxon Kingdom of England, to become King William I. To most Britons he is remembered mainly for his victory at the Battle of Hastings in 1066; his vicious 'harrying of the north' to suppress rebellion in 1070; and the accounting of what his new kingdom was really worth in the *Domesday Book* of 1086. For many casual readers, their own British history begins with William the Conqueror. Everything before him is hazy, everything after him is documented and comprehensible.

Some old established British families enjoy this thought and boast that their ancestors 'came over with the Conqueror'. Others retort that this is nothing to be proud of. The Normans were little more than a bunch of ex-Viking pirates who seized a sudden opportunity for fame and fortune and went on to suppress an older and richer culture than their own. William managed to elevate into an issue of holy honour his spurious claim to the throne. It disguised a simple land-grab.

Modern historians have eschewed the 'conqueror/pirates' dichotomy and pointed instead to the ways in which Saxon England in the mid-11th century was related and even merging in social and political terms with its neighbours in France and among the continental dukedoms. The Battle of Hastings was not so much a clash of two societies, in this view, as a struggle between the insecure, half-Danish Godwin dynasty of King Harold II of England and the insecure, quarter-Danish Norman dynasty of Duke William of Normandy. And they competed for the spoils as England fell into a political succession crisis when King Edward 'the Confessor' died, childless, on 5th January 1066.

Nevertheless, it would be a mistake to assume that the Battle of Hastings was merely about overlordship or somehow irrelevant to the general trajectories of British and continental history. William's victory and King Harold's death that day changed many things. The whole of Britain would henceforth be a different sort of 'transmarine domain' – not British/Scandinavian, but rather British/continental, as England, Wales and Scotland became more deeply entwined with affairs in Normandy, Brittany, Anjou, Maine and Aquitaine. The Battle of Hastings changed the futures both for England and for all its continental neighbours. By the time of William's death in 1087 some 15,000 of his Normans had ended a respected, 600-year-old Anglo-Saxon dynasty and taken control of ninety-two percent of the land of a rich English society of well over two million people, imposing on it their own feudal system. The drama of the upstart Norman Duchy making a success of such an outlandish adventure reverberated loudly across all of Europe.

This was an achievement considerably beyond mere piracy, even though Duke William's acquisitive eye was a strong driving force. If William displayed a piratical Viking streak, it was nevertheless honed by inbred survival instincts, an austere, sometimes cruel religiosity and a warrior outlook which assumed that victory and conquest were the only ways an inheritance could be defended; sooner or later, everything must be fought over. His place in history is defined by the Battle of Hastings. But in truth Hastings was only the greatest of the battles he fought. William was fighting for his life from the age of ten and he died fifty years later, still fighting on the borders of Normandy, after becoming ill while reducing the town of Mantes to ashes.

William was born in unpropitious circumstances; the illegitimate child of Duke Robert of Normandy, to a local working girl, Herleva of Falaise, around 1027. 'William the Bastard' was nevertheless acknowledged by his father and brought up in Robert's household. As a child he must have impressed his father because in 1034 Robert named William as his chosen successor and made the magnates of Normandy swear oaths of allegiance. Robert was setting out on Crusade, and in 1035 like so many others, he died of illness on the return journey, when he had reached Nicaea. The eight-year-old William became the next Duke of Normandy, with the aged Archbishop of Rouen acting as regent. But when the Archbishop died two years later, Normandy fell into chaos and William was in immediate danger. His father had provided for a number of guardians to protect his illegitimate son but relentlessly, one by one, they were murdered. The assassins didn't want to kill William, though he later claimed to have made narrow escapes when they killed first his tutor and then his personal steward even in his own chambers. In reality, the assassins were staging a gradual coup for control of a dukedom that was now up for grabs, and they were supported in their efforts by the King of the Franks who saw in it the chance to bring the upstart Norman domain under his direct control.

The effect on the young William of being surrounded by so much violence and death in his boyhood can well be imagined. He grew up to be, apparently, of average height but stockily built and was evidently a strong and robust teenager. As a young Norman nobleman, he was trained endlessly in the arts of the warrior – horsemanship, swords, shields, lances and spears, not to mention toughness, stoicism, leadership and the ruthless execution of battlefield requirements.

Just over a century since the Viking chieftain Rollo had accepted Christianity in exchange for control over his 'North-man' domain, four generations of Norman dukes, formally owing allegiance to Frankish kings, had built their own, strong, dukedom. Norman society maintained a thoroughly spartan outlook and prized warriorship and conquest more highly than most of its neighbours. France and its subordinate dukedoms existed in a constant state of turmoil and competition. Wars were limited but frequent; and peace for and in Normandy, it was assumed, could only be based on the dominant military power of its Duke. And if the men of Normandy harked back a little too much to their Viking forebears, they tried to make up for it in the eyes of the Frankish peoples by strong adherence to the Church in Rome and a grandiose religious piety, giving full expression to their ambitious architecture and showy church culture.

This was the society that shaped the young William into a tough, religiously committed and single-minded warrior-Duke. He was knighted at the age of fifteen, after which he was in full control of his Dukedom. He had been shrewd enough to gather around him during the dangerous years a trusted 'band of brothers' – some of whom appear to have been the assassins of his guardians, since contemporary chroniclers feared to name them. But if they became trusted comrades, they still had to be regularly rewarded; and they stayed beside him throughout his campaigns and certainly received their due when together they won the greatest prize of all.

Normandy's fears and ambitions were traditionally directed towards the rich dukedoms to the south – particularly Anjou – but when he was nineteen, William had to face a serious rebellion in the north of his dukedom, forcing him to flee for his life. He enlisted the help of the French King and then led and won a decisive battle at Val-es-Dunes, tearing down his opponents' castles, sharing out their wealth among his band of brothers and summoning a Council at Caen to lay down new terms for a peaceful Normandy. The young Duke William was not to be underestimated and Normandy, for all its doubtful pedigree, would assert itself among the continental dukedoms. He went on to bolster his growing political base in 1051 with a marriage to the 'very beautiful' Matilda, the young daughter of Count Baldwin of Flanders. And he worked hard in these years to increase the cultural and religious reputation of Normandy, attracting scholars, nurturing clerics and promoting revolutionary, new cathedral architecture.

But the struggle for survival was an existential condition for William. Between 1051 and 1060 Normandy was invaded twice by Geoffrey of Anjou, and by the French King who seems now to have decided to bring William down, joining coalitions of Anjou, Aquitaine and Blois to reduce Normandy to true vassalage. Revolts were fomented in both north and south Normandy, and even after they were put down, another war with the French King followed in 1058. These were campaigns of feint and manoeuvre, punctuated by short, sharp engagements. William proved indefatigable and brutal in his own defence. His instincts seemed to tell him unerringly when to attack and when to screen opposing forces. He also seemed to know how to avoid over-extending himself and would cash in his military gains at the right moment. He used his hastily built castles to great effect and punished severely those who tried to build their own unauthorised defences. In the event, it was the death in 1060 of both King Henry I of France and Geoffrey Martel, Count of Anjou that left William exhausted but still standing; and with his Normandy intact. When the Count of Maine died in 1062 William claimed it and used his excellent mounted knights to bring Maine under his own control.

Other than being driven by a deep instinct for military expansion as the means of survival, it is not clear quite when William set his sights on Anglo-Saxon England – a monumental risk, a much bigger prize, an ambition so manifestly audacious that its success changed European history forever.

The audacity of his ambition is indicated by the thin nature of his claim to the English throne – despite all that Norman historians subsequently wrote. As a second cousin to King Edward the Confessor, William's own dynastic claim was distant. His great aunt Emma of Normandy had married, first, King Aethelred 'the Unready', and then later, King Cnut. But Emma offered no blood line to the Saxon royal family. There were at least three others with closer blood-line claims – two of them French. Instead, William relied on more personal arguments. He claimed to have visited King Edward in 1051, though even the fact of a visit is uncertain. It is possible (and there is even more reason to doubt this) that Edward told William on that occasion he should succeed to the throne. The following year William of Jumieges seems to have reinforced this idea in William's mind, though only on the basis of gossip around the court. But after 1060, when William could enjoy a brief period of relief from constant campaigning, he seems to have watched events in England with special interest. When Harold Godwinson, quite fortuitously, became his 'enforced guest' in Normandy during 1064 William obviously made him swear some sort of oath that Harold subsequently ignored. In fighting against Harold's kingship two years later, William made much of his God-given right to deprive a holy oath-breaker of the English crown.

William certainly acted as if he truly believed in his own legitimate claim. Perhaps he did. If so, he was falling for his own propaganda. Edward the Confessor had been inclined to exploit his childless status by hinting to different people that he was minded to name them as his successor. He may have said this to King Sweyn Estridsen of Denmark; he may have said it to William in 1052. He certainly said it unambiguously, on his deathbed, to Harold Godwinson.

In fact, no fewer than five men had some claim to Edward's throne. Young Edgar the atheling had been deliberately placed by Edward in direct line of descent, when he was old enough, to succeed him. Sweyn Estridsen claimed he had been promised the throne over twenty years previously. Norway's Harold Hardrada thought he had a claim, dating back nineteen years via a promise King Cnut had made to his father. Against these, William claimed the throne had been promised to him fourteen years previously. And Harold knew that, less than a month previously, Edward had finally given the throne to him. The Witan confirmed it. William's claim, even if it were true, was far from the strongest. In reality, Edgar the atheling had the most legitimate dynastic claim; Harold the most legitimate political claim. Duke William's claim was merely more recent than Estridsen's or Hardrada's. And bolstering it so elaborately with Harold's alleged oath-breaking was an embellishment that just emphasised its central weakness.

William was taken by surprise at King Edward's death and Harold's immediate coronation in January 1066. If he had foreknowledge of Edward's decline, he would surely have placed an emissary at the English court. Nevertheless, he acted immediately and gathered his supporters and the wider Norman aristocracy together to outline an invasion plan. The obvious risks were so great that he had trouble convincing even these acquisitive magnates as his preparations got underway. But he was also attracting mercenaries and adventurers from across Europe as his intentions became public. It was not until late July, however, that William could rely on a sufficient force, around 8,000–10,000 troops – some estimate as many as 12,000 – and a fleet of 500 or more ships that had been built or hastily adapted.

From this point until he sat on the English throne, William's approach as a commander was characterised by remarkably inconsistent behaviour. He displayed the bold strategic imagination to attempt the venture and to convince (repeatedly) even his most loyal followers that it was worth one do-or-die effort – for they would assuredly face death or ruin if they didn't succeed. He drove meticulous and imaginative preparations for a cross-channel landing. Over the last two thousand years many cross-channel military expeditions have been mounted, to and from the Continent. But in relation to their own historical eras, none exceeded this one until D-Day in 1944 – cavalry embarkation for 2,500 horses, prodigious stores and disembarkation procedures, mobile smithies, three pre-fabricated castles, engineers and equipment, seaman/foot soldiers and much more. He maintained an almost manic leadership and commitment to the project and held its central strategic purpose steady.

Yet William's military tactics on the ground were tentative and hesitant both before and after Hastings. He put his own forces under pressure where they were facing the decisive battle in unfavourable conditions, and for which he relied too heavily on the strength of his Norman cavalry. But then again, as a commander he was personally brave to the point of recklessness and above all, he was lucky when it mattered. He was lucky when he appealed to the Pope for support to dispossess Harold the oath-breaker. The Vatican was shocked at the prospect of sanctifying the invasion of a Christian country, but Archdeacon Hildebrand (later to become Pope Gregory VII) saw advantage in it and persuaded Pope Alexander II to give William a sacred banner to take into battle. William was now able to justify his project as a holy war, even wearing round his neck at Hastings the saintly bones on which he claimed Harold had sworn his oath.

This curious pattern of great strategic determination, tactical hesitancy but favourable luck characterised William's campaign throughout the year. The progress of the campaign and the battle have been described from King Harold's perspective in another chapter. From William's perspective, he spent the months from July to September waiting for the freakishly long spell of northerly winds to change so that he could attempt a crossing. He set out around 12th September from the river mouth at Dives-sur-Mer and nearly lost his whole fleet when he was driven 100 miles further east into St Valery at the Somme estuary, where he waited again. By the time the winds really swung round to the south-west, it was late in the season and setting off on the evening tide on 27th September to get the fleet safely onto English soil in twenty-four hours was already a considerable risk. But he took it.

His forces landed at Pevensey on 28th September, probably unsure where they were. A cavalry force raced to Hastings to secure the town and one of his flat-pack castles went up immediately at Pevensey. He probably did not know when he left St Valery that Hardrada and Tostig had already landed to invade northern England, and he certainly couldn't have banked on an unopposed landing, or seventeen days' grace before Harold arrived. On 29th September he moved his force to the better site of Hastings. In the eleventh century Hastings occupied a narrow neck of land surrounded by marsh and water. It was a good position for defence and for his fleet. But it also bottled William's forces up. Unaccountably, he stayed there and waited;

sitting in a trap that Harold would surely close as he approached down the road from London. Seeing Harold coming so swiftly onto him late in the afternoon of 13th October, William's tactical nous seems to have returned. He had his troops stand-to overnight in case of a surprise attack, and then before dawn moved his army out to meet Harold and forced the King to take up his strong defensive position on Senlac Ridge. The initiative was now with William. But Harold had only to survive the battle to win, even if he lost most of his English force that day. William had to win decisively, there and then – and kill the King – or he would lose everything. William had no prospect of reinforcement, no hinterland into which he might retreat, no sympathetic population to allow him to regroup and try again. This was the do-or-die moment. And yet he had now committed his force to a frontal attack, uphill against a strongly defended ridge, over broken and boggy ground that would make life difficult for his cavalry. His attack began around 9-o'clock in the morning and he made up in sheer self-belief, bravery and good luck what he had lacked in tactics.

He had a force of at least 3,000 foot soldiers, perhaps 2,000 sailors/light infantry, 800 or more archers and, critically, 3,000 or more cavalry that he personally led with his half-brother. He had French and mixed forces on his right wing, Bretons on the left and his strongest Norman forces in the centre. There was little scope for any tactical innovation. William began with archers, firing at a difficult angle uphill; then foot soldiers having to attack uphill – both taking fire from higher ground – and then with cavalry, uphill, over a boggy surface to confront a porcupine of spears in the English shieldwall. Not surprisingly, this was unsuccessful, but William had no choice but to repeat the same pattern of attack, in the hope he could eventually shake the nerve of those on Senlac Ridge.

William is said to have had three horses killed under him that day – entirely believable given his style of leadership. He was everywhere around the battlefield and remained in full control of his forces, even though they were making no headway. The crisis moment for him, and for the battle, was the event around noon when the English right wing pursued retreating Bretons on his left and the Normans in the centre suddenly faltered. We don't know which of his three horses he had lost at that moment, but William was down, possibly injured, and rumour ran through his troops that he was dead. He mounted another horse, took off his helmet so all could see his face, and rode through his cavalry yelling at his men to reform on him. He then led the counterattack on the English right wing and cut down those caught in the open.

And so it went on, into the fading light of an October afternoon. Whether the Normans then tried feigning retreats to catch undisciplined opponents, or were just nibbling away at the English flanks, the tactics didn't – couldn't – change much. As Harold's shieldwall shrank towards its centre it could still remain defensively effective and William was losing many troops on both his own flanks. Eventually he united the remaining two thirds of his force into a single unit and tried again. That produced the key moment late on when William's cavalry was finally able to get up onto the ridge as Harold's flanks reduced. Now they could attack on level ground, swinging cavalry, archers and foot soldiers together in a big, combined, left hook against the shieldwall. Nevertheless, the attackers were rapidly running out of daylight. But this was when, sometime between five o'clock and five-thirty, Norman cavalry finally broke through – though it was probably from the other wing that Harold's own position under the royal standards was breached – creating mayhem across the whole ridge.

But William spurred onwards. In the chaos, he couldn't be sure whether Harold had escaped or was dead. Fighting was continuing back along the escarpment behind the ridge. Perhaps English reinforcements were arriving; certainly, Norman knights were falling into a trap created by English housecarls about a mile back, amid the muddy depressions around the escarpment. William took control again to overcome the last of the housecarls and then sent his knights in pursuit of the fleeing English, realising only then that the day was finally his. It was the end of a uniquely long, nine-hour battle. In the enfolding dusk, William turned his fourth horse of the day back towards Senlac Ridge where his tent was pitched for the night.

The English reacted to the news of Hastings by crowning the atheling Edgar as King, while the Godwin family planned guerrilla resistance across the south. William became remarkably cautious again, moving slowly along the south-east coast and then onto London. He was not able to fight his way across London Bridge; burning Southwark and withdrawing again, moving as far west as Wallingford before taking his forces onto the north bank of the Thames. But – luckily again – English command then fragmented when the northern earls decided not to fight for London and pulled their forces out. Saxon magnates bowed to the inevitable and surrendered to William at Berkhamsted. William entered the capital and was crowned on Christmas Day 1066 in Westminster Abbey, even as his Norman troops ravaged the populace of London into sullen acquiescence.

It may all have seemed like a triumph of divine providence for the Duke, though as King William I, it brought him little respite. He was immediately back on campaign for three years to suppress local uprisings in the west-country, Wales, the midlands and repeatedly across the north. In 1072 he invaded Scotland to demand the allegiance of King Malcolm III. Indeed, over the twenty-odd years until his death, he spent his time in England largely suppressing regional revolts and successively longer periods back in Normandy fighting, with diminishing success, to preserve his domains against avaricious neighbours. William's biggest challenges in England turned out to revolve around renewed Danish attempts to get another foothold in his turbulent kingdom.

The famous northern revolt against William in 1069–70 was based around the arrival of King Sweyn Estridsen's Danish forces in York, harking back to the days when northern England could be a Scandinavian colony. William – old style – eventually bought the Danes off, who departed in 1070 and left the region to the King's vengeance.[1] William's brutal 'harrying of the north', laid waste for generations the lands north of the Humber. This was certainly intended as punishment, but it was also to deny any further attractions of the region to Scandinavian marauders. His brutality even shocked the Pope and William's construction of Battle Abbey at Hastings was all part of a public penance the Vatican then imposed on the Norman invaders. Sweyn

---

1. This was the same King of Denmark to whom King Harold's eldest daughter had fled after the failure of anti-Norman revolts in the years after Hastings.

Estridsen wasn't finished, of course. He briefly teamed up with the thegn, Hereward of Bourne – 'Hereward the Wake' in popular stories – in 1071 to oppose the Normans in the Fenlands around Ely. William personally took charge of the siege and then the final assault on Hereward's last, marshland redoubt. By then, King Sweyn Estridsen had already departed, having been bought off again by William and taking with him the sacred booty that had already been removed from Peterborough Abbey.

Even the 'domesday survey' of 1085 was driven by the threat of another serious invasion; this time jointly from Denmark and Flanders. Major taxation was required for England's defence, but the old tax system was obscure and had become chaotic with so much land transfer since 1066. The *Domesday Book* began as a tax survey, but it evolved to become a grand bargain between the King and his new landowners – permanent, legal recognition in return for taxation and military service. It became an audit of Norman feudalism; which was practised in England in a purer form than anywhere on the Continent.

The *Domesday Book* also stood as a documentary monument to the transformation that William, 'the Conqueror', had brought about. He was acknowledged a magnificent hero in Normandy, but he struggled for the rest of his life to hold his transmarine domain together. The new King of France and the Count of Anjou tried to take advantage of his over-extended commitments and William spent more of his remaining years fighting in Normandy than in England. Yet England was never secure, no matter how harshly his Norman forces tried to control it. William became prodigiously fat. His wife and eldest son regularly betrayed him. And he died in 1087, isolated, depressed and ill, still fighting endless wars – fearful of his imminent meeting with God.

Two sons and a grandson became the next three Kings of England, before his dynasty was superseded by the Plantagenets of his great grandson. Henry II and Eleanor of Aquitaine created, briefly, a dazzling Angevin empire that well-illustrated the depth of the change that the Conquest had wrought; the end of Anglo-Saxon England and several new chapters in English and continental history. William had risked everything and sacrificed a great deal for it.

6

The Empress Matilda

Popular history consigns Matilda to a shared place with Stephen – King Stephen – who usurped her rightful claim to be the first Queen of England and against whom she fought a bitter civil war for eighteen years to wrest the crown from him. It left England on its knees. 'The anarchy', as the period has since been known, reduced the country to penury and history conflates 'Stephen and Matilda' together as the chief perpetrators of the disaster. Stephen seized the crown and just about held onto it, despite all that Matilda could do. He won the military victory; but Matilda ultimately won the argument and history's victory. Her son, Henry II, succeeded Stephen and presided over a new and glamorous Plantagenet dynasty; an Angevin empire that spanned England and more than half of France. Stephen became a footnote in royal history, whereas Matilda, an empress on the continent, but never Queen of England, was mother to a straight succession of seven English kings over the next 223 years.

And yet, Matilda herself was ever fortune's fool – a plaything of the heavens that repeatedly demanded she rise to a challenge, that tempted her with honour and glory, only to snatch them from her even as she reached for the prize. She was not a skilful military tactician, nor an astute strategic campaigner. But that probably made little difference to the final outcome. It was Matilda's fate to see all the natural good fortune of her royal birth repeatedly overshadowed by the better fortune of others on the political and military battlefields of England and Normandy. In fighting with such grim determination for what she knew should be hers, Matilda might be forgiven for believing she was fighting fate itself, as well as the usurper King Stephen.

Her father, Henry I, son of William the Conqueror, had made the best of his own opportunities in taking the English throne after his brother, William II ('Rufus') died in a hunting accident. Henry I was a powerful figure who ruled for thirty-five years, but curiously for someone who fathered a host of illegitimate children, he seemed content with only two legitimate off-springs; Matilda, who was born in 1102, and her younger brother, William Adelin, who was thereby the only male heir to Henry's – never entirely secure – throne.

On the continent, the cash-strapped Emperor of Germany[1] spotted the opportunity that the daughter of a rich English king presented and arranged a betrothal to Matilda when she was six. An alliance between Henry I and the Emperor would help to contain French kings, so it represented a good deal for them both. At the age of eight, leaving the Norman French of Henry's court, Matilda was dispatched from England to the stiff formalities and the high German of the Empire to meet the twenty-four-

---

1. Only later to be known as the Emperor of the Holy Roman Empire.

year-old Heinrich V who would be her husband. Heinrich immediately dismissed her retinue, leaving her almost completely on her own. Too young yet to be married, she was immediately crowned Queen of the Germans in 1110, married to Heinrich when she turned twelve and then crowned Empress in 1117 when she was fifteen in lavish ceremonies at the Vatican. We can only wonder at the fear, and then the determination, with which the young Matilda faced these events. She had travelled through the Brenner pass over the Alps in late winter, accompanying her new husband on his progress into Italy to intimidate the Pope.[2] And when Heinrich had to return quickly to Germany to deal with rebellion, he obviously trusted his sixteen-year-old wife enough to rule the Empire's Italian territories in his absence.

The young Matilda was evidently rising to all challenges. She had become popular in Germany as an intelligent young queen, and now as Empress, she seemed to use her advisers well and wielded power responsibly as she presided over the imperial territories of Italy. Her own pedigree to do this was unrivalled. Her mother had been an excellent consort to Henry I and her maternal grandmother was the pious and widely admired Queen Margaret of Scotland. Indeed, her grandmother not only connected Matilda to the ancient Saxon house of Cerdic, but was so revered in the memory that in the thirteenth century she was declared a saint. Perhaps it was not surprising that Matilda wore the mantle of power with apparent ease. She stood in the midst of a bloodline that went from a mythical king in the past to a saint in the future.

But fickle fortune began to beckon Matilda away from the good life she was establishing in the Empire, married as she was to a powerful husband she admired and who, in turn, respected her. Her mother in England died in 1118. Matilda was back in Germany by 1119. And in 1120 the '*White Ship* disaster' changed the course of English history and with that, Matilda's place in it.

Henry I's court was travelling back to England from Barfleur on 25th November that year. The king's fleet set off, but his heir, William Adelin, and young nobles, friends and retainers – the smart young set of the English court – packed into the *White Ship* for a riotous party before they left. Some three hundred crew and passengers got roaring drunk and then decided to set off late on a moonless night, determined to get up enough speed to overtake the King's fleet. At the harbour entrance they ran onto submerged rocks and quickly sank. There was only a single recorded survivor (though one noble, Stephen of Blois, had shown the good sense to leave the party earlier). Henry I's wife was dead and now too, with this disaster, was his only and beloved male heir (not to mention two of his, equally beloved, illegitimate sons). Amid his personal anguish, Henry was now faced with a succession problem. He took a new young wife – Adeliza – but no children resulted from the union. The *White Ship* disaster forced Henry to think differently about the English succession, and his daughter Matilda – popular Empress of extensive continental territories – featured ever more prominently as he worried about securing the Conqueror's dynasty for the future.

---

2. Not as extreme as his previous expedition where Heinrich V had kidnapped His Holiness Pope Pascal II until his demands were agreed.

In 1122 Henry wanted to meet Matilda personally, presumably to discuss the succession issue confidentially with her. He travelled to Kent to meet her, but the Count of Flanders would not grant Matilda safe passage from Germany to any of the channel ports, and the meeting never took place. It was to prove the first of a lifetime of frustrations in the matter of Matilda and the English succession. Three years later Heinrich V died unexpectedly, at the age of thirty-eight. Matilda was suddenly bereaved, childless and a twenty-three-year-old dowager Empress. She resigned her dower lands in Germany, handed over her imperial insignia and travelled to Normandy, keeping only a few, suitably fabulous personal treasures – alongside the mummified hand of Saint James the apostle.

Henry I could now plan afresh for his succession. It had to be Matilda. In 1127 and again in 1131 he twice had the nobles of England swear oaths to recognise her as his legitimate successor. Her cousin, Stephen of Blois, tussled for the right to be the first among them to swear it. And the King had already decided Matilda should marry again – Geoffroi of Anjou, a beautiful and feckless youth of fifteen. Matilda argued against it but allowed herself to be over-ruled. She despised the callow boy but married him in 1128, and separated within a year. It became an interesting relationship. King Henry more or less commanded the couple back to their marriage bed to produce some heirs. Matilda met the challenge completely. She gave birth to three boys between 1133 and 1136; Henry (to become Henry II), Geoffrey and William. Geoffrey's birth almost killed her – preparations were being made for her burial while she lay haemorrhaging – but she nevertheless survived and delivered another boy less than two years later. Her relationship with husband Geoffroi evidently improved; at least they were prepared henceforth to behave cooperatively, if separately.

But the key moment arrived in December 1135 when Henry I died. Matilda was ill and pregnant with William. On news of the King's death she had moved quickly north to secure disputed territories in Normandy. But Geoffroi was preoccupied with a rebellion in Anjou. Matilda established a secure base in Argentan but could go no further. Had she been beside her father when he died, or in Rouen, London or Winchester, it might all have been very different. But she was pregnant, and ill, in Argentan.

December was a bad time to attempt any channel crossing. But Stephen of Blois seized the moment, crossed to England handily from his wife's county of Boulogne, rode hard to London to proclaim himself king among the wool merchants who so valued the Boulogne link; and then made hell-for-leather for Winchester, where his younger brother was Bishop and just as handily-placed to hand over the royal treasury to him. Only three weeks after Henry I's death, Stephen was crowned King of England in Westminster Abbey. Matilda's throne had been usurped in a breathless coup.

Matilda's reactions to this news seemed to leave her uncertain. Henry I's death had plunged Normandy into more chaos than England. Matilda could secure her inherited lands by maintaining her strong base in Argentan. Geoffroi was fighting in Anjou and Maine, with incursions into Normandy, but they were both tied down. In October 1136 Matilda personally led fresh troops to La Sap to reinforce her husband in what proved to be an unsuccessful siege. Geoffroi was evidently committed to being a Count in Anjou and a Duke in Normandy rather than a Queens' consort in England. So, while the couple consolidated their continental lands, Matilda was powerless to do much about events across the Channel. She personally seemed caught between two priorities. She realised that she and Geoffroi could lose everything. They were already, in effect, fighting Stephen and his followers for influence across Normandy and Maine. In regard to England, perhaps she felt that the manifest legitimacy of her claim to the throne and the brazen style of Stephen's coup would create a groundswell of support if she just stayed on the Continent. But having spent years at the centre of political power in Germany and Italy she must also have realised that her lack of presence in England was debilitating.

Stephen had already been raised to wealth and prominence by Henry I and he was a competent and brave military leader. Despite sporadic rebellions against his coup, he seemed to be steadily consolidating his position. The Pope upheld Stephen's claim in England, finding a formula to overlook repeated, multiple oath-breaking. King David of Scotland opportunistically invaded south – twice – on behalf of Matilda, his usurped niece, and on the second occasion was roundly defeated at Northallerton. It was only after 1137 that Stephen began to overreached himself. He was suppressing many rebellions, but there were powerful figures disappointed by him who considered themselves 'dispossessed', and many other supporters who held lands on both sides of the channel. In 1137 Stephen took forces to Normandy to secure their key territories.

Up to this point, Matilda's hopes for her English crown were dead in the water. But Stephen's Normandy campaign was a miserable failure. Most important of all, in the following year Robert, Earl of Gloucester and Governor of Caen, one of Henry I's illegitimate children and thus a half-brother of Matilda – a considerable fighter and military leader who had reluctantly allied with Stephen – declared himself for Matilda. Suddenly, she was a credible contender again. If Matilda represented a dynastic focus for the growing number of the 'dispossessed', Robert of Gloucester was a military figure that her supporters could rally round. On 30th September 1139 Matilda and Robert landed in England with a small force to launch their offensive to regain Matilda's crown.

The landing was risky. Stephen's forces had all the southern ports guarded – except for Arundel, five miles inland up the River Arun. They disembarked there and Robert led his force of knights in a madcap ride across country to reach his stronghold of Bristol before they could be intercepted, there to raise the standard. Matilda couldn't be part of this and repaired to Arundel Castle where Queen Adeliza, Henry's second wife, now his widow, and a friend to Matilda, resided quietly. Stephen and his formidable forces duly arrived at Arundel to confront Matilda and her small infantry force in the castle. There the two women – stepmother and stepdaughter, both in their mid-thirties with less than a year between them, the dowager queen and the dowager empress – simply dared Stephen to do his worst. In reality, Stephen held all the cards, but he was stumped. Astonishingly, he then allowed Matilda and her troops to move peacefully to Bristol where she joined up with half-brother Robert. With that, an all-out civil war was set to begin in earnest.

It was a war of castles and sieges rather than manoeuvrist battles. In a fractured England, the allegiance of few could be taken for granted and as it went on, the war became a series of personal power games among the barons themselves. The forces of Matilda and Robert couldn't deliver a decisive blow against the stronger armies of King Stephen, but they could keep Stephen constantly on forced marches to besiege, or counter-siege, rebel strongholds as they arose. In truth, neither side had much of a strategy. Stephen was merely reactive. Wallingford, an erstwhile rebel stronghold in the east of Matilda's territory, became a constant threat to London that diminished his other options. For their part, Matilda and Robert had some excellent tactical leaders – Miles of Gloucester and Brian Fitz Count in particular – but they never linked their tactical skill to a discernible political strategy for a satisfactory outcome, other than Matilda's simple claim to what was rightfully hers.

Matilda's own sense of entitlement was real enough. She was a dowager empress and the legitimate claimant to the English throne. To that, she was entitled. But she seemed to express that entitlement by taking the loyalty of others for granted. Loyal subjects might accept that an anointed and uncontested king could behave imperiously if he chose. But in a civil war a (female) claimant to the throne risked alienating too many supporters by assuming an attitude that was described by many contemporaries – though not all – as 'puffed up', 'insufferable', 'arrogant'. Whether accurate or not, her absolute claim to legitimacy was not a sufficiently broad political objective to justify all the military risks that others took on her behalf. And for the first two years the prospects of victory appeared bleak.

But in 1140 it seemed as if the heavens were finally prepared to let events run for Empress Matilda – from victory that began as farce, and took her to within twelve hours of a ceremonial entry into London, before her full coronation at Westminster. In the autumn of that year the Earl of Chester, nominally a supporter of King Stephen, used his wife's social visit to Lincoln Castle to seize the stronghold for himself in a piece of comical trickery. So far, so typical. But when the citizens of Lincoln appealed to Stephen, the King marched a force to Lincoln to restore the castle's previous owners. The Earl of Chester immediately slipped away and loudly declared for Matilda – as if he had always meant to. It was a wonderful opportunity for Matilda and Robert. While Stephen was besieging Lincoln Castle Robert marched, for once, a much larger force to counter-siege Stephen's troops inside the city. Instead of withdrawing, Stephen – brave and foolish – insisted on making a stand. On 2nd February 1141, facing Robert outside Lincoln's west wall, Stephen's forces disintegrated and he was left with just a few men around him, fighting ferociously with sword, and when that broke, with an axe, until he was felled by a rock and captured.

Everything now ran swiftly in Matilda's favour. With the King captured, and latterly held in chains, his support rapidly evaporated. The knock-on effect in Normandy was dramatic, as English nobles strove to safeguard their possessions on both sides of the Channel, allowing Matilda's husband Geoffroi to negotiate, fight and subdue the whole dutchy. Matilda travelled to Winchester where she took command of what little was left of the royal treasury. More important, she got the senior clerics to decide that she was the legitimate successor after all; that Stephen had merely been an interim choice while she was detained in Argentan, and not a very good interim choice at that. Discerning God's third position on the matter within ten years, the Church at Winchester declared Matilda to be 'Lady of England and Normandy'. It only now remained for her to be crowned and anointed at Westminster.

But in victory, Matilda was ungracious to her opponents, probably feeling that she had to stamp on her new kingdom the sort of authority her father would have imposed. But times had changed. She offended many potential supporters and demanded copious finances from the London merchants who had already funded Stephen's war. She seemed indifferent to their hostility as she made preparations for her coronation. King Stephen, chained in Bristol, had accepted his defeat. But his own wife, Queen Mathilda of Boulogne, had not. She rallied the pockets of pro-Stephen opposition to Matilda and brought mercenaries into London who ransacked parts of it and created widespread disorder. And then, on 24th June 1141 as Empress Matilda sat down to a banquet in Westminster Hall on the very eve of her ceremonial entry into London, a riot against her was organised within the city and a mob came surging across the river Fleet and along the open ground of the Strand to attack the royal party in the Hall. They fled for their lives, leaving tables of warm food for the mob.

The ultimate prize had been snatched from Matilda yet again. She fled to Oxford to regroup her forces. She still held King Stephen in captivity – her trump card. In August she and her commanders set out once more for the royal treasury in Winchester, where the Bishop had betrayed her and changed sides yet again. Just as victory at Lincoln had been a vicious comic opera, so Winchester turned into a mirror-image of it. The Bishop fled and Matilda's forces settled in to besiege the garrison he had left behind in the castle, Matilda and Robert occupying Winchester city. But Stephen's Queen Mathilda then led her mercenaries in a rapid march to counter-siege them. They were soon all but encircled and Empress Matilda was in real danger of being captured by Queen Mathilda. Empress Matilda's closest supporters, Robert Earl of Gloucester, Miles of Gloucester and Brian Fitz Count, were all experienced military leaders. But they seemed paralysed in the city until they, and Matilda, were firmly trapped and low on supplies. Did the Empress not heed their judgement? Or overrule them? Possibly. They certainly delayed until there was no option but a fighting breakout. On 14th September they tried it – Robert's men engaging in an eight-mile running fight to buy time for Matilda's party to escape in a desperate two-day chase to Devizes and thence to safety in Gloucester. But the whole column had to cross the River Test at Stockbridge and by the time Robert finally reached the Test his troops were congested around the crossing. He made a last stand on the eastern side of the river and in what became 'the rout of Winchester' the respected fifty-year old warrior was beaten and captured.

The only thing that could have made the disaster of London worse for Matilda was to lose the presence, the troops and the lands of Robert, Earl of Gloucester. Without him, she could not carry on. Now each side held a vital trump card over the other. The answer was as unpalatable as it was inevitable. After some elaborate choreography, King Stephen was exchanged for Robert, and both sides were back where they had started in 1139.

In truth, Matilda was near the end of the road in any case. Bereft of any strategy and now, presumably, fully aware of how unpopular she was with the English, it was only her grim determination that kept the campaign alive in a miserable and increasingly chaotic war of attrition. She appealed to husband Geoffroi to bring fresh forces from Normandy, but he was unwilling to dilute his strength when he was closing in on victory. By September 1142, again in desperate straits, she found herself surrounded at Oxford Castle by King Stephen's forces, with Robert unable to protect her. Stephen was certainly not going to be magnanimous this time. The Oxford garrison faced starvation. In mid-December Matilda was famously forced to escape through the besieging pickets, on foot with just three guards, and covered in white sheets as camouflage against the thick snow as they picked their way across the frozen River Thames and escaped the city in a seven-mile trek to Abingdon and then safely by horseback to the haven of Wallingford.

This was effectively the end of active campaigning for Matilda, though the conflict continued, incredibly, for another ten years. Her son Henry inherited her war and after a foolish false start in 1147 became steadily more influential in representing his family's claims to England, once his father had completely secured Normandy. Miles of Gloucester had already been killed in an accident in 1143 and in 1147 the indispensable Robert of Gloucester died of fever. The following year Matilda left England for Normandy, never to return. As Matilda's eldest son, Henry maintained the hostilities against Stephen's eldest son, Eustace, while King Stephen, not unlike Matilda, went steadily into decline. In 1152 Henry became a very powerful nineteen-year-old indeed when the rich and vivacious twenty-eight-year-old Eleanor of Aquitaine grabbed him as her next husband just three months after her divorce from King Louis VII of France.

So, when young Henry crossed back to England in 1153 to continue the war, two vital things had changed. Political power was inexorably flowing his way on both sides of the Channel. And after eighteen years of warfare, the barons were doing private deals, either not to fight each other, or else to offer only token hostility and then withdraw. Battles at Malmesbury and then Wallingford that year resembled battlefield re-enactments; fighting had become ritualistic and simply ineffective for the commanders. In August Eustace predeceased his kingly father, and in November the final deal that had long been foreshadowed was codified by the Treaty of Winchester. Stephen would remain King for his lifetime (which turned out to be merely eleven months more) and Henry would rule after him. Thus it was that in December 1154 the twenty-one-year-old Henry, Duke of Normandy, Count of Anjou and Maine and now through his exciting marriage, also Duke of Aquitaine, became King Henry II of England. It consolidated a new Anglo-Norman dynasty and founded an Angevin Empire, stretching from Northumberland to the Pyrenees.

His mother Matilda didn't witness any of this herself. She had retired to Rouen where she was widowed for the second time, and played the respected Dowager Empress, mother to the English king, and shrewd advisor on European politics to her son, among many others. She strenuously advised her son against raising Thomas Becket so high – ordained priest one day and consecrated Archbishop of Canterbury the next – but did not live to see the sad outcome of Henry's impetuosity. Matilda suffered a probable stroke in 1160 and was evidently less influential thereafter. Her robust health was failing, even though her mind was ever active, and she was increasingly committed to her beloved Abbey of Bec, whose monks in the Priory of Notre-Dame-du-Pre looked after her with great devotion before she slipped away on 10th September 1167.[3]

Matilda had lost her English war but eventually secured her own royal legitimacy, without ever becoming Queen. It was a triumph of sorts, though England had paid dearly for it. Matilda ended her life in a glow of respect from many across Europe and surrounded by the deep affection of those close to her. Perhaps she died contented. But if she did, it's also a good bet that when the ultimate audience took place, she probably gave God a real piece of her mind.

---

3. The priory was to be burned down no less than three times by the English forces of the successor kings of her line; the final time by Edward III's forces in 1346.

William Marshal – the 'greatest knight'

He was the landless younger son who was led to be hanged as a hostage at the age of five. Yet he rose to be acknowledged by his contemporaries as 'the greatest knight' of his generation. He stood close beside five different kings and witnessed the rise and fall of the sparkling Angevin Empire. He was central to the events that produced Magna Carta in 1215 and – at the age of seventy – made the key political call and personally led the forces that triumphed in a civil war which thereby guaranteed a definable English identity among the aristocracy. The alternative would have been a continuation of the strong Anglo-French aristocratic kinship networks that prevailed during the disastrous reign of King John. At so many key moments William Marshal was *there*; and his presence mattered.

Yet since William Marshal did not begin life near the top of the aristocracy, his story was barely understood until 1861 when a manuscript that had not been read for 600 years was auctioned at Sotheby's as part of a job lot. It remained unread until 1881, when its extraordinary account – the first contemporary biography of a medieval knight – was finally published in three volumes between 1891 and 1901 as the *History of William Marshal*. There had been glancing references to him in other sources. He made a perfunctory appearance in Shakespeare's *King John* as Earl of Pembroke. But neither his story nor his historical significance was properly assessed until the early twentieth century.

William Marshal was born in 1147. His father, John Marshal, was a minor west-country Norman aristocrat who found the desperate civil war between King Stephen and Empress Matilda very much to his personal advantage. He campaigned eventually for Matilda and within his accumulating possessions, built a castle at the small, prosperous town of Newbury. King Stephen besieged it in 1152, while John Marshal was miles away. John sued for an armistice and offered his youngest son, the five-year-old William, as a hostage to his peaceful intentions. But his intentions were never peaceful and as soon as he was back in control at Newbury castle, he began to fortify it strongly, indifferent to his son's fate. In fact, young William was taken to be hanged, then reprieved by King Stephen, then led to the bucket of a trebuchet to be catapulted into Newbury castle, then spreadeagled as a human shield as Stephen's forces prepared for a frontal attack on the walls. William survived the gruesome theatricality of all these successive threats because his father genuinely didn't care and wouldn't respond, but King Stephen was not a naturally cruel man. William remained the King's hostage until the following year when the Treaty of Wallingford finally ended Stephen and Matilda's war. Young William was returned to his family. At least his mother, it was reported, 'was overjoyed to see him'. And he grew into a tall, strong and formidable fighting man who was not easily frightened.

From the outset, William Marshal was nothing if not a knightly figure. At the age of thirteen he was sent to Normandy to take up a household position at the castle of baron William of Tancarville. There he was trained in the profession of arms, horsemanship and competition. He was always destined to become a fighting knight – a member of that emerging military elite across Europe that began to take very specific forms in the twelfth century. Knighthood embraced a romantic attachment to early Arthurian ideals of martial skill and chivalry, alongside all-important horsemanship. The Church in Rome had moved – perhaps only half-consciously – to co-opt this new military elite. The declaration of the First Crusade in 1095 provided an unchallengeable Christian rationale for the pursuit of a fighting, chivalrous life among the growing ranks of battle-winning cavalry. William Marshal was trained to join them and imbued with their spiritual and religious core; though with no great personal wealth behind him, he was dependent on patronage and would have to live on his wits.

He was knighted by Tancarville at the age of nineteen and in the same year fought impetuously and well for him, defending Tancarville territory from its neighbours in upper Normandy in a confused border engagement at Neufchatel-en-Bray. He returned to England and entered the household of his maternal uncle, the Earl of Salisbury. Within two years he was fighting in Normandy again when the Earl was summoned to help Henry II's campaign in Aquitaine against the Lusignans of Poitou.

William's military campaigns were never uneventful. In 1168 he found himself among the Earl's retinue escorting Queen Eleanor of Aquitaine through the forests of Poitou when they were ambushed by a large group of Lusignan horsemen. In fighting a rear guard to ensure the Queen's escape, the Earl of Salisbury was killed in the mêlée – a shocking outcome that immediately rendered the attackers outlaws – and William, wading in lightly armed and unsupported, was severely wounded in the thigh and captured. He was of little ransom value to the Lusignans but, bleeding profusely, he was taken with them as they became fugitives from Angevin troops among the wooded hills of Poitou. For the second time in his life William was a hostage. After some months, and still wounded, a ransom was arranged for him by Queen Eleanor herself. He was released into her care to recover and thence to join her own military retinue. In a dramatic turn-around, William Marshal now found himself near the very centre of events.

His growing military skills, however, were not matched by any increase in his independent wealth. Fortunately, he was ideally placed to prosper on the twelfth century tournament circuit. Not to be confused with the more structured sport of jousting, tournaments were altogether bigger affairs. They would begin with a 'mass joust' between two large competing syndicates made up of multiple individual teams – that was the opening spectacle that supporters would witness – before dozens, often hundreds, of knights would split up into a series of running skirmishes that would cover a wide area of pre-designated countryside, including villages where the mayhem would flow through the fields and lanes. Knights would unhorse their opponents or compel some submission to guarantee a ransom or confiscation of horse or armour;

payable after the event. Knights did not aim to do more than bruise each other, but it was all inherently dangerous, not least to the peasants who lived within the designated area; and hugely destructive to agriculture and property. Tournaments were, in effect, full-scale cavalry battles, without the intention to kill. They were banned in England for precisely these reasons, but tournaments were extremely popular on the Continent.

Immediately on becoming a knight in 1166 William Marshal had begun to accumulate valuable experience and some independent assets on the tournament circuit. He was around six feet tall (in an era when men's average height was 5ft7in) well-built and evidently handsome.[1] His horsemanship and weapon-skills were good and his close-quarter handling of horse and weapons must have been superior to most, and were doubtless further honed as he developed a personal reputation on the circuit. He spent perhaps a year in tournaments as one of the Tancarville knights before moving to the service of the Earl of Salisbury and his fateful campaign in Poitou.

But following that campaign and Queen Eleanor's patronage, William was appointed by Henry II to be military tutor and mentor to Henry, his dashing eldest son, known thereafter as 'Young King Henry'.[2] William was eight years older than Young Henry – a gap that allowed him to be both mentor and close friend. Young Henry effectively ruled in England for a couple of years while his father was preoccupied in Aquitaine. And on that basis, he joined in the first great family rebellion against Henry II. William Marshal stood by his younger charge in the rebellion. He probably could not afford to do anything else. It drew William into the destructive intra-family war of 1173–4 where Young Henry allied with King Louis VII of France to depose his father and proclaim himself the true Angevin king. A family revolt was already in progress in Aquitaine. So the new allies invaded Normandy (three times) but were beaten back, twice in the north, once in the south. In between, they assembled a full-scale force to invade England, to be launched from Flanders direct into East Anglia to raise revolt, while Scottish armies continued to attack northern English shires. A small bridgehead for this invasion was even established at Norwich. But the winds would not swing round in time for Young Henry's force to sail, and the 'Old King', Henry II, was simply too fast, too clever and too ruthless to be outfought merely by three of his sons, his wife, and the Kings of France and Scotland.

A political settlement and a (temporary) family truce was established by the Treaty of Tours in September 1174. Henry II's sons were forgiven – though not his wife – and William Marshal's awkward loyalty was apparently understood. Young Henry, still mentored by William, would subsequently be kept on a very short leash at the Old King's court. But the tournament circuit beckoned for them both and the Young Henry – direct heir to the Angevin empire – was always a glamourous celebrity on it.

From 1176–79 Young Henry and William Marshal led a charmed and riotous life riding around the tournaments of Europe. William was effectively the business manager and coach of Young Henry's team, as well as its star performer. His tournament

---
1. His height was determined from his skeleton in Temple Church.
2. The Young Henry was crowned in 1170, though still the heir, in order to stabilise King Henry II's intended succession.

party-trick was to get inside an opponent's reach, grab the horse's reins and whip them forward, out of his adversary's grasp and simply ride off towing the horse behind with the unfortunate rider grimly holding on as best he could. William became a star of the circuit and immensely rich on it, while a cult following developed around Young Henry in the courts of Europe. The grandest tournament of all, on the occasion of the coronation of Philip II of France, was held at Lagny-sur-Marne in 1179, where some 3,000 knights careered across the lands now occupied by Disneyland Paris. Young Henry and William naturally added lustre to the proceedings by their participation.

By the end, William was also leading a top team in his own name, he had partnership arrangements with other stars, a clerk to administer it all, and he had declined at least one offer to ride for Philip of Flanders despite a generous transfer fee. He is reliably estimated to have captured more than five hundred opposing knights in the three or four years he was fully active on the circuit. Images of knightly chivalry, of course, were constantly burnished in these contests and William's personal stock rose with it, though the reality was that he was also a tournament bully who practised all the gamesmanship of the habitual champion.

The glamour and ambition surrounding Young Henry could not to be contained merely by the tournament circuit, however. In 1182 he very publicly 'took the cross' – committing himself to go on Crusade – but in the meantime decided he could oust younger brother Richard ('the Lionheart') from Aquitaine where his appalling behaviour had created loathing among local barons. In 1183 William was again campaigning on Young Henry's behalf – against Richard in Aquitaine and, reluctantly, Henry II as well. But Young Henry fell ill on the campaign and died at the age of twenty-eight. His early death changed everything for the Angevins. And it left William Marshal isolated and on the wrong side of the dynastic struggle.

He chose a shrewd course of public virtue by going on Crusade in fulfilment of his master's pledge to take the cross. William became a crusader. He travelled with just a squire and perhaps two servants and arrived in the Holy Land late in 1183; in time to be involved in the campaigns following the Second Crusade in Galilee to protect the Christian Kingdom of Jerusalem against Saladin's latest probing. In fact, Saladin was mainly preoccupied against Mosul during these years. Jerusalem was relatively safe. But the Kingdom of Jerusalem that had come into being with the First Crusade was now in a parlous state of bickering and vainglorious disunity. It was obvious to all that it was in manifest crisis, while Saladin was working steadily to unify Muslim forces for the great assault that would finally conquer it in 1187. But William discharged his obligation to the Young Henry at the Church of the Holy Sepulchre. And he evidently made a personal religious commitment while in Jerusalem and arranged in great secrecy with The Templars that when the time came, he would take the vows and be buried as a Knight Templar.

William was back in Europe in 1186, just a year before the final disaster unfolded for the Kingdom of Jerusalem. His absence from Court had been well-judged and he went straight into Henry II's household, fighting for him across Angevin territories, against King Philip of France, allied now with the ever-rebellious Richard 'Lionheart', Henry II's eldest surviving son. In a rapid retreat from the burning city of Le Mans,

William, yet again mounting a near-individual rear guard so the King could escape, confronted Richard 'Lionheart' directly with lance and shield in the pursuing mêlée along the road north from Le Mans. William could have killed him but prudence dictated he should only unhorse the heir to the empire, buying precious time along the King's escape route. Henry II's time was indeed precious. Less than four weeks later he died; William Marshal standing vigil as the King lay in state at Fontevraud Abbey.

Richard I, as 'the Lionheart' now became, and notwithstanding his recent unseating, immediately required William's loyalty and sent him to England to look after state matters while Richard consolidated his continental territories. And he rewarded William with a marriage to the very eligible Isabel de Clare, Countess of Pembroke, the wealthy, sole heir to Leinster in Ireland, Chepstow in Wales and Longueville in Normandy.[3] With this, and in addition to several English lands the Old King had already granted him, William became a very powerful baron in the Anglo-Norman world and subsequently Earl of Pembroke in his own right.

Isabel was eighteen in 1189. William was forty-two. In dynastic terms it was a perfect match. Isabel bore him ten children; five girls, five boys. She was bright and determined. *The History* bears out many instances where she was an intrinsic part of his inner council when important decisions had to be taken. In 1207–8 she successfully resisted a siege inside Kilkenny Castle and ran the defence of Leinster's territory against invaders when William was forced by royal command to stay in England. She outflanked the invaders politically and then moved onto the offensive and beat them decisively in the field. All the indications point to a respectful and stable thirty-year relationship between William and Isabel; both uniquely strong characters. William was not a contemplative or spiritual man – he was a fighter, top to bottom – but he radiated an image of chivalrous Christianity. There is no evidence of mistresses or illegitimate children either before or after his marriage, and when it was later reported that the forty-eight-year-old Isabel was completely distraught at the time of William's death, there is no reason to doubt it.

In the troubled decade from 1189 to 1199 when Richard I was preoccupied with the Third Crusade and Prince John (Henry II's youngest son) was trying to displace Richard's authority in England, William Marshal was serving as one of the four co-justiciars of the English realm, appointed by the absent king on his behalf. He navigated his way through exceptionally treacherous waters, including working with Queen Eleanor to see off yet another French invasion (invited by Prince John who would have been content to be a client king to the Capetian dynasty in Paris). Then in 1194 King Richard was back in England. John fled to Normandy and William Marshal rode with the King to extinguish the last stronghold of John's English ambitions and his endless machinations by subduing Nottingham Castle. Then it was back to the Continent with Richard to recover control of his Angevin lands, particularly in Normandy. They

---

3. William Marshal married into lands in Normandy, Pembroke and Leinster. He acquired eight castles inside his Irish lands, and outside his lands in Wales and Normandy, other castles at Cardigan, Usk, St. Briavels, Goodrich, Gloucester, Chepstow, Bristol, Hampstead Marshall, Chichester, Orbec, Dinan, Lehon and Becheral.

became brothers in arms, running a fast and intense campaign against the Empire's Enemies that lasted best part of four years – sieges, manoeuvres, envelopments. At the siege of Milly Castle, and now in his fifties, William reversed a failing attack by dashing alone up a spare scaling ladder himself and assaulting the parapet – an act of reckless instinct that further excited the admiration of his entourage. He was always a soldier's soldier.

Everything changed for William in 1199, however, when Richard the Lionheart died at Chalus after being wounded by a crossbow bolt. It was at this point that William Marshal – the classic knight, the darling of the tournament circuit, the soldier's soldier and a natural leader – stepped up a level to be a national commander in ways that affected English history thereafter.

Faced with yet another succession problem, William's voice was *primus inter pares* among the three most decisive opinions.[4] And in deference to dynastic legitimacy, he plumped for John as the next Angevin monarch. King John, as was his avaricious wont, both rewarded William Marshal for his support and proceeded to treat him appallingly. Yet William stayed loyal. He fought for King John in Normandy against Philip of France in 1202, but could not stop him losing control in Anjou, Poitou and then right across Normandy. He tried to protect his own family lands in Longueville but John, visibly paranoid, then effectively banished him from Court. So for some years William concentrated on his own dynastic affairs; interestingly, giving up two of his sons to live at Court as hostages to his loyalty. Basing himself largely in Leinster, William observed the King's weakening hold over disillusioned English barons; it was only a matter of time before he would be deposed. In 1212 King John decided that he needed William Marshal back as an ally and adviser and asked him to return to Court.

William could do nothing to prevent John losing virtually all the crown's continental territories, which he duly did in 1214, but he could help him hang onto his crown in England by recognising the need for a political solution. Working with the Archbishop of Canterbury, William became the trusted intermediary to represent the King's position to suspicious barons – meeting at Brackley and four times in seven months at the New Temple beside the Thames – as they edged towards the settlement that would conclude with Magna Carta. When the barons took control of London in May 1215, John had finally run out of options. He retired to Windsor Castle while five days of negotiations went on in the meadows of Runnymede.

William Marshal was officially named in the Great Charter, later to become 'Magna Carta', as first among the magnates of England who had advised the King to accept this settlement. The document was sealed on 15th June (it was never actually signed) and William's eldest son was named among the twenty-five barons who were charged with overseeing its implementation. There is no clear evidence that William drafted any of the Great Charter, but there was no doubt that, above all others, he had cajoled the King to accept the inevitable and present himself at Runnymede on the 15th to set his seal on it.

---

4. In addition to William, the support of Archbishop Hubert Walter in Rouen and Justiciar Geoffrey FitzPeter in London settled the matter.

The settlement was an immediate failure, since John and some of the barons promptly violated it. By the autumn the country was plunged into a new civil war. The rebellious barons invited Prince Louis of France to invade, and his advance guard duly arrived in London in January 1216, then his main force at Sandwich in May with some 1,200 knights and accompanying foot soldiers. John's military campaigning was as disastrous in England as it had been on the Continent; manoeuvring his dwindling forces and Flemish mercenaries and 'punishing' territories the length and breadth of England with gruesome atrocities, but never pitting himself against the military core of the rebel barons.

William tried to mediate with the French King and may have offered advice to John but he largely watched from his own operations around the Welsh marches as the southeast, eastern and northern England were lost and some two thirds of the aristocracy renounced John as King. In October 1216, exhausted and increasingly ill on the campaign, King John died at Newark. Another moment of national decision had arrived.

Now, William Marshal, the powerful Earl of Pembroke, made the call that changed the course of English dynastic history. His own interests would have been best served by lining up the diminishing residue of King John's England with the majority of the barons and their French ally. A Capetian King Louis in Westminster, son of King Philip II of France, would have created a new Anglo-French transmarine empire – different to the Angevins, but not different in principle; and in the long run probably more powerful. That was the political logic of events in 1216 and the Earl of Pembroke would have been richly rewarded for engineering it.

But William Marshal's loyalty to the Angevins was instinctive. He moved to champion a near-hopeless position. King John had specifically asked that his young heir, Henry, be put in William's care. William met the nine-year old boy, anxious for William's protection, on the road at Malmesbury and lost no time in having him crowned King Henry III at a makeshift ceremony in Gloucester (since Westminster was in the hands of Prince Louis). By unanimous consent, William Marshal was made 'guardian of the realm' – in effect regent to the boy king. There was no historical precedent for this 'guardian' position and he had no hereditary pedigree for the role. It was a purely meritocratic decision taken in dire circumstances.

William's best military supporter was Ranulf of Chester, and he also had the important backing of the church through the papal legate, Guala of Bicchieri. But he had precious little else. The royal treasury, much of which John had carried around with him, was empty. Based in Bristol, the royalists held a few castles but occupied little reliable territory, and Alexander of Scotland was already on the rampage in the northern shires. The royalists were short of money, troops, allies and prospects.

William knew they could not sustain a full campaign against the rebels. He would have to bring matters to a head quickly. He and Guala re-issued a shorter Magna Carta (forty instead of sixty-three clauses) under their personal seals with the most objectionable anti-royalist commitments removed. And – since Prince Louis and his entourage were making themselves unpopular in London – he made it clear that magnanimity would be shown to rebel barons coming back to the royalist cause. In April 2017 Prince Louis brought fresh reinforcements into England. But he split his forces – to besiege Dover and strengthen the existing siege of Lincoln. William saw the sudden opportunity for a decisive blow and grabbed it. It was a risky and decisive move on the part of the royalists, untypical of the war strategies of this era. But it probably represented the only opportunity they would ever have; an all or nothing moment.

Lincoln Castle was the western bulwark of Lincoln city's wall, placing the castle as at '9 o'clock', inside the oblong curtain wall that enclosed the city. The castle was held resolutely for the royalists by the redoubtable castellan and joint Sheriff of Lincolnshire, the Lady Nicola de la Haye. She had been holding out in the castle since March 1217 against rebel forces who were inside the city walls, occupying the rest of Lincoln. The rebels were defending the city walls whilst simultaneously attacking Lady Nicola's castle inside them.

William gathered what forces he could and marched from Newark to relieve Lady Nicola's siege, making a wide detour to approach Lincoln from the northwest, at the top of the incline where the city sloped steeply down to the river Witham and the marshy ground beyond the southern gate. William could easily get his troops into the castle by its external postern gate to augment Lady Nicola's forces, but that would not lift the siege. The royalists had about 600 knights and, with Lady Nicola's forces inside the castle, upwards of 1,000 foot soldiers and archers. He somehow had to outflank the rebels inside the city, not least because they outnumbered his own force by about two-to-one. The city's northern gate – Newport Arch[5] – was the obvious entrance point, but that was what the rebels expected. Instead, a disused Norman west gate (at about '10 o'clock') in between the castle and the north gate had long been blocked with rubble and masonry. This was William's way in. Before dawn on Saturday May 20th the royalist forces moved within range of Lincoln's walls.

Ranulf of Chester set up a diversionary attack on the north gate while Lady Nicola's archers inside the castle, augmented by William's own crossbowmen, released torrents of bolts at the rebels in Lincoln's streets below, and William's engineers worked to remove enough rubble to open a passage through the old west gate. By noon it was clear enough to be a viable entrance and William – now seventy – led his knights to attack through it. He famously set off, forgetting to don his helmet and a squire had to gallop to him to remind the Earl to put it on. But he led them through the west gate, just where the famous *Strugglers Inn* pub now stands, charging east along the modern-day Westgate Street with the castle walls along their right flank, then turning ninety degrees south, still skirting the castle onto modern-day Danesgate and Bailgate, careering down Steep Hill between the castle and the Cathedral. It was a classic cavalry hit on fractured infantry – unstoppable and devastating. Some rebels made a tough stand within the courtyard in front of the Cathedral, but by then Ranulf's forces were through the north gate and added their weight in a second hammer blow. On down the hill the royalists swept, on and down modern-day High Street towards the river. There may have been another brief stand around the foot of Steep Hill. But it became a complete rout when fleeing rebel troops congested around the Stonebow Arch (part of the Guildhall today) in a bid to escape over the bridge and into the countryside to

---

5. Newport Arch is a 3rd Century gateway into Lincoln, reputedly the oldest such arch in Britain still used by traffic.

the south. History has no real idea of the casualties in either camp. But this was no tournament, and all the accounts agree that it was a vicious one-sided slaughter in a battle the royalists simply had to win.[6]

Within two weeks of the battle, more than sixty rebel nobles had returned to the royalist camp and lined up behind William's leadership. The outcome at Lincoln was devastating for Prince Louis, besieging Dover. But the royalists were still in poor shape to fight a long war. The most realistic objective was to remove the French prince from England. In August reinforcements for Prince Louis set sail from Calais, under the command of Eustace the Monk – famously, the cleric turned pirate. William was down at the coast, having hastily assembled a makeshift fleet, crewed by many of his erstwhile sergeants. On 24th August the French fleet was intercepted and efficiently destroyed off Sandwich, while William Marshal watched from the clifftops. At the end of the month William's forces surrounded Louis and his men occupying London, and by September he was able courteously to escort Prince Louis from London to Dover where the Capetian prince took ship for France, never to return.

It was over. The Angevin empire was gone, but the royal dynasty would survive in Henry III, and it would henceforth be based on the kingdom of England and Ireland. An English political identity would emerge from it. William Marshal continued as guardian of the realm until 1219, shoring up the finances as best he could; getting the Scots to relinquish their wartime gains in the northern shires, working less successfully to subdue Welsh rebellion, and always doing what he could alongside the papal legate to consolidate the loyalty of the barons and smooth the path of Henry III towards adulthood.

At the age of seventy-two William's body was failing though his mind remained fully active on state affairs until the very end. Towards his last days he was surrounded by his family at his home in Caversham, and attended by his closest knights. He held an entirely personal conversation with the young King. His good friend Aimery of St Maur, master of the Templars in England, travelled to Caversham to admit William to the Order of the Knights Templar. And he spent his final hours on 14th May 1219 with his wife, sons and daughters and the Abbot of Notley around his bedside.

Two years to the day after the Battle of Lincoln, on 20th May 1219, he was laid to rest in the beautiful Temple Church, which now lies just down a little ally off modern Fleet Street. He was incommoded somewhat by the *Luftwaffe* in 1941, but otherwise has lain peacefully there alongside two of his sons and Aimery St Maur. And an easily-overlooked statue of him, just on the left above the royal throne, stands in the House of Lords. His left-hand rests on the pommel of his sword. In his right hand he holds a copy of Magna Carta – revised and re-issued several times in the years following, until it became one of the foundations of modern democracy. He looks down on the monarch in silent insistence that they don't forget it. In a tumultuous warrior life, he rose to command when it really mattered and probably did more than any other single person to bring it about.

---

6. Much of Lincoln had become a pro-Louis VIII city and was therefore well-plundered afterwards, creating the epithet that the battle was 'Lincoln Fair'.

Edward I – 'hammer of the Scots'

Few English kings commanded armies as frequently, as personally, or for as long, as Edward I during his sixty-eight-year life. For most people, Edward I represents the classic medieval English monarch – a leader in war, builder of monumental castles and subsequently dubbed 'hammer of the Scots'. He was also styled the 'English Justinian' who translated a great deal of existing law into formal statutes. As his reign progressed, he convened more and bigger Parliaments until, by the time of his death in 1307, Parliament had become an enduring part of English government.

For some of his contemporaries, he was the greatest Christian king of his European generation; 'a great and terrible king…a flower of chivalry'. For others, he was cruel, driven by rage and vengeance who, in the words of a Scottish chronicler, 'troubled the whole world with his wickedness'. In truth, he was a more complex character than many a Plantagenet king. And since he reigned for thirty-four years and, with only brief interludes, was fighting wars for thirty of them, it is hardly surprising that he had different and changing personas as both commander and king.

Edward I is also credited as the monarch who partly created, and certainly represented, a growing identity of Englishness within Britain during the late thirteenth century. Between the reign of his father, Henry III, and his son and grandson, Edward II and Edward III, there was a sea change in English political identity that revolved to a significant extent around Edward I's wars. He bequeathed a legion of troubles to his successors; but they were distinctly English troubles. It has often been observed that the nation of England, and subsequently the nation of Britain, were both overwhelmingly forged by war. This was certainly true of the thirteenth and fourteenth centuries. Whatever the personal character of the man, Edward I's role as a military commander had an effect greater than most commanders in British history, for good and bad, on the underlying society over which he presided.

The long reign of Edward's father, Henry III, was characterised by naivety and genuine foolishness. Disastrous campaigns in France to regain the old Angevin territories left Henry III with little more than a reputation for military incompetence. At home, his tax demands, subservience to the Pope, his corruption and abuse of government and his favourites from Poitou, not to mention his deeply unpopular foreign queen, Eleanor of Provence and her Savoyard cronies, all coalesced into another revolt of the nobles in 1258, not unlike that which had confronted his own father, King John, less than half a century earlier.

This was the increasingly fraught reign into which Edward was born in 1239. His sixteen-year-old mother, Queen Eleanor, reputedly beautiful and doted on by Henry

III, gave birth to Edward in the Palace of Westminster – an interesting portent for the future. He grew into an unusually tall man, at 6ft 2in, hence his nickname 'Edward Longshanks'. He was naturally strong. He had a commanding presence and an incisive manner of speaking. He also had a way of thinking pragmatically when faced with difficult political – and personal – choices. He seemed to have all the best attributes for a national commander in that age. He also absorbed, and then enlarged, a highly romantic self-image. His father had named him Edward in reverence to the sainted Edward the Confessor – still an important figure in the Plantagenet dynasty's constant search for legitimacy.

Edward himself was quite capable of unsaintly rages – 'much given to swearing', it was said – alongside personal cruelty. But he was also very taken with contemporary romantic notions of chivalry. He revelled in the Arthurian legend and drew constant inspiration from what most thirteenth century people took as legitimate history. Geoffrey of Monmouth's, *History of the Kings of Britain*, written in the 1130s, was an elaborate confection of little fact and much myth that painted the peoples of these islands as a noble race that traced its ancestry (just like Virgil's Romans) to the fall of Troy. Their successors, like the ancient King Lud, King Leil, Old King Cole, and above all, King Arthur, were the founders of a Britain that enthusiasts took as the alternative – heroic – model for the troubled and lawless society they saw around them.[1] Like the vast majority of his contemporaries, Edward had no doubt about Arthur's place in history, conveniently glossing over the fact that Arthur was said to have fought to preserve Romano-Britain against Anglo-Saxon invaders. Edward was an avid follower of the Arthurian stories of chivalry. He constructed his own version of the Round Table – now hanging on the wall of Winchester's Great Hall – and in 1278 he paid homage to his great Arthurian predecessor at Glastonbury, re-interring King Arthur's bones and those of Queen Guinevere amid elaborate ceremonies in a new tomb he had specially designed and which became the model for his own – which these days sits in front of Edward the Confessor's shrine in Westminster Abbey. His is a direct imitation of Arthur's mysterious, largely plain marble tomb.[2]

As a young man Edward constantly clashed with his father. Henry III devolved extensive lands on him around the time of young Edward's marriage, at the age of fifteen, to the thirteen-year-old Eleanor of Castille. His father even made him Duke of Gascony – territory roughly consistent with the old Aquitaine that was so central to the Angevins. But his father would not allow him personal discretion to run any

---

1. King Lud was thought to be a Trinovante chieftain who founded London and whose grave was even marked by Ludgate. King Leil was supposedly an ancient King of Briton who founded Carlisle. 'Old' King Cole was asserted by Geoffrey of Monmouth – reproducing a story from Henry of Huntingdon – to be the grandfather of the Roman emperor, Constantine the Great. At least it chimed with the pleasing notion that the ancient Britons were refugees from Troy.
2. It is, of course, all based on a series of hoaxes. King Arthur never existed – at least not in a single individual – and his bones, tombs, courts and kingdoms were all cheap fakes. The tomb that Edward I had constructed for Arthur and Guinevere's re-burial sadly did not survive the dissolution of the monasteries in the sixteenth century – else with modern science we might have known something about the two humble peasants who presumably lay inside it.

of these extensive territories independently. Henry III was desperate to hold onto Gascony. It was the last remnant of the royal inheritance in France after King John had managed to lose most of it. He cared deeply that French kings should not absorb it. But Henry III conducted a typically unsuccessful campaign in Gascony in 1254 against French encroachment and again – this time alongside his son – in 1259. These were salutary lessons for Edward in the dangers of casual military thinking. In 1256 he had accompanied his father on an abortive expedition into Gwynedd in Wales to suppress Llywelyn ap Gruffydd and that must have demonstrated to him the importance of getting the right logistics in place before military expeditions began. He observed at first hand his father's military failures – the father who constantly thwarted and enraged him. Meanwhile, in between these campaigns he acted like many a frustrated princeling heir – behaving badly, sometimes very badly, with his retinue of two hundred or more knights in a dissolute life punctuated by the occasional distractions of continental tournaments.

Edward's first major statesmanship challenge came in 1258 with the family crisis and the intermittent civil war which then spanned the next seven years.

On 30th April of that year a group of knights and barons – in armour – marched in on Henry III as the King sat in Westminster Hall with Edward standing beside him. The nobles flatly demanded some disagreeable reforms and the expulsion of foreign cronies from the Court. More than this, they demanded a new Magna Carta, involving regular parliaments, a permanent 'King's Council' of twenty-four to guide him, and some control over future appointments. These were huge demands; a scheme of government that would not actually arrive for another four hundred years. But the royal family were in no position to argue. The demands were enshrined first in the Provisions of Oxford in 1258 and then again in the Provisions of Westminster in 1259. Henry III had no choice but acquiesce, but schemed constantly to evade the Provisions. A civil war became inevitable. It broke out in 1264. Simon de Montfort, the King's brother-in-law, emerging to lead the rebellious nobles against the royal family and their Savoyard and Lusignan associates in an outright struggle for control of the crown.

Edward was frankly equivocal during these troubled years, hopping in and out of court matters between France, England and some attractive continental tournaments. Given his dysfunctional father, Edward was a disciple of the need for reform and a good nephew to his charismatic uncle, Simon de Montfort – who constantly preached reform, albeit in draconian and brutal terms. But Edward was also naturally sympathetic to his other Lusignan half uncles – even to many of the Queen's Savoyard cronies – and most of all to a troubling sense that royal legitimacy was paramount, even in the case of Henry III.

Edward first backed his royalist Lusignan uncles, then in 1260 flirted with outright revolt against his father alongside Simon de Montfort's 'reformers', but then reconciled with his father. The following year he did the same again, returning from France to align with de Montfort, before yet again standing alongside his father. By the time unrestricted fighting began in 1264 Edward had evidently made his choice. He realised that he was better served, and probably more reconciled, in supporting his father and his king.

Already, by 1263, the crisis was so severe that Henry III and Queen Eleanor had found themselves trapped in the Tower of London, surrounded by anti-royalist, anti-foreigner mobs. Edward had scandalously raided the considerable coffers of the Templars just nearby and dashed off to Windsor to establish a strongpoint. Queen Eleanor set out by boat from the Tower to join him but was pelted by Londoners as she tried to pass under London Bridge. With her life in danger, she hastily withdrew to the Bishop of London's palace. This incident – comical and serious – seemed to have a lasting effect on Edward's lifelong and heartfelt hostility to any acts of *lese majeste*.

A helter-skelter campaign developed into the spring of 1264, the royalists gathering power as it progressed. Edward joined his father in a showdown against de Montfort on 14th May at the battle of Lewes in Sussex. By then, the royalists considerably outnumbered de Montfort's forces. De Montfort was acting in desperation. Nevertheless, Lewes was a disaster for the royalists, largely due to Edward's own actions. Edward commanded forces on the right of the royalist line, his uncle Richard of Cornwall in the centre, Henry III on the left. De Montfort had seized the higher ground in a surprise night deployment and the large royalist forces had to arrange themselves quickly from the positions they had awoken in.

Edward's own cavalry charge against de Montford's left wing was brilliantly successful, as was his own murderous presence leading it. They were quickly into de Montford's infantry – mainly Londoners whom Edward now despised. Edward's cavalry pursued them mercilessly, leaving the royalist right wing wide open. De Montfort was far too good a commander to ignore the opportunity, and by the time Edward returned toward Lewes in mid-morning, he suddenly had to fight for his own life, his uncle had been captured, and Henry III had barricaded himself inside Lewes Priory. It was a miserable defeat – mainly Edward's fault – that left de Montfort to dictate his own terms.

England now had a taste of de Montfort's reformist rule. The first recognisably modern English parliament met in January 1265 near Kenilworth Castle. De Montfort led a council of fifteen, set above the King's Council of twenty-four, and Henry III was under house arrest while Edward was kept hostage first at Wallingford and then in Hereford. But De Montfort had no natural legitimacy other than his own leadership of the revolt, and his autocratic parliamentarianism became quickly unpopular with the aristocratic rebels he had recently led.

In May 1265 Edward escaped from his minders in Hereford through outrageous trickery and the war was on again. Only fifteen months after Lewes, Edward led a bold cavalry dash overnight to catch many of de Montfort's infantry napping in the town of Kenilworth – rather than inside the castle where they should have been. De Montfort was on his way from the south to try to unite with his Kenilworth forces. But Edward then pushed his men ruthlessly south-west for thirty miles and used subterfuge to trap de Montfort at Evesham in the loop of the river Avon. The only escape for de Montfort was to the north; and there Edward's forces, at least three times larger, were waiting.

There was to be no chivalry at Evesham. Edward made clear that no quarter would be given to anyone, and a special squad of a dozen knights was tasked to get to de Montfort quickly and kill him outright. In the event, it was Roger Mortimer who delivered the blow before de Montfort was hacked to pieces. The casual killing went on through the afternoon into the streets of Evesham itself.

Edward I is most associated in the popular mind with his later campaigns in Wales and Scotland. But it was the decade after Evesham that really made him the sort of commander, and king, that he became. He had finally committed himself unequivocally to legitimate kingship. After the disaster of Lewes he had taken command at Kenilworth and Evesham and conducted operations with single-minded clarity. He spent two years in a mopping up campaign; by turns magnanimous, as he followed his own instincts, but also ruthlessly complicit with Henry III's unwise approach to disinherit all de Montfort's followers – a policy which undoubtedly kept rebellion alive in centres as far apart as Alnwick, Lincoln, London and Ely.

Then in 1268 Edward made the grand gesture and 'took the cross', as the Pope had been requesting Henry III to do for some years. Edward raised the money for a small force of knights and followers – perhaps 1,000 in all – to go to the Holy Land as part of what was characterised as the Ninth, or 'Lord Edward's' Crusade. As always, after much wrangling between French and English crusaders and diversions elsewhere in the Mediterranean, he finally arrived with his force in 1271 to try to lift the siege of Acre, by then the only significant crusader outpost left in the struggle to preserve the Kingdom of Jerusalem.

Edward was now the warrior prince, heir to a powerful kingdom, a veritable ball of energy, the personification of chivalry, fighting the good fight in lands of huge symbolic importance to medieval Europe. He strengthened the defences of Acre and led raids against Mamluk forces, distinguishing himself in some of the fighting. His numbers, however, were far too small to make much difference to Acre's plight, faced as it was by multitudes of Mamluk warriors. But Edward had a grand strategy. He got reinforcements from England and Cyprus, and he aimed to combine with the Mongol forces in the Il-Khanate (the Persian province of the Mongol empire) then ruled by Abaqa Khan, great-grandson of Genghis Khan. Edward's emissaries persuaded Abaqa Khan to send horsemen southwards against the Mamluks while the crusaders would strike out east from the coast.[3] Large forces of Mongol horsemen did in fact come as far south as Aleppo, but they then withdrew as the Mamluks geared up to confront them. Simultaneously, Edward's grand expedition eastwards was showy and destructive but failed to capture its main objective – Qaqun – and was forced to withdraw back to Acre.

Given this setback, Acre's defenders, in May 1272, negotiated a long truce with Mamluk Sultan Baybars I. This ten-year truce enraged Edward. He regarded it as a breach of sacred faith. Within his own quarters he was attacked and seriously wounded

---

3. While Europe fretted over successive crusades in the near east, the greatest geopolitical changes of the age that were to affect Europe were occasioned by the rise and astonishingly rapid conquests of the Mongol armies from the Russian steppes.

in a stabbing by a Muslim assassin. In September, when he had recovered sufficiently from the wound, he decided it was pointless to continue and began a circuitous journey back to England.

In reality, he had accomplished next to nothing on crusade. Yet it had as profound an effect on him as on his international reputation. He developed skills in logistics and tactical campaigning, operating over large areas. He moulded a band of brother warriors around him who were all infused with the same spiritual mystique of crusader knights. Notwithstanding the truce, he had also shown political skill and at least seemed to have a grand strategy to win back the Holy Land. He was *primus inter pares* among crusading leaders and his personal reputation stood as high an anyone's in Christendom.

The climax came when news reached him in Sicily, during his protracted journey home, that Henry III had died. At the age of thirty-three his moment had finally arrived. Yet Edward's elevation to the throne was so assured that he didn't hurry back. In fact, it was another eighteen months before he arrived at Westminster, to be widely acclaimed as the great crusader and joyfully crowned as England's next monarch.

As King Edward I he subsequently fought major and prolonged campaigns in Wales, Scotland and Flanders (to take French pressure off Gascony). Yet the campaign he always wanted to fight was to return to the Holy Land at the head of a united force of Christendom to win back the Kingdom of Jerusalem. This is how he now saw himself; the powerful warrior king, the great European strategist, and the embodiment of Christian chivalry. Yet this self-image also had the effect of drawing him into three expensive wars – two of which he didn't need to fight – and rendering his grand crusader project no more than an ever more distant dream.

Initially, he worked hard to establish his own distinctive kingship after Henry III's miserable later years. He pushed back at all the recent encroachments on crown rights. He reinforced the Tower, for example, inserting his own sheriffs at Guildhall and outlawing many of the Guilds' restrictive practices. He was, from the first, a reformer against much of the crony corruption and maladministration that had taken hold across England. He made himself popular by trying to formalise common law and property rights and getting 'oral rights' either written down or written off. He put royal claims and demands into statutes that went through more frequent Parliaments, rather than merely into royal writs. For over fifteen years he ruled with growing administrative ability, both centralising and yet legitimising power through his own person, hence the sobriquet that he was the 'English Justinian'.

This was also the period in which he embarked on two Welsh campaigns that were, for him, unavoidable. The first, in 1276, had been coming for some time. Llywelyn ap Gruffydd had accepted Henry III's overlordship of Wales and agreed to pay regular tributes in return for being acknowledged by the English as Prince in Wales. But the regular payments had dried up and the English Marcher Lords were increasingly involved in territorial clashes along the Welsh Marches. Llywelyn refused to attend Edward's court in Chester to pay homage, and even arranged to marry the daughter of Simon de Montfort – a young woman who was Edward's own cousin. Edward would not allow the English crown to be disrespected in such ways. He had the bride's ship intercepted off the Scilly Isles on its way from France to Wales and kept his cousin under house arrest in Windsor. And he made preparations for the conquest of Wales which – unless Llywelyn both paid homage and paid up – he now regarded as unavoidable.

By January 1277 he had assembled a large force at Chester and another at Worcester and Carmarthen. He entrusted the campaign to some of his band of brothers – Roger Mortimer, William de Beauchamp, Roger Clifford, Otto de Grandson, John de Vesey – all veteran crusaders. While they pushed into Welsh territory Edward went on a pilgrimage through the shrines of East Anglia. And while he contemplated his Christian destiny, he kept a close eye on all the weapons and transports he was even then ordering to the Welsh border for the full campaign. It began in earnest during July when he resumed command with impressive forces – even thirty-five ships sent from Dover and Gascony to Chester to bring war-making and building materials to the campaign. So it was that Edward, fighting against Llywelyn's guerrilla forces, began his determined campaign to create the castles and strongpoints that would facilitate his grinding conquest of Wales. His victory was as much a feat of military engineering as fighting and when Edward's forces occupied Anglesey – the Welsh granary – in September, Llywelyn was immediately forced to settle. The King let Llywelyn keep some of Gwynedd and reoccupy Anglesey (so long as he paid annual rent for it). And he was slyly magnanimous, even financing Llywelyn's adjourned wedding to his cousin, a year later.

English demands made the Welsh situation unstable, however, and in 1282 Llywelyn's younger brother, Dafydd, led a popular uprising that Llywelyn felt obliged to follow. In 1282–83 Edward conducted yet another campaign, mirroring the first. Llywelyn was killed in a skirmish. His brother Dafydd, the last independent Prince of Wales, was eventually captured, found guilty of a new charge called 'high treason' – in light of open rebellion – and then hung, drawn and quartered for it in 1283 at Shrewsbury.[4] The campaign laid down some truly monumental castles to establish English strong points which still stand magnificently at sites such as Harlech, Conwy, Caernarfon, and then later at Beaumaris. The castles were the focus of deliberate English settler colonisation around them, from which the Welsh were excluded. It was all testament that Wales would henceforth come under direct – and unchallengeable – English rule.

The campaign left Edward, without any doubt, as an impressive king in matters of both war and peace. European princes looked to him as a power broker and a natural leader within Christian Europe. He appeared sincerely pious and observed all the religious and kingly rituals. He was personally tough on his sons, though indulgent to his daughters. He put his daughter Mary of Woodstock into holy orders at Amesbury Priory, but ensured she had a generous clothing and wine allowance and regularly paid her considerable gambling debts. He worked assiduously on domestic matters, spent time in Gascony and tried seriously to raise enough money via Papal arrangements to finance the great crusade he assumed to be his real God-given destiny.

---

4. Dafydd ap Gruffydd was the first named individual in Britain to be executed in this way.

It all began to go wrong in 1290. Eleanor of Castille, with whom he had fourteen children, died near Lincoln. Though she was thoroughly unpopular in the country, Edward was devastated and severely depressed to lose her.[5] His domestic reforms were starting to run out of steam and his ability to raise the money he needed was being heavily circumscribed. Over the next seventeen years his military instincts began steadily to override his otherwise good political judgement.

He did not need, nor did he originally intend, to invade Scotland. For Edward, Wales was a barbaric territory that was all the better for being colonised. But he saw Scotland as a civilized country within the European mainstream and there was no need to try to incorporate it if he could have peaceful relations with Scottish kings. But he was drawn into the problem of the Scottish succession. King Alexander III of Scotland had died in a riding accident in 1286. It led to a bitter succession contest in Scotland between John Balliol and Robert Bruce. Edward was asked to arbitrate in a dispute that had begun with fourteen different claimants to the throne. He had previously arranged, cannily, for Alexander's little three-year-old granddaughter, living in Norway, to marry his own six-year-old son. It was a brilliant piece of dynastic politics that might, in due course, have peacefully united the royal families of England and Scotland three centuries earlier than subsequently happened. But in the fateful year 1290 the little girl died on the voyage to Scotland. So now Edward had to choose. In a series of high legal debates – the 'great cause' as it was known – Edward then swung round to back John Balliol, Lord of Galloway, for the succession, whilst requiring him to do homage and recognise Edward as his feudal overlord on behalf of Scotland. He wanted Balliol as a puppet king. This high-handedness was partly driven by his increasing need for authority – and troops – in his attempts to hold off French claims in Gascony, which were rapidly moving towards another war.

Edward's efforts to hang onto Gascony, while fighting for what he now regarded as his royal due north of the border, became completely absorbed in a series of military campaigns that dominated the rest of his reign. It increased the powers of parliament – and the City of London – as he tried to raise ever greater sums for his war chest. And it eventually reduced him to an angry invalid raging against the collapse of his body when the army needed his commanding presence.

He made repeated attempts to form anti-French alliances with European princes but could never create a really useful military coalition from them. His military needs led him to recruit criminals into his army. He made increasing tax demands on all his territories while his credit arrangements with Italian bankers all but collapsed. Ireland was bled dry for supplies. After already harsh measures to extract more money from the Jewish community, he cravenly expelled all the Jews from England in 1290

---

5. Over some two weeks her body was brought in procession from Lincoln to Westminster Abbey, and twelve stone and marble monuments, surmounted by a cross, were constructed at each of the places where the royal party stopped overnight. The three least grand of these monuments – nevertheless impressive – still stand at Geddington, Hardingstone and Waltham Cross. The last stop on the journey in London was marked by the grandest of the twelve monuments, in a place henceforth known as Charing Cross. A Victorian replica of an 'Eleanor Cross' now stands in front of the mainline station there.

to satisfy Parliamentarians who were thereby relieved of their outstanding debts to Jewish financiers, and duly granted him a whopping tax for his proposed holy crusade.

But the treasure he was accumulating for crusades was spent instead on simultaneous military commitments to meet what emerged as an unsustainable three-front strategic challenge. Philip IV of France unsubtly tricked him – possibly turned his fifty-four-year-old head with the prospect of marriage to Margaret, his teenage sister – and confiscated Gascony. In 1294 Edward went to war with France to retrieve it. The crusade would have to wait. But a serious revolt in Wales then forced Gascony to wait while he deployed his available forces, yet again, in a three-axis thrust into the territory to suppress revolt and restore Caernarfon, which had fallen. It was, as ever, a short but tough campaign. Then in 1295 what became the 'auld alliance' between France and Scotland was born at the Treaty of Paris, and a two-front problem took real shape before him. The Scots crossed the Tweed and began destructive raiding into Northumberland.

French forces were already attacking the south coast. In August 1295, Dover was raided and burned, then Winchelsea and Hythe. The south of England went into invasion fever. But Edward concentrated on Scotland. In 1296 he moved against Berwick-on-Tweed with a huge army, destroyed it and then went on to a decisive victory over the Scots at Dunbar, moving and conquering as far north as Elgin on the Moray Firth. By the end of the year Balliol was captured and Edward thenceforth ruled the country directly from Berwick.

Part of his forces were already, belatedly, back in Gascony from early 1296 under the command of his brother, who was clearly bogged down. Brother Edmund died on campaign and Edward was by then haemorrhaging money on both fronts. He tried to intimidate the aristocracy and the church to stump up funds; but he was also failing to cajole most of his nobles to fight for him in a territory as far away as Gascony – an interesting indication of their evolving loyalty. He ordered them, raged against them, promised them, almost humiliated himself before them on a dais outside Westminster Hall in an unprecedented public meeting. In the end, Edward was saved from imminent civil war when news arrived that his forces in Scotland had been heavily defeated at Stirling Bridge by two obscure nobles called Andrew Murray and William Wallace. The aristocracy rallied to the King, another version of Magna Carta was devised, and Edward, already landed in Flanders to campaign against France, raged that he had to give so much for the loyalty he felt was merely his due.

The Scottish revolt grew and spilled over into a huge expedition led by Wallace to strip Northumbria and Cumbria of as much wealth as his forces could carry away. Edward had no choice but to accept a truce in France so as to redeploy his main forces against Wallace. In 1297 he led another massive force into Scotland, defeating Wallace (who escaped) at Falkirk and was drawn into an indecisive campaign that only exposed the brittle loyalty of his military magnates. He withdrew for the time being. Edward managed a political settlement over Gascony when the Pope's arbitration found in his favour. He finally married Philip's teenage sister, and then prepared for an impulsive winter campaign against the Scots in November 1299. But Edward's political instincts were now very wayward. His domestic support was collapsing again; he couldn't garner sufficient forces until he had been seen to keep some of his earlier promises to his nobles. And while he delayed into 1300, English footholds in Scotland – like the critical Stirling Castle – were falling.

In summer 1300 he launched a new invasion from Carlisle but was immediately facing a classic guerrilla war where it was impossible to draw the enemy into another Dunbar or Falkirk. Scottish forces had learned some hard lessons. Edward's campaign ground to a halt; his temper as short as his money and his numbers. He was forced to agree a brief truce with the Scottish rebels whom he utterly despised.

In 1301 he tried again, attempting a pincer movement from both Berwick and Carlisle, but didn't quite manage to close the circle north of Glasgow. He nevertheless struck out for Stirling but was held, within sight of the besieged castle itself, for lack of supplies and money to pay his soldiers. But he managed to keep his weakened forces camped in Scotland and despite losses in Selkirk and Roslin launched yet another offensive in 1303 – leaving Stirling Castle in enemy hands and pushing directly north, yet again as far as the Moray Firth and Kinloss. But Scottish forces behind him were attacking in central Scotland, through the borders and into Cumbria. It was an attritional stalemate.

Nevertheless, Edward's dogged persistence paid off in 1305. For separate diplomatic reasons both Philip of France and the Pope dropped their support for the Scots and, in a state of exhaustion only a little worse than that of their English (and Irish) adversaries, Scottish leaders capitulated. A fairly magnanimous settlement was agreed for them, Stirling Castle was subjected to the earliest recorded use of gunpowder in Britain as it was finally taken, thanks also to a massive trebuchet named 'Warwolf' (that Edward was determined to test). And William Wallace was handed over by his countrymen to be tried in Westminster Hall, executed and quartered, with his limbs being distributed between Newcastle, Berwick, Sterling and Perth, his head, of course, adorning London Bridge.

At his Christmas court in 1305–6 Edward I was King supreme in England, Wales and Scotland. He had (somewhat luckily) retained Gascony regardless of his military campaigning. At sixty-seven he had fathered a second child with Queen Margaret. But impressive as all this seemed, and much as England had gained through his reign, it did not represent stability for the kingdom.

In February 1306 Robert Bruce, grandson of the Robert Bruce who had claimed the throne when Edward found for John Balliol, broke his pledge to Edward. This second Robert Bruce murdered the Guardian of Scotland, was excommunicated by the Pope but nevertheless had himself crowned at Scone as King Robert I of Scotland. He was to have a turbulent but spectacular military career against the English that places him in history as the king who led the 'first Scottish war of independence', the turning point of which was at Bannockburn in 1314.

But for Edward, the emergence of King Robert I in 1306 was a complete outrage. He became obsessed not just with restoration but cruel vengeance. Yet another big campaign was put in hand. By now, however, the King was being carried around in a litter. His English forces, led instead by Edward Prince of Wales, campaigned initially with some success while, at the King's orders, no mercy was shown to any Scottish rebels.[6] And though Robert I kept losing battles, his cause was steadily gaining hearts and minds as a result. The English cause in Scotland was suddenly slipping away, while English government and its finances were again tipping towards chaos.

Now sixty-eight and gravely ill, the King made slow progress from Westminster as far as Hexham and thence to Carlisle. He had developed dysentery, but still he judged his own presence was essential and he painfully mounted a horse, leading forces westwards out of Carlisle to join the campaign. But after ten days they had only advanced six miles and at the Burgh Marshes in Cumbria, on the Solway Firth, he died on 7th July 1307.

Edward I had taken English kingship to new levels of administration, international prominence and conquest. But after 1290 his reign began to spin out of control and his strategically unsuccessful Scottish wars came to define much of his legacy. As modern writers have observed, Edward was not 'hammer of the Scots' so much as hammered *by* the Scots, in open-ended guerrilla campaigns that would be well-understood by modern twenty-first century commanders. On the other hand, if he didn't prevail in his later wars, he didn't lose them either, and he avoided the opprobrium that attached to Henry III or King John. In an era when kings were expected to be leaders in war, his personal standing and royal legitimacy were – and remain – correspondingly high.

Perhaps, through his iron will and determination, he shaped history. Or perhaps he was the victim of it. Fate was cruel to him in 1290. He provoked the 'Scottish wars of independence' and his wars with Scotland and France created the two-front dynamic that thirty years later underlay the 'Hundred Years War' which his feckless son and then his fierce grandson and great-grandson all walked into. Until very near the end, Edward was still talking about leading the grand crusade to recover Jerusalem. It was said by some that on his deathbed he requested his heart be carried to the Holy Land. It was a delusion that said much about the 'great and terrible' king who was ultimately unable to escape from his own wars. His successors all lived with the consequences.

---

6. The Prince of Wales was to succeed his father as Edward II. His reign was regarded as a disaster, but it appears he was no mean fighter and a competent enough military leader.

Edward III – warrior King

Edward III was the first English king – arguably since King Harold II in Saxon times – to create a national sense that the English were fighting their enemies in their own defence and for the sake of their own country and society. After the incessant wars of his grandfather Edward I, and the disastrous reign of his deposed and murdered father, Edward II, this Edward emerged as a genuine national leader; a celebrated warrior king, successful in battle, courtly and charismatic, and an inspired military commander. He was the darling of subsequent historians who so liked to describe 'our island story' as if it were a narrative of ever-growing British consciousness and accumulating greatness. Edward III certainly fits the picture. He ruled for fifty years and made diminutive England one of the greatest military powers in Europe. Over thirty years he built an empire of conquest against France. But then lost it all in less than five – and lived long enough to see the denouement for himself.

Unlike his grandfather, Edward III was not a complicated man. He lived for war and he was very good at it. But he was not very good, and nor were those around him, at thinking about what war was for; what he imagined it would achieve for him or for England. These, of course, are modern perspectives. For most among the medieval elites, war was its own reward – expressions of masculine nobility, status and chivalry and a means to greater wealth and power. This was even true – at least in matters of wealth – to increasing numbers of those lesser men who fought alongside their elite leaders. Even the meanest English bowman or foot soldier might hope to return from Edward III's grand campaigns all the richer for the fighting.

Still, we might have expected so grand a king as Edward III and his famous eldest son, Edward Prince of Wales – the 'Black Prince' – to have shown a better grasp of some of the strategic fundamentals if they were prepared to fight so incessantly for conquests they would always struggle to retain. In 1337 Edward III drifted into what history now characterises as the 'Hundred Years War' between England and France. It lasted until 1453. This pitted England's six million people into open-ended conflict against the greater territory of an immensely richer society of eighteen to twenty-one million people, making demands on the French aristocracy, not to mention its royal family, that could never ultimately have been met.

The Hundred Years War rumbled on through the fourteenth and fifteenth centuries and is remembered in popular British history chiefly for the three great English victories at Crecy, Poitiers and then Agincourt; commanded respectively by Edward III, the Black Prince, and Henry V – without much reference to the fact that France eventually triumphed in those 116 years of cross-channel conflict. These were undoubtedly great military victories, but all three of them were forced on English and Welsh troops who had got themselves trapped on military expeditions with no achievable, or sometimes even clear, strategic aims. They were all last-ditch escapes in defensive actions which followed a remarkably similar pattern on their respective battlefields. Of the three, Edward III's victory at Crecy was the greatest, since it was the first to display the innovation that subsequent commanders adopted, and it set up the decade of high military triumph for Edward III that brought him the accolades which contemporaries were all too ready to bestow. But Edward effectively squandered his battlefield successes through lack of interest or understanding of the international politics surrounding them.

There is, though, a reasonable point in his defence. In an era of all-embracing Christianity following the end of the 'Holy Land Crusades' (there were many subsequent crusades in different lands) the concept of a holy and just war remained very strong throughout European society. The influential Thomas Aquinas in the late thirteenth century had drawn extensively on St Augustine's early fifth century philosophy which defined the conditions under which wars could be fought justly for the sake of peace and holiness. More than that, it was a key legal principle in the Middle Ages that only a sovereign could authorise a just war; and conversely, any war pursued by a sovereign must, by definition, also be just. 'It was the criterion by which public war was distinguished from mere criminal violence', says historian Jonathan Sumption. The Plantagenets' dynastic claims against French kings were therefore matters of justice in themselves and thus legitimate interests for the rest of the country. Military leaders throughout the Hundred Years War would, on the eve of battle, submit themselves to the will of the Lord, and God would decide the outcome. It was a substitute for what modern analysts might call grand strategy. Kings and princes went to great lengths to assert their religious justification for war. If God then decided the outcome, 'might' was automatically 'right' and whatever flowed from that was evidently His will. It was, admittedly, easier than making difficult strategic choices, particularly during the fourteenth century when England's tactical and technical superiority in military affairs allowed it to go consistently onto the offensive. And for decades, battlefield success and faith in the divine judgement disguised England's foolhardiness in taking on a neighbouring power three or four times bigger in a struggle for ultimate control. But Edward III, and the sixty or so noble English families who loyally followed him to pursue God's arbitration in the matter of the Hundred Years War, might have been better served by thinking it through more carefully. They certainly had plenty of time to consider.

Edward III was born in 1312 at Windsor Castle in the middle of the chronic instability of his father's reign. As the male heir to Edward II, his father had him created Earl of Chester when he was only twelve in an attempt to bolster the monarchy against baronial opposition. In 1325 he was sent to France, in lieu of the King, to perform homage to Charles IV of France for the Duchy of Aquitaine. It would prove a fateful trip. Aquitaine was held by kings of England in their personal capacity as peers of France and it was a permanent source of instability between the two kingdoms. France had invaded Aquitaine in 1323. Edward's mother, Queen Isabella, had already arrived in France, apparently to mediate over the territory. But when Edward arrived, he found himself immediately in the midst of extraordinary family politics. Far from mediating, Isabella was conspiring against her husband with the exiled Roger Mortimer, whose predecessor had struck the first blow against Simon de Montford at the battle of Evesham on behalf of Edward's royal grandfather. Mortimer was Iabella's lover. It was clear that a usurping invasion of England was being planned by the Queen and Mortimer, using young Edward as their claim to legitimacy.

At the age of thirteen Edward presumably had no choice but to go along with it. In 1326 the invasion took place and provoked an immediate revolt against Edward II who was summarily imprisoned in Kenilworth Castle. In January 1327 Parliament agreed to depose him in favour of young Edward who was immediately crowned Edward III in Westminster Abby. The ex-King died – evidently murdered – in September that year.

The Isabella/Mortimer regime proved as dysfunctional as the one they had deposed and young King Edward III was their puppet – virtually a prisoner in his own court. He was forced to sign a humiliating Treaty with Scotland following military failures to repel Scottish raids as far south as Durham. He was sent again to France to do grudging homage to the new King of France following the death of Charles IV. He opened a secret line of communication to the Pope as a fallback against his inability to communicate anything independently. When rumours swept the court that Isabella was pregnant with Mortimer's child, the possibility of Edward's eventual usurpation could not be discounted. In October 1330 Edward and his few trusted friends acted. They moved through an underground culvert of Nottingham Castle to get into the inner bailey and then burst in on Isabella and Mortimer, killing their immediate attendants and arresting them both. Mortimer became the first person to be executed at Tyburn, and Isabella was banished for the remainder of her life. Edward III summoned Parliament, repudiated all that had been done in his name, and at the age of eighteen took full control of his kingdom.

Edward had by then been married for two years to Phillipa of Hainault. They were expecting their first child – the man who would grow up to be the Black Prince – and she would subsequently bear him thirteen children. In fact, the year of their marriage was to mark two fateful events that would figure greatly in Edward's subsequent wars. His 1328 marriage meant that the Count of Flanders became his father-in-law, giving him some dynastic influence with a principality that was not only critical to England's wool economy but a natural ally against French influence across the Continent. And when Charles IV of France died without a direct heir in the same year, it was apparent that Edward of England had a plausible claim to the French throne itself. He was a grandson of King Philip IV who had died in 1314. That made Edward III the closest direct heir (though via a female, since his mother was Philip's eldest surviving daughter). This stood against the claim of Philip of Valois, a descendant through an unbroken male line to Philip III who had died in 1285 – making Philip another generation distant but with no females to complicate his claim. Edward of England's claim might have been plausible, but in political terms it was a non-starter. Philip would always be the choice of the French court (citing 'Salic law') whatever the blood lines suggested. National European kingdoms had emerged sufficiently by the fourteenth century to transcend most of the dynastic struggles that characterised their leaderships. At that stage there was never a chance that the French establishment would willingly put an English king on the throne. And it has never been clear quite how seriously Edward III and his advisers ever took the dynastic claim that emerged, unbidden, in 1328. But it remained there – a political gauntlet that he might be tempted to pick up in the future – the ultimate, unachievable ambition to rule simultaneously and legitimately in both France and England.

Like his grandfather, Edward III felt he had to turn his immediate attention to Scotland. In 1332 Edward Balliol, the son of his namesake whom Edward I had supported, launched a war to grab back the Scottish crown that Robert Bruce – King Robert I – had assumed. He was defeated, and appealed to Edward III for English help, offering allegiance and territory. For Edward III it was an opportunity to avenge not just the humiliating treaty he had been forced to sign but his father's own disaster at Bannockburn in 1314. Edward marched into Scotland with Balliol and laid siege to Berwick-on-Tweed. When a Scottish army arrived to relieve it, the English took station to meet it on Halidon Hill two miles away.

This was the battle which created Edward III's tactics that would prove so successful at Crecy thirteen years later.[1] It also chimed with Edward's own understanding that his father had lost so disastrously at Bannockburn because of the vulnerability of cavalry to well-drilled pikemen. At Halidon Hill he tried a new formation which became the characteristic English force deployment for set-piece battles for many years to come. It was completely successful. Halidon Hill was Edward's first significant military victory and marked a portent for his future as a warrior king. But in a less welcome portent of the future, Halidon Hill also marked the return of Edward I's old strategic challenge.

Edward Balliol was chased off the Scottish throne in 1334. Edward III led yet another army into Scotland that year to restore him, and had to do it again in 1335, and again in 1336. The Scots went back to guerrilla tactics. They would not cooperate with another English Halidon Hill formation, and the English were once more chasing shadows. But the 1336 campaign was undertaken under the threat of a major French expeditionary force designed to land in Scotland to support their 'auld alliance' partner. To forestall this Edward III made a clever dash to Stirling with just a few men, thence to Perth, collecting English garrison troops, and as far north as the Moray Firth, from where he began a brutally destructive procession down the east coast, denying all port facilities and supplies to any French force that might appear.

But he was back in his grandfather's old three-front trap; Scotland, Aquitaine and Flanders. Returning to England, Edward found the country in the grip of French invasion fever. Coastal towns were being raided, Gascon and English ships were being seized, warning beacons being prepared and county levies were being mobilised. In fact, Philip VI of France had already called off the expedition to Scotland and would never have attempted a serious invasion of England. But the new situation was worse for Edward, because Philip had decided to concentrate his anti-English energies

---

1. In fact, before his defeat, Edward Balliol had achieved a dramatic local victory at Dupplin Moor with these tactics and had presumably shared his experience with Edward III as he advanced with him into Scotland.

against Aquitaine. Edward had almost certainly intended to go back to Scotland to finish his campaign once and for all. But now he had to turn to his Aquitaine problem. Aquitaine was a crown possession but it was Gascon, not English. Keeping it supplied from England was almost impossible, requiring long sea journeys across the Bay of Biscay or else transit over hostile French territory. It was impossible to defend directly. So the answer was, as in Edward I's day, to campaign against France in the north – in Flanders (only nominally French) or the Low Countries and into Normandy – to keep pressure off Aquitaine and gain territory elsewhere to trade against its safety from French invasions.

Scotland was therefore saved in 1337 by Edward III's need to address Aquitaine. He launched a campaign into Flanders and so began a three-year obsession with events in the Low Countries. This marked the beginning of what turned into the intermittent conflict characterised as the Hundred Years War. In the following year, Edward was in full war mode against King Philip VI and in 1339 he was campaigning inside France itself. Then in January 1340 the die was cast as a matter of cynical political and legal calculation. Edward made the pronouncement that defined his life and his historical legacy. He formally claimed the French throne as his by right. Europe was puzzled. The Pope was reportedly 'stupefied'. The French court was furious.

It must have seemed that at least God approved the audacity of the claim. In that year Edward III triumphed in the fierce naval battle at Sluys. The King was trying to land a significant force on the Continent – sailing some 120–150 ships up the Zwin to Bruges to relieve his hard-pressed ally in Flanders. A large French fleet of 213 ships barred his way, lashed and chained together to create a three-layered barrier against any passage up the estuary. But after initial fighting the French fleet became disorganised by westerly winds and strong tides. The chains were a hindrance and were soon discarded as the English attacked from upwind in groups of three ships; a central vessel packed with men-at-arms and flanked by two ships full of archers. It was a devastating tactic that made the most of the range and rate of fire of the longbow. As with all such naval battles, it was a brutal process – hand to hand combat with ships locked together and no prospect of withdrawal or escape for anyone. No quarter was offered either during the battle or after it. The King was in the midst of it all and took an arrow wound in the thigh. But it was a dramatic victory. The English fleet seems to have lost only two ships and between 400 and 600 men, but captured 166 French vessels and sank or burnt another twenty-four. There were almost no prisoners and French losses were estimated somewhere between 16,000 and 18,000 men. It was one of the most significant naval victories of the medieval period and gave England's young king a massive boost in prestige.

In strategic terms Sluys allowed Edward III to land English troops on the continent – though he was never able to deploy enough to make much difference to the struggle for territory. And his victory still did not give him unchallenged control of the Channel – something that was never achieved during the Hundred Years War. French raids on the south coast continued. Not least, Edward was also facing the characteristic financial and political crisis that was the natural concomitant of waging these wars. In Aquitaine, France had already occupied about a third of his lands. In Scotland most of the territory south of the Forth and the Clyde was back in Scottish hands. In Flanders he was in hock to continental creditors. He returned from Sluys with his warrior reputation greatly enhanced, yet was beset on all sides by the financial troubles characteristic of a small country. Edward used his new prestige to assert himself among his nobles and then jumped at a chance to intervene in the Breton Wars of Succession when the Duke of Brittany died without leaving a direct heir.

Brittany was a gateway across both land and sea routes to Aquitaine. Effective control of it was certainly useful in any Anglo-French conflict, and having future Breton rulers depend on English support and pay homage to Edward as their sovereign lord would strengthen his claim to the French throne. But possession of Brittany still did not solve the three-front problem he had inherited from his grandfather. Edward campaigned across Brittany during these years but his available forces were always too small to take major strong points or secure decisive victories. Philip VI of France was content to let him campaign across large areas and run down his war chest. Edward was forced into a truce, leaving significant forces in Brittany, while his undisciplined soldiers sustained themselves by running amok through the countryside.

Given Edward III's character, the next turn of events was all too predictable. He fell into the 'one last push' syndrome; so often the death-knell of a failing strategy. Ironically enough, it almost worked in a perverse way, and produced his greatest military triumph – which might have made all the difference in the long run if he were possessed of that strength of mind to quit while he was ahead. In 1344–45 he got Parliament to make one last financial effort for his war and planned a very ambitious three-pronged invasion of the Continent. He would land forces in Bordeaux in Aquitaine, and in Brittany, and, under his own leadership, in Normandy. These armies would link up with local forces who were believed to be ready to join the campaign. With the exception of some gains in Aquitaine, it all fell apart very quickly; not least because Edward put so much faith in chancers and adventurers in foreign lands who promised what they could not deliver.

But in 1346, resorting again to conscription and a massive feat of logistics, Edward III led the biggest expeditionary army of the Hundred Years War, in 750 ships, across the Channel to Normandy. It landed on the Cotentin peninsula, next to the beach best known to modern generations as D-Day's 'Utah beach' of 1944. The English assaulted and savagely sacked Caen, though were not able to occupy the citadel, which left a powerful French garrison at their rear when they moved on. Edward decided to march on Paris and thence to move north, eventually to withdraw, ordering his English fleet to embark his forces near the mouth of the Somme. But he was unable to provoke the French to a pitched battle by threatening Paris. He got to within ten miles of the city but he was not strong enough for an assault, and could not provoke the French to come out and fight for it. French forces kept him south of the Seine and collapsed the bridges. Eventually, with supplies running very short he had no alternative but to withdraw and head for the mouth of the Somme to meet his fleet.

Philip VI had gathered his forces and was unwisely provoked by the humiliation of Edward's march into racing towards the Somme to trap the English on the south side of it. His forces got to the Somme bridges first. Near the estuary, the English discovered a marshy ford at Blanchetaque and fought their way across it in a brave and clever engagement. They took up defensive positions just outside Crecy. It is impossible to say whether or not Edward welcomed this situation. It would be the pitched battle he was looking for, but at that stage he may have preferred escape, given the hungry and exhausted state of his forces. Nevertheless, he had found a good defensive position even though he was outnumbered two-to-one.

Edward III was also confident of his tactics. They had worked at Halidon Hill in 1333. His forces were on rising ground with their backs protected by a forest. They had found enough time to dig trenches and traps against advancing cavalry. The archers – about a third of the whole force – stood in protective triangular formations on each wing of a broad crescent, surrounded by the baggage wagons for protection. Underneath these wagons were over a hundred light cannons, making their debut in open battle. In the centre, knights were dismounted to fight on foot, in three divisions ('battles' in the terms of the day) their horses held at the rear for pursuit if events turned towards the offensive. The Black Prince was given command of the leading battle, Edward led the rearmost to act as a mobile reserve. The principle behind the formation was that the archers could break up a cavalry attack and prevent any classic cavalry-on-infantry hits, and men at arms, foot soldiers and pike men would hold their own in the melee that followed.

The topography gave the English the classic advantage of a narrow front against superior numbers that would funnel French cavalry attacks riding up the slope at them. It was mid-afternoon on 26th August as French scouts coming up the road from Abbeville realised that their English quarry was finally about to stand and fight. Philip VI should have waited until the morning when his whole force would have been drawn up. He seemed uncertain, but then discovered at about five o'clock, just as rain began to fall, that some French cavalry were moving forward to attack anyway. He ordered the *Oriflamme* to be unfurled. Edward responded with the Dragon banner – 'no prisoners' in both cases.

The English waited, in their crescent formation, to receive the French attack. Philip's Genoese crossbowmen were no match for the quick-firing English and Welsh longbowmen, and they fell back in confusion, hampering advancing French cavalry. Long-range fire from Edward's archers, and then crossfire as the French closed with the English crescent proved devastating. It was the first time French forces had faced the sheer power of massed longbowmen. The pits and traps that had been prepared, the mud created by rain that had now become fierce, and the primitive canons, all blunted the impact of Philip's charging cavalry in the diminishing light. The resulting melee between unmounted men in the chaotic muddle of attackers rapidly came down to individual contests of skill and courage. Philip VI had two horses killed under him and received an arrow in the jaw before he was pulled away from the fighting. The sixteen-year-old Black Prince was in the midst of it all and Edward finally had to commit his whole reserve battle. French attacks continued until around midnight, varying tactics between mounted and unmounted men, trying to break into Edward's position. Following several failed charges, the first and second English battles seem to have gone forward to attack survivors and loot the bodies, but were still disciplined enough to reform in line before the next attack. But it was a chaotic night all round before fighting eventually subsided. Next morning French infantry was still arriving at the battlefield and English knights now mounted up to break them with cavalry charges and a pursuit that extended for some miles.

By noon on 27th August, it was evident that the 10–14,000 English and Welsh troops had won a decisive victory over a force twice its size. They had humiliated the French nobility who were truly shocked at the outcome. Edward's losses seem genuinely to have been no more than about 300 men, whereas over 2,200 French nobles are reliably believed to have perished in the battle and the pursuit, and somewhere between two and four thousand other troops.

Events were flowing Edward's way. His finances now allowed him to keep his army in France for another year. He moved on immediately to capture Calais, looking for a permanent centre for English trade and a bridgehead for continental campaigning near his Flemish allies. Calais, however, proved a very tough nut to crack. The English settled in for a winter siege. After Crecy, France could not raise a credible army to relieve the port city, and English reinforcements were flowing in. Philip VI appealed to the Scots to invade England to distract Edward from Calais. They did, and in October that year were dramatically defeated at Neville's Cross near Durham by entirely local forces under the command of the warlike Archbishop of York. King David II of Scotland was taken prisoner. Almost a full year after Crecy, and near starvation, Calais finally opened its gates and its famous six burghers emerged to offer their own lives to spare the citizenry. Only with difficulty was Edward persuaded by the Queen to be magnanimous. After such hard campaigning he didn't appear to see the political benefits of mercy. The king sat on the dais constructed specially for him to receive the Calais supplicants and condemn them to death, and the politically more astute Queen Philippa, there and then, argued and pleaded with him – successfully – for their lives. Still, the French population of Calais was immediately expelled and English settlers brought in to colonise it. Calais became a rich English city for the next two centuries. In September 1347 the King returned to London for triumphal celebrations.

With France internally riven and militarily weak, Edward now enjoyed a decade of power and prestige. The miracle of Crecy had confirmed God's approval of his claims and most of what followed only increased them. In memory of that battle he founded the Order of the Garter – the most famous chivalric order in Europe – and officially established the ever-popular St George as England's patron saint. Over the New Year of 1350 he and the Black Prince personally sprang an audacious trap for over 5,000 French troops who tried to retake Calais in a treacherous 'throw the gates open' plot. Then in August, father and son were both at sea in the Channel, ambushing armed Castilian merchant ships – allies of France who had been attacking English shipping and menacing the east coast. It was a tough and brutal fight, but King Edward and the Black Prince were a formidable command team. Meanwhile, English and Gascon troops were skirmishing, generally successfully, against French forces in Brittany and Aquitaine.

The climax of these years came in 1355–6. France was in turmoil under Philip's successor, King John II. Edward sent the Black Prince with an elite group to Gascony, to be supplemented by larger local forces. His original plans for a grand pincer movement against France were naïve, however, and quickly unravelled. He raided in Picardy, had quickly to re-take Berwick in another Scottish campaign, but then looked to exploit the massively destructive march the Black Prince was conducting right across southern France, from the Atlantic to the Mediterranean and back again. The booty his son's forces were gathering was unprecedented. Edward tried to organise yet another north/south pincer movement, sending an expedition south from Normandy that would join up with his son. The forces that Edward could send, however, were never big enough to make it work. The Black Prince had set off northwards from Bergerac towards the Loire in August 1356. But the northern force could not get nearer than sixty miles from the prince to make the vital link-up. The Black Prince was forced to turn back, pursued now by John II's much larger French army which, in September, trapped him east of Poitiers. The climactic battle that followed is described in another chapter, but among many French nobles taken prisoner at Poitiers, King John II of France was himself captured and brought to London.

In the spring of 1357, therefore, Edward III of England could parade the Kings of France and Scotland, and a great many others, as his prisoners. He held all the cards. And he finally had some real control over England's three-front problem; he could make choices over Scotland, Gascony and Aquitaine, and now also in relations with the kingless French court. France was on its knees, losing fortresses to the Duke of Lancaster who garrisoned them, and many towns to the 'free companies' and brigands who emerged from the fragmented and neglected armies that operated across French territory after the 1356 campaigns.

Edward did not think wisely. Demanding full sovereignty over the Duchy of Aquitaine seemed a natural demand. The French throne itself might still be a stretch but his claim to it nevertheless remained a powerful bargaining chip. By 1359 he was claiming, as of right, about half the territory of France – more than restoring Henry II's old twelfth century Angevin empire in the Frankish kingdom. He also felt he was now in a position to dominate Scotland once and for all.

Over the next three years his triumphalist demands on both Scotland and France only deepened political turmoil in both countries as their kingless establishments rejected them. Exasperated by the political realities of this, Edward finally went for an all-out attempt to capture the French throne in October 1359, with a direct invasion of northern France aimed towards Reims, where he intended to have himself crowned King of France. To subdue, and then rule, in France would break the 'auld alliance' with Scotland and, finally, leave Edward and England dominant in northwest Europe. Since 1337 he had allowed himself to be drawn steadily onto this moment.

It was a grand invasion, setting off from Calais, in three broad columns led by himself, the Black Prince and the Duke of Lancaster. It was the most glamorous army of that era, packed with famous English names. The campaign was always a pipe dream, of course, even if Edward had managed to have himself crowned. The French locked themselves securely inside their fortresses and followed a classic scorched earth policy, while also trailing Edward's forces to keep them moving ever onwards, struggling for supplies. Reims proved impregnable and the English were left to ravage their way, pointlessly, back and forth south of Paris and around Chartres for more than six months. There would not be another Crecy or Poitiers. The whole campaign was a bleak failure. In May 1360 Edward settled for treaty terms he had previously rejected, returning to London 'in triumph' with an army that was, in truth, beaten and exhausted.

Unequal treaties – signed by one side under severe duress – tend not to last, and Edward's Treaty of Bretigny – the 'great treaty' as it was called for years afterwards – was certainly unequal, giving England a good deal more than Edward's miserable Reims campaign really deserved. When King John II died in England during 1364 he was succeeded by Charles V, who immediately began a powerful fightback against the English and a restoration of France's inherent, underlying power. Edward's attempts to encircle France diplomatically all came to nought, while Aquitaine fell into mismanagement under the control of the Black Prince who was as politically inept as his father. England's influence over events in France, and Scotland, slipped steadily away.

Edward's queen died in 1369. His erstwhile mistress, Alice Perrers, emerged in public as manipulative, greedy and conspiratorial. She was heartily detested. Her influence increasingly cut the king off from the English political establishment and Edward became withdrawn and distracted, presiding over a visibly corrupt government.

By 1372 most of Aquitaine was lost, then Poitou and almost all the territories the Treaty of Bretigny had ceded to England. Edward's forces and allies across Aquitaine, Brittany and Normandy were steadily over-run or else just hanging on at their strongpoints. At least two grand attempts to mount expeditions to reverse these losses turned into expensive fiascos. Edward's military empire was crumbling in front of him. The 1376 Parliament was outraged by the financial strain and the crony corruption and opposed the king's government outright. In the same year his beloved son, the Black Prince, died of illness. Edward III died on 21 June the following year. Within days of his death the armies of France and Scotland were on the march again. By the end of that month 4,000 French troops were burning Rye, Lewes, Hastings and as far west as Plymouth; though fought off in Southampton and Poole. It was symbolic revenge for what the English had long been doing in France. An anticlimactic end to a tumultuous reign. Many said Edward had 'ruled for too long'.

As a military commander Edward III certainly deserves his place in British history. He was a classic soldier's soldier who led by example and inspired his country and his forces. He inherited the most centrally-governed society in Europe, which greatly helped Edward mount his military campaigns. 'War created the state' it is said, 'and the state created the nation'. There was a close-knit nobility and a Parliament who generally felt that Crown and English interests were in harmony. They cared about Scotland, France and Calais, if not always much about Aquitaine. More than any of his Plantagenet predecessors, the king was thought of as 'Edward III of England'. He inspired genuine national loyalty. He was an instinctive battlefield tactician. He saw the great potential of the longbow and he promoted excellent innovative defensive tactics using it. His campaigns also created something close to a modern-style, all-volunteer professional army; a multitude of captains and their own groups of neighbours and friends who were prepared to sign up for loyalty, maybe patriotism – certainly adventure and booty.

In a strategic sense, however, Edward never seems to have appreciated just how much he was taking on in his French wars. Not appearing to understand France's underlying strength, he never seems to have considered cashing in some of his gains during the years of dominance. Nor did he appear to appreciate the depth of the challenge in trying to subdue Scotland and simultaneously protect English possessions in Aquitaine. He had a golden opportunity in 1357 to resolve, or at least escape from, his grandfather's strategic bind, the two- to three- front grumbling, persistent war. In his religiously-fuelled triumphalism, Edward didn't appear even to recognise it. He was, by his own estimation, a king born for wars in which God would decide who would rightly prevail.

10

Edward, The Black Prince

Edward, Prince of Wales, eldest son of Edward III, was not known in his lifetime as 'the Black Prince'. Some of his armour may, or may not, occasionally have been black. The name was in common use, however, by the time of Holinshead's *Chronicles*, which were a major source for Shakespeare's history plays. And it was, in any case, a fitting sobriquet to represent the terror he instilled in England's enemies during his relatively brief forty-six-year life. For the French, the sobriquet was also indicative of the shameful darkness of his deeds on French soil. Shakespeare has King Charles VI of France describe him as being, 'bred out of that bloody strain That haunted us in our familiar paths: Witness our too much memorable shame…Of that black name, Edward, Black Prince of Wales.' For the English, however, this 'Edward, Black Prince of Wales' was foremost among the most celebrated and chivalrous English commanders of the Hundred Years War. His contemporaries saw him as one of the noblest knights of the age. It was, in fact, an age in which a prince might be counted chivalrous as a knight but still behave like the very devil himself as a commander.

Edward, Prince of Wales, was the heir to the English throne who died just a year before he could inherit it; never a king but always a warrior, and part of a chivalric, romantic, father-and-son command combination that for a while seemed to be truly unbeatable. They both understood the power of propaganda and played on it relentlessly as England's 'invincible' father and son. And like his father, before his life ended in chronic infirmity and weakness, Edward was to see all they had conquered together lost in the hiatus of his final few years.

He was born in June 1330 at Woodstock. His father, Edward III, was himself only seventeen at the time and just about to assert himself as the young king who was determined to take full control from his mother and her lover. King Edward was also anxious to consolidate the position of his son and natural heir. Before he was three, little Edward was created earl of Chester, then Duke of Cornwall when he was seven. In those early years he and his sisters would spend Christmas at the Tower of London and when threats of French invasion seemed more immediate, the young royals would be moved to Nottingham Castle for safety. Assessing his formal education is guesswork – though it is certainly untrue that he attended Queen's College Oxford, whatever the institution claimed to the contrary. But his training for knighthood was a matter of course and far more important to him. Unlike many of his predecessors, Edward III wanted his young heir to assume genuine responsibilities. When he was seven his father had him clad in purple velvet robes to lead a papal delegation into the City of London. He was designated 'Guardian of the Realm' on three separate occasions when he was eight, ten and twelve, during his father's campaigns in France. Unsurprisingly, the young Duke of Cornwall operated a lavish and expensive household and by the time he became Prince of Wales at the age of thirteen, sizable debts were already racking up in his name.

Then in one tumultuous year he sprang from 'heir-to-the-throne' to 'famed English warrior' when he accompanied Edward III on his 1346 campaign. His father knighted him as soon as they landed in France and the Black Prince, as we shall call him, with the earls of Northampton and Warwick as his experienced commanders, immediately led forces to burn and ravage the countryside through Cotentin. He was prominent in the brutal capture of Caen, impetuously attacking it from the north before his father had his forces properly deployed in the west and south. He subsequently led the vanguard column in Edward III's destructive, exhausting, and ultimately fruitless procession towards Paris; and thence to dash to the coast for a rendezvous with English ships to rescue them. The Prince continued to lead the forward column on the army's forced march towards safety. In fact, the Prince's vanguard slowed the whole force down by assaulting – against the king's orders – insignificant villages and the suburbs of Beauvais on the way. The French got ahead of the leading column and cut them off at the Somme. The vanguard nevertheless managed to fight skilfully across a marshland ford it found near the Somme estuary and the pursuit ended at Crecy where the Black Prince faced his first pitched battle.

He was just sixteen and his father put him in command of the leading formation (a 'battle') that would face French forces first and for the longest period. Of course, the Prince would rely greatly on old warriors like the earls of Warwick and Oxford, Geoffrey d'Harcourt and John Chandos. But the French were approaching English positions obliquely as they climbed the slope and the initial shock of each wave of attackers would fall first on the Prince's formation, in front and to the right of the English line.

Crecy has been described in another chapter. It was an outright triumph for Edward III's tactics. But the young Black Prince was given full scope by his father to show himself a brave and murderous fighter as he 'led', and certainly inspired, the leading battle. Like other knights, he fought on foot at Crecy and led at least parts of his battle forward to attack the French second line just as the Count of Alencon's cavalry attacked his position. He went down in the fighting and was rescued by the Earl of Arundel's men, continuing to scrap fiercely against successive attacks until Edward's reserve forces arrived to relieve some of the pressure. By the end of the night the Prince was battered and exhausted but much honoured.

The Prince had played no strategic command role in the campaign but he certainly proved himself a fighter. Like most of the men of Plantagenet royalty, with his mop of blond hair, he was by then a naturally strong, tall and striking figure – a feature, it seems, of his father, grandfather, and great-grandfather – all men who looked as if they were born for battle and command. (Indeed, even his grandfather, the lamentable Edward II, was said to be a good fighter in close combat.)

It was natural that after Crecy, the Black Prince began to share command decisions with his father, who clearly trusted him. He was closely involved in the long siege of

Calais which lasted during an exceptionally cold winter, before the city capitulated. He eventually returned with his father to England more than twelve months after Crecy to enjoy together their years of triumph, during which a truce lasted, and was progressively extended, between dominant England and enfeebled France.

For the Prince, these were the years of ceremony and fine clothing, hunting, tournaments, womanising and illegitimate children; to the point where monastic chroniclers had something to say about the Black Prince's behaviour and his extravagance. They were also years of virulent plague in England, especially during 1347–1348, when war and foreign diplomacy were effectively on hold.

Both Edward III and his son were nevertheless itching to press their advantage over France, either through their diplomatic demands or else by a resumption of fighting in which they felt such confidence. A relatively small incident over Calais in 1349–50 reveals much about their bellicose approach. They learned of a plot, to be triggered amid the New Year revels of 1350, to throw open the gates of Calais to a force of 5,500 French troops who would then enter and recapture the city.

King Edward learned of the plot on Christmas Eve 1349. But rather than simply exposing and frustrating the plot, in great secrecy King Edward and the Black Prince took a small elite force of knights – all totally incognito – over to Calais on 30th December and laid a trap. They hid in cellars, vaults and chambers and even constructed a false wall near the city entrance to conceal some knights, and sawed partly through the timbers of the main drawbridge so it would take an armed knight but could be quickly broken by a big boulder levered off the high wall above it. Early on New Years' Day a party of fifteen French scouts stole into Calais to check the coast was clear and found nothing amiss. That night the gates were opened and a good number of French soldiers dashed into the city. Right on cue, the drawbridge was smashed, the inner portcullis dropped, and English troops emerged and overcame the invaders in a fierce, brief fight. After much confusion, French forces now stranded outside the gates fled. But King Edward, very foolishly, pursued them with about thirty knights and a handful of archers, only to find himself suddenly confronting some eight hundred French troops in the marshes to the west of the city gates. His position was near hopeless. But the Black Prince, anticipating his father's predicament, led reinforcements from the city's seaward gate toward the marshes where Edward was now making a stand as the French attacked along the causeway. According to Jean Froissart's *Chronicles*, the King was by then fighting hand-to-hand with Eustace de Ribbemont. The Prince arrived in time to turn a losing fight in the King's favour – probably the closest Edward III ever came to death in battle, since without any royal regalia he could hardly rely on being captured as a prize.

It wasn't a campaign, it was a caper; the stuff of soldiers' stories and legendary retelling. The King and his son, incognito until the very end, had pulled off an audacious trap against a treacherous plot. Glorious derring-do – and completely unnecessary. But both the King and the Prince instinctively understood the power of such incidents to cement their place in the hearts of the English people. And it speaks volumes for their natural preference for violent action over cool strategic calculation.

In the same year both King and Prince were again leading troops from the very front – again unnecessarily – in a dangerous naval engagement. Castile, ally of France, was a longstanding enemy of Gascony. Powerful Castilian fleets had for some time been menacing trade routes between Gascony and England, attacking English shipping and raiding the east coast, to the point that Edward III was forced to put men on coastguard duty along the North Sea coast and at Channel ports and beaches. In August, a fleet of improvised English ships – most of them cogs with fighting forecastles and afterdecks hastily added – set out from Winchelsea to intercept a powerful Castilian fleet laden with booty on its way home. The military value of this single interception, however, might be set against the assets Edward III was prepared to risk for it. The King and the Black Prince embarked in their own ships, as did the earls of Warwick, Salisbury, Lancaster, Arundel, Gloucester, Huntingdon and Northampton, accompanied by some of England's most distinguished knights.

The two fleets of roughly equal size – around a hundred ships in all – clashed on the evening of 29th August within sight of those lining the clifftops along the Sussex coast. Sea battles involved exchanges of missiles and arrows before ships rammed or laid alongside each other to fight hand-to-hand in the most brutal of circumstances, where breathers, still less retreat, was simply impossible. Ships would be burned, sunk, captured, or else survive victorious. In this case, the Castilian ships were significantly bigger and higher than the English ships, some were manoeuvrable galleys, and all were heavily armed with powerful catapults and packed with armed men. They were also better-handled by experienced Spanish sailors bearing powerfully downwind on the English fleet. Their commander, Charles de la Cerda, didn't fear this battle. With the wind astern, he could have avoided it altogether if he had wished.

According to Froissart, it was a ferocious affair. The essence for the English was to brave the storm of arrows from the Castilian mast-tops, get their cogs in close enough to grapple and then board the high-sided Castilian ships, using rope ladders slung across the enemy's gunwales. The King's ship, badly damaged in its first collision, was sinking. Another enemy vessel urgently had to be grappled and captured while the King's ship remained afloat. The Prince's ship was also sinking fast, badly holed in being grappled and battered by a big Castilian vessel that resisted all attempts to board it. Lancaster brought his own ship to the other side of the Castilian, boarded and captured it – hauling the Prince's crew (including the Prince's own ten year-old brother, John of Gaunt) aboard just as their own ship finally foundered and sank. Everywhere, English archers were making the difference, but boarding was always difficult against taller ships. The fighting was savage; Castilian troops were tossed into the sea, dead or alive. By the time darkness fell, the Castilians had lost some twenty-six ships, at least fourteen captured and possibly another ten or twelve sunk or burned. Around twenty surviving vessels scattered towards French ports during the night.

It was a clear tactical victory, achieved at considerable cost in lives, if not so heavy in ships. It was also achieved at great risk of royal losses. It could have been a dynastic catastrophe for England. Even in an era that presumed kings should be warriors, leaders were not expected to be downright reckless. And victory in the Channel brought precious little strategic advantage. Indeed, in the years immediately after Winchelsea, the Channel remained effectively closed to English maritime traffic by French ships sitting regularly offshore, and a convoy system had to be adopted to get English ships across the North Sea, in both directions. Neither this victory, nor Edward III's earlier triumph at the battle of Sluys, gave England any maritime control of the Channel or the western approaches during the Hundred Years War.

Still, the English loved their King and the Black Prince for it all, and the following year Parliament gave Edward III the absurd title, 'King of the Seas' in recognition. The battle had achieved little but was wonderful propaganda.

The episodic war continued in Gascony, Picardy and especially in Brittany, where England became deeply embroiled in its 'war of succession'. The Black Prince attended to his own estates, and took no part, and little interest, in any of the ongoing diplomacy between England and France. To be fair, neither did his father. Lancaster was effectively Edward's foreign minister, while the King blew hot and cold about military campaigns to gain the French crown that was 'legitimately' his – and which would be inherited by the Black Prince, even if Edward III himself died in the process.

More insecurity in Gascony led the King to send the Prince there as his lieutenant in 1355 in one of his several attempts to create a north-south pincer movement; supporting Gascony from either Brittany or Normandy. That grand design evaporated, but left the Prince to take the war to France by raiding powerfully eastwards from Gascony in three columns spread widely enough to loot and destroy a big swathe of territory, as it went. Bold as ever, the Prince took the expedition six hundred miles in eight weeks from his Atlantic base at Bordeaux as far as the Mediterranean at Narbonne and back again. French forces, as usual, barricaded themselves inside their main towns and let him do his worst to the rest. Everything they came across was looted and destroyed; everyone they encountered was killed. The Pope sent to him to desist, but papal envoys were ignored. It constituted a strategy of sorts; hurting the French economy and depriving it of taxes from a region that provided more than half the French King's revenues, while collecting spoils themselves. England was awash with fine French booty during this period.

The following year King Edward was keen to follow up on the Prince's success and sent him reinforcements, trying again to create a three-front attack on France and maybe a north-south pincer movement, where the Prince would move north and link up with Lancaster coming south. In truth, the strategy being communicated from England was so shifting and confused, that the Prince concentrated his six or seven thousand men – mainly Gascon cavalry with about a thousand English archers – at Bergerac. From there he could take any one of three possible routes. Then in July 1356 he moved north towards the Loire to try to link up again with Lancaster. It was never likely to work. Lancaster's small force was around Angers, sixty miles from the Prince, when very large French forces moved out of Orleans to intercept his march. The Prince was urgently trying to locate Lancaster's force, but faced by this considerable threat, he turned his army abruptly south near Tours. Yet again an English army was force-marched a long way towards safety while a French army twice its size tried to get ahead of it. The English were still over a hundred miles north of Bordeaux when the confrontation occurred, just outside Poitiers. There was a day's pause for fruitless

Papal mediation during which the French received further reinforcements and the English dug pits and planted obstacles.

The Prince's army made the most of its defensive position. But his men were already exhausted, without food, water or supplies. Even their stocks of arrows were low. In the confused battle that followed on the morning of 19th September the Black Prince was undoubtedly lucky. Nevertheless, he was a naturally talented battlefield commander – probably the best among all the Plantagenets – and in the characteristic style of a natural battlefield winner, he also had the instincts to recognise his good fortune and exploit it to the full.

French forces planned to launch an armoured cavalry spearhead – its horses in part armour – against the Prince's archers on the flanks to neutralise them before moving on foot in three battles, up the hill and onto the small plateau where the English centre stood. They had learned from Crecy that the prerequisite for success was to deal with the feared English longbow before trying to close with the bulk of the enemy's troops. But the Earl of Warwick's vanguard suddenly moved some distance back from the left flank, accompanied by the baggage train. The baggage train is the giveaway. Despite what the Prince subsequently said, it seems he was attempting a frankly dangerous – eleventh hour – withdrawal, probably south of the river Miosson, covered mainly by his archers. Misinterpreting this move, undisciplined French cavalry then launched uncoordinated attacks first against Warwick's withdrawing forces who swung in a big circle behind the position to come back towards the English centre, while other French cavalry then pointlessly attacked the Earl of Salisbury's forces on the right. English and Welsh archers had been left alone and though everyone's movements were confused, neither flank had been turned. The French had achieved nothing and the prince's dispositions were suddenly looking stronger.

All this was hidden from the French infantry by the brow of the hill, and unaware that the English archers were still at full strength, the first French battle, led by the Dauphin, then engaged the centre of the English force but had to contend with the great clouds of arrows and numerous obstacles that channelled their attack into a few gaps in the big hedges and vines which dominated the site. Even so, the Black Prince had to commit everything he had to hold this powerful attack in a two-hour struggle. But the Dauphin's failure and retreat seemed to confuse the duc d'Orleans' second battle who then half-withdrew and half-fled as the first battle got tangled up with it. The English were reprieved and able to regroup and recover after three hours of fighting before the third, biggest, enemy battle, led by the French King, began their advance, trudging on foot up the slope towards the English position. The Prince and his chiefs decided it was better to go onto the offensive than face an even heavier attack on the line. They had enough time to send a force of sixty knights and a hundred mounted archers in a big circle north east to get behind the third battle – raising a large cross of St George to show they were in position – to mount up themselves with every man-at-arms who could be spared, and then launch a fierce cavalry charge against the French who were by then engaging on foot against the English lines. French forces were attacked front and rear, shocked by the charge and driven down the slope to the west at the river Miosson which lay behind the original English starting position. The whole struggle fragmented and wheeled around. It was here that the French King himself, John II, was overwhelmed and captured.

For the Black Prince and his troops, Poitiers was another crushing English victory against a force double its own size. It represented the triumph of a small and cohesive force that had campaigned together for the last two years, where communication within the army was good, commanders were experienced – most had been at Crecy – and where the Prince's ability to think quickly and communicate efficiently with his forces was unparalleled. The army's morale was naturally high; if not a band of brothers, they were certainly a band of neighbours. And the confidence, the verve and the imagination of the Black Prince as their talented commander was probably the most critical single factor. It wasn't a battle he sought, nor a battle he controlled. But it was a battle he won nevertheless. He marched his men back to Bordeaux with carts of French treasures and booty piled high, ahead of column after column of disconsolate prisoners.

Another near-miraculous victory confirmed for Edward III that God obviously approved his claim to the French throne. That throne was, after all, now empty since John II was his honoured (and genuinely respected) prisoner spending most of his time at the Savoy palace beside the Thames. The Black Prince had returned to a hero's welcome in England and took no part in any negotiations for a 'permanent peace' now that England could dictate terms. The Prince attended to his estates, his tournaments and ceremonies while his father over-played his diplomatic hand with France and decided in 1359 – not unwillingly – that he would, after all, have to mount a great invasion to move on Reims and have himself crowned King of France.

The King and the Prince assembled the biggest military expedition to leave England's shores up to that time; around 12,000 troops – including, as it happens, a teenage Geoffrey Chaucer[1] – to join with perhaps 6,000 or more from other garrisons and allies on the Continent. King Edward hoped that the majesty of his power and the justice of his claim would persuade the French nobility to accept his demands without a fight. But both king and Prince over-estimated their political influence. Reims would not agree, nor open its gates, and the prince was soon leading, yet again, one of three English columns within a foraging army in a wayward progression around northern France before Edward ended the expedition with a new treaty in 1360 and the exhausted troops took ship from Calais to go home.

The following year the Black Prince married the vivacious and wealthy Joan, Countess of Kent. He was thirty-one. She was thirty-four or five and twice married already. One of her marriages was dissolved, in another she was a widow, but for a couple of years in the 1340s two living husbands had contested over which of them was really married to her. For the Prince, it was evidently a love match. There was no dynastic advantage in it, and in personal letters years later he called her his 'truest sweetheart', his 'dearest companion', his 'beloved companion'. Her influence certainly reinforced his natural style and extravagance, and she bore him two children, the younger of whom became King Richard II, who succeeded to Edward III's throne as a boy.

---

1. In fact, he was captured and held prisoner, before getting back to Calais after the Treaty of Bretigny.

Joan accompanied the Black Prince when he was made Prince of Aquitaine, now that the whole of the traditional province – not only Gascony – was made a sovereign English possession by the 1360 settlement. It was the perfect setting for their lavish lifestyle as Prince and Princess of Aquitaine. But Aquitaine was not Gascony and required, in any case, more political finesse in its governance than the Prince had ever possessed. By 1366, only a couple of years after their arrival, France's new king, Charles V, was actively conspiring in Aquitaine.

The Prince was, it seems, encouraged from London to intervene across the Spanish border in restoring the pro-English King Pedro ('the cruel') to the throne of Castile after he had been deposed by his pro-French half-brother Henry ('the bastard') of Trastamara; and allying again – in a triumph of hope over experience – with the endlessly duplicitous Charles ('the bad') of Navarre. The scheme should have had very little to recommend it. But it promised a campaign and seemed a good idea to the Prince. It turned into another strategic blind alley. It was seven months of campaigning in Castile during 1367 that brought English and Welsh archers into Spain for the first time. There was a decisive victory at Najera over Henry, who lost more than half his force to sheer fright, so great was the reputation of an English army, followed by an accumulating debt to pay for it all. Pedro regained his throne, couldn't pay his war debts, and was murdered two years later. More important still, the Black Prince was ill on the campaign, where dysentery became endemic and he began to suffer progressively with debilitating ill-health; constant fevers and dropsy.

It was all a distraction from the real threat. In 1369 Charles V had made his diplomatic preparations well and simply 'confiscated' Aquitaine as he found grounds to declare war. The English response was chaotic and brutal – punishing city after city without managing to bring French forces to battle. In 1370 the Prince, carried now on a litter, supervised the angry destruction of Limoges and its associated massacre – his last battlefield command and probably his most shameful. In 1371, sick and distressed, he returned to England and resigned the Principality of Aquitaine and Gascony. Intermittently bed-ridden, he saw English possessions fall one after another to Charles V while his father grew progressively more distracted and ineffective. The Prince tried briefly, at the end, to identify with reformers in Parliament and get a grip on the drifting state. But before this came to anything, and a year before his father's own demise, the Prince died at Westminster in April 1376.

The Black Prince – the Prince of Wales – was made for the fury of the battlefield, but not for the more subtle art of war. His honoured tomb in Canterbury Cathedral, in a way, encapsulates that legacy; a truly gifted battlefield commander, the best of his age, but never a national leader, either in fact or natural ability. Above his tomb was hung his surcoat, helmet, shield and gauntlets. And they can still be seen in a glass case in the Cathedral's Trinity Chapel to this day.

Henry V

Thanks to Shakespeare, Henry V is probably England's most popular medieval monarch; the hero of Agincourt in 1415 who snatched a fabulous victory over the French with his poor and battered army against fearful odds. It remains a classic story characterised by mud, blood, steel, cruelty and courage. Fewer people are interested in what happened in the years afterwards – far more intriguing than another triumph for English battle tactics and the longbow.

Agincourt sent shivers through France and Europe, but it settled nothing. Henry V continued to fight and scheme and ride his luck over the following five years until, in 1420, an astonishing moment arrived. It was agreed he would marry the French king's daughter, Catherine of Valois, and so become the rightful heir to the French throne. On the death of Charles VI – which actually followed in 1422 – he would become king both of France and England and bequeath a united crown to his successors. Meantime, he would act as regent to the ailing French king. It was what five English monarchs before him had dreamed of, but never got close to achieving. At a stroke, the strategic problems that had dogged them all – caught between operating against Scotland (and Wales), in Aquitaine and Flanders, with France as the hub of all England's foreign challenges – would be resolved. The unity of the two greatest crowns in northern Europe under an English king would change the history of the continent. And he, Henry V, had achieved it in just seven years since he ascended the throne. There was more than a whiff of Arthurian Camelot about it. It was a moment – a bright, shining moment – that left romantics constantly musing about what might have been.

But though history takes many startling turns, the deeper strategic truth was that this moment encapsulated a political illusion. Whatever happened to the Plantagenet and Valois crowns, the Hundred Years War had by 1420 become a fierce national struggle between the English and French peoples, where an inherently weaker England pitted itself for the ultimate prize against an inherently stronger France. And the outcome would not lie in a courtly vision of unity between a conquering English king and his beautiful young French queen, but in the mud, blood, steel, cruelty and courage of another thirty-three years of war.

The King Henry who created that illusory historical moment was born in Monmouth in September 1386. He was the first grandson of John of Gaunt the powerful 'king-maker' and founder of the House of Lancaster. His father, Henry Bolingbroke, Earl of Derby, was John of Gaunt's eldest son, which gave Bolingbroke great status but no direct line to the succession. As such, young Henry was therefore high and famously born, but never remotely destined for the throne. Perhaps for that reason he was able to absorb a sophisticated education and a great deal of clerical scholasticism, in which he revelled. He was good in Latin and French in addition to his appreciation of literature in his native English. For all his knightly training, he was thought to be a 'bookish' young man.

As a boy he evidently got on well with his father's cousin, King Richard II, even when his father, Bolingbroke, was ruthlessly exiled. King Richard had young Henry accompany him on his Irish campaign; knighting him there, but also making him an implicit hostage to his father's good behaviour in his Paris exile. It was nevertheless just then that his father brought his quarrel with the King to a head. Bolingbroke landed on the Yorkshire coast in June 1399. Young Henry was imprisoned in Ireland while Richard II returned to meet the challenge. The country prepared for war. But Bolingbroke immediately began to peel forces away from Richard's side. In September that year Richard II agreed to abdicate – always a mistake for medieval kings since he was murdered in captivity (probably starved) within five months. Henry Bolingbroke became King Henry IV and as his eldest son, Harry of Monmouth was brought back from Ireland to become, overnight, the Prince of Wales and heir to the kingdom.

Of course, their House of Lancaster was immediately challenged and both father and son found themselves staving off assassination plots and outright revolts. The most famous was in 1403 when the Percy family turned on them. Henry IV and his son, found themselves at Shrewsbury, up against the Earl of Northumberland and *his* son, 'Hotspur', (the young Sir Henry Percy).[1] The battle of Shrewsbury was the first time that longbow archers had fought each other on English soil. There were fierce arrow barrages with commensurate losses on both sides.

It was here that the sixteen-year-old Prince of Wales was hit in the face by an arrow. It appears that he refused to leave the field; the shaft was broken off and he had the wound packed with honey and continued fighting with the bodkin tip lodged in his face. (It was only removed many days later when the doctor had devised a special instrument to extract it without killing him.) At the end of the battle, only the Prince of Wales's vanguard division on the left was still in good shape and two of the three senior members of the Percy family, including Hotspur, were dead. It didn't resolve the Lancastrians' legitimacy, but Shrewsbury certainly showed what sort of warrior leader the young Henry was likely to be.

He was exceptionally tall for a medieval man, some 6ft 3in with a rangy rather than a muscular frame. Reportedly very fast of foot and with good balance, Henry had some of the natural advantages of reach and agility for fighting both on horseback and dismounted. He had thick brown hair, cut in the basin shape then fashionable among knights, and a long, clean-shaven and expressive face forever carrying the permanent scarring from his arrow wound.

---

1. It was quite a turnaround. The Percy family had been supportive of Bolingbroke's bid for the throne and Harry Hotspur had acted as a mentor and battlefield instructor for the young Harry of Monmouth during his boyhood. Even after Shrewsbury, the family managed to create northern uprisings in 1405 and again in 1408.

By then, some of the depths of his character were becoming very evident. Extremely pious, he displayed his religiosity with great ceremony. There was no hypocrisy here – he took his responsibilities to the faith very seriously. But he took preparations for his kingship very seriously too. From the moment of his investiture as Prince of Wales (and, to make the point, also Duke of Aquitaine) he increasingly identified with all the virtues his ailing father seemed to be losing; thrift, good management, respect for Parliament and serious attention to the affairs of state.

He was involved in, then personally commanded, significant campaigns in Wales against Owain Glyndwr almost continually after 1400 – not least because Glyndwr claimed to be the true Prince of Wales and latterly had the backing of French troops (who, in a Franco-Welsh force confronted the English in 1405 as far east as Worcester). But frustrating as these campaigns always were for English commanders, Henry was absorbing an unparalleled military education during these years. This included the battlefield innovation of ensuring a three-to-one ratio of archers to men-at-arms, whilst also understanding their tactical integration – highly dependent on command clarity and unit discipline. This was to dominate England's military thinking for the next forty years and fundamentally change the nature of its armies.[2]

By 1407 Henry was playing a greater role in government, attending the Royal Council even while preoccupied with Wales; and emerging as a dominating presence on it by 1410. He addressed with all his youthful energy and no little dedication most of the governance issues the failing Henry IV was ignoring. He worked hard to make native English the official language of the state, and he championed many other governmental reforms. But he over-reached himself with his father and fell into direct confrontation with him in 1412. For a few months that summer it was rumoured that young Henry was prepared to usurp him if his seriously ill father would not abdicate. His father would not, and lurched decisively towards recognising his second son as heir. It was a tense moment for the Prince of Wales, until Henry IV obliged him by dying in March 1413.

It was during these years before Henry IV's death that we may detect something of Shakespeare's Prince Hal in the real Henry, exasperated and struggling for dominance against his overbearing father. There is contemporary evidence that Henry was no stranger to dissolute behaviour – not particularly at odds with deep religiosity for medieval princes. And he seems to have had a number of unsuitable friends – certainly some he could not take with him into his own reign. After his coronation there was no role, or further mention, for fourteen of his erstwhile retainers to whom he had apparently been close. He obviously dropped people if he thought it politic.

As he matured, Henry was felt to be a man who listened to advice, who could be persuasive, generous, and fair in his own judgements. But equally, he could be entirely ruthless and downright cruel. He was meritocratic, often rewarding ability over status. Henry was a warrior, a charmer, a fanatical religious prig, a wise leader, a ruthless

---

2. Recruiting far larger numbers of skilled commoners as archers and developing the semi-professional volunteer army that had been foreshadowed in Edward III's time.

executioner. He was a chameleon to whom *raison d'etat* was all. If policy required it, Henry could be anything.

In his religiosity he burned heretics. He personally oversaw at least one Lollard blacksmith burned alive in a barrel at Smithfield. Henry had him pulled out and offered a pension when he thought he detected some recantation in the poor man's screams, but when he realised he had misheard, had him returned to the barrel. And with that same instinct for religious absolutism, Henry put himself under a vow of complete celibacy from 1413 until his marriage in 1420, as an offering to God – a spiritual price – for his success in war. He kept to it. He was driven, obsessive, full of self-belief; a man of ruthless charm and, probably for that reason, naturally charismatic.

He was also tormented by the weakness of his natural legitimacy as the son of a usurper. The plots against his father and himself had been continuous, and though he swatted them away, he appeared to be quietly neurotic about his own legitimacy. What modern scholarship can infer from many historical sources, Shakespeare arrived at by intuition. His Henry V knows there is nothing he can do before God to atone for 'the fault my Father made in compassing the crown'. But he also knows that war *will* atone for that fault here on earth as long as he is successful. And neither Shakespeare's king nor the real Henry V lost any opportunity to give God full credit for English victories under his command. There was some real fatalism in his attitude to military success, and indeed to his own survival in battle. He would rather die than be captured and ransomed at Agincourt. It was all part of his covenant with God.

The accession of Henry V at the age of twenty-seven had immediate impacts in Parliament, in the country and in the erstwhile preparations for a resumption of conflict with France. There were plenty of minor reasons to break the latest truce with France; French support for piracy in the Channel, sending troops to fight for Owain Glyndwr, commercial disputes, open warfare in Gascony and endless clashes over the observation of Edward III's 'Great Treaty' of Bretigny in 1360. And yes, the Dauphin does seem to have sent young King Henry an insulting gift of tennis balls, though probably in 1414 while he was celebrating Lent at his beloved Kenilworth Castle.

But the real motive for Henry's resumption of hostilities was that, despite its bellicosity, France was already slipping back into civil war. Two branches of the French royal family, the Burgundians and the Armagnacs, were both negotiating with the English for support. It seemed a perfect time for a dramatic intervention. Henry offered the French King a deal whereby he dropped his own claim to the French throne in return for all the territories ceded under the Bretigny treaty, and a great deal more besides, plus the hand of Catherine of Valois in marriage – and a huge dowry. But Henry's audacity produced a swift reconciliation between Burgundians and Armagnac family branches of the French crown, rejecting his offer outright and then insulting English envoys for good measure. Henry could not have been surprised. Perhaps he was pleased; since Parliament, the clergy and a good number of London merchants happily entertained war fever.

Henry's strategy for his French invasion was clever but dangerous. It was a closely guarded secret that he would attack Harfleur in Normandy, then strike down the Seine at Paris. This would not be just a raid. His expedition was large at about 12,000 troops and included builders, engineers, siege engines and cannons. He intended to conquer towns and occupy rich territories in Normandy and the Ile de France. He would campaign for a full year, leaving him to form a winning alliance with the powerful Duke of Burgundy and thereby dictate events between France's warring factions.

But he only had enough revenue to pay his army for the customary three months.[3] He borrowed copiously. Dick Whittington, in between his second and third stints as Mayor of London, lent £2,000 to the expedition. In order to have his all-important captains enter into indentures to serve beyond the first three months, Henry gave them jewels from the royal collection as surety against repayment to be made by January 1417.[4] He was pawning his wealth for the war and he would have to be successful in extracting cash from his conquests.

Henry's 1415 campaign rested on two major assumptions. The first was that the Burgundians and Armagnacs would not be able to sustain their family reconciliation and would again split the government, so that he could play them off while still allying with the Burgundians. But that didn't happen. Intra-dynastic politics took second place to a threat to the national homeland and Charles VI – weak, disrespected and visibly deranged – nevertheless stood at the head of a kingdom that would fight back. And secondly, Harfleur had to be taken quickly. It was a good strategic objective, allowing for easy supply from England into Normandy and would act as another Calais, providing a shorter route into the French heartlands and to Paris. But Henry had to capture it immediately to get his ambitious campaign moving; and this he singularly failed to do.

The siege of Harfleur began soon after Henry's expedition arrived at the mouth of the Seine on 14th August. But its defences were impressive and its garrison well-commanded. Mining and counter-mining, ponderous artillery duels and extensive engineering works failed to breach the walls. Only on 22nd September, when it was clear that Paris could not mount a relief effort, did Harfleur surrender and open its battered gates. Henry, with his unerring instinct for the theatricality of command, walked barefoot to the church of Saint-Martin inside the town to give thanks, before ordering that the residents be expelled and English colonists brought in to make it, like Calais, an English city.

In truth, Harfleur's defiance had wrecked his campaign. He lost many men in the five-week siege, his army had become riddled with disease and he would have to leave a strong garrison there to guard against attempts to recapture it. Paris was evidently holding itself together. A lightning push south was now out of the question so there would be no rich pickings from Normandy. But a straight return home would leave him facing the Crown's creditors with nothing to show for so expensive an expedition. He persuaded his commanders that they should make for Calais by the quickest route. That would be something at least – traversing part of the lands he claimed, whilst appearing to seek battle with a French army that was steadily building to his north-east, but nevertheless outmarching it to safety in Calais.

---

3. Men-at-arms received a shilling a day, archers sixpence.
4. He had pawned his personal jewels before in the Welsh campaigns but not directly to his lowly captains. This was a first.

With that, the Battle of Agincourt took shape. The army abandoned its artillery and most of the baggage train, moving out of Harfleur on October 8th for what should have been a direct one hundred and sixty-mile march. Down now to about 8,000 active troops, increasingly tired and hungry across a stripped landscape, losing more men to illness, they hugged the coast up to the river Somme. But the bridges were down, the fords guarded and the French were waiting on the northern side. Henry turned east along the south bank of the river while the French tracked him from the north. For six days they marched in parallel either side of the river until, in a final forced march, the English outpaced their trackers, making a cross-country dash at a long bend in the river, to converge at a pair of damaged causeways that got them across the Somme. They had marched two hundred miles in twelve days. The army turned north west again towards Calais, still almost a hundred miles away. And on 24th October, in pouring wet weather and still two days' march short of safety, powerful French forces blocked their path just between the villages of Tramecourt and Agincourt.

By then, Henry had fewer than 7,000 soldiers. The French had a notional number of around 28,000, and growing all the time as their nobles converged on the area. But it is likely that perhaps 14,000 French troops actually confronted the English army from their ridge the following day, though another 10,000 'mounted and armed servants' were available behind them. More important was the structural disparity. Henry's forces were eighty percent archers – more than 5,000 of them – unprotected and very lightly equipped, apart from their longbows, against well-armed French cavalry and professional men-at-arms fighting on foot.

The difference in forces spoke for itself and Henry's army, outnumbered by a minimum of two-to-one, was certainly in poor physical shape. English defensive battle tactics were tried and trusted, however, and Henry sent out patrols overnight to scout out favourable conditions over the ground ahead. But the moral component of so beleaguered a force was down to him. There is no clear evidence that the king walked among his troops that night, but it would have been unlike him not to have done so. He could be a soldier's soldier when the need arose. In his unbending faith, he believed in his soldiers, and as long as he remained alive, they seemed to believe in him. The rain continued all night. In the pre-battle hours, Henry heard three masses, one of them among his troops.

When the wet, cold morning dawned on 25th, the English lined up around 9 o'clock in the defile between two woods not more than seven hundred yards wide with large contingents of archers on the wings of their usual crescent formation and more archers in wedges among the dismounted men-at-arms in the centre. Long sharpened staves were driven obliquely into the ground in front of them to impale charging horses. But the French waited. Henry needed them to attack since he couldn't break his small formation or give up his narrow front between the two woods. He had to move forward. Shakespeare's Henry V was making speeches all morning, but according to one witness he simply said 'Felas, let's go', and they quietly moved up to within bowshot of the French lines – three hundred yards – where they re-planted their defensive staves and immediately provoked the attack they wanted.

The French knew English tactics well by now. Their cavalry charged the archers. Modern plate armour had made arrow strikes much less effective on riders, but their horses remained vulnerable. The charges not only failed, but in the mud of the ploughed fields, dead and wounded horses created havoc among the dismounted men-at-arms advancing behind the cavalry towards the centre of the English line. The cavalry in plate armour were humbled as much by the impact on their horses of mud and sharpened stakes as they were by the arrow storm they fully expected. Nevertheless, the first of the unmounted French divisions – pitting 5,000 men-at-arms against 1,500 – pushed the English centre back, even as they were cramped towards the middle and struggling in the cloying mud. Henry ordered his archers on the wings to drop their bows and join the battle at the centre. The preference for plate armour over chain mail meant that stabbing and slashing weapons were now outnumbered by more bludgeoning instruments – maces, hammers, axes, falcon beaks, bill-hooks. The archers grabbed whatever was to hand and set about fallen or unsteady French men-at-arms to help blunt the power of the attack. That this tactical switch could happen at all spoke volumes for the communication and unit discipline Henry could expect within his small force. Denied the space to operate, French troops following up in the next division added to their own problems and compacted into a killing zone where more nimble English fighters could outnumber them in detail. The French inability to neutralise the archers, and then the nightmare of the crush, the mud and the bludgeoning was devastating within that first hour.

Henry commanded in the centre and was fighting on foot. At one point he straddled the wounded body of his brother, the Duke of Gloucester, protecting him while he was down. At another he was seen to be beaten briefly to his knees by no lesser person than the Duke of Alencon wielding an axe – effectively Alencon's last blow before being cut down, probably by Dafydd Gam, among the King's bodyguards.[5] Henry's gem-encrusted, crowned helmet, on which he was wearing the Black Prince's ruby, saved him.

Not long after midday the English thought they had won. They were looting bodies and collecting prisoners. But another French division in the rearguard seemed to be organising itself to attack just as the Duke of Brabant's forces, arriving late, began somewhat feebly to engage. A random, largely peasant-driven, attack on the lightly-guarded English baggage train had already occurred. Henry was nervous, fearing that they might now be attacked from front and rear with released French prisoners on the loose. He ordered the prisoners be killed and sent two hundred archers to the rear to see it done. But in fact, French forces were steadily withdrawing from the field. Henry reversed the order when it became clear, at about 3 o'clock, that the day was finally his – though around seven hundred prisoners had been killed in the meantime – an

---

5. John I de Valois, Duke of Alencon, was the grandson of Count Charles Alencon who had led cavalry attacks sixty-nine years before against the Black Prince's battle at Crecy, and died there. Before he died at Agincourt, Duke John had killed the Duke of York. Contrary to popular belief, the dented helmet above Henry V's tomb in Westminster Abbey is not the one he wore that day, though the Black Prince's ruby that he proudly wore in his crown circlet at Agincourt remains among the British crown jewels.

act that attracted condemnation only in more modern times. French losses overall were around 6,000 men with perhaps 2,000 more captured; English losses were in the low hundreds, maybe fewer.

On 29th October an army of hollow men trailed into Calais. But if Agincourt had settled nothing between England and France, it changed everything for Henry V. He returned to London in glowing triumph – with his customary appearance of absolute humility – as if the whole campaign had been a glittering success. Now there was money from Parliament and clergy, enthusiasm and political commitment to carry the war forward.

In 1416 English Harfleur had to be defended by sea against an attempt to recapture it. Then in 1417 Henry led 10,000 fresh troops to Normandy to resume hostilities. It turned into one of the great ironies in the history of the Hundred Years War – or perhaps just God's way of keeping Henry grateful. Agincourt had been the battle Henry was trying to avoid. It was his lucky escape from a failed campaign. But now, the very conditions that had made his 1415 campaign a failure were reversed in three helter-skelter years.

Henry took Caen quickly and immediately struck south, cutting Normandy in two. He now styled himself Duke of Normandy and kept his troops completely disciplined as he crossed 'his own lands'. He created a Norman conquest in reverse, giving territory to his English supporters as he went. He took Rouen after a long siege in 1419 and was menacing Paris itself by August that year. This was exactly what had been impossible in 1415.

And, most crucially, the reconciliation between Armagnac and Burgundian branches of the royal family that had kept French government together throughout Henry's campaigns now fell disastrously apart. In September 1419, a henchman of the Dauphin murdered John, Duke of Burgundy. It was part of an old blood feud that did not surface in 1415. But it did so now. Poor Charles VI, under outraged Burgundian influence in his makeshift capital at Troyes, suddenly had no other option but to agree Henry's terms – exactly the political outcome that Henry might originally have hoped for in 1415.

At the Treaty of Troyes on 11th May 1420, that most astonishing moment of the Hundred Years War occurred. Henry seemed to have united both the Plantagenet and Valois crowns. He had long since offered to renounce his claim to the French crown in return for a generous deal. Now it would be his anyway through right of conquest as soon as Charles VI died. He had wanted to marry Catherine of Valois since 1413 for good political reasons. But after meeting her in person during 1419 he was an eager bridegroom, as a thirty-three-year-old king who had been genuinely committed to his celibacy vow for the past seven years. Troyes was the victorious and happy pinnacle of his life. He could claim to have created permanent peace and was already turning his thoughts towards leading both kingdoms in a new great crusade to win back the Holy Land.

As regent for the ailing Charles VI, Henry conducted himself carefully and sensitively towards his new French subjects. Indeed, there were loud mutterings in Parliament that they had lost their victorious king to the blandishments of an effete French court. In reality, however, he was now drawn into the French civil war against the forces of the outlawed Dauphin who was disinherited by the Treaty of Troyes. Henry had continuously to bolster his own succession, with the Duke of Burgundy's support, and to gain full acceptance for the Treaty. There was a brief interlude when he brought his young Queen to England in early 1421 and they spent an idyllic break at his 'Pleasance' in Kenilworth Castle, where their only son was apparently conceived.

There followed campaigns in Chartres and Meaux with the Duke of Burgundy, whose support was critical to the new order. But in 1422 Henry was clearly ill while still campaigning in Charenton. He arrived in Vincennes, greatly reduced, and died there on 31st August 1422. Poor, mad, Charles VI outlived him by less than eight weeks. On his deathbed, and still lucid, Henry had made it clear by his final wishes that he well understood how fragile England's triumph in France might turn out to be if it were not vigorously defended.

He was quite right. There was an immediate French uprising against the English succession of Henry VI – just a nine-month-old baby – with the able Duke of Bedford named as regent. The English held their own against a joint French and Scots army at Verneuil. It was a second Agincourt in fact. But by 1426 the writing was on the wall for the English conquerors in France. The tide finally turned decisively for French forces in lifting the siege of Orleans in 1429, just days after the arrival of an infuriating young mystic calling herself Jeanne d' Arc.

By 1453 northern France was in a state of devastation and the English occupation had completely collapsed. England finally lost the war and became a genuine offshore island to the Continent for the first time since 1066. Henry VI's chronic personal weaknesses not only contributed to that loss but stimulated a powerful dynastic challenge to him in England. Henry V's neurosis about his Lancastrian legitimacy was probably not misplaced after all. The House of York openly opposed his son and in 1455, not two years since losing its last foothold in France, England was plunged into what became thirty years of desperate civil strife. England capped its defeat in the 'Hundred Years War' by immediately entering its own 'Wars of the Roses'.

Could it all have been different between England and France? Yes, of course, in any number of details and turns of quixotic fortune. But perhaps not in the broad outlines of European history.

Shakespeare wrote seven extremely popular history plays about the Plantagenet kings, spanning the whole dynasty until – very much out of sequence – he finally wrote *Henry V*. It was the last of his Plantagenet plays. So his audience knew very well the full story of the Hundred Years War and the Wars of the Roses. He concludes his version with Henry V and his bride, Catherine of Valois, on stage looking towards the glittering future that in 1420 seemed to stretch before them. 'Fortune made his sword', says Shakespeare's Chorus, 'By which the world's best garden he achieved, And of it left his son, imperial lord.' But the romantic Shakespeare was also a hard realist. 'Henry the Sixth, in infant bands crowned King of France and England, did this king succeed', he informs us, 'Whose state so many had the managing That they lost France and made his England bleed. Which oft our stage hath shown; and, for their sake', he says, nodding to the betrothed couple centre stage, and almost as an afterthought, 'In your fair minds let this, acceptance take.' Quite so.

12

Sir Francis Drake

The popular image of Sir Francis Drake casts him as a patriotic rogue; a corsair, privateer – sometime pirate – an adventurer, slaver, explorer, implacable opponent of Spain whom Queen Elizabeth I liked and encouraged while pretending to disapprove, and who shared command of the English fleet when it famously defeated the Spanish Armada in 1588, saving the realm from invasion. Somewhat unusually for popular historical images, this is all substantially true. Hyperbole around the life of Drake only really applies in casting the defeat of the Spanish Armada as so dramatic a saviour of the realm. Whatever the wild intentions of Philip II of Spain, his 1588 campaign was far from an effective invasion plan. In fact, there were five 'armadas' – attempts at amphibious landings – between 1588 and 1601; four Spanish, aimed at attacking England; and one English, aimed at attacking Spain. They all failed, some more miserably than others.

The character we have come to know as Sir Francis Drake was a born seaman, with a natural leadership personality, an instinct for adventure and a taste for its rewards; a committed Protestant, or at least a staunch anti-Catholic. Stocky, fair-haired, persuasive in his own unrefined way, he also proved to be ahead of his time in coming to understand the emerging nature of sea power in the sixteenth century. The precise date of his birth is unknown but is generally estimated to be around 1540–41. He was certainly born in Tavistock, Devon into a farming family; perhaps illegitimate, as the eldest of twelve children. He was made a very young apprentice – another hint of illegitimacy – to the household of William Hawkins in Plymouth where his seagoing experience, with a large dash of privateering, began immediately.

In 1548 his family fled to live on the Medway in Kent, after Drake's father was arraigned for assault and robbery. The boy was then apprenticed to the master of a local barque that plied the coastal routes and traded along the coasts of France and Flanders. He made a good impression on all his employers and was back working for the Hawkins family – this time for John Hawkins – by the time he was eighteen. John Hawkins's ships were traders which also prowled the French coast looking for easy plunder. And of course, they ventured to the new world. During his twenties, Drake was a seaman on board Hawkins's ships on at least some of their longer voyages to Africa and the West Indies.

The Atlantic slave trade between West Africa and the Caribbean was an official monopoly run by Portuguese merchants. In 1562 John Hawkins forcibly broke into it, backed by a friends-and-family consortium and made himself instantly rich. He immediately planned a second slaving voyage for 1563–4, backed by a bigger private consortium and now by Queen Elizabeth herself. Drake may have been a crew member on that second Hawkins voyage, and if so, would have had a commensurate share of any profits.

Inevitably, the Queen was pressured by Spain and Portugal to stop these expeditions and forbade Hawkins to undertake another one that year. So Hawkins furnished Captain John Lovell with a fleet that went anyway in 1566–7. Lovell attacked Portuguese settlements and ships on the African coast taking their slave cargoes to the Spanish plantations across the Atlantic – failing, it seems, to make a sale of them. It was an unprofitable expedition, but Drake was undoubtedly serving on one of Lovell's ships. We have no idea whether he thought much about what he was doing, but Drake was a willing, early English slave-trader.

John Hawkins immediately sought to recoup his losses with another voyage. On this trip there is good evidence that Drake was either an officer aboard the flagship, or possibly even given his own ship in the course of the expedition. It was ill-fated from the start. There were active Spanish attempts to intercept it, heavy fighting on the African coast, bad weather that reduced the fleet and then an Atlantic hurricane that forced their badly damaged ships into Vera Cruz in Mexico. No mention was ever made, of course, of the effects of all this on their imprisoned slaves. Having agreed that Hawkins could repair his ships at Vera Cruz, the Spanish then fell suddenly on them with overwhelming force. Only two badly damaged vessels escaped in the confused fighting that followed. Drake himself had to swim for it to make for a ship, and Hawkins subsequently accused him of desertion and theft. It appears, however, that Drake genuinely thought Hawkins lost in the fighting and so had distributed their treasure among surviving crew as they ran for safety.

This incident in 1568, however, lifted Drake's ambitions to a different level. No longer interested in slaving, or for that matter in conventional trading, he became implacably anti-Spanish after Vera Cruz. As a religious zealot, he hated Catholic ascendancy and everything the Vatican represented. He also realised just how easily Spain's looted American treasures could fall to a skilful predator as they passed overland. Now in his late-twenties, Drake had long demonstrated his sailing acumen. But he also had confidence in his command abilities – across more than a single ship and also in land operations. British maritime history is studded with some brilliant captains who were nevertheless poor leaders of a squadron or a regiment of marines, or who failed to master the personal politics of shared command that any group of ships involves. Drake's self-confidence, his religion, and his acquisitive instincts obviously drove him on.[1]

In 1572 he created an independent enterprise to attack the Spanish Main, specifically the Panama Isthmus where gold and silver from Peru was moved through the jungle to the Caribbean Sea for transhipment to Spain. He left Plymouth with two small ships and a crew of 74 men and made for the Spanish Main. He allied with the 3,000 or so

---

1. His acquisitive instincts were not exclusively personal. Defending the Elizabethan realm was beyond the revenues of the Crown and always involved cooperation between the state and private magnates who would invest in their patriotism in the expectation of a fair return.

Cimarrons – escaped Spanish slaves who survived as jungle guerrillas – and working with them, attacked and occupied the port of Nombre de Dios. It became his Spanish Main base for almost a year, launching forays against Cartagena and Spanish shipping and intercepting overland treasure convoys around Panama. He enriched the expedition and made the Spanish Main a much less secure place for the empire's operations.

He returned to England, rich and (in)famous but had to lie low, since his success was now politically embarrassing. He was asked by the first Earl of Essex to assist with some naval power in support of the earl's ill-fated attempts to colonise parts of Ulster. Drake served the earl's chaotic campaign in blockading Rathlin Island while its defenders and inhabitants were massacred. It did him no credit and little good, but was a service, of sorts, to the state.

In 1577, however, Drake was given permission by the Queen to undertake an expedition against Spanish shipping along the Pacific coast of America.[2] With this voyage, he was to become the first English sailor to circumnavigate the world. He set off in December with five ships and 164 men and boys, and added a sixth ship when he captured a Portuguese merchantman near the Cape Verde islands. Very soon, the journey tested Drake's powers of command. It was a difficult Atlantic crossing; his crews falling sick, and ever fearful of the unknown. He was voyaging in a deeply religious age that included implicit beliefs in witchcraft and magic and in which the weather always seemed to be an expression of these unknowable forces. By the time he reached the coast of modern-day Argentina, Drake had been forced to scuttle two ships for lack of men to crew them, and then to burn another, so badly were its timbers rotted. His leadership was a critical element in keeping the voyage alive. As a commoner, he was not much bothered by hierarchies, but he was a disciplinarian in the matter of ship-handling. He was ever-cheerful in adversity and could fire up his men to almost any attacking challenge. He seemed to listen to all advice, but then did – always – what he himself thought best. He was possessed of a charming brutality. From the beginning of this voyage, he had constantly quarrelled with his high-born co-commander. Thomas Doughty, previously a close friend, now seemed to Drake to have a brief from conspirators at Court to scupper the whole – unofficial – expedition. When they reached Patagonia in June and were preparing to take on the terrors of the Magellan Strait, Drake finally snapped and accused Doughty of witchcraft, then of mutiny and treason. Following a trial by ships' crew, and a sentence of death, Drake joined convivially in a banquet for him ashore before Doughty was led to the block – in the manner of a gentleman – and beheaded.[3]

---

2. Though not with a royal patent, to which the Spanish had already furiously objected two years previously. Drake was setting off officially to enter the Mediterranean, with a royal wink to go the opposite way.
3. Eighteen months later, when the doomsayer chaplain criticised all this as the ship lay grounded, in mortal danger – the chaplain claimed it was God's judgement on them – an exasperated Drake had him chained to a hatch cover and declared him excommunicated.

In September 1578 Drake's three ships tried to enter the Pacific via the fierce Magellan Strait.[4] But one ship was lost with all hands immediately and another was badly damaged and gave up, returning to England. Unaware he was alone, Drake pushed on through the strait, now in his single ship (renamed from *Pelican* to *Golden Hind*). He was driven south, probably as far as latitude 55°S around Tierra del Fuego. Finally giving up on any rendezvous with his other ships, he turned north along the Pacific coast of the Americas, attacking Spanish settlements and what ships he encountered. His was the first hostile vessel the Spanish and Portuguese had ever encountered in the Pacific. From his conquests, crucially, Drake obtained more accurate navigation charts. He was seriously injured by native people on Mocha Island, off Chile, but still went on to sack Valparaiso. Then he was into the Spanish and Portuguese trade routes in the Pacific. He captured a Spanish ship loaded with Peruvian gold, and heard of an even bigger prize bound eventually for Manila. He gave chase and captured it off the coast of Ecuador, winning a huge haul of looted treasure – gold, silver, jewels and chests full of royal plate. He lavishly dined the officers of the captured crew and set them ashore in Ecuador with personal gifts and letters of safe conduct.

He was now concerned to avoid Spanish vengeance and prepared for a homeward journey. It was generally believed that the power of Atlantic swells rendered the Magellan Strait a one-way passage, and Spanish ships were already cruising in the Atlantic looking for him. So Drake explored the possibility of a north-east passage from the Pacific to the Atlantic in the icy extremes of North America, but around 48°N was forced back.[5] The *Golden Hind* made landfall in what is now Oregon and then slipped south towards California, anchoring near modern-day San Francisco. Drake claimed it as 'New Albion', with a fort and a suitable brass plaque in the name of Queen Elizabeth and her successors.

Now there was nothing for it but to keep on westwards. After some months of preparation, they set sail south-west in July 1579 to pick up the winds that – they hoped – would take them to the Indies. With very imperfect instruments for measuring latitude and none at all to calculate longitude they plunged on a roughly southwesterly line, ignoring the tentative routes further south that Portuguese traders were exploring. They saw no land for sixty-eight days until they sighted the Caroline Islands, then ran along the Philippine coast to make a grateful landfall in the Moluccas, in modern east Indonesia. After several months – dealing diplomatically with Sultan Babullah – Drake then tried to beat north through the Malacca Strait but was forced back. In the closest the voyage came to complete disaster, the *Golden Hind* ground hard on one of the unknown reefs south of Peling Island (modern Sulawesi). Guns and equipment were jettisoned overboard to lighten the ship, but to no avail, and after three days of pounding Drake and his crew took the sacrament together in preparation for its inevitable disintegration. But the wind swung round and slowly, painfully, the hull slid

---

4. Modern research regards it unlikely that he rounded the tip of Cape Horn a little further south, despite the fact that the channel where Atlantic and Pacific oceans meet is nevertheless named 'Drake's Passage'.
5. Though this is only around the latitude of Vancouver.

off the reef. For two more months they battled difficult winds, driven into the Banda Sea and along north Timor before, yet again with grateful praise to the lord, they put into Tjilatjap in southern Java – the first Europeans ever to sail the south coast of Java. Repairs and revictualling followed before they struck south-west for the Indian Ocean.

In England, it was known at Court that Drake had entered the South Sea, but that he was dead, he had been caught and hanged, he had been lost in storms, killed by natives; his ship had simply disappeared, and so on. In fact, he was by then ploughing through vast but more settled waters, making for the Cape of Good Hope, and in July 1580, exactly a year after leaving the American coast, he made landfall in Sierra Leone in West Africa. In September, laden with treasure and spices, the *Golden Hind*, rotting and clogged with weed, laboured into Plymouth Sound with fifty-nine survivors of the 164 crew who had set out three years previously. Queen Elizabeth was entitled to a half share of the cargo – a share which was worth rather more than the Crown's annual income. She had always maintained to the Spanish ambassador that she thoroughly disapproved of Drake's activities, but she took her cut and immediately decreed that all documentation from the voyage be impounded as state secrets. Drake was knighted aboard *Golden Hind* at Deptford on 4th April 1581.[6]

On the basis of his fame, Drake made dubious claims to some ennobled kin, who loudly denied him. But given his new wealth, he purchased Devon's Buckland Abbey in 1580, which became his ancestral home for several generations. His wife of twelve years, Mary Newman, died the following year and in 1585 he married Elizabeth Sydenham, the only daughter of the High Sheriff of Somerset. He became a Member of Parliament on three separate occasions, for different constituencies, between 1581 and 1593, but took only fitful interest in a few issues. One suspects that becoming Mayor of Plymouth may have meant more to him, since he always worked hard for the city. But if he was a local hero in Devon, he was regarded as a vulgar upstart by most of his contemporaries, with his west-country accent, poor manners, boundless boasting and the disreputable stories that seemed to follow him around. Richard Grenville and Martin Frobisher – two of the most noted mariners in England – disliked him intensely. Indeed, Buckland Abbey had belonged to the Grenville family and they would never have sold it to him had he not dishonestly used an intermediary to purchase it. He was an early tax-evader, too, keeping deliberately vague records of his wealth, particularly in respect of his seizures from the Spanish. But Drake had the goodwill of the Queen, whether she thought him a vulgar tax-evader or not.

Though clearly an outsider, strategic events were to propel Francis Drake along as outright war with Spain became all but unavoidable. The counter-reformation was sweeping across Europe, driven largely from Philip II's wealthy Spanish court, with determined papal backing. Protestant England was too small and weak to be one of its main European targets, but Queen Elizabeth had already been excommunicated by Rome and the heretics in London would have to be dealt with sooner or later. English attacks on Iberian shipping hardly made the empire tremble, but it added to

---

6. Though not by the Queen herself, despite romantic Victorians wishing otherwise. To help deflect Spanish anger at Drake's predatory behaviour, she persuaded a French diplomat to do it.

a Spanish belief that England should be subdued all the sooner. By 1585 Spain had united with Portugal, France was weakened by civil war, and Spain's Duke of Parma was successfully reducing the rebellious Protestants in the Spanish Netherlands to submission under the all-powerful Hapsburg dynasty. In 1585 the key port of Antwerp was finally surrendered by the Dutch rebels to Parma.

The Dutch appealed to England for help, just when Philip's secret deals with Catholics in France raised again the overblown fear of a powerful anti-English alliance between the two biggest powers on the Continent. It drove Elizabeth to conclude the Treaty of Nonsuch in 1585, providing troops and aid to the Dutch rebels. It was the first international treaty concluded with what would shortly become the Dutch Republic – a risky move, aiding anti-royal rebels. Elizabeth and her closest advisor, Lord Burleigh, were doubtful, but both Leicester and Walsingham – Elizabeth's famous spymaster – persuaded them.

Philip II thought this sufficient cause for war against England and duly declared it. The Queen would not embrace it, however, and constantly dithered between trying to appease Philip II, clinging on to straws of peace talks wherever she saw them, whilst authorising her naval captains in an on/off series of campaigns to neutralise Spanish sea power. Her vacillation drove Drake, Hawkins, Grenville, Frobisher and the rest to distraction. Thus it was that in July 1585, only months after his second marriage, Drake was served with a Queen's Commission to undertake some pre-emptive action against Spain. He was given overall command of a fleet of twenty-one ships and a considerable force of 2,300 soldiers led by Christopher Carleill, who, despite the nepotism of being Walsingham's stepson, was in fact an excellent leader and the perfect soldier foil to the sailor, Drake.

This sort of potent striking force – both a privateering and a strategic venture – was ideal for Drake's tactical dash and self-confidence. More than that, Drake's plans showed he was beginning to appreciate what few of his contemporaries in the age of laissez-faire trade and exploration really understood; that fleet actions were the key to maritime control. If a battle fleet could dominate a wide area of sea-space, or a crucial trade route, friendly merchants and everyone else could go freely about their own business, without being half-trader, half-warship. The seas could be made secure 'for the state' with effective battle fleets.

He immediately took his force to occupy Vigo in Spain and held it for two weeks, then sacked Santiago in the Cape Verde islands. Then across the Atlantic with his ships and soldiers to capture Santo Domingo in Hispaniola, the old seat of Spanish power in the Caribbean, followed by the occupation of the key trading city of Cartagena in present-day Columbia – releasing slaves held by the Spanish and recruiting some of them into his forces. He was in control of Cartagena for two months while he scoured the surrounding territories. Then attacks on Spanish Florida, a relief trip to Walter Raleigh's beleaguered Roanoke colony in the Carolinas, and back into Portsmouth to a hero's welcome after a ten-month expedition that had been less financially successful than hoped, but which had genuinely strained the sinews of Spain's American empire. He was, by some measure, the most famous sea captain in Europe. To the Spanish he had become 'El Draco' – 'the serpent', in league with the devil – the pirate who seemed possessed of dark powers to turn up anywhere and disappear quickly, leaving fear and destruction in his wake. Even Lord Burleigh, who heartily disapproved of him, conceded that Drake was 'a fearful man to the king of Spain'. Indeed, Philip II had put a price of 20,000 ducats on his head, dead or alive.

Queen Elizabeth seemed fearful of what she had unleashed. Drake's raiding had Spanish merchants clamouring for restitution and Spain's lines of communication with the Caribbean and the Spanish Netherlands were obviously threatened by English expeditionary fleets of this sort. An invasion of England moved to the top of Philip II's crusading agenda and he pursued it with a fevered personal commitment. Pope Sixtus V promised him a million crowns once a Spanish army landed in England. Philip's 'Armada' of ships, troops and supplies was forming; and all Europe could see it.

In February 1587, after one too many Catholic plots, the Queen had Mary Queen of Scots executed. Now the die was cast. The following month Drake was given a new commission that effectively allowed him a free hand to hinder Spanish designs however he judged best. He took a fleet of twenty-four ships straight to Cadiz where more than sixty ships for the Armada were assembled and only awaiting favourable winds. He brought his force to attack immediately and in a fierce raid – not really a sea battle – braved passage under all the shore batteries to gain the outer harbour. He then personally led a flotilla of small ships' boats into the inner harbour during the night of 20th April, to board vessels and set them alight. Other Spanish vessels in the outer harbour were destroyed with gunfire wherever they tried to take on his ships. It was an audacious, highly risky raid that could have cost him the fleet. But it succeeded through sheer astonishment and the fact that England's purpose-built, new-design warships, up close and well-commanded, were almost invincible. Drake claimed to have destroyed thirty-nine enemy ships. Many Spanish sources only admit to a more plausible twenty-five, but either way, such losses were more than enough to delay the Armada for a year. Drake withdrew quickly and, in a procedure anticipating Nelson over two hundred years later, patrolled up and down the Iberian coast from a temporary base he captured at Cape St Vincent, his ships fanning out to intercept Spanish supplies and disrupt stockpiling for the Armada. He even blockaded Lisbon for a few days to make his point. And with the luck of the devil that El Draco could expect, he captured the massive Portuguese carrack, the fabled East Indiaman and the King's own ship, the *San Filipe*, near the Azores with its double cargo of oriental riches. It was a sensation when he brought it back to Plymouth.

Still, the Armada would be coming. As a commoner, Drake could not be appointed Lord Admiral of English naval forces. That was given to the Queen's cousin, Lord Charles Howard of Effingham, sailing in *Ark Royal*. But Drake became his Vice Admiral in the *Revenge* and Howard was an experienced sailor and shrewd enough to defer to Drake's judgement in matters of battle tactics. Their instincts were to take the offensive and go looking for the Armada as far away from the Channel as possible. The Queen again prevaricated. Drake twice took forces to Finisterre at the end of June and almost got just the weather gauge he needed for another pre-emptive attack as the Armada ventured out, then was driven back. But the English arrived too late to catch the core of the Spanish fleet and were themselves forced back to Plymouth as the winds veered round in early July. So they would just have to wait. Within two weeks, the Armada had reformed and was finally on its way.

The epic of the Armada was both more and less than it seemed at the time. It had been years in gestation and when finally launched, it was certainly impressive; 124 ships and 8,000 sailors, manning 2,500 guns, carrying 19,000 troops, to sail to England, link up with the 17,000 men of the Duke of Parma's army ready to invade from Flanders, with another 63,000 waiting in the Spanish Netherlands, to land in Kent and release the Catholic faithful of the country to rise up, aided by a Scottish invasion, against the government of Protestant heretics. Against this, Elizabeth had fewer than 6,000 professional soldiers to defend England if the fleet failed to defeat the Armada. Then, too, Elizabeth had executed Mary Queen of Scots and thereby opened the way for Philip himself to assert his personal right to the English throne.[7] When the Armada got into the western approaches its 'forest of masts' was said to be truly awe-inspiring. The rest of Europe, dominated by the fabulously wealthy Spanish empire, did not expect troubled England to be able to resist the grandeur and sheer might that Philip II could bring against it.

On the other hand, Philip's plans were very poorly thought through. And the one man who could make them work – the Marquis of Santa Cruz – died suddenly in February and was replaced by the depressive and fatalistic Duke of Medina Sidonia, who certainly couldn't. Santa Cruz seemed to understand modern sea power, but Medina Sidonia never did. If the Armada was intended to destroy Queen Elizabeth's fleet and therefore allow Parma's army an unhindered crossing of the English Channel in its 200 barges, then neither its tactics nor its armament were suitable for a battle of annihilation. Or if the Armada was intended to land Spanish troops somewhere along the English coast – Plymouth, Portland or the Isle of Wight were the possibilities – creating a pincer movement with Parma's forces landing from Flanders, then an undefeated English fleet would be able to destroy at least one of these armies in the vulnerable process of landing, and leave weakened Spanish forces still apart from one another. Or if – as it turned out – the Armada tried to link up with Parma to shepherd his army across the Channel, the simple topographical fact was that Parma's troops assembled along the Zeeland coast near Dunkirk, could never be properly protected by Armada ships. They were waiting in shallow waters, whereas the Armada had no deep-water port available and would have to ride offshore at Calais, where it would be vulnerable. Parma's men were already being attacked by Dutch rebels whose flyboats could have cut them down immediately if they set off, undefended, in open invasion barges. And the English fleet would quickly have been in among both ships and barges if Parma had ever been foolish enough to try it. While the English fleet remained in existence, the manoeuvre was simply impossible, at least without some divine intervention. There is some reason to believe that's what Philip assumed.

---

7. No matter that Philip had been an unloving husband to Queen Mary I, though she had adored him up until her death in 1558; his marriage now became the basis of his claim. When Mary died, he proposed to Queen Elizabeth I. Upon polite rejection, he managed to scrape some happiness with the fourteen-year-old Princess Elizabeth Valois of France, in the third of his four marriages.

Not least, Philip's strategy massively overestimated the possibility of a Catholic uprising in the England of 1588. There was conspiracy and treason aplenty, but the nationalist, Protestant resolve of England was one of the most remarkable features of Elizabeth I's reign. The prospect of conquest by the Spanish empire, with Catholic France in tow, sparked a patriotic response – among English Catholics too – that could be seen across all the forts, militias and beacon fires that ringed the English coast that summer.

The real importance of the 1588 battle, partly understood it seems by Drake, though very few others, was that it was a battle for sea control. As such, it would have to take place between battle fleets, not a mixed Armada that was more a massive convoy than a maritime striking force. As he viewed the Armada, Drake shrewdly estimated that fewer than half the vessels were battleships, immediately spotting the weakness of that magnificent forest of masts. He understood the simplicity of the equation; if one side or other controlled the English Channel with its battle fleet, then an invasion would either succeed or fail because of it. In the event, neither side managed to establish their control over the waters that mattered. The Spanish had an armed convoy that reached its eventual objective near Calais and the English had a battle fleet that was still functioning to the end. Only when both sides had effectively failed in their initial strategic intentions did the events of 1588 resolve themselves into a fleet action that decided the outcome.

Experienced sailors often say that maritime control is essentially about coping with the problems of the sea itself; the enemy are just one more damned nuisance. As it played out, the battle of 1588 was undoubtedly a complex contest between wind, tides and ships, and the skills of those manning them.

The winds that prevented Drake attacking the Spanish fleet from Finisterre were the same southerly winds that brought the Armada quickly and unmolested into the western approaches on 19th July, taking English commanders by surprise. There is no evidence that when the Armada was sighted Drake was playing bowls on Plymouth Hoe and refused to be rushed. The simple truth was that the tide was running strongly against English ships in harbour and for several hours they could not have got out. But then, as dusk fell, Drake and Howard led the fleet in a superb piece of collective seamanship, towing and warping themselves against the westerly wind into the open sea, sailing their manoeuvrable ships exceptionally close-hauled, to pass north and south of the Armada during a day and night of rain and squalls. They appeared at dawn on 21st July, upwind near the Eddystone Rocks, behind the Armada and in a natural attacking position. The Spanish were dumbfounded. El Draco seemed to have lifted the fleet bodily out of Plymouth and placed it right behind them.

The resulting battle of Plymouth set the pattern. Armada ships formed a huge crescent facing west, even as they proceeded eastwards up the Channel, waiting for English ships to close so they could use their size and soldiers to grapple and board them. But that was exactly what the English were determined to avoid, and they stood off and bombarded the Spanish with their heavier calibre, cast-iron guns, as opposed to Spanish bronze guns that quickly over-heated. English gunners were good in that they fired at twice or thrice the rate of Armada gunners, but poor in that they consistently aimed high, bombarding superstructures but doing little damage around the waterline. As the days went on, Armada ships became increasingly battered with many casualties aboard, but none were sunk. The English had some luck when Drake and others fortuitously captured the *Nuestra Senora del Rosario*, which turned out to be carrying about a third of all the treasure Philip sent with the Armada; and the *San Salvador* caught fire and was set adrift before the English took it in tow. But apart from that, English ships could not afford to get in close enough to sink any enemy vessels. The Armada kept inexorably on.

Admiral Medina Sidonia may have contemplated getting his ships into the Solent to seize the Isle of Wight as a base for operations. Howard and Drake were anxious to forestall this as the Armada approached Portland Bill, and Drake hoped to trap the enemy fleet against the Owers Shoals he knew so well just off Selsey Bill further east. But the summer wind was capricious. It first trapped Frobisher's squadron with Spanish ships having the weather gauge, then swung around and rescued Frobisher but frustrated Drake's hopes. But it put the Armada downwind, having to head south-southeast away from the Solent. That was their last alternative option. From then on, Medina Sidonia had no prospect of landing along the English coast and no choice but to proceed towards Calais for the impossible rendezvous with Parma in Flanders. Howard and Drake, while shepherding the Armada past Selsey Bill, were yet again out of powder and shot and had to reprovision quickly. And Howard seemed to be out of any better ideas, other than waiting for Seymour and Wynter to arrive with reinforcements from the Dover Strait.

On 27th July the Armada limped to anchor off Calais and Medina Sidonia and Parma began angry exchanges as to why neither could help the other. Dutch fighters effectively pinned Parma's army in place among the waterways of the Flemish coast. Seymour and Wynter's reinforcements had joined the fleet, bringing Howard's force up to a full strength 140 ships. Unable to unite their forces, and caught – downwind again – at anchor, Spanish commanders knew full well how vulnerable they were. The English lost no time, and just after midnight on 29th July, sent eight fireships drifting towards them on a brisk wind, running with the strong tide. Most Armada captains immediately slipped their cables, abandoning anchors (actions they would profoundly regret in the storms they subsequently faced) to manoeuvre away from the fireships. Without anchors, many were swept along on the tide, colliding and entangling themselves. None caught fire but the dislocation was all the English needed. By dawn everything was set, at last, to close with the enemy for a fleet-on-fleet battle as the Spanish tried to reform outside the small port of Gravelines. The battle of Gravelines would be for control of the Dover Strait.

Inexplicably, Howard made a massive error in taking his ship, and about twenty captains who followed him, off on a chase after the *San Lorenzo* which had no bearing on the outcome. But Drake's leadership persona with the rest of the fleet was far more influential, and his instincts remained implacable. He led them in a headlong, helter-skelter downwind attack on the bulk of the Spanish fleet as it was still reforming. 'It was the hour', said Drake's great Victorian biographer, Julian Corbett, 'for which Francis Drake had been born'. He pitched his *Revenge* against Medina Sidonia's flagship. Frobisher in the *Triumph* and Hawkins in the *Victory* followed him with their squadrons into the impenetrable, rolling smoke. Once the smaller English battleships were in among the big Spanish galleons, galleys, galleasses, armed merchantmen and freighters, there was only one plausible outcome; though aristocratic Spanish captains fought long and courageously against the English heretics. Howard eventually managed to bring his wayward group back into the real battle and over six hours the English dismantled the Spanish fleet as more of them sank, foundered or fled, until both sides were out of ammunition. The majority of Armada ships used the north-westerly wind to push north-east up the coast but found themselves caught between Drake's ships and the treacherous shoals of the Zeeland banks. None dared turn decisively to port to gain more sea room with the English within sight, upwind, waiting to pick them off. As the day passed their position became more desperate and their foundering more inevitable. Drake watched during the following night from the quarterdeck of the *Revenge* as his most complete victory over Spanish naval power took shape before him among the shallow waters of Zeeland which he had first known as a young apprentice seaman.

But the gods of the sea have many different ways of commanding respect. At the very point late the next morning, when most of Medina Sidonia's fleet would have grounded, the wind swung round to the south-west and gave them the blessed power of a wind on the beam to escape northwards. The English followed for a few days, but then just north of Dogger Bank, all were scattered in the first of a series of August storms. What the gods had prevented Drake from enjoying in a single, victorious spectacle, they now visited piecemeal on the battered and sickly Armada as it was forced round northern Scotland and south down the wild Atlantic coast of Ireland. Badly damaged ships were wrecked in successive storms, sailors and soldiers drowned, or casually murdered when they struggled ashore. During September the remnants of the Armada arrived back in different Iberian ports, led by a broken Medina Sidonia, so ill he had to be carried ashore at Santander. Only sixty of his ships are known for certain to have got back and some 15,000 men were lost.

Queen Elizabeth, clad in armour and riding a fine horse, made her famously defiant speech at Tilbury on 8th August, when the sea battle was actually all over. Her gesture nevertheless expressed both the national defiance of Spain and the reality that London didn't know for some months that, in fact, the danger had already passed.

So too, it seemed, had Drake's disproportionate share of warrior's luck. At the height of his renown, he led an English counter-armada against Spain in 1589; a great war-syndicate shared between crown and commerce that fitted out 180 ships and embarked many troops. This enormous force was too hurriedly assembled, did not exercise together, and suffered repeated bad weather and more royal vacillation which created unachievable objectives. Drake ran his own strategy. His fleet visited great destruction on Corunna and along the Portuguese coast but then failed to create an opportunistic land and naval link-up at Lisbon, intended to extract Portugal from Spain's control. The Atlantic storms that scattered and destroyed his fleet were as nothing to the Queen's fury at having her orders reinterpreted. It was all a political failure that cost twenty ships and perhaps 12,000 troops. Almost in petulance, Drake sacked Vigo, before slinking home to face a court-martial. His enemies at Court made the most of it and he was denied an expedition command for the next six years.

When he finally embarked on his 1595 expedition it was a joint commission with the elderly John Hawkins and it quickly descended into acrimonious, old-style privateering with no obvious strategic purpose. He attacked Puerto Rico, played hide and seek in the waters around Tortola – in the modern British Virgin Islands – and went back to his old haunt at Nombre de Dios; all for very little gain. He was without those elements of surprise, tactical speed – and devil's luck – that had always been his hallmarks. Older, depressed and very ill with dysentery, he made for Puerto Bello off Panama in yet another attempt to siphon off some of its riches. He died in January 1596 and was buried with great reverence, in his armour, six leagues out at sea, inside a lead-lined coffin that reputedly contained personal treasures.

Drake's coffin has been sought many times around Puerto Bello. In beach bars across the Caribbean modern chancers and fanatics will regale any visitor with the certainty that they know exactly where it is. The mystery fits his semi-mythical status in British history. But his achievements were far from mythical. Julian Corbett credits him with saving the English reformation. Less grandiose, he was undoubtedly a remarkable commander; a ball of energy, courage and ideas, a leader who could inspire his men to follow him – literally – to the ends of the earth. And his growing awareness of fleet actions, amphibious land/sea operations (sometimes, of course, unsuccessfully executed) and his instinct for sea control, nevertheless laid one of the foundation stones around which Britain's naval power would develop in the following century.

13

Sir Walter Raleigh

Sir Walter Raleigh was ten or twelve years younger than Sir Francis Drake, and their stories overlapped in many ways during the reign of Queen Elizabeth I. They both sailed to defend England from Spanish invasions and fought on land to loot Spain's empire in the Americas. But they were very different sorts of individuals and commanders. Drake was a natural warrior and remarkably successful in the national cause. Raleigh was a natural courtier, with a different sense of mission and vision of glory. And he was not very successful, at least as a military commander, though still one of the most popular men of his era. It is difficult to pin down quite what is genuinely true in Raleigh's life, so much did he elaborate and obfuscate around his own actions. He has come down to us through history in some very curious ways.

He was thrown into the Tower three times, and came out twice, after living incarcerated there for several years with his wife. Among other projects, he began a celebrated *Historie of the World*, while in the Tower. He was close to the great poets of the age, and both Ben Jonson and William Shakespeare wrote plays that were thinly veiled discussions of his alleged treason against King James I.[1] It is not true that he brought tobacco to England, though he popularised its use after John Hawkins introduced it. Nor is it true that he 'discovered' the potato; the plant already grew in other parts of Europe. He founded colonies, and has cities, counties and mountains named after him in the United States; but he never set foot in North America. And no serious historian believes that he came to the notice of Queen Elizabeth by spreading his cloak across a puddle she was about to step into. The story only resonates because it embodies his craven and ingratiating behaviour around her.

Raleigh was born between 1552 and 1554 at East Budley in Devon into an established county family of gentlemen farmers, in which he had a brother and three half-brothers. He grew up naturally imbued with the protestant cause in England and – since his father had to hide from Queen Mary's catholic agents to avoid execution – became fully committed throughout his life to its defence, even if his own intellectual development led him more towards humanism than religiosity. Like Drake and many others, he was thoroughly loyal to Queen Elizabeth and had no less keen an eye for the commercial opportunities of patriotism.

Well-educated and highly articulate, Raleigh attended Oriel College, Oxford, though apparently with an expensive social life that prevented him completing his

---

1. Ben Jonson's *Sejanus His Fall*, and Shakespeare's *Measure for Measure* were presented in 1603 and 1604 respectively. Shakespeare was one of the actors in the first performances of *Sejanus*. Its second performance was at the Globe Theatre.

studies. Instead, he spent two or three years on the Continent, fighting with Henry Champernowne's hundred horsemen for the Huguenot Protestants in the French civil war, surviving, it seems, two pitched battles. When he returned to England he was eventually admitted to the Inns of Court at the Middle Temple; a good career move, though he never intended to practise law. Now in his early twenties, Raleigh's persona was well-formed; charming, witty, writing some well-regarded poetry and embodied with a perceptive instinct for fashion – in both dress and politics. He was a young man on the make and he shared the fashionable taste among such men for profitable adventure. In 1578 he joined his half-brother, Humphrey Gilbert, in an attempt to take an expedition to explore a North-West passage somewhere up in the arctic waters of the Americas. Raleigh commanded one of the Queen's ships in the flotilla, the 100-ton *Falcon*, taking care to have an experienced Portuguese master mariner with him. Since there was no North-West passage, the expedition was doomed to fail, but it failed while still en route to America. England and Spain were conducting an undeclared mercantilist war against one another's shipping and it appears that Gilbert and Raleigh were not above some well-judged piracy – Philip II of Spain later rated Raleigh as a pirate second only to Francis Drake. But a single confrontation with Spanish ships became a fierce sea battle off the Cape Verde islands in which many were killed and young Raleigh only narrowly escaped death. But he survived, he learned important lessons regarding planning and provisions, and he managed to re-tell the story of the expedition in ways that got him noticed by the Queen and described in contemporary history books. He emerged from the whole miserable affair as an intrepid, natural sailor and young hero. In fact, he was neither. He was never a good sailor and for all the many miles he voyaged, he disliked being at sea and did not command a ship with much skill in stormy weather, when it mattered most. And though he was certainly not lacking in personal courage, his instinct for heroic leadership was always tempered by a stronger instinct for pragmatism. He was a conscientious and talented administrator and a natural fixer – not the same Drake-like attributes of confident, impetuous heroics.

After Cape Verde and in the wake of half-brother Humphrey Gilbert's savage reputation in Ireland, Raleigh found himself as a captain of a hundred men he had raised to help quell the Desmond rebellions in Munster – catholic rebellions against protestant England as much as they were struggles to retain dynastic feudalism against Tudor colonisation. Successive and characteristically brutal campaigns between 1579 and 1583 left the south of Ireland ravaged. At the siege of Smerwick Raleigh's men slaughtered at least 600 Spanish and Italian papal troops who had been sent to assist the Earl of Desmond. As the revolt was steadily supressed, Raleigh, like his commanders, was rewarded with long-term and profitable land-holdings in parts of Munster.

Through these attritional campaigns Raleigh's organising skills were recognised and he was solicitous over the welfare of his own men. And he was clever enough to open a private line of communication to Francis Walsingham – the Queen's spymaster – providing local intelligence and some shrewd judgements on the direction of events. In truth, Raleigh hated Ireland and as much as he contributed to England's immediate military success, he constantly looked for preferment back at Court.

The Irish campaign also provided the first example of what Raleigh intended as his great legacy to English history. He enthusiastically endorsed the policy of Walsingham and William Cecil to push English colonisation in Ireland as a way of pacifying the country. He tried over many years to colonise his Munster estates with English settlers. Recognising the potential of potatoes as crops, he introduced them into Irish agriculture in the 40,000 acres and fortified towns he now controlled. But his potatoes took more easily than his settlers. It was never a success, but he saw in it the essence of a greater mission than the pacification of troublesome Ireland. Colonisation as a concept, for Raleigh, was the key to a change in the strategic balance between England and its continental rivals. During the same years he was simultaneously trying to colonise the Americas just as earnestly as Ireland. Dreams of overseas colonisation represented a mission appropriate to a man of his widely varied talents.

With the back of the Irish rebellion broken, in December 1581 Raleigh managed to be sent with dispatches to Elizabeth's Court at Greenwich. Affecting a 'plain soldier' charm and offering his candid views of the campaign, he certainly caught the Queen's eye. She bid him remain. He was tall, swarthy and handsome, personable, dashing and assured. The antiquary, John Aubery observed that Her Majesty always liked to have 'proper men' around her. Raleigh was certainly that, and he spoke with studied eloquence on history, science, exploration, seamanship and military campaigning. With the fall from grace of Robert Dudley, Earl of Leicester, Raleigh fortuitously slipped smoothly into the favourite's role. As with a succession of royal eye-catching favourites, many wondered about his real relationship with the 'virgin queen'. We will never know the truth. They exchanged complimentary love poetry each had composed, and for long periods she would not allow Raleigh to leave Court. He was made Captain of the Queen's Guard, responsible for her personal safety – in effect, her bodyguard – and was near her most times. He offered advice on all matters of policy as one so close naturally would. Many assumed that Elizabeth's head had been thoroughly turned by Raleigh. But if so, and however attractive a man she found him, they didn't reckon on her shrewd judge of character. Raleigh was given wealth and privilege by Elizabeth, but never one of the great offices of state; never one of the important military commands. He was only ever an adviser, never a policy-maker. And she never made him a Privy Councillor; a lack of political weight within her circle that constantly gnawed at him.

But in 1585, in his early thirties, and as the slide towards war with Spain began to seem irreversible, Raleigh's star was rising. He became Member of Parliament for Devonshire. The Queen knighted him and awarded him properties; he was appointed warden of the tin mines in Devon and Cornwall and Lord Lieutenant of Cornwall. He was granted taxes from vintners and cloth merchants; even a patent on the manufacture of playing cards. Now he had real wealth and status. Not least, for his self-image of glory, he had been granted in 1584 a Royal Charter allowing him – on a twenty percent cut for the Crown – to explore and colonise any 'remote heathen and barbarous lands, countries and territories not actually possessed of any Christian Prince or inhabited by Christian Peoples'. The charter would be valid for seven years. It was designed to authorise the establishment of English colonies that would be capable of mining precious metals from heathen lands, and establish bases from which privateering raids on Spanish ships might be mounted.

Raleigh seems to have appreciated the strategic significance of these intentions. It is an exaggeration to claim, as some writers have, that Raleigh was founder of the British Empire. But some of the elements were certainly there. Whereas Drake had used his military acumen to attack Spanish power wherever he saw it, Raleigh instinctively took a wider view of England's national interests and believed not only in the 'Christian mission' of colonisation but saw it as a source both of national protection – from the Spanish – and what would be termed today as 'power projection'. The Queen never quite shared these visions however, and tended to view all overseas operations as little more than risky commercial ventures. Like everyone else, Raleigh had only a hazy notion of what might lie in the Americas. But his vivid imagination and his passion for science, history and geography, seem to have constructed in his own mind the near certainty of the wealth and future power of the Americas that others barely grasped.

If Raleigh appreciated the significance of his Royal Charter, however, he did not manage to raise the requisite money from investors, or provide sufficient chattels, or gather enough colonists to overcome all the natural difficulties of setting up a sustainable society in strange lands. Unlike the Pilgrim Fathers of a future generation, many of Raleigh's colonists were paid to participate in the experiment. For them, it was a high-risk opportunity, not a sacred calling. And Raleigh did not lead them, since he was forbidden by the Queen to leave her side. Had he done so, there would almost certainly have been more direction and clarity to their confused endeavours in the new world. Immediately he received the charter, however, he dispatched a small reconnaissance mission to investigate the south eastern coast of North America and it returned with good reports and two agreeable Algonquin warriors who were an immediate sensation at Greenwich.

In accordance with his Royal Charter, Raleigh immediately named North American territories (not already Spanish or French) as 'Virginia' and styled himself thereafter 'Lord and Governor of Virginia' – a title that infuriated his rivals at Court. In 1585 he sent an expedition under his cousin, Richard Grenville, who built a fort and established a small colony on Roanoke Island, leaving 107 settlers there when he returned home – nabbing a Spanish prize on the way back.[2] But the settlers were soon in trouble. In 1586 at the end of his famous raiding expedition to the Americas, Drake took off a number of Roanoke colonists who had had enough. Raleigh sent another expedition in 1587, which found Roanoke deserted but they tried again with about 120 settlers.[3] Plans for replenishment and reinforcement were frustrated by the immediate danger to

---

2. Under the terms of the Charter, Raleigh could claim a boundary of about 600 miles in all directions from any colony he established, which meant that in modern terms Roanoke gave him claim as Governor from Florida in the south to Maine in the north and as far west as Kentucky *provided* the Roanoke colony thrived. Its long-term commercial potential was immense; a fact evidently appreciated by Raleigh but not actioned by him with consistency.
3. The colony consisted of 90 men, 17 women and 11 children, including Virginia Dare the granddaughter of expedition leader John White, who became the first English child to be born in North America.

England of the Armada and it was not until 1590 that a relief mission finally arrived. All the remaining settlers had disappeared – no trace, or bones or bodies – it became known simply as the 'lost colony of Roanoke Island'. Years later, Raleigh dispatched three expeditions to Virginia, perhaps to try to find some answers; more practically to bring back valuable woods and plants from the wider area. None of them found anything and the final attempt in 1602 never even made it to Roanoke, turning back in the face of bad weather.

The failed Roanoke colony was partly a victim of the distractions caused by the imminence of the Armada during those years. It is interesting that such an acknowledged seafarer as Raleigh was not at sea during the campaign, alongside Howard, Drake, Grenville, Frobisher, Hawkins and the rest. Instead, Raleigh was made responsible for the land defence of Cornwall, Devon and Dorset, particularly given the possibility of an attempted Armada landing somewhere around Plymouth, Portland or Weymouth. It was a role for which his organisational flair was ideally suited. And as a non-aristocratic courtier, Raleigh was one of the few west-country figures on whom Elizabeth could genuinely rely; there were too many great families in western England whose loyalties were not certain and many with barely-concealed Catholic sympathies. Raleigh was highly competent, vigorous in the way he undertook such tasks and he could have no other allegiance; he owed everything to his Queen. Others resented him, but coastal defence was a key element in England's preparations and Raleigh was an important member of the Council of War as it considered how the Spanish threat might actually play out.

As a wealthy man Raleigh also had ships built. Drake's *Revenge,* and the *Roebuck* that fought in Drake's squadron in 1588, were his ships. His *Ark Raleigh* had been sold to the Crown in 1587 and renamed *Ark Royal*, becoming Lord Howard's flagship in the battle. There is inconclusive evidence that Raleigh might have taken part in the fighting off Portland Bill on 23rd July; but if so, it was unremarked by others. Nevertheless, he could share in the collective pride of the government and the military establishment that defeated the Armada, and in the edgy, tenuous salvation it seemed to have brought the realm for a while.

Perhaps it marked the high point of Raleigh's rise to power. He certainly received many rewards from Elizabeth in the next couple of years. But his chameleon life began to take a series of more bizarre turns thereafter. In 1591 he secretly married – that is, without the permission of the Queen – Bess Throckmorton, one of her ladies-in-waiting. Feisty and resourceful, Bess had become pregnant by Raleigh some months earlier. The couple eventually had three children together over their twenty-seven-year marriage. When the Queen discovered the marriage, and child, she had them all sent to the Tower – though it didn't stop Raleigh maintaining some of his administrative duties while he was there. The Queen's anger at secret marriages was not merely personal, though in Raleigh's case it might have been. In an era of religious plots and deadly intrigues, any marriage at Court might turn into a security threat to the state or the Queen herself. Like top civil servants in the modern era, courtiers' lives had to be vetted. Raleigh and his wife were released after a couple of months when he bought himself out after the fortuitous capture of a Spanish prize by his own Panama expedition ships. But Bess never returned to Court and, out of favour, the couple concentrated on their own wealthy and admired private lives at Sherbourne Castle.

But political power is addictive and Raleigh still craved access to it. His scheme to redeem himself was at once fantastical and entirely pragmatic; another Raleigh venture where image and reality became hard to separate. He would set off to that part of Guiana that is now Venezuela, to discover the legendary site of El Dorado – the fabulous city of gold somewhere (he believed from fanciful Spanish accounts) around Lake Parime in the highlands. In 1595 he led six ships to Guiana and began mapping and searching for El Dorado. Like the North-West passage, it didn't exist. But the discovery of some 'fool's gold' in river basin ores was enough to keep the El Dorado dream alive for many years.

In fact, there was also some characteristic Raleigh strategy behind the dream. He believed that the fabled city of Manoa, possibly in the Orinoco lowlands would either be, or hold the key, to El Dorado itself. If he could find it, the English exchequer would enjoy a massive windfall. He hoped, in any case, to extract gold and silver from mines 'he knew' to exist in the area – though the number of mines 'he knew of' was always elastic. But he also believed in establishing a strong English colony that could reach into the southern hemisphere to compete with Spain and simultaneously diminish the internal commerce between native and Spanish traders. His imagination was fired by the glittering prospects of gold, but his pragmatism could see a good mercantilist rationale for a strong presence south of the Caribbean. If he could find El Dorado, England would assuredly establish a powerful base to defend it.

The expedition became an epic quest as he led his ships up unknown tributaries of the Orinoco delta, observing a new world of jungle wildlife, stunning vistas, exotic peoples, naked and impressive Amazonian women – his subsequent account lost nothing in the telling. In the end, his expedition returned with only enhanced promises of success for the future. But Raleigh was feted nevertheless as an intrepid explorer and a visionary. His 1596 book, *The Discoverie of the Large, Rich, and Bewtiful Empyre of Guiana* was – apart from 'bewtiful' – an overstatement in every respect. But it convinced many in England, and he produced another pot-boiler on his Guiana travels in 1606.

Meanwhile, as urgent as the quest for El Dorado was, the war with Spain provided Raleigh with other opportunities for redemption if he was prepared to go back to sea commands. Like Drake, he constantly pressed for more maritime privateering operations against the Spanish in the wake of the Armada victory. But the Queen was always cautious and Philip of Spain was able to prepare another Armada designed to land an army possibly in England, or more likely in Ireland, in support of yet another major revolt.

When he returned from the Orinoco, Raleigh was made third in command in 1596 of a force that would again attack Cadiz. Charles Howard, who had commanded against the Armada, and the Earl of Essex were to lead a big Anglo-Dutch force of, eventually, 170 ships and 16,000 troops. Raleigh devoted enormous personal effort to get the force prepared in time to sail. When it did, the operation turned out to be surprisingly easy. Though Spanish forces could certainly overwhelm any English attempt to occupy Cadiz permanently, they were too dispersed and disorganised to prevent it being held briefly in a two-week raid. The Spanish immediately lost ships, and to prevent others falling into English hands, burned thirty-two vessels themselves and had to stand by while the enemy sacked and incinerated Cadiz; not attacking citizens, but holding them for ransom. It was another major blow to Philip of Spain and a cheeky victory for the Anglo-Dutch force. Raleigh was seriously wounded in the leg during the early action, but his chief concern was to be the first to get his own version of the affair back to England. His letters to Court were a study in false modesty, with carefully judged praise for his most bitter rival, the Earl of Essex. They skated over the fact that the force had failed to really stymie Spain by capturing its merchant fleet at Cadiz, or seize its treasure ships.

No matter. Raleigh was one of the new heroes of the sea. In October that year a second Spanish Armada against England came to grief in storms off Finisterre, so that none of the force even reached the Channel. The following June, controversially, Essex and Raleigh were jointly embarked on the 'Islands Voyage' to the Azores, to destroy the Spanish fleet, occupy Ferrol, displace Spanish power in the islands, and intercept the next huge treasure convoy as it passed through. The over-ambitious expedition, led by the two over-weaning rivals, failed on every count, incurring significant losses in both ships and troops. The personal rivalry between Essex and Raleigh had been toxic. Again, in October 1597, Raleigh got his account of the whole sorry affair to the Court first. But the eventual truth was stark enough.

That very month, the third Spanish armada was on its way. It was another large force – 136 ships, almost 9,000 troops, plus 300 horses. And the English coast was wide open, its depleted and battered fleet still trailing in from the Azores after its failures. As usual, however, this third Armada's objectives were as ambiguous as the previous ones – help revolt in Ireland, or land in England – and if so, to raid English ports, or actually invade to provoke a catholic uprising. The objectives kept shifting. And, as ever, older designs of that era's warship were easily scattered in autumn storms as the force reached the Western Approaches. Some Spanish ships made involuntary landfalls on the Welsh coast; there was a brief landing at Falmouth, but most Spanish vessels milled around, failing to be intercepted by the returning English fleet. Raleigh was in the *Warspite* and though he didn't engage any major ships, he gathered from one smaller captured vessel vital intelligence about the size of Spanish forces. Only then was the real extent of the threat clear; and how lucky the English could count themselves, having taken the fleet so far west to the Azores. Raleigh immediately set out again with Howard from Plymouth to look for the enemy. But by then, most Spanish vessels were almost back in Corunna. The danger had passed. Since the 1596 Cadiz raid, both sides had been less than competent in their naval campaigns. They had effectively bankrupted Philip of Spain, and England's strategy in those years showed that its leaders were still only groping towards an understanding of sea control as a way of defending the realm.

Raleigh's own prestige – like that of Essex – was now highly equivocal, since the Islands Campaign had been a dangerous disaster. He became an MP twice more, was excluded from Court when he was sent as Governor of Jersey to strengthen its defences, and he organised the final expedition for the Roanoke colony in 1602. When the Queen died in 1603 there were precious few to support him at Court and Raleigh was left exposed to the whims of her successor, James I. The new king saw Raleigh as a dangerous intriguer and abhorred everything about him.

Raleigh's longstanding connections with Lady Arabella Stuart gave James I the opportunity he needed to have him arrested quickly in 1603 – at the *Old Exeter Inn* at Dartmoor – on charges of treason. There had been a genuine conspiracy in favour of Arabella Stuart against the incoming King, but the case for Raleigh's involvement in it was extremely weak. Nevertheless, he was taken to the Tower for a second time, convicted, sentenced to death, then spared; but not before, in despair, he had stabbed himself in a botched attempt at suicide. After recovering from his depressive state, he spent the next twelve years in the Tower; presiding, in fact, over a tolerable literary and scientific salon, and becoming a celebrity, sighted on his regular walks along the inner walls. Bess joined him and a third child was born inside the Tower in 1605. Even incarcerated, he became tutor to the Prince of Wales – which should have been his ticket out of imprisonment. But the Prince succumbed to typhoid in 1612 and that hope was dashed. Meanwhile, James I had stripped Raleigh of his official sources of income and confiscated much of the rest. Raleigh regularly petitioned the King and offered advice on everything he could conceive, but to no avail. Eventually, the parlous state of James's finances offered Raleigh a final opportunity to argue, once again, for the El Dorado scheme.

James allowed him out of the Tower on license and Raleigh sank what money he and Bess still possessed into a final expedition to find the legendary city, or at least its – unnumbered – gold and silver mines. Of course, he didn't. James I and Philip III of Spain were observing a fragile peace after the turbulence of the Elizabethan years. But while exploring up the Orinoco River, Raleigh's force (though not him personally) ended up fighting with Spanish troops and thence sacking San Thome, in direct contravention of James I's most explicit instructions. Raleigh lost his volatile and headstrong son who was in command during the engagement – suckered into a fight the Spanish seem to have provoked to have Raleigh condemned once and for all. Raleigh himself was devastated to lose his son; he was already ill, and broken by the whole failed venture. Raleigh was not the first, nor the last, to be ruined by El Dorado.

He returned to England, knowing he would immediately be arrested; thought about escaping, but decided against it on grounds of honour. He was brought to London and held under arrest at his wife's house in Broad Street, but then threw in his lot with a foolish French plot to spring him from arrest and meet a ship at Gravesend. He was betrayed and captured as, heavily disguised and armed with four pistols, he attempted to leave Tower dock in a rowing boat. He went back to the Tower for the third time. He was tried again for treason and this time the sentence would not be commuted. But the King understood that Raleigh was a national hero and now, too, a political martyr. Raleigh's beheading was carried out on 29th October 1618 in Old Palace Yard outside Parliament. To distract attention, it was timed to coincide with the Lord Mayor's show a couple of miles away. Raleigh was buried in St Margaret's church, inside the grounds of Westminster Abbey – except for his embalmed head, which was carried around in a bag by his wife for almost thirty years. It was eventually reunited, at least proximately, with his body in 1667. Nothing about Raleigh was ever straightforward.

Walter Raleigh was not a prominent military commander in any conventional sense. He was counted among that band of sea-dogs that Elizabeth relied on for national survival in troubled times. But he was, in the phrase of the age, a 'man of parts'; a genuine scholar, poet, soldier, scientist, explorer, cartographer and fashionista. He was not a popinjay – though he could behave like one – but immensely gifted and resourceful. He showed strategic vision ahead of his time. Before his execution he was anxious that his wife should retrieve notes he had for a book, *The Art of War by Sea*. And his constant interest in the potential of the Americas suggests it was based on more than a lucky guess on his part. His failures lay in the restless spirit that wanted to do too much; that lacked the single-mindedness to make one thing a life's work; and which was always slave to the public acclaim which blurred the lines between truth and image. As a gentleman, rather than an aristocrat, he rode a tidal wave of glamour and approval while he could. But the post-Elizabethan Court was immediately different under James I and he found himself increasingly out with the times, and out of significant friends when his persuasive powers were failing him. He was guilty of venality in many respects, and foolishness in others. But he was never a traitor; rather, a man of moderate birth but considerable intellect who flew too high in royal circles and was brought down partly by Court jealousy but mainly because under James I of England and Philip III of Spain, the political ground had shifted under him. King James certainly didn't like him, but that hardly explains his eventual determination to have Raleigh executed. The fact is that after all the confrontation and opportunity of the Elizabethan era, James I was untroubled to sacrifice Raleigh – in his mid-sixties – for the sake of his rapprochement with the new Spain that was emerging.

Oliver Cromwell, Lord Protector

Oliver Cromwell is one of the most astonishing figures in British military history. Born at the less fashionable end of a Huntingdon country family, he did nothing to distinguish himself until he was forty-one. But by the time he was fifty-eight – and in an age that believed in the divine right of monarchs – he was offered the crown of the combined kingdoms of England, Wales, Scotland and Ireland. He declined the crown, but exercised its powers anyway, until he died only eighteen months later. If ever the fate of one man was entirely determined by the outbreak of war and the exercise of military command, it was Oliver Cromwell. And since it all happened as a result of civil war and the eventual execution of an anointed king, it was characteristically merciless and brutal. Cromwell was, and still is, both revered and reviled across the length and breadth of the British Isles, wherever his ferocious energy took him. Indeed, though his body is long-since lost and his head secretly buried, some biographers have noted that he is never at rest; Cromwell remains Britain's busiest ghost – in manors, castles and old houses everywhere.

His extended family was socially prominent when he was born in Huntingdon in 1599. Oliver was, in fact, the great-great-great nephew of the infamous Thomas Cromwell – the blacksmith and brewer's boy who became Henry VIII's chief minister prior to his fall and execution. Oliver's father had been a Member of Parliament for Huntingdon and his prominent uncle was a substantial landowner. But while his branch of the Cromwell family was certainly well-connected, they were not well off. At the age of eighteen, while Oliver was studying, not very effectively, at Sidney Sussex College, Cambridge, his father died. Overnight, he had to assume the role of head of a household, consisting of his mother and seven sisters. He was quickly able to make an advantageous, and apparently happy, marriage to Elizabeth Bourchier in 1620, with whom he subsequently had nine children surviving into adulthood.

Cromwell took appropriate roles in local politics but he was a pugnacious individual who got embroiled in fierce personal disputes, one after another. His finances suffered and when he felt compelled to move from Huntingdon a few miles away to St Ives, he no longer owned any property and had become no more than a tenant farmer. In 1636, however, he was fortunate to inherit land and money from Thomas Stewart, a childless uncle, and the Cromwells moved with their growing family to live rather more comfortably in Ely.

By then, it was clear that Cromwell's edgy character was fundamentally shaped by a sense of his own personal relationship with God. He had not merely grown up as a dedicated Puritan with a visceral distaste for catholicism, or any manifestations of 'popery'. He had, according to his own later account, undergone some sort of religious epiphany around 1630 and felt the overwhelming power of 'providence' – either as its servant or its personal instrument. He would deliberate long and hard in private over important decisions, wrecking himself with the moral agonies of choice until he felt the will of God revealed to him. And then he would be resolute in his course.

Cromwell was a complex man. A Puritan, yes, but not without a lively sense of humour. He was a practical joker on social occasions, not always in control of himself. He abhorred catholicism but believed in general toleration among the different sects within protestantism. For many years he was tentative, quite ambiguous, in his political stances; but a man of iron will and clarity of thought in matters of military command. When Parliament offered him the crown in 1657 he spent over two months thinking about it before declining; not – as his detractors claim – as a matter of cynical calculation, but because he seems to have been genuinely uncertain what he *should* do, until God gave him guidance. His strong convictions did not make him insufferably priggish, and yet he was not embarrassed to claim, as he constantly did, that he was God's instrument. Like Alfred the Great and the medieval kings of England, he sincerely believed that God ultimately gave military victory, and legitimate power, to the righteous.

On the basis of patronage, Cromwell became Member of Parliament for Huntingdon in 1628–9, making no impression on anything. Elected again a decade later in 1640 as member for Cambridge in the 'short', then the 'long', parliament he was, by the standards of the day, in later middle-age. His appearance in the House of Commons was still inauspicious; plain clothed, somewhat dishevelled and little versed in the capital's manners. He spoke in public during all those years with a kind of ineffectual sincerity. Never a man of evident physical stature or robust health, he sought treatment more than once for his depressive states of mind. He was a hypochondriac whose weaknesses took him off the political front line quite regularly. Yet he subsequently pushed himself to the very edges of exhaustion in his relentless military campaigning and in the miles and miles he rode. He always understood and loved horses; just as well, since he spent so much of his later life in the saddle.

But arriving in Parliament that April in 1640 he witnessed at first hand the latest humiliations of Charles I; the bankrupt King's high-handed demands in trying to raise taxes, the Scottish occupation of Newcastle-upon-Tyne and the demeaning Treaty of Ripon that followed, the beginning of another serious insurrection in Ireland, and above all, the King's botched attempt in January 1642 to invade the Commons chamber and arrest five MPs on the spot. Cromwell was not one of them, but he was more outraged than most by Charles's attempt at a constitutional coup. As Crown and Parliament drifted into a muddled antagonism over the following months, Cromwell was an industrious follower, rather than a leader, of Parliamentary opposition to the monarch. He had always worked hard on procedures and committees on behalf of individuals such as John Pym, John Hampden or the Earl of Essex. By 1642 it was clear that he grasped more incisively than most the emerging logic of the situation. Parliamentarians must prepare to fight the King. He had no idea where this would take them – he certainly did not then even contemplate regicide. He did not believe in removing the King, but rather in making him, or a successor, a monarch subject to a more godly constitution, in a more godly country. But the time for posturing was over; Parliament would have to take to the field.

He returned to Cambridge on his own initiative to give effect to Parliament's desire to prevent the Cambridge colleges – naturally Royalist – donating their plate and treasures to Charles I. Cromwell had no authority but raised an informal armed band in his own home territory and took it to Cambridge to prevent any transfer of treasure, creating a blockade of anything leaving for the Royalists. Then he seized the arms magazine at Cambridge Castle (with its precious gunpowder) and guarded the crossings of the Rivers Cam and the Ouse, to stop any aid reaching the King from East Anglia. While others were confused by events, Cromwell acted instinctively and decisively.

Parliament was impressed and commissioned him to raise a troop of horse to serve with the Earl of Essex's cavalry. Partly with his own money, Cromwell recruited and equipped sixty horsemen to his troop which, by default, he commanded as a captain. He had no experience of military life, still less of campaigning. He had never commanded anything or anyone. He read the military manuals on procedure and took his troop to muster at Northampton. He was inventing his own command techniques as he went – learning quickly. His personal ability with horses probably helped him gain respect. He was no elitist, he believed in his men, he had manifest personal convictions, and once free of the political arena, he became a natural leader in the military world where clarity of action pays such dividends among soldiers.

Nevertheless, Cromwell's military role was still peripheral in the autumn and winter of 1642–43. In October, Charles was leading his Royalist troops from Shrewsbury to take London, when the forces of the Earl of Essex, moving from Northampton to Worcester, blundered into them at Edgehill. The resulting battle was a confused stalemate, with Parliamentary forces too widely scattered to engage properly. Cromwell's troop, along with Hampden's brigade, seem to have arrived when it was too late to contribute much. The Royalists continued their march on London. But in other ways, the outcomes of Edgehill would have critical effects on the war. Cromwell became convinced thereafter of the need to recruit only godly men of real conviction into Parliamentary forces. Their commitment mattered more than their numbers. 'If you choose godly honest men', he said, 'honest men will follow them'. It was to be his guiding principle for recruitment into the brief, unique and unbeatable army that came to serve him until his death.

And the political outcome of the war – the execution of the King and all that followed from it – in a way, was settled in the weeks immediately after Edgehill by the battle that never was. Cromwell joined the bands from Hertfordshire, Essex and Surrey in scrambling to oppose the continuing Royalist advance from the west towards London. The confrontation took place in November at Turnham Green. Parliament's defence line ran from south to north, finishing just where today's Piccadilly Line tube station stands. The Royalists baulked when they saw the number of spontaneous volunteers standing beside the regulars ready to fight; they decided to avoid battle and turned away towards Oxford. In the event, Charles had squandered his first and last chance to win the war quickly. He never again got close to the capital. And without it, he was condemning the country to a prolonged struggle and his own forces to ultimate failure. If he were to win, it would have to be by occupying London, and quickly. The longer the war lasted, the stronger Parliament – in London – would become.

And yet, Charles's dismal fate in the war created the very issue that tortured Cromwell's conscience as much as any other Parliamentarian. He struggled with it for the rest of his life. The Earl of Manchester famously expressed the problem during his angry confrontations with Cromwell two years later; 'If we beat the King ninety-nine times,' he said, 'yet he is King still, and so will his posterity be after him'. Very few Parliamentarians were fighting for a republic; certainly not the highly conservative Oliver Cromwell. Parliament could defeat the King in the field, but it could not replace his legitimacy, or that of a successor. It was a dilemma that only increased for Cromwell as his meteoric rise continued; it overshadowed his every triumph on the way.

But in 1643 he was promoted to command a regiment as Colonel of Horse, and he operated vigorously across the Eastern Counties, taking effective command in securing Cambridge, Lincolnshire and Nottinghamshire while his Major General was fully occupied elsewhere. He led constant operations and raids around the region; he was swift, tough-minded and uncompromising. He had his horse shot from under him leading his cavalry at the battle of Winceby. In a year when the Royalists made many gains across the west and the midlands, eastern England became secure Parliamentary territory. Parliament was again impressed with Cromwell, and before the end of 1643 he was promoted straight to Lieutenant General, responsible under the Earl of Manchester for the 'Eastern Association' of forces. By early 1644 he was a member of the Parliamentary Committee directing the whole war effort.

Cromwell was quickly involved in the long siege of York that year, which was being held for the Royalists by the Marquess of Newcastle. The most effective of the King's generals, his flamboyant nephew, Prince Rupert of the Rhine, arrived in July with Royalist troops to break the siege. The Parliamentarians withdrew towards Tadcaster, but there they turned to face Rupert while other allied units began to converge on the area. Having relieved York, Rupert foolishly decided to 'pursue' the Parliamentarians southwards until he found, six miles north of Tadcaster, a superior enemy force of about 22,000 Parliamentarian and Scottish forces waiting for his 18,000 Royalists at Marston Moor. It would mark the biggest battle of the Civil War.

Marston Moor, fought in the early evening of 2nd July, ended in overwhelming victory for the Parliamentary army. And it marked a watershed in Cromwell's rise to power. The Parliamentarians, now with their Scottish Presbyterian allies, were commanded jointly by the Earls of Lieven and Manchester and by Lord Fairfax. The latter's son, the redoubtable Sir Thomas Fairfax, commanded cavalry on the right wing. Cromwell commanded four or five thousand cavalry and troops on the left wing. Cromwell's first charge was ruthlessly effective in driving the outnumbered Royalists opposite him – Rupert's previously unbeatable cavalry – back in confusion. The Royalist centre was open to a flank attack. But Cromwell was wounded in the neck and had to withdraw for treatment. Meanwhile, the Parliamentary centre was being steadily defeated by the veteran northern foot soldiers of Prince Rupert and the Marquess of

Newcastle. Thomas Fairfax's cavalry on the right had only achieved a pyrrhic victory. By late evening, around half of Parliament's army was on the run and Lieven, Lord Fairfax and Manchester had already abandoned the field in the expectation of defeat. Cromwell returned to the battle, to meet the wounded Thomas Fairfax who had ridden across to him. The two junior commanders understood each other. After consulting his own English and Scottish leaders, Cromwell swung his whole force – still cohesive after their earlier victory – round to launch a vigorous attack on the centre and rear of the Royalist lines. Outnumbered and losing their cohesion as losses and looting diminished them, the Royalists became easy victims to a whirlwind of killing; 'God made them as stubble to our swords' as Cromwell famously put it. Eventually, even Prince Rupert was forced to hide before escaping. His trademark poodle was found abandoned, and killed in case it had satanic powers.

Cromwell was lauded as the hero of the battle, to the intense irritation of many others. Certainly, he was prepared to take the plaudits for it (at least after God), all enhanced in the public mind by the explosion of printed pamphlets and tracts that became a feature of British politics for the first time during this era. But Cromwell's real problem was that so decisive a victory was not followed up with alacrity. Parliamentary factions became more antagonistic – he was firmly in the more moderate camp of the 'independents' over the absolutist Presbyterians, whose influence was key to keeping Scottish forces allied with them against the nascent 'popery' of the Royalists. A series of military blunders by Parliamentary generals in the south west allowed Charles to regroup his political and military forces after Marston Moor, and at the second battle of Newbury in October 1644 the Parliamentarians failed to nail their opponents when they had them caught inside a pincer movement. Cromwell was there, and for once, seemed to misread the battle and brought his own cavalry in too late to clinch the outright victory that seemed probable.

But his chief battle was with the Earl of Manchester in Parliament. After Sir Thomas Fairfax, Cromwell was the most respected military commander in the Parliamentary army. He rounded on Manchester and his associates for the lacklustre way the war was being prosecuted. In truth, their 'lacklustre' was the constant hammering of the central problem – 'if we beat the King ninety-nine times, yet he is King still'. Cromwell's logic was becoming persuasive, however, and Parliament found for him and against Manchester. If he would not relent, the King must somehow be captured or driven into exile and the war must go on at a greater level of intensity.

Parliament began to form a 'New Modelled Army' which was to prove decisive on the battlefield.[1] The New Model Army was created in February 1645. It was disbanded after only sixteen years with the restoration of Charles II. But in that short time the 'NMA' reshaped military thinking both in Britain and across much of Europe. It became the hinge between the ad hoc, localised armies of medieval wars and the professional, standing army, for both war and peace in modern times.

---

1. The term 'New Model Army' was not used until 1845 by Thomas Carlyle, but it has since become the accepted name.

Cromwell did not create or initially command it. Sir Thomas Fairfax was made Lord General. But Fairfax and Cromwell had great respect for each other and both pushed hard against Parliamentary traditionalists who resisted its relentless demands for professionalism over privilege. Cromwell's whole approach to war was embodied in the NMA and he had growing influence in its use; after 1650, he was its supreme commander. Though he was later confronted with many political clashes between the New Model Army and other demands on a ruler's loyalty, he always came down eventually on its side. It became, for good or ill, *his* army.

NMA troopers were liable for service anywhere, rather than only around their local area. Senior commanders were required to observe the 'Self-Denying Ordinance' which forbade them occupying a post in Parliament alongside one in the army (Cromwell was famously an exception), so there would now be a separation between political eminence and military judgement. The forces of the Earl of Essex, the Southern Association and Cromwell's own Eastern Association were merged into an establishment authorised for 22,000 troops – divided into fewer, but larger, regiments with fewer officers. There would be 14,400 foot soldiers – musketeers and pike-men – 6,600 horse (cavalry), and 1,000 dragoons (in effect, mounted musketeer infantry). The regiments of horse – Cromwell's 'Ironsides', as they became – were key, not just for mobility and impact but because they were highly disciplined. On the Royalist side, Prince Rupert's experienced and fearsome cavalry was generally restricted to one effective charge during a battle, because riders all drifted away to their own devices afterwards. But the NMA's horse regiments were trained to regroup and go again, and again, as commanded. Among the foot army, the NMA would deploy two musketeers for every pike-man. The 16-foot pikes were principally to defend against cavalry attack. Muskets were evolving to become the lethal edge of the army in battle and musketeers were trained to fight six ranks deep, so that front ranks could fire, retreat to the sixth rank and have time to go through the laborious reloading drill before they again became the front rank. That, at least, was the theory. Artillery, interestingly, was not so well used on either side, despite the endless sieges of the war, but NMA artillery was at least properly supplied.

Most important, the New Model Army was regularly paid, properly equipped and well-provisioned by efficient quartermasters. The NMA was not the totality of the parliamentary forces; there were other less mobile formations available to Parliament under different commanders, as before. But it was the fighting core of Parliament's military power and was feared by Prince Rupert and the Royalists even before it was fully ready. Thomas Fairfax also willingly took on Cromwell's conviction that the NMA should recruit, and conscript, only from committed, godly, men. It was uniquely strong in what today is termed the 'moral component of military power'. Perhaps that sense of shared conviction could not have lasted indefinitely, but while the NMA existed, it was overwhelming. Cromwell's aphorism that 'a man must know what he fights for, and love what he knows', has been quoted down the years at staff colleges and management courses the world over.

The spring months of 1645, however, were difficult for the NMA as it shook itself down for battle. It failed in the south west and Royalists launched a furious assault to take Leicester, causing some panic in London. Parliament gave Fairfax, in

Oxford, and Cromwell in the eastern countries, leave to campaign as they thought best. Fairfax immediately brought Cromwell to him and put him in charge of all the NMA's cavalry. Then, gathering reinforcements wherever he could, Fairfax set out to confront the King and Prince Rupert as Royalist forces withdrew northwards. They caught up with them at Naseby.

On midsummer's day at Naseby the King played into Fairfax's hands by launching an attack with inferior numbers, up a slope, against a strong Parliamentary position. In fact, Royalist foot soldiers did very well and Rupert's fierce cavalry broke through Parliament's left wing – but then failed to follow up so that Henry Ireton's surviving troops on the left were able to re-organise themselves. Cromwell's cavalry on the right was again decisive. Facing a strong Yorkshire Royalist cavalry charge himself, he let it come on to him, then timed the moment perfectly. Crashing through the Royalist horsemen and – as at Marston Moor, though now in a seamless manoeuvre – he swept round against the Royalist centre. Still, it was a tough fight but the superiority of Parliamentary numbers, which might have been as high as two-to-one, eventually told until Royalist forces were virtually surrounded. The King's soldiers and commanders had been brave – Charles I almost insanely so – but disciplined Parliamentary units had manoeuvred and engaged with a speed and purpose never before seen on a British battlefield.

After Naseby, Fairfax took his troops to the west-country and destroyed the remainder of the Royalist field army, then reduced one stronghold after another in the west and south of England. In April 1646 Charles I finally gave up, fleeing from Oxford and surrendering himself, not to Parliamentary forces, but to their Scottish allies based at Newark.

Parliament's military victory, however, could not be turned into commensurate political capital. Parliament paid the Scottish army to turn the King over to them and go home. But still, Charles rejected outright all Parliament's demands for a reformed framework of kingship. Parliament became even more factionalised along sectarian lines. It also now feared its own army and wanted to disband it. For its part, the army was sorely neglected once victory had been achieved and was accused (in truth unjustly) of turning politically radical, even republican. Parliament wanted to send it to Ireland to suppress rebellion – and get it out of the country. The army wouldn't disband, and nor would it be ordered to Ireland.

Cromwell was again ill and missed some of these immediate struggles. But when he returned to the fray, his influence was very evident. In May 1647 he was almost certainly behind a bold, crack-of-dawn stroke to snatch the King from Parliament's captivity in Northamptonshire and make him a captive of the army, first at its headquarters in Newmarket, and eventually at Hampton Court. And while he tried to negotiate with Charles over the future of the monarchy, Cromwell was attempting to mitigate the growing anger of the army in the 'Putney debates', held in St Mary's church at the army's encampment beside the Thames. In rhetorical terms, these famous discussions represented the beginnings of modern democratic demands. In reality, they were more about conditions for those who had fought for an ungrateful Parliament. By then,

Cromwell would have no truck with 'the levellers' in the army who attacked the whole social hierarchy of the country.

Still, Cromwell – unlike some in the army – was not a willing regicide. But in November Charles I forced his hand with a typically inept ploy; 'escaping' to Robert Hammond, Governor of the Isle of Wight. But (since he had misjudged his man) he actually put himself neatly back into the army's custody at Carisbrooke Castle. Nevertheless, Charles I's conspiracies to engineer a foreign invasion were now crystal clear, and his standard was raised again, via Scottish Royalists, to provoke a second civil war.

That was Cromwell's Rubicon and suddenly the old argument reversed itself. The King had now committed treason. But if 'yet he is king still', then treason against whom? The answer was unavoidable; against the state, as embodied in Parliament and upheld by the army. Many were squeamish at this logic but Cromwell had finally embraced it. He took the NMA to suppress Royalists in Chepstow and Tenby, then to Preston where, over a number of disciplined campaigning days, he defeated a large, invading Scots army whose disorganised verve was no match for these new Parliamentary soldiers.

He was in Pontefract on 6th December 1648 when Colonel Thomas Pride – with Cromwell's knowledge and almost certainly his approval – arrived at Parliament with soldiers. There and then, under the shadow of troopers, he 'purged' it of all those who still believed in negotiating with the King. It now became the 'rump Parliament' of merely seventy members, obedient to the newly emergent leaders of the army.

Events careered on. Charles I was put on trial on 20th January in Westminster Hall. This was too much for Sir Thomas Fairfax who chose to absent himself – though Lady Fairfax barracked the court from the gallery for its temerity in putting the King on trial. Cromwell remained resolute and took the lead in seeing it through. The axe fell at ten-past-two on 30th January 1649, as Charles knelt on a scaffold erected outside the present Banqueting House on Whitehall.[2] At that fatal stroke the crowd seemed to groan rather than cheer. What had they done? And surely, if the King was now dead, his heir had claim to rule? Parliament's only possible answer was the long-heralded republic. The rump Parliament passed 'An act declaring England to be a Commonwealth' in May 1649. That was now the constitution.

At least for the army and the rump, this second civil war was much less ambiguous than the first. It was a war to defend the republic from the embittered Stuarts – from the heir, Charles II (as he would become), who now led forces, somewhat quixotically, to invade the realm and grab back his family's throne. Charles made it clear that his campaigns would be launched both from Ireland, which had been in revolt since 1641, and also from Scotland. So now Cromwell was made Lord Lieutenant of Ireland and the army was deployed under him – the only commander it would accept for the

---

2. The precise timing is preserved by a little black square indicating the time of 14.10 on the clock atop the Horse Guards building that stands just a few meters opposite the execution site today. Interesting, that at its historic headquarters the army that executed a king should mark that particular moment.

role – to suppress rebellion and snuff out the popery that was an ever-growing part of Charles II's support.

Ireland witnessed Cromwell's darkest period as a commander. He had always been personally courageous in battle, and showed an instinctive ability to read a struggle, hour by hour. He was ruthless in doing what was necessary to tip the scales towards victory. But as one battle followed another, he also seemed to revel in the easy killing that followed – once an enemy had cracked and the event degenerated, as most did, into a free-wheeling pell-mell of personal violence. His self-righteous confidence and his arm, being the very arm of providence, perhaps made his own pitiless cleaving entirely guilt-free. And in Ireland – though in truth his campaign ended up killing very many English Protestants alongside Catholics – his hatred of popery seemed to put an almost joyful edge on his cruel efficiency; a 'holy glee' in the phrase of his contemporaries.

He was in Ireland for only nine months between 1649 and 1650, where the rebellion continued until 1653, but the tide turned irrevocably during Cromwell's command. There were 'no quarter' assaults on Drogheda, Wexford and, after a brutal setback, against the escapers from Clonmel; all accompanied by widespread casual murder amid units of out-of-control Parliamentary troops. Many Irish atrocities laid at his door were not ordered by Cromwell, and the colonialist land-grabbing of Parliament afterwards was not his responsibility. But he said nothing to indicate that he disapproved and seemed to assume that the occupation of a brutal army was Irish Catholicism's just desserts. It was no more than had been visited on many parts of the Continent during the religious spasm of the Thirty Years War, which ended only in 1648. Five times more were killed at Magdeburg than Drogheda, ten times more than at Wexford. Such comparisons may be odious, but all Europe was in violent religious turmoil during Cromwell's lifetime. Perhaps it helps explain his own battle-weary blood-lust.

In 1650 Charles II duly arrived in Scotland to prepare an invasion over the border into England. Cromwell returned from Ireland and was pleased immediately to be made Lord General of the army – supreme commander – to take the campaign into Scotland; pleased also to be fighting a dubious combination – something less than an alliance – of Scottish Presbyterians, neo-Catholic Royalists and outright papists. At Dunbar, Cromwell's New Model Army (for once, outnumbered) won a complete victory over predominantly Presbyterian forces. Cromwell's force of around 11,000 demonstrated its discipline and spirit by launching an attack at night, in bad weather, quickly outflanking the confused Scots, and putting them to flight not long after dawn.[3] After so many tough battles, this was Cromwell's greatest and most straightforward triumph. He reportedly kept laughing out loud at the one-sided nature of the fighting.

Hard-line Royalists, freed by Dunbar from their Presbyterian partners, went for broke and crowned Charles II king at Scone Abbey. Events paused, since at fifty-one, Cromwell was falling ill again with dysentery and kidney stones. But he was still able to direct his forces to draw Charles and his Scots onto another defeat at Inverkeithing

---

3. This was not the first time the NMA had fought at night. It had done so, very effectively, in storming Bristol in September 1645. Like the modern British army, the NMA knew that night is a great friend to disciplined forces.

and then block their access to the east coast, denying the Royalists any reinforcements. Charles now had no option but to cross the border with his army of around 12,000 Royalist Scots and push south in a crazy invasion, merely hoping for the best. He picked up very little support as he moved through England; chased all the way, being forced ever westwards, away from London. He drew breath at Worcester. And there, Cromwell arrived in early September with a Parliamentary force of close to 40,000 men. So, at Worcester, where the first battle of the English civil war had begun in 1642, it finally ended there in 1651. It was over. Royalism was dead, at least while Cromwell lived and commanded his extraordinary army.

And yet, and yet, the country might have felt itself driven into a republic, but was still not comfortable with it. The war was over but the realm was obviously still in political and moral turmoil. Sir Thomas Fairfax had withdrawn from national politics. Cromwell was Lord General of the army and the dominant voice in the governing 'Council of State'. Yet he was not embarked on some single-minded quest for supreme power; he was still not sure what God wanted and, like many others, still toyed with the idea of a 'mixed monarchical' government sometime in the future.

In fact, both Cromwell and England were struggling with one of the classic political dilemmas of modern history, played out in many countries around the world since then. Military organisations take power from dysfunctional or corrupt governments on behalf of the nation, promise they will rule only for a transitional period while some better government is created, then find themselves both unable to rule properly, or effect a transition back to legitimacy. Military governments become trapped in their own dictatorship, usually succumbing to a special sort of corruption all their own.

So it was for Cromwell. Even the rump Parliament became a barrier to the godly transition he now thought inevitable, and he dissolved it – forcibly – in 1653. It was replaced by an assembly of 140 members nominated by the army, laughingly known as the 'barebones Parliament', until that was dismissed after five months. The only course left was that Cromwell must now be proclaimed 'Lord Protector', England's legitimate Head of State – not anointed in recognition of a divine right, but obviously chosen by God, as revealed through his victories in war. It was so done in December 1653. Cromwell ruled what turned out to be a (brief) United Kingdom of England and Wales, Ireland and Scotland. From 1655 to 1657 the Lord Protector embarked on a disastrous experiment in dividing all three kingdoms into twelve regions and putting each under the rule of a Major General. It was straight military dictatorship. It immediately became the most joyless expression of Puritan rule that finally reached deep into every town and village in the realm, causing sullen resentment everywhere.

Now a significant European leader, Cromwell also devised an assertive foreign policy. He took a mercantilist approach to growing Dutch trade, revamping and professionalising the navy. He had already pitched the country into the first of the Anglo-Dutch wars from 1652–54, which ended in stalemate. He allied with France and against Spain, sending the NMA to help France capture Dunkirk, still within the Spanish Netherlands. And he created a 'Western Design' to colonise the New World, in a vision derived very closely from that of Walter Raleigh half a century before. He sent forces to capture and claim Nova Scotia. He aimed to take Hispaniola from the

Spanish, but when that failed, the force took Jamaica instead, which became the centre of Britain's western empire for the next two centuries. He officially re-invited the Jews, expelled from England by Edward I, back into the country; for good commercial reasons and because they were, self-evidently, a godly people.

Cromwell declined to be crowned king, but he and his family took on all the finery of the Stuart monarchy. And like almost all dictators the world over since, he named his son as successor. When Cromwell died, ill and exhausted, in September 1658 he was buried in Westminster Abbey with all the trappings of a monarch. But his death prompted another turn of the wheel. After a year of crisis, the solid and much-respected General George Monck, who had been a Royalist, then a Parliamentarian, now turned Royalist again and left Coldstream with his troops (to become thereafter the Coldstream Guards) and marched on London to hold it for the popular return and 'restoration' of Charles II. Monck might have tried to take power for himself – a continuation of military dictatorship was certainly possible – but he didn't. Instead, he paraded some 30,000 Ironsides and foot soldiers on Blackheath to meet Charles II as the King prepared to enter London. They laid down their arms, took a few paces back, then came forward and picked them up again 'in the name of King Charles the Second', as Monck shouted the orders. As other writers have observed; if there was a single moment when the British Army came into existence, it was there on Blackheath on 29th May 1660.

The restoration was selectively vengeful. Cromwell and other family members were turfed out of their tombs in the Abbey and the mouldering bodies of him, Henry Ireton and John Bradshaw were ceremoniously hung and dismembered at Tyburn, before their heads were spiked atop Westminster Hall. The subsequent fate of Cromwell's head is a saga of its own. But the head, reliably proven to have been his, was eventually buried in 1960 in the grounds of Sidney Sussex College, Cambridge, its precise location still a closely-guarded secret.

The English civil war gave the country a brief taste of republicanism which fundamentally affected the way its monarchy would henceforth operate. Though the process had been traumatic, there was a completely new, and healthier, relationship between Parliament and the monarch thereafter. It would not have played out as it did without the New Model Army. It was a 'model' to other armies not for any great tactical innovation but for the fact that it was a national professional force, properly organised and disciplined, well-supplied, and which above all, paid attention to that 'moral component of fighting power' – in this case the commitment to a patriotic Protestantism. And it became a standing army, paid for by the state, to exist in peacetime as well as in war. It was officially replaced in 1661, but like Cromwell, its ghost didn't sleep; its influence and some of its units persisted into the army that emerged over the next century. Unlike the modern Royal Navy or the Royal Air Force, the British Army is not designated as 'royal', even though it is pledged to the monarch as its commander-in-chief.[4] The modern British Army was founded through Parliament,

---

4. In contrast, for example, to the 'Royal Armies' of other monarchies such as the Netherlands, Denmark, Sweden, Thailand or Saudi Arabia.

thence to serve a monarch. It thus serves 'the King in Parliament', representing that balance of loyalties that bolsters a flexible but surprisingly robust British constitution.

Oliver Cromwell was instrumental to that taste of republicanism and to the early foundation of Britain's modern army. Over the tumultuous sixteen years of his politico-military life he never seemed to be sure whether he was the servant or the instrument of divine providence – only that divine providence was hard at work in seventeenth century Britain. Perhaps it didn't matter. He was swept along by the momentum of events, and more than most, was both shaping and being shaped by them. For all the deaths he had caused from the darker reaches of his soul and through his own tortured personality, he never seemed to waver from the certainty that he was firmly engaged in God's work.

15

John Churchill, Duke of Marlborough

John Churchill was elevated to become the 1st Duke of Marlborough, and – not without significance as it turned out – he also became a Prince of the Holy Roman Empire. He was Britain's single most successful military commander in virtually every major aspect of command. He and Wellington take the accolades as the best battlefield leaders Britain has ever produced. He shares with Nelson and Collingwood the plaudits for grand strategic vision, and perhaps with Douglas Haig for his appreciation of what was necessary in coalition warfare when the future of Europe was at stake. Among military historians he is judged, by general consent, the most complete and personally accomplished of British military commanders.

Discounting the battles in which he was involved as a young man, John Churchill fought as commander in ten consecutive European campaigns. As one of his contemporary captains famously expressed it, 'he never fought a battle, which he did not gain, nor laid siege to a town which he did not take'. He ultimately fell foul of domestic political machinations in Britain, and he certainly had his detractors who viewed him as rapacious, untrustworthy and dishonourable. But his reputation across the Continent remained immense. He won battles, he generally prevailed in campaigns, and he used his campaign success to a grand strategic purpose. He arguably did more than any other single individual to maintain some sort of balance of power in Europe and prevent it falling under the dominance of a single country – in this case, Louis XIV's France. When he was old and infirm, he reputedly paused in front of one of the many paintings of him in his pomp. 'That was once a man', he said sadly. Indeed, that was.

Like General George Monck, who in many ways he succeeded as the great architect of the British Army, John Churchill was a west-countryman. He was born in May 1650 into that stratum of the gentry that lived in genteel austerity rather than inherited wealth. His father was Member of Parliament for Weymouth and John Churchill became a pupil at St Paul's School in London. While still a schoolboy his elder sister, Arabella, was appointed a maid of honour to the Duchess of York and was very quickly involved in an affair with the Duke of York – the man who would ascend the throne as James II.[1] On that basis, John was taken on as a page to the Duke and begged him for an ensign's commission in the Foot Guards, which he was granted in 1667. He obviously saw the army as a means to some advancement and as a seventeen-year-old began his lifelong profession as a soldier. He was subsequently involved in politics but was never a politician; he was highly involved at Court but was never a genuine courtier. He managed to survive in these fraught arenas, but it

---

1. Though it was no passing fancy. Over the years she bore him four children.

was his destiny and his inclination to be a soldier and a military commander. Few other commanders achieved anything close to the social or historical prominence of John Churchill – to become the Duke of Marlborough – exclusively through their military achievements and reputation.

Over the next four years with the Foot Guards, Churchill may have served in the Tangier garrison, and he was certainly part of the Lord High Admiral's Regiment of Foot, embarked at sea as a supplement to below-strength marines, under command of the Duke of York. In 1671 he returned to England, a handsome, well-built, charming, intelligent and confident young ensign on the make. He fought a sword duel – presumably over some matter of honour – that raised his profile in royal circles. Barbara Castlemaine (later Duchess of Cleveland) was one of Charles II's rejected, but still respected, mistresses, having been installed in a house right opposite St James's Palace. Her lovers in 1671 included a rope dancer, an actor and William Wycherley the playwright. Young Churchill became one of her regulars at a time when her residual power at Court was still great. She underpinned his meagre capital and gave him social influence, though on at least one occasion he was forced to escape through Barbara Castlemaine's window – some say only naked into the wardrobe – when the King made an impromptu visit. Churchill had a daughter by her – Barbara Fitzroy – whom he never formally acknowledged.

Thanks to Charles II, and the endless shifts in Stuart foreign policy, England was temporarily allied with France at the time. Churchill fought on the Duke of York's ship when the King's forces were defeated by the Dutch in Southwold Bay. He became a captain in the Foot Guards as a result. But having a daughter with Barbara Castlemaine had lost him Charles II's approval, and in 1673 he took himself off with the Duke of Monmouth's gentlemen volunteers to fight for Louis XIV's forces at Maastricht, where he was even part of a 'forlorn hope' attacking force. He returned quickly to royal favour with reports from the Duke of York of his personal courage at Southwold, and from the Duke of Monmouth, who told the King that Churchill had 'saved his life' in the trenches of Maastricht. And serving once more alongside French forces in 1674, again as a volunteer, Churchill watched General the Vicomte de Turenne, the greatest master of battle tactics in Europe, beating the army of the Holy Roman Empire at Sinsheim and then Ensheim. He was learning quickly. In 1675 he became a colonel in the Foot Guards and now had some significant personal income.

At the age of twenty-five, he had reached a key moment in his career, poised between the Court and the army. He was a conscientious and serious-minded man, not greatly given to humour, but with considerable emotional intelligence. He could get on with people of all ages, nationalities and social status. Churchill the young officer was no more dissolute than most others in his position. And as David Chandler delicately puts it, for someone at Charles II's court, 'he was not transformed into a voluptuary'; though clearly, his affair with Barbara Castlemaine had given him a head start in restoration society.

In 1675 he fell completely in love with the tempestuous and vivacious fifteen-year-old Sarah Jennings. They were discreetly married two years later. She enriched his life over the years as Sarah Churchill, driving on his own personal ambition, even as she created ever greater political difficulties for him at Court. Though he spent most of his later life 'on campaign' he was devoted to her and the five children they had together. John Churchill was inexorably drawn into the toxic politics of the day as James, Duke of York, declared himself Catholic and as a result was effectively exiled to live in Scotland, taking John with him as his assistant and adviser. The two men became genuinely close and when James eventually returned to London, Churchill was rewarded with a peerage. Sarah found her own rewards in being close to Princess Anne, younger daughter of James, Duke of York. The Princess was destined to become Queen Anne and was already competing vigorously for political influence with her elder sister, Princess Mary, destined to become queen before her. The clique around Anne lodged in the cockpit part of Whitehall Palace. They became the 'cockpit circle', fiercely whiggish as the struggles for influence intensified.[2]

This was one of a number of threads that were to weave in and out of John Churchill's career for the rest of his life. Sarah loved the intrigue of being an intimate friend of Anne and drew both her and John to the in-fighting between Anne and Mary. Sarah was hard to handle. John Churchill was a committed Anglican. So was Sarah, but violently anti-Catholic into the bargain. John was a moderate Tory, Sarah a visceral Whig who saw party, and royal, politics in largely tribal terms. She dominated Anne with her highly intelligent intimacy, her didactic opinions and her determination to shape royal politics around her own views on every conceivable matter. When Anne became Queen in 1702, Sarah's personal influence was immense, both over Anne and the government's Whiggish policies – inclining to war with France. She and John Churchill were, for a while, the two most prominent figures in the realm even among the immediate royal family. With the Lord Treasurer, and hence governmental leader, in the person of Earl Godolphin – a great ally of them both – they seemed to be guiding the country on all matters of foreign policy; and in Sarah's case, a good deal besides.

But times, and favourites, change. Sarah so overplayed her hand – eventually treating Queen Anne with undisguised contempt – that the relationship was fractured beyond repair by 1710. For John Churchill, involved in constant campaigning abroad during Anne's reign, it became a political roller-coaster ride at home that he could do little to influence directly. He loved Sarah to distraction, but increasingly found himself trying to defend the indefensible to the Queen and to Tory grandees as resentment and hatred against his wife mounted. Sarah's own fate as a courtier first gave him some of the opportunities that propelled Churchill to fame and success; and then effectively halted his career before his grand foreign project could be completed.

Another constant thread in Churchill's story was that even before his sponsor and friend, the Duke of York, ascended the throne as James II in 1685, Churchill could see at least some of the writing on the wall. James was not just privately Catholic; he was inflexible, apparently tin-eared to the growing concerns of Anglicanism – to which

---

2. The cockpit was one part of Henry VIII's palace originally created for sport. The subsequent prominence of Downing Street, just a few metres away, was based on its proximity to the cockpit of the Stuart era. Part of the cockpit still exists in Whitehall's current Cabinet Office, where Cockpit Passage opens to offer views of the Downing Street garden; a space originally given over to cock-fighting and bear-baiting, among other amusements.

Churchill was genuinely devoted. And James was foolish, even stupid in the way he dealt with political issues. Churchill owed everything to James, but during the 'Scottish exile' he seems to have realised that his mentor was heading for disaster and that his own genuine personal loyalty would be stretched by his even more genuine personal ambition. Churchill was not willing to end up on the losing side and he was astute enough to see his own treachery coming. His Anglicanism, his wife, and his sense of political self-preservation seem to have decided him to betray James long before it became public. And when it came, his silver-tongued duplicity was such that the next three monarchs he served as a military commander – William III and Queen Mary and then Queen Anne – never really trusted him. His influence at Court increasingly relied on his tangible military abilities that could not be gainsaid.

Thus it was that he defended James II in 1685 from the immediate intrigues surrounding his accession, and displayed his tactical command ability at the Battle of Sedgemoor in Somerset, where he stoutly snuffed out an invasion attempt in the Monmouth rebellion. Yet three years later in 1688 he was among those who actively conspired to invite William of Orange to invade the country and seize James's throne, to rule jointly with Princess Mary, William's wife.[3] It was the 'Glorious Revolution' and Churchill's somewhat inglorious role in it was to advance with James's troops towards Axminster to confront the Dutch invasion then, on 23rd November, to defect overnight with 400 officers and soldiers to join the forces of William of Orange. The royal army had been melting away to join William for several days, but Churchill's defection was the greatest military and psychological blow to the King, who struggled – always – to understand what was going on. During the hiatus, Princess Anne and Sarah Churchill were put under house arrest at the cockpit, but escaped with the connivance of the Bishop of London and fled to Nottingham. Losing the loyalty even of his own daughters, James disappeared to exile in France.

It is said that 'treason never prospers', since when it does 'none dare call it treason'. Had James II defeated William of Orange on Salisbury Plain, it would certainly have been called treason. But though '1688' succeeded (easily), it was nevertheless an exercise in treachery by many, and John Churchill was rewarded for his by being made Earl of Marlborough and a Privy Councillor. His role in the 'Glorious Revolution', however, created a remembrance of uniquely personal treachery on his part that hung on his reputation for the rest of his life. He even reinforced it by trying to justify himself with weasel words to James II in exile and by maintaining tenuous links with Jacobite groups on the Continent. Many at Court wondered where his real loyalties lay.

From 1689 onwards, however, it is possible to see 'Marlborough', as he now became – later elevated from Earl to Duke after Blenheim in 1704 – in his guise as an accomplished military commander, albeit with the toxic politics of the Court and his own family issues as a constant accompaniment to his professional life.

He became heavily involved in re-modelling the Army, purging it of Jacobite officers and working to restore some morale after the shame of desertions and inaction

---

3. The excellent biographer Richard Holmes makes the point that Churchill was not just drawn in – he 'was at the very centre of the plot'.

in 1688. When King William III was in Ireland winning the iconic but indecisive victory at the Battle of the Boyne, sending James II scuttling back to exile in France, Marlborough was thinking about ways to make a strategic difference to the Jacobite invasion threat through Ireland. He led forces to take Cork and Kinsale in the south, to make it impossible for French troops and equipment to be landed in the Jacobite cause – though in the event his clear victories were not followed through adequately – and already, there were those at Court who were waiting for Marlborough and his wife to come crashing down.

Such risings against William and Mary became subsumed in the muddled and global affair generally known as the War of the League of Augsburg, which began in 1689 and spanned the next nine years. Though confused, it set the pattern of continental conflict – and Marlborough's involvement – thereafter, revolved around a shifting coalition of England, the Dutch Republic, the Holy Roman Empire, Spain, Savoy and Portugal, all resisting the power and encroachments of 'the single dominant power' that European leaders always feared. In this case it was France under King Louis XIV.

Domestic issues also intruded dramatically in these years. The rivalry between the two sisters – Queen Mary, as she now was, and Princess Anne, as she still remained, turned to complete estrangement and swept all before it at Court. Marlborough was accused of treason in 1692 on some very thin evidence and an acknowledged forgery, and spent a month in the Tower. He was implicated again in renewed Jacobite plots in 1696 – unfounded, though he only had himself to blame given his ongoing correspondence with Jacobite groups – a foolish sort of political insurance policy with a uniquely high premium.

Queen Mary died of smallpox in 1694. The war was ended by the Treaty of Ryswick in 1696. By then, poor Anne had endured seventeen pregnancies but would be leaving no direct heirs when her time to rule arrived. And by 1700, King William III was obviously dying. England's protestant succession was in danger, and Jacobitism was still very much alive in Scotland, Ireland and in France, much encouraged by Louis XIV. Queen Anne ascended to the throne in 1702. The Marlboroughs were then an intrinsic part of her close circle and John, alongside Earl Godolphin, were both decisive players in her foreign policy.

That was the situation when Marlborough embarked on his purple patch of command that secures his enduring military reputation in British history. In 1700 the feeble-minded Carlos II had died in Spain. Louis XIV tried to replace him with his grandson, making the Bourbon branch of the Hapsburg family in Spain a natural ally to an already mighty France. Immediately, a new coalition between England, the Dutch Republic and the Holy Roman Empire's (alternative) Hapsburgs came into being to contest the Spanish succession. French armies had not been defeated in Europe for over forty years, but the immediate future of the Continent would be decided over whether it would acquiesce in a demarche that would, at a stroke, create long-term French hegemony.

The 'War of the Spanish Succession' from 1701–14 was a more focussed and consequential version of the nine years of war that the Treaty of Ryswick had ended. And it spanned the union of England and Scotland in 1707, after which Marlborough was fighting for Great Britain. The war progressed essentially on an annual cycle, from fighting season to fighting season across Europe, with armies resting at winter quarters and commanders like Marlborough going home for a while before returning each spring to assess the next prospects.

Marlborough had become a natural manoeuvrist commander. He is credited with creating eighteen battle situations in these years, through speed, manoeuvre and deception. On seven of these occasions he fought and won. On six occasions he was thwarted by the caution and hesitation of his allies. On three occasions he decided not to press to battle and twice French forces simply escaped his manoeuvring clutches. None of this would have been possible had Marlborough been anything less than a commander of all-round accomplishment. And while it would be inadvisable to try to describe all his victories during these years, one or two examples illuminate the range of his command talents.

Even before the 1701 war, Marlborough's command of the 8,000 English troops sent to the Low Countries in 1689 had showed, as Richard Holmes puts it, 'Marlborough in miniature'. At the age of thirty-nine he spent three months training and drilling his post-1688, disheartened, troops. He drove them hard, no less than himself, in feeding and equipping them properly, exercising them and paying special attention to their needs as soldiers. Not for nothing would the Duke earn the sobriquet among his troops as 'Corporal John'; he knew his men and looked after them. In this case, the small English force came to impress his superior allied commanders in the campaign. At the Battle of Walcourt that year he personally led the Life Guards and the Blues in a fierce charge that quickly broke six French infantry battalions and decided the engagement.

Towards the other end of the battle spectrum, the enormity of the Blenheim campaign fifteen years later, demonstrated Marlborough's skills at the highest level of military consequence. He was then Captain General of the combined allied forces and by 1704 was managing the vicissitudes of a multinational alliance, dealing principally with the Dutch determination not to have coalition forces diverted anywhere that might leave them exposed to a French offensive in the Low Countries. But Vienna was under severe threat of capture jointly by French troops and Louis XIV's ally, the elector of Bavaria. Another French army in northern Italy could also threaten the city and a Hungarian revolt to the east offered Louis XIV a further pressure point. Quite simply, the fall of Vienna would have knocked the Empire out of the anti-French coalition and would present Louis with the prospect of outflanking the remaining allies. Marlborough immediately appreciated the strategic equation. The war could rapidly be lost in southern Germany, regardless of any allied success in the Low Countries in the meantime. Many could see the logic of this situation but coalition politics would not entertain a new and different strategy.

Marlborough got Queen Anne's agreement to a daring response, however, and told very few of his officers his real intentions. The gritty Prince Eugene of Savoy, an ally whom he had not then met, was also brought into his plan. But to his Dutch allies, and his French enemies, Marlborough created the illusion that he would launch a limited campaign in the Moselle valley – not too far away for Dutch nerves – intended merely to draw French and Bavarian forces away from Vienna. In fact, he worked himself to exhaustion planning a different and huge campaign with commensurate risks. For the benefit of French intelligence, he fed all around him with evidence that he planned a limited offensive, while his own intelligence officers worked hard to place French and Bavarian forces precisely. This was to be no speculative probe south-eastwards; he was taking a big force in a dangerous campaign to save Vienna. He would march his army 250 miles to the Danube, leaving two French armies in his rear, easily able to threaten his line of march if the deception failed that he was only going as far as the Moselle valley.

On May 19th 1704, his force of 21,000 – of whom 16,000 were British – set out from Bedburg, just north-west of Cologne. It picked up other coalition reinforcements en route. On 26th they reached Coblenz where the Moselle meets the Rhine. Instead of moving down the Moselle Valley, the force crossed to the east bank of the Rhine and carried on south. Now French commanders wondered if he was moving into Alsace to attack Strasbourg. Marlborough had bridges built across the Rhine to reinforce that idea. French armies began to trail south after him but he continued to outpace them, out-think them, and exploit their inflexibility, since he knew that Louis XIV had personally to approve their deployments. On June 10th Marlborough met up in person with Prince Eugene north of Ulm, and they immediately became brothers in arms and firm friends. Prince Louis, the Holy Roman Empire's imperial field commander, joined them on 13th. After five weeks of well-planned, pre-provisioned and disciplined marching, Marlborough arrived at the Danube, storming the fortress of Schellenberg to use as a base and a secure river crossing. His coalition forces now sat between Vienna and advancing French forces, Eugene on the north side of the Danube, Marlborough on the south. Marlborough was 350 miles south-east of his escape point at Antwerp.

On 10th August French forces pushed hard against Eugene's smaller army, but Marlborough was able to link up with it and form a good defensive line east of the river Nebel which flowed into the Danube near the village of Blenheim. French and Bavarian forces occupied Blenheim and sat in a secure position west of the Nebel. Since French forces in that part of the operational area were some 56,000, as opposed to the 52,000 of the allied forces, and had superior artillery as well as marshy ground in front of them, they were confident that Marlborough would not attack. Any assault against well-prepared defensive positions with other than far superior numbers, let alone inferior numbers, is risky in the extreme. And in this case, the defenders had much the better of the topography over the four miles of battle front stretching north-west from the Danube at Blenheim along the line of the Nebel. The French assumed Marlborough would withdraw north in the face of superior forces

But Marlborough was adamant that this was the right moment and he had a sophisticated plan of attack. He knew full-well that his tactics would create a bloody affair. In that respect he foreshadowed later commanders like Wellington, Haig – above all, Napoleon – who knowingly traded their men's lives for local advantage in a complex geometry of battle tactics. Marlborough wasn't casual about this. His nerves made him genuinely ill before most battles – migraines, nausea and stomach upsets. He was never at rest during fighting, he kept his forces moving with some fluidity because he rode everywhere around the battlefront and had trained an excellent staff to operate around him. He was forward enough to put himself in significant danger on a regular basis.[4]

At Blenheim he began moving his troops up towards the Nebel in the early hours of 13th August. He required the faithful Prince Eugene to move through the northern woods and streams towards Lutzingen on the extreme right wing and hold out against troops and cavalry that would otherwise act as an enemy reserve. He required the Prussian and Danish infantry on his right to neutralise French infantry at Oberglauheim. He set his own left wing to attack Blenheim and in between, on the Hochstadt Plain, he would use his larger cavalry force – interspersed with infantry lines to lure the enemy into a trap with further cavalry waiting behind them – to destroy the concentrated French cavalry in the centre. The allies lost the element of surprise because it took so long for Eugene to get into position in the difficult ground to the north. And the attacks on Blenheim were repelled with heavy losses. For a few hours it was a desperate struggle. Marlborough's forces got across the Nebel relatively easily, the Danes and Prussians crossed but were later pushed back over it. Eugene's forces were launching repeated attacks but being beaten; and the village of Blenheim still held.

The breakthrough occurred when the French General, Philippe Clerambault, alarmed at the scale of the attacks on Blenheim, and without consulting the overall commander, the duc de Tallard, ordered all the reserve battalions into the village – which took them out of the centre just when Tallard needed reserves and couldn't draw them away from Eugene's fierce assaults on the opposite wing.[5] Marlborough immediately saw the opportunity of a weakened centre. He reorganised his forces and in the late afternoon led a strong fresh assault across the whole front, which finally cracked French resistance, isolating groups and pushing more than 3,000 troops (including Clerambault) to drown in a curve of the Danube. The French infantry in Blenheim village held out to the end. It was a blazing ruin against the night sky before 10,000 French infantrymen finally laid down their arms and surrendered. In the following couple of hours, Marlborough's first note announcing the remarkable victory was written on the back of a tavern bill and sent to Sarah, asking her to share the news with the Queen, whom he would write to properly 'in a day or two'.

This was battle on a new scale; bigger in numbers, territory, organisation and casualties. Some 14,000 allied troops were killed or wounded; perhaps 30,000 French and Bavarians and a further 14,000 captured. Such epic clashes distinguished those commanders who could extract success in them from the majority of commanders in that era, who couldn't. The aura of French military invincibility had been dispelled; the coalition was saved and the whole of Bavaria, with its important resources, soon fell under allied control. Blenheim was the most decisive single victory of the war. From then onwards it was the terms on which Louis XIV would have to settle, rather than the likely victors, that was chiefly at issue – though it all dragged on for another decade.

---

4. And unlike almost every commander of the era apart from Wellington, he advised his men to lie down to reduce the dangers in an artillery barrage.
5. Eugene had already shot two of his own troopers to prevent any incipient flight.

Marlborough was to win another significant major battle at Ramillies in the 1706 campaign in an even more emphatic demonstration of his command superiority, and then again in 1708 at the Battle of Oudenaarde, which recovered almost all of the Spanish Netherlands for the allies. Notwithstanding the myriad frustrations and setbacks of coalition warfare, the military tide continued to run in Marlborough's favour. France was on the point of collapse and England – now Great Britain – was the foremost continental military power, at least for a while.

But the political wind had changed. Whig influence was being replaced at Court, as was Sarah the Duchess of Marlborough, and war-weariness had set in at the prospect that Louis XIV – against all the interests of France – might hold out indefinitely. Marlborough's victory at Malplaquet in 1709 was extremely bloody and his enemies at home used it against him, arguing that he wanted to prolong the war for his own rapacious ends. The Tories argued for a global maritime policy rather than worry too much about the European balance of power, and when they won a landslide victory in the 1710 general election, Britain was looking urgently for a way out.

In the 1711 fighting season Marlborough created the very antithesis of Malplaquet. The only fortresses then standing between the allied armies and Paris itself were Bouchain and Cambrai – Bouchain the toughest obstacle since it was defended by powerful outer lines. Marlborough completely deceived and outflanked French forces opposite him in a spectacular, eighteen-hour night march to get behind them and occupy the impregnable French lines without losing a single man. French General Villars could only watch helplessly from outside while, inside its own powerful defensive works, Bouchain was calmly put under siege by Marlborough's troops. Villars had no choice but to order its unconditional surrender. In the art of war Marlborough could be a true artist. Though by then, he was drawn, ill and deeply stressed by all that was happening at Court.

Later that year he was accused by Tory politicians of misappropriating military funds – marginally accurate but hugely exaggerated – and in December was peremptorily dismissed by Queen Anne. His continental allies were stunned by the turn of events. Marlborough went into voluntary exile on the Continent in December 1712, where he was feted almost everywhere both as the greatest general of the age and a Prince of the Holy Roman Empire. Sarah joined him in Frankfurt in 1713. Two months later the long war was ended by the Treaty of Utrecht. It brought peace but left the country still viscerally divided between Whig and Tory, Jacobite and Hanoverian factions. Coincidentally, the Marlboroughs returned to Britain on the very day in 1714 that Queen Anne died.

There was some rehabilitation for him at the end, under King George I – the sixth monarch he served. Marlborough formally presided from London over the defeat of the Jacobite rebellion of 1715, though William Cadogan, his erstwhile and exceptional old chief of staff, directed operations in the north for the Duke of Argyle. In 1716 Marlborough suffered two strokes but recovered somewhat. He and Sarah got to live for a while in the east wing of the unfinished Blenheim Palace, though he was living at Windsor Lodge when he suffered his fatal attack in 1722. His children, grandchildren, and Sarah were with him on his last evening. Sarah predictably had a row with her daughters, sent them all out, and lay down beside John Churchill while he slipped away in the early hours of June 16th. He was honoured, and buried, in Westminster Abbey. But he was eventually moved, on Sarah's instructions, to the vault beneath the chapel at Blenheim, where he lies with her.

Marlborough had stood head and shoulders above all his contemporary commanders. He understood battles, movement, tempo, combined arms, intelligence and morale issues better than anyone. At the lowest level, for example, he understood that with flintlock muskets, *platoon* volley fire would be far more impactful than (larger) company volleys and could be repeated more quickly as rolling fire along the line. Or again, at the operational level, he had an excellent eye for ground and learned how to move troops and equipment around quickly and efficiently when the need arose. Above all, he was a natural strategic commander. He is sometimes criticised for expending too much energy in the Low Countries when the Spanish succession issue began to revolve around Iberia and the Mediterranean. But the Low Countries held the allied coalition together, and though he could not do very much about it for coalition and domestic political reasons, he certainly understood in his own mind how the dynamic of the war was changing after 1708. At least the grandiose prospect of a Bourbon super-state in Europe, drawing on all the overseas territories it would have inherited, was snuffed out by the wearying war.

In a strange historical irony, Britain's best ever commander was never genuinely required to fight for his country's survival or its political freedom – history didn't bend that way during his lifetime. But he fought long, hard and bravely for Britain's interests. And in so doing he contributed more than most to preventing Europe's domination under a single power and to its survival as a continent of plural and independent countries who would work out their international relationships in their own ways.

16

John Jervis, Earl of St Vincent

The life of Admiral John Jervis is intimately bound up with the development of the Georgian Navy, from its emergence after the Treaty of Utrecht in 1713 – by which Britain acquired the gem of a maritime outpost in Gibraltar – to its triumph at Trafalgar and thereafter. He lived his life under three Georgian kings, actively serving George II and George III as a seaman, and dying during the reign of George IV. In one way or another he served and commanded in four separate wars from 1756 to 1815; the Seven Years War, the American War of Independence, the French Revolutionary Wars and then the Napoleonic campaigns. Admiral Jervis, Earl of St Vincent, took his title from the 1797 battle where he commanded and which was enthusiastically celebrated in Britain.

In fact, the great victory at Cape St Vincent which made him so popular with the public was effectively won for him by Nelson, Collingwood and Troubridge after it was slipping through his own fingers. It was a famous victory that made only a limited strategic difference to the defence of Britain at the time. Conversely, his greatest contributions to Britain's defence were won largely ashore and within the Royal Navy's tangled bureaucracy, making him extremely unpopular within the Service. Almost certainly, his bureaucratic victories had a greater strategic effect than Cape St Vincent and contributed more significantly to the Trafalgar triumph and much that followed from it.

The story of John Jervis suggests great experience as a wartime sailor but not necessarily great achievement at the highest levels of military command. His is not a study in failure, however, but more in the facilitation of others' success, in the interests of the Service he loved. Jervis put the Royal Navy above everything else. By contrast, Horatio Nelson, a subordinate who owed Jervis so much, was a natural and spectacularly successful battle commander, but he clearly did not put the Royal Navy above everything else. Ironic, then, that Jervis died in his bed in Brentwood, Essex at the age of eighty-eight, always devoted to his navy; while Nelson made the greater sacrifice and died painfully for his navy on the orlop deck of HMS *Victory* when he was forty-seven.

Jervis was born into a long-established family at Meaford Hall near Stone, Staffordshire. He was second son to a successful barrister. His mother was well-connected and a cousin to Admiral of the Fleet, George Anson, who had circumnavigated the globe and emerged as another architect of the Georgian navy. The family moved to London when Jervis's father was appointed an Admiralty solicitor and Treasurer of the Royal Hospital for Seamen at Greenwich. His father intended him for the legal profession but after running away to Woolwich for three days 'to go to sea', Jervis was helped by a family friend, Admiral George Townshend, to a post as a fourteen-year-old able seaman abroad the *Gloucester*, bound for Jamaica. In the way of boy seamen, he shuttled around many different ships over the next eight years – sloops, frigates, brigs, yachts – studying conscientiously. He became a midshipman at the age of seventeen and then, after the obligatory six years' service and an examination, a lieutenant in 1755. He was immediately embarked on the *Nottingham*, which was involved in Admiral Edward Boscawen's ill-fated expedition to Nova Scotia. He was lucky to escape the rampant sickness that ran through the squadron before it was forced back home, having failed to achieve anything.

Jervis reached officer rank just as the Seven Years' War was breaking out in 1756. That conflict is sometimes described as the real 'first world war'. It pitted Britain against France in India, East Asia, North America, the Caribbean, Europe and in the Atlantic. It was a fitful, on-off ground war wherever British and French soldiers confronted each other. But it was a constant war at sea during those years, each side seeking the benefits of maritime control to dominate the most lucrative trade routes.

Throughout his life, Jervis insisted fiercely that he had never enjoyed any wealth or preferment in his career. In later intra-service battles he would stand on his prickly dignity as the example of a meritocratic officer all too rarely found in the Royal Navy of his day. This was not entirely true. His family connection to Lord Anson certainly helped, and evidently secured him a post in June 1756 as Third Lieutenant on the flagship *Prince*, under Captain Charles Saunders. Nevertheless, Jervis proved to be well worth his place and when Saunders moved his flag to the *Culloden* for an expedition to capture Quebec, he took Jervis with him as Second Lieutenant. Saunders was impressed with the twenty-three-year-old Jervis, giving him temporary commands, including sailing a prize to England and then bringing him back to his new flagship, *Neptune*, for the famous Quebec attack. Saunders would lead the maritime component; the youthful General James Wolfe, the troops.

French forces thought Quebec virtually impregnable from the St Lawrence River, since its powerful currents and natural hazards – including the fearsome 'Traverse' downstream of Quebec – made it so risky for warships, let alone troop transports, making it to the foot of the Heights of Abraham. Saunders took time to get the navigation right. On 12 September 1759 young Jervis commanded the sloop *Porcupine*, guiding troop transports at night through the shoals and rapids of the St Lawrence River, for their landing below the Heights of Abraham. The troops scaled the cliffs in the dark, to line up along the Plains the following morning, beating French defenders and capturing the garrison. It was a successful example of what were recognised as 'amphibious operations', though it cost the life of General Wolfe, as well as his French counterpart. Wolfe had reportedly given Jervis his last letter and some personal effects which Jervis subsequently delivered to Wolfe's fiancé in Britain. Within three months of the Quebec operation Canada was British and Jervis was so well-regarded in the Admiralty that at the age of twenty-five he was made post captain of the 44-gun frigate, *Gosport*.

In the *Gosport*, Jervis was part of the Channel fleet, but also fended off French attacks on a convoy he escorted to North America, and he was involved in the seizure of Newfoundland from French control. He returned home as the 1763 Treaty of Paris concluded hostilities. The end of the war confirmed Britain's growing imperial status – alongside a glimpse of how onerous 'imperial commitments' might turn out to be. But for now, British power was confirmed in Canada, Louisiana, in Florida and the lands east of the Mississippi, together with islands in the Caribbean. It was the sort of American empire that Walter Raleigh had groped towards over a century and a half earlier. Elsewhere, it extended to territories in India and Africa and to more British outposts in the Mediterranean, which would play an important role in the Georgian navy.

Like most naval officers in peacetime, Jervis was pensioned off on half pay until he was needed again. As a dedicated sailor, these fallow years reveal something of his driven personality. He was as interested in pretty young women as any post captain in his early thirties might be, but he was not wealthy and seemed to have no thoughts of marriage and no candidate fiancé in mind. He had ample opportunities for romantic dalliance but there are only coy references in his surviving letters. If he was bored in a land at peace, however, he was certainly not indolent. He became a close friend of the Whig politician Charles James Fox and was much influenced for a time by the fiery radicalism of John Wilkes. With Lord Grafton's Whig ministry briefly in power in 1769, and doubtless through his own growing reputation, Jervis was given command of the *Alarm*, a new design 32-gun frigate. For three years he had an eventful command, and notwithstanding his radical friends, he was made mentor to one of George III's younger brothers – the first Duke of Gloucester – who was sent round the Mediterranean courts in the *Alarm* to prize him away from an illegitimate lover (to whom, in fact, he had been secretly married for five years). Pointless as it was, the exercise took Jervis as the Duke's companion to some of the best courts and salons in Europe. In 1772, however, the *Alarm* was paid off and Jervis was back on half pay again.

Always in pursuit of self-improvement and with an eye to naval intelligence, he visited France and learned the language. He teamed up with a more senior captain, Samuel Barrington, who had become a friend during service, and together they went to Kronstadt and St Petersburg, to Sweden, Denmark, Germany, and the Netherlands, keeping extensive notes on local shipbuilding techniques, on harbours and coastal navigation. They went along the continental coast of the Channel, improving existing charts as they went, paying particular attention to Brest – which Jervis would later blockade very successfully as commander of the Channel Fleet. If nothing else he became painfully aware during these years that the endemic corruption in British shipyards and within the armaments industries rendered British ships inferior both in design and sailing characteristics to their French equivalents. And he understood just how much the navy he had known up until then was in need of fundamental reform if it was to match the growing competition throughout Europe.

In 1775 the outbreak of the American War of Independence brought Jervis back into service in command of the *Foudroyant*, a captured 80-gun battleship of the most useful 'third rate' classification. It was the biggest two-decker in the navy. The *Foudroyant* would be the making of him as a captain. For three years it was the guardship for Plymouth operating with the Channel Fleet. But in 1778, France declared war on

Britain in support of the American colonists. Within six weeks the *Foudroyant* was sailing behind Admiral Augustus Keppel's flagship in the confused skirmish that became known as the First Battle of Ushant. Keppel's failure to nail a victory at Ushant led to a series of acrimonious courts martial and a national controversy that pitted Whigs and Tories behind particular Ushant captains. Jervis provided a respected voice in defence of Keppel, which turned out to be decisive. But the affair was a symptom of the deeper malaise and outright politicisation that gripped the navy. The following year Jervis was part of Admiral Charles Hardy's fleet that simply retreated in the Channel off Plymouth in the face of a superior French and Spanish force. Jervis felt shamed by it.

Nevertheless, in 1782 he was part of a squadron led by his old friend Samuel Barrington, pursuing a French convoy defended by six warships, bound for the East Indies. Barrington's twelve ships gave chase, but only the *Foudroyant*, with its French design, aggressively sailed by Jervis – hoisting topgallant sails on all three masts (a considerable strain) – could catch the convoy. He took on the *Pegase* and captured it after an hour of fighting. The convoy completely escaped Barrington but Jervis got prize money and a knighthood out of his action, and public acclaim at a time when it was in short supply for the Royal Navy.

It was politic for Sir John Jervis, as he now was, to marry. An arrangement that had been mooted for a decade was realised in 1783 when, at the age of forty-eight he married Martha Parker, his forty-one-year-old cousin. Through her aristocratic mother he inherited a small estate in Essex. There were no children, though the marriage was apparently affectionate and entirely proper. Martha appeared to accept that no family commitments should distract her husband from his duties to the navy.

Increasingly at the centre of discussions about the future of his Service, Jervis became a Member of Parliament, first for Launceston, then for North Yarmouth in 1784 and finally in 1790 for Wycombe. He was fully involved in important strategic debates about the defence of the country. The Royal Navy was at the cutting edge of Georgian technology; it was the principal instrument of military power. It was also ruinously expensive – all the more so given its endemic corruption. William Pitt the Younger first became Prime Minister in 1783, committed to putting the public finances in order. He was not a navy man and engaged in a fierce debate in cabinet and Parliament over whether the country was better defended by strong coastal fortifications than by roving, very expensive, battlefleets designed for sea control. It harked back to those dimly-understood strategic choices that previous mariners like Drake and Raleigh had confronted. The Channel was exposed as alarmingly vulnerable during the American War of Independence; how best now to defend it? Jervis threw himself into the argument, vehemently and personally against Pitt's proposal to build shore defences. Parliament eventually rejected Pitt's plan only by the casting vote of the Speaker. This, and his growing agitation for fundamental reform in the navy, began to earn Jervis some powerful enemies. He drew his bureaucratic battlelines more clearly with each controversy.

In 1793 revolutionary France declared war on Britain. Now as a Vice Admiral, Jervis was given command of the naval elements of a large expedition to capture French possessions in the West Indies. His 1794 campaign demonstrated drive and courage, if not any great strategic appreciation on his part, and its outcome added to growing opposition to him at home. The expedition attacked and, after some difficulty, occupied Martinique, then St Lucia. Guadeloupe surrendered quickly and San Domingo was taken. But inadequate forces were left at Guadeloupe and French troops retook it easily. Jervis and his army commander seriously weakened their force in repeatedly trying and failing to reoccupy Guadeloupe. Jervis went down with yellow fever and by the end of the year he had to leave the campaign to other commanders – to whom he had bequeathed endless difficulties. New commitments in the West Indies were expensive. Both French and British entrepreneurs were incensed that Jervis and his joint army commander had imposed a levy on all estates on Martinique to pay for the occupation.

Nevertheless, Jervis was promoted to full Admiral in 1795 and given command of the troubled Mediterranean fleet. It was in a precarious position, thanks mainly to French victories in Italy and the Franco-Spanish peace of 1795, which rapidly evolved into an anti-British alliance. Gibraltar was the only established, secure British base. And mutiny was breaking out in ships throughout the fleet. By the standards of the time, Jervis's approach to this problem was sound. He enforced discipline with great vigour and little mercy; but he also expected his officers to meet exacting professional standards. He did all he could to clear women off his ships (with only partial success) and he paid great attention to diet and the legitimate welfare of his sailors. He was constantly at war with corrupt suppliers and contractors to the fleet. He was, it may be said, exceedingly unpopular but few could doubt that he was even-handed.

His chief military objective was to maintain critical blockades at Toulon and Cadiz. It was now strategically vital that French fleets in the Mediterranean and at Brest and the Spanish fleet in Cadiz were prevented from joining forces, either to mount an invasion of Lisbon, or to facilitate landings somewhere in Britain. In addition to everything else the Mediterranean theatre demanded, Jervis maintained these two close blockades, despite being constantly short of ships, full crews for them and every category of supplies. Blockade duty was exceptionally hard both on ships and crew – at sea for long periods, staying just off the coast with constant close haul sailing to hold a given position, almost no opportunity for the crew to earn prize money, still less for a run ashore. Jervis wrote acerbic reports to the Admiralty describing the meagre resources he had to maintain this vital maritime objective, but to little avail. The role of the Mediterranean fleet became increasingly unsustainable.

In late 1796 the government decided to cut its diplomatic losses in southern Europe and withdrew the Mediterranean fleet altogether. Jervis's ships were sent to anchor just west of Gibraltar and in the River Tagus at Lisbon, where, at least in theory, they could still stop French and Spanish fleets from escaping together into the Atlantic. For Jervis, it appeared as another shameful retreat provoked by a near-treasonous government in London.

The weakness of this strategy became apparent immediately. In December 1796 a French fleet of forty-three ships and 14,000 troops made an attempt from Brest to invade Ireland, as a bridgehead for an attack on England. Only a fierce storm prevented it landing. Simultaneously, a Spanish fleet of twenty-seven ships of the line and ten frigates left Cartagena in Spain and was through the Straits of Gibraltar on a strong easterly wind, to escort four merchant ships carrying high-value mercury from Malaga to Cadiz. It was then to link up with the rest of the French fleet in Brest and sail into the Channel to convey an army waiting on the Dutch coast to invade Britain. But the wind – a Levanter – blew the Spanish fleet far out to the west and it had to head back towards Cadiz to deliver its merchantmen. Meanwhile, Jervis had led an emasculated British fleet out of the Tagus to escort a small merchant convoy safely out into the far Atlantic and was on his way back towards Cape St Vincent and thence to the Tagus.

This was the disposition of forces as they famously converged on 14th February 1797, in dense overnight fog, near Cape St Vincent. The Spanish fleet was about thirty-five miles to windward of Jervis, heading north. He closed with them, coming south and guided by the sound of Spanish signal guns in the fog. Jervis commanded fifteen ships of the line and seven others. The Spanish had twenty-seven ships of the line and eleven smaller warships. Jervis had no idea how outmatched he was. The fog-bound, chilly dawn revealed not only the daunting numbers opposing Jervis but also that he was then too close to break off contact. His ships, moving south, were shortly to sail straight between two loose Spanish columns both heading north. The bigger and nearer Spanish column, with eighteen ships of the line, had the upwind advantage against the British who would be passing to the east of it.

Jervis could not help but order battle stations, though there is no evidence he would have done otherwise even if he could; he never shied away from an engagement. And though the wind and the dispositions were unfavourable to him, the British fleet could quickly arrange itself into line astern to pass in a three-mile gap between the windward and the leeward Spanish columns engaging them both almost simultaneously. But visibility was poor and Jervis could not see until too late that the windward Spanish column was turning north-east to cross behind the British ships so that it could link up with its leeward column, once Jervis's fleet – edging south-west – had passed through the gap between them. Eventually seeing this, Jervis ordered his line of ships to go about, in turn, also to sail north-east, bringing them alongside the Spanish windward column to prevent both Spanish columns from uniting – when their combined firepower would be overwhelming. Snake-like, the British line would reverse direction and then come parallel with the Spanish formation sailing on the same heading. But going about *in turn* was now too late and the snake would be left trailing behind the Spanish column as it continued north-east. Third from the back of the snake, in HMS *Captain*, Nelson could see the futility of the manoeuvre and rather than wait his turn to go about, he disobeyed orders and broke away to attack the leading ships of the Spanish column that were just then sailing past the rear of the British snake. The two ships behind Nelson followed his lead, and they were joined by the *Culloden* which, as the leading ship of the snake, was the only one whose turn brought it close enough to engage at about the same time.

It was fierce and dangerous – some say outright reckless – but Nelson, alongside Collingwood in the *Excellent*, Towry in the *Diadem* and Troubridge in the *Culloden* were exceptionally good commanders. With the *Captain* nearly wrecked, Nelson famously laid it alongside the *San Nicolas* which was already entangled with the *San Jose* and boarded both in turn. By his initial disobedience, Nelson and three other captains had created the battle mêlée that was to prove so advantageous to British ships in this, and many subsequent, actions. From further down the line in HMS *Victory*, Jervis could only watch as Rear Admiral William Parker ordered his own division to 'fill and stand on' in support of Nelson. More British ships were able to join the fray once the Spanish manoeuvre to unite both columns had been frustrated.

The Spanish leeward group fired on the British snake as it reversed itself close to them but was slow to engage in what had become the main battle further north. By dusk, all British ships had been fully engaged. The Spanish fleet was badly mauled and broke off. Four British ships were disabled, but there were four Spanish prizes and the biggest battleship in the world, the four-decker *Santissima Trinidad*, was reduced to a floating hulk as it crept away.

Cape St Vincent was clearly a victory for the smaller British force. The Spanish fleet had mounted almost twice the number of guns but had come off much the worse. On the other hand, it had escaped. Jervis didn't pursue the defeated enemy; the valuable merchant cargo of mercury – fundamental to the production of Spanish and French gold coins – had remained safe with the leeward squadron; and the prospect of a joint Spanish and French fleet leading an invasion of Britain remained a realistic threat. There was still no alternative to containing that threat through more blockades.

But after years of defeat and disappointment Cape St Vincent was a victory to be celebrated at home and in Parliament. The public thrilled to Nelson's exploits and Jervis was duly lauded as the architect of a great triumph. He certainly deserves credit for the way he embraced the confrontation. But he was lucky to have his battle orders disobeyed at just the right moment by a junior commander of greater flair. He also deserves credit for his faith in Nelson. Jervis embodied traditional beliefs in sea power and battle tactics, not to mention having a very conventional cast of mind. He might have been expected to dislike the sort of wilful, popinjay self-promotion of a man like Nelson. But he recognised the outstanding talent that Nelson brought to sea power and his ability to manufacture victories when it mattered. He trusted Nelson with many difficult assignments and shielded him from criticism and jealousy that, privately, he probably shared. They were never friends, but a strong mutual respect grew between them. So, too, with other talented commanders – he clashed with Cuthbert Collingwood, Thomas Troubridge, Edward Pellew, and famously with Thomas Cochrane – but he always recognised their talent while he was unsparing with those commanders he thought deficient. And though many captains who were to become Nelson's 'band of brothers' disliked Jervis, few failed to recognise how much the navy needed his dedication to it.

After Cape St Vincent Jervis was back on blockade duty off Cadiz. Mutiny was breaking out everywhere, from Spithead and the Nore to Jamaica, driven by the tensions and iniquities that had plagued the Service for more than a generation.[1] Jervis

---

1. They included the intolerable conditions on board so many ships, the political influence of the American and French revolutions, the multi-national nature of most of the crews and the fact that US ships were offering attractive terms of service. Not least, too many captains and officers were simply not worthy of their crews' respect.

was determined it would not spread to the Mediterranean fleet. His approach to the problem embodied those same elements that lay behind his lifelong campaign to reform the Service. They were based on a combination of iron discipline and obedience; the application of it to all ranks; constant training and useful activity, and attention to the genuine welfare needs of the crews.

There are vignettes a-plenty of all these instincts. He lost no time in hanging potential mutineers in his fleet. When there was real tension on the *Marlborough* over a particular death sentence, he had boats from across the fleet armed with carronades surround it with orders to bombard the ship if the execution was even delayed, let alone cancelled. He kept ships apart so that recently arrived crews could not mix with established crews. He bombarded Cadiz virtually every night to keep his blockading ships busy. He couldn't hang any officers, but he publicly punished and humiliated them in some celebrated events seen and heard by all. He could publicly humiliate an errant midshipman, shaving his head and putting a notice around his neck in front of the whole crew. At the same time, he worked hard to get better food onto his ships and was successful in reducing all the usual causes of illness at sea. He knew when a streak of theatricality would help and could show generosity. In one case he reimbursed from his own pocket the considerable sum of £70 to Roger Odell who had lost it in the water. Roger Odell had been one of his 'captains of the tops' in the *Victory* (a dangerous role in battle requiring nerve and skill) and Jervis ceremoniously made a practical joke out of his gift to restore the man's fortune – putting him on trial for crying, then telling Odell he was 'one of my best men', so here's £70 and 'no more crying, mind'.

Of greatest long-term significance, Jervis was indefatigable in improving the victualling and fresh-water facilities in Gibraltar, alongside its ship-repair yards. The subsequent successes of the Mediterranean and Atlantic fleets would have been impossible without it. Gibraltar was the foundation of Britain's growing power across the Mediterranean and the eastern Atlantic. Meanwhile, the Admiralty was anxious to see action to follow up Cape St Vincent, though resources were still too scarce to do more than maintain the most important blockades. The Adriatic was considered and rejected. London then decided on an expedition to capture Tenerife in the Canary Islands, though there was little strategic logic in it. Jervis seemed agnostic over whether it was worth the effort, but gave the task to Nelson and Troubridge. Tenerife turned out to be Nelson's most singular failure. It cost him an arm and (briefly) a crisis of confidence.

Of much greater significance, Napoleon was gathering a massive expeditionary force in Toulon and London worried where it might be headed. Jervis was one of the very few who thought a French expedition to Egypt was a real possibility. He sent Nelson and Troubridge, again, with fifteen ships and three frigates he could barely spare, to try to locate and engage it. He not only kept faith with them both, but he caused himself endless subsequent trouble by appointing Nelson above more senior fleet commanders, particularly William Parker and John Orde. He gave Nelson virtually open-ended orders to do whatever he thought appropriate.

Jervis was holding off scepticism at his decisions and abusive criticism from London when news of Nelson's triumph at the Battle of the Nile came through. It effectively gave Britain the Mediterranean and turned the tide, at least in that theatre of war. Jervis's judgement was emphatically vindicated. But his Mediterranean success also wrecked his health, bringing fresh responsibilities to watch over the seas around Cadiz, Naples and Sicily, Minorca, Acre, Alexandria and Malta. He retired on grounds of illness in 1799 and went home. But in a mixture of vanity and duty he then agreed to take over the Channel Fleet in 1800 and set about reforming it in his characteristic ways. He forbade officers to sleep ashore, improved all the sick quarters, applied ruthless economies and produced a smaller force of more deployable ships with better crews, and so on and so on. It was tough work, and he was hated for it.

Significantly, Jervis blockaded Brest more closely than his own captains thought possible, leading ships himself deep inshore thanks to the excellent charts he had made many years before. Napoleon later admitted that the Brest blockade was a big factor in his decision to offer peace in the Treaty of Amiens of 1802.

Jervis was tired and ill, but he had become First Sea Lord in 1801 and carried on his crusades. He attacked the outright nepotism in naval dockyards, bringing them directly under Admiralty control and introduced better machinery for ship-building. He broke the power of the Navy Board – civilians who were all part of the merchant builders' corruption in the dockyards. He championed the essential functions of the marines and got them designated as Royal Marines. He was mercilessly attacked by Pitt, opposing the Addington government, for running the navy down with economies. But under Jervis's stewardship, the navy then had more than 1,500 *operational* ships of all types and 80,000 sailors – still inadequate for crewing, but more than ever before. He prevailed on the government in 1801 to send a fleet to Copenhagen in a straight act of aggression to break the nascent power of Denmark, Sweden, Russia and Prussia – the 'League of Armed Neutrality'. His unpopularity with all and sundry both in the navy and in Parliament seemed only to strengthen his resolve. He was under siege, and his judgements became erratic even if his reforming strategy was sound.

In 1804, when Addington's government fell, Jervis stepped down as First Sea Lord. Surprisingly, he agreed to take command again of the Channel Fleet. His approach hadn't changed and his unpopularity was by then legendary. He was commanding the Channel when his protégé Nelson triumphed at Trafalgar. In 1807 another change of government led him finally to retire from the sea at the age of seventy-two.

For all he had done, Jervis still thought he had failed to reform the navy sufficiently. Notwithstanding Trafalgar, he told George III that the Service was worse than he had ever known it. Perhaps illness and exhaustion led him to such depressive conclusions. It was not true, though his record in the upper house in the years following suggests an ex-military Lord with very fixed and peppery views. His wife died in 1816 and he moved to France for the sake of his health. He died peacefully at his estate in 1823 and was buried in Stone, Staffordshire, in the family mausoleum. He is named by history after the battle he almost lost. But he won for the Royal Navy some of the most important battles that are seldom even named.

17

Admiral Cuthbert Collingwood

The reputation of Admiral Cuthbert Collingwood, second in command at Trafalgar, is always overshadowed by that of Nelson. Without doubt, Jervis, Nelson, Collingwood and Wellington were the four most strategically significant British military commanders during the French wars of their era. But Nelson's star shines so brightly that Collingwood is most often overlooked among them. In his 1970 play, *Bequest to the Nation*, Terence Rattigan traduces Collingwood's professional reputation, as dramatists will, to highlight Nelson's military genius by comparison. But Collingwood was a remarkably successful commander in battle and displayed a politically sophisticated outlook that Nelson either lacked, or didn't live long enough to develop. Collingwood fought in the American War of Independence and then three major fleet actions in the French Wars, for which he was – with Nelson and Edward Berry – among only three captains to be awarded three Naval Gold Medals during those years.

Yet 'Old Cuddy' as he became known, has acquired a popular reputation as a dull tactician and a cantankerous old Admiral. Both characterisations are unfair. His command style was certainly different to both Jervis and Nelson. William Makepeace Thackeray spoke of 'Collingwood's gentle glory'. There was not 'a nobler, kinder, more beautiful life of duty, of a gentler, truer heart', he said. One of Collingwood's ordinary sailors wrote that 'a better seaman, a better friend to seamen – a more zealous defender of the country's rights and honour, never trod the quarterdeck.' Clearly, Collinwood's virtues as a commander were more subtly practised than Jervis's iron ferocity, or Nelson's charismatic genius.

He was born in 1748 in Newcastle-upon-Tyne into the extensive Collingwood family. But his father was a bankrupted trader and, along with his younger brother, Collingwood joined the navy. In 1760, at the age of twelve, he got a post as cabin boy on a frigate commanded by one of his cousins. From then until his death in 1810 he would be officially 'at sea' for all but three years of his life. From first to last Collingwood was a sailor's sailor.

Like most successful commanders, his early rise through the ranks was boosted by some gallantry as a young officer. For Collingwood, it was at Bunker Hill during the American War of Independence. But prior to that he was at sea for five years before he could even be rated a midshipman – the lowest officer rank – and served in six different ships in his first fourteen years of service. He was a master's mate in 1770, which is to say, a midshipman with extra responsibilities. By the time Collingwood was on the *Preston*, sent to Boston in 1774 to suppress the incipient revolution among American colonists, he certainly knew his business around every inch of a ship.

The battle of Bunker Hill in 1775 was a moral victory for the 1,500 colonist amateurs who held out in their trenchwork blockade around Boston harbour before being overwhelmed by 3,000 British regulars. They didn't succumb to a naval barrage and General William Howe was forced to land troops at the foot of the peninsula to overrun them. Even then, it took three assaults and the burning of Charlestown before the exhausted colonists ran out of ammunition and fled. Master's mate Collingwood was responsible for the boats ferrying troops onto the peninsula and going back and forth all day to bring supplies, evacuating the large number of wounded. It was a dangerous role, particularly as American marksmen tried to target the reinforcements and supplies. But Collingwood displayed the nerveless calm for which he was to become well-known. His own laconic, understated letters described it as 'fierce'. Having already passed his promotion examinations, his superiors noted what they called his 'conspicuous personal deeds' that day – we don't know what they may have been – and made him a lieutenant there and then.

Lieutenant Collingwood was given command of a brig, and made a post captain of the *Hinchinbrook*, a small frigate, then of the *Pelican*, in which he was shipwrecked in a powerful hurricane. His career and his personal life began to take turns of greater consequence, however, between 1783 and 1786 when he was posted to the West Indies.

In September 1783 he left Spithead in the frigate *Mediator* bound for English Harbour in Antigua among the Leeward Islands. He was required to take as passengers the ageing Royal Commissioner for English Harbour, John Moutray, his thirty-one-year-old wife Mary, and their young twins. During the voyage they all became good friends. Mary Moutray broke down Collingwood's inscrutable correctness to discover the witty and emotionally intelligent man beneath. And within a few months, Nelson also arrived in Antigua on his own posting. They were glad to see him, not least because Nelson's enthusiasm lifted the morale of the whole dockyard. The Moutrays, Collingwood and Nelson were to form an intimate little salon of their own, at 'Windsor', the Commissioner's house, in the otherwise godforsaken Leeward Islands.

Nelson and Collingwood were already good friends. They had met first in 1773. Collingwood, the master's mate, was ten years older than the fifteen-year-old midshipman Nelson. They instinctively liked one another and the tall, well-built young man helped the slightly built teenager of more delicate health, at sea for only two years, to adjust to the life. They were completely different characters. Nelson was the best sort of 'Type-A' personality; Collingwood the best sort of 'Type-B'. In addition to his precocious natural talent, Nelson was more well-connected than Collingwood and his career rapidly overhauled that of his older friend. He was a lieutenant at eighteen and a post captain at twenty-one. Collingwood never resented it. There is not a word or a hint in any of his letters that he was jealous of Nelson. He recognised Nelson's flair and wild courage and he was canny enough to see Nelson's growing influence with the Admiralty. As he wrote years later, 'Whenever Lord Nelson got a step in rank, I succeeded him. First in *Lowestoffe*, then in the *Badger*...and afterwards the *Hinchinbrook*...which made us both Post Captains.' Nelson's career began to pull Collingwood's along in its wake.

Thus, in 1784 they were both commanding frigates on the West Indies station. Collingwood felt committed to upholding the Navigation Acts, which meant that America – now an independent country – could no longer sail its ships in and out of British colonies to trade freely. It was his initiative, but Nelson backed him up in the *Boreas*, and Collingwood's younger brother, Wilfred, also sent on station in the sloop *Rattler*, added his weight to the campaign. The three captains shared the considerable political heat that their enforcement created. They were very unpopular with governors and entrepreneurs who wanted to turn a blind eye and threatened to sue all three of them. But Collingwood knew the law in detail and gave the Admiralty no option but to support them – though, of course, Nelson subsequently got most of the credit.

In 1785 the Moutrays returned to Britain when John took seriously ill. Both Collingwood and Nelson wrote how bereft they felt, deprived of Mary's vivacious company. They had both fallen in love with her. John died in Bath that November. If Mary Moutray had become a widow while they were still in Antigua both Collingwood and Nelson would almost certainly have proposed to her; and she might well have accepted one of them. As it was, all three went their separate ways but they maintained a warm, triangular relationship for the rest of their lives with gossipy letters, indiscreet observations and very occasional visits.[1] They understood one another very well. Mary outlived both her admirals by many years, living to the age of ninety-two.

In 1786 Collingwood was back in Britain and his ship paid off, leaving him on half pay without a command. He returned to Newcastle, but like all post captains, stayed close to the Admiralty on the matter of another command. He got one voyage out and back to the West Indies, but then in 1791 he married Sarah Blackett, daughter to the mayor of Newcastle. They settled into a modest house in Morpeth, which he treasured, and very quickly they had two daughters to whom he was devoted. He loved his family, but could not have known how little of his subsequent life he was destined to spend with them. His nearest beating heart companion almost until the end of his days turned out to be a puppy he acquired sometime during these years. He named him Bounce. In the event, Bounce lived to be a very old dog. From the mid-1790s Bounce went through every voyage with Collingwood, every battle, every run ashore. He turned out to be a contented sailor, taking his exercise by swimming behind Collingwood's barge in anchorages. The admiral and his dog were inseparable.[2]

With the French declaration of war against Britain in 1793, Collingwood was given command of HMS *Prince*, Admiral Bowyer's Channel Fleet flagship, and when Bowyer moved his flag to the better sailing *Barfleur*, he took Collingwood with him as his flag captain. And it was in the *Barfleur* that Collingwood would participate in the first of his three great fleet actions.

---

1. Mary's son, John Moutray, subsequently served under Nelson, and was lost to fever in 1794.
2. Sadly, we don't know Bounce's breed. He was once included in a portrait of Collingwood by an artist who had never seen him and Bounce is rendered as a fashionable and anaemic-looking Jack Russell, which is impossible. We know that he was 'the height of Collingwood's table'. His longevity, and swimming in tidal anchorages, suggests a much bigger and stronger dog. The best guesses have been a Newfoundland or perhaps an Old English Sheep Dog.

By this time, Collingwood's approach to ship command had become well-established and he would follow it with demonstrable success for the rest of his career. By the standards of the time, he was a remarkably modern man-manager. If he was awkward with most women, he understood men very well. He was a disciplinarian who hated flogging and thought it counter-productive. It was generally believed throughout the navy that he had banned flogging on his ships. He hadn't and he didn't speak against flogging; he just didn't do it. It was the same with impressment. He didn't ban pressed men on his ships, as was popularly believed; he just didn't have them. Having risen from a cabin boy over many years he was somewhat indulgent to what he referred to as the 'uncontrolled eccentricities of sailors' and he ruled through encouragement and disapproval more than fear. He abhorred swearing and discourtesy, one man to another, of whatever rank. Having served for a long time both below and above the rank of midshipman, he was notably hard on any midshipman who displayed a sense of entitlement or was less then fully committed to his duties. Over the years his crews came to refer to him as 'father', and he chivvied them, insisting on full ventilation, exercise and fresh food to the point where virtually no one was lost to illness on board his ships.

His most uncompromising demands on the crew were in the matter of ship handling and gunnery – always gunnery – which he insisted on practising whenever the opportunity was available. He would set up competitions between gun decks to encourage their rates of fire. He never quite achieved a shot a minute, but the *Excellent* was seen to deliver a truly phenomenal three broadsides in three and a half minutes. At one shot every seventy seconds, the work of the gun crews must have been Herculean. During that era, British ships could expect to get one broadside off within three minutes; in Nelson's fleet it was sometimes nearer to two minutes. But no one could match Collinwood's crews, where even the biggest 32-pounder guns, almost three tons apiece, were worked by a fifteen-man crew to such a level. Most French and Spanish ships needed four minutes or more to fire a broadside. Under his influence, Collingwood's ships were the fastest firing units within any fleet he joined. This effectiveness was based fundamentally on a crew's sense of duty and personal loyalty to him. For Collingwood, they were anyway synonymous.

Senior captains could often take many crew members with them when they changed ships and Collingwood had a core of Tynesiders – his 'Tars of the Tyne' as he called them – who joined to serve on his ships. Navy manpower was always chronically short and his wife and friends would put the word out around Newcastle that Captain Collingwood 'was recruiting'. Some groups who joined up to serve with him found themselves dispersed around different ships. They complained, and Collingwood did all he could to get them transferred while he was serving on the *Prince* and the *Barfleur* – ships he commanded before he became nationally famous.[3] It was to this

---

3. One seaman on the *Royal Sovereign*, Collingwood's ship at Trafalgar, observed that it seemed to be crewed overwhelmingly by Geordies – surely incorrect, but indicative of a sense of identity on board. A significant contingent of Tynesiders had been transferred from the *Dreadnought* to the *Royal Sovereign* when Collingwood moved his flag to it.

core of Geordies, waiting on their gun decks during the morning of Trafalgar that he is believed to have said, 'Let us do something today which the world will talk of hereafter.' Collingwood was not an outwardly demonstrative man. Those in the navy who didn't serve with him thought him dull. He didn't make any effort to create something akin to Nelson's 'band of brothers' among fellow captains; he expected them to do their duty without having to be patted and praised. But for the crews on his own ships, though he set very exacting standards, he loved them, looked after them, and they knew it.

For Collingwood, his first major fleet action as a flag captain was a frustrating affair, where the calibre of his crew was difficult to demonstrate. The Fourth Battle of Ushant, more popularly known as the 'Glorious First of June' was a five-day cat and mouse engagement in 1794 where the excellent French Admiral Villaret-Joyeuse was trying to get a massive food convoy of 127 merchantmen from America into Brest to relieve the French famine. Admiral Richard Howe's fleet was probing, but failed to locate the convoy until 28th May, 350 miles west of Ushant. The target was huge, but all Howe was certain of was the French escorting battle fleet he had just spotted. Villaret-Joyeuse took his warships south and dangled the end of his formation close enough to be engaged by the British. Howe took the bait and followed for three indecisive, foggy days while the merchantmen proceeded in safety in the opposite direction far to the north. On June 1st a full fleet action finally occurred. Admiral Bowyer's *Barfleur*, captained by Collingwood, was in one of the two squadrons in the central division. The British broke through the French lines and created the general mêlée to which they were becoming accustomed. Bowyer was seriously wounded early on and Collingwood took over tactical responsibility. The central division was less heavily engaged in the fight but the *Barfleur* helped out the *Invincible* against the much bigger *Le Juste* and captured it, among seven prizes taken that day. No British ships were lost. The British had won the clash of battle fleets; the French had won the strategic engagement in getting their food convoy through. Both sides lauded their heroic commanders.

Neither Bowyer, Collingwood nor the *Barfleur* were recognised for what they had done in the battle. Collingwood was deeply affronted by the omission until it was finally put right with the award of a Naval Gold Medal years later. But at the time, he was hurt and depressed. He made the long journey from Portsmouth to Morpeth, just to spend two days with his young family – 'his blessings'. His wife met him on the road. In late 1794 he was given command of the 74-gun third-rate *Excellent*, which made some small amends for the slight, and before it sailed in the New Year, he was able to snatch another visit home, 'eight or nine days among my darlings' as he wrote to Alexander Carlyle.

Excellent went on convoy duty in the Mediterranean, where Collingwood would serve again with his friend, Nelson. But the entry of Spain into an anti-British alliance with Napoleon effectively banished the Royal Navy from the Mediterranean in 1796. Britain's war was going badly both on land and at sea. Sailing from the Tagus in Portugal in 1797, the *Excellent* was with Admiral John Jervis's fleet of fifteen ships of the line when it encountered twenty-seven Spanish warships off Cape St Vincent. The nature of the Battle of Cape St Vincent has been outlined in a previous chapter, but Nelson and Collingwood's own roles in it have always commanded attention.

Nelson, in the 74-gun *Captain*, was third from the end of the line of British ships going south west that were about to fail to engage with a loose formation of Spanish ships going north east and soon to cross behind the British line. Collingwood was following Nelson in the *Excellent*; George Towry bringing up the rear in the *Diadem*. Nelson disobeyed orders and turned directly into the ships at the front of the Spanish line, plunging the *Captain* into a desperate fight with the biggest warship afloat, the *Santissima Trinidad*, and its three consorts, each of which out-gunned him. Collingwood and Towry followed Nelson into the fray; it would have been unthinkable to leave him so exposed. The battle was thereby transformed into the classic 'pell-mell' encounter in which Nelson so believed.

With his 74 guns Collingwood immediately engaged the 112-gun *Salvador del Mundo*, then the 74-gun *San Isidro*, less than five yards away. The *Excellent*'s gunnery was so devastating they both struck their colours in less than twenty minutes. Collingwood could have taken them both – they had struck to him. But he left them for other British ships coming up. Nelson would be overwhelmed unless the *Excellent* could relieve the pressure on the *Captain*. He joined the *Culloden* to engage the *San Nicolas* at less than three yards – at one point, in all the smoke, he thought 'we were fast to her'. But his quarry tried to sheer away, and got tangled with the *San Jose*. The *Captain* was by then a hulk and Nelson pulled up against the other side of the *San Nicholas*, caught fast to the *San Jose*. These were the two ships that Nelson then boarded, one tangled with the other, in his famous exploit. By then, Collingwood was on to the *Santissima Trinidad*. Against its 130 guns and four decks, his two-decker simply didn't have the height to allow for an attempted boarding. But he pounded the *Santissima Trinidad*, which was in very poor shape by the time it withdrew. In the final analysis, all four of the enemy ships taken at Cape St Vincent were the victims of Collingwood's gunnery on the *Excellent*.

Of course, Nelson won the adulation of the country and deserves credit on many counts. But the navy knew what Collingwood had done. Nelson acknowledged it immediately, if a little diffidently. He spoke of Collingwood's 'assistance in nearly a critical moment'. Far from 'assistance' it was actually a rescue at an overwhelmingly critical moment for which Collingwood had ignored two prizes. But the action cemented Collingwood's reputation within the Service, gave him some wealth and made him one of the growing band of British naval heroes.

He was back on Cadiz blockade duties in the *Excellent* when Nelson triumphed at the Battle of the Nile in 1798 and was mortified not to be there – an omission he blamed on Jervis. That aside, the *Excellent* had been at sea almost continuously for three years and Collingwood now longed to get home. At the age of fifty-one he could enjoy the fruits of his success. He turned down command of the 90-gun *Atlas*, he was promoted to rear admiral, and he went home with Bounce to enjoy celebrity status in Northumberland.

There, he was caught between a genuine desire to retire, and a sense of duty – and some vanity – to have another command. After three months at home he was back with the Channel Fleet and detached in the *Triumph* on a fruitless chase into the Mediterranean under the command of the indecisive Lord Keith, trying to intercept French ships escaped from Brest. Then he was in and out of Plymouth in the *Barfleur* during 1800 and 1801 in the endless blockade of the Brest peninsula. Sarah and his eldest daughter travelled the 425 miles from Morpeth to Plymouth in January 1801 to take rooms there and spend days with him when he had some shore time. Nelson was regularly ashore too. On one occasion Collingwood wrote to Mary Moutray telling her how he, Sarah and his daughter were 'by the fireside cosing' with Nelson at Plymouth's Fountain Inn. Nelson may have been a national hero, but his personal life was by then a public scandal, his eye and head wounds were troubling him and he was prone to bouts of black depression. Collingwood disapproved of Lady Hamilton but he seemed to understand Nelson too well to be judgemental. And Nelson took comfort in relaxing with his old friend and the Collingwood family he had come to know. The Treaty of Amiens, when it was concluded in 1802, felt like a blessed relief. Sarah took her daughter home, while Collingwood had some tedious duties to perform before returning to Morpeth to experience a country at peace.

In truth, though he loved his navy, Collingwood had now had enough of the sea. He took country walks with Bounce, always with a pocketful of acorns, planting them in any likely spot, so 'the navy would never want for oaks to build fighting ships', as Dudley Pope put it. He always had an acute grasp of politics, however, and he could see before the year was out that the peace would break down. When it did, and the call came, he genuinely didn't want to return to sea. But he never contemplated shirking the obligation. Britain, he knew, needed his experience.

In May 1803 Collingwood and Bounce travelled through Newcastle on their way back to war. The *Newcastle Courant* offered a guinea to all those already signing up to serve on his ship. He would never see his beloved family or his home again. It was back to soul-destroying blockade duty off Brest, hoisting his flag – now as a vice admiral – on a number of different ships, including the *Culloden*.

The Trafalgar campaign of 1805 will always belong to Nelson and is described in another chapter. But fate decreed that Collingwood would both set up Nelson's battle at Trafalgar and carry it through for him. As part of his plan to invade Britain, Napoleon intended to use his Mediterranean and Atlantic fleets to draw British ships away to the West Indies before doubling back in time to protect invasion barges crossing the channel from Boulogne. It was never a feasible plan but Nelson had chased Admiral Villeneuve's fleet across the Atlantic and back without encountering it. During that time, Collingwood was blockading eight Spanish ships in Cadiz. He flew his flag in the 98-gun, second rate *Dreadnought*, and he had two 74-gun third raters, a frigate and a bomb ship in his tiny squadron.

At dawn on 20th August Collingwood suddenly saw Villeneuve's twenty-six ships of the line coming over the horizon, not having gone into the Channel but approaching his squadron, evidently intent on getting back into the Mediterranean. Besides the obvious danger, Collingwood also saw the considerable opportunity of the situation. He manoeuvred to protect his bomb ship, then disposed his force in a way that indicated he was relatively indifferent to the massive fleet bearing down on him, edging south-east towards Gibraltar. He hoisted signals, that Villeneuve would see, to a non-existent British fleet further south-east that might – if it had existed – be coming through the Straits of Gibraltar into the Atlantic. Then he turned his ships to face the French fleet and sent one of his 74s to get close enough to reconnoitre them as if in anticipation of a major fleet action. Villeneuve may have suspected it was all a bluff, but wasn't prepared to call it. He turned round and sailed his fleet into Cadiz. And Collingwood put his tiny squadron back on blockade duty, now bottling up thirty-four major enemy warships inside a port that struggled to accommodate them all. Collingwood dispatched his frigate with the news and then endured an agony of suspense waiting for reinforcement as British ships converged on him. John Knight arrived a few days later with the *Queen*, *Tonnant*, *Minotaur* and the *Bellerophon*. That relieved him a little, and on 31st August Calder, thankfully, came in with eighteen ships of the line. Then on 28th September the *Ajax* and the *Thunderer* arrived, along with HMS *Victory*, carrying Nelson who had come to assume command. This was what they had waited for. Throughout their careers, Nelson and Collingwood had always discussed naval strategy. Now, they went over the battle plan in great detail and shared a locked 'trunk' with two keys so that no one else could access messages between them. All it required was that Villeneuve and his Spanish counterpart, Admiral Gravina, come out to fight.

They did so on 19th October, and after two days of fruitless manoeuvring towards Gibraltar then back towards Cadiz, the thirty-three French and Spanish warships arranged themselves in a crescent of partially doubled up ranks to receive the two lines of British ships, coming at them from the west at right angles to pierce the formation and set up another 'pell-mell' battle.

Nelson would lead the northernmost line of ships, Collingwood the southern line. Nelson had previously asked Collingwood to transfer his flag to the 100-gun *Royal Sovereign* for the battle. It was partly a practical joke. The lumbering *Royal Sovereign* was known as the 'west-country waggon'. But Collingwood didn't know it's hull had just been re-coppered before arriving on station. Rather than take it for himself, Nelson had given his friend the fastest ship in the fleet. The effect was that as the two lines of British ships headed towards the enemy crescent in light winds, the *Royal Sovereign* pulled a long way ahead. Normally, ships going into battle would hold some speed in reserve, partly to stay in formation. But in light winds, with the French and Spanish fleet almost within reach of safety again in Cadiz, this was a straight charge to grab the one opportunity on offer.

Collingwood headed for the Spanish flagship, *Santa Anna*. He decided to cut into the enemy line further north than had been planned, leaving his division outnumbered in the 'pell-mell' clash against a greater portion of enemy ships comprising the rear of their line. As the *Royal Sovereign* approached, with no significant guns facing forwards, it simply had to give the Spanish and French ships free shots against its oncoming bows. Collingwood fired off some starboard guns to create smoke that would roll ahead of them in the gentle breeze, but the decks of the *Royal Sovereign* were quiet as it received the first salvos, closing the final mile. At 400 yards six enemy ships opened up on the *Royal Sovereign*. Six minutes later it was crossing the stern of the

Santa Anna. The *Fougueux* behind the flagship tried to push up to close the gap. It did, indeed, become very narrow, but at twelve-twenty the *Royal Sovereign* unleashed a huge double-shotted broadside, at point blank range through the towering stern of the *Santa Anna*, almost disabling it in one exchange. Then Collingwood was round onto the starboard of the flagship and was quickly surrounded by four of its consorts and the (French) *Neptune* further away.[4] Behind the *Royal Sovereign* the *Belleisle*, the *Mars*, *Tonnant* and *Bellerophon* were strung out over a quarter of a mile back. For twenty minutes the *Royal Sovereign* engaged six enemy ships before the *Belleisle* arrived. It was a fearsome first hour. The Master was cut in half by shot as Collingwood was speaking to him. Another shot was so close, its slipstream spun him around and threw him across the quarterdeck. He was splattered in blood and bruises and took a large splinter in the leg, which he left untreated throughout the day, and which troubled him for the rest of his life. After that first hour, only Collingwood, his flag captain and his secretary were left standing on the quarterdeck.

The battle around the southern line of attack was the more intense of the two centres of fighting. Fifteen ships in Collingwood's division took on nineteen of the enemy's combined fleet. His leading eight ships engaged seventeen enemy ships in the first phase, and by the end, only five out of the original nineteen enemy ships escaped back to Cadiz.[5] Around two-thirty Collingwood was informed that Nelson was wounded, probably dead. He was shocked but can hardly have been surprised. The *Royal Sovereign* was by then shattered, so he moved his flag to the frigate *Euryalus* to command the battle. Collingwood ordered six ships to form a gun line to windward, having his frigate tow the *Royal Sovereign* into place to join it. The enemy's unscathed northern division had finally turned about and launched a two-pronged counter-attack to try to rescue its admiral and some of his failing ships. By five-thirty it was all over, when the *Achille* exploded. The French counterattack had been pushed westward, away from the battle area and didn't attempt to return to it, where both the victors and the prizes wallowed in a rising swell.

But the sea never makes life easy for mariners. A ferocious storm was arriving, the greatest in the memory of several captains. In modern terms, it was somewhere between a Storm Force 10 and 11, with steady fifty-knot winds, gusting much higher. Many ships were by then incapable of anchoring – as Nelson had originally intended – and the treacherous shoals off Cape Trafalgar lay to leeward. Collingwood confronted the storm with responsibility for twenty-seven damaged British ships of the line, four frigates, a schooner and a cutter and a record-breaking fourteen war-wrecked prizes. He decided to ride out the storm, standing westwards to the open sea. Another ferocious battle against the elements was fought over the next four days, to maintain the fleet and deal with the prize ships. It became an epic in itself; many warships were no more than floating hulks, British prize crews and enemy sailors

---

4. The *Royal Sovereign* was engaged by the *Santa Anna, Fougueux, Indomptable, San Justo, San Leandro* and *Neptune*.
5. If Collingwood had cut the line where Nelson intended, he would have enjoyed a fifteen to twelve advantage in ships.

worked together to keep their ships afloat to avoid foundering; frigates worked hard to take ships in tow; and Collingwood was as anxious to save French and Spanish seamen as British.[6] But in the midst of the emergency, some enemy ships were retaken by their captured crews and escaped to Cadiz, four were lost with all hands on the reefs off Trafalgar. And there was one sortie by enemy ships from Cadiz, emerging to grab back a couple of the prizes but losing three of their own ships in the process. Further attacks on the enfeebled and encumbered British fleet remained a possibility as it struggled to get north of Cadiz. On 24th October, with the storm still raging, Collingwood controversially ordered that crews be taken off all but four of the prizes and have them sunk. Whether or not he over-reacted, there was no doubt in his own mind that this was the inescapable strategic logic. The whole point of the carnage was to 'annihilate' – in Nelson's own words – the enemy battle fleets, whether or not they became prizes. Several large fortunes, not least Collingwood's own, were sent to the bottom. The captured prizes were worth, in modern terms, somewhere between £100 and £220 million.[7] And just as none of Nelson's ships struck their colours at Trafalgar, so not a single British ship was lost in the storm. From 28th October, jury-rigged or towed, they began to limp into Gibraltar. The crews were exhausted and – in contrast to the country's unrestrained joy – battle-shocked and sullen.

Collingwood longed to get home, but couldn't. He was the only man the Admiralty trusted to run the Mediterranean theatre. He became Vice Admiral and Commander-in-Chief of the Mediterranean Fleet. From his headquarters in Menorca he was responsible for British relations from Cadiz to Constantinople, dealing with kings, queens, pashas and sultans, over eighty ships and 25,000 men. He proved to be a skilled diplomat and his political antennae remained as acute as ever. When Arthur Wellesley (before he became Wellington) landed troops in Portugal, Collingwood had already taken steps to support the 1808 Spanish uprising against Napoleon and to strengthen relations with Lisbon. From the sea he secured Cadiz on behalf of the Spanish uprising, captured the French ships sheltering there, and worked constantly in getting supplies both to Wellesley in Portugal and to the Spanish insurgents – something Wellesley always appreciated. But increasingly, in this unbroken seven-year operational tour, Collingwood's health was failing. He twice asked to be relieved of his command, only to have the Admiralty insist he must stay, playing on his sense of duty and his vanity.

Collingwood's vigorous campaigning prevented the French fleet holding onto any part of the Mediterranean. He was desperate to lure the French into one final Trafalgar – another fleet action where he could finish them off as a naval power. He was once close to it in 1808 chasing a French fleet from Toulon to Corfu and back, with an innovative battle plan clearly drawn up.[8] But the weather was against him; and in reality the focus of the war had switched to Napoleon's land operations. The

---

6. For which he was held in high regard by the Spanish government, and remembered in later years when it mattered politically.
7. An average seaman might have expected about £30 as his share of the likely prize money; equivalent to three years' pay. A captain could have expected around £10,000 – enough for a country estate.
8. It revolved around a variation on the Trafalgar strategy that would protect British ships for longer against enemy broadsides, during the dangerous run-in.

maritime war was now dominated by frigate actions and strategic raiding. Unable to engineer another fleet action, he became cantankerous and distracted by the volume of other work.

Much of his popular reputation as 'old Cuddy' derives from his behaviour in these final years; trying to run his wealthier (and now very status-conscious) family by correspondence, ill and exasperated by the increasing demands of his post. Eminent petitioners complained that he spent more time in meetings discussing issues with his damn dog than listening to them. So he did. In August 1809 Bounce, old and rheumatic, fell overboard from the flagship one night and was lost at sea. Collingwood was devastated; they had sailed thousands of miles and grown old together. 'Wiser than many who hold their heads higher, and grateful to those who were kind to him', he wrote sorrowfully. The Vice Admiral became so exhausted and ill that in February 1810 he felt there was no option but to resign his commission. Collingwood's secretary wrote to Sarah advising of her husband's condition, hoping she might arrive in Portsmouth or Plymouth as quickly as possible. In March 1810 he was virtually carried onto his flagship and on the first day of the voyage home he expired peacefully at sea. Collingwood died of a range of ailments of old age, though he was only sixty-one. But on that final day, still lucid, he professed himself content and reconciled with fate that he had always done his duty. He loved his family, his navy, his country and his dog – though in which order is not entirely obvious.

Collingwood was given a ceremonial funeral and laid to rest just a few feet away from Nelson's ornate tomb in the crypt of St Paul's Cathedral. There is a florid monument to him in the nave of St Paul's, but in the crypt his tomb is completely plain; merely a stone sarcophagus. There are faintly etched words inscribed at one end of the lid; 'Cuthbert Lord Collingwood, Died 7th March 1810, Aged 61'. Tourists crowd around Nelson's tomb in the centre of the crypt without noticing the plain stone box behind them. It seems like a symbolic injustice in the national memory. Perhaps, as a generous spirit, the ex-cabin boy wouldn't have minded too much.

Admiral Horatio Nelson

Admiral Lord Nelson is probably the most celebrated military hero in modern British history. He was also a key commander at a significant time in the country's affairs. His decisions were both dramatic and consequential. All the 'great British commanders' in this collection are notable for their historical significance in some way. But not many of them were manifest battle heroes while also being commanders of sufficient rank to make a political or strategic difference. Edward III, Henry V or Francis Drake spring to mind, but popular heroism and political consequence don't occur together very often. Leaders tend to become heroes in the teeth of battle and not infrequently get others around them killed. Commanders who make a strategic difference can normally only be effective if their seniority keeps them above the battle.

At the time of his death in 1805, Nelson was a Vice-Admiral, as appropriate to his command at Trafalgar. But his heroic influence on the Royal Navy goes far beyond his rank in life; dying at Trafalgar at the age of forty-seven. On 21st October every year, on every ship, at every shore base, the modern Royal Navy celebrates Trafalgar Night with some grand and traditional dinners. The dessert course is always modelled into 'ships of the line' and paraded in. Drink is taken, tables are thumped, admirals roar, and junior officers are sucked into the family of the Service. It's all based on Nelson; the spirit of the Royal Navy he embodied, the great victory at Trafalgar, and the dominance that victory gave to British naval power around the world, not eclipsed until the 1930s.

Bearing the weight of more than two centuries of adulation, Nelson's own character was as flawed as anyone else's, and rather more than some. In contrast to Jervis or Collingwood, who led men through the example of their own dutiful devotion, Nelson exuded leadership charisma. He had that something extra – quite a lot in fact – in dealing with those he led. He was a complex man; naturally god-fearing, instinctively patriotic and aggressively anti-French. He was egotistical and by turns highly manipulative yet courteously accommodating; hard-hearted and foolishly romantic. Most of those he commanded later in his career genuinely loved him; he was a winner and a charmer. He was both reckless and strategically astute, gambling on fate and making himself appear the master of it. Nelson was never physically robust. He was frequently ill, famously sea-sick throughout his career, and yet full of perseverance, insanely brave, no stranger in actual fact to failure, and often wounded. Through his illnesses and serious wounds, he confronted death on several occasions. It seemed to have an almost mystical effect on him. Even as a young captain he embodied a growing self-belief that became serenely embedded in his confident, assertive leadership. And that self-belief drove him towards what he came firmly to believe was his date with destiny in 1805. He had everything to live for after Trafalgar; he just didn't believe he would.

Nelson was born at Burnham Thorpe into a comfortable Norfolk family in 1758, the sixth of eleven children. He was well-enough connected through his mother to give him some advantages as a young mariner. His early career followed a path similar to other such officers, going to sea first as a boy in the role of ordinary seaman and coxswain, then midshipman and promotion to lieutenant, after which he could be given his own command. From 1771 to 1779 his service took him to the West Indies, the East Indies, and to look, yet again, for a North-West passage in the polar Atlantic. In these years he first contracted malaria which stayed with him, then dysentery and scurvy, and he was more prone than most to suffer with parasites whenever in tropical climes.

He showed verve and commitment in even the smallest tasks and studied hard for his lieutenant's exam. But he also benefited from the influence of his first captain – and his maternal uncle – Maurice Suckling. Having become Comptroller of the Navy, Suckling subsequently presided at Nelson's interview for his lieutenancy. With this particular connection it is no surprise that Nelson was a lieutenant at eighteen and a post-captain at twenty-one. His link to Suckling ensured that his genuine talent and commitment was fully recognised. More than one visitor to his ships after 1779 observed that this slight figure seemed no more than 'the merest boy', as the Duke of Clarence put it, in charge of 28-gun sixth or fifth rate frigates with crews of 200. He commanded four of them before 1787 and his fresh, officer style was already brave and enthusiastic, authoritative and imaginative – dreaming up entertainments and diversions for his crew – anxious to get his ships into whatever action was at hand. He made a habit of personally running up the ratlines into the tops, alongside his new midshipmen, to offer them reassurance and encouragement. He spoke loudly about 'heroism' and 'duty to the navy' and only a little more quietly about his own 'destiny' in it all.[1]

Even as he championed obedience to the Service, however, Nelson was headstrong and impetuous. On the West Indies station, he appealed for support to the Admiralty, the Prime Minister and government ministers in London over the heads of local officials and Leeward islanders on matters large and small, making him very unpopular in Whitehall. He exceeded his authority on judicial matters and was twice censured by the Admiralty. He would never be directly insubordinate, but he acted on his own best judgement and used his growing influence with the royal family, through his friendship with fellow captain, the Duke of Clarence – subsequently William IV – to shield him from the consequences.

Nelson fell in love easily. He wanted to marry Mary Simpson in Quebec, but was refused permission as she was only sixteen. He wanted to marry the daughter of an English clergymen he got to know in St Omer on a brief sojourn in France. He wrote to another, more wealthy, Suckling uncle asking for money to make him a marriageable

---

1. Though this was only partly successful at the time. In these years he commanded the frigates *Hinchinbrook, Janus, Albermarle* and *Boreas*. In the last two of these ships the crews declined to offer to serve again with him when the ships were paid off.

prospect, stating it was fundamental to his happiness. In any case, the young lady refused him. In Antigua he fell in love with Mary Moutray – as did his great friend Collingwood with whom he served on the same station for a while. When she was compelled to go home to England Nelson was genuinely heart-broken. But almost immediately, he fell in love with the young widow Frances (Fanny) Nisbet, who kept house as niece of a powerful slave plantation owner on the island of Nevis. He again asked his rich uncle to provide him with enough to marry, though even then, Fanny took some persuasion before they wed in Nevis in 1787. He brought Fanny and her young boy, Josiah, to live at Burnham Thorpe later that year. It was not a successful move. After the first flush of Caribbean romance, the relationship between them steadily soured in the windy Norfolk winters.

He was five years back in Britain, frustrated and unhappy with his domestic life, without a command and not very popular at the Admiralty. But war with France in 1793 kick-started the tumultuous and passionate twelve years of his life that was to define Nelson in British history and propel him to his hero's death and a huge plinth in Trafalgar Square.

He was given the 64-gun *Agamemnon* and sent to the Mediterranean. For four years he was busy in the service of a slowly failing British strategy against young Napoleon's rising star. It led eventually to the navy's complete withdrawal from the Mediterranean in 1796. He chafed against the caution of his commanders, William Hotham and then Hyde Parker, until the arrival at Mediterranean command of John Jervis, who was prepared to give Nelson more discretion and trusted in his judgement. He exceeded his authority again in trying to get troops from the Kingdom of Naples to support Britain's attempts to keep Napoleon's revolutionary army out of Toulon. Nelson performed a number of diplomatic tasks with great charm and intelligence. At sea, he showed considerable tactical skill, and though at the time he could not influence it much, he also had an astute grasp of Britain's broad strategic situation, not just in the Mediterranean but in the war as a whole. He appreciated how maritime and land operations should complement one another and – more than Napoleon ever did – how much land operations could be made dependent on what happened at sea.

Ironically, it was when operating on land that he was least tactically successful. He was full of elan and offensive spirit in contrast to more wary army commanders and would make prodigious efforts to have his naval guns dragged across awful terrain to bombard inland objectives. He had already performed small logistical miracles in 1780 during a canoe-based assault against the San Juan fortress on the mosquito shore of Nicaragua. He was the same in the assault on Bastia in Corsica in 1794, taking Bastia and moving immediately on to Calvi. During the Calvi siege he was cut across his back and the following day wounded in his right eye. He felt his presence had been intrinsic to success and was angry that his efforts in the Corsica campaigns were not acknowledged. In July 1797 he was almost killed in a clash of assault barges off Cadiz, fighting sword to sword with Spanish boats countering his reckless attack towards the harbour. Less than two weeks later Jervis sent him as commander, accompanied by the excellent Thomas Troubridge and over 1,000 troops, on an amphibious operation to capture Tenerife.[2] It was a complete disaster. Nelson and Troubridge, who also wanted for nothing in courage, failed to appreciate the strength of the city of Santa Cruz and then reinforced failure, finally attempting a hopeless assault against it in the dark. That attack cost Nelson his right arm, which was amputated that night on board his flagship. He was depressed and morose after Santa Cruz. He had several wounds. He had lost the sight in one eye and an arm. But Jervis buoyed him up and didn't blame Nelson for the debacle – though in truth he should have. When the final collapse of British naval power in the Mediterranean came, Jervis sent him to supervise the evacuation of Bastia and Elba, which he performed with good judgement and incisive action.

If his seabound judgement was always sound, Nelson's emotional judgement was, as ever, quixotic. He had dalliances while ashore. In particular, he began a very public affair at Leghorn (Livorno) with Adelaide Correglia, an Italian opera singer notorious in matters of romance. She may also have acted as a local spy for Nelson as well as being his mistress. She was derided by fellow captains as 'his dolly'. Even the generous Captain Freemantle said that Nelson 'makes himself ridiculous with that woman'. And while he was in the Mediterranean, Nelson had got to know Sir William Hamilton in Naples along with his youthful wife, Emma. The story of Emma Hamilton is, in itself, an epic of a young woman's fortitude, intelligence and survival in eighteenth century society. It seems certain there was a spark between her and Nelson during these years. When they met again in 1798 it would burn very hot indeed and, like his affair with Adelaide Correglia, in public. It became a scandal across Europe; Fanny in Norfolk being humiliated; Nelson, Emma and the ageing William Hamilton in a *menage a trois* they made little attempt to conceal. But by then Nelson and Emma were meeting deep emotional needs in each other, and Nelson had become a celebrated national hero.

Nelson's path to national heroism transcended the navy's regard for him through a series of fleet actions that began before the Cadiz and Tenerife episodes and followed hard on each other after that. Some of them are described in previous chapters.

His first major fleet action had been at the battle of Cape St Vincent in February 1797. On that occasion, Admiral John Jervis engaged a much larger Spanish fleet but was about to see it slip through his fingers as he led his ships in a laborious manoeuvre to reverse course while maintaining an orderly line. Nelson, third from the rear of the line in the 74-gun, third-rater *Captain*, could see the initiative was about to be lost. He disobeyed orders and cut out of the line, attacking the massive 120-gun, four-decker *Santissima Trinidad*. The *Captain* was quickly surrounded by Spanish ships and could only be supported by Collingwood and Towry who followed behind Nelson, and by Troubridge in the *Culloden* who was then close enough to get into that first engagement. It was exceptionally risky; surrounded by seven enemy ships, most of them bigger than the British 74s. But Nelson's manoeuvre created the mêlée between

---

2. Nelson's relations with Troubridge were in some ways a microcosm of his character. They had been young lieutenants together and great friends who trusted one another. But as Troubridge moved with Jervis towards the Admiralty, and for reasons that seemed to begin with protocol and jealousy, Nelson not only became estranged from him (to Troubridge's great dismay) but he came to regard Troubridge as an avowed enemy, apparently behind every slight or setback Nelson perceived.

the fleets that proved to be so advantageous to the Royal Navy's superior seamanship and gunnery. After an hour the *Captain*, almost completely wrecked, was starboard of the *San Nicholas* when the *San Jose* collided and got entangled with the *San Nicholas*'s port side. Seeing a unique opportunity, Nelson had the *Captain* ram up alongside the starboard quarter of the *San Nicholas*. Now all three ships were locked together and British boarders swarmed onto the *San Nicholas*. Nelson broke through one of its stern windows and skirmished with Spanish officers in the dark as he made upstairs for the quarterdeck. The ship surrendered to him, though he had picked up another minor wound with a shell splinter. Taking the next opportunity, he then led a second boarding attack straight onto the *San Jose*, a first-rater that towered above them. It was ready to surrender as soon as he arrived on its quarterdeck. No matter that his first manoeuvre had to be effectively rescued by the devastating gunnery of Collingwood, Towry and Troubridge; Nelson had personally led attacks that captured two Spanish warships. This was fighting courage, risk-riding and leadership of the highest order. His exploits immediately made Nelson the darling of the nation. It was probably due of this fighting success that he became so cavalier in the battles at Cadiz harbour and Tenerife which followed soon after. He had become fatalistic.

In spring 1798 Napoleon had amassed a major expeditionary force at Toulon, but few in the Admiralty had any idea what he intended to do with it. Ignoring the claims of more senior captains, the First Lord of the Admiralty gave Nelson to Jervis; and Jervis was happy to give Nelson a fleet and great discretion to find Napoleon's force and do whatever he thought best when he intercepted it. For three anxious months Nelson criss-crossed the Mediterranean, trying to intercept Napoleon. In fact, Nelson and Jervis were two of the tiny handful of people who realised that a big French landing in Egypt would make perfect sense for Napoleon – establishing a base for a march to India to make common cause with the powerful Tippu Sahib of Mysore, who continued fighting the British in the Anglo-Mysore wars (where young Arthur Wellesley was then winning his spurs).

Though he had to be wary of French landings anywhere, Nelson was certain in his own mind that Napoleon was going for Alexandria. He was quite right. On 1st August 1798 he saw the French fleet anchored in line of battle in a good defensive position at Aboukir Bay. Nelson sent his ships to attack immediately, though it was sunset; splitting his force into two lines, one line going perilously inshore to create a cross-fire, as the other line passed along the seaward side of the vanguard and centre of the French ships. By midnight, the French vanguard and centre was broken and the French flagship, *L'Orient*, blew up in a stupendous explosion. Over the next day, other messy engagements occurred; only two out of thirteen French ships escaped. By 3rd August, Napoleon's fleet support for his grand expedition was totally destroyed, and the Royal Navy was back in the Mediterranean – never to leave.

Nelson had received another penetrating head wound above his damaged right eye in the engagement. He was concussed and suffered debilitating headaches and nausea. It left him ill and surly with battle stress. He took his flagship back to Naples, specifically it appears, to renew his acquaintance with William and Emma Hamilton. From their first – very public – reunion on the main deck of *Vanguard*, Nelson and Emma were scandalously besotted with one another. For all his impetuous romanticism and all her intelligent vulgarity, they became the love of each others' lives.

He was busy again, both at sea and in allowing himself to be drawn into the vicious politics of the Neapolitan Court and its enemies in Italy, caught up in the ferment of revolutionary war. He was cruel in executing Francesco Caracciolo, a noble Neapolitan who had served with distinction in the Royal Navy, but effectively been forced to turn republican. Nelson showed signs of great mood swings. He kept finding reasons to remain in Naples and decided which Admiralty orders he would faithfully obey and which he would reinterpret. In 1800 he was back in Britain, with the Hamiltons, the object both of adulation and censorious ridicule. He was promoted Vice-Admiral and joined the Channel Fleet.

Nelson's third great fleet action followed in April 1801. Second in command to Hyde Parker, he was sent to threaten the Danish fleet at Copenhagen in order to hobble the 'League of Armed Neutrality' which opposed Britain's blockading activities. Hyde Parker reluctantly agreed to let Nelson attack the Danish fleet directly. Leading the group of experienced captains he would come to call his 'band of brothers', Nelson took the fleet into a fierce inshore action against Danish ships backed by powerful fortress guns. Nelson deployed the fleet – again – into hazardously shallow waters. When it came under sustained fire from the shore batteries, Hyde Parker hoisted 'signal 39', to 'discontinue action'. Nelson famously claimed he couldn't see the signal, putting the telescope to his defective right eye, and bore on in. In fact, the engagement was less successful than it later appeared. Both fleets were badly damaged and six of Nelson's ships had grounded. Instead, it was Nelson's muscular diplomacy in Copenhagen after the battle, and then in Tallinn, that took Denmark out of the equation and killed the nascent League. Nelson's celebrity status wherever he went was persuasive.

By then, Emma had had his child – Horatia – and William Hamilton was gravely ill, dying two years later. Still, Nelson remained unwell and personally erratic. He was wildly jealous of the Prince of Wales, convinced that while he was at sea, the Prince would seduce Emma. He became viciously estranged from Troubridge and was less than fair to the efforts being made at the Admiralty by Jervis, to whom he owed so much. Nevertheless, by the time he was made Commander-in-Chief of the Mediterranean he was giving thought to the sort of tactics that could bring about the 'annihilation' – a word he used many times – of an enemy fleet. He believed that a big enemy fleet had to be broken up and disorganised if it were to be completely destroyed. The innovation of attacking a fleet by cutting through its line to segment it rather than sailing parallel to it, had already proved successful elsewhere – at the Battle of the Saints in 1782, at Cape St Vincent in Nelson's own action in 1797, and particularly in Admiral Duncan's actions against the Dutch later that year at Camperdown. It depended entirely on the superior quality of Royal Navy ships if they were to win the resulting mêlée. Nelson was thinking about how to refine the idea in detail – minimising the risks and maximising the flexibility of any collection of ships a British commander might have on the day.

By 1805, like everyone else, Nelson was convinced the country was facing a full-scale French invasion. He instinctively understood the real nature of the threat. Napoleon had 200,000 troops camped at Boulogne and a flotilla of 2,000 craft to get them onto the south coast. Characteristically, Nelson grasped the strategy better than Napoleon himself, who only belatedly accepted the need to ensure that the French fleet would dominate the Channel prior to launching his invasion. Nelson, however, immediately understood that the vagaries of wind and weather could tip an invasion attempt either way. So destroying the French fleet – not just holding it off in the Channel – was critical to end any prospect of invasion. He was determined to be the instrument of 'annihilation' of any fleet that could make Napoleon's plan work.

By then, Nelson had been continuously at sea for almost two years, blockading and patrolling the Mediterranean, trying to maintain his meagre force of ships. He was much the worse for the gruelling regime this imposed, and desperate for some domestic comfort with Emma and his young daughter. He wrote that he was torn between his duty and his happiness, though it seems just as likely he was torn between his ego and his exhaustion. But in January 1805, suddenly, the game was afoot.

Napoleon (who continued to misunderstand maritime strategy) devised a plan that might just have worked on land, but was simply impossible at sea. It began as an elaborate scheme for different squadrons to slip through the British blockade from several ports simultaneously, attack African trade routes, then sail across the Atlantic to harass the West Indies. This would draw the biggest British fleet away to the West Indies – Cornwallis's force around Brest – after which the French fleets would then combine into a truly grand fleet to sail straight back to Europe, land an invasion force in Ireland, then overwhelm any residual British ships in the western approaches and sweep the Channel clear for the invasion barges waiting in Boulogne. Napoleon was nothing if not optimistic. 'Let us be masters of the Channel for six hours', he said, 'and we are masters of the world'. In an age of sail and rudimentary communications, he was hostage to almost 10,000 miles of sea and months of changing weather. It was a ridiculous plan.

Admiral Villeneuve, in Toulon, was tasked to make the fantasy work. He never believed in it, but all the same he left Toulon at the second attempt in May. He failed to pick up Spanish ships at Cartagena, since they weren't ready, but then combined with a Spanish fleet from Cadiz led by Admiral Federico Gravina. The Rochefort fleet had already slipped past the blockade and sailed to the West Indies, but not finding Villeneuve waiting there, had returned to Rochefort. The Brest fleet was unable to defy the blockade and stayed where it was. Napoleon's plan was already unravelling, but Villeneuve set off for the West Indies with what he had.

At least Villeneuve had been able to slip out of Toulon, and had Nelson searching for him somewhere in the Mediterranean. But hearing that Villeneuve had gone through the Straits, Nelson – commander only in the Mediterranean – didn't wait for orders from London. He intended to be the nemesis of French naval power and he simply took his Mediterranean fleet to chase Villeneuve across the Atlantic and screen the Caribbean. His instinct was that the French would go to Martinique, in the north. But Admiral Alexander Cochrane and the governor of the Leeward Islands insisted that Villeneuve was more likely around Trinidad, to the south. Nelson followed their advice, though as usual, his own instincts were spot on. Villeneuve was in Martinique and

Nelson had missed him. It was unusual for Nelson not to act on his own judgement, though he later claimed he was virtually ordered by his superiors to go south. If he had maintained his normal headstrong confidence, the great sea battle of 1805 would have occurred somewhere off Martinique on the other side of the Atlantic, where the French and Spanish combined fleet was at least in better shape than when it returned to Europe in July.

Fearful now that this evident decoy plan might actually be working, Nelson didn't stay long in the Leewards and chased back across the Atlantic. In fact, he overtook Villeneuve – only fifty miles apart – without any of the scouting frigates spotting each other. He arrived in Gibraltar, exhausted, on 19th July. With nothing to do but await developments, he went back to Britain and spent a poignant twenty-five days, mainly at his Merton home with Emma Hamilton and Horatia.

As it turned out, Villeneuve was screened from entering the Channel by Admiral Robert Calder, who then fought an indecisive action with him off Cape Finisterre on 22nd July. Then on 2nd September news arrived that Collingwood had Villeneuve's French and Spanish fleet bottled up in Cadiz. The nation knew what was going to happen next. Nelson travelled to Portsmouth to board the *Victory* and take command of the British fleet that was even then converging on Collingwood's position. In Portsmouth, the crowd was so great that Nelson couldn't reach the jetty to board his barge and he had to divert it to Southsea beach. Still they flowed with him, shouting and cheering. Like a messiah setting forth to win their salvation, the crowd parted for him as Nelson approached his barge. Some dropped to their knees and blessed him. Of course, he loved it. Though he also took yet another sign; he was sailing to his destiny, unlikely to return.

When he arrived on station Nelson's presence was electrifying. He was a whirlwind of activity and resolve. He immediately got his captains together over dinners on his flagship – something Collingwood had not done – enthusing them and sharing his thinking on the coming battle. He pulled the fleet fifty miles offshore to tempt the Combined Fleet out of Cadiz. Collingwood had stayed close to the coast, anxious to keep the enemy bottled up. But now, the British were spoiling for battle and wanted the enemy to venture out. Nelson had his frigates on picket in a relay system to keep watch and stay in touch with his battleships cruising far offshore. This was only one of the many risks Nelson was accepting for this engagement.

He had finalised his battle plan at home in Merton, assuming two lines of sixteen ships and a further squadron of eight ships behind them to act as a reserve – forty ships of the line in all. But as events unfolded off Cadiz, he would only have twenty-seven against the Combined Fleet of thirty-three. So he would be outnumbered for this battle of 'annihilation' and there would be no reserve squadron. Then too, he had to offer Villeneuve a realistic prospect of escape to lure him out of Cadiz. Cruising fifty miles away gave Villeneuve a sporting chance and ran the risk that the Combined Fleet might still slip through his fingers.

Nevertheless, by every contemporary account, there was complete confidence throughout the British fleet that this battle would take place, that it would be decisive, and that they would certainly win it. Nelson's 'band of brothers' were less in evidence at

Trafalgar than is popularly supposed. He had commanded only eight of his Trafalgar captains previously. But the powerful influence of Jervis over many years had created a core of real leadership among this generation of captains. And Nelson's personal effect on all those he commanded, at every level, was simply astonishing. They would follow him into any battle he devised.

The *Victory* had been on station exactly three weeks when events moved suddenly. On 19th October Admirals Villeneuve and Gravina brought the Combined Fleet laboriously out of Cadiz. Nelson's first risk would now be tested. Would the fleet turn north, and even now head for Brest and the Channel? Or play safe, turn south and slip into the Mediterranean? If Nelson waited until he was sure, he would be chasing without intercepting. He had to guess.[3] Being Villeneuve, he played safe and turned south. And being Nelson, he guessed right and set course to intercept around the Straits of Gibraltar.

Nelson knew there would be no second chance when the interception happened and he sailed his fleet in battle order to make sure he could engage immediately. Sunday 20th October was a frustrating day, in rain, fog and squalls, as the Combined Fleet tacked south-west to position itself to turn south-east and run through the Straits, while Nelson's fleet made cagey progress to cut it off. Around six-o-clock on the morning of 21st Nelson gave the order to prepare for battle. Villeneuve now saw he wouldn't make it through to the Mediterranean before Nelson caught him. He then made a fatal mistake. Villeneuve decided to withdraw back to Cadiz, commanding the fleet to reverse itself, each ship turning about so that the rear of the column became the front and the front became the rear division. This caused confusion, leaving the Combined Fleet caught between Gibraltar and Cadiz, against a lee shore in a west-north-west breeze, with the British fleet to windward in a natural attacking position. It also left his observation squadron in a muddle at the rear of the column and stymied its ability to act as his tactical reserve. It was confusion rather than battle tactics that created a four-mile defensive line that was two ranks deep in some places and not in others, and it formed a crescent shape because the centre was pushed leeward by the swell since the wind was too light to counteract it.

On the other hand, the Combined Fleet had some strengths in addition to superior numbers. Its tight line of ships, some now doubling up, showed that the French and Spanish intended to make a close-range fight of it. Both Villeneuve and Gravina fully expected Nelson to attack in the way he did. They had seen the tactic before and knew it relied on British sailing and gunnery. Their answer was to grapple the British ships and board them; making the coming clash as much of a land battle as possible. For that reason, there were 30,000 sailors, marines and troops on board the Combined Fleet, as against 17,000 on Nelson's ships, and many Spanish and French captains had devised particular ploys and trained their men specially in boarding manoeuvres.

By eight-o-clock on the morning on 21st October the battle was set up, though the fleets would not come within range of each other until almost noon. The day was

---

3. Though from intelligence he had received before he left Britain, he was inclined to believe that making for the Mediterranean would be Villeneuve's intention.

crisp and sunny, the wind very light, though every experienced sailor could also feel an Atlantic storm swell developing. Moving slowly north, the French and Spanish arranged themselves as best they could to receive a British attack. Nelson could not afford the time for precise adjustments to his order of battle; the Combined Fleet was within reach of Cadiz and at a speed of only two to three knots in the prevailing breeze this battle would be a laborious sailing affair. The two British columns would simply charge the enemy line more or less at right angles from the positions they were in at dawn that morning. His two columns were somewhat disorganized but it conformed to the essence of Nelson's plan, without some of its earlier refinements.

But that plan now involved another huge risk. As experienced mariners who had spent years sailing those waters, Nelson and Collingwood both knew that light winds off the treacherous shoals of Cape Trafalgar could swing round capriciously or drop altogether. As the fleet approached the enemy's four miles of broadsides at an agonizing walking pace, there was always the possibility that British ships might become entirely becalmed, front-on, under the 2,568 guns of their enemy. If their tactical positions that morning had been reversed, Nelson's fleet could probably have destroyed each oncoming enemy ship as it came within effective range, so superior was British gunnery. But if Nelson could be confident that the Combined Fleet could never achieve that against his ships coming in line astern towards them, it would have been a very different matter if the light wind suddenly vanished. Four ships behind *Victory*, on the *Conqueror*, Lieutenant Humphrey Senhouse feared exactly that outcome as the fleets closed on each other. As it was, the two British columns were propelled as much by the rising swell as the breeze.

Accepting the risks, Nelson's *Victory* led the northern column; Collingwood the southern column in *Royal Sovereign*. The battle around Collingwood's southern column has been outlined in a previous chapter. And though the battle in the north was less intense (a relative term!) the fate of the ships around the *Victory* and the French flagship, *Bucentaure* had a critical bearing on the outcome. Nelson's attack with the northern column had a greater impact than Collingwood's because more of Nelson's ships hit the enemy line closer together and were able to support each other from the outset.

Then too, Nelson adjusted his final line of attack to approach more obliquely, keeping the enemy guessing as to where he would try to break into its formation. The *Victory* sailed past the *Heros* and the huge *Santissima Trinidad*, suffering broadsides as it went, before turning sharply to port to break the enemy line across the stern of Villeneuve's *Bucentaure*. This may not have been entirely intentional. *Victory* had already had its mizzen top-mast shot away and it hung dangerously over the poop deck. The ship's steering was also wrecked and the crew had to rig lines on the orlop deck for twenty men to haul the tiller round. Nelson may have ordered Hardy, his flag captain, to break in at that point, where *Victory*'s battle proper would commence, because steering damage would be less important once the ship-to-ship slogging match began.

In cutting the enemy line behind the *Bucentaure*, the 12th ship from the front, Nelson isolated the central and rear divisions of the combined fleet, putting the lead division out of the battle and unmolested. His calculation was that the British fleet would be able to defeat the two thirds of the fleet they had engaged –twenty-one ships – outnumbering them before most of the eleven other enemy ships sailing north were able to come round and join the fray. This, too, was quite a risk. In the south, Collingwood's division certainly didn't outnumber the enemy during the hours that mattered most. But Nelson's essential manoeuvre was emphatically vindicated. The French Admiral Dumanoir, commanding eight powerful French ships among the leading northern division of eleven – 630 guns in total – didn't turn about and join the fighting until it was too late to make a difference.

Nelson had based his Trafalgar thinking on the conviction that any battle of annihilation needed new tactics and a full day to achieve victory. A brush in the fog or a battle at dusk would never do it. Very few ships of the line actually sank or blew up; it took time to batter a ship into submission to the point where its crew struck the colours. Ironic, then, that at this final vindication of all Nelson's tactical genius, the battle was effectively won between noon and two-o-clock. The late entry of Dumanoir's division led to a sudden intensification in the fighting about an hour later which died away quickly. By then, the result was not in doubt; only the margin of victory.

But that margin of victory was coloured by Nelson's own destiny. He had told several people that he didn't expect to survive this battle, even as it began. Of course, he had thought himself likely to die, or was dying, on many previous occasions. But this time was different. His manner was relaxed; his fatalism serene. Some writers criticize his appearance on the *Victory*'s deck in full admiral's uniform with decorations, as if inviting a sniper's musket-ball. But this is mistaken. All captains did the same; every ship decked itself out in its full regalia as it went into battle. Bands played, pennants flew, sailors cheered. The whole fleet was e*n fete* for the occasion and ships didn't quieten until the commencement of the dangerous run-in from around 1,000 yards.

Nelson wrote a moving prayer in his cabin less than an hour before the first salvos were fired; 'To Him I resign myself and the just cause which is entrusted to me to defend. Amen. Amen. Amen', he concluded, before kneeling for a while at his writing desk. By then, he had set up the battle he wanted and his work as a commander was over. The last decision he would have to make was to cut across the enemy line astern of the *Bucentaure* and after that he would simply remain on deck while Hardy fought the flagship in the pell-mell affair Nelson had created.

Perhaps that final decision was his most fateful. Behind the *Bucentaure* was the *Redoutable*, captained by the impressive Jean-Jacques Lucas. It came up to support the flagship and became entangled with the *Victory*'s starboard yardarms as the gap closed. Both ships swung away, locked together. Lucas was determined to board the *Victory* and had his rigging, shrouds and tops festooned with marksmen. He had rehearsed his sailors and troops regularly for boarding operations. *Victory*'s gunners were surprised to see *Redoutable*'s gun ports snap shut after a couple of broadsides. Lucas had ordered everyone onto the deck to prepare for the imminent boarding of *Victory*. The mainyard was unslung and lowered to act as a bridge; the bowsprit was crowded with troops preparing to leap across to the British flagship as the bows swung round.

The *Redoutable* carried more troops than almost any other ship in the Combined Fleet. Their fire had already cleared *Victory*'s upper decks. The Quarterdeck was always the most dangerous place to be in sea battles of this era. Adam Nicolson calls them a 'killing zone'. And it was while Lucas's boarding preparations were unfolding, in the midst of a real crisis for *Victory*, that Nelson was shot by someone in *Redoutable*'s mizzen-top, thirty feet above and only fifteen yards away from him. We will never know who was responsible for the most famous musket-ball in British history. But whoever fired the fatal shot almost certainly missed. Their aim would anyway have been obscured by *Victory*'s mainsail. Nelson was wounded by a downward ricochet, probably off the mast behind him, walking with Hardy near the quarterdeck hatch, just as he turned to face the stern. Nelson was taken below where the extent of the injury was very evident – the ball had entered his left shoulder, punctured a lung and shattered his backbone before lodging below his right shoulder blade.

With its upper decks now only thinly manned, *Victory* was seconds away from the impact of *Redoutable*'s boarding. But out of the thick smoke that obscured it from friend and foe alike, the drifting *Temeraire* emerged, fired at *Redoutable* then rammed it midships. This turned the hunter into the hunted and in that exchange saved the *Victory*. The *Fougueux*, detached from the southern battle, drifted up alongside the starboard side of the *Temeraire*, and for some forty-five minutes four ships locked together almost in parallel – *Victory*, *Redoutable*, *Temeraire* and *Fougueux* – to bludgeon each other with whatever they could muster in the state they were in. The *Fougueux* had drifted away from an identical situation less than half a mile south where the *Santa Anna* was still locked with Collingwood's *Royal Sovereign* on one side and the *Mars* on the other.

The battle took on a similar character all across its two and a half miles of fighting. Nelson and Collingwood had each remarked that it was too hot a contest to last for any length of time. The *Bucentaure* submitted at about one-forty-five, having been attacked not just by *Victory* but then by *Conqueror*, *Agamemnon* and the *Britannia*. One after another, French and Spanish ships in the teeth of the action struck their colours. Others, severely damaged, made their escape. Down on *Victory*'s orlop deck, Nelson lay dying, receiving news of his triumph as it unfolded. The leading division of the Combined Fleet that had been excluded from the action hesitated, misunderstood Villeneuve's signals, then eventually turned to enter the battle around three o'clock. Captain Cyprien-Infernet made a suicidal effort in the *Intrepide* to rescue the already captured flagship – more a matter of honour than effectiveness – while Dumanoir sailed his ships past a hastily assembled British gun line to the west of the battle area and was evidently deterred from getting further engaged. In fact, he was caught with his squadron exactly two weeks later by Richard Strachan off Cape Ortegal and lost all four of the intact ships that withdrew from the action at Trafalgar. It was a telling postscript to the whole affair.

Lying secure below the waterline in the *Victory*, Nelson spoke a number of important last words, many of them about his hopes for the nation's treatment of Lady Hamilton, before lapsing into fitful muttering. At four-thirty, just as Dumanoir's counterattacking ships were breaking away, Nelson finally expired. The concluding moment of the battle occurred at five-thirty when the *Achille*, on fire for some hours, blew up against the sunset in an explosion that was seen in Cadiz.[4]

---

4. An injured, near-naked woman – wife of an *Achille* sailor – was picked up and rescued, and she lived. A black pig was also seen swimming away from the explosion. It was rescued and then butchered and eaten that evening.

Though the gains of the Trafalgar triumph were somewhat dissipated by the effects of the violent four-day storm that arrived within hours, the immediate scorecard told its own story. None of the twenty-seven British ships were lost or struck their colours. Eighteen of the Combined Fleet were lost, fourteen of them taken as prizes. Eleven escaped to Cadiz, though none ever put to sea again. Four were led away by Dumanoir, to be captured by Strachan on 4th November. On the day of Trafalgar, Nelson certainly achieved 'annihilation'.

The strategic effects of Trafalgar were more subtle. The victory did not prevent a French invasion of Britain – though everyone in the fleet assumed that was why they were fighting that day – because the invasion had already been called off. Napoleon had decamped his army from Boulogne and marched against the Austrians, defeating them at Ulm two days before Trafalgar occurred. And he went on to his greatest victory against the combined forces of Austria and Russia at Austerlitz on December 2nd that year.

The real strategic importance of Trafalgar lay in the fact that it guaranteed Britain would not lose the war. Whatever happened next – and most of the other war news was bad for the allies – Britain was the one major European power that could not now be conquered. That was a huge psychological boost, shifting the European balance of expectations that anti-Napoleon coalitions were feasible, even though the Third Coalition collapsed with Austerlitz. Trafalgar destroyed French naval power in the Mediterranean and put an end to Napoleon's most grandiose global designs. From then on, the conflict would be a series of major land battles underpinned by economic warfare between Britain's global empire and Napoleon's continental empire. Defeat at Trafalgar effectively cut Spain off from its colonies in Latin America and increased the tension between Madrid and Paris, which exploded three years later in the Spanish uprising against Napoleon. Trafalgar itself did not stop an invasion, but it safeguarded Britain and guaranteed the country could continue the war and play for the long term.

All this could be credited to the strategic acumen and tactical genius of one man. He took on each successive risk, embracing the destiny he saw for himself, failing only to overcome the final risk as he turned near the mast on his quarterdeck. Nelson's body was brought back to Britain, laid in state in the Painted Hall of Greenwich Naval Hospital, then at the Admiralty, and after a state funeral, given to rest in an ornate tomb at the centre of the crypt in St Paul's cathedral.

HMS *Victory* later became a troopship, a depot and a prison ship and was due to be broken up in 1831. But after a public outcry it was retained and remains in its Portsmouth berth, a fully commissioned ship of the Royal Navy. As a wooden ship first laid down in 1759 it has required constant refurbishment and replacement since it was saved in 1831. The public love it and the navy use it for diplomacy and VIP receptions and dinners. This author once asked the senior officer on *Victory*, how much of this magnificent construction we see all around us actually went to Trafalgar in 1805 and came back? The officer thought for a moment and then replied, 'most of the orlop deck – probably'. The twenty-first century *Victory* is, in a way, very like Nelson's reputation. He was lauded as the ultimate national hero in the imperialist nineteenth century, re-examined for his personal character flaws in the Freudian twentieth century, then castigated for his associations with slavery, empire and oppression in the self-conscious, guilty, twenty-first century. His reputation and historical significance are constantly remodelled. And yet despite all, there is an irreducible core of Nelson; the man, the spirit, the leader who went to Trafalgar. And though the living man never came back, much else did. It remains as tangible for the Royal Navy as HMS *Victory* sitting magnificently in Portsmouth.

Thomas Cochrane – the Sea Wolf

It was Napoleon himself who coined history's description of Admiral Thomas Cochrane, 10th Earl of Dundonald, as 'le Loup de Mer' – the Sea Wolf. It was true enough. First Sea Lord Admiral John Jervis, Earl of St. Vincent, said he was 'mad, romantic, money-getting; and not truth-telling'. And that was true, too. Admiral Keith said he was, 'wrong-headed, violent and proud'. All true. Thomas Cochrane was the most outrageously successful frigate commander of his age. But he was outrageous in other ways too.

Cochrane was famously a model for C.S. Forester's Horatio Hornblower and Patrick O'Brian's Jack Aubrey. In fact, the real Thomas Cochrane was a more colourful and controversial character than either Hornblower or Aubrey. The difference between the real and imagined characters was that the fictional heroes had to move up the ladder towards Admiral status as their series of books progressed. The real hero, by contrast, was too flawed and controversial to be promoted above post captain. He didn't behave himself as well as Hornblower or Aubrey and was denied the promotions he felt were his due.

Nevertheless, though he never commanded a Royal Navy first rate ship of the line, and only had a flotilla of them under his command when he was seventy-two, even his enemies could not deny Cochrane's brilliance as a young frigate captain. Other famous frigate captains, like Sir Edward Pellow, excelled during that period when the Napoleonic War moved from grand fleet encounters towards strategic raiding and support to the land forces around the fringes of Napoleon's empire. But Cochrane was something else again.

His experience offers an interesting perspective on command. He won audacious tactical victories. He was an inventor and well ahead of his time. He had innovative military and technological ideas that might have been strategic game-changers. But for most of his career Cochrane was at war with the Admiralty and the navy didn't trust him, or most of his inventions. For all his talent and fame, Cochrane had no reliable strategic instincts and made little strategic impact on Britain's behalf. He took his services to Latin America – he advertised in the press that he was available – and during seven dramatic years from 1818 to 1825 his role turned out to be historically decisive in bringing no fewer than three Latin American countries to independence.

Two centuries later, Cochrane's story of leadership is both captivating and comical. In three successive small ship commands, he captured many enemy vessels bigger than his and he attacked powerful shore defences and inland fortresses with breath-taking affrontery. He developed both the tactics and the right vessels for 'strategic raiding'.

He was captured by the French, and exchanged. He was imprisoned in Malta, but escaped. He was imprisoned in London, but escaped. He was a troublesome and populist Member of Parliament, hated by most of the establishment, yet adored by the public. He was dismissed from the navy in 1814 following a financial scandal. He was sentenced to the pillory in Threadneedle Street. He married his young wife no fewer than three times and they adventured together, until after twenty-seven years, decided they could no longer live together, and separated apparently amicably. He was desperately mercenary, but gave a good deal of his own money to deserving causes and to his crews and friends. He was widely regarded as a liar and a cheat. He certainly played fast and loose with the laws of war in his many crafty victories against steep odds over French, Spanish and Portuguese ships. But he showed rock-solid personal integrity in dealing with his sailors, supporters and friends. He went to his grave obsessing that his personal integrity should be put beyond any doubt.

Not least, in becoming an admiral in three other navies Cochrane's contributions were critical in gaining independence from Spain for Chile, and hence for Peru, before performing the same service for Brazil against the colonial administration of Portugal. Without him, they would not have achieved independence at the time or in the way they did. Eventually, he commanded the insurgent Greek navy during its war of independence against Ottoman Turkey. He was finally reinstated in the Royal Navy, as rear-admiral, responsible for North America and the West Indies – something of a harmless sinecure by then. With the outbreak of the Crimean War in 1853, Cochrane, almost eighty, begged the Admiralty to give him the Baltic fleet for operations against Russia so he could implement his longstanding 'secret war plan'. The Admiralty refused, fearing he might risk the whole fleet in one harebrained operation. Not much had changed over the years.

Cochrane was born in 1775, eldest of seven children, including a half-sister, to the eccentric and stony-broke 9th Earl of Dundonald.[1] He also had six uncles. These included a hero who died at Yorktown in the American War of Independence, a scoundrel with the East India Company, an even bigger scoundrel profiteering and slave-trading in Dominica, and the respected Admiral Alexander Cochrane of the Royal Navy who is remembered chiefly for his role in burning the White House down in 1814 during the United States-British War of 1812–15.[2] Cochrane's formal education was very poor. His mother died when he was nine and his father was indifferent to him. As a neglected and quick-tempered, six-foot tall, strapping young man, Cochrane was inclined to settle arguments with his fists. He grew into a pugnacious and charismatic leader whose world was divided into followers, for whom he would do anything; and all others, who were liable to become adversaries or enemies, and on many of whom he swore lasting vengeance.

---

1. He was known as Lord Thomas Cochrane from the age of five, but didn't inherit the title as 10th Earl of Dundonald until 1831 on the death of his father.
2. Cochrane transported the troops and marines up the river towards Washington and advised Major General Robert Ross to extend the 'punishment' burning to private property in the city as well. Ross demurred.

In 1793 he went to sea as a midshipman on the frigate *Hind*, captained at the time by his respectable naval uncle, Alexander. He was a lieutenant on Lord Keith's flagship *Barfleur* by 1798. In a pattern to be repeated many times, he got into a feud with the *Barfleur*'s first lieutenant and was court martialed. And in another oft-repeated pattern, he personally saved the prize ship *Genereux* in a fierce storm when he was detailed to command it into a safe port. He climbed aloft himself to lead the crew, who were unwilling, some wounded and unable, to reef the sails amid the storm and fend off disaster. As a young Lieutenant he spent some time talking to Nelson – a shining celebrity following the Battle of the Nile – while the *Barfleur* was in Palermo. Nelson liked the young man and saw in Cochrane the fire of battle he himself was inspiring around him. They talked of maritime tactics; the need to get in close and keep an enemy off balance, or the advantages of the lee side in a fight. Admiral Rodney had established years before that the optimum use of conditions was to approach an enemy from windward but then exchange shot from the leeward side, where enemy ships would naturally heel over in the wind towards the lee, reducing the elevation of their guns and hence their range. Cochrane was dazzled by Nelson; he absorbed everything the national hero offered.

Cochrane's own derring-do reputation began when he was given command of the brig-sloop *Speedy* – barely a warship at all – in 1800. He escaped a Spanish ship of the line by pretending to be Danish and plague-ridden. He escaped a French frigate by setting stern lamps adrift on a raft and then heading the other way in the darkness. He developed excellent tactics for shore raiding, getting close inshore during the night – risky – then attacking in the early dawn. Cochrane achieved immediate fame when his 14-gun *Speedy* captured the Zebec frigate *El Gamo*, whose crew outnumbered his by six-to-one. He pretended to be American to get close, getting underneath the frigate's gun elevation before boarding it, then fooled its crew into thinking they were about to be overwhelmed by his tiny force. He accounted for fifty-three assorted vessels in less than eighteen months. In that time his ordinary seamen were earning more in prize money than officers on other ships. And he had managed to go to a fancy dress party in Malta clad as one of those ordinary seamen, been challenged by the French host who tried to throw the seaman out, started fisticuffs with the host, then with the picket guard, and as a result fought a pistol duel at dawn where both he and the outraged host were injured.

His luck ran out in 1801 off Alicante when, trapped in a bay, he tried to evade three major French ships of the line closing in on him. He was captured, exchanged after a while, and made a post-captain on his return home. In 1803 he created an international incident with the United States in the miserable HMS *Arab* (a 'haystack') he had been given to keep him quiet, and as a result was sent out of the way as the Orkneys' guardship on whaling protection.

But in 1804, with St Vincent no longer First Sea Lord, he was rehabilitated and as a post captain was given the 32-gun frigate *Pallas* and in 1806 the impressive 38-gun *Imperieuse*. In these two ships he cemented his popular reputation. He left Plymouth in January 1805 in the *Pallas* with an arrest warrant chasing him for personal assault in the process of press ganging. Within eight weeks, cruising off the Azores, he had made every member of his crew extremely rich with prize money. A couple of weeks later the *Pallas* was pursued in a storm by three French ships of the line. Running before the wind, it was a thirteen-knot chase. With so much more sail, a ship of the line would always overhaul a frigate in a brisk wind. But Cochrane had his well-trained crew drop all sail suddenly, put the helm hard over, and swung into the path of the storm. The three French ships shot past him and the *Pallas* was away before they could turn. They chased him through the night and early next morning, when they caught up again, the *Pallas* turned out to be another raft bobbing along with a stern lantern burning on it.

In the *Pallas* and the *Imperieuse* Cochrane developed his shore-raiding tactics to become the era's most effective exponent of coastal warfare; these days more generally known as 'littoral operations' in which the Royal Marines specialize. He used the power and mobility of his ships as effectively as he managed and led land battles – of which there were many. He had a natural ability to think clearly and quickly amid the fearful chaos of battle; displaying an instinctive feel for the momentum of a fight, even as he put himself in mortal danger. Interestingly, he planned all his operations very carefully and lost remarkably few of his own men in them. It was all in sharp contrast to his reckless approach to more personal challenges. Young midshipman Frederick Marryat, later to become the novelist Captain Marryat, wrote, 'I never knew anyone so careful of the lives of his ship's company as Lord Cochrane, or any who calculated so closely the risks attending any expedition. Many of the most brilliant achievements were performed without the loss of a single life.' In this period he operated successfully all around the Iberian Peninsula, the Azores and the Bay of Biscay, earning Napoleon's particular epithet at the time that he was 'le Loup de Mer'.

In 1809, as part of a grand raid commanded by Admiral Gambier, he led twenty-two fireships and three 'explosive vessels' (entirely of his own design) into the Basque Roads off the port of Rochefort, where eleven major French warships and several frigates were sheltering. They were protected by a two-mile long wooden boom, secured by chains. On the night of 11th April Cochrane himself sailed the first explosive ship into the boom. He and his small crew made their escape after setting the fuses – then went back for the ship's dog they realized had been left behind – finding themselves then so close to the huge explosion it went right over them. The boom was destroyed. But only four of the British fireships actually got into the anchorage; their cautious captains abandoning most of them over a mile out to sea. The effect was nevertheless dramatic. French captains cut their cables to avoid the fires, ships collided, and many ran their vessels aground to allow crews to escape. In the dawn Cochrane signalled Gambier that eleven French ships were aground, lying on their sides at low tide. Only two, he said, were afloat.

The action opened up the French fleet to complete destruction at the hands of Gambier's warships, at least until they could refloat on the incoming tide. But the cautious Gambier, eight miles offshore, wouldn't bring his ships any closer than three miles. In practice, Gambier was waiting for the tide to rise, but in so doing was burning through the hours in which the French lay at his mercy. In frustration, Cochrane took his own *Imperieuse* into the anchorage to do what damage he could. It was a huge missed opportunity for the navy and it effectively ended Cochrane's immediate career. He denounced Gambier – who was guilty only of a commander's moral cowardice – in vitriolic terms and in public. There was a Court Martial. The navy establishment united to protect Gambier, even falsifying charts where rocks sitting a hundred feet deep in the Basque Roads were shown at depths of merely thirty feet. Cochrane was deprived of a command and suspended from the navy on half-pay for his increasingly intemperate attacks on the service.

By then he was also MP for the constituency of Westminster and Cochrane lost no opportunity to use his status in the feud with Gambier and others. He was a fierce parliamentary reformer as well as scourge of the Royal Navy. When his political friend, Sir Francis Burdett, was resisting arrest in his barricaded house in Piccadilly, Cochrane turned up to help Burdett. He had a plan and rather a lot of explosives with him – sufficient to blow up most of Piccadilly as it then was. Burdett quickly gave up the siege, mainly because he feared Cochrane would enact his plan and destroy most of the neighbourhood.

But after the Basque Roads controversy Cochrane was left at a loose end with no ship and no goodwill at the Admiralty. In 1811 he arrived in Malta to root out more naval corruption in the operation of the 'prize court' there, which he believed had defrauded him of legitimate rewards. He stole incriminating documents from the back of the judge's robing room, pinned to the lavatory door, where he had found them. He was arrested, refused bail, and was imprisoned. He quickly escaped using the classic 'file and rope' tools. Back in Parliament to reveal all the evidence, it was said that his account had the House of Commons convulsed.

In 1812 he eloped with the underage, orphaned, penniless and beautiful Kitty Barnes – daughter of a Spanish dancer – to marry secretly in Scotland, thereby disinheriting himself from his one wealthy uncle.[3] Unlike her husband, Kitty grew into a woman who enchanted all those she met, and she quickly became a considerable social asset alongside Cochrane's own brutal magnetism. Kitty was no trophy wife. She bore him seven children. She didn't just tolerate his principled belligerence but seemed to love him for it; fiercely defending his reputation. She was alone for long periods during their subsequent years in Latin America as he campaigned. She fought off a kidnapper. She crossed the Andean mountains at 15,000 feet in winter to take confidential dispatches to her husband in Peru. She escaped capture by the Spanish, clutching her son while she crossed a swaying cane-rope and hide bridge over a swollen gorge. She stood by one of the guns on Cochrane's flagship as he bombarded Callao. Perhaps it was inevitable that two such spirited characters could not remain united forever. Much later, at the age of forty-three, when Thomas was sixty-four, and having developed expensive tastes, Kitty separated from him and went to live in Boulogne. They met on several occasions, though never again lived together. Cochrane always provided generously for her.

---

3. Concerned, in due course, about the legality of their first marriage and the legitimacy of their eldest son, they married again in the Anglican Church in 1818 and then again in the Church of Scotland in 1825. Katherine Barnes was also known at Katy, but most called her Kitty.

During the early years of his marriage, however, Cochrane's career in the Royal Navy – and hence his trajectory as a significant British commander – all revolved around his involvement in the 'great stock exchange fraud' of 1814. The fraud was a classic of insider trading. It was based on a complete hoax that Napoleon was dead. The Stock Exchange shot up for a while until the hoax was disproved. The Government's Omnium securities, in particular, peaked at the news and six individual holders of Omniums had made a lot of money selling them at – very brief – peak prices. Cochrane, his uncle (of Dominica slave-trading fame), and his stockbroker were three of the six. And it turned out that the hoaxer – a disreputable Prussian aristocrat – was not only known to Cochrane but had been in his London house on the day of the hoax. Cochrane had acquired Omniums only a month before selling them at the peak. The circumstantial evidence seemed overwhelming. Cochrane's uncle absconded before the sentence, and Cochrane himself was duly found guilty, fined, sentenced to a year in prison, stripped of his knighthood in a ceremony at Westminster Abbey, dismissed in disgrace from the Royal Navy, expelled from Parliament, and for good measure, sentenced also to the pillory opposite the Royal Exchange (though this was later rescinded when the government feared a riot if he were pilloried).[4] From Elba, even Napoleon said this was no way to treat a hero. And in the best traditions of British populist democracy, Cochrane was immediately returned to the Commons, unopposed, by his Westminster constituents in the subsequent by-election. By then, however, he was in the King's Bench State House prison in Borough Road, Southwark. True to form, in March 1815 he escaped through a high window, using ropes to get across the rooftop before abseiling above the prison wall to the street outside and thence to a safe house. Two weeks later he appeared again in the House of Commons and was carried out after a spirited struggle with the Bow Street Runners. He was returned to prison to finish his sentence.

No wonder he advertised his services in the press to any other government that might appreciate him more. But he added to his feud with Gambier and the Admiralty a relentless new campaign that went beyond the grave to prove his innocence in the great stock exchange fraud. It has split opinion since, though the general consensus is that he shouldn't have been found guilty on the basis of the actual evidence presented in a trial that had the nation agog.

So it was that in 1818 he and Lady Cochrane, along with two children, sailed for Valparaiso and a new life. In Chile they rapidly became a celebrity couple. Working on behalf of Bernardo O'Higgins, leader of the Chilean nationalist movement and Chile's first recognised head of state. Cochrane took command as Vice Admiral of a mixed fleet of seven ships as against the fourteen major warships and several other vessels of the Spanish authorities.

Cochrane's campaigns in Latin America opened another chapter of command for him. He was involved in wars on a smaller scale but with far larger stakes than had been the case in Europe. Relatively small fleets could make big differences to the balance of military power and the tenuous hold Spain and Portugal had over their colonies.

---

4. Which was the last time a sentence of pillory was ever handed down in Britain.

O'Higgins was an inspirational strategist and politician who realized what Cochrane could achieve; working, too, with a number of British soldiers and sailors who, in the years of peace, were also plying their trade in the new world.

Spectacular tactical success now had strategic impact. Attacking Spanish control in neighbouring Peru was necessary for Chile to win the war it was fighting to consolidate its earlier, shaky declaration of independence from Spain. The campaign was a series of strategic raids by land and sea. In the most successful of all Cochrane's lifelong exploits, leading just 250 men in small boats, he stole the Spanish flagship *Esmeralda* from under Spanish noses in the centre of its fleet, inside the heavily defended anchorage of Callao harbour. American sailors in the anchorage whispered encouragement from the gunwales of their own ships as Cochrane's small boats slid past. The *Esmeralda* was the most powerful Spanish ship in Latin America. With that in his force, Cochrane blockaded Callao and – in his own flagship *O'Higgins* – had control over the Peruvian coast. Spanish forces could only be supplied by sea. Momentum shifted immediately and Peru successfully declared independence in 1821. With one campaign, Peru's independence was achieved and Chile's independence made secure.

Two years later, in 1823 Cochrane was commanding the eight ships of the Brazilian fleet of Dom Pedro, ruler of an independent Brazil from Rio de Janeiro in the south, against strong Portuguese power in the north based around Bahia. A series of raids, more bluff and deception, and one fleet action – the 'Battle of 4th May' off Salvador, Bahia – pushed Portuguese forces out of the country altogether. Modern Brazil was created and the political map of Latin America changed forever.

Those successful years were, of course, also characterized by Cochrane's personal failings. He fell into lasting enmity with many he worked with, outraged by a lack of resolve, even 'cowardice', in their own cause. His *bete noire* in Peru was General San Martin, whom he accused of every possible perfidy. But San Martin's strategic instincts were better than his. Cochrane constantly complained that he was defrauded of prize money and due payments. When he left Brazil in 1825, he disobeyed orders to return to Rio, pocketed public money he judged should be his, plundered a merchant ship for the balance, and returned to Britain in a captured Brazilian frigate. After a series of dramatic campaigns that both he and Kitty had prosecuted in their own distinctive ways, it was a dispiriting end to what might have been a more triumphant conclusion.

In typical Cochrane fashion, the whole adventure had begun as a madcap vision to sail to Chile via St Helena, rescue Napoleon (whom, despite all, he much admired) and help set him up as the emperor of an independent United States of Latin America. Indeed, on his outward journey to Valparaiso in 1818 Cochrane was detouring to St Helena to meet Napoleon. But he was diverted in mid-Atlantic by urgent events in Chile. Nevertheless, he kept the scheme alive and didn't give up plotting such foolishness until Napoleon's death in 1821. The ironic truth is that – finally – Cochrane's fleet command as Vice Admiral had begun as a strategically ridiculous fantasy, and ended in a curiously successful ignominy; messy but politically crucial to Latin America's future.

Back in Britain, Cochrane was in danger of another arrest warrant being served under the Foreign Enlistment Act. Moving swiftly to France, a French arrest warrant was also threatened for one of his seizures in Chile. But he had signed up to command the Greek navy in its war of liberation from Ottoman Turkey. This was probably the most innovative, but certainly the least successful, of all his campaigns. He had been working on a range of 'inventions' including gas lighting, bitumen for ships' hulls, high-pressure and rotary marine engines and propellers, among many entrepreneurial 'schemes'. And he now commissioned the building of six military steamships for the Greek war, and added two more steam frigates already building in the United States. He aimed to create a modern battle fleet that could go anywhere, regardless of wind and currents.[5] Such a fleet might have made a huge difference and it anticipated the next innovation in maritime warfare by at least thirty years. But the ships were not ready on time, costs ran out of control, and two uncompleted ships eventually just rotted on the Thames at Deptford. Cochrane put some of his own money into the venture but the maritime engineer responsible for the steam engines was a charlatan and may well have been working for Turkey and Egypt to frustrate the arrival of Cochrane's ships in Greece. His revolutionary fleet never materialized and he was left as a celebrity commander with a few makeshift vessels, appearing frankly foolish to many contemporary observers.

But, true to form, Cochrane nevertheless led a successful infantry charge at the age of fifty-two against heavy Turkish positions in a doomed attempt to break the siege of the Acropolis. He rescued a ship full of women and children destined for the slave markets of Turkey and Egypt. And he tried an unsuccessful re-run of his Basque Roads attack against the Egyptian fleet in Alexandria. As a commander, however, he became increasingly superfluous to Greek independence, which was finally settled by Admiral Edward Codrington at the Battle of Navarino in 1827, where Turkish and Egyptian power in Greece was finally broken by the joint fleets of Britain, Russia and France. Cochrane left the scene, disgusted with everyone involved and arguing with the Greek nationalists over payments due to him.

In 1829 he returned to Paris, taking up again the crusade to restore his good name after the Stock Exchange scandal. He was still liable for arrest in Britain and was heartily detested in the Admiralty. But the accession of William IV – the 'sailor king' – helped rehabilitate him. When his father, who had long since disowned him, died in 1831, Cochrane succeeded as 10th Earl of Dundonald. He pestered an unenthusiastic government with his case, but garnered support from the Royal Family and certainly from popular opinion. In 1832 he was graciously pardoned and restored to the Royal Navy list as a Rear Admiral. But he then refused to take any command until his knighthood was also restored. That stand-off lasted fifteen years. In that time Cochrane continued developing his many new ventures and scientific innovations, not to mention revenge on his enemies. In the end, Queen Victoria intervened to reappoint him to the Order of the Bath, and with that he took on the command of the North America and West Indies station in 1848, his final naval role until retirement in 1851.

---

5. The steamship *Savannah* had crossed from America to Liverpool in twenty-six days during 1819 and in 1820 steamships could be seen regularly on the Thames. In designing his rotary steam engine, Cochrane borrowed George Stephenson's 'Locomotive No 1' – the *Rocket* – for his trials.

He died in October 1860 of complications following operations for gallstones. The Royal Navy wanted to leave it there. But Victoria and Prince Albert were determined that his heroic status should be recognised. They wanted him buried in Westminster Abbey. Neither the government nor royalty were officially represented at his grand funeral, which wound its way slowly from his Kensington home to the Abbey. Chilean and Brazilian officers stood guard of honour at his tomb, decorated as it is with the arms of Chile, Peru, Brazil and Greece. To this day, annual tributes are offered at his tomb by the Chilean government – now normally accompanied, thankfully, by the First Sea Lord.

From Boulogne, Kitty – herself unwell – blamed him for squandering the family's fortunes in dubious schemes and had thought of him towards the end as 'deaf, miserable and senile'. Official controversy around Cochrane followed him in death; about the legitimacy of his first marriage, the outstanding money owed by the government to his estate (eventually paid in 1876) and the wretched 1814 Stock Exchange scandal which was still rumbling a century afterwards in 1914.

Cochrane, we might say, was a wonderful leader in battle, but a deficient commander, given the range of talents 'command' really requires. But he had a significant effect on Latin America as it embraced decolonisation. And his long and eventful life is one of the most colourful skeins in the already rich tapestry of Royal Navy culture and history. He was born in the year of the American War of Independence. His direct experience went from his conversations with Nelson to the dawning of the steam age. Cochrane's grandson, the 12th Earl of Dundonald, eight years old when Cochrane died and the last member of the family known to him, commanded in the Boer War and finally, as a Lieutenant General, took the 2nd Life Guards to the trenches in the First World War. In his exuberant, turbulent and exasperating way, Thomas Cochrane linked them all.

20

General Sir John Moore

General Sir John Moore will be forever associated with the desperate 'retreat to Corunna' over the winter of 1808–09 during the first phase of the Peninsular War. John Moore was a good Lieutenant-General and his efforts to get his army to Corunna and then defend it while the troops escaped by ship, was regarded a classic of survival against the odds. He became a hero both for his command of the operation and because he was killed in the final stages of the action. It was, however, a curious episode altogether. British and allied policy in Spain, opposing Napoleon's domination of the country, was both controversial and unsuccessful in 1808. And being chased to Corunna by a French army and scrambling out of the country on Royal Navy ships, represented a humiliating failure. But like the evacuation from Dunkirk in 1940, it could have been a great deal worse, and the action kept Britain's only available field army intact, which at least retained some strategic leverage for the nation in the ongoing land war with Napoleon. Victory at Trafalgar established the fact that, with the Royal Navy defending it, Britain would remain unconquered and could stay in the war for as long as it chose. Rescue at Corunna at least preserved an army capable of going back to the Continent to fight again. Critical historians have continued to wonder, however, how Moore's force came to be so exposed as to need such a desperate escape in the first place.

John Moore had a good upbringing and a smooth rise into the highest ranks of the British Army. Like almost all officers who became prominent in their late-30s or early-40s, fate gave him opportunities to show some personal gallantry in the early phases of his career and catch the official eye.

He was born into a well-connected family in Glasgow in 1761 and had a friend in the young Duke of Hamilton, who was close to him in age. As an adolescent he was taken, along with the Duke, on the classic 'grand tour' and then spent two years living in Geneva. At the age of seventeen he joined the army as an ensign and saw action in the American War of Independence. His early moment for gallantry arrived in 1779, during the American naval and ground force siege against Fort Majabigwaduce (later Fort George) in Maine. The Redcoats inside the fort were heavily outnumbered, but as a young lieutenant Moore commanded the most critical bastion at Dyce's Head, fending off attacks against it by American marines – the most formidable part of the rebel force. Marshalling his men, Moore was lucky to escape death on more than one occasion at Dyce's Head. But the fort held on until it was relieved. Fort George was the very last military post to be abandoned when the British withdrew from United States territory following defeat in the War.[1]

---

1. Fort George was reoccupied again during the United States-British War of 1812–15.

Returning to Britain in 1784 he became a Member of Parliament, as did many aspiring military officers, in his case with the support and involvement of the Duke of Hamilton. He spent six years in Whiggish politics, though often supporting Tory Prime Minister William Pitt on specific issues. In 1790, given the inevitability of war with revolutionary France, he resumed his military career and went to the Mediterranean as a major with the 51st Regiment of Foot. He was part of the British invasion of Corsica. Moore was fighting in the same campaign as the young Nelson in 1794, and like Nelson, was wounded in the attack on Calvi, again distinguishing himself leading forces in the storming of Mozello Fort. His commander was impressed and took him on as his Adjutant General. William Pitt had liked him, and so had the Duke of York. He was becoming both well-regarded for his prowess as an officer and was well-connected following his period in Parliament. To his own surprise, Moore was made a Colonel and given a brigade to command. He was then sent with General Ralph Abercromby to the West Indies in 1796. He got on very well with the excellent Abercromby who acted as a mentor to him into the higher ranks.

In the West Indies Moore showed he could command and manage big forces with conscientiousness and competence. He played an eye-catching role in the recapture of St Lucia – lost after John Jervis had captured it in 1794. He led the 27th Inniskilling Fusiliers, who were later to achieve a tragic fame at Waterloo, in a fierce two-day assault on French forces holding Fort Charlotte; a powerful strong point atop a natural defensive promontory. Both he and the Inniskillings were honoured for it. He was made Governor of the island when Abercromby departed, though he was soon forced to return home when he contracted yellow fever.

The steady qualities of his leadership, alongside his own personal courage, seemed to emerge at virtually every action in which he was involved during those years. In 1798, as a Major-General, he was sent to Ireland as part of the force charged with suppressing the Wexford rebellion. Though brief, his campaign again revealed the soldierly correctness that was to form the basis of his reputation. The Wexford rebellion was an indigenous Irish revolt, but it was in part fomented and acted as cover for French forces in Ireland. It was viewed as another front in Britain's ongoing continental war. Moore had landed in Dublin with Abercromby in December 1797 to deal with the incipient rebellion. But Abercromby resigned his role as British commander at the brutality of the response that was expected of him, and was replaced by the harsh General Gerard Lake.

Moore was in a difficult position, but when it came to the main confrontation at the Battle of Foulksmills, and lacking contact with Lake's troops, who should have formed a pincer with his own, Moore nevertheless used his small force of 1,500 regulars against some 5,000 Irish rebels to clear the road into Wexford. He personally rallied his troops who were on the verge of a chaotic retreat when they faced being outflanked, and then led them in good order in a successful counterattack into Wexford. His success in a formal battle, rather than a guerrilla pursuit, helped save lives on both sides, and putting a quick end to the rebellion probably saved Wexford from a brutal sacking, since he kept Lake out of it while tempers were hot. Unlike other commanders in the campaign, no accusations of mistreatment were ever laid against Moore either before or after Wexford.

Again working under Abercromby, Moore was then sent on the Anglo-Russian expedition against the Dutch and French at Helder in the Netherlands. It was, at best, a partial success. But he was with Abercromby in the expedition to Alexandria in March 1801, attacking Napoleon's army in Egypt. The Battle of Alexandria was a chaotic engagement that British forces seemed about to lose and which cost Abercromby his life. But Moore led storming parties against French batteries which made a critical difference. He was wounded once more, this time seriously. He eventually recovered well enough the following year to lead the 52nd Foot in subsequent campaigning until the fall of Alexandria, which finally thwarted Napoleon's military designs on Egypt. Moore returned to Britain in 1803.

He was called by many 'an unlucky man' given the frequency of his wounds. But Moore wasn't so unlucky. The fact was, he led from the front in a succession of brutal assaults against fortress walls and battalion formations. He was a tall and athletic man who was said to be graceful and well-balanced as he moved, not gangly or awkward. In his own drills, he is recorded to have been able to get off five musket shots a minute – an astonishing rate of fire with a muzzle-loading Brown Bess. As a youngster he had been noted for his fiery temperament and he was said both by contemporaries and later historians to 'enjoy' close quarter fighting. 'Enjoy' is a strange term in this context for all but an abnormal few military fighters. More likely, he was just good at it, and must also have had a powerful survival instinct. Probably more important, he was both a self-disciplinarian and a fair disciplinarian of others. From early in his career he seemed to understand the need to channel the fighting spirit and he was to control and develop this instinct into something valuable and lasting for the British Army.

Maturing as a commander, he came to embody that command spirit which modern military training now seeks to nurture in all British officers – cool aggression. He had sound judgement of his tactical position and was able to lead his forces in incisive manoeuvres, even outright aggression, without succumbing to the bloodlust that naturally accompanies extreme fear and exertion. He was very much the soldier and – whatever his inner fire – never the warrior. It was for these reasons that he became so admired among the soldiery. He was a winner who they could see was prepared to put his own life on the line, and he didn't waste theirs.

It is not surprising then, that in addition to his fame at Corunna, Moore is known for one other great achievement as a commander; a new and better approach to soldiering and the creation of Britain's much-admired light infantry. His thinking about the true nature of good soldiering had begun over a decade before when he took over the 51st Foot in Cork and immediately began to do something about the pervasive drunkenness among both its troops and officers. He understood that soldiers – and officers – needed to behave in a soldierly way whether or not they were on operations. And with better quality individuals, he saw the advantages of operating more flexibly with self-sustaining units that could be smaller than a battalion.

Having just returned from Egypt, and with the breakdown of the Peace of Amiens and renewed war with France, Moore was given a brigade to train at Shorncliffe, near

Folkestone. He had been speaking to his well-connected friends about his ideas and was invited to train the 52nd into something lighter and more flexible. But the nation was mobilizing again and Moore had tacit permission to experiment. He added to the 52nd, the 4th, 59th, 70th and the 95th line regiments for his new light brigade. Such was his reputation that the desperate and unruly 43rd was also added, so he could rescue them as a regiment.

He had learned a lot from Abercromby, whom he much missed, and his extensive personal involvement in close quarter fighting gave him some clear ideas about efficient tactics. At that time battalions of foot soldiers were designed to form 'the line', the several hundreds of them in the line creating a strong core of fire and courage that compensated for the natural failings of the individual. But Moore had come to understand the advantages if some battalions deployed skirmishers out in front, with support and reserve elements, able to create more flexible fighting units. Any battalion could have a company – around a hundred men – of skirmishers working with it. Skirmishing had been used for over a century in front of British forces, but Moore organized and professionalized a force for it. Well-trained skirmishers could operate with Baker rifles – harder and slower to load but with range and accuracy that smoothbore muskets would never have. He was drawing inspiration from French *voltigeurs*, but his creation of organized skirmishers and more flexibly structured battalions created the British light infantry that was better than the *voltigeurs* and added a powerful new element to all British infantry forces. And in Moore's thinking, soldiers and officers had to be more sober, fitter, and more mobile to be able to move quickly and look after themselves in smaller units. He drilled his troops hard and practiced manoeuvre until they could operate, if necessary, in new ways.

It isn't, therefore, just for the creation of light infantry that Moore is given such credit, but rather that he evolved at Shorncliffe a template for the modern professional soldier – how he should behave and how he could expect to be treated. Some writers have said simply that Moore was the greatest and most humane general the British Army ever produced, though it would be a long time before his template was standard across the whole army. Others have observed more laconically that from Shorncliffe he gave the Duke of Wellington what became the famous Light Division, without which the Duke would never have prevailed in his Spanish Peninsular War some years later. The 95th and then the 60th Rifles, in particular, emerged as the foundation units for what is currently the amalgamated and much-admired 'Rifles' regiment within the modern British Army.[2]

During the repeated French invasion scares after 1803 Moore had already applied his energy to important defensive works for which he was made responsible. He recruited 340,000 members of a militia to stand in a secondary defensive line along the South Downs if the regular army should be beaten at the coast by Napoleon's army. He was the initiator of the Martello Towers, having seen how effective they were in Corsica,

---

2. The Rifles is currently the largest infantry regiment in the British Army with four regular battalions, descendants of some of the army's most prestigious infantry regiments. Alongside its various special forces units, the modern army considers itself especially good at 'light infantry' tasks.

and he began the cutting of the Royal Military Canal in Kent and Sussex. He was a whirlwind of structured military thinking.

Moore never married, and though a dashing and decorated officer, seemed to have little time in his life for personal matters. There is, thankfully, some evidence from his correspondence and one of her nieces, that he may have been secretly engaged to Lady Hester Stanhope. It would be nice to think he was. The vivacious Lady Stanhope was unmarried at the age of twenty-seven, was hostess and private secretary to her uncle, Prime Minister Pitt, and a dedicated and formidable romantic. After Moore's death she left England, spent time with Lord Byron in Greece and had a series of colourful adventures around the Ottoman Empire, in which – among many other achievements – she was the first archaeologist to explore any sites in Palestine. She became both famous and infamous, then very eccentric, as 'Queen Hester of Sidon' where she held court among Pashas and visitors alike. We might hope that she and Moore spent a few of their younger years in a discreet relationship together.

After Shorncliffe, Moore was sent as commander to take over forces in Sicily and then to a politically fraught mission to command British troops aiding Sweden. King Gustavus IV was demonstrably insane, and Moore argued against his fantasy offensives. In the event, the King arrested him and Moore had to escape from Stockholm dressed as a peasant. Back in London he was commanded to take some British forces to the Iberian peninsula, landing them near Lisbon. But in the very act of landing his troops, the controversial Convention of Cintra was concluded. French forces in Portugal had been heavily defeated by the British at Vimeiro, but the three commanders – including Wellesley (who later became the Duke of Wellington) who was very unhappy about it – agreed at Cintra to let the French withdraw unmolested from the country rather than press the advantage. The government was furious when it saw the details of the deal that had been negotiated and in October 1808 commanded Moore, sitting just outside Lisbon, to take over British forces in Iberia, while it recalled the offending commanders.

It was to be this campaign which would define Sir John Moore in British military history. He was given command of the field army, and it was to operate from Portugal, a secure British base following Vimeiro, moving into Spain to help the Spanish Patriots fight Napoleon's invasion.

At this point Moore's story begins to take some rather strange, and more human, turns. The conventional hagiography of Moore lists his considerable battle honours and the influence of Shorncliffe as if they were all preparation for this greatest, and last, of his commands. But his incisive tactical thinking was also accompanied by strong views on strategy and a dismissive attitude towards political leaders in London who were responsible for it. His fame was such that he was increasingly testy and regarded by many people as having become difficult and touchy. He had complained bitterly before being sent to Lisbon at serving under commanders, unlike himself, with little or no field experience. He had no time for Foreign Secretary George Canning or British diplomats in Spain, and didn't think much of the orders he was then given as he took command of the British force. The government was clear that it expected Moore to establish footholds for his 40,000 army in Galicia and Leon, basing his operations around Burgos in north-west Spain, from where he would work out ways of helping the Spanish Patriots in their war against Napoleon.

Napoleon had personally assumed command of French forces to put right the reverses his troops had recently suffered at the hands of the Patriots. He re-conquered Madrid and prepared to move south and west to overrun the whole Iberian peninsula. John Moore, trying to draw together during November the forces he now commanded in the midst of Napoleon's offensive, was slow to bring his army to action and the poor roads of Spain left them strung out in three columns with one force in the north and all his cavalry and artillery making a huge detour to reach him from the south. Meanwhile, his Spanish allies could produce nothing of what they had confidently promised. Moore was anxious to act decisively and, thanks to Spanish guerrilla activity, had excellent intelligence of French dispositions. But he seemed caught between conflicting desires – his natural *elan* for the offensive, but yet anxiety that he was now in command of the only field army Britain possessed.

He ignored his orders to centre British forces around Burgos and instead went to Salamanca, some 150 miles further south-east and only 130 miles from Madrid. He intended to threaten French lines of communication by venturing so far into central Spain. On 28th November, however, disillusioned with Spanish efforts and feeling exposed where he was, Moore decided to move. He considered moving east into Old Castile to help distract French forces from Madrid, but within days Madrid had fallen anyway. He then realized that he could surprise Marshal Jean-de-Dieu Soult who was struggling with a widely dispersed French corps further north at Carrion. Moore concentrated his forces and on 11th December began to move against Soult. On 21st December his cavalry overran Soult's picquets at Sahagun. But Moore didn't follow up immediately and allowed the alarmed Soult to reinforce his position. It was a fatal pause. Two days earlier in Madrid Napoleon had only then discovered, to his great surprise, that a British army was operating to his north-west. Immediately realizing Moore's vulnerability, Napoleon shelved his grander plans for Iberia in order to pursue the British to a destruction he felt would be certain. On 23rd December Napoleon was on the march north to cut Moore off from any route back into Portugal. Moore saw what was developing. He withdrew from any prospect of battle with Soult and took the decision on 28th December to run for the sea.

In his letters Moore tried to rewrite history, maintaining that the government had left him in this mess. But the mess was largely of his own making. He had not been content with the government's gradualist strategy of support for the Spanish or in playing a containment role against French forces in the north, merely pinning them in place. He had an extremely low opinion of the abilities of the Spanish Patriots, yet deployed his forces as if a dramatic victory might somehow be achieved on the back of their success. Fierce defenders of Moore's reputation argue that he skilfully trailed his coat in front of Napoleon to set him on a chase to the extreme north-west of the country in order to prevent the Emperor driving south to conquer Andalucia and then Portugal. But though Moore's campaign did have the effect of buying some time for the Spanish Patriots to draw breath after their recent shattering defeats, the claim that the British were executing a clever piece of distraction is completely unconvincing. If it were a ruse, Moore almost sacrificed the whole army for it, and the political and psychological damage of the retreat was at least equal to the advantage it incidentally created.

The whole 250-mile scramble took Moore's army through the mountains of Galicia, in the teeth of appalling winter weather. Victorious and seasoned French forces were snapping at their heels as the British tried to make it to the coast before disease and the enemy overtook them. It turned into a brief epic of suffering and endurance. It was also an epic of contrasts. Moore and his commanders, and particularly his cavalry, conducted tactically skilful rearguard actions as the army trailed through the mountains in freezing rain, then driving snowstorms. Moore was meticulous in organizing the retreat as best his circumstances would allow. His own creation, the Light Brigade, maintained its unity very well and gave his rearguard some essential flexibility. But the army as a whole became strung out and military discipline – so revered by Moore – simply broke down. He could do nothing about it. The army became a rabble; its route all the way to Corunna marked by a swathe of theft, arson, rape and murder. It fostered widespread hatred of British forces within Spain which the Duke of Wellington, later on, could do little to mitigate.

Many expected Moore to offer battle when they reached Astorga, where Spanish forces joined them, and conditions might have been favourable. But he kept moving. There was an attempt to offer battle further on at Lugo, but by then Napoleon had departed, leaving the chase up to Soult, and the French were not concentrated enough to close on British positions. Moore thought he might make more advantageously for the coast at Vigo further south west, but realized that his army might simply disintegrate before it got there, so opted to keep on for Corunna which was nearer – though the final stages of the retreat over that shorter distance proved the most brutal of all.

Eventually, and much reduced by sickness, Moore's army reached the sea at Corunna on 12th January. Moore had lately ordered the 250 British ships from Vigo to rendezvous there but they were late arriving and didn't appear until 14th. By then, there was no alternative but to fight a rearguard action on the heights that overlooked the town and protected the port, while the guns and the sick were hastily embarked. Fortunately for Moore, Corunna was packed with British stores meant for the Spanish army and his men could at least ready themselves for the attack he knew must follow. Nevertheless, 6,000 horses from the cavalry and artillery trains were slaughtered, multiple tons of supplies and fixed guns were destroyed and a massive explosion was created when 4,000 barrels of powder that couldn't be saved were detonated.

British forces arranged themselves across the high ground above the port and on 16th January French forces launched fierce attacks on them, looking for a weakness that might turn one of the flanks. Much of the fighting centred around the village of Elvina. It was lost briefly and, as ever, Moore personally led a counter-attack to retake it. It was after that in late afternoon, while mounted on his horse, that Moore was hit full on his left shoulder by cannon shot and fatally wounded. By the end of the day, none of the British defences had been breached and more troops and guns were embarked. The following day French gunners launched salvos of shot from the cliff tops as British ships weighed anchor and the Spanish garrison in the citadel maintained a courageous final redoubt, resisting surrender until the British ships had escaped.

In Britain, the heroism of the march and the death of Moore – like Nelson in the very act of victory in battle – allowed the nation to lionize the whole episode. But many could see that what arrived in Portsmouth a few days later was 'the mere wreckage of an army'. More than a fifth of the troops had been lost along with all the horses. The guns had been saved but the vast majority of the stores were gone. And the campaign had achieved very little. Britain had been kicked out of the most heavily populated area of Spain in the north-west and had given up important towns like Lugo and Corunna. British-Spanish relations were badly damaged and the whole idea of a British presence in the peninsula to fight Napoleon was doubtful. The retreat created a full-scale political crisis for the government of Lord Portland. In the end, all that can be said with confidence is that the retreat saved Britain's only field army from almost certain destruction, had Napoleon caught up with it.

The place where Sir John Moore fell is marked by a stone which these days stands in the grounds of the University of Corunna, and the house of a local trader where the dying General was taken became a modern *Banco Popular* building with a commemorative plaque above its doorway. Marshal Soult had Moore buried the following day on the southern ramparts of Corunna and a small and tasteful sarcophagus was built at his tomb that still stands, overlooking the bay. As Moore lay dying his final, intriguing, words were to ask to be remembered to Lady Hester.

21

The Duke of Wellington

By most estimates, the Duke of Wellington and John Churchill, Duke of Marlborough, are the two greatest and most successful ground force commanders in British military history. It is hard to disagree. Their campaigns were a century apart and they were men of a very different character, but their virtues as commanders – their tactical acumen, strategic vision, their political and organizational abilities and their ruthless streak in pressing to win – speak for themselves. The Duke of Wellington participated in sixty-two different engagements over a period of twenty-one years, commanding either a significant proportion of the force, or the whole force, in almost all of them. There were reverses and rebuffs, of course, but he never lost a battle.

Cynics, both in his lifetime and occasionally in later writings, sometimes called him the 'sepoy general' because he gained his reputation with easy victories in the Mysore and Maratha wars in India before 1805. But those victories were against much larger numbers and they only appeared easy because they were so decisive. In more than thirty large and small engagements during the Peninsular War, Wellington was up against seasoned French troops and some of Napoleon's most experienced marshals.

And then there was the Battle of Waterloo. Ah, Waterloo – forever to be associated with the name of Wellington; the battle that most defines him in the popular mind. In reality, Waterloo was not the most strategically significant battle he fought. Though it was unavoidable, Waterloo was peripheral to the European balance of power in 1815. Nor was it his best performance as a commander. But it was undoubtedly the closest and most brutally dramatic battle he ever fought and it ended in total victory. Napoleon was finished by it. So was Wellington. It is doubtful whether the Duke had it in him to take responsibility for another battle after more than twenty years of warfare and the awful carnage around the Mont St Jean ridge that June day in 1815. If the political significance of Waterloo doesn't really define Wellington's reputation, the drama of it certainly does.

He was born in Dublin in 1769, son of Lord Mornington and part of the 'protestant ascendancy' – the natural establishment in Ireland. Arthur Wesley was the fourth born among six children and, given that the Earl of Mornington's properties were mortgaged to the hilt, not well-favoured by circumstances among the British aristocracy.[1] He was not a dull child, but lonely and taciturn; about as well-educated as minor aristocracy

---

1. Arthur was born 'Wesley'. The family changed it to 'Wellesley' in 1798 and his various promotions led him from being General Wellesley to a Field Marshal and in a series of related dynastic promotions to a Dukedom, as 'Wellington' in 1814. For the sake of clarity, this chapter will refer to him throughout either as 'Wellington' or later on, 'the Duke'.

usually were, which is to say, fitfully. He seemed to have little ambition. His mother referred to him as 'my awkward son Arthur'. Fortunately, brother Richard, nine years older, was his idol and mentor and Richard inherited the Mornington title in 1781. With Richard's influence, Arthur bought himself a number of ranks in Britain's moribund army – an ensign then a lieutenant at eighteen and a position as military aide to Lord Buckingham, a captain at twenty-two, a major then a lieutenant-colonel in 1793 by the age of twenty-four. Though he had been in uniform for some years, he never had a day of formal military training in his life and he was now in command of the 33rd Regiment of Foot. It speaks volumes about the state – and the status – of the army in British society at the outbreak of the French revolutionary wars. As a complete military amateur, all Arthur had were a young buck's social life, the inevitable debts, and a seat he really didn't want for the constituency of Trim in the Irish Parliament.

He also had the pain of romantic rejection which much affected his subsequent attitudes. He had proposed to the lively and attractive Kitty Packenham in Dublin during 1793, but her family wouldn't allow her to marry someone with such limited wealth or prospects. He took the rejection to heart and seemed to resolve to take soldiering far more seriously. In any case, he had no other calling and few obvious skills. He threw himself into military literature and campaign histories, learning earnestly. When, later that year, the 33rd was sent to Flanders to join the Duke of York's disastrous campaign against revolutionary France, amateur that he was, Arthur conducted his regiment very well. As British forces were ignominiously withdrawing, he found himself in temporary command of a brigade. Though, as he said later, the whole sorry affair didn't teach him what to do as a commander, it certainly taught him what not to do. He was impressed by the importance of combining naval support with whatever the army was doing ashore. Above all, he took from the campaign the importance of supply and logistics and the responsibility of any commander to attend closely to them. It was to become the most notable hallmark of his lifelong military success.

Arthur's life changed fundamentally in 1796 when he was sent with the 33rd to India. He spent ten years continuously in the sub-continent. Here he gained wealth, military experience, political status and a degree of fame. His career was carried along on the basis that elder brother Richard had become Governor General in Calcutta only a few months after Arthur arrived there in February 1797. The brothers, along with younger brother Henry, pushed for war against the Tipu Sultan of Mysore, to protect the East India Company's interests, expand British India and expel residual French influence backing the Tipu Sultan. Richard's driving ambition and his subtle manipulation changed the political map of India, and though Wellington was only then a colonel, he was privileged by his brother's influence (and often resented for it) within the military establishment. The successful Mysore War was followed by the Second Maratha War – inevitable yet provoked – in 1803. By 1805 the conquest of the Maratha Empire put more swathes of Indian territory under Company and governmental jurisdiction. Wellington was then a Major General and Richard officially delegated to him full military and political control in Central India during the conflict.

He had already served as governor of Seringapatam and Mysore. Between them, the Wellesley brothers had become a dominant force in British India.

In a succession of campaigns during these two wars Wellington commanded government and Company troops in many different types of battle – Seringapatam, Gawilghur, Conaghul, Argaum – ranging from open-ground contests, sapper campaigns against dug-in defences, even running fortress assaults with escalading ladders. He undertook powerful political roles but personally led at least one cavalry charge and operated near all the front lines of the fighting. And he created multiple miles of bullock-cart columns to supply and sustain his forces. They became almost his wonder weapon, since their ubiquity and effectiveness so surprised both allies and enemies.

His most notable triumph was against the cosmopolitan troops and vastly superior artillery of the Maratha's army at Assaye in September 1803. It outnumbered his 9,000 troops by more than five to one and was camped securely across the Kaitna river. Wellington was nevertheless determined to take it on. He was told definitively that all the Kaitna fords were well-guarded. But he insisted on seeing for himself. And he observed that at Peepulgaon there was another village, Waroor, on the other side of the river. He reasoned it was likely the river must be fordable between two adjacent settlements. Indeed it was, and he got enough of his army across it before the Maratha's huge force could fully react. It was a dangerous manoeuvre but once on the northern bank, he set up an aggressive flanking attack on slowly wheeling enemy lines and led his forces in a bloody triumph. He had one horse shot and another stabbed from under him in the heat of the battle, fighting sword in hand at close quarters for some of it. Assaye brought Wellington to the public's attention in Britain. Though when he came home in 1805 – he'd had enough of India by then – his prowess as a commander was still in some doubt at Horse Guards.[2] In 1807, he was given command of the brief expedition to coerce the Danes at Copenhagen, but with a second in command – a role he never believed in – to keep an eye on his battle-management. For many, he was still the 'sepoy general'.

By then, his personal life had become complicated. He had departed for India with the solemn declaration to Kitty Pakenham that, 'My mind will remain the same'. He came back rich, famous, an experienced man of the world. But he had cooled on Kitty in the meantime, while she seemed to have aged and to have become staid. He felt he had promised, nevertheless, so they married in April 1806. Though they had two sons, Wellington treated Kitty with growing indifference over the years and he was a distant and intimidating father to both his young boys.

As he grew in military stature, Wellington revealed himself a complex character. He was austere, disciplined and demanding of his officers and soldiers. He didn't explain himself to others very much, but his orders were always crisp and he expected them to be obeyed, not reinterpreted. His correspondence was voluminous. He had endured

---

2. On the way home his ship put in at St Helena, where Wellington stayed in the house that Napoleon would first occupy in his exile there ten years later. Apart from the field of Waterloo, this was the nearest contact history ever provided them. Wellington abhorred Napoleon but showed great respect for his generalship and studied it closely – something Napoleon never did of Wellington's campaigns.

enough hardships in military service and put his own life on the line often enough to have the moral authority to require the same of his regiments. But he was far from a killjoy. He was an excellent rider and lived for hunting in his leisure time. He was frugal in his food, and in what he provided his dinner guests, but throughout his life served and drank excellent wine. When occasion arose, he was a natural party animal, and as a lean and fit young General he basked in the adulation of the ladies. He was serially unfaithful to Kitty throughout his career and brazen about being seen with obvious courtesans. He was noted for inviting 'ladies of loose character' to his various parties in Brussels. He remained haughty and indifferent to moral condemnation and his status eventually placed him largely above it. If there was something of the libertine about him, there was also comparatively little of the public scandal that had surrounded Nelson's private life. Only much later in 1831, when Kitty was dying, probably of cancer, at 'Number One London' – Apsley House – did he really seem to reconnect with his wife. He was genuinely distressed at her illness and tried his best to nurse her through the final decline. All too late? Probably.

In 1808 he was sent to Portugal to assist in the burgeoning Peninsular War campaign. He quickly defeated French forces in an aggressive attack at Rolica and then conducted a masterly defence when his forces were heavily attacked at Vimeiro. But those victories were won while he was in process of being superseded in command by Hew Dalrymple and a number of senior officers who out-ranked him. Dalrymple drew up the Convention of Cintra that let French forces leave Lisbon with their weapons and all their loot on Royal Navy ships, no less. At least it got them out of Portugal. The government and public were appalled by Cintra. Wellington had been pressured to agree the Convention but didn't put his name to it. Nevertheless, he was recalled to London with Dalrymple to answer for it. While he was in London, General John Moore was trying to rescue British forces in the Peninsula from Napoleon's pursuit in what turned out to be a heroic fiasco. The retreat to Corunna put the whole idea of British operations in the Iberian Peninsula in doubt.

Wellington himself was cleared of blame by the Cintra enquiry and he then took the bull by the horns with a strategically astute memorandum to Secretary of State for War, Robert Castlereagh. He argued that 30,000 men, along with artillery and cavalry, and putting the Portuguese army under British command, would be sufficient to defend the country regardless of what the French did in Spain. And defending Portugal properly would be the first step in helping the Spanish Patriots expel their invaders.

The government agreed and this became the bedrock of Wellington's own Peninsular War – the war that represents the essence of his success and his importance as a British commander. He would defend Portugal at all costs and work more gradually with his Spanish allies as occasions arose. Wellington would not be driven towards risky glory like Moore. He would bide his time, pitting his small core of fighting infantry against French forces – over 320,000 of them across the Peninsula at their peak in 1810 – but working from a secure base around Lisbon.

He arrived in Lisbon in April 1809. In his immediate area of operations he faced Marshals Soult and Ney with some 40,000 troops occupying northern Portugal and Galicia, and over 50,000 French troops under Marshal Victor poised further south in

Spain ready to enter central Portugal through the Tagus or the Guadiana valleys. It was from this inauspicious position that Wellington's five-year war in the Peninsula developed. It was characterized by a long list of battles and engagements, marches, retreats and sieges, the names of which are captured on many battle honours among modern British regiments; Busaco, Badajoz, Salamanca, Vitoria. Some were more successful than others; some proved to be indecisive or simply confused. But though his allied commanders sometimes suffered defeats in the war, Wellington never did. It does a disservice to the Duke and the military staff he drove so hard to skip across five years of constant struggle – summer campaigning, winter quarters, coalition politics, arguments with London, and supply and logistics – always supply and logistics. Nevertheless, some moments were pivotal.

Wellington discovered the unreliability of his Spanish allies almost immediately in July 1809 at Talavera – a desperate victory he was unable to exploit and which cost him over 5,000 troops – more than a quarter of his available force at the time. He was compelled to retire to the border town of Badajoz with the supply situation becoming critical. He knew that Napoleon would further reinforce French armies in Spain after beating the Austrians at Wagram and smashing the 'Fifth Coalition' against him earlier that month. But Wellington was planning for the long term and he spent the autumn and winter constructing the lines of Torres Vedras – a triple-layered defensive barrier of forts, rivers and trenches to protect Lisbon and give his forces a safe haven. In addition, he incorporated Portuguese brigades into each British division to strengthen their fighting qualities, and organized the Portuguese irregulars so they could lay waste the countryside ahead of any French advance. These measures in the autumn of 1809 were probably the most important initiatives Wellington took to create his ultimate Peninsular War victory.

His foresight was just as well. In spring 1810 Marshal Andre Massena entered Spain with 138,000 fresh French troops to conquer the remainder of Portugal. Massena advanced from Almeida in the north-east and the Duke met him with a joint British and Portuguese force at the formidable strong point of Busaco. It was another important moment. The French were thrown back but the allied force nevertheless had to withdraw into the lines of Torres Vedras. Massena came on but simply couldn't penetrate allied defences. After a fruitless eleven months, Massena was forced to retire back to Almeida, having lost some 30,000 men, mainly to sickness. Wellington was secure behind his Torres Vedras lines and would not move until he was ready. Meanwhile, he sent home for his pack of hunting hounds so as to have some diversion from the draining burdens of the campaign.

The war then moved to a series of battles along the Portuguese-Spanish border, guarded by fortresses at Almeida, Ciudad Rodrigo and Badajoz. Wellington's troops worked hard to dislodge big French contingents from these fortresses, but tough, indecisive battles followed, since Soult and Marshal Marmot could always summon up enough troops to march against any besieging forces of the allies. Wellington was anyway short of the heavy guns he needed for sieges, and it was not until reinforcements arrived – with a proper siege train – at the end of 1811, that he could move eastwards more effectively.

Ciudad Rodrigo and Badajoz were the principal border gateways in either direction, depending on who controlled them. In January 1812 Wellington took Ciudad Rodrigo and immediately the army moved on to besiege – for the third time – the almost impregnable Badajoz. This was another strategic turning point. After a hurried bombardment, and with French troops approaching from the north to break Wellington's siege, the multi-pronged attack on Badajoz began during the night of 6th April.[3] The assaults – more than forty of them around the city's numerous bastions – were clearly failing. Grim and unbending, Wellington sent more regiments into the barely viable breaches, until the dead in the wide ditch between the breaches at the Santa Maria and Trinidad bastions – these days a municipal garden – were piled high, one on another, before they had even reached the rubble of the breached walls. In the event, it was Tom Picton's 3rd Division that finally got into Badajoz, using scaling ladders against the thirty-foot-high old castle walls on the opposite side. And once they were in, the troops went berserk in an orgy of violence and theft that went on for two days. Not for the first or last time, Wellington struggled to maintain order among his soldiers. He was fashioning in the Peninsular War the best infantry in the world, and in relative terms, probably the finest – certainly the most dominant – that Britain has ever fielded. But even he, with his strong disciplinarian instincts and his willingness to hang looters, could not prevent the bloodlust and drunken frenzy that gripped his soldiers after some of their toughest victories.

The Duke's relationship with both his men and their officers was never a relaxed one. He was always a patrician; never a soldiers' soldier. Unlike those who served under Moore or Nelson, his men didn't love him; nor he them. But they respected Wellington and wanted to serve under him because he won his battles. And if he didn't love them, he nevertheless hated to sacrifice their lives. Notwithstanding his dispassionate comments about necessary losses among his soldiers, he was often tormented by them. Some of Wellington's officers became his good friends, but many others reacted rather in the way of the soldiery. His anger was cold, his disapproval consequential. His political instincts were quite acute in dealing with his military allies, with Horse Guards in London, and those among his own staff who gossiped endlessly about him to their parliamentary friends back home. Nevertheless, he never lost sight of the bigger picture, so he put up with persistent personal aggravations. But they separated him from many of his men. Only reluctantly did he trust his officers to act without his explicit instructions. As the responsibility told on him, he became more secretive, pernickety and controlling. Only much later in the campaign did he show enough confidence in his seasoned officers to let them act truly independently.

By 1812, Wellington commanded about 60,000 allied troops. French forces in Spain then numbered at least 230,000, spread between five separate armies, all now struggling with a vicious Spanish guerrilla movement. That guerrilla movement was as important in defeating Napoleon in Spain as were the allied armies; more so in the earlier phases. Wellington managed to keep large French forces apart and with

---

3. Popular stories have it, poignantly, that the agony of Badajoz occurred on the night of Easter Sunday. But Easter Sunday in 1812 fell on 29th March.

Napoleon setting off to invade Russia and a weak French government holding on in Madrid, the initiative was shifting towards the allies. In June 1812, immediately after Badajoz, Wellington won a huge victory at Salamanca, moving skilfully onto the offensive after cat and mouse manoeuvring against Marmot's forces. Marmot's army was smashed, the road to Madrid was open and Wellington entered the capital in triumph, becoming overall commander of British, Portuguese and Spanish forces in the Peninsula. But there were a series of setbacks. He underestimated the strength and resilience of French forces as he pushed towards the French frontier. He was unable to take a refortified Burgos, then was forced to abandon Madrid allowing the French army and 'King Joseph' – Napoleon's elder brother – back into the capital. Wellington was compelled to settle for winter quarters again in Portugal. He was in a foul mood. He blamed himself for the expensive failure to take Burgos and all that had happened since. He had over-interpreted his victory at Salamanca. He was angry, careworn and completely overworked, given his reluctance to delegate. All Wellington could do was prepare the army, in his meticulous way, for the coming campaign season, re-equipping his forces for rapid movement. He still had to prevent French forces from combining, but he had the instinct that the time had come to move aggressively onto the offensive.

The key moment arrived in May 1813 when he left Portugal 'forever', as he said, to venture further into northern Spain. A French army under King Joseph and Marshal Jourdan left Madrid with the intention of combining with large French forces in the north-west to overwhelm Wellington. But Wellington's forces, and his supply lines, had reached peak effectiveness. They moved 400 miles in forty days using deception to lure the French column on.

The French column was, in any case, encumbered by a king, a royal court, a civilian administration and, apparently, a 'walking bordello' of camp followers. As John Fortescue remarked of the manoeuvring forces, 'Wellington's supplies were always hunting for his army; Joseph's army was always hunting for its supplies'. That comment encapsulated the Duke's greatest achievement in the Peninsular War. On 21st June Wellington caught Joseph's column at Vitoria. His forces pinned French troops in place from the west while a powerful flanking force – led again by Picton's 3rd Division – attacked from the north. It was the most decisive victory of that war; King Joseph's troops were routed. The French abandoned all but three of their guns and wagonloads of dazzling treasure and baggage. Yet again Wellington's army – men and officers alike – went on a looting spree whose extent and riches had no parallel in earlier campaigns. The Duke was predictably furious, but the victory definitively broke France's grip on Spain. It was merely a matter of time before the British, Portuguese and Spanish allies would be up at the Pyrenees.

Even then, San Sebastian proved a very tough nut to crack. Again, the army went on the rampage when it fell, and again, Wellington was forced into winter quarters after more engagements along the Nivelle river, Neve and St. Pierre. It was obviously frustrating. Wellington was having to achieve his campaign victory the hard way. But he crossed the Pyrenees in the west, and in spring 1814 the allied army was in Bayonne. On April 12th, after a brief and fierce siege, the Duke rode into royalist-inclined Toulouse. And it was there, in the afternoon, that news reached him that Napoleon, badly beaten at Leipzig and unable to prevent a massive invasion of France, had finally abdicated. At a grand dinner in Toulouse that evening the news was confirmed; King Louis XVIII was restored as King of France. Reportedly, the dinner erupted in ten minutes of sustained cheering and applause for the Duke, while he sat, reflective, 'bowed and confused' by the adulation, before he brusquely called for the coffee.

Wellington was immediately offered the Paris Embassy and he lived a high and discreetly promiscuous life in the French capital for a few months from late August 1814. He was no fan of the restored Bourbons though he strongly championed their legitimacy. A lot of his energy in these months went into trying to persuade the new government to follow Britain's lead in abolishing the slave trade. In January 1815 he was sent as Britain's representative to the Congress of Vienna, which would re-make Europe after the fall of Napoleon's revolutionary empire. And in Vienna there were yet more grand events, society ladies and hunting.

But on 7th March news reached the delegates that Napoleon had escaped from Elba and by 20th that he was triumphantly back in the Tuileries. The allies immediately assembled a 'Seventh Coalition' of forces to deal with it, drawn from Russia, Prussia, Austria, the Netherlands, Baden and Wurttemberg, Hanover and Britain. Wellington would command British, Netherland and some other allied forces and converge with a Prussian army under Marshal Gebhard von Blucher. Total allied numbers – over 700,000 troops – and the determination of the European powers to see off Napoleon once and for all, meant that the ex-Emperor's 'Hundred Days' would never be more than a footnote in European history. The Congress of Vienna didn't even interrupt its work while it dispatched four separate armies to put an end to Napoleon's nonsense. For all the considerable glory and power Napoleon's campaigns had won for France, the country was on its knees in 1815. Napoleon could win a battle, which indeed he did against the Prussians at Ligny, but even winning a second, or a third, battle would still leave him facing the stark reality that France was exhausted and the other Europeans were no longer frightened of him. The allies would not be divided. They were determined that this time there would be no quarter; France would be invaded, Paris occupied again, and Napoleon killed or captured.

Wellington and Blucher, along with the Prince of Orange leading his Netherlanders, were in a position to be the first to engage French forces. With all his strategic cunning, Napoleon planned to move quickly to hit the closest allied armies hard and push them apart, relying on his proven strategy of bludgeoning opponents into making a separate peace with him. But pyrrhic victories in present-day Belgium would keep weakening Napoleon while the rest of Europe closed in from several directions to occupy his country. Napoleon's own strategic illusions would not be shattered until he was beaten, yet again, fair and square, on the battlefield. It is as certain as anything in history ever can be that had it not happened at Waterloo it would have happened somewhere else. But time and chance determined it was Waterloo; a battle of little strategic importance that nevertheless had to be fought.

The Duke was based in Brussels; Blucher and the Prussians arriving further to the east from Liege and Maastricht. They were watching carefully the French frontier to which Napoleon had brought his 'Army of the North'. Wellington had his forces widely dispersed to the west of Brussels because he thought it likely Napoleon would try some grand left hook – swinging his army round to cut Wellington off from his supply bases (and his line of retreat) at Ostend and Antwerp, and then to approach Brussels from the west, perhaps before Blucher's Prussians could offer any help. It's what he himself would have done. And Napoleon fed Wellington enough clues to make a left hook seem inevitable. Then before dawn on 15th June, Napoleon had his whole force cross the River Sambre at Charleroi heading directly north towards Brussels to fight whomever appeared in front of him. Blucher took up a position at Ligny and Wellington gathered his forces and rushed them south as best he could to the crossroads at Quatre Bras, blocking the road to Brussels and near enough to Blucher to force Napoleon to fight them both. Wellington's forces were only just in time getting sufficient numbers to Quatre Bras to hold the position during the 16th, but Blucher was being heavily beaten at Ligny and that night had to withdraw north to Wavre to preserve his army to fight another day. Though Quatre Bras was by then secure, this left the Duke no option but to withdraw too. During Saturday 17th he fell back on a good defensive position along the Mont St Jean ridge, just south of the village of Waterloo. There he would make a stand on Sunday 18th June, holding the position until Blucher, further east, could bring the remainder of his mauled Prussian army the eight miles from Wavre to the ridge.

The Battle of Waterloo is the most studied battle in British history and there is no attempt here to describe it adequately. From the perspective of Wellington as a commander, two features stand out. One is that, unlike Napoleon who stood for most of the battle on the opposite ridge around the inn at La Belle Alliance, issuing frequently unclear and ambiguous orders, Wellington was everywhere across the ridge during those long hours of daylight. He kept the ebb and flow of the battle constantly in view, riding on 'Copenhagen', around every part of his defensive lines. He irritated some of his commanders with the unnecessary detail of his many orders. Wellington had some 92,000 troops under his command, with up to 50,000 Prussians expected to arrive at some point on his left flank. Again, Wellington was worried that Napoleon would be clever and try a left hook to get round his more exposed right flank. So he stationed more than 17,000 of his troops further west to guard against some rapid flanking move. In reality, Napoleon was determined to batter through the middle and the Duke's blocking force took no part in the battle, but it reduced his manpower in what turned out to be the actual battle area. On the morning of Waterloo, the Duke arranged about 68,000 allied troops on and around the Mont St Jean ridge, as against 73,000 French troops assembling opposite. He would have little depth and few reserves until Blucher arrived.

A second prominent feature is that Wellington was consistently lucky throughout these days. He was lucky on Friday 16th, since between them, Napoleon and Marshal Ney had managed to confuse Marshal D'Erlon and keep his 1st Corps marching and counter-marching all afternoon between two battles at Ligny and Quatre Bras without firing a shot in either of them. If D'Erlon's corps had fought at one or other of Friday's two battles it would have made a real difference to French fortunes, and Wellington's stand at Mont St Jean the following Sunday would very likely have been either meaningless or impossible. Then too, Wellington was lucky because it rained so ferociously on Saturday as his forces were withdrawing from Quatre Bras. The ground around Wellington's position on the ridge was so wet, the local streams so flooded, that Napoleon's artillery took time to drag their guns into place for the 'Grand Battery' opposite Mont St Jean, and his cavalry wanted to let the ground dry on Sunday morning rather than risk being bogged down in the valley between the two ridges. So it was that Napoleon didn't begin his attack until after 11.30. Wellington's only intention was to hold the ridge until Blucher arrived. He held it – eventually by the skin of his teeth – for almost nine hours once the battle commenced. Had it not been for the rain, the battle could have begun much earlier and Wellington might have had to hold the ridge for many more hours. The weather had been exceptionally hot until Friday; then driving rain from late Saturday morning which didn't finally stop until dawn on Sunday, after which the weather was sultry. On any other day during that mid-summer week, it would have been different, but the torrential crack in a heat-wave at that precise time on that particular Saturday, significantly reduced the hours available to Napoleon to try his battering ram tactics the day after.

Wellington remained calm and composed as he rode his luck on the day itself. His immediate right flank – potentially vulnerable – was held mainly by units of the Coldstream and the 1st and 3rd Foot Guards at the chateau of Hougoumont. He made it clear there could be no significant reinforcement – he simply didn't have the numbers. Indeed, Hougoumont was attacked first and it turned into an epic battle within a battle, effectively 1,500 troops – guardsmen and allied contingents – holding off over 10,000 attackers in their grim struggle to maintain the right flank of the allied line. The chateau almost fell about 1 pm in the afternoon when the north gate was forced open. But luck was with the defenders who managed to wrestle the gate closed again before more than a few dozen attackers had got inside.

Wellington cantered back and forth as Napoleon's main attack then went forward; D'Erlon's 1st Corps – this time at the front of the fighting – sweeping up the incline toward the centre left of the allied line. It was nearly through, getting ready to wheel left and scour along the ridge. Without time to refer to Wellington, Picton set his 5th Division against the French corps, at least to slow it down. He was felled after his first step. But the move worked and hindered D'Erlon's troops. Lord Uxbridge, as cavalry commander, also acted on his own judgement and immediately brought his heavy cavalry against D'Erlon's Corps, timing the attack to perfection. D'Erlon's 19,000 troops were attacked by 2,500 heavy cavalry of the Household and Union Brigades. The impact – the heaviest cavalry hit on an infantry formation in British military history – was devastating. D'Erlon's corps was destroyed by it. But the British cavalry didn't stop. Battle-crazed with success they swept onwards to attack Napoleon's Grand Battery, deep in the midst of French lines. Having therefore ridden into a death trap and now with their horses blown, they were counter-attacked by French lancers and cavalry, on fresh horses, who simply eviscerated them in the mud, cavalry troopers and senior officers alike struggling to get back to their own lines.

Wellington watched it all with cold anger. He had seen too much of this in the Peninsula. The heavy cavalry's first impact had eliminated Napoleon's most effective formation and taken it out of the reckoning. But then long-standing failures of cavalry officer-ship had led his 'heavies' – his principal strike weapon – to wanton self-destruction against the Grand Battery. For the rest of the battle Wellington's cavalry played only marginal roles, rather than being his instrument of victory as the enemy weakened. Uxbridge reproached himself for the rest of his life for the debacle.

The Duke frequently watched Hougoumont from the ridge above as its own epic struggle continued. The chateau was on fire by mid-afternoon. He kept a close eye on the strongpoint of La Haye Sainte, too, just below the ridge in the centre of his line. It was held by 400 members of the excellent King's German Legion, who repelled repeated attacks as the French tried to establish a foothold at the base of the ridge. Later in the afternoon he was riding up and down the allied infantry squares – twenty-two of them – as they repelled 6,300 French cavalry in ill-judged, through brave and persistent, attacks. By most accounts, there were around twelve concerted cavalry assaults on the squares and many skirmishes. All the squares were becoming smaller and tighter as the fighting continued. On at least two occasions Wellington was in danger of being shot or captured out in the open by French horsemen. He galloped for the nearest square, waving at the infantrymen. They dropped to the ground and, hunting-style, he leapt over all four ranks.

Infantry squares were nearly impregnable against cavalry as long as they remained steady. But when the cavalry withdrew, squares offered a concentrated target for artillery. Much depended on where they had been placed. Having been heavily involved at Quatre Bras, the 27th Inniskillings had been moved up to the ridge only later in the day and placed above and to the east of La Haye Sainte. As French artillery units edged further forward, however, there was nothing the Inniskillings could do about enemy guns working only 270 yards away. Losses mounted alarmingly. Major General Colin Halkett, commanding the nearby 5th Brigade, and already wounded three times, had suggested earlier to Wellington that his units needed some relief for a while. Wellington's reply was well-noted; 'Tell him', he said to the messenger, 'what he asks is impossible: he, I and every Englishman on the field, must die on the spot we now occupy'. Apart from referring to his multinational force as 'English', that was a pretty accurate summary of the Duke's position. Any other options had long since disappeared. Halkett understood and resolved that his brigade would stand regardless. To Halkett's left, the Inniskillings – an Irish infantry regiment raised in the late seventeenth century – under constant artillery attack, never fired a shot all day. But long before the end of the battle they famously lay 'dead in square' after the wounded had crawled away and the survivors had drifted into other units.[4]

The culminating phase of Waterloo was played out about seven-thirty in the evening. La Haye Sainte had finally fallen. Forty-three of the four hundred King's German Legion soldiers survived to scramble back up to the ridge. It was clear there would be one more major attack on the ridge now that Napoleon was in possession of all the ground below it. They were still fighting at Hougoumont. With evident anxiety, Wellington was waiting for Blucher to arrive through the wooded ground to

---

4. Their losses were officially recorded as 478 officers and men out of a total of 698.

his left. He was only dimly aware that the Prussians were actually putting their main attack into the area of Plancenoit, a village almost behind Napoleon's vantage point at La Belle Alliance; creating a potential encirclement. Napoleon had been steadily feeding his reserve troops into Plancenoit to hold Blucher and the Prussians off while he disposed of Wellington. The back and forth fighting around Plancenoit during late afternoon was every bit as fierce as anything happening on the ridge, and by evening it was clear to Napoleon that he would run out of time, as well as reserves, if he didn't finish it now. He put everything he had left into this final attack as evening drew on. Meanwhile, Wellington reorganized his remaining forces out on the ridge – about 35,000 men still standing – knowing too, that the next hour would settle it one way or another. For both commanders, the equation had become very simple. Whichever force was first to break would lose, and there would then be a rout. There were no reserves left on either side to prevent it. The battle would now be decided, as it were, on the turn of a card.

And when the French attack came, first on the centre left, where the 27th, the 30th, the 33rd and the 69th had effectively disintegrated, Wellington's lines were immediately pushed back. Halkett's brigade was again bearing the brunt of the first wave. At that moment the Duke was standing further west above Hougoumont with the Guards, but he galloped across to Halkett to find him waving the colours of the 33rd aloft to call fleeing troops to him, putting some order back into small groups of men. Halkett took a musket ball full in the face. The Duke got two fleeing battalions of Brunswickers back into position and brought Light Dragoons up to block any further flight. He kept watching Halkett's line as order was restored. Wellington's presence itself was usually enough. Many soldiers saw him close up during these moments. He was sitting fully upright on Copenhagen. They said his face was very pale. He was gaunt and strained. But his voice was even, authoritative and calm. Within a few minutes Halkett's brigade had counterattacked and taken back the ground it had lost.

As soon as that sector was stabilized, Wellington was off across the ridge again to rejoin the 1st Foot Guards, where he knew the next pressure point must come. Napoleon's Imperial Guard – his 'Immortals' – were marching up the hill to confront the British Foot Guards, arranged in fighting lines but lying down some way behind the ridge. The French Chasseurs and Grenadiers of the Imperial Guard approached in column – a fearsome prospect but not a good fighting formation when only those at the front and sides could use their muskets. In all the smoke and confusion they could not have realized that the Foot Guards were lying down so near to them. Certainly, they made no attempt to get into a firing line as they came on. Wellington, wrongly but as usual, took command of the Guards while three columns of French Chasseurs tramped closer. He waited until they were effectively at point blank range, then called to Colonel Maitland 'Now's your chance!' And 1,500 Guardsmen sprang up in full formation and delivered one, maybe two, devastating volleys into the French columns directly ahead. Then they lowered their muskets and bayonet charged. Almost simultaneously, the dashing Colonel John Colborne of the 52nd Oxford Light Infantry had used his own initiative to take his men forward beyond the ridge to outflank the leftward French column as it came up the incline, and the 52nd were now exchanging fierce volleys with the flank of the Imperial Guard columns. Under this intense close-quarter firepower, in front and from the side, Napoleon's 'Immortals' cracked and began to run. For the first and only time in its distinguished history, the Imperial Guard retreated without orders. 'La Guarde Recule'. The effect all across the French line was electrifying.

For the first time that day the Duke became animated. Standing in his stirrups, waving his hat above his head, he shouted at the battalions ranged along the ridge to pursue the breaking French. 'On boys, on', he kept shouting, 'they won't stand, they won't stand'. After fighting defensively for over eight hours, his depleted force swept down into the valley in an offensive that lasted less than an hour. Prussian units that were just now emerging from the woods east of the ridge added weight to the growing rout. The Duke followed close to the edge of the broken fighting. 'The battle's won', he called back when he was warned, 'my life's of no consequence now'. He followed the chaotic retreat up to the position Napoleon had occupied for most of the day at La Belle Alliance, and a few hundred yards further on he ran into Blucher and his staff, coming from the direction of Plancenoit. It represented the moment of total victory. The two commanders spent only a couple of minutes together, since there was a complete language barrier between them. But they shook hands across their horses, the Prussians agreed they would continue to pursue the French into the night and Wellington's troops would bivouac on the battlefield wherever they found themselves. With that, Wellington turned Copenhagen around and in the midsummer dusk retraced his steps across the length of the battlefield from La Belle Alliance back to the Mont St Jean ridge. By most estimates, some 47–52,000 men and more than 10,000 horses lay dead or dying around the shallow valley through which he now picked his way.[5] He went back up to the ridge, then along the road less than two miles to the inn at Waterloo which acted as his headquarters.

During the fighting Wellington had ridden around the battlefield with an entourage of about twenty people – his commanders, staff and messengers. At the end of the day he was, astonishingly, the only member of that command posse to emerge completely unscathed. All the others were dead, wounded or missing. 'The finger of providence was on me' as he said more than once, in some wonderment. Back at his headquarters he was joined by his old friend Miguel de Alava. In stunned and complete silence they ate a frugal meal together at a large table laid for many others. The Duke rose from the table about midnight to get some rest. He collapsed onto his bed and, like his soldiers in the field, fully clothed and filthy from the battle, surrendered immediately to the sleep of nervous exhaustion. About three o'clock in the morning Dr Hume visited him with latest reports from the battlefield and a list, a long list, of all the dead and missing among his fellow commanders. He sat impassively while Hume went through the names. Then, in what evolved to become one of his many celebrated aphorisms, Wellington said, 'Thank God I don't know what it is to lose a battle. But it is a pitiable

---

5. The battle site is remarkably small – just two-and-a-half-miles from west to east and less than a mile-and-a-half between the two opposing ridges. During less than eleven hours, 200,000 troops using some 47–60,000 horses fought within and around that space.

thing to gain one with the loss of so many of one's friends.' He suddenly put his hand out to the doctor. Hume took his hand. Wellington was silent; then he began to sob, the tears, said Hume, coursing down his face that was still almost completely black from the smoke and dirt of the battle.

This kept happening to Wellington in the weeks and months following Waterloo. He was very reluctant to speak about it. And when he did, he would begin to cry again. He said repeatedly, 'I have fought my last battle'. He wrote exactly those words in a letter to his brother; and again, in another letter to at least one of the adoring young ladies with whom he habitually corresponded. 'I have fought my last battle'. It was a cry from the heart as much as a statement of fact.

In the event, Wellington had thirty-one years of national politics ahead of him before he retired from public life in 1846. He died peacefully in 1852 in a decline of gentle melancholy. But there can be little doubt about the effect of Waterloo on his role as a military commander. As the man who had taken responsibility for more than twenty years in battle after battle, he had nothing left to give by the time that June day in 1815 had ended.

He was never as successful in politics as he had been as a military commander, but in his long life he bestrode British history from the 1780s to 1852, deep into the reign of Queen Victoria.[6] His most important contributions to allied victory over Napoleon lay in the tough campaigns of marching, sieges, skirmishes and battles in the Peninsular War – the campaigns that drained Napoleon's Empire while it was being pressured by other allies in Russia and Germany. In a way, he had already earned the right to administer, along with Marshal Blucher, the final coup de grace to Napoleon at Waterloo.

In a personal letter to the Prince Regent, Napoleon tried to place himself under the protection of British law as he abdicated for the second time. The 'British people', he wrote, were 'the most powerful, the most constant, and the most generous of my enemies'. He might have had Wellington in mind.

---

6. Nevertheless, his political life was eventful and worthy of the many studies devoted to it. He served twice as Prime Minister, led the Tory opposition, drove Catholic emancipation through Parliament, fiercely opposed electoral reform, served as Foreign Secretary under Robert Peel, and then maintained a pragmatic approach from the Lords to the new 'Conservatism' as Peel steadily developed it.

Queen Boudica. (*Painting, John Opie (1761–1807)*)

Alfred the Great. (*Bronze statue, Hamo Thornycroft, erected at Winchester 1899*)

Aethelflaid of Mercia. (*Statue by Edward George Bramwell 1913, in front of Tamworth Castle, depicted with her arm around nephew Aethelstan*). Tamworth Borough Council

Harold II. Statue at Waltham Abbey Church, Waltham Cross.

Harold II. Detail from the Bayeux Tapestry.

William I. Portrait, circa 1597–1618, unknown artist.

Empress Matilda. Detail in an image from the Gospel of Henry the Lion, circa 1188.

Edward I. Erected in Westminster Abbey, 1272-1307, thought to be a likeness.

William Marshal. Baron William Marshal Earl of Pembroke c 1146–1219 Appointed to Secure the observance of Magna Carta. (*Fully rounded cast, gilding by John Evan Thomas, heritagecollactions.parlaimant.uk*)

Edward III. Detail from bronze in Westminster Abbey.

Edward, Black Prince. From an engraving reproduced in Thomas Pennant's *A Tour of Wales*, 1781.

Henry V. From an anonymous Sixteenth Century portrait.

Francis Drake. Miniature, 1581, Nicholas Hilliard (1547–1619). (*Kunsthistoriches Museum*)

Walter Raleigh. Miniature, circa 1585, Nicholas Hilliard (1547–1619). (*NPG*)

Oliver Cromwell. Unfinished miniature, circa 1653, Samuel Cooper (1609-1672). (*Bowhill House*)

John Churchill. Portrait, circa 1685–1690, John Closterman (1660–1711). (*NPG*)

John Jervis. Portrait, undated, George Peter Alexander Healy (1813–1894).

Cuthbert Collingwood. Detail, undated painting by Henry Howard (1769–1847). (*Greenwich Hospital*)

Horatio Nelson. Portrait, 1800, Lemuel Abbott (1760/61- 1803). (*Royal Museums Greenwich*)

Thomas Cochrane. Portrait, 1830, James Ramsay (1789–1854).

John Moore. Portrait, undated, Thomas Lawrence (1769–1830). (*Gordon Highlanders*)

Arthur Wellesley. Portrait, 1815–16, Thomas Lawrence (1769–1830). (*Wellington Collection*)

FitzRoy Somerset. Watercolour, 1818, William Haines (1812–1884).

Herbert Kitchener. Photograph 1899, Alexander Bassano (1829–1913).

Douglas Haig. Photograph 1920, The Literary Digest History of the World War, NY, 1920.

John Jellico. Photograph 1925(?).
(*Library of Congress Bain Collection*)

David Beatty. Detail from image, HMS Queen Elizabeth 1916(?), unknown photographer.

John Gort. Photograph 1939. (*War Office Official Photographer*)

Hugh Dowding. Photograph, circa 1935. (*Ministry of Information Official Photographer*)

Harold Alexander. Photograph 1948. (*Nationaal Archief, Nederlands*)

Dudley Pound. Photograph 1939, Bassano and Vandyk Studios. (*NPG*)

Bernard Montgomery. Photograph 1944, E.G. Malindine, 5th Army Film & Photographic Unit. (*IWM*)

William Slim. Photograph, undated (1939–45), No 9 Army Film & Photographic Unit. (*IWM*)

Arthur Harris. Photograph 1941, unknown photographer. (*Crown Copyright*)

22

FitzRoy Somerset, Lord Raglan

Those who know of Lord Raglan usually associate him with the disastrous 'Charge of the Light Brigade' in 1855 during the Crimean War, and more broadly with the whole, poorly conducted operation in the Crimean Peninsula from 1853 to 1856. He was Commander-in-Chief of British forces in Crimea for most of that time. Those who know of him simply as Lord FitzRoy Somerset, before he was elevated to become Lord Raglan, would probably have a more positive view of his military career. At the age of twenty, he was a dashing and gallant young officer in Wellington's army that went to the Iberian Peninsula in 1808, serving with intelligence and distinction. At the age of twenty-seven, after many fierce engagements, he fought his last active battle at Waterloo. It cost him his right arm. Thirty-eight years later, he had just turned sixty-six when he was sent as British commander to the Crimean War, for which neither he, nor the nation that sent him, was remotely prepared. His demonstrable success as a young soldier is overshadowed by history's judgement that he was a tragic failure as a commander. That sense of failure almost seemed to kill him while he was still in the Crimea.

It is possible to explain, but hard to excuse, the way the British army conducted itself in the Crimea. As commander, Raglan must certainly take responsibility for what happened. But the blame for it is both shared and systemic in the British army after the triumph of Waterloo. Indeed, his great role model and mentor, Wellington, was one of those who held back military reform in the years when it should have gone ahead while the country basked in its victory over Napoleon. Raglan's career is a story of personal triumph and tragedy that encapsulated the two different eras in which he lived.

He was the ninth and youngest son of Henry Somerset, the Fifth Duke of Beaufort, born at Badminton House in Gloucester during September 1788. At the age of sixteen he was commissioned as a cornet in the 4th Light Dragoons and became a cavalry lieutenant in 1805. He was a smart and charming young man, going with Sir Arthur Paget – who as Lord Uxbridge was to command the cavalry at Waterloo – on a diplomatic visit to the Ottoman court in 1807. He was not particularly well-read nor a culturally rounded personality. He lived for the military and applied his undoubted intelligence predominantly to that. He was quick to see the military implications of anything that unfolded. He was made a captain in the 43rd Regiment of Foot and in that capacity was taken onto the staff of Arthur Wellesley – to become the Duke of Wellington – as aide-de-camp in July 1808. He was then, according to Elizabeth Longford, an 'apple-cheeked young man of nineteen' who quietly became respected for his intelligence, truthfulness and a certain 'exactitude' in the way he understood, and conveyed, orders.

It was in this role that FitzRoy Somerset was to distinguish himself both as a young fighting officer and a high-flier for the army of the future. He served Wellesley closely during all five years of the Peninsular War, becoming one of the three officers regarded by others as Wellesley's 'military family'.[1] He fought at Rolica and Vimiero, and at the battle of Porto in May 1809 and then in the ferocious battle of Talavera in July. Being on the general's staff didn't exempt a young officer from fighting with his own regiment during a battle itself, and FitzRoy Somerset did more of this than most. He was wounded at Busaco in September 1810. The following year he was moved from aide-de-camp to become acting military secretary to Wellesley and was riding beside him in four dreary engagements at Pombal, Sabugal, Fuentes de Onoro and El Bodon. After that he was promoted brevit major.

Then in 1812 his military star rose spectacularly at the ferocious storming of Badajoz. Wellesley pressed home the assault by sheer force of numbers attacking several dubious breaches simultaneously. When the cracks in French defences finally appeared, FitzRoy Somerset was first to the top of the San Vincent bastion, leading men into the streets behind the walls. In the resulting chaos, he was instrumental in finding the French governor of the city – quickly, while he was still alive – to secure the surrender. Three weeks later FitzRoy Somerset was promoted to lieutenant-colonel and was then forever back and forth among the front lines with Wellesley in a series of engagements that became famous names of the Peninsular War; Salamanca, Burgos, Vitoria, San Sebastian, Nive, Orthez, and finally in the siege of Toulouse. He was a close member of the general's staff at all of them and one of the few staff officers Wellesley genuinely liked and trusted. He emerged as a moderating influence on Wellesley's periodic irritation and anger. FitzRoy Somerset would smooth his commander's acerbic language and disguise some of the more insulting tones to other officers as he conveyed Wellesley's missives.

The relationship became even closer. Wellesley became the Duke of Wellington and FitzRoy Somerset, already taken to the Paris embassy to act as the Duke's secretary while he served as ambassador, married Wellington's niece in the joyful and celebratory atmosphere of peace in 1814. Lady Emily Harriet Wellesley-Pole was, by all accounts, a delightful young lady and certainly well-regarded by her uncle. The first of the Somerset's five children was already on the way in May 1815 when both Wellington and – now 'Sir' – FitzRoy Somerset were riding back to war to face Napoleon again, who had escaped from Elba and was embarked on a speculative 'Hundred Days' adventure to somehow grab his empire back.[2]

That campaign has been described in another chapter. In the scramble to occupy and hold Quatre Bras on Friday 16th June, Wellington and FitzRoy Somerset both

---

1. The other two were said to be Lord March, eldest son of the Duke of Richmond, and Captain Burgh, later Lord Downes.
2. The youngest of their five children – Katherine – witnessed the outbreak of the First World War before she died in 1915.

had to gallop for safety into the square of the 92nd Regiment, steeplechasing over the crouching infantrymen to get inside as French cavalry charged. On Sunday 18th FitzRoy Somerset was part of the command group that rode with Wellington back and forth across the Mont St Jean ridge as the duke fought his monumental battle of Waterloo. Like all Wellington's command group riding along the ridge, FitzRoy Somerset was wounded during that desperate day. As the farm at La Haye Sainte finally fell to French attacks in late afternoon, Napoleon's skirmishers were able to swarm towards the foot of the ridge to cover French artillery being dragged closer to allied lines. FitzRoy Somerset was riding beside the duke as they assessed this new crisis in the battle. His left arm was pressed against Wellington's right arm as they spoke to each other over the noise of battle. A musket ball shattered FitzRoy's right arm. Depending on the angle of the shot, possibly from one of the skirmishers with powerful rifles, it might otherwise have hit Wellington.[3] But FitzRoy Somerset was taken away and had all but a stump of his arm amputated. Afterwards, he was fit enough to participate in the Army of Occupation in France until May the following year.

Like many a rising military star, he decided to dabble in politics and had two relatively brief periods as Member of Parliament, from 1818–20 as member for Truro and again from 1826, before standing down in 1829. But he had returned to the British Embassy in Paris for a while, and then followed Wellington as his secretary when the duke became Master General of the Ordnance, and then again when Wellington was made Commander-in-Chief of the forces in 1827.

FitzRoy Somerset's military credentials were impeccable; an extensive and gallant battle record, years of experience as a staff officer at the highest level and a growing career in the peacetime army – all in the reflected glow of Wellington's patronage and approval during the peak years of the duke's military prestige. When Wellington became prime minister in 1829, he stepped away from his military career completely. Sir FitzRoy Somerset was then a substantial military figure in his own right. He was made lieutenant general in 1838 and when Wellington died in 1852 – though not without some official reservations – FitzRoy Somerset was confirmed as his successor Commander-in-Chief of the forces. It must have seemed like a fitting tribute to them both. FitzRoy Somerset was elevated to become Baron Raglan of Monmouthshire. It seemed just as logical that, as Lord Raglan, he should command the force sent to war with Russia in 1854. It would be a joint British, French and Turkish expeditionary force, with Britain as the senior allied partner, though there was no overall coalition commander. Someone with diplomatic skill as well as military pedigree was obviously required.

The conflict began as a dispute between Russia and Turkey. The Russian orthodox church claimed guardianship over the Holy Places in Jerusalem, and then extended its protection to all Orthodox Christians within the Ottoman empire. Britain and

---

3. In February 1820, James Ings, one of the Cato Street plotters, had followed Wellington as he walked towards Green Park, intending to stab him once he entered it. But Fitzroy Somerset happened to bump into the Duke just then and they changed direction and walked together instead up to Apsley House. Unwittingly, Fitzroy Somerset had this time almost certainly saved the Duke's life.

France realised, correctly, that this was a manoeuvre by Russia to further undermine the foundations of the staggering Ottoman empire, probably to take Ottoman territory in the Danubian principalities and move on towards Constantinople for a bridge from the Black Sea into the Mediterranean – an erstwhile Russian geopolitical objective. To protect the existing balance of power in Europe and keep Russia out of the near east and the Balkans, London and Paris allied with Turkey to stall a Russian army that had already moved down the Danube valley as far as Bucharest. The allies sent their joint force to Varna on the Black Sea coast, barring the way to Constantinople. Russian forces quickly withdrew. At that point, the operation could have been regarded as having achieved its objectives.

But the western allies had long wanted to neutralise Russia's Black Sea Fleet and this seemed the perfect opportunity; invade Crimea, seize the major naval port of Sevastopol and destroy the Russian fleet in the process. Raglan himself, and the more professional soldiers near him, were openly sceptical about the prospects. Was the force intended to occupy the significant territory of Crimea – in which case it was far too small? Or was it merely a 'grand raid' to destroy the Black Sea fleet and its base – in which case, what was the force supposed to do once Sevastopol was in allied hands amidst hostile territory? No one was able to offer an answer and politicians in both London and Paris were keen on the idea. No version of a general staff then existed in Britain which might have considered the viability of the whole plan. Sitting in Varna, Raglan first expressed, but then suppressed, his own doubts as the force moved from the Black Sea coast to an invasion further south deep into the Crimea.

Raglan was a man of even temperament, cool under pressure. He spoke excellent French and was a model of courtesy with allies. He had a lifetime of military experience behind him. But he was now sixty-six, his mental capacity was not what it was, and for all his years at Wellington's side, he had never himself commanded a formation larger than a battalion. Though his military judgements during the campaign were certainly not all faulty, at key moments he seemed to veer between over-caution and reckless risk-taking.

His own limitations, however, were symptomatic of the greater sclerosis that had gripped the British Army after its triumphs over Napoleon's forces. Wellington had believed in the innate quality of key people in the command chain, but was not a natural reformer of the system that produced them. His most significant victories in India and the Iberian Peninsula were won through manoeuvre warfare – moving quickly, fighting flexibly, supplying efficiently. The battle of Waterloo, in contrast, had been a grim, attritional affair, emphasising drill, discipline and character. And it was the Waterloo experience that seemed to influence the army most in the following years. There was minimal reflection on where the technologies of warfare might be heading, or the implications, for example, of the more powerful Minie rifle that was replacing the faithful Brown Bess musket among the British forces in Crimea. At about 100,000 men, the army had long since been reduced to a quarter of its 1815 strength, and half of it was stationed permanently abroad. This was the portion of the army that had up-to-date operational experience, in India, Kandy, Burma, the Cape Colony, in the Ashanti wars, or in China. There was almost no rotation of units and the other half of the army left in Britain, a good proportion of whom were in Ireland, had already lost most of the organisational cohesion it had developed under Wellington. It had fallen back into a collection of semi-autonomous regiments, raised and paid for by prominent aristocrats. The purchase of commissions had therefore become rife again and meritocratic promotion was even harder to obtain. There had seldom been so great a social distance between officers and soldiers. And the quality of the soldiers declined steadily amid their poor living conditions. For the officers, the small field army in Britain seemed to become more sartorially magnificent in direct proportion to its operational inexperience.

This, not to mention the precipitous decline in the efficiency of logistical trains to accompany troops going abroad, were all part of the legacy that Raglan, with his own high reputation, took with him to the southern shores of the Crimean Peninsula. His headquarters were barely competent and proper staff work within the army had more or less ceased. Raglan's five young aides-de-camp were there to perform the role in which he had excelled as a young man. Four of them were his nephews; the other related to him by marriage, and none of them had any previous experience of staff work. Five of his six divisional generals were over sixty. One was thirty-five and Queen Victoria's cousin, but had never been in a war. Of the other five, only two had ever commanded brigades in action – nothing larger. Within the cavalry, Lords Lucan and Cardigan, who were to be so involved in the debacle of the Light Brigade, were brothers-in-law and for years had heartily detested each other. Keeping them physically apart actually influenced the way Raglan sited his cavalry bases. More to the point, both Lucan and Cardigan were sticklers for cavalry drill and parade ground manoeuvres. But both were complete amateurs, neither with any previous experience at all of commanding in battle.[4] Raglan did have one or two good professional commanders, like the incomparable Sir Colin Campbell who had served for many years with Moore and Wellington, and in India and China, but who could not escape the fact that he was a Glasgow carpenter's son. Campbell was only a brigade commander. But Raglan would have been well-served to have him directly at his side. Instead, Raglan's aides were young and inexperienced; his senior commanders old and inexperienced. Raglan himself had been through five years of campaigning in situations just like this with Wellington, but his own lack of practical command over comparably large forces merely emphasised the limitations that age and infirmity were now placing on him.

Nevertheless, the Sevastopol campaign began well enough when allied forces landed in September 1854 and after a hard-fought engagement, defeated the Russians who occupied a good defensive position across the Alma River. At that point, it would have been possible to go straight for a weakly defended Sevastopol that lay to the south and take the north shore, leaving the port at the allies' mercy. But French forces imposed continuing delays and Raglan was making tactical decisions by consensus rather than

---

4. The nearest Cardigan had come to real gunfire was in a duel in 1841, where he had used a specially made pistol with concealed rifling and a hair trigger – no more illegal than anything else in dueling, but widely regarded as dishonourable. Lord Lucan had never faced an enemy in battle, but was nevertheless popularly known as 'the exterminator' since he was so ruthless a landlord during the Great Famine in Ireland.

Wellingtonian diktat. The allies went in for a 'flank march' eastwards around Sevastopol, putting themselves to the south and south-west of the port from where they began a siege bombardment. British forces took the small port of Balaclava as their supply base further south and defended it with a thin screen of 4,000 cavalry and some troops and guns facing to the north and north-east from where any Russian forces marching to the relief of Sevastopol would emerge. The forces defending Balaclava were thin because most were involved in the siege and the anticipated infantry assault on Sevastopol, six miles away.

On 24th October Raglan received intelligence from a native Crimean spy that the Russians were approaching to attack British communication lines north of Balaclava with 25,000 men. Unlike Wellington, though like many others of his era, Raglan didn't set much store in spying and intelligence and did not react one way or another to the information. The following day Raglan's position was attacked by substantial Russian forces which quickly took the Causeway Heights, cutting British communication lines to Sevastopol and overlooking Balaclava itself. Raglan ordered two infantry divisions around Sevastopol to come up in reinforcement. But for the time being all he had to defend the position was the cavalry, alongside a weakened Highland Infantry battalion plus an already shaken Turkish battalion. In fact, his outnumbered forces fought very well. The understrength 93rd Highland battalion, commanded by Colin Campbell, repulsed a strong force of Russian hussars, and then the Heavy Brigade, outnumbered three to one, charged the bulk of the Russian cavalry and drove it off the Causeway Heights. So far, the day had been a great success in repulsing attacks by vastly superior forces. And the Heavy Brigade, in particular, have seldom been credited for their notable victory up to that point. Raglan's problem, however, was that while his 'heavies' could chase Russian cavalry off the Heights, he nevertheless needed to send infantry up there to win it back and secure the ground. And the reinforcing infantry had still not arrived – indeed, not understanding the vulnerability of Raglan's position – they were positively lethargic in responding to his orders. They put breakfast first.

Like most military disasters, the 'Charge of the Light Brigade' that followed was the result of a cumulative series of mistakes and misunderstandings which drove the folly onwards. Raglan had taken his command position on the Sapun escarpment, the highest ground about two miles opposite Causeway Heights and well over a mile from the valley below where his cavalry was now assembled. With his single left arm he was swinging his telescope from horizon to horizon as he waited anxiously for his two infantry divisions to arrive from Sevastopol. But each order to his cavalry commanders below took around thirty minutes to arrive, as riders picked their way down the steep and treacherous path from his command position. But Raglan was keen to exploit the success the heavy cavalry had just enjoyed at Causeway Heights and ordered Lord Lucan, commander of the cavalry division, to take his troopers back up there and hold it, pending the arrival of his late-running infantry. But the wording of the order was ambiguous and Lucan thought he was to wait until the infantry arrived before he moved off – a safe enough assumption, since sending cavalry to *occupy* the Heights without infantry support, when Russian numbers were so superior, was a dangerous game. In fact, Raglan wanted to act precipitously, in the hope that British infantry and artillery would arrive in time to support the otherwise vulnerable cavalry on the Heights.

The British had already placed several heavy naval guns in six big redoubts along the line of the Heights. Four of the redoubts had been taken by the Russians and now, just as Raglan was worrying about bigger enemy movements, his staff spotted groups of Russian horsemen preparing to haul away the British guns lying unattended in the redoubts they occupied. Raglan immediately sent an order to Lucan to 'advance rapidly to the front – follow the enemy and try to prevent the enemy carrying away the guns'. It was marked 'immediate' and Raglan stressed to young Captain Louis Nolan – an excellent horseman who reckoned he could get down to the cavalry faster than any of the other riders around Raglan just then – 'tell Lord Lucan the cavalry is to attack immediately'. But when he received it, some twenty-five minutes later, Lucan, who was positioned at an elevation more than three hundred feet below Raglan, was simply non-plussed by the order. He could not see the British naval guns Raglan was concerned about. The only guns he could see were Russian guns on the higher ground as he looked to his left at the end of the two-mile long valley that stretched in front of him. While his cavalry had been deployed at the western end of the valley for some hours, he had not thought to send out scouts to see what was happening on the other sides of the many hills that surrounded him. The excitable and insolent Captain Nolan, trying to goad Lucan with the implied authority of Raglan himself, made vague gestures both at the valley where Lucan could see no guns, and the one where he could see far too many of them.

Sending unsupported cavalry to recover British naval guns from the redoubts on the Causeway Heights was risky in any case. Sending them down the valley (though it was actually more of a depression) in a funnel held by the enemy between Causeway Heights and the Fedioukine Hills on the other side, was pure suicide. Nevertheless, Lucan determined without further clarification that this must be Raglan's intention and that logically, the Light Brigade would lead the charge with his Heavy Brigade in support. He rode over to Lord Cardigan, commanding the Light Brigade, to convey the order in person. Lords Lucan and Cardigan were each severely deficient in many human qualities, but physical courage was not among them. Their exchange has been preserved for posterity. Lucan said, 'Lord Cardigan, you will attack the Russians in the valley'. 'Certainly my Lord', replied Cardigan without hesitation, 'but allow me to point out to you that there is a battery in front, a battery on each flank, and the ground is covered in Russian riflemen'. 'I cannot help that', said Lucan, 'it is Lord Raglan's positive order that the Light Brigade is to attack the enemy'. Cardigan didn't reply. He simply rode away, determining that he was facing his own near-certain death in the next few minutes. It was all a tragi-comic failure of command from two vain and inexperienced popinjays who couldn't use their common sense in the confusion of war. Even then, the tragedy might have been averted, since Captain Nolan spurred forward as the Light Brigade began trotting down the wrong valley, shouting and waving his sword toward the Causeway Heights. He rode across Cardigan himself, presumably trying to recover the situation. But Cardigan ignored him and Nolan was suddenly caught in a shell-burst which killed him instantly. He appears to have been the first casualty of the charge.

The numbers in the Charge of the Light Brigade tell their own story. Officially, 676 riders set out from the 17th Lancers, the 4th and 13th Light Dragoons, and the 8th and 11th Hussars. Twenty-five minutes later, 195 of them rode back. Killed and wounded numbered 247, most of the others were captured. At least 470 horses were lost. During that twenty-five minutes, the Light Brigade had trotted, cantered and then galloped through the gauntlet of fire, only charging flat out when they were very close to the guns in front of them. They took the Russian artillery position. The survivors rallied and then charged the Russian cavalry waiting behind the guns, forcing them in shock to withdraw to the far end of the valley. But Russian lancers had closed in behind the Light Brigade along the gun line they had just taken, barring their escape. Smaller groups of survivors had to fight their way out of the position again, the same way they had broken in, extricating themselves from the hopeless position their action had created.[5] Cardigan had disappeared. Having shown undoubted courage, riding out in front of his troopers and first to reach the gun line, crashing through the space between two guns firing directly at him, he decided he should not be mixing it with the common soldiery in the vulgar brawl that followed. He had led the charge, was still alive, and had done his job; so he left his troopers to look after themselves, retracing his steps, straight back to lunch on his yacht moored in Balaclava harbour.

The infantry, who might have supported even so crazy a charge, were still not in position. More to the point, Lucan did not commit his Heavy Brigade in the way Cardigan had assumed he would. Lucan held them back early in the action, reasoning that there was no point in sacrificing the heavies just to compound the blunder of committing the Light Brigade. The commanders immediately fell to fierce argument over responsibility for the massacre. It hinged on the understanding of poorly drafted orders. And Captain Nolan was dead, so it must have been his fault.

It was, of course, a systemic failure. Contrary to popular mythology, British forces won at Balaclava – and against the odds. But the loss of the Light Brigade was indefensible. The Highland Infantry and then the Heavy Brigade had fought magnificently earlier in the day against vastly superior numbers, and the Light Brigade had pressed home a suicidal attack in a way that profoundly shook their Russian counterparts. The Russian push against Raglan's position effectively ended at that point. But Raglan's cavalry commanders were simply incompetent and then lacked the moral courage to face the truth afterwards.

Naturally, the buck must stop with Raglan. He didn't have time to correct the most egregious defects of the army he took to the Crimea, but there is no evidence that he ever tried. He was slow to appreciate his own tactical position and slow in adjusting to the movement of forces. After Alma, he twice had Sevastopol at his mercy, once immediately after the battle, and again, in one of the early stages of the siege. But he kept giving shaken Russian forces time to recover. The famous 'flank march' on

---

5. Though, in fact, Russian lancers were surprisingly ineffective in this role. Four of them surrounded Cardigan and he just swung his sabre at the lance points and they more or less let him pass.

Sevastopol, rather than a straight occupation of its north shore, was a major strategic error. And when the Causeway Heights were attacked, he seemed to panic and resort to risky tactics that turned into catastrophe when they were misunderstood.

Still, the following month his forces won at the battle of Inkerman, a confused affair over seven hours after Russian forces launched a powerful, surprise attack on the outskirts of the weakened allied siege lines. It was called 'the soldiers' battle' because much of it was in fog, and lines of command on both sides were tenuous and more confused than usual. Units simply fought what was in front of them, applying their own tactical good sense. In the end, Inkerman was a triumph of dogged defence by British and French forces. The upshot was that the Russians would not attack allied forces in open battle again and France became thereafter the senior partner in the alliance. By April 1855 there were 110,000 French troops in Crimea, compared to 30,000 British. Nevertheless, Raglan was made a Field Marshal, while his troops were still stuck outside Sevastopol for the winter.

Everything was lacking in his army, and in particular hygiene. Cholera became rife among the poorly clothed and under-nourished ranks. At the height of the health crisis only 9,000 British troops were reported fit for duty; 23,000 were reported sick. Over forty percent of them were dying in the military hospitals, where Florence Nightingale and her volunteer nurses didn't at that stage fully appreciate the importance of maintaining good hygiene standards. Virtually every aspect of logistical provision remained appalling. Raglan was not the man to take the supply situation by the scruff of the neck. The whole expedition became a scandal in Victorian Britain. Cardigan had unilaterally returned home, and while he was basking in the adulation of having led the Light Brigade's heroic charge, Raglan was being roundly condemned in Parliament and the press.

On 18 June 1855 – forty years to the day after Waterloo – Raglan launched an all-out assault on Sevastopol. It was a complete failure. Suffering already with cholera, and in a deep depression, Raglan died outside Sevastopol ten days later. The war went on. Sevastopol was eventually taken by the allies and Russia's Black Sea Fleet effectively destroyed. There was a peace treaty, signed in Paris in March 1856, which restricted Russia's influence along the Black Sea coast and facilitated the withdrawal of the allies from the most pyrrhic of pyrrhic victories in Crimea itself.

Raglan's body had long since been returned to Britain and interred in the church at Badminton. Over the years, his family and supporters have tried to rescue his reputation from the shadow of the Crimea, and particularly from that day of both success and fiasco at Balaclava.

Raglan's memory certainly deserves some relief. He was a good and dedicated lifelong soldier. But as Commander-in-Chief he was no reformer when the army desperately needed reform, and as a battlefield commander – thirty-nine years after he had last been on a battlefield – he failed to provide the right sort of leadership when it suddenly mattered most.

23

Field Marshal Lord Kitchener

Lord Kitchener is forever associated with a famous 1914 recruiting poster at the outbreak of the First World War where, with his luxuriant, curving moustache he stares determinedly forward and points an accusing finger straight at the viewer. The slogan the government intended was that, 'Britons, Lord Kitchener Wants You'. But in visual terms the poster nowhere names Lord Kitchener himself. It simply says 'Britons' above his stern face and 'Wants You' below it. His image alone served for his name. The only other words below that, in smaller print are, 'Join Your Country's Army. God Save the King'. It was enough. And variations on that iconic theme appeared for many years; imitated in many other countries around the world.

Kitchener was dead less than two years after the appearance of that first image. But the fact that he was a famous enough soldier not to need a name on his poster is an indication of his national importance. The influence Kitchener had over Britain's war effort in the twenty-two months left to him could not guarantee that Britain would win its war against Germany and the Central Powers. But his influence was critical in guaranteeing that Britain would, at least, not lose it. He created a citizens' army that first went into action on the Somme just twenty-five days after his death. In 1914 the professional army – the 'old contemptibles' – had fought Britain's battles on the western front long enough for Kitchener's new citizen army to arrive in numbers in 1916 – the first and most tangible result of the full mobilization of society fighting the total war that now engulfed the European powers. Without 'Kitchener's Army' of miners, butchers, bakers, clerks, barrow-boys, bus-conductors, teachers, servants and solicitors, Britain could not have sustained the effort to see the war through to the end.

Horatio Herbert Kitchener was a complex man; idolized in public by the time of the First World War, respected by many for his military skills and judgements; heartily disliked, indeed detested, by many more. He was a man of great personal accomplishment and natural ability. He could be sensitive and politically astute. But he was driven by relentless ambition, a bully to his staff, ruthless and emotionally repressed to the point where – even when it mattered in command terms – he was an uncommunicative loner who didn't care whether he was understood or not. Kitchener was a tall man, 6ft 2in with a mop of blonde hair that he plastered down and, it was said, an intimidating gaze. One journalist said he had 'steady passionless eyes…his face is harsh, and neither appeals for affection nor stirs dislike'. He grew a large moustache to increase the gravitas of his persona, particularly with foreigners in mind. He was a lifelong bachelor – a source of constant but unsubstantiated rumours about his sexuality – who had one very close young friend all his professional life and showed general indifference to everyone else, regardless of rank or status.[1] Lloyd George said that Kitchener's mind operated like a lighthouse, sending out a penetrating beam for a few moments before moving on and leaving utter darkness behind it.

He was set in the classic mould of an imperial officer of the time, serving in the Levant, in Cyprus, Anatolia, Egypt, the Sudan, South Africa and in India. His first and only European command post was when he was made Secretary of State for War in 1914, which in fact was a political post. Kitchener was born in County Kerry in 1850 to English parents, but then lived in Switzerland as a boy, educated in Montreux, before he went to the Royal Military Academy at Woolwich to train as a Royal Engineer. He had a scientific and intensely practical turn of mind. He spoke French fluently, and when he was sent to western Palestine in 1874 as a mapping survey officer, he learned Arabic. Indeed, his Arabic became so good, he could adjust his dialect between the Bedouin tribes of Egypt as opposed to those in the Sudan. With fellow officer Claude R. Conder, he produced an eight-volume map survey of Palestine west of the river Jordan, which provided the grid system still in use today and marked out some of the geographical features that became modern political borders. In 1878 he was sent to survey Cyprus and was made vice-consul in Anatolia the following year.

There followed fifteen years in Egypt and the Sudan which established Kitchener's military reputation, for good and bad, and made him a national figure in Britain. In 1883, as a captain, he was made second in command of an Egyptian cavalry regiment and tasked with helping to reconstruct Egyptian forces. This was necessary after Britain intervened to administer Egypt in 1882, under the nominal sovereignty of the Khedive, who was himself operating under the relaxed overlordship of the Ottoman Sultan of Turkey. Working through British administrators with just over a hundred British officers to re-make the Egyptian army, Kitchener became part of an imperial 'arrangement' in Egypt, which lasted over seventy years, though it was never a formal act of colonization. But it suited Cairo, Istanbul and London alike, displacing French influence in the region. Further south, the Islamic state of the self-proclaimed Mahdi ruler, leading Dervishes and many Hadendoa warriors, was a grumbling threat to Ottoman/Egyptian authority, such as it was, over Sudan. Rudyard Kipling wrote admiringly of their fearsome effectiveness.

In 1884 Kitchener was a staff officer on General Wolseley's unsuccessful expedition to rescue General Charles Gordon, willfully besieged in Khartoum by the Mahdi's forces late in 1884, after the frankly mad Gordon tried too hard to civilize Sudan in the name of aggressive Christian imperialism. He paid for it with his head. But the next year Mahdi died and was succeeded by Abdullah al-Khalifa, whose even more fundamentalist beliefs began genuinely to worry the British and outrage popular opinion at home, particularly in light of the jingoistic emotion triggered by Gordon's death.

In 1886 Kitchener was 'Pasha' (Lord or General), leading Egyptian forces against Mahdist rebels at Handub, where he was wounded in the face. He had a natural squint that was made worse by this injury with the result that he seldom made direct eye-

---

1. That friend was Captain Oswald Fitzgerald, who drowned with him on *HMS Hampshire* in June 1916.

contact with others; another element in his aloof mannerisms. However, his methodical approach to command was effective and drew admiration from the authorities in both Cairo and London. Sir Evelyn Baring (Lord Cromer), Britain's man in Cairo, described Kitchener's soldiering as 'the most able I have come across in my time'. By 1892, as a British brigadier, he had become 'Sirdar' – Commander-in-Chief – of the Egyptian army.

In 1896, European imperialism reached a critical point in Egypt and Sudan. Prime Minister Lord Salisbury made a shrewd geopolitical decision. Italy was trying to seize Abyssinia (Ethiopia) as an imperial possession, a policy of which London approved. But Italian forces were losing badly against local Mahdist forces who now threatened to take Eritrea and move into the Horn of Africa.[2] Simultaneously, an ambitious French expedition had set off from Dakar on the Atlantic coast, to march right across Africa with the objective of conquering Sudan, taking control of the upper Nile waters, and thereby pressuring the British out of Egypt. Salisbury now ordered Kitchener to take a force and invade northern Sudan. This was designed to take pressure off the Italians and satisfy the public's growing appetite to 'avenge General Gordon'. But the mission also involved secret, sealed orders to Kitchener, to be opened only when he had captured Khartoum.

In contrast to the failed Wolseley expedition twelve years previously, Kitchener's march to Khartoum was not the dash of a relief column. He had time to prepare properly to take a force of 15,000 Egyptian troops, later augmented by almost 9,000 British regulars, over 580 miles south of Wadi Halfa (the border between Egypt and Sudan) across the Nubian desert and into the upper Nile. In the best traditions of Marlborough and Wellington, Kitchener prepared his logistics with great care. He secured Dongola province en route and then paused for a year while the Sudan Military Railway was built over two-thirds of the distance to Khartoum. Disassembled gunboats were brought up by rail, to operate along the Upper Nile where it became navigable around Khartoum during the summer. Telegraph lines were built in all directions as the army advanced. By July 1898 Kitchener brought up his reinforcements and was ready to make his move on Khartoum, which stood on the east bank of the Nile. But the Khalifa left only a small force in Khartoum and instead assembled most of his large army ten miles away on the western bank of the river north of the sprawling Mahdist capital and site of the Mahdi's sacred tomb at Omdurman. It was here, on 2nd September that the Khalifa's 52,000 warriors would confront the 20,000 of the Egyptian/British force.

In fact, the numbers were irrelevant. The Khalifa had a clear battle plan for his forces as well as a fallback option that made the best use of the ground he had chosen for the confrontation. But it was all for nothing. Kitchener's gunboat and land artillery were hitting the Mahdist forces at 3,000 yards, their shells fused for airbursts; the

---

2. The Horn of Africa was the most sensitive part of Britain's whole Egypt/Sudan imperial policy, namely the need always to protect the route to India. The 'fit of absent-mindedness' by which the peak of the British Empire was said to be formed, was built around an obsession to protect all access, whether from Africa, the near east or central Asia, to India, the greatest jewel in the imperial crown.

infantry, firing new Lee-Metford rifles with their ten-round magazines, opened up inside 1,800 yards, and at something around 1,700 yards the new Maxim machine gun, and some older Gatling guns, fired ten rounds a second at oncoming warriors. The Mahdists launched themselves in disciplined ranks, suicidally, at the crescent of Kitchener's thin line. At 800 yards all battalions were fully engaged in rapid fire. Not a single warrior made it as far as the Egyptian/British crescent – just as well since Kitchener had nothing in reserve and his whole force had their backs to the river. His battle line was strung out and tactically vulnerable. He never explained whether he realized this, or simply had such faith in modern firepower to know the Mahdists would never reach it. It might have been a different story if they had. Then Kitchener moved his units forward to complete a series of local encirclements and prevent survivors falling back into the defences of Omdurman. The 21st Lancers, to which a young Lieutenant Winston Churchill was attached, engaged in the last full-scale cavalry charge in British military history. It was a ferocious dash incurring significant losses that had scant tactical value and took the Lancers out of the reckoning as a reconnaissance asset to discover where the Mahdists were trying to reform – cavalry yet again, and for the final time, 'galloping at everything' as Wellington had sourly observed many years previously.[3]

The Mahdists had attacked all out and directly into the rising sun. By 8.30 that morning it was all over. Some 30,000 of the Khalifa's 52,000 force were dead or wounded, as against fewer than fifty dead and 382 wounded among Kitchener's men. To this day, it isn't clear how much encouragement Kitchener gave to his troops – wittingly or otherwise – to murder the Mahdist wounded, apparently 'to remember Gordon'. Inside Omdurman thousands of Christians and enslaved women from all over Africa were freed, before Kitchener commanded that the Mahdi's tomb be blown up, the Mahdi's body disinterred, beheaded (tit-for-tat for Gordon), and thrown into the Nile. Many professional soldiers, including Churchill, were ashamed to be associated with Omdurman's aftermath. Even Queen Victoria was tearful and appalled when she heard about it. Kitchener wrote her a personal letter of apology. But Mahdist power was broken, though there followed some months of nasty follow-up operations before F.R. Wingate finally defeated the remnants of the Khalifa's forces at Umm Diwaykarat in November 1899.

Meanwhile, there were Kitchener's sealed and secret orders from Lord Salisbury. These now instructed Kitchener that, if successful at Khartoum, he was to enact the real reason for the expedition; to move south and occupy all of Sudan, forestalling, and if necessary, confronting the French expedition marching from Accra. By then, the French had established themselves in the fort at Fashoda, after the considerable feat of marching from west to east across Africa.[4] Kitchener's force arrived at Fashoda (present day Kodok in South Sudan) on 18th September, barely two weeks after Omdurman,

---

3. Though it should be noted that a young Churchill wrote an extremely perceptive and mature account of it all in *The River War*, published in 1899.
4. It was quite a march. It took two years, fending off local attacks, fever and the privations of traversing both forests and mountains. The troops had spent five days and nights crossing swamplands in which they had to remain upright at all times.

and he instructed the tiny French force – which he easily outnumbered – to leave immediately. Thence followed the famous 'Fashoda Incident' which brought Britain and France to the brink of open war. The troops swapped pleasantries and exchanged gifts of jam and champagne, whilst keeping their weapons trained on each other's camps. Kitchener followed his orders but dealt very diplomatically with his French counterpart general – complimenting him on the logistical feats of his force and not objecting to the flying of the French Tricolor alongside British and Egyptian flags. For almost three months both camps lived 'in polite antagonism' as Churchill put it at the time. In truth, Fashoda was a pestilential camel stop, reduced to an island during the flood season. But it was the basis of an extraordinary French territorial claim that set off much rabble rousing in both Paris and London. In the end, Paris had too much to lose by a colonial war with Britain at that moment and backed down, agreeing to leave Sudan completely. From then onwards, Egypt and Sudan would operate under Egyptian (and formally also Ottoman) suzerainty and tight *de facto* British control.

Kitchener was a national hero and in the public mind, a natural winner. His driving ambition was nourished by the adulation and he had actively been cultivating at least some of the press. Correspondents from *The Times*, *New York Herald*, *The Manchester Guardian*, and *The Daily Chronicle* all accompanied his Sudan expedition. In particular, he worked with G.W. Steevens of *The Daily Mail*, who sent back immediate and very perceptive first-hand accounts of the campaign that became a best-selling book in 1898.

In his own individualist way Kitchener also set about reshaping the governance of Sudan, since he was now appointed Governor-General. He set up a college to train for government, open to all-comers He improved communications, initiated more irrigation schemes, rebuilt mosques, guaranteed freedom of religion for all and actively tried to prevent evangelical Christian missionaries flooding into Sudan to convert the heathen. Notwithstanding the lasting distaste for the aftermath of Omdurman and the relentless pursuit of Khalifa's Mahdists, Kitchener's whole campaign in Sudan represented the high point of his success as a military commander, before his subsequent strategic importance took on more political aspects.

At the other end of the continent, the Second South African War – the Anglo-Boer War – from 1899 to 1902 that followed hard on the Sudan campaign could hardly have been more different. Kitchener's role in it, however, suggested some familiar parallels.

The war arose out of a long-standing and increasingly bitter power struggle for colonial dominance between British authorities in Cape Colony and Natal as against the Boer settlers mainly in the self-declared republics of Transvaal and the Orange Free State. In 1899, buoyed with the sudden wealth of diamond and gold mines in Transvaal, Boer leaders felt sufficiently provoked to push their case to outright military confrontation. They declared war on Britain in October, gambling – not unreasonably – that the British empire might simply lack the political will to prevent a series of *faits accompli* by self-sufficient farmers who could now afford to buy weapons from anywhere. The Boers were a good deal more hostile to indigenous and incoming tribal peoples – not to mention the white British 'Uitlander' settlers – than the British colonial administration in Cape Colony and Natal, but they were not fighting to build themselves a mere colony, but rather a national homeland. And their gamble seemed a good one, at least until the end of 1900. They had German and French support and London's initial military response was largely incompetent.

Within eight weeks, British tactics were ruthlessly exposed by expert Boer marksmen using Mauser rifles, smokeless cartridges and their own 'komando' techniques. Boer forces out-manoeuvred the British almost at will. Ironically, as Allan Mallinson points out, the British plight would have been even worse had the Boers not created famous sieges at Ladysmith, Mafeking and Kimberley. For British commanders were very experienced at running besieged settlements, and sieges tied up large numbers of Boer fighters who would have been better employed elsewhere, while the sieges gave Britain time to mobilise reinforcements. The siege of Ladysmith brought British attempts to relieve it by taking the high ground at Spion Kop in January 1900. That famous defeat to a smaller Boer force was the low point for the British army.

But by then the strategy was already swinging in London's favour. The very experienced Field Marshal Lord Roberts was sent out to run the war at the beginning of 1900, along with considerable reinforcements. Kitchener was sent with Roberts – who always thought very highly of him – as his second in command. With a four to one superiority in troops and a ten to one dominance in artillery, the British simply overwhelmed Boer forces in a series of conventional engagements, invading and annexing first the Orange Free State and then the Transvaal, sweeping through Johannesburg before entering Pretoria. The war was effectively won by autumn 1900 and Roberts went home to become the Army's Commander-in-Chief, leaving Kitchener in command. But if conventional operations were finished, the 'bitter-enders' among Boer fighters, led mainly by Christian de Wit, then began a powerful guerrilla campaign against British forces that extended deep into the spring of 1902.

The military response to the bitter-enders had been designed by Roberts before he went home, to deal, as he thought, with the remnants of the conflict. But Kitchener actually faced a full-on guerrilla challenge – over a hundred komando groups accounting for some 25,000 men – in a new phase of the war. Kitchener tried to buy them off with generous terms but when that failed, he carried through the Roberts plan on a grand scale, applying his characteristically cold logic. He created a command train and a mobile HQ for his staff, and embarked on a huge scorched earth campaign – burning 30,000 farms, destroying crops, poisoning wells – to deprive the guerrillas of supplies. He employed armoured trains, laid thousands of miles of barbed wire, built chains of some 8,000 blockhouses, driving guerrilla forces up against them as he 'cleared' one area after another. Most controversially, he created 'camps of refuge' for the families of those whose farms had been destroyed and whose men were 'on komando'. Kitchener was uncharacteristically vague as to whether these camps were merely to take Boer families out of the war, or to punish them for their husbands and fathers. Either way, concentration camps, as they undoubtedly became, were overwhelmed, undersupplied, and the breeding ground for disease. They were chronically overcrowded and witnessed shocking death rates. At the peak, they held some 111,000 people, 38,000 of whom died, 26,000 of them women and children. When humanitarian campaigners in Britain expressed their outrage, Kitchener used martial law provisions to prevent his critics returning to South Africa. Quite quickly, responsibility for the camps was transferred from the military to civil authorities and the situation improved dramatically. But the effects of the camps could not be undone and the moral stain was permanent.

By the beginning of 1902 as more guerrilla leaders 'came in' from the Velt, the Boers were being steadily forced towards a peace treaty; eventually concluded at Vereeniging in May. And Kitchener was now arguing fiercely with Alfred Milner, the Governor of Cape Colony, and the government in London that the Boers should not be humiliated or forcibly Anglicized – as Milner fully intended. Kitchener was sympathetic to Louis Botha's demands that the Transvaal and the Orange Free State be recognised as sovereign but with a special relationship under overall British administration. London wouldn't go along with this, but Kitchener argued the case and was clear that the Boer community must be offered some future prospects of self-government.

In London there was grim satisfaction in a messy victory. It had cost over £270 million, by far the greatest war expense since the struggles against Napoleon, and had eventually involved over 300,000 troops. The government abolished the Boer republics and retained them as British colonies instead, but nevertheless offered limited self-government within five years along with compensation for lost livestock and some financial help with reconstruction. London was looking towards a Canada-style dominion, which in fact was achieved in 1910 with the creation of the Union of South Africa. It even made a crucial concession to the Boers over black African representation in their self-governing entities. The 'Kaffirs' in Transvaal and Orange Free State would only be enfranchised *after* representative government had been established. London knew full-well that this meant 'never'. It was a single word, said Thomas Packenham, 'that would echo and re-echo down the years'. The Boers had lost the war but certainly went on to win the peace – a shameful peace in the view of many liberals in Britain.

In fact, the Boer War stimulated a major realignment in British global policy. The empire had sent volunteers to the British cause in South Africa, but the empire was militarily over-extended and not politically coherent. The Royal Navy was no longer pre-eminent on its own; industrial competitors were emerging strongly, and Germany – staunch supporter of the Boers – rather than France was evidently the empire's most dangerous challenger. Lord Salisbury's policy of 'splendid isolation' now looked downright dangerous and Britain began to create alliance and 'entente' relations with Japan, France and Russia, even direct staff talks with Paris, as it felt a new world emerging around it. In 1914, barely a decade after the Boer War and only four years after the creation of the Union of South Africa, its Prime Minister, Louis Botha and former komando and Defence Minister Jan Smuts, pledged the allegiance of the Union to the British empire and to Britain's war against Germany.

Meanwhile, Kitchener – satisfied with Vereeniging – had returned to Britain in the summer of 1902 to a hero's welcome everywhere, becoming a Viscount in the process. By the end of the year he was back on imperial duty, as Commander-in-Chief, India. He set about reorganizing the bloated Indian Army and preparing it for a range of more modern operations than it had anticipated. Characteristically, he founded the

Indian Staff College in Quetta – these days the Pakistan Command and Staff College, where his portrait still hangs.[5]

Kitchener understood colonial armies better than his own. His instincts in reorganizing the Indian Army were naturally centralizing and he clashed repeatedly with Lord Curzon, Viceroy of India, to the point where Curzon resigned in November 1905. His reforms were partly successful but also disruptive and many subsequently had to be reversed. While Kitchener was struggling with British military policy in India, the British army at home was undergoing some vital post-Boer War reform under the influence of the Esher Committee, creating a new General Staff and an enhanced Committee of Imperial Defence. And a new Secretary of State for War, Richard Haldane, drove through the fundamental reforms that would allow the peacetime army to be mobilised swiftly and sent to the continent in the event of conflict with Germany. While Kitchener performed high-profile ceremonial duties in India, touring the empire as a Field Marshal in 1909, military affairs were changing quickly at home.

Kitchener was now a senior politician as much as a soldier and he desperately wanted to be named Viceroy of India. He lobbied hard for it in Parliament and Whitehall, even pursuing the dying Edward VII to support the idea. Prime Minister Asquith seemed sympathetic, but Asquith was running a reforming Liberal government. John Morley, Secretary of State for India, was adamantly opposed to having such a controversial and conservative military officer in the post, and Lord Curzon was whispering loudly against Kitchener to anyone who would listen.[6] It was not to be. At least during the 1911 coronation of King George V, Field Marshal Lord Kitchener commanded the 55,000 British and imperial troops brought into London from across the world to celebrate the event.

When war broke out in August 1914 Kitchener happened to be on leave in Britain. Asquith immediately named him Secretary of State for War. It was a popular appointment with the public but it made Kitchener a senior politician and took him, at least constitutionally, out of the military command chain altogether. But he insisted on wearing his uniform as a Field Marshal and at the grand strategic level his voice in cabinet was always influential, and sometimes decisive. He was out of touch with the modern British army but he had certainly applied his practical intellect to an understanding of the political and technological drivers of this war. He and Douglas Haig were almost alone in government circles in predicting that the war would last at least three years, would require the ramping up of industrial production and would involve the clash of armies numbered in the millions. Kitchener understood that the Royal Navy could no longer guarantee Britain's defence and that nothing less than a full, and long, commitment to a continental campaign would be necessary.

Thanks to Haldane, Britain was in a position to send the British Expeditionary Force (the BEF, Britain's only field army) to France in short order. It would sit on the left

---

5. Among its graduates, the College can boast several eminent alumni, including Field Marshals Wavell, Montgomery, Auchinleck and Slim.
6. A serving military officer would not be appointed Viceroy until Lord Wavell in 1943 in the circumstances of the world war.

flank of the French Fifth Army. The German plan was to create a rapid hammer blow with a right hook through Belgium into France, encircling Paris within six weeks. So it was that the 160,000 men of the BEF sat on the left flank of the 254,000 men of the French Fifth Army and found themselves more or less opposite the combined 580,000 cream of German forces in its First and Second Army who were the hammerhead of the wide swinging blow they aimed towards Paris. If the BEF was at least the right idea, it would have to be made much, much bigger.

Kitchener argued that the BEF, as it was, should be sent to Amiens to prepare for a counter-attack, not wasted in fruitless forward defence against overwhelming German force, particularly when he had such a low opinion of French staying power against German pressure. But Sir John French, commanding the BEF, disagreed and Asquith backed his commander and over-ruled his Secretary of State for War. The result was the retreat from Mons – an event that might have been worse but for Kitchener's reluctance to commit the full force to it which would have risked losing everything.

From then onwards, Kitchener was locked in a desperate struggle for strategic influence with Sir John French (as well as Sir Henry Wilson and the rising Douglas Haig). Kitchener didn't believe a conscript army would be effective in the new warfare. He was building his 'New Army' of free and patriotic volunteers. He didn't believe in doing it through the Territorials, in whom he had no faith.[7] Nor was he prepared to have his new army committed in dribs and drabs to immediate tactical offensives. He directed the western front generals to operate conservatively until his citizen army was ready for a decisive, war-changing, offensive when its numbers, equipment and training were right. The recruitment of 500,000 men – to become 2 million by mid-1916 – was a huge societal undertaking but his personal influence on it remained considerable.[8] For most of the young men flocking to the colours, and the public left behind, they were the soldiers of 'Kitchener's Army', and they assumed they would somehow be fighting under his command.

In fact, by 1915, his practical grip on military command had become frankly eccentric. He now insisted on holding his New Army back at home to guard against a German invasion of Britain. His battles with the volatile Sir John French eventually ended with French's removal from command of the BEF and his replacement by Douglas Haig in December. Early in 1915 Kitchener favoured a Mediterranean strategy to take pressure off the western front and buy more time, and his voice was decisive in backing Churchill's enthusiasm for the Dardanelles/Gallipoli campaign. When that failed at the end of the year, his standing inside government was considerably reduced and he had already been blamed for the 'shells crisis', where munitions shortages became critical. The shells crisis brought down the Liberal government and forced a Coalition. Kitchener was kept on in the new government for the sake of public assurance, but in truth, he was being 'managed' by those around him as he became erratic, secretive

---

7. He was completely wrong in this. His experience of reserve forces in other armies convinced him they were structurally deficient. He had no appreciation of how good the British territorial forces had become by then.
8. That total included about 1 million infantry and 1 million gunners, logistics and various supporting troops.

and frequently dishonest. He partly broke his own rule by allowing some of his new divisions to be committed first to Gallipoli and then the Loos offensive in September 1915, but this, it was later officially admitted, was connected to his manoeuvring to be appointed Supreme Allied Commander. He didn't believe in having too many machine guns per battalion, nor in new-fangled armoured tractors mis-named as 'tanks'. By 1916 the government was happy to give him some latitude on matters of recruitment and supply to the New Army, but otherwise constrained his influence as best it could.

Russia was in trouble on the eastern front and Kitchener and his staff left Britain to hold direct talks with Russian leaders on the most urgent problems. He sailed on *HMS Hampshire* on 5th June 1916. Later that day just west of the Orkney Islands, the *Hampshire* hit a mine, only recently laid by German U-boat, *U-75*. Only twelve survived. Among the 737 who perished were all ten members of Kitchener's staff. He was seen standing on the quarterdeck during the twenty minutes the *Hampshire* took to sink, though his body was never recovered.

For the public, Kitchener's death was a desperate blow and as untimely as it could possibly be. Many in the press, reflecting public dismay, wondered openly how the country could possibly win the war without him. For the Cabinet and the high command, of course, his death was undoubtedly tragic but extremely timely. His New Army went fully into action on 1st July on the Somme. That first day and the subsequent, prolonged offensive was famously a disaster. But his great volunteer citizen army was in being. It learned and adapted, and it was the core of the great conscript army that followed it onto the Western Front. And eventually it prevailed, as an equal partner to the French army, as the historic wheel of the western front turned remorselessly on troop numbers, industrial production, innovation and the endless competition of prosaic human courage. The great 'imperial soldier' had genuinely understood all that, even if he hardly commanded in it.

Field Marshal Douglas Haig

Douglas Haig's popular reputation as a commander has waxed and waned as society's views of the First World War have changed. For more than a century, opinions about that titanic struggle have gone through cycles of relief and triumphalism, disgust, incomprehension, and then greater contextual understanding by a new generation of military historians. Though the First World War was a global conflict, the prevailing British image of it is dominated by the Western Front. As British commander for most of the war on the Western Front, Haig's reputation is forever shackled to the shifting interpretations of that campaign.

Haig was a successful cavalry soldier and, throughout his career, an excellent staff officer at all levels, with a flair for administration and military organization. Most writers would not bracket his innate generalship alongside Cromwell, Marlborough or Wellington. But he led the largest British army in history, he oversaw its biggest battles, its greatest single defeat and then its final triumph in 1918; the most extensive military victory Britain has known. The cost in lives – the whole distasteful strategy encapsulated in the ugly word 'attrition' – was staunchly accepted by Haig as both inevitable and justified. His subsequent military reputation rests on whether later historians have agreed with him. It rests, too, on the question of how much difference Haig's generalship actually made to the outcome of such big campaigns; massive movements that could be influenced by the commander, but hardly controlled by him. Haig certainly presided over more than two and a half million men fighting Britain's war on the Western Front. But did he mould them into the instrument of victory they subsequently became; or did he, rather, just oversee processes of learning and adaptation taking place much further down the line?

Haig was not loquacious or highly articulate, unlike many of his political opponents. He was naturally reserved in the manner of many late-Victorian figures. He did not seek to justify himself in public and had no interest in writing newspaper pieces, still less any personal memoirs. He let his actions speak for themselves. A deeply religious man, Haig also had an innate and growing conviction that he was working to enact God's will on the Western Front. But since God was keeping his opinion to himself, others were not slow to step in, offering theirs. Haig died in 1928. His public reputation has been a battlefield ever since.

Douglas Haig was born into Edinburgh's Haig & Haig scotch whisky dynasty in 1861. He was ever a shy and largely inarticulate boy, neither clever nor particularly well-educated, but well-loved by his mother as the youngest of her eleven children. From the first, Douglas absorbed the strong presbyterian instincts of the Church of

Scotland alongside his mother's doughty sense of dutiful resilience. His father was distant and an alcoholic, though Douglas's eldest brother provided a male role model. The boy was plagued by ill-health. He was a lifelong asthmatic, and became punctilious, then faddish, about food, which he believed caused the asthma. Given his father's alcoholism, he was always frugal in his own drinking. Illness prevented him from graduating from Brasenose College Oxford, but he was, anyway, more determined to enter Sandhurst to begin a career in the army, which he did in 1884. If he expressed a distinctive youthful character at all, it was not in his restrained socializing or his timidity with young women, but rather in excellent horsemanship. He loved hunting and was a very good polo player. It was his one serious sport, though he later became keen on golf.

As a young army officer he was picked out, not for any obvious flair or personality but rather for his conscientious application; a determination to master the tasks at hand. In an age when it was not fashionable for British junior officers to apply themselves much to military matters, still less the art of war, Douglas Haig thought about it a good deal. After Sandhurst he was gazetted with the 7th Hussars, based in India. But he first got to observe French cavalry exercises and as a result of his talent for staff work, spent a while as aide-de-camp to the Inspector General of Cavalry. Ten unspectacular but diligent years later, he used some time in-between postings travelling in Germany to make a careful study of the German army, which had impressed him greatly. His insights proved to be pretty accurate and they influenced all his subsequent thinking on German military prowess. He spoke good French and tolerable German and in 1896, at second attempt, got himself into Staff College at Woolwich, where he made the most of his opportunities. At the age of thirty-five he was regarded as an army high-flier.

Staff College recommended that Haig should accompany Kitchener in his 1898 expedition to the Sudan. He joined Kitchener's Anglo-Egyptian force at Wadi Halfa as it was preparing to cross the border into Sudan, thence southwards to destroy the Mahdi's power base at Omdurman, and re-establish Egyptian-British control. Haig was brave and resourceful in upholding the discipline of Egyptian cavalry when it was under pressure. And though he was critical of Kitchener's highly autocratic style of command, Kitchener was impressed by Haig and promoted him brevet major. At the battle of Omdurman the cavalry's role became awkward, looking after the flanks and then leading the somewhat chaotic push against the city of Omdurman itself. Haig had used his cavalry squadron cleverly and flexibly, having them dismount to join the infantry where necessary, riding them carefully under crossfire and then riding hard when it mattered.

He left the Sudan with both his staff work and his fighting qualities much admired and was immediately posted as Chief of Staff to Sir John French, who was sent to command British cavalry during the Second Boer War. In October 1899 French and Haig were in Natal. French launched a surprise and successful attack on Elandslaagte – the only victory for British forces during that early period of many defeats. A month later, both men came under fire aboard the last train out of Ladysmith as the Boers surrounded the city and besieged it. For the first few months, French and Haig were seen as the only effective British command team in the war. The tide began to turn in 1900 and Haig was promoted and given command of the 3rd Cavalry Brigade. In early 1901 he was responsible for clearing Boer guerrilla fighters from the northwest of Cape Colony. Throughout a frustrating counter-insurgency campaign which began in a lacklustre way, Haig injected dynamism and ruthlessness to his part of it – exactly as Lord Kitchener, who was by then in command of the war, had wanted. Haig's leadership was not flawless and he fretted over command mistakes that had cost the lives of his troopers. Nevertheless, in September 1902 he sailed home with his regiment and his own reputation high. He now had successful command experience at senior levels and had established personal relationships during the war with many of the commanders who would work under him on the Western Front a decade later.

A stint with the cavalry in India followed, working with Kitchener to try to reform the Indian Army and update its methods and thinking. He supported Kitchener when his lordship was embroiled in a 'him-or-me' tussle with the Viceroy, Lord Curzon – a row which led to Curzon's resignation. Haig's loyalty to his boss was based on the merits of the issue, but it did his personal relationship with Kitchener no harm. In fact, Haig was increasingly critical of the limitations of both his mentors, Kitchener and French. He made harsh judgements about their command abilities, but kept his views largely to himself and remained safe in their shadow – particularly as he already had good family connections to the Prince of Wales, who became Edward VII, and also with the Duke of York, subsequently George V. He was a popular invitee to royal social events; a distinguished officer with an impressive record. In 1905 Edward VII described his friend, Colonel Haig, as his 'best and most capable general'. All this gave Haig both protection and some useful political influence.[1]

In June 1905, on leave at home, Haig met the Hon. Dorothy Maud Vivian, one of Queen Alexandra's maids of honour. Their paths had crossed briefly, though wordlessly, two years previously. But now he was invited to Windsor Castle, staying for the Ascot races. On Thursday he was introduced to the attractive twenty-six-year-old Doris – as she was known to friends – and then played golf with her on Friday. On Saturday he proposed to her on the golf course, standing up, tongue-tied and abrupt, and she accepted. They were married in the Chapel Royal at Buckingham Palace a month later. Some writers have thought this wonderfully romantic; others simply cynical. It doesn't matter. It was a perfect marriage for a general. Douglas and Doris were a devoted couple throughout their lives. They had four children together and his family life during the strain of command in the world war was a personal escape for him during his regular visits back to London. It was undoubtedly one of the blessings that kept him going through thick and thin. Doris dedicated her whole life to her husband, his command responsibilities and to their family. By the standards of the time, when military protocol didn't really know what to think about the private lives of its commanders, she was perfect.

---

1. They were to prove important attributes for Haig during the First World War when Lloyd George increasingly tried to undermine him.

Back in India, Haig took more interest than Kitchener in how the army in Britain was reforming itself after the shock of the Boer War. Like his boss, he foresaw Britain becoming engaged in a serious land war in Europe that would likely last for some years. By 1909 he was convinced of it, and that Britain was running out of time to prepare itself for a conflict that would involve 'the whole resources of the nation'. It was around then that Haig began to write about the necessary sacrifices that would later become known as the policy of 'attrition' on the Western Front. That characterization has dogged his reputation for over a century. But attrition was not some casual post-hoc rationalization, driven by an inner sense of guilt. His conviction in 1909 that Britain would 'win by wearing the enemy out', was based on a clear analysis of the emerging nature of war – not clever, but intellectually honest – from which he drew the hard conclusions.

He certainly went along with, and tried to help, Richard Haldane's critical military reforms during these years. In 1907 he had become Director of Staff Duties and had compiled some rudimentary military doctrine for the army. He worked with Haldane to create a new 'Territorial Force' of volunteer auxiliaries, which – despite Kitchener's dismissal of their value – proved essential in 1914–15. Haig did another brief tour back in India, but was then given the prestigious Aldershot Command in 1912 where he made an immediate reforming impact on its two divisions and its cavalry brigade. Most of his fellow officers and his soldiers didn't know quite what to make of him. He exuded military competence and dedication, but he was brusque, socially gauche, prone to what Gary Sheffield calls 'thunderous silences', and difficult to like except among those who worked closely with him, and sometimes not even then. But this was the man who would lead a corps, and soon the whole army, as it went to war in August 1914.

Haig was given command of I Corps, alongside Smith-Dorrien of II Corps, which together made up the British Expeditionary Force – the BEF – shipped hurriedly to the continent.[2] It was a tiny force, merely 160,000 troops among a British army, even including the new 'Territorial Force', of only 400,000 (about a third of which was garrisoned in India). In comparison, France and Germany had built armies of around 4 million each. Germany mobilised 2 million to the western front in 1914; France about 1,700,000. Like Kitchener, Haig wanted to deploy his forces rearwards – around Amiens – so they could counter-attack, rather than go immediately toe to toe with the 580,000 of the German First and Second Armies bearing down on them, which would naturally force them to retreat. Understanding German operational thinking better than most, Haig worried that they would try large encircling sweeps to outflank allied forces, and that one of the two British corps, or the whole of the BEF, might be encircled and defeated there and then. But as junior partner to the massive French force, Prime Minister Asquith, along with Sir John French who was commanding the BEF, felt they had to send it to Mons in Belgium, holding the French left flank

---

2. Horace Smith-Dorrien was one of the very few British survivors of the disastrous Battle of Isandlwana during the Zulu War in 1879.

from the great swinging right hook that German forces were executing. At Mons, the BEF fought heroically and then duly retreated in a state of exhausted confusion.

Smith-Dorrien's II Corps was under greater pressure than I Corps. Haig nevertheless conducted the I Corps battle with great assurance and no little skill as it engaged, knocked German forces back, then withdrew in good order 160 miles in thirteen days. Haig, the man with the diffident personality, put his commander's stamp on his corps with cool and incisive decisions. On 23rd August he was crawling on his stomach to the crest of a hill to see for himself the advance of massed German forces against his battalions, all firing furiously. A few hours later he almost drove straight into German lines at Givry, looking for 6 Brigade HQ, to give his orders directly.

Both allied and German forces came close to losing the whole campaign in those chaotic weeks. On 5th September the French Fifth Army and the BEF stopped retreating, regrouped, then attacked in what became known as the First Battle of the Marne. That battle stopped the German advance from encircling Paris and for a short while, left them wide open. If the allies had followed up strongly, their enemy might well have cracked, but German forces held on just long enough to re-establish their lines.[3] With prompt reinforcements, the BEF then moved over towards Flanders, to safeguard its vital channel ports. The First Battle of Ypres, a fierce attempt by BEF and German forces both to take the offensive, became known as the 'race to the sea' – a desperate British action to prevent the BEF being outflanked along the coast and cut off from its supply ports. On 31st October the BEF – I Corps now leading the battle – came closer to outright defeat than at any other time in the war. Only a battalion of the Worcestershire regiment was left in front of Ypres when German forces took Gheluvelt on the Menin Road. Haig's defensive generalship was already admired, but never more so than in those dangerous days around Ypres at the end of October and early November. The 'first Ypres' cost the BEF 58,000 men. By the end of 1914 the BEF had incurred 96,000 casualties (the French almost a million), and the regular army, the 'old contemptibles', had effectively been destroyed.

On the evening of 16th September John French had commanded BEF units to dig trenches and hunker down, in expectation that they would shortly be moving forward again. But that night proved to be the beginning of four years of trench warfare on the Western Front. Haig, at least, had quickly recognised that they were involved in 'a kind of siege warfare'. This new kind of warfare was a continuous process; an ongoing and endless firefight punctuated by big offensive pushes from one side or another. Along the British sector, German forces had the better of it, occupying most of the higher, and drier, ground facing the BEF. They could see more and dig deeper and further than the British opposite them, whose Flanders trenches were characteristically wet.

The remorseless nature of trench warfare was determined by a number of inescapable realities. The trench line ran from 'Kilometer Zero' in the south-east, at the intersection of the French, Swiss and German borders, in a continuous line all the way to Nieuport

---

3. Haig shares some responsibility for the failure to follow up. John French ordered 1st Corps to seize the crossings over the river Aisne, but Haig chose instead to occupy the safer high ground short of the river.

on the Belgian coast.[4] So along the whole front there were no flanks to turn; no way round except somehow through the middle.[5] The sheer density of troops crammed into that battlefield middle was another ineluctable fact. It was determined by the railway networks behind them and the number of motor vehicles pressed into military service. In any breakthrough, the bulk of attacking troops had to move forward on foot, while the opposition's reinforcements could be rushed to the area by rail and road to plug defensive gaps as retreating troops were falling back on their own lines of communication. Many breakthroughs were made by both sides; none were ever sustained until September 1918.

The war between the front lines was dominated by artillery fire which continually wore down the troops, huge tangles of barbed wire which impeded all movement in no-man's land, or else created killing grounds around the gaps, and machine guns which could operate in intersecting arcs of fire to create a wall of bullets that attackers somehow had to struggle through. As the war went on, artillery learned better how to operate 'creeping barrages' that would land shells just ahead of attacking troops moving across no-man's land. Even so, almost every attack turned into a race for the parapet once the artillery barrage had stopped – whether the attackers could get to the edge of enemy trenches before the enemy could emerge, shocked and shaken from their deep dugouts, and reach the parapet first to get their machine guns working. Communication via flags and runners was extremely poor at the beginning and didn't improve very much even with the use of wireless. Horse-mounted cavalry was used in various ways right up to 1918, but never to achieve a breakthrough or turn a breakthrough into a rout. Aircraft became increasingly useful as artillery spotters and later as reconnaissance and intelligence gatherers – something Haig had appreciated before the war – and aircraft, battling each other for 'control of the air' above the conflict zone became a new feature of warfare. The Western Front imposed its own remorseless logic on commanders just as much as the common soldiers who fought there.

Over Christmas 1914 Haig was promoted to become a full general, and I and II Corps were enlarged to become the First and Second Armies of the BEF as it expanded. Offensives involving First Army followed in 1915; almost successfully at Neuve Chapelle, poorly at Aubers Ridge, expensively at Festubert and disastrously at Loos. The Loos offensive and the chronic munitions shortage dubbed the 'shells scandal' led to the removal of the clearly inadequate Sir John French from command of the BEF. In December 1915 Haig was appointed Commander-in-Chief in his place. After sixteen months of war Haig was certainly well aware of all the prevailing tactical conditions and the numerical strength of the German opposition. Like Kitchener, he believed that Britain would have to hang on for two or three years before troops from the Empire would give them a numerical advantage as Germany weakened. He was right; in fact more right than he knew, when troops from the United States also

---

4. The blockhouses of three countries still exist today at Kilometer Zero, looking at each other in an area of pleasant woodland.
5. Which was why politicians in London became attracted to more grand outflanking manoeuvres in campaigns such as Gallipoli and Salonika.

began to arrive in numbers during the final weeks of the war. He later claimed that his conviction, of hanging on until the balance decisively tipped against Germany, was something he had always appreciated. His critics doubt it, and the BEF under his command didn't always conduct its operations as if that was really the intention, even if it was the eventual result.

But consistency is never easy to maintain in war, for soldiers or politicians, and Haig's reputation as BEF commander hinges on the three greatest battles Britain fought during the conflict; the Somme in 1916, at Passchendaele in 1917, and in defence against the great German attack – the Ludendorff offensive – in spring 1918. They were pivotal to the final outcome.

The Somme offensive of July 1916 brought the new form of warfare home to Britain as a shocking realisation. It pitched Kitchener's New Army of volunteers into battle for the first time.[6] But it also ushered in conscription for the first time in British history.[7] The battle was run by a General Headquarters (GHQ) that now presided over an unprecedented five armies within the BEF.[8] The GHQ became bigger than anything Britain had created before. Over 1,000 officers were moved by Haig from St. Omer to a new GHQ base at Montreuil where, under his supervision, it eventually looked after the flow of 2,700,000 troops going back and forth, 400,000 horses and mules, many millions of artillery shells, millions of tons of food and supplies – 400,000 tons a week – and all the strategic level planning for the grand offensives which the allies, having halted the invasion of France, now pursued to push the Germans back behind their own frontier.

After fighting defensively during 1915, the Somme offensive was the long-anticipated 'big push'. But it was also an improvisation in response to events. A major joint allied offensive for mid-1916 had been agreed by Haig and Joseph Joffre, his French counterpart, the previous December. Preparations were ongoing but in late February German forces launched a major attack on French positions at Verdun. That battle became an agony of attrition for both French and German armies. Immediately, Joffre insisted on a British offensive further west to relieve the pressure. Still the junior partner in the alliance, Haig had to accept that the grand joint offensive would now have to be a largely British affair, with some French support on the British right along the allied trench line. There were other imperative factors. Joffre thought that the French army would only be capable of one more big push after Verdun before it became 'combat ineffective'. In the east, Russia was weakening and the Tsar's forces also needed some release of pressure. If Russia collapsed, even more German troops would soon be streaming towards the Western Front.

---

6. Notwithstanding that some had previously been committed to the Gallipoli campaign and the Loos offensive.
7. Conscription had begun from January 1916 with the passage of the Military Service Act.
8. Technically 'Army Corps', within which individual 'Corps' existed. 'Army' is always an ambiguous term referring both to a formal command level, alongside 'army' as one of the three great military branches or in its intuitive use as any large collection of ground forces doing the fighting in a particular campaign.

So Haig was boxed in. Far from hanging on until help arrived, the British now had to lead one big effort to break through and force a decision on the Western Front that year, or else risk the balance tipping sharply against the Allies. Still, he was confident that after so much careful preparation the offensive would work. This encapsulated the ambiguity of his strategic approach – an ambiguity he smoothed over in his post-war account. He constantly thought that significant breakthroughs could be made and that preparations should be in hand to move quickly to exploit the ground behind the enemy's trench lines. He found Henry Rawlinson, commanding Fourth Army which led the Somme offensive, far too cautious. Haig always wanted more momentum. But when it didn't happen, he rationalized with a clear conscience, that these setbacks were all part of the 'wearing down' process necessary to defeat the enemy in due course. 'Breakthroughs' were about capturing territory. 'Wearing down' was about defeating the German army, and they were two different things. He hoped for one – and many thousands died for it – but had to keep settling for the other.

In a way he was quite right. Attrition worked. Within two weeks of the start of the Somme the Germans suspended their offensive at Verdun and by the end of it, the invading German army – superior until then – had been fatally undermined, to the point where it began to construct the heavily defended 'Hindenburg Line' over fifteen miles rearwards to fall back on. Erich Ludendorff had taken over and reorientated German forces to a 'defence in depth' approach. The Somme offensive failed to create an allied breakthrough, still less a 'decision' on the Western Front, but it laid the foundations for a victory by attrition – the hardest way.

It could scarcely have been harder. On 1st July, after a continuous seven-day artillery bombardment 120,000 men rose from the British trenches to assault German lines in the first attack.[9] At French insistence the attack began at 7.30 – broad daylight instead of the early dawn always favoured by British troops. The bombardment had not cut the wire. British artillery was too dispersed. A third of its shells were duds. Its creeping barrage was a mess. Communications collapsed immediately. Intelligence had vastly underestimated German strongpoints in farms and buildings behind the trenches. It's not true that British troops were instructed to walk across no man's land; it was simply that they made no more than walking speed across the wire and shell holes. But it *is* true that their commanders thought this citizen army would be incapable of tactical sophistication and was therefore sent across no man's land in massed waves, rather than detachments. It was a fatal miscalculation. In the end, they lost the race for the parapet almost everywhere, usually before they had reached the first German trench line. As the Official History put it, 'There was no wavering or attempting to come back, the men fell in their ranks, mostly before the first hundred yards of No Man's Land had been crossed.' Haig didn't make that awful miscalculation. He had argued for detachment attacks, having already seen German and French troops use them effectively. But his subordinate commanders all favoured waves, and on the principle that an operational leader should respect the view of the 'men on the ground', he assented to it. Was that weakness? Or negligence? It's hard to imagine Marlborough or Wellington deferring to their subordinate commanders over something so important.

---

9. Britain devoted fourteen divisions to the attack, backed up by six French Divisions on their right.

It wasn't just German machine guns that made the difference. The German artillery barrage into no man's land was just as devastating and German forces launched fierce counterattacks on almost every part of the line where they lost ground. In fact, it was the human cost of their own expensive counterattacks that did most to undermine German strength by the end of the Somme offensive.

Haig was often angrily criticized for being a 'chateau commander' during the fighting. But in reality, there was little alternative. Like other commanders, Haig did go forward regularly to meet troops in rear areas for the sake of morale and information. But going much further forward in the prevailing conditions took a lot of time and removed the theatre commander from the communications and inputs he needed to do the job at his particular level of responsibility. At GHQ in Montreuil Haig was noted for leading a very regular day, making few variations to his routine, even in the midst of offensives like this. That was his style and it kept him sharp. Nevertheless, in the chateau his incoming information in early July was very poor. He thought initial British losses were about 40,000 over two days, when in fact they were 60,000 in one day, and he ordered his commanders to keep pushing. He probably would have anyway.

In the British centre the Fourth Army did well and had the front open for several hours. But the advance took it between the infamous triangle of woods – High Wood, Delville Wood and Bazentin-le-Petit Wood, full of German strong points that turned the space between them into a killing ground. Again, nothing could be achieved for the loss of so many men. Across the whole front the Somme became a long battle; 'never silent, never still anywhere' as John Terraine put it. There was another big push on September 15th with useful gains, but nothing critical. It was the last chance that year to create some 'decision' in the struggle. The first objective on the first day of the battle had been to take Beaumont Hamel at the northernmost end of the attack line. On November 13th, four and a half months later, Beaumont Hamel was finally captured. On November 18th the offensive was, in the euphemism of the time, 'closed down' as the uniquely cold winter of 1916–17 tightened its early grip under Picardy's snow-filled skies. The offensive had hinged on Beaumont Hamel to swing a right hook from the south into German positions. At its furthest extent that punch had forced German lines seven miles back, for which the allies together had lost 624,000[10] troops and caused Germany around 680,000 casualties.

Mons and the race to the sea in 1914 had destroyed the Old Contemptibles. The Somme now destroyed Kitchener's citizen army. But morale was never broken and despite all, the remains of both forces acted as the core of Britain's first ever conscript army which began to arrive in France over the winter into 1917. Haig's own religious faith, and his belief in the divine adjudication that would bring final victory on the Western Front, grew only stronger for the sacrifice.

The following year, many similar factors were evident in the 1917 Passchendaele offensive. The imperatives for the Allies were just as compelling. The quixotic General Nivelle replaced Joffre as French Commander-in-Chief, promising much. But he delivered only a disastrous spring offensive and the French army mutinied after its

---

10. 420,000 of them were British casualties.

failure. Fully half of its Western Front divisions were in uproar. Britain now became the dominant party in the relationship and only a big, British-led attack could give French forces some breathing space to recover. Haig had already launched a strong attack at Arras in support of Nivelle's brief fiasco and was then left with an ongoing battle that merged into the messy Passchendaele offensive two months later.

London's own motives for the 'big push' of 1917 were anyway becoming urgent. Britain occupied the vital channel ports of Calais and Dunkirk, but Ostend and Zeebrugge were in German hands and the U-boat base at Zeebrugge was believed by the Admiralty – wrongly (and some in the Admiralty knew this) – to be the source of ever more severe shipping losses in the Atlantic. First Sea Lord, Admiral Jellicoe told the Cabinet in June 1917 that Britain would be finished by 1918 if it didn't neutralize the threat of Germany's U-boats. 'There is no good discussing plans for next spring', he said, 'we cannot go on.' Nor was that view a secret. Charles Repington of *The Times* observed, 'it was at present a question whether our armies could win the war before our navies lost it'. So an ambitious campaign in Flanders, pushing to the coast alongside an amphibious operation to sweep German forces away from the Belgian ports, appeared to many, though not all, to be a matter of national survival.

But 1917 also turned out to be the year that ushered in much bigger twentieth century trends. The Russian revolution had commenced in February and the prospect of Russian military collapse was now very real. It would only be a matter of time before hundreds of thousands more German troops would redeploy to the Western Front. The United States had been provoked into the war by Germany's U-boat campaign, but US troops would not be arriving in numbers for at least a year, and in the meantime, US demands for Allied shipping imposed an extra strain. Bolshevik ideas were at large across Europe and no one knew, including their commanders, how much longer French armies would continue to fight. The Italians were throwing themselves into a major offensive against Austria-Hungary that led them to the disaster at Caporetto which then required support from forces that had to be detached from the Western Front. And Lloyd George had become Prime Minister in Britain. He was profoundly antithetical to Western Front advocates and looked always for the time and chance to replace Haig and those who thought like him.

As part of the scheme to clear the Belgian coast, Haig planned a big Allied push in a 'Third Battle of Ypres' using the Passchendaele Ridge of high ground lying from south to north towards Roulers as the right flank. With that key transport hub attained, the forces could swing westwards and push on. An offensive up the coast from Nieuport and an amphibious operation could then capture or neutralize the enemy ports some forty miles away. It was hugely ambitious, but this seemed increasingly to be a win-or-lose moment in the struggle. Again, Haig based his planning on significant French support, but with more mutinies, that was repeatedly delayed as the summer months drained away.

He gave the tactical direction of the offensive to General Gough of the Fifth Army. He was not the right general to lead it. Gough changed the main objective of the attack from Roulers, ignoring the ridge of high ground (a decision he was profoundly to regret) and instead pointed the attack north-west, more directly at the coast but across low-lying country. Astonishingly, Haig did not intervene, though he had repeatedly stressed the importance of the ridge. Haig and Gough seemed continually to misunderstand each other as the offensive drew nearer. Hostilities began with a very successful attack by Plumer's Second Army on Messines Ridge on 7th June, preceded by the detonation of nineteen huge mines in an explosion that was felt in London.[11] There was then a frustrating delay of thirty-seven days before 5th Army's artillery was able to open the preliminary bombardment and another seventeen days before the main attack began just before dawn on 31st July.

In fact, the greatest obstacle to success had begun over a week before in a little swirl of cloud more than a thousand miles away in the Atlantic. A deep depression began to form and a cool airstream headed towards northern Europe. The rains began within hours of the attack starting; more than double the average for Flanders, more than five times what had fallen in 1915 or 1916. It was near continuous, with very few days when the ground might dry. Mud quickly overwhelmed the attack. Many soldiers drowned in deeply flooded shell craters. Horses and mules disappeared completely, as did the frontline railway tracks; some of their small steam engines were buried as they seized up. Instead of two men, it required sixteen to carry a stretcher the 4,000 yards back to solid ground – four teams of four men in relay to wade through it all. The Passchendaele Ridge became essential, no longer as a springboard to attack Roulers, but because it was more solid than any ground around it as winter set in.

On 6th November the Canadian corps captured Passchendaele village and six days later the offensive was closed down. Planning for the amphibious operation was cancelled. After three and a half months Roulers still lay beyond the advance. The offensive had gained less than six miles at a cost of 245,000 British casualties. German forces had suffered grievously as well, and the effects of Passchendaele in Berlin should not be underestimated. Germany was getting desperate but knew that the Russian revolution would provide a now-or-never moment to redeploy forces from the Russian front to defeat the Allies in the West before the Americans arrived. In Britain that same desperation expressed itself in a longer time-frame. Britain would have to survive the U-boat menace; there would be no breakthroughs, and the war would go on into 1918, 1919 and perhaps 1920 before the Allies, their empires, and their American friends could overwhelm German defences.

The army that emerged from the mud of Passchendaele was certainly not broken, but it was sullen, disillusioned – perhaps just philosophical – and had stopped expecting anything but more of the same. Haig had believed in the ambitious 'Belgian ports' strategy, but seemed content with yet another 'wearing down' exercise. He was as convinced as ever of ultimate victory, but he was at a low ebb that winter, his credibility draining away, Lloyd George removing close military allies and relentlessly undermining him. In late November the Third Army won a lightning, innovative victory at Cambrai, then lost it all within a few days. The BEF kept innovating under Haig's influence, but it was never enough.

The year 1918 began in the same grim mood and preparations for the inevitable German offensive were evident enough in GHQ. German deception operations worked

---

11. Herbert Plumer looked remarkably like the cartoon character, Colonel Blimp. But he was the shrewdest and most successful of Haig's British generals, and Second Army turned out to be Haig's best formation.

well, however, and Haig's staff only anticipated half the picture. On 21st March the 'Ludendorff offensive' launched itself at Gough's under-strength and poorly prepared Fifth Army in the south, making big inroads on a thirty-five-mile front that quickly became 200 miles wide. Eighteen days later a second attack began in the north against the Second and Third Armies near the coast. German forces operated skilfully and fast, anticipating some of the manoeuvre warfare of the 1940s. The allied situation was dire, particularly for Haig, since Ludendorff had decided that his offensive must destroy the British first as prelude to addressing the more vulnerable French army. On 11 April Haig issued his most famous order to each man in the BEF, 'Every position must be held to the last man', he wrote, 'With our backs to the wall and believing in the justice of our cause, each of us must fight on to the end'. In similar circumstances the Duke of Wellington would at least have given that one an approving nod. In the atmosphere of crisis Marshal Ferdinand Foch was made supreme commander of all Allied forces and Haig, putting aside national pride and personal ego, loyally supported him. British and French forces were very close to being split apart by Ludendorff's thrust. Haig made plans, in the worst eventuality, to withdraw the whole BEF to Dunkirk.

But by May, they had weathered the worst of the storm and the German offensive finally ran out of steam – for all the usual reasons – in mid-June. With Allied reinforcements rushing into the theatre, just in time, it suddenly became a war of movement. At the Second Battle of the Marne the tide turned. The BEF benefitted from fresh and well-commanded dominion troops from New Zealand, Australia, Canada, and South Africa. And US troops were now operating as independent units, in ever-growing numbers. The BEF had certainly learned and was now operating in combined arms style – infantry, artillery, aircraft, tanks and communications all working together with greater efficiency.

In reality, this steady evolution in tactics had taken place within Army and Corps, one or two levels below Haig at GHQ. Most of his subordinate commanders, like Wellington's in the Peninsular War, had become very competent and knew what had to be done, first in desperate defence and then in counter-attack. But Haig had nurtured and encouraged them for two years, he had kept his nerve at the moment of greatest crisis and he now urged his commanders to drive forward as one objective after another became plausible. The 1917 targets of the Passchendaele offensive suddenly fell into his hands. The Allies breached the Hindenburg Line in late September and then it was a helter-skelter advance. Haig had deliberately kept London in the dark, since he didn't trust in the discretion of Lloyd George's cabinet, and it was not until then that the penny dropped for the government; events might be going beyond yet another slogging match. By the second week of October British forces were finally into open country beyond the devastation of the war zone. Even then, the expectation among many, including Haig, was that this run of success must come to an end at some point.

In truth, the German Army was not defeated by its tumbling retreat – it could well have rallied with what it still had – but rather by the psychological blow of seeing so many new American and Dominion troops entering the fight. It created a sense of hopelessness in German ranks. Not least, at home Germany was in the grip of Bolshevik-inspired revolution. A new German government looked urgently for a peace deal, but right up until late October, there was no certainty that the fighting would end. The BEF fought its last battle crossing the Sambre river on 4th November. The twenty-five-year-old poet Wilfred Owen was killed in that final encounter. The German government would now take an armistice on any terms, and a week later it was all over. The fighting ceased at 11 o'clock on 11th November. At that moment Haig was meeting his five army commanders and staff in Cambrai. They were the top team, says Gary Sheffield, that had 'just won the greatest series of victories in British military history'. All but Haig were in a celebratory mood. But he was entirely matter of fact that morning, worrying already about the march into Germany and keeping a vast army occupied and disciplined when it was no longer fighting.

After the war Haig was honoured and rewarded, but never offered a civilian public role. Lloyd George's subtle vilification of the whole Western Front strategy went into high gear. In one respect, Lloyd George had a point. It was true that the war would ultimately be won or lost on the Western Front, but Britain was involved in a global conflict and there were much wider considerations weighing on the government to which Haig had accorded scant importance.

Haig and Doris devoted themselves almost exclusively to help establish, and then develop, the British Legion both at home and across the Dominions. He was revered by ex-servicemen everywhere and he made their post-war welfare his principal concern for the rest of his life. He had written his *Final Dispatch* as BEF commander in March 1919. In it, he eschewed any personal praise for his role and repeatedly commended the courage and fortitude of his troops. The essence of his thinking – the way he saw himself in British history – was as the commander of one long, continuous campaign from 1915 to 1918. In particular, he wrote, operations during the two years from the Somme to the Sambre should be viewed as 'one great and continuous engagement' – a single battle. And as in most battles, there are likely to be phases of pressure, pulling and pushing, simply trying to exhaust the enemy, looking for openings, and then, a breaking point where one side gains unstoppable momentum. That was his view, his own justification, for the battle of the Western Front where 2.2 million British and Empire troops were killed or seriously injured. It was rather too neat a view and not entirely consistent with the record; but it was not obviously wrong either. Haig wasn't prepared to say more or discuss it further.

In January 1928 Haig had a fatal heart attack at the age of sixty-six. The nation mourned and put on an elaborate public funeral in Westminster Abbey before he was buried at Dryburgh in the Scottish borders. In November that same year Erich Maria Remarque's classic *All Quiet on the Western Front* first appeared, triggering a popular – and populist – anti-military mood that castigated the leadership of Haig and all his contemporary generals. The politician and amateur historian, Alan Clark, rode another wave of that mood in his best-selling 1961 book, *The Donkeys*, based on a telling German opinion his research had uncovered. German commanders, he claimed, saw the BEF as an army of 'lions led by donkeys'. Under considerable pressure from professional historians, Clark later sheepishly admitted he had actually made it up.[12] Haig would probably have been too proud to challenge the insult, even had he been alive to hear it.

---

12. In fact, it was an anonymous *bon mot* that had circulated around many armies from the nineteenth century onwards. Clark claimed it was in contemporary German memoirs, which it wasn't.

25

Admiral John Jellicoe

Admiral John Jellicoe will forever and rightly be defined by the Battle of Jutland in 1916. Jutland was the first and only clash of British and German battlefleets during the First World War. For the Imperial German Navy that battle should have represented *'Der Tag'* – 'The Day' – for which Berlin had waited impatiently for over a decade. For the Admiralty in London, the British public, and certainly for the sailors in the fleet, it was to be the new 'Trafalgar' which they assumed was inevitable. There was immense disappointment in Britain that the outcome of Jutland fell far short of another Trafalgar, and a mountain of criticism descended on Admiral Jellicoe that he had squandered the opportunity to create one. But the fact is that if Jutland was only an arguable victory, as seemed to be the case at the time, it actually had greater strategic value to Britain than Trafalgar.

Jellicoe was a naturally bright man with a carefully considered attitude to all professional decisions. He was below medium height, a devotee of physical fitness, a gifted cricketer, and a good shot. As a young officer, he developed an unfailingly polite charisma in the way he moved through the Service. Unlike David Beatty, his battlecruiser commander at Jutland on whom he had to depend for so much, Jellicoe was not impetuous. And far more than Beatty, Jellicoe bore a huge weight of responsibility at Jutland in 1916, not to sacrifice the central core of the navy for this battle. The Royal Navy was the vital instrument for Britain's survival during the world war and the means of blockading Germany in order to go on and win it. Jellicoe despised Winston Churchill as First Lord of the Admiralty, and Churchill was correspondingly hostile to him. But writing in 1927 Churchill was generous enough to reflect, in a phrase always quoted when Jellicoe is discussed, that he 'was the only man on either side who could lose the war in an afternoon'. Typically Churchillian in its pithy brevity, but it was true enough. As the two great battle fleets converged in the North Sea to fight it out in May 1916, the stakes were considerable for Germany, but quite immense for Britain.

John Jellicoe rose to be an earl, but he had no particularly elevated family connections. His intellect and personal qualities took him a long way. He was born in Southampton in 1859, the son of a Royal Mail steam packet captain. He went to train as a cadet at HMS *Britannia*, graduating second in the class. He went from midshipman to sub-lieutenant in four years, coming third out of a class of 103 and was a twenty-one-year-old full lieutenant by 1880. Two years later, in the way of British imperial forces, he found himself with the infantry, commanding a rifle company of the Naval Brigade in Ismailia during the British intervention in Egypt in 1882.

He became a natural gunner – interested in the science and art of naval gunnery that was fast developing at the time. He attended the navy's gunnery school at Whale Island in Portsmouth and went onto its directing staff the year after he graduated as a gunnery officer. He grew close to John (Jackie) Fisher who commanded the school at that time. Fisher liked him and marked him out for the future. Fisher became the most influential and powerful British naval strategist of his era and Jellicoe absorbed Fisher's evolving ideas on the fundamentals of modern sea power and the reforms the Royal Navy would have to face if it was to maintain its global dominance. Jellicoe was back at sea in 1886 as gunnery officer, winning a Board of Trade medal for rescuing the crew of a stricken steamer off Gibraltar. When Fisher became Director of Naval Ordnance, he brought Jellicoe back in 1889 as his Assistant Director.

Four years later Jellicoe was serving in the rank of a commander, looking after gunnery on HMS *Victoria*, the powerful flagship of the Mediterranean fleet, when Vice Admiral George Tryon managed to manoeuvre his fleet so that the *Camperdown* collided with it and tore a hole in the bows. Tryon would brook no questioning of any orders and had his two lines of ships turn inwards towards each other while going onto a 180-degree reciprocal course. It was a bewildering act of command incompetence close to the Tripoli coast. The *Victoria* went down quickly, losing half its crew of more than 700. From his station in the ship, Jellicoe was lucky to be among the survivors.

After the Mediterranean Jellicoe was able to use his technical skills, sitting for a while as a captain on the Admiralty Ordnance Committee. Then in 1900 he was again in a land command, as Chief of Staff to Edward Seymour leading British forces in an eight-nation alliance against the Chinese nationalists of the 'Boxer Rebellion'. As Seymour's deputy, Jellicoe played the organising role within the improvised force trying to push from Tientsin to relieve westerners besieged in the Peking Legation. The force failed to reach Peking and was itself besieged both ahead and behind it. Seymour broke out of the trap by attacking Peitsang, but it was a confused affair. Japanese troops led with great determination, British cavalry didn't arrive in time to support them, Russian and French forces were unable to get across flooded flanks, and American infantry failed to find the battlefield until too late. Nevertheless, led by Japanese foot soldiers, the attack was pressed home though Jellicoe, leading a British party, received a severe wound in his chest and left lung. He was expected to die within hours and quickly wrote out a will. But he survived, and Seymour's force was eventually relieved by another contingent out of Tientsin.[1] Jellicoe's leadership and personal gallantry were recognised both with the German Order of the Red Eagle, and a British Companion Order of the Bath.

Back in Britain after his recovery, Jellicoe now had command experience, recognised expertise in armaments, gallantry awards, and Jackie Fisher as a mentor – who was First Sea Lord from 1904. Jellicoe was then thought to be one of the smartest and most

---

1. The relieving force included young Commander David Beatty with sailors from HMS *Barfleur*. Future US president Herbert Hoover was involved in the defence of Tientsin, as were Hugo von Pohl, who would go on to command the German High Seas Fleet in the First World War, and Togo Heihachiro who would go on to command Japanese forces at Tsushima in 1905 and who was 'firmly convinced', apparently, that he was 'the re-incarnation of Horatio Nelson'.

capable men of his generation in the Service. In 1902 Jellicoe had married Florence, daughter of the shipping magnate Charles Cayzer. They had a son and five daughters. His family gave Jellicoe great personal stability and inner strength.

In 1905 Jellicoe was put in overall charge of Naval Ordnance, and sat on Fisher's committee that guided the design of the era-defining Dreadnought battleship. He was also made aide-de-camp to King Edward VII and was able to use his growing influence to push in several quarters for greater naval funding. As a rear admiral he was a vigorous member of the Fisher clique who saw the inherent naval advantages offered by the Dreadnought class of ships – and the urgency of creating a fleet of them.

Navies across the world could see that HMS *Dreadnought*, the first battleship of its class launched in 1906, was a revolutionary advance in naval warfare. It was not distinguished by a single novel element, but brought together in one ship all the new technologies of the time. Steam-driven rotary turbine engines made it fast – twenty-one knots in 1906 – while its five pairs of 12-inch guns provided fearsome firepower at long range. By 1914 the newest Dreadnoughts had 15-inch guns. Given that shells at that range would now fall almost vertically onto a target, it was heavily armoured on its main top surfaces as well as along the sides. A Dreadnought-class ship might be untroubled by many direct hits. In short, Dreadnoughts set new standards in propulsion, protection and firepower, rendering all pre-Dreadnoughts obsolete and suicidally vulnerable if any should try to take one of them on. A more lightly-protected version was developed as the Invincible class battlecruiser that would be faster – 25.5 knots – but still carry four pairs of 12-inch guns. HMS *Invincible* was launched as a cruiser class of Dreadnought technology in 1907. In fact, Fisher believed that the future lay with the battlecruiser, and by 1916 the most modern battlecruisers did twenty-eight knots and carried 13.5-inch guns. Nevertheless, the Admiralty was ever convinced of the superiority of the biggest ships, and Invincible battlecruisers – with armour that turned out to be too light, traded-off for their speed – were used to reconnoitre and sweep ahead of the battleships which would be guided and protected before they came to deliver their killer blows against an enemy.

In the decade after 1904 Jellicoe championed all the rapid gunnery and scientific targeting advances that went into the Dreadnought. He was keen to promote armour-piercing shells and saw the value of airships, and then aircraft, for fleet reconnaissance. He was a Dreadnought man to his fingertips and seemed to grasp their full potential rather better than many in the Admiralty. He worried about vulnerabilities, too. Other new innovations such as torpedoes, sea-mines, and submarines getting in among the Dreadnoughts, were new and potent counter-threats. He became convinced, rightly, that Dreadnoughts lacked enough armour and protection below the waterline, and Britain's own development of torpedoes and sea mines lagged behind that of other powers, especially Germany.[2]

---

2. British Dreadnoughts also lacked the same beam width as their German equivalents, making them less stable as gun platforms and less able to contain damage by compartmentalizing below decks. Whereas Germany built new docks to accommodate building its ships, the socially-reforming Liberal government in Britain would not spend money widening its long-established docks. So British Dreadnoughts were built only within the dimensions existing docks could accommodate.

Some foreign powers gave up trying to compete with the Royal Navy when they saw the Dreadnought. Others, like the United States, took it up as a challenge, and for Germany it began a fierce competition in which the Imperial German Navy felt it would now be able to compete on nearly equal terms. If Britain could exert naval dominance by fielding fewer than thirty of the new Dreadnoughts, then Germany trying to compete with the sixty-two capital ships and over 350 other significant vessels of the 1900 Royal Navy – a preponderance that had been two centuries in the making – was now irrelevant. Germany could be a comparable power simply if it could produce a new high-tech fleet of a dozen or more ships like *Dreadnought*. Germany entered into what was characterised as the 'naval race' with Britain to build Dreadnoughts. In fact, by 1912 it had lost the race; Britain had outbuilt it. But in losing, the Imperial German Navy had still grown into a force to be reckoned with, and it certainly worried the Admiralty.

During these years Jellicoe's rise in rank and responsibility was as impressive as it was seemingly inevitable; second in command, then later commander, of the Atlantic Fleet; Controller of the Navy as Third Sea Lord; second in command of the Home Fleet while commanding the 2nd Battle Squadron within it; then Second Sea Lord in 1912. At the outbreak of war in August 1914 Admiral George Callaghan was commanding the Home Fleet. The new First Lord of the Admiralty, Winston Churchill, immediately removed him from the post, beefed up the Home Fleet, renamed it the Grand Fleet, and appointed Jellicoe as an Admiral and its commander. Jellicoe was appalled at Callaghan's treatment and tried more than once to decline the post in protest. Many were up in arms about it, but Callaghan went quietly and discouraged any revolt over his removal. Commanding the Grand Fleet, Jellicoe now took over the single mightiest instrument that would guarantee Britain's wartime survival. It also became, along with Douglas Haig's army in France, the ultimate instrument of victory.

After flirting with audacious and risky Nelsonian alternatives, the Admiralty had come up with a strong and practical strategy by 1912 that would meet Britain's most pressing wartime needs. It could not afford to let German ships raid the trade routes on which British supplies depended, or interfere with the passage of its forces back and forth to the Continent, the Mediterranean and the Middle East. It was too hazardous to blockade the German High Seas Fleet close to its bases in northern Germany around Wilhelmshaven. Any significant fight with German capital ships should be well out into the North Sea. The strategy was therefore to block the High Seas Fleet's routes into the Atlantic via the Dover Straits and the Orkney-to-Norway passage. So with a large force of older cruisers and destroyers at Harwich to look after the narrow Dover Straits, the battlecruisers at Rosyth and Cromarty and the Grand Fleet spread between Cromarty and its new base far north at Scapa Flow, the German fleet would not be *able* to escape the North Sea in any direction without a major fight.

For their part, the admirals of the *Kaiserliche Marine* knew that having the High Seas Fleet take on Britain's still larger Grand Fleet in a single action would probably end badly. Admiral Tirpitz had toyed with *Risikogedanke* – risk theory – that if the German navy could inflict heavy losses on the British, even at the expense of its own fleet, British naval power could be so diminished as to end its global dominance and allow Germany to graduate from being a 'world power' to a 'great power'. But Kaiser Wilhelm II, who was solely responsible for the German navy through the *Kaiserliche Marine*, hated the thought of sacrificing his beloved fleet for a theory. Nevertheless, the inner belief that *Der Tag* would arrive sooner or later was persistent throughout a German fleet that showed immense pride and confidence in itself. The result was that Berlin's admirals looked for opportunities to destroy parts of the Grand Fleet piecemeal and even up the unfavourable odds. There was an element of risk theory in this as well. If the German navy could chip away at the Grand Fleet, it would anyway have the effect of stretching British naval power elsewhere in the world. But *Der Tag* never seemed too far away either.

From the beginning of hostilities, naval engagements occurred in several theatres – in Heligoland Bight, at the Falkland and Coronel Islands, and in the battle of Dogger Bank. But the two great fleets played a cat and mouse game across the North Sea, trying to lure parts of the opposition onto their own big guns over the horizon. The High Seas Fleet raided Britain's east coast, to lure the Harwich Force into a trap before battlecruisers could come racing down from Scotland to intercept. But after a mauling at Dogger Bank the Kaiser was reluctant to risk his ships again in the midst of the North Sea. The Grand Fleet, meanwhile, made regular sweeps from Orkney to Norway and south towards the Skagerrak, patrolling Germany's escape route into the Atlantic. Admiral Pohl, commanding the High Seas Fleet, was jabbing at the Grand Fleet, cautiously looking for an opening to land a heavier punch. Jellicoe in the Grand Fleet was keeping the gates to the Atlantic firmly shut. But whatever opportunities might arise for a full fleet action, he would never risk his force to the submarines, mines, and torpedo-carrying fast destroyers he knew were always out there. Early on he had made it clear to the Admiralty – who had agreed with him – that, if necessary, he would refuse an action if it threatened his fleet with too much exposure to mines and torpedoes.

Thus did both great fleets approach each other in thickening mist south-west of the Skagerrak on 31st May 1916, neither of them seeking, or expecting, the major fleet action that actually followed. Some 151 British ships approached ninety-nine German ships – 250 vessels in a small part of the North Sea. The Battle of Jutland is described from the perspective of David Beatty, leading the battlecruisers, in another chapter. John Jellicoe came upon the action in the second phase of the battle with his mighty force of twenty-four Dreadnoughts along with the vast fleet of light cruisers and destroyers sweeping ahead and protecting them. Jellicoe's force, even without Beatty's scouting group, was the most powerful naval fleet that had ever sailed. It constituted almost the totality of Britain's maritime power. As naval theory postulated, the Grand Fleet was arriving behind the scouting battlecruisers to strike the decisive blows. As he approached the ongoing battle, however, Jellicoe was poorly served by almost all the information given him. He was commanding in the most important naval action of the war and, in the absence of accurate information, was thrown back on his instincts and experience to make the most consequential tactical decisions any commander could confront. Historians tend to agree that for the most part he got it right.

British naval intelligence had captured all the cipher codes for the High Seas Fleet (and much else besides) and knew that Admiral Reinhard Scheer, the new and more dynamic German fleet commander, had a plan. Scheer intended to put a screen of U-boats close to the British coast, then take his fleet north towards the Skagerrak, enticing the Grand Fleet out, first to tangle with his U-boats and then, with luck, create for him a chance to lure David Beatty's scouting battlecruisers into a dangerous trap under his own big gun battleships, close to the German coast. By 16th May Admiralty intelligence knew that eighteen U-boats were on their way to take station off the Scottish and English coasts. Forewarned, the Grand Fleet and Beatty's battlecruisers put to sea from Scapa Flow, Cromarty and Rosyth several hours before the High Seas Fleet left Wilhelmshaven, passing over the U-boat screen unmolested before the German crews were in position. So far so good. But then, in an indefensible example of arrogant ignorance, Jellicoe was informed by naval intelligence that the High Seas Fleet was still in harbour over nine hours after it had sailed.[3] He proceeded towards the Skagerrak at only fifteen knots with his fleet in a tight box of six parallel columns of Dreadnoughts, keeping his big ships together and conserving fuel. He increasingly assumed this operation would now turn into yet another routine sweep. His seaplane carrier, *Campania*, had shown straight incompetence – simply missed the departure – and was not with the fleet at all, depriving Jellicoe of his only means of aerial reconnaissance. He was informed by naval intelligence, incorrectly, that German destroyers were capable of sowing minefields – which were always on commanders' minds. He was also led to believe that superior German torpedoes left very little trail in the water and were all the harder to detect. That, too was incorrect; but all this faulty intelligence played directly into his tactical decisions.

When Beatty's scouting battlecruisers encountered the 1st Scouting Group of the High Seas Fleet, a vigorous battle began from 14.20 in which the British ships took significant losses as they ran south, chasing the German battlecruisers who were luring them towards Scheer's big battleships coming north – exactly as Scheer had hoped. At the point where Beatty realised the whole High Seas Fleet was at sea and turned immediately north-west – now switching from pursuer to quarry to draw Scheer's biggest ships towards the Grand Fleet further north – Jellicoe was fifty miles away over the horizon. Beatty's first, urgent wireless report to Jellicoe at 16.30 misreported the position of the High Seas Fleet by seven miles. Jellicoe ordered his ships to full speed and plunged south. Commodore William Goodenough leading the 2nd Light Cruiser Squadron in the *Southampton* risked everything to stay within range of the German fleet to keep reporting its position. But ten enemy ships had engaged him and in taking violent evasive action to dodge the shells falling all around the *Southampton*, his position reports to Jellicoe were not precisely accurate. At 18.00 Beatty's battlecruisers now

---

3. Because Scheer always changed his fleet's normal wireless call sign (which was 'DK') when he sailed, allocating it to a shore base. Civilian analysts in 'Room 40' at the Admiralty knew all about this. But Capt. Thomas Jackson, Director Naval Operations, who had very little time for civilians in the Admiralty, walked into Room 40 and simply asked where they had placed the 'DK' callsign. 'Wilhelmshaven', he was told. And without further curiosity he walked out and had it reported to Jellicoe and Beatty.

running north-east finally converged with the Grand Fleet speeding south. Jellicoe twice signalled Beatty, 'Where is the enemy's battle fleet?', but both times got only imprecise answers. On the flagship *Iron Duke*, Jellicoe's officers were looking into the deepening haze. Beatty seems not to have realised that Jellicoe could not see what he himself could see more clearly from the bridge of his own flagship, HMS *Lion*. Jellicoe's ships were still in tight formation. Minutes were now critical and Jellicoe still had no accurate fix on his German opponents; indeed, some of the reports from across the fleet now flooding into the *Iron Duke* were flatly contradictory on how the High Seas Fleet was manoeuvring.

Jellicoe ordered his ships to form line astern – a hazardous high-speed manoeuvre, which took fifteen minutes – bringing his fleet into a battle line where all guns could be brought to bear simultaneously. He was right both in timing and direction. At least he knew by this stage that the High Seas Fleet would be appearing very soon; and he guessed enough about Scheer's probable heading to sail his own fleet so as to get between Scheer and his line of retreat towards Wilhelmshaven. Scheer, by contrast, was still not certain what was out there as he chased Beatty's force further north, then north-east; but on he went. As they came in sight of each other Jellicoe's Grand Fleet was positioned exactly to 'cross the T' in front of Scheer's ships and at 12,000 yards had them silhouetted against the western horizon for his range-finders and gunners.[4] It was a real shock for Scheer and a considerable act of judgement on Jellicoe's part. Before they had sighted the German fleet, it seemed to Jellicoe's officers and fellow captains, and certainly to Beatty, as they prepared to shake down into a battle line that turning the fleet to starboard, as they did so, was the natural manoeuvre to make. But Jellicoe stood at the compass and studied it intently; he looked around at the weather horizon down to about five miles, then he stared back at the compass. The bridge on the *Iron Duke* was hushed as he pondered. Then he issued crisp orders to his signals officer to hoist for the fleet to turn to port as it went into a battle line. Much later, in 1934, a team of analysts at the Naval Tactical School spent many days examining every scrap of information germane to that order and concluded it was the most ideal manoeuvre the Grand Fleet could have made at that particular moment. Jellicoe had spent less than thirty seconds amid the silence on his bridge thinking it through.

At last, and in the fading daylight, this was the long-anticipated encounter between the major ships of two great battle fleets. Jellicoe had much the better of it. After ten minutes of pummelling in which Jellicoe's own ships remained unharmed, Scheer broke off the action and disappeared into the gloom. He had inflicted a good deal of damage on Beatty's battlecruisers but none on Jellicoe's main force. From the rangefinders amid the tops of British ships, the German adversaries suddenly disappeared over the horizon. Jellicoe guessed, again correctly, that Scheer would go west or south-wards to escape British fire, taking him out of danger but further away from the safe waters around Wilhelmshaven to his south-east.

---

4. 'Crossing the T' meant that one fleet was in a line across the top of the T, bringing all its guns to bear on an enemy coming onward, and only able to open fire with the guns of its leading ships.

In one of the decisions for which Jellicoe was later much criticised, he didn't turn his fleet sharply south-west to pursue Scheer. Instead, with night approaching, he took the Grand Fleet due south towards Wilhelmshaven to block more decisively Scheer's eventual route to safety – where he would arrive, Jellicoe anticipated, sometime in the following dawn. That allowed the gap between himself and his enemy to increase, because Jellicoe was also wary of following a retreating force that might draw him onto mines or coordinated torpedo attacks from Scheer's destroyers. It was unlikely that German submarines could have been sent to the random part of the North Sea where battle had actually been joined, but on *Iron Duke* Jellicoe was receiving constant reports of U-boat sightings as lookouts saw periscopes when they were actually looking at debris in the water. In fact, just before 19.00 hours, *HMS Marlborough* of the Grand Fleet was hit and badly damaged by a torpedo launched by a German destroyer.

A few minutes later Scheer turned his whole fleet around and began sailing due east towards the Grand Fleet that was heading south. He later claimed this was a deliberate manoeuvre as part of his bold battle plan. But that is very unlikely. Almost certainly, he was trying to sail behind the Grand Fleet as it steamed southwards, passing to the north of it, thence to turn south himself and dash straight down to Wilhelmshaven and safety. Instead, he miscalculated and blundered straight into the middle of Jellicoe's ships. Without any manoeuvring, Jellicoe had 'crossed the T' again – having his ships in line, with most guns able to bombard the German fleet as it came towards him.

Once more, Scheer broke off after ten minutes, instructing Hipper's battlecruisers and older ships to make what became known as 'Hipper's death ride'. They sailed suicidally straight at the Grand Fleet, accompanied by a big torpedo attack from German destroyers, covering the escape of Scheer's big ships who disappeared westwards again. Thanks to the bravery of Hipper and his commanders and sailors – which their opponents genuinely admired – Scheer's ploy worked. Jellicoe might have welcomed the chance to destroy Hipper's battlecruisers charging towards him, and it would have turned him to face the torpedoes as his fleet combed them. But instead, he turned away at high speed, outrunning many of the torpedoes and giving his captains more time for combing manoeuvres, while the 4th Light Cruiser Squadron was sent to deal with the oncoming destroyers. Even so, there were some narrow escapes as his fleet dodged the running torpedoes. Hipper's battlecruisers were then able to turn away too, escaping the destruction they must surely have anticipated.

Again, Jellicoe had spurned the prospect of a close chase and a decisive fleet action against Scheer's force which had now twice shown it would not stand up to a Grand Fleet bombardment. But true to his own doctrine, Jellicoe would not expose the fleet to unknown threats that night in favour of some risky nocturnal Trafalgar. Instead, there followed several chaotic hours of ad hoc encounters as both fleets converged on roughly southerly courses, six miles apart, towards Wilhelmshaven, each uncertain of the position of the other. During that confusion there were nine separate actions in the dark between British and German light forces causing losses and sinkings on both sides. In one case British destroyers found themselves attacking German Dreadnought battleships at merely 1,000 yards. In another, the destroyer HMS *Spitfire* involuntarily rammed the giant battleship *Nassau*. It lost almost all its superstructure, but made it back to port with pieces of the *Nassau* strewn across its deck. By 03.30 the following morning Scheer had finally passed behind the faster British fleet and was inside the minefields in relative safety off the coast of Jutland. Jellicoe was waiting for Scheer to appear somewhere from the west as the Grand Fleet straddled his route home to Wilhelmshaven. But it was all too late. At 04.40 Jellicoe's ships turned for home.

Within hours, Germany was *en fete* celebrating a fabulous victory over the Royal Navy. Its full losses were not immediately reported but the High Seas Fleet had certainly sunk more British ships than it had lost itself. The Royal Navy lost three big-name frontline battlecruisers, three older armoured cruisers, eight destroyers and endured a human cost of almost 7,000 casualties. The High Seas Fleet had lost one battlecruiser, one pre-dreadnought heavy cruiser, four light cruisers and five destroyers, incurring just over 3,500 casualties. British ships arrived back at their Scottish bases a day later, when news of a famous Royal Navy defeat was already more than half-way across the globe. The world believed it. Britain, and the Admiralty, were depressed by it. Pride was taken in the many acts of individual valour, of course, but it was impossible to deny that Jutland was no Trafalgar.

Indeed, it wasn't. It was better than that. After Trafalgar, the victorious British fleet had limped, or was towed, into Gibraltar for an extensive process of rebuilding. But when the Grand Fleet arrived back in Scapa Flow that evening, Jellicoe signalled the Admiralty that the fleet was ready to steam out again at four hours' notice. The gates to the Atlantic remained firmly shut to Germany, while the High Seas Fleet – the survivors much battered – underwent long repairs and refits. Germany's losses at Jutland were proportionately greater than the Royal Navy's. The heavy imbalance of maritime power in favour of Britain remained completely unchanged; Jutland hadn't altered it at all. 'Risk theory', not to mention '*Der Tag*' both remained ephemeral. The High Seas Fleet had been unable to go toe-to-toe with the Grand Fleet – just two ten-minute contests from which Scheer had pulled away, escaping to safety – and it was never to try again. There were two short, ineffective forays towards the British coast once the High Seas Fleet was reconstituted, in August and October that year, and some commerce raiding in Scandinavia in April 1918. But there was no appetite in any of these excursions for another major confrontation. On 21 November 1918 the whole seventy-strong fleet finally sailed en masse across the North Sea to Scapa Flow – to internment; after which German captains scuttled the fleet in June 1919 in a last, sad gesture of defiance.

John Jellicoe was duly honoured after Jutland and became First Sea Lord in November that year. But he was increasingly suffering from his bullet wound in the lung; he was depressed, and depressive. He was depressed by the loss of Field Marshal Kitchener when the *Hampshire* went down, just days after Jutland. And he was depressive about the U-boat threat to Britain's survival in the war. With the High Seas Fleet rendered strategically irrelevant by Jutland, Berlin turned again to unrestricted U-boat warfare to starve Britain – just as the Royal Navy planned to blockade Germany to the point of starvation. As First Sea Lord, Jellicoe was primarily concerned with the U-boat threat and his mood veered from sombre to complete despair. Neither he, nor the Admiralty in general, believed that convoys were the answer, but were morosely unable to come up with any other ideas. He told the War Cabinet in spring 1917 that the country would be finished by 1918, so effective was the German U-boat campaign. The threat was certainly serious but, in truth, Jellicoe had lost his perspective on the overall maritime picture and his cool analytical brain seemed to have deserted him. He was prickly and defensive. Others in the government observed how the Admiralty seemed steeped in fatalistic gloom under his leadership. After a year in post, he was summarily removed in a letter sent to his London home at six-o-clock on Christmas Eve 1917.

Not least, he was being constantly attacked for his handling of Jutland. David Beatty and his supporters became increasingly vocal in an inquest on the battle that dominated the navy for years and has continued ever since. Jellicoe's service after the war – as Admiral of the Fleet and then in 1925 as 1st Earl of Jellicoe – were effectively consumed by the feud that Beatty and his supporters wilfully stoked. Did Beatty's battlecruisers let the big ships down? Or did they, rather, deliver the High Seas Fleet to a destruction that Jellicoe failed to execute? There was real personal bitterness between them as the arguments raged back and forth. Jellicoe tried to maintain his dignity, at least in public, but was worn down by it. It would be fair to say that Jellicoe won the argument among serious naval historians. But in a way, Beatty won the subsequent argument about battle tactics. In the Second World War the Royal Navy was far more influenced by Beatty's tactics and his Nelsonian attitudes than by those of Jellicoe.

Jellicoe died of pneumonia in November 1935, the bullet from his old wound still lodged in his left lung. Beatty, himself very ill, insisted on being one of the bearers carrying Jellicoe's coffin. He kept to himself whatever he was thinking as he did so, knowing for sure he was very soon to follow. Beatty died four months later. They are both interred in the crypt of St Paul's Cathedral – like Nelson and Collingwood just a few yards away – laid to rest right next to each other. One wonders sometimes what their ghosts must talk about.

26

Admiral David Beatty

David Beatty's name is always associated with that of John Jellicoe. They were the two admirals who commanded British ships at the Battle of Jutland in 1916. Jellicoe was the superior officer leading the Grand Fleet, and Beatty commanded its associated fleet of battlecruisers. The battlecruisers had a crucial role to play in Grand Fleet operations, scouting ahead of it and, in the case of Jutland, acting to deliver the German High Seas Fleet to its nemesis under the guns of Jellicoe's mighty force of Dreadnoughts. The battle didn't go that way; it was a confused and frustrating affair. The German fleet escaped and claimed Jutland as a historic victory, and the names of Beatty and Jellicoe have forever after been linked within the fierce arguments over whose fault it was that the outcome of Jutland seemed so disappointing. In fact, Jutland was a strategic success for the Royal Navy, but that was not how it felt on the day, or indeed the days after. And the personal bitterness of the subsequent arguments over command responsibility at Jutland only served to weld Beatty's name firmly to Jellicoe's for more than a century afterwards.

Beatty and Jellicoe had completely different personal characters and vastly different private lives. Nevertheless, their respective careers wove a series of figure-of-eight patterns as they acted, and interacted, one in the wake of the other for some thirty-five years. It began in the Chinese Boxer rebellion of 1900 and ended in their deaths within four months of each other in 1935 and 1936. Beatty's personal attacks on Jellicoe's reputation during their later years only reinforced the popular association of his name with that of his superior officer. Beatty's reputation in history is better served, however, when it is not. Because he made some important contributions to the Royal Navy that emerged from the First World War and later served a longer stint than anyone as First Sea Lord when the balance of global power was inexorably shifting away from Britain in the 1920s.

David Beatty's father was a tall and powerful Irish officer with a chequered history in the British Army. His mother was a strong-minded Irish beauty married to someone else. After her divorce, they married and settled in Cheshire, but by then they had two sons, Charles and David, both illegitimate, and relevant dates were obscured to disguise it. David was born in 1871 and he spent his childhood and youth allied to elder brother Charles (with whom he was always extraordinarily close) against the overbearing behaviour of their father.

Young Beatty was possibly relieved to become a naval cadet at the age of thirteen. He went from midshipman to lieutenant via a family-influenced post on HMS *Alexandra*, flagship of the Mediterranean Fleet, and a course at the Royal Naval

College, Greenwich. His early naval career was humdrum, mainly because he didn't take it over-seriously. He was middle of all his classes and managed only indifferent assessment marks. He did, however, score rather more highly on the social scale. He cheerfully misbehaved and established good friendships with the daughter of the Commander-in-Chief Mediterranean Fleet, with fellow officer Lt Stanley Colville, and with an impressive number of London actresses and performers during his studies at Greenwich. Their signed photographs, it was said, adorned the walls of his cabin at the naval college.

From the very first, Beatty had an ambiguous attitude to authority. Unlike his father, he was barely of medium height, but just like him, was wilful, he could be aggressive, and was driven by personal objectives – in which the navy didn't always figure pre-eminently. He perched his naval cap at a jaunty angle over his left eye. In photograph after photograph for the rest of his career, even in later official portraits, that carefully arranged symbol of non-conformity was his trademark. As the cap acquired more gold braid with promotion, its studied impropriety was a challenge to the rest of the establishment.

A greater character contrast between Beatty and Jellicoe could hardly be imagined. The first of the figure-of-eight loops his career did with Jellicoe's occurred when he served as a lieutenant on the *Camperdown* in 1893 – the very ship that had collided with, and sunk, the *Victoria*, flagship of the foolishly autocratic Admiral Tryon three months earlier, and from which Jellicoe had been one of the lucky *Victoria* survivors.

If Beatty was an establishment rebel and a glamorous poseur, he was also a young man of innate ability. As he matured, he showed he had the knack of motivating others and they, in turn, trusted his judgement. His big chance came in 1896, oddly enough, with Lord Kitchener in the Sudan. From then onwards, he began regularly to leapfrog other officers in the pecking order as he stamped his strong personality on every command. At the end of Beatty's life the Archbishop of Canterbury opined that, 'In him something of the spirit of Nelson seemed to have come back'. Beatty would certainly have inclined to that view. That return of the Nelson spirit, if such it was, began in the Sudan. Beatty's good friend on the *Alexandra* and then his commander on the *Trafalgar* had been Stanley Colville. Kitchener appointed Colville to command his flotilla of gunboats as he made his way slowly up the Nile to defeat the Mahdist rebels of Omdurman and Khartoum. Colville asked for Beatty as his second in command for the gunboats, and when Colville himself was wounded in the first action at Dongola, Beatty took over the flotilla. He handled the gunboats well in the push to Omdurman and during the battle itself. There were several difficult challenges and he seemed not to put a foot wrong in providing naval support to Kitchener's ground force. After Omdurman Beatty steamed on to Fashoda to support Kitchener in the quaint standoff between British and French forces in Sudan. Kitchener was impressed with Beatty, who was awarded the DSO for his leadership and promoted to the rank of commander, ahead of four hundred more senior lieutenants. On that campaign he also met an even more youthful cavalry officer, Winston Churchill, with whom he shared a bond through the 4th Hussars with whom his scandalous father had also served.

As empathetic personalities they liked each other, and that particular connection was later to save Beatty's naval career.

The following year he was on the vast China station in the *Barfleur*. Like Jellicoe, he was involved in operations to supress the Boxer Rebellion of 1900. Jellicoe was deputy in Edward Seymour's column trying to move from Tientsin to relieve the foreigners' Legation Quarter in Peking. But Seymour had become surrounded, Jellicoe was seriously wounded in a major action at Peitsang and was expected to die, and Tientsin itself was under attack. Beatty led 150 naval personnel from the *Barfleur* to join a cobbled together naval brigade to help defend Tientsin. He was wounded in the left arm, but then discharged himself from hospital to take part in the relief operation that Tientsin was eventually able to mount to extricate Seymour's force. The wounded David Beatty was in the action that brought the more badly wounded John Jellicoe to safety. He returned to Britain with a damaged left arm that required complex surgery.

Beatty was promoted to captain on his return and acquired warrior status after the Sudan and China, living with his brother in Suffolk and engaging in the worlds of hunting and London high life. He had rank and recognition and he clearly applied himself more than before to matters of naval technique. If his progress was beginning to parallel that of Jellicoe, however, his personal life showed increasing shades of Nelson. Before he went to the China station he had fallen hopelessly in love with Ethel Tree, a fabulously wealthy American heiress, who inconveniently was married to Ronald Tree at the time. There seems to have been an illicit affair, followed by some volatile declarations while he went to war and then returned, wounded, to an uncertain emotional future. His personal letters to her were full of dramatic Nelsonian angst. But Ethel obtained a divorce from Ronald Tree and she and Beatty were married in May 1901 in Hanover Square with none of their families present, both of which thoroughly disapproved. The following year, Jellicoe was married in what would turn out to be a long and happy union for him. But Beatty, twelve years younger than Jellicoe, was embarking on the stormiest relationship of his entire life.

Nevertheless, with Ethel's wealth behind him, Beatty had an independence that did not rely on his naval career. When he was sent to command a cruiser in the Mediterranean Fleet, Ethel rented the Capua Palace in Malta so they could pursue the social high life ashore. The first of their two sons was born in the palace. Luxurious marriage to Ethel saw him through his rapid rise to real naval seniority, but their relationship became an increasing trial to him – her demands, her wealthy eccentricity (many thought her mentally ill), their mutual jealousies and her promiscuity simply wore him down. It was indicative that on the outbreak of war in 1914, Ethel donated her personal steam yacht to the navy as a hospital ship, kitted out at her expense, but then seemed to assume she would command the vessel herself and determine its locations. Beatty was increasingly driven to distraction by Ethel's behaviour. His letters indicate he adored her beauty and spirit, but he began to indulge his own infidelities. His valued friendship with Eugenie Godfrey-Faussett, wife of a fellow naval officer whom he had known for many years, turned into a decade-long affair that was half-way discreet but evidently precious to him. Still, when Ethel pre-deceased him in 1932 Beatty requested that on his own death, he be buried alongside her at Dingley Hall, their home in Northamptonshire – a request the nation subsequently denied since he was then a prominent war-leader and belonged somewhere more public.

For the time being, these years of rapid naval expansion gave Beatty lots of opportunities. He commanded cruisers from 1902 to 1905. He was personally good at ship handling, he ran his commands with drive and efficiency and promoted gunnery that excelled at least in the rates of fire if not always in marksmanship. And he was popular on the mess decks; they liked his blend of buccaneering discipline. He took over the battleship *Queen* in the Atlantic Fleet in 1908 and then leap-frogged promotions again to become a rear-admiral in 1910; at thirty-eight the youngest flag officer in over a century, just as Nelson had been. He then almost sabotaged his own career when he was offered second-in-command of the Atlantic Fleet – a highly prestigious role – but declined since he wanted a post in the Home Fleet to be nearer his social life and family. It was a gesture of high-handed arrogance from a young and wealthy senior officer and it was too much for many at the Admiralty, though he himself felt aggrieved at the way he was treated. For some months his career hung in the balance. But then in June 1912 Churchill became First Lord of the Admiralty and took Beatty on as his naval secretary. Just over a year later Beatty approached the pinnacle of his command career when he was appointed rear-admiral commander of the 1st Battlecruiser Squadron. And he was late taking up that particular appointment because he didn't choose to cut short his Monte Carlo holiday.

With the Invincible-class battlecruisers, Beatty was taking on some of the Dreadnoughts that would determine the outcome of the First World War at sea. In 1914 Admiral John Jellicoe was given command of the Grand Fleet (a reinforced version of the old Home Fleet) at Cromarty and Scapa Flow, with Beatty as his subordinate commander controlling the lighter, faster battlecruisers that could act alone with great power, but whose role with the Grand Fleet was to scout and protect the heavier Dreadnoughts and Super-Dreadnought battleships as they went into action. Beatty's was a weighty and exciting role for any senior officer; to command a potent force big enough to conduct major naval engagements in its own right, but also to act as the leading edge of the most powerful naval force the world had ever known whenever the Grand Fleet emerged from Scapa Flow.

The revolutionary power of the Dreadnoughts has been described in another chapter and the Battle of Jutland has already been viewed from Jellicoe's perspective. Commanding the battlecruisers, Beatty had a fair amount of leeway and his nature was to use it to the fullest extent. With less strategic responsibility than rested on Jellicoe's shoulders, Beatty could try to create his own 'Nelson touch' with his battlecruiser squadron. He laid great stress on high-tempo gunnery and his ships' manoeuvrability. From the beginning of this command his intentions were clear. At that time the Royal Navy was preoccupied with the need to instil manoeuvre discipline and adherence to higher orders as its heavier, powerful fleets sailed and ordered themselves for battle. That obsession had created George Tryon's collision tragedy in 1893 since none would query his disastrous orders even when the collision was unfolding in front of them. But Beatty issued very different standing orders to his battlecruiser captains. He said they should display 'initiative, resource, determination, and no fear of accepting responsibility'. He said that his instructions to them 'will be of a very general character', and he relied on them 'using their own discretion as to how to act in unforeseen circumstances'. This was not what most commanders of battle squadrons were saying at the time, but this approach went deep into Beatty's own psyche.

If Beatty's intentions were very clear, however, his own signals protocols were not. His greatest drawback in this respect was his appointed signals officer. Ralph Seymour was a young lieutenant who, to put it kindly, was inexperienced in signalling. But he was very well-connected and his sister was a close friend of Churchill's wife. Beatty had no acquaintance with him when Seymour was made flag lieutenant on his own flagship, HMS *Lion*, but he was apparently impressed by the connections. Compounding the problem, Beatty's standing orders added that he would not necessarily wait for acknowledgement of his signals from following ships before acting on them in the flagship; speed of response was too important. Both of these drawbacks were to cost him dearly in the battles to come.

The first naval clash after the outbreak of war occurred at the end of August 1914. The commander of the Harwich Force got Admiralty agreement to let him set a trap for German cruisers and destroyers that patrolled with great punctuality inside the Heligoland Bight, protecting the High Seas Fleet's main bases in northern Germany. It was actually a very risky raid and Jellicoe, who had not been informed of this caper until forty-eight-hours before it began, immediately sent Beatty with three battlecruisers to give it some long-range cover. It was just as well since the whole raid could have been a disaster. But the battlecruisers were decisive and German forces were surprised and outnumbered, losing three cruisers and a destroyer and having six others badly mauled. Beatty had no role in planning the operation and only a marginal one in the battle itself, but his Dreadnoughts were the margin that made the difference, and he was immediately a public hero as British ships returned home to cheering crowds.

In January the following year there was a great opportunity to inflict serious damage on the German High Seas Fleet at Dogger Bank. With German naval codes in British hands, Beatty's battlecruiser squadron was in a position to turn the tables on Franz Hipper's own battlecruiser squadron as it ventured across the North Sea towards the Harwich Force. Suddenly fearing a trap, Hipper headed for home and Beatty's ships began a fierce stern chase after them from 35,000 yards. But it was indecisive. British fire was too concentrated on one ship, the *Blucher*, which was eventually sunk, and British gunnery (characteristically at the time) was poor, allowing German ships to escape. Beatty's *Lion* was badly damaged and pulled out of the chase, after which his signals caused confusion among his captains, seeming to encourage them to concentrate on the already doomed *Blucher* rather than make the most of the distress of the *Seydlitz* and the *Derfflinger* as they fled.[1] The escape of the badly damaged *Seydlitz* taught the Germans quite a lot. The destruction of the *Blucher* taught the Admiralty nothing. Dogger Bank was a British victory and convinced the Royal Navy

---

1. Beatty signalled his ships to 'attack the rear of the enemy', but Seymour had left a previous 'north-east course' signal still flying, so Beatty's captains read it as 'attack the rear of the enemy bearing north-east', which directed them to the *Blucher*.

that it would eventually catch and destroy the High Seas Fleet. But the fate of the *Seydlitz* convinced the Germans that they had to modify their gun-turret design to prevent flash fires inside the turret going straight down into the magazines. It was an unrecognised lesson for the Royal Navy that it would learn the hard way.

Beatty had shown characteristic elan, if not great clarity, at Dogger Bank and was again lauded for it. His 1st Battle Squadron was designated a 'battlecruiser fleet' and after much nagging, four of the Queen Elizabeth class Super Dreadnoughts were taken from Jellicoe's fleet and added to it – the *Barham*, *Warspite*, *Valiant* and *Malaya* – a little slower than his battlecruisers, but more formidable in every other respect. These Super Dreadnoughts became the core of the 5th Battle Squadron within Beatty's strengthened fleet, and its role at Jutland was to have a significant effect on the outcome.

In May 1916 the long-awaited showdown off the Jutland coast arrived, as outlined in another chapter. British intelligence knew the Germans planned a High Seas Fleet sortie into the North Sea, so set sail first to try to spring a trap as it emerged. Beatty's battlecruiser fleet was in the forefront of the action. Unfortunately for him, it also made his fleet the exemplar of so much that was not right about the Royal Navy at that time, and it exposed the limitations of his own Nelsonian approach to conflict at sea. Some have thought the element that most deserved Beatty's own 'Nelson touch' was just the outrageous good luck of his famous predecessor. But he doesn't escape the judgement of history so lightly. Beatty's thinking and actions at Jutland were deficient in several respects.

His fleet consisted of the 1st and 2nd Battlecruiser Squadrons accompanied by his new 5th Battle Squadron – ten Dreadnoughts and Super Dreadnoughts in all – and their screening forces of three light cruiser squadrons and two destroyer flotillas alongside elements of two other destroyer flotillas and one seaplane carrier for reconnaissance. They set out from Rosyth while Jellicoe's Grand Fleet sailed from Cromarty and Scapa Flow, going some 200 miles eastwards intending, if they didn't locate any German forces, to turn north and rendezvous with Jellicoe about ninety miles off the Skagerrak entrance. No fewer than 151 British ships were at sea for this engagement, and they would eventually confront some ninety-nine German vessels. Beatty's scouting group consisted of over fifty ships; Jellicoe's Grand Fleet of another hundred. Between them, they deployed thirty-seven Dreadnoughts and Super-dreadnoughts, thirty-three armoured and light cruisers and eighty-two destroyers, plus other specialist and aircraft elements. The two most powerful navies in the world were rapidly converging in the North Sea.

Both forces of British and German battlecruisers – their scouting groups – were out ahead of their main fleets. Franz Hipper's 1st Scouting Group was probing northwards, while Beatty's ships were moving steadily eastwards, based on a faulty intelligence report to both him and Jellicoe that the High Seas Fleet hadn't yet left port. The opposing scouting groups actually arrived within fifty miles of each other on 31st May and discovered their close proximity by accident at 14.20 hours when their own light screening forces clashed. Beatty realised something was afoot and turned his force south-east to intercept.

And this is where Beatty's own battle began to go wrong. Not anticipating immediate action, he had his 5th Battle Squadron, with its slower Super Dreadnoughts, sailing five miles behind his 1st and 2nd Squadrons. He was anxious always to have his racy battlecruisers lead any action. The whole force had been steadily zig-zagging as a precaution against submarine attack. But when Beatty signalled the decisive turn towards the south-east, the 5th Battle Squadron didn't see his signal flags clearly at that distance and amid the extra smoke created by his ships moving to full steam ahead. HMS *Tiger* should have been repeating every flag signal by searchlight but didn't replicate this one. Wireless communication was unreliable and not used consistently in Beatty's force.[2] Most importantly, Beatty's *Lion* hauled down its flag signal quite quickly, which was the sign to execute the order, and then he was off to the intercept, without waiting for acknowledgement that his signal had been received. Beatty sped away with the 1st and 2nd Battlecruiser Squadrons while his 5th Battle Squadron turned the other way onto its next routine zigzag course. His fleet was now split and heading in opposite directions as the interception approached. In the eight minutes it took for this mistake to be corrected by searchlight, the 5th Battle Squadron was then ten miles behind Beatty's main force. Whatever happened next, the big guns would be arriving late at the interception.

At 15.30 the two opposing battlecruiser fleets saw each other directly. Beatty immediately manoeuvred into an aggressive position to close with Hipper's ships and cut him off from his line of retreat. Hipper did an about turn and headed towards Admiral Scheer's main High Seas Fleet forty miles behind him. The battle was running to the south at high speed, twenty-five knots – Beatty chasing Hipper, who was drawing the British onto the big guns of Scheer's main fleet coming north, while Beatty's own big guns in the 5th Battle Squadron were labouring still seven miles astern. Even so, Beatty's 12-inch and 13.5-inch guns outranged Hipper's 11-inch and 12-inch guns and the British could have opened fire some minutes before the Germans were able to. But they didn't. British range-finders were inferior to German designs and in high-speed manoeuvring the ranges constantly changed. British gunnery officers consistently over-estimated the distance and when he might have given the orders himself, Beatty was pre-occupied with sending vital wireless signals to Jellicoe. As the range closed, with British ships silhouetted clearly on the western horizon, the German battlecruisers opened fire first. Five minutes later, Beatty's flag captain on the *Lion* took it upon himself to return fire at 16,000 yards, since Beatty had still not returned to the bridge. For several minutes the British had given up a natural range advantage when they could have struck the first blows without reply.

Faulty British range-finding continued uncorrected. German targets laying eastwards and obscured by the smoke of British destroyers passing between the fleets, also rendered Beatty's gunnery less effective than it should have been. There were many other reasons for poor British gunnery, not least in the poor quality of British shells. But within fifteen minutes both sides were certainly hurting each other. Then, famously, the *Lion*

---

2. Though it was part of Jellicoe's standing orders that every signal should be hoisted, and then repeated by searchlight and wireless.

was severely hit by the *Lutzow* in its midships Q-turret. The flagship almost blew up right there, and again later on from more fires in the same turret. It staggered out of the attack for a while before rejoining the fray. After twenty-five minutes Beatty's 5th Battle Squadron had finally arrived and was in action. Now the Germans were seriously outnumbered and out-gunned by the Super Dreadnoughts' 15-inch shells. But fatal flaws in British turret design then cost it three valuable ships. British anti-flash barriers were too few and inadequate if a turret was hit directly. The flash of a cordite fire inside some turrets passed down through the trunk and hoists and straight into the magazines. Keen to achieve a maximum rate of fire, Beatty's gunners had also stockpiled opened cordite charges near the hoists and doors. Unaccountably, it seemed, the *Indefatigable* just disintegrated after being hit. Then the *Queen Mary* – pride of the battlecruisers – simply blew up and sank rapidly. Two hours later another of Beatty's battlecruisers, the *Invincible*, was blown in half in the same way. It was the *Queen Mary*'s demise that prompted Beatty's famous and quite superfluous comment, 'There seems to be something wrong with our bloody ships today.'

All this was taking place while the destroyers of both sides were engaged in a running dog-fight of their own, trying to get torpedo attacks off against any of the enemy's big ships they could close with. At 16.50 Beatty was informed by his screening ships that Scheer's High Seas Fleet was coming toward him. Until then, he had been the hunter, giving chase with superior forces. Beatty's situation was now reversed. He would surely lose most of his battlecruisers if he kept on towards Scheer's High Seas Fleet. But this was also the opportunity the British wanted. Beatty turned away to the north-west, timing his move perfectly, and luring the whole German force to chase him due north and then north-east leading them towards Jellicoe's Grand Fleet which was still fifty miles away, plunging south at top speed.

Even so, more flags-only signalling from the *Lion* was missed again by Beatty's 5th Battle Squadron. As he headed north, he passed his big battleships still going south. There was a delay before the 5th Battle Squadron received specific instructions to follow him. The 5th Battle Squadron then did the maritime equivalent of a handbrake turn, presenting itself – in procession – as side on targets in front of the big guns of Scheer's battleships chasing north. For thirty minutes the squadron was pummelled by Hipper's and Scheer's combined force while Beatty's 1st and 2nd Squadrons ran beyond German range.

Jellicoe, coming south to support Beatty, didn't know the position or course of the High Seas Fleet. As Beatty reached Jellicoe, he seems not to have realised that his commander-in-chief would not be able to see what he himself could easily observe from his vantage point nearer the enemy. He didn't give Jellicoe an immediate report and when he was prompted, his reports were imprecise because he assumed Jellicoe could see the whole picture anyway. Jellicoe couldn't, and had already been forced to make some accurate guesses before Beatty's signals arrived. Beatty had, however, been tactically astute in pulling his pursuers across Jellicoe's path as he approached, so his own commander-in-chief would see them before German commanders knew that the Grand Fleet was closing in. As Beatty's and Jellicoe's forces combined, the Grand Fleet turned into a line of twenty-four Dreadnoughts and Super Dreadnoughts, six miles long, 'crossing the T' of Scheer's fleet and giving German commanders a nasty surprise as their ships emerged from the gloom.[3] German tactics, to draw Beatty's battlecruisers under the guns of the High Seas Fleet's big ships had been completely turned round. Now Beatty had drawn the whole High Seas Fleet to emerge under the even bigger guns of the Grand Fleet. He had achieved exactly what was intended. Now it was up to Jellicoe, and Beatty watched and manoeuvred in increasing irritation as he saw Jellicoe playing safe – always concerned to preserve the Grand Fleet rather than risk it for a 'new Trafalgar'.

All battles are far more confusing than they seem in retrospect. As Beatty manoeuvred his ships to join the front of the main British battle line he seems to have executed a complete circle, losing touch with the enemy as he did so. Until the end of his life Beatty vehemently denied that this peculiar manoeuvre ever happened; but the logs of those ships following him round show that it did. Young Jack Cornwell VC, badly wounded, famously worked his gun alone on HMS *Chester* as it was being demolished by four German cruisers. In truth, he was almost certainly dead before his heroics are supposed to have happened. But he showed that a sixteen-year-old boy was prepared to stand by his gun, wounded and alone if necessary, and his VC and the 5.5 inch gun in question are still displayed in the Imperial War Museum to record the fact.

Other reputations were made in the chaos. Lt Commander John Tovey in the destroyer *Onslow* had already tried a torpedo attack on the battlecruiser *Lutzow*, then the light cruiser *Wiesbaden*. Out of the mist, the rest of Hipper's battlecruisers suddenly appeared, closing at 8,000 yards. Tovey was determined to keep trying while he still had torpedoes left. Already badly damaged, and making barely ten knots, Tovey had to take *Onslow*'s helm himself, launching a suicidal attack with his last two torpedoes – both of which he thought had hit but which actually missed. Surprisingly, the *Onslow* made it out of the maelstrom of shells, towed to safety by HMS *Defender* and thence hauled back to Aberdeen. Twenty-five years later in 1941, John Tovey – Admiral Tovey – led the task force that finally cornered and sank the *Bismarck*. Other commanders also behaved with a Nelsonian heart, if not with the same tactical head. As the combined British force sailed across 'the T' ahead of Scheer's ships, Rear Admiral Robert Arbuthnot, whom Andrew Gordon describes as, 'in a colloquial if not a clinical sense, insane', led his light cruisers across the bows of Beatty's line to get at the wallowing *Wiesbaden*. His manoeuvre forced the battlecruisers away from their targets, his smoke obscured their view of them, and he put his own poorly-armoured ship in exactly the spot where the well-armoured battlecruisers had intended to operate. The end was quick, and Arbuthnot's *Defence* was split in two by a terrific explosion before most German ships could even train their guns on it.

The main action, however, became increasingly indecisive as darkness approached. Beatty's battlecruisers were about six miles ahead of Jellicoe's leading ships, but Scheer had escaped over the horizon to the west and no one was sure where the next contact might happen. In some frustration Beatty signalled to Jellicoe, 'submit that the van of

---

3. The Grand Fleet's order of battle was still awaiting the late arrival of the big ships in the 5th Battle Squadron to add to its numbers.

the battleships follow me: we can then cut off the whole of the enemy's fleet'. Jellicoe was already heading warily west before turning the fleet south, but Beatty wanted more big ship support to take his battlecruisers hunting aggressively due westwards. Since Beatty had lost contact and was only guessing at the enemy's position, that was a risk. Was the signal some bravado presumption from an arrogant subordinate commander, or something intended for the historical record by a man who could see the battle slipping away? Either way, it presaged the future because fierce arguments about Jutland – letting the Germans escape the great reckoning – commenced as soon as British ships returned to port.

Jellicoe became First Sea Lord after the battle and Beatty was promoted into Jellicoe's role commanding the Grand Fleet. He was not short of ideas. Ahead of most thinkers, he pressed to use the navy's growing air power to launch torpedo-bomber attacks on German ships in Wilhelmshaven, but the Admiralty shelved the plan for lack of resources. Above all, he itched to show how he would not fail to create the new Trafalgar once another opportunity arose. But as he sat and chafed in Scapa Flow, that opportunity for a shot at real glory never came. And as it failed to arrive Beatty became all the more vehement – and personal – in his criticisms of Jellicoe's tactics; more defensive, too, about his own command of the battlecruisers at Jutland. It must have been a bitter sort of satisfaction for him to escort the High Seas Fleet to Rosyth and thence to Scapa Flow for its internment in November 1918. In an act of apparent malice, he unlawfully forbade the flying of the German flag in its fleet – unlawful because the fleet was interned; it had not surrendered and it eventually scuttled itself rather than do so.

In 1919 he again followed Jellicoe, becoming a five-star admiral and First Sea Lord in November that year.[4] Beatty did eight years in the role; the first officer to do so and an indication of his influence and competence in it, and in contrast to Jellicoe's frankly depressive, brief, performance as '1SL'. As such, Beatty was presiding over a post-war navy that was subject to inevitable downsizing, coupled with a steep decline in Britain's national finances. He fought against the trends on behalf of the navy, got the Singapore naval base underway – a matter of some strategic importance – and frequently threatened to resign. He played a key role in the negotiations for the Washington Naval Treaty of 1922, which agreed specified limits for the navies of the United States, Britain, Japan, France and Italy. It marked the end of Britain's unchallenged naval dominance which had been unbroken since 1815, but it recognised the new reality. Britain would henceforth accept parity, at least with the US navy. There followed a decade and a half of further limitations, however, which Beatty found very hard to accept and pushed Britain's naval power further down the scale. He was fighting a series of losing battles for the navy both domestically and internationally, but he fought hard. He retired from the Service in 1927 and roundly denounced the 1930 London Naval Treaty from his seat in the House of Lords. Nevertheless, he had also done a great deal both through administration and his own force of personality to

---

4. Though Jellicoe had been peremptorily sacked at Christmas 1917 and replaced by Roslyn Wemyss in the meantime who was First Sea Lord until November 1919.

maintain the morale of the Service during difficult years of transition. At least he had the pleasure, as he retired, of seeing the entry into service of the sister ships, *Nelson* and *Rodney*, which were to play significant battleship roles in the Second World War. For a man who had once commanded Kitchener's Nile gunboats against the Mahdi in Sudan, this must have given him some personal satisfaction. He had kept alive the sort of Nelsonian strut that he thought had let the navy down at Jutland.

But he would not let Jutland go. The Royal Navy was obsessed with it while Beatty was still in the Service. His attitude encouraged division among naval officers into supporters and detractors and a blizzard of often foolish books and articles appeared. When Captain John Harper's official report on the battle landed on his First Sea Lord's desk, Beatty destroyed it with constant demands for revisions until it was scuppered in 1920, then replaced with a highly mendacious account of which he approved.[5] He tried to influence Sir Julian Corbett's official history of the Royal Navy at war, but then Corbett died, so Beatty had a 'Dissenting Preface' – undermining Corbett's Jutland section – inserted into a book he could not then change. Jellicoe, of course, was not guiltless in the personal animosity all these arguments generated, though he avoided writing any personal commentaries about them, save in his memoir, *The Grand Fleet*; though he was not above private prompting among friends. But Beatty was relentless about Jutland and always on the attack.

Which was a shame. Because though Jellicoe increasingly won the argument among historians, Beatty's approach to battle and operations quickly found greater favour, and more success, within the Royal Navy. The navy realised it would have to develop more decentralised command at sea, giving captains more discretion, better tactical training, and better signalling. Even in a major battle like Jutland, it must be able to fight in smaller units. It absorbed the imperative for better fire control and realised it would have to be capable of fighting at night, perhaps very aggressively. Gunnery had to improve alongside a more open approach to embracing rapid innovations in weapons systems. Beatty vigorously championed engineering skills and the more willing embrace of science throughout the Service. The Royal Navy needed to get more of the Nelson spirit back, not just in its innate aggression, but in tandem with its inventiveness, vision and all the technologies of sea power.

As Beatty was laid to rest in the crypt of St Paul's Cathedral in 1936 – next to Jellicoe – many felt, like the Archbishop of Canterbury, that he had provided a modern link to the navy's great nineteenth century hero. Winston Churchill had already weighed in with personal letters and in his own war memoirs, most warmly if not with great factual accuracy. 'I never cease to proclaim you as an inheritor of the grand tradition of Nelson', he had written to Beatty. Even those critics who subsequently thought Beatty a dilettante would probably agree that he had certainly tried.

---

5. That, in itself, provoked Admiral Reginald Bacon to write a book referring to Beatty's Jutland politics as a 'scandal'.

Field Marshal John Gort

Field Marshal, as he became, John Standish Surtees Prendergast Vereker Gort, born into an Irish viscountcy to become the 6th Viscount Gort, is one of the more curious examples of British commandership. The American General George C. Patton, no shrinking violet himself, called Gort 'the bravest man in the British Army' and on the battlefield, he almost certainly was. During the First World War he was wounded five times in four separate incidents, mentioned in dispatches eight times, won three DSOs, the Military Cross and the Victoria Cross, all for quite different and separate achievements throughout the conflict.[1] He was an excellent soldier, a leader and a warrior to his very core. In the Second World War his seniority and fighting reputation placed him in command of the British Expeditionary Force (the 'BEF') that went to France in 1939. But his tactical excellence and courage did not translate into the same sort of excellence at the operational or strategic levels, and Gort presided over the BEF's defeat in May 1940 and its wildly improvised evacuation from Dunkirk. Along with relief at that deliverance, the immediate inquests were harsh, and Gort didn't come out of them well. But so much had been against him in 1939–40 that, notwithstanding his strategic limitations, it is doubtful anyone else could have done better. Nevertheless, he was sidelined and virtually ignored, until he served the country once again in holding Malta together during its grimmest months of siege in 1942–43. That brought him some redemption, at least in the public's mind, if not in his own.

It is simplistic to regard Gort as one of those great fighting commanders – as say, the Black Prince, John Moore or Thomas Cochrane – who were unable to make a success of strategic command when their fighting reputations propelled them into it. Generals who habitually refer to themselves as 'nought but a simple soldier' are normally consummate politicians; that's why they say it. But Gort really was a simple soldier. He displayed exceptional levels of military competence, enormous personal integrity and more moral and physical courage than innate imagination. One of his enemies spoke for a few others, insulting him as 'utterly brainless and unable to grasp the simplest problem'. He was certainly limited in his outlook but far from 'brainless'. His thinking worked literally rather than laterally; he kept both body and mind to a strict discipline, didn't see the point of religion except as a morale-booster, and showed typical patrician compassion for his soldiers along with a self-awareness of the sort

---

1. The partial exception is the Distinguished Service Order, awarded for conspicuous leadership. His first DSO was awarded for his tireless staff work at GHQ rather than at the front – an award he felt ashamed to win at the time.

of person he was. He rationalized his own character because it moulded the military leaders he thought the country needed in times of war. He seemed to realise he could only be a man for his own cataclysmic era; he didn't fit into any other.

He was the son of the 5th Viscount Gort, of Ireland. Born in 1886, he had little home life, packed off to Malvern and Harrow and then straight into Sandhurst in 1904. His father had died in 1902, whence Gort became the 6th Viscount. His mother re-married and he didn't get on well with her, still less his new stepfather. He was, of necessity, a self-sufficient young man, but shy and socially awkward. His one passion, from boyhood until the end of his life, was soldiering. He joined the Grenadier Guards as an ensign in 1905 and was a lieutenant in 1907. From the beginning he was determined and conscientious to a degree that made him unpopular with his more languid and confident fellow-officers. He read extensively, but exclusively, about military affairs. He simply had no other intellectual hinterland, either then or later in life, save that which he gleaned by experience.

In 1908 he arrived in Ontario, Canada to visit his disgraced uncle, Jeffrey Edward Prendergast Vereker, and went moose-shooting.[2] Gort had the reputation of being a rotten shot and it was written, even by an admirer of his, that he missed the moose and shot the local guide, who subsequently died. A more plausible alternative version was that he was chasing the moose which he had only wounded – Gort being a rotten shot – and slipped, accidentally discharging his rifle. If so, his firearms discipline was as poor as his shooting.[3] Either way, he tried to make financial amends to the guide's family and scuttled back to New York for the first ship home and never returned to Canada. After that he did a stint at Trinity College Cambridge, though without much intellectual reward.

He may have been gauche and socially uninteresting, but Gort was certainly a very eligible bachelor. His second cousin, Corinna Vereker – known as Kotchy – set her cap at him. She was beautiful, clever and lively, an extravagant socialite at twenty; and serially unfaithful. They married in 1911 and Kotchy achieved the status of viscountess. It was obvious how ill-suited they were. Nevertheless, they had three children, but his marriage never made him, or her, very happy. However hard John Gort may have tried with his limited reservoir of personal charm, it left him isolated.

His military career progressed as expected, however, and in 1914, as the war broke out, he was promoted captain when he got himself transferred as ADC to the commander of the 2nd Division of the British Expeditionary Force embarking for France. On 22nd August, he moved with the divisional HQ up to Mons and two days later was helping organize its inevitable retreat. He was wounded in the groin, though not seriously, before the division turned to make a stand at the river Marne on 5th September. Even as a junior captain, Gort's command style was distinctive. He was meticulous in administration, but more than that he tried to place himself at

---

2. His uncle had resigned his commission in the army after an affair with another officer's wife and moved to Kenora in north western Ontario.
3. His reputation as a rotten shot seemed genuine. Years later in India he wounded, then chased and shot, a tiger. His fellow officers were of the opinion that it probably died of fright.

the heart of the action – partly, it appears, for the excitement of it – but so as to see the situation for himself. His 'eye for ground' was well-educated and he showed an instinctive grasp of what the enemy were probably doing. Surrounded by soldiers, he was upbeat and ever-cheerful about their situation. Young Gort took to the battlefield that particular brand of carefree aristocratic eccentricity under fire that probably reassured, but maybe just puzzled, his own troops.

When his divisional commander was promoted to command I Corps he took Gort with him as ADC and by spring 1915 Gort was Brigade Major of the 4th Guards Brigade, in the front line of the trenches. This was where he really wanted to be, looking after the safety and fighting quality of the men and exerting his growing authority. If he had not been a very popular Grenadier officer in languid peacetime, he was certainly valued by the guardsmen now; he embodied the combat attributes they truly respected. He had already been mentioned in dispatches several times and he won the Military Cross in June. His own long family tragedy was beginning to unfold, however, with the news that his second child, Joscelyn, had died that spring. He was deeply affected by the news but he suppressed the grief because, he reasoned, he was surrounded by so much of it elsewhere and he had no right to indulge himself.

Just a few hours before the Somme offensive began in 1916 Gort was summoned to serve on Douglas Haig's staff at GHQ in Montreuil. He did his staff job with the customary gusto but he was tormented to be away from the action alongside the guardsmen he had helped nurture towards this great offensive. But he was shrewd enough to learn as much as he could from ten months at GHQ. He formed the firm opinion that it was too far away from the front to be fully effective – a conviction he would take to France with him commanding a different BEF from his own GHQ in 1940.

The great offensives of 1917 and 1918 gave Gort the opportunities he craved and won him the nickname 'tiger Gort' doing what he was best at. In April 1917 he was appointed Commanding Officer of 4th Battalion, Grenadier Guards where his style of leadership found the perfect platform amid the hard-bitten professionalism of the Guards Division. In classic warrior fashion, he would do everything himself before he would require it of his men, and he shared all their privations and discomforts – though he didn't need to. He would conduct his own reconnaissance patrols across no-mans-land before wandering around it during an attack, walking-stick in hand, meerschaum pipe in mouth, encouraging his guardsmen forward. He went through Arras, Passchendaele and Cambrai from spring to autumn 1917, achieving his battalion's objectives time and again, chiefly through attention to detail, personal stalking of enemy positions, and what was becoming an uncanny knack for spotting tactical advantage. He was wounded in the arm on the first day of Passchendaele, but carried on commanding until the position was secured. He was more seriously wounded in the side and shoulder in the latter stages of Cambrai, where the Guards had to attack, unsupported, the village of Gonnelieu to stem a German counterattack. As ever, having achieved the objective, this time at considerable cost, Gort was off alone to find out what was happening on the left of his besieged troops when he was caught in a burst of machine-gun fire. He was returned home for treatment and did not rejoin the Guards in France until March 1918, as commander of the 1st Battalion. That was less than two weeks before the great German attack – the 'Ludendorff offensive' – was launched.

It was Germany's last throw on the Western Front; a furious offensive to break the deadlock before the country was overwhelmed on all sides. The Guards found themselves conducting fighting retreats as the sixty-four German divisions got to within forty miles of Paris, and failed – just – to split the French and British armies and get between them. But the German offensive ran out of steam, and became short of men. At Blairville, Gort took over a section of the line where German behaviour seemed curious; active at night but not during daylight. He watched for a couple of days, then simply walked across no-mans-land with his orderly to confirm his suspicion that the trenches were only manned at night. His battalion occupied them immediately. From early August 1918 the allied counter-offensive began to roll forward. It quickly became fast, open country fighting and Gort's natural tactical skills didn't let him down, though after more than three years in the trenches a great deal of improvisation was required. Of course, his success was facilitated because he was commanding Guardsmen, the most disciplined and elite of the BEF's infantry units, but he certainly handled his force well – making them train whenever out of the line, and integrating new recruits immediately into the standards he expected. Like most troops, the Guards would follow their commander anywhere if he were a natural winner. Viscount Gort evidently was.

Gort won his Victoria Cross as the troops crossed the Canal Du Nord – part of Germany's Hindenburg Line – in September 1918. It was a multi-layered defensive obstacle and Gort spent most nights with his senior company commander quietly watching the front before leading his battalion at dawn to their company starting points for the push forward. On 27th September, with Guardsman Ransome – his soldier servant – beside him, Gort finally led his battalion across the canal itself towards their objective of Premy Ridge. But the flanking attacks had failed and his battalion was exposed. He personally led his companies to improvised positions around woods and houses protecting them from flank attacks. He was wounded in the eye but continued after Ransome applied a dressing, then got help from some Welsh Guards whom he directed to the flanks. He strode into the open to commandeer a lone tank that was already under fire, then commanded the attack on Premy Ridge itself. He was struck again in a shell burst which severed an artery, had Ransome apply a tourniquet, and continued until he collapsed. In and out of consciousness, he commanded from a stretcher until the battalion had secured the ridge, capturing two hundred prisoners and two full artillery batteries. Gort and Ransome were moving away from the fighting line when they were caught in another artillery strike and Ransome was badly wounded. Gort stumbled on alone to find an Irish Guards medical officer and brought him back to Ransome. Between them they tried to treat Ransome and get him away, but he died within minutes. Gort later wrote movingly about Guardsman Ransome and his loss. But, as ever, he was philosophical as he recovered in hospital at home and received all the plaudits for what was widely acknowledged to be a richly-deserved VC, as much for his continual acts of valour as for the Canal Du Nord.

During peacetime, his war record made Gort something of a celebrity within military circles but his lack of wider interests also put him on a career course that was rewarding but hardly spectacular. He was a naturally modest man, but still, he didn't lack for military ambition. His peacetime roles, however, showed how the army assessed him, not as a future national commander but as a valuable trainer. He was an instructor at the Staff College and returned to it later on as Commandant. In 1926 he became chief instructor at the Officers' School in Sheerness. He was made director of military training in India and was then entrusted with re-writing the *Infantry Training Manual*. But he also got the chance to be Commander of the Guards Brigade in 1930 and he established a long friendship with the influential – and heretical – Captain Liddell Hart, *The Times* military correspondent, during the years when battle tactics were under the microscope.

His family tragedy continued to spin out. His eldest son, Sandy, rejected everything about his father and the army, and was all but estranged. In 1925 Lady Gort broke up the marriage after too many trips to the nearby Spanish Embassy. Divorce was embarrassing enough at that time but the details in this case were scandalous too, since Kotchy's love life had long been joked about in the London clubs. Gort didn't disappear. He sat stoically in the mess at Wellington Barracks, next to Buckingham Palace, while his fellow officers devoured every salacious newspaper report of the divorce. Kotchy disappeared from his life completely. He was later delighted that Sandy had finally joined the army and thought him 'doing well', but in 1941 Sandy committed suicide. Gort took immense pride in his daughter Jacqueline, however, who was very like him and always instinctively supportive. And he formed a deep, entirely platonic, friendship with Lady Marjorie Dalrymple-Hamilton around the time of his divorce. Like the Duke of Wellington and Mrs Harriet Arbuthnot, Gort found in her a confidante, a confessor and an endless source of personal encouragement in his darkest hours. 'Cis' Dalrymple-Hamilton and Jacqueline were the only non-military companions of any real importance to him.

He could at least indulge his love of sailing along the south coast, and he learned to fly. Above all, he defined himself within the tribal brotherhood of the Guards. Most young officers, being close to boyhood themselves, get up to boyish games and pranks, and senior officers usually join in to help cement tribal bonds. But Gort was ever the ringleader in endless rags, practical jokes and bizarre competitions. It was (arguably) less dangerous than the trenches but it obviously kept alive for him the spirit of soldiering.

His career suddenly took on a new significance, however, when Leslie Hore-Belisha made him Military Secretary at the War Office and then the youngest ever Chief of the Imperial General Staff in 1937. He became a full general, leap-frogging many more senior officers. Hore-Belisha thought that Gort would be the ideal man whose drive and popularity would help him reform the army, working with Ronald Adam as deputy to provide the intellectual fire-power Gort evidently lacked. Gort injected unfussy urgency into Britain's war preparations and greatly improved the staff work around him. But the wider results were disappointing. Gort couldn't reconcile himself to Hore-Belisha's feline political stratagems and after two years was barely on speaking terms with him. He did absorb some of Liddell Hart's reformist views but was unable to do more with them. He pressed the case for greater mechanization among the infantry and the concept of organic armoured divisions, but he didn't manage to bend the army, or its tank design, to be more than an infantry support arm. Similarly, he knew the value of air-ground cooperation but couldn't make the Air Ministry budge in its opposition to creating more squadrons to support it.

Notwithstanding the force it had been under Douglas Haig two decades previously, the army didn't shake off its imperial policing mentality. The British Empire, on the very eve of its progressive decolonisation, was nevertheless at its greatest geographical extent by 1921 and imperial policing seemed a natural imperative. Above all, the service was not structured, and did not think, as a big continental army. In the 1930s it was more tactically adept than strategically literate. Engaged with Liddell Hart's thinking and despite his own perceptive understanding of what it would need to do in a war against Germany, Gort had made small impression on the army in the two years before it faced its great continental test. In autumn 1939 the army was sent, as a new BEF, to help defend France from German attack. As ever in British history, it was the country's only field army. Somewhat unexpectedly, Gort was given command of it. Some had doubts about his command abilities but he was popular in the army, he knew northern France very well, and he was delighted to be demoted from CIGS to Commander-in-Chief BEF and get away from Hore-Belisha and Whitehall. He was 'thrilled', in his own words, to be going back to war.

His force eventually grew to 330,000 men, but as in 1914 the BEF was still the junior partner being only one army alongside nine French armies and a Belgian and a Dutch army defending the whole front in the west. Gort willingly accepted that he would be subordinate to the supreme French commander, Maurice Gamelin. The French plan, when the German attack came, was to hold along the Maginot Line while pushing the British and the strongest French forces to the river Dyle running roughly north-south through Belgium. The nine divisions of the BEF would have the First French Army on its right flank to the south, the Ninth Army further south again down the line of contact and the Seventh on its left to the north. So thirty-eight divisions in total would line up north to south, facing eastwards across Belgium.[4] Gort thought the plan foolish – another Mons in the making – since it was far better to fortify the French frontiers than take major forces into a northern offensive. But after the 1914–18 experience Paris wanted to fight as far away from French territory as possible.

Gort loyally went along with the plan and continued to try to build up the BEF's readiness. He wasn't helped by London diverting BEF forces to other theatres or indulging sundry political interference, though he got rapidly bogged down in detail and seemed to be waiting for the German offensive before he could address the bigger issues. He was both Commander-in-Chief of all British forces in France and the army commander too. One role required him to stand back, the other to keep close to the

---

4. Total allied and German numbers were very evenly matched; the allies fielded 135 divisions containing 3.3 million troops, the Germans 141 divisions containing 3.5 million.

fighting line. It was a thankless task and his subordinate army commanders, men like Bernard Montgomery, Alan Brooke and Harold Alexander, were frustrated at his small scale, pernickety attitudes. He was variously referred to as 'the best platoon commander in France', a 'battalion commander', even the 'lance-corporal'. Montgomery later wrote imperiously that Gort 'did not see very far, but as far as he did see he saw very clearly'. Meanwhile, the BEF remained committed to a French plan over which it had grave doubts.

When the German western offensive eventually began on 10th May, the allied plan could not have been more helpful to it. Allied forces had been made strongest along the northern and southern flanks and weakest in the centre, exactly where the main German thrust began – cutting through the Ardennes forest and racing towards the channel coast at the Somme estuary. French reserves were virtually non-existent. The BEF with the First and Seventh French Armies duly moved north to the Dyal in Belgium and in three days the German *blitzkrieg* had crossed the Meuse at Sedan behind them. By May 13th the French plan was in tatters and the enemy breakout from Sedan was followed by a week of relentless German advances, all accompanied by fearsome close air support to German armoured columns as they raced westwards.

The BEF was not the main target. German commanders needed to cripple the French army first. That army certainly didn't collapse immediately, but its command structure did. The German *blitzkrieg* took considerable risks in thrusting forward so quickly, but its speed of manoeuvre effectively out-thought the ability of French Headquarters, with almost all its forward communications cut, to respond effectively. And von Rundstedt's racing panzer divisions did not all keep on relentlessly westward, as Paris expected, but then turned north to cut the BEF and the Seventh French army off from the coast. By May 15th the BEF had been under real pressure for forty-eight hours. Gort insisted on being close – too close – to the front lines and kept shifting his own command centre from his GHQ at Arras to other locations. Coherence was lost and staff officers and commanders were shuffled around and mixed in ad hoc ways Montgomery later criticized as 'amateur'.

Gort constantly awaited clear orders but got very few as French command froze under the assault, so he relied, as ever, on his tactical instincts. He was rapidly losing his out-gunned tanks and by 17th May he had lost faith in his French allies too, aware that his counterpart commanders had given way to simple despair. Meanwhile, his BEF was being reduced to a disorganised infantry force. Gort was a bit player in the unfolding drama; destined always to be a loser in this campaign. The BEF could never save France if France could not save itself.

On 19th May, in desperation, Paris replaced Gamelin with General Maxime Weygand as supreme commander and Weygand demanded all-out offensives. French and BEF forces would push against German forces from north and south simultaneously. On 21 May the BEF launched a surprisingly successful offensive to clear German forces from Arras, but the big supporting French effort failed to materialize. Even so, General Erwin Rommel received a nasty shock at Arras and assumed he was up against fully five divisions instead of the scratch force scraped from Alan Brooke's II Corps that actually assembled.

It was a glimpse of what might have been. But the allied counter-punch was simply too late; the German offensive had already split the allies apart, the French Ninth Army had been shattered and its First army, which had fought resolutely on the right flank of the BEF, had been suddenly withdrawn on 18th May, forcing Gort to pull his main forces back to cover the flank. And already, on 20th May, von Rundstedt's panzers had reached the coast at Calais and cut Gort's supply line to the south. Weygand was by then living in his own world of fantasy offensives. On 25th May he commanded Gort to use his only two reserve divisions – those available to keep his last escape route open to the coast at Dunkirk – to sustain the attack southwards on the following morning, still trying to reunite the two allied forces. Gort was, by then, convinced it was all fantasy. But he was under unambiguous orders, and the War Cabinet in London, having only a hazy idea of the changing situation on the ground, had already commanded him to do the same. From Paris, Churchill had repeated the instruction again in a personal telegram seventy-two hours previously.

Gort faced the absolute loneliness of command. During the afternoon of 26th May Lt-Col Templar arrived at Gort's HQ in Premesques to report to the deputy commander, Henry Pownall. He had to go via Gort's office to reach Pownall's next door. He crept past, finding Gort alone, quiet, staring at large wall maps. Sometime later he was still staring at them. Gort's lifelong instincts were to attack; to never-say-die; to obey orders – from his French commander, the War Cabinet and now his Prime Minister. At five-thirty that afternoon he took another call at his desk confirming more French disintegration and he re-considered an intelligence report from captured documents that suggested the direction of the next German push.

At six-thirty his voice quiet, he disobeyed orders and gave his own orders instead to use his two reserve divisions to hold open the corridor that would get the BEF to Dunkirk to withdraw. It was a personally courageous act of complete defeat, and it would leave the shattered remnants of the French army to fight on alone. The BEF was the only field army Britain possessed. It was the professional core of a new conscript army that would have to be built around it before this war was over. It had to be saved. If General John Gort never had, or never again would, make another national strategic decision, this one was enough for a lifetime. His biographer said that without it 'there might have been no Stalingrad or Alamein and the breaking of the Axis might long have remained a daydream in the imaginings of a captive Europe and a helpless America'. That rather overstates the case, but there is no doubt Britain's war would have gone very differently if Gort had decided otherwise. The following morning he received a message from London that reversed its previous instructions and now told Gort to do what he had already, urgently set about.[5]

And so followed the deliverance of the BEF from Dunkirk. It wasn't as chaotic as most of the images associated with it suggest. Holding on to Arras for a bit longer

---

5. The fact that London was already thinking about the withdrawal option and came to the same conclusion as Gort a few hours later should not obscure the fact that if Gort had obeyed his original orders that day, he would have committed his only two available divisions to an attack further south and would not, therefore, have been able to hold the corridor to Dunkirk open for the BEF. London would have performed its volte face just too late.

and hard resistance by the Franco-British garrisons at Boulogne and Calais led to German miscalculation and enough delay to give the BEF good access to Dunkirk on the uncontested English Channel. The maritime evacuation – 430 'little ships' and all – was extraordinarily well organized from beneath Dover castle by Admiral Bertram Ramsey. The numbers speak for themselves. In the ten days of 'Dunkirk' some 860 allied vessels of all sizes were involved.[6] Churchill and the Admiralty thought they might rescue 40–50,000 of their troops; Gort hoped for 100,000. In the event, they got 338,000 back, 225,000 of them BEF, alongside more than 100,000 French and Belgian troops, while more made their escape from French ports in Normandy and Brittany. Not least, it was all facilitated by the quiet heroism of French and British rearguard units who were instructed to hold the perimeter around Dunkirk with very limited chances to escape themselves. Eventual capture seemed their best prospect.

Nevertheless, the BEF came back as a thoroughly beaten force, its discipline already breaking down.[7] Yet the country greeted the bewildered servicemen as heroes, the public buoyed by events to face more resolutely the challenges to come. But like the army that returned after John Moore's retreat from Corunna in 1809, the BEF had abandoned an army's-worth of equipment; 64,000 vehicles, 2,500 guns, 76,000 tons of ammunition and 400,000 tons of food and stores. However the public reacted, and rather like Corunna, it was a disaster for the BEF and personally for Gort. As the evacuation drew to a close and the Dunkirk beaches were emptying, he ordered his subordinate commanders home. He intended to stay till the end and then join his beloved guardsmen still holding the perimeter. He assumed it would mean death or capture but he couldn't imagine what else a Grenadier Guardsman General should do. Churchill, alarmed at the blow to morale of exactly that prospect ordered him home in no uncertain terms; 'no personal discretion is left to you in this matter', he thundered. On June 1st Gort, quite distraught but correct, handed over command to Harold Alexander with three divisions still to be rescued. He was brought back to Dover in a fast motor launch while soldiers still queued up, chest deep in the water, for the next little ship to take them to a destroyer offshore.[8]

Formal tributes, but no more than formal, were paid to Gort on his return. He was shunted off to be Inspector of Training and the Home Guard. As his loyal deputy Pownall put it, Gort couldn't shrug off the mantle of, 'The commander of the BEF that was driven into the sea in three weeks!'. He was heavily criticized by many prominent figures in public, and a number of military colleagues in private. He felt humiliated and aggrieved that Churchill and the War Cabinet had demanded the impossible. But he was never a pompous man and he dealt stoically with his own sense of failure, though desperate to have all his dispatches from France published. He was made Governor of Gibraltar, a role he didn't want, but accepted as a matter of public duty.

---

6. The 'little ships' accounted for about a third of those rescued. Most embarked on the destroyer force that shuttled back and forth from the mole at the harbour's breakwater.
7. No medal was ever struck for the 1940 campaign in France, though it involved 68,000 British casualties and 40,000 who became prisoners for the duration of the war.
8. In fact, Alexander brilliantly managed to extricate all the British rearguard from the perimeter, though some 35,000 French troops had no alternative but to surrender on 4th June.

With all his usual energy he made significant improvements to its defences. Then in May 1942 he was sent as Governor to Malta, and here he made a real difference.

During that year Malta was so besieged it was perilously close to starvation and never far from falling. By summer, its rolling 'surrender date' was calculated as two or three weeks hence. Gort shook up the lacklustre defence organisation, got sixty Spitfires safely delivered, concentrated the anti-aircraft batteries and saved the *Welshman* supply ship, reorganized the dwindling food supplies and the air raid procedures. In true Gort fashion, he shared all the hardships, gave everything of himself, went everywhere by bicycle with fuel so short, and was immensely popular with the islanders. In August the most famous supply convoy of the war – the *Pedestal* convoy – passed through the Straits of Gibraltar with more than seventy Royal Navy ships escorting fourteen merchantmen. Five of the merchantmen got to Malta and the island was reprieved, long enough for Montgomery's victory at Alamein in October to turn the tide of war in the Mediterranean. Gort flew immediately to Cairo to report *Pedestal's* results personally to Churchill. Churchill's doctor remarked that Gort 'is hardly recognizable, stones lighter …years older, with sunken cheeks and tired eyes'. Churchill himself fell to tears at this new and latest deliverance. Malta had survived. Gort never saw it as personal redemption, but others did. The Maltese believed that he 'saved Malta' and his military colleagues agreed he had done more than any other Governor to defend the island. For a generation of historians who tended to ignore Gort, it seemed his most successful command.

Cis Dalrymple-Hamilton remained his psychological rock and Jacqueline had married the perfect son-in-law for Gort; Major William Sidney, a Grenadier. Astonishingly, Sidney won his own VC at the Anzio landings in February 1944. Gort glowed for his daughter and her husband. In October 1944 Gort was sent to Palestine and Transjordan as High Commissioner. Since he was completely apolitical he was a great success for a while, but his health was failing and he had to give up the post in November 1945 – convinced the territory was on the verge of a stable future. Of course, it wasn't, but he had been well-respected on all sides before tensions in Palestine really spun out of control.

He was now a Field Marshal and was made an English viscount – which only duplicated his inherited Irish peerage. But he had no home of his own in Britain. It hardly mattered. He spent his remaining four months in Guy's hospital suffering from liver cancer. He died at the end of March 1946, still feeling the nation's eyes on him as a defeated and disgraced commander. Perhaps his happiest moment in later life was in March 1944 when he flew to Naples to see General Alexander pin the VC on his son-in-law's chest – with a ribbon cut from one of Gort's own uniforms. Both officers, holders of the Victoria Cross, then stood either side of Alexander while a battalion of Grenadiers marched past in honour of two such courageous guardsmen.

Air Chief Marshal Hugh Dowding

Hugh Dowding – 'Stuffy' Dowding as he was known from the age of thirty – was not a very good pilot. Nor was he a particularly popular squadron commander or wing commander. He was at odds with many of his contemporaries and superiors, not least with Hugh Trenchard, 'father of the Royal Air Force' and its first Chief of Air Staff. Hugh Dowding was tall, gaunt, austere and preoccupied with his own concerns; hard to get to know and even harder to like. He was rather different in private and among family and close friends. But in his professional life as an RAF officer, he was not 'clubbable' in the image of the youngest of the three armed services. He never fought in more than one, confused, air battle himself. He never rose to the very top of his service as the RAF's chief. He was sacked at the very point where he had achieved undeniable success, and was bitter about the way he was treated, whatever he later said to the contrary. And yet, he has long been recognised as the man who more than anyone else created the victory in what was known, even while it was being fought in the summer of 1940, as 'the Battle of Britain'.

That particular battle, like the 'miracle of Dunkirk' which preceded it by just a few weeks, has been eulogized in Britain's twentieth century national story. In the grim, hot summer of 1940, with 2,400 invasion barges and two German Army Groups assembled on the French coast, the RAF and the *Luftwaffe* fought for control of the air above any attempted invasion. The RAF didn't defeat the *Luftwaffe*, but fought it to a standstill, forcing a change in German strategy. It was the first time the German war machine had been denied outright victory since the occupation of the Rhineland in 1936. Historians have long debated the strategic significance of the Battle of Britain. But while many have sought to debunk the romantic drama that surrounds it, none have seriously argued that it was anything other than a significant battle. And Dowding won it, not just in the four months his pilots in Fighter Command were fighting it, but in the four years before that when he created the foundations to conduct just such a battle. He had long anticipated the challenge and knew that as and when a struggle for air control over Britain took place, there would be no prizes for coming second. Like 'Trafalgar Night' in the Royal Navy, 'Battle of Britain Night' in Royal Air Force bases everywhere is celebrated as one of the foundation stories of the Service. It remains the RAF's Trafalgar.

The RAF was fortunate to have such a clear thinker and strategic visionary as Dowding in the right place for long enough before the clash of 1940. His RAF promotions that brought him to that point had always been somewhat grudging. He became an Air Chief Marshal essentially for the quality of his staff work, in an organisation that prided itself more on flying skills and dashing leadership among its senior officers. He achieved what he did in spite of the RAF hierarchy rather than because of it. Indeed, he was due to retire before 1940 and was extended by a few months at a time to keep him in post while things were 'difficult'.

His youthful career gives a fair indication of Dowding's subsequent trajectory. Born in 1882 to a professional English family living in Scotland, he was educated at St Ninian's in Dumfriesshire and then Winchester College. He was keen on an army career and enrolled at the Royal Military Academy Woolwich, instead of Sandhurst. RMA Woolwich concentrated on the technical and engineering skills of the army, rather than the more elitist leanings towards infantry and cavalry training at Sandhurst. He became a serious-minded artillery officer and saw early service with Royal Garrison Artillery in Gibraltar, Ceylon and Hong Kong. It was a steady career in which Dowding didn't have the opportunity of service or displays of youthful gallantry in any active operations. He attended Staff College at Camberley in 1912, where he earned his epithet 'stuffy' among contemporaries. He lacked characteristically Edwardian social skills in his earnest approach to everything. The only obvious departures from this pattern were his enthusiasms for polo, and for skiing, at which he became a British slalom champion. He also developed an interest in aviation at Staff College and the following year obtained an Aviator Certificate and then went through the Central Flying School's course to become eligible as a Royal Flying Corps pilot. Typical of him, he was not bitten by the flying bug. He was interested in aviation for its benefits to the artillery – obvious to him if not to most others. And having become a reserve RFC pilot, he was happy to return to his artillery duties on the Isle of Wight.

At the onset of war in 1914, however, an RFC role was more valuable than artillery, and as a thirty-two-year-old novice pilot – absurdly old compared to most RFC novices – Dowding joined No. 6 Squadron in the British Expeditionary Force sent to France. As an army captain he was quickly made a flight commander with No. 9 and then back at No. 6 Squadron; a tribute to his maturity and organisation more than any flying skills. He quickly became interested in the potential of getting air-ground wireless communication established in RFC aircraft and was sent back to Britain in 1915 to work on it. When he returned to France as commanding officer of No. 16 Squadron, Dowding almost immediately crossed swords with Hugh Trenchard, commander of RFC forces in France. Hugh 'Boom' Trenchard was the antithesis of Dowding; loud in voice, in opinions, a big personality who instilled relentless 'offensive spirit' in his airmen. 'Stuffy' and 'Boom' were never likely to get on, and Dowding was quietly and irritatingly pugnacious in pushing his professional judgements against Trenchard's natural assertion.

Dowding was back in Britain leading the experimental '7 Wing' at Farnborough before returning to France to lead 9 Wing at Fienvillers during the 1916 Somme offensive. It was from here that, as Wing Commander, he was engaged in his only significant air combat, flying an outclassed BE2c where he and his observer were lucky to survive.[1] Again, he clashed with Trenchard with what seemed to the commander

---

1. As wing commander Dowding was forbidden to fly on operations but obtained permission for this sortie as a gesture to his men.

as a risk-averse attitude, asking permission to rest No. 60 squadron who had suffered severe casualties. Few of Dowding's own pilots naturally took to him, but both then and later many expressed their appreciation for his professionalism, judgement, and his consistent reluctance to risk their lives unnecessarily. If he was not a natural leader in battle, many recognised he was nevertheless a good officer. By 1917, however, Trenchard was happy enough to see 'a dismal Jimmy' shunted off to an RFC training brigade in Britain. Dowding was made chief staff officer for the Service's organisation in York. It was there that he transferred to a new equivalent rank when the Royal Air Force, the first independent military air service in the world, was founded on 1 April 1918 – April Fool's Day – with no apparent sense of irony.

At the end of the war, Dowding was duly honoured with a CMG and received a letter retiring him from the Service. It was his superior officer at York, Sir Vyell Vyvyan, who launched a persistent campaign to persuade a reluctant Trenchard to reverse the decision and offer Dowding one of the scarce permanent RAF commissions as a Group Captain. Dowding thus became one of the few first-generation staff officers who served in senior positions – 'air rank' – from the establishment of the RAF though to the Second World War. Though Trenchard was sceptical and Dowding always felt his lack of combat experience, he nevertheless became one of the real founders of the infant service, bringing his sense of technical professionalism to studying the new science of air power. The RAF, however, was being shaped by Trenchard's dynamic leadership and Dowding's emerging understanding of the fundamentals of twentieth century airpower steadily diverged from the view taken by most of his contemporaries. The importance of Dowding's influence on the RAF's nascent professional culture was not greatly appreciated at the time and often passed over afterwards. But he was one of the handful of service leaders who created the highly technocratic RAF that triumphed in the Second World War and set standards for other air forces as they integrated science and technology in the use of aircraft. Small packets of air power can make big differences in combat, and to a greater extent than in ground or maritime forces, successful air forces are inherently high-tech in operation and technocratic in organisation. Dowding seemed naturally to grasp this.

In 1918 he had married Clarice Vancourt who was the widow of an army officer and who already had a seven-year-old daughter. Dowding and Clarice also had a son of their own – Derek – who went on to be one of his father's young Battle of Britain pilots.[2] But Clarice died suddenly in 1920, a little over two years into their marriage. Dowding didn't share much of his grief but his sister helped look after the two children as he ploughed doggedly on in his career. He didn't enjoy much of a home life until he remarried, very happily, in 1951 when he was sixty-nine.

During the interwar period Dowding spent two years from 1924 as chief of staff to Iraq Command in Baghdad. He was involved in 'colonial air policing' where unsupported bomber aircraft and a few armoured cars could suppress disorder and revolt with a fraction of the forces that might otherwise be necessary. Iraq was a

---

2. Derek Dowding survived the battle and the rest of the war, retiring from the RAF in 1956 as a Wing Commander. He died in 1992.

big country, a land-bridge for the British to imperial India and a source of oil for which the Royal Navy was becoming increasingly thirsty. Air policing in Iraq gave airpower an independent measure of political effectiveness it never enjoyed either before or since. Dowding and his commander, Josh Higgins, refined 'air policing' to a degree that singularly impressed the Air Ministry and elevated it to the status of a pseudo air power doctrine. But Dowding's reaction to this success was interesting. He worried about the humanitarian effects of bombing rebel villages and got Higgins to change the policy so that no villages were bombed without warning. More than that, while London warmed to the whole coercive approach, Dowding assessed that it was very unlikely to work in a European context. People wouldn't be coerced so easily and bombers wouldn't be given free run of the skies to coerce them. While the RAF's tactical achievements in Iraq (not to mention on the North West Frontier and Somaliland) were reinforcing a growing consensus in London around the potency of aerial bombing, Dowding was realistic enough to detach himself from his own success and came home more attuned to its limitations.

Nevertheless, it did his career some good and Trenchard thought him best employed with promotion to the Air Ministry as Director of Training. Thus, at the age of forty-four Dowding achieved his first genuinely influential appointment. If he was old to be a novice pilot, he was now young to be so significant a staff officer. In 1929 he was sent to Palestine and Transjordan to report on the security problems posed by growing inter-communal unrest. His report was prescient, hard-hitting and boosted his reputation again.

That year became pivotal to Dowding. Trenchard retired. His staff reputation was undisputed and as he left the Service, Trenchard had the honesty to say directly to Dowding that he had been wrong in his previous assessment of him. That left Dowding bemused and grateful, though it didn't stop Trenchard, in retirement, joining repeated conspiracies to undermine him. Crucially, however, Dowding was now appointed to that part of the airpower task that was to cement his place, and that of the RAF, in British history; the 'Air Defence of Great Britain'. He became 'Air Officer Commanding, Fighting Area, ADGB'. He also joined the Air Council, responsible for 'supply and research'. That gave him a voice on the RAF's policy-making executive and the seniority to influence the new science of air power in Britain.

But it was always an uphill battle. Notwithstanding Trenchard's valedictory comment, others like Sholto Douglas and John Slessor at the Air Ministry, or Donald Stevenson in Home Command thought 'Stuffy' was just that, and frankly a drag on RAF thinking – which in the Trenchard legacy, was both gung-ho yet also remarkably conservative. Dowding was no more prophetic than anyone else about the approach of war with Germany, but as the likelihood grew, he became ever more clear in his foresight of what it would mean for British airpower. The cumulative judgements he made in the crucial years from 1935 to 1939 were proved overwhelmingly right, both tactically and strategically, though he was still fighting for them in both the Air Ministry and Downing Street deep into 1940.

One series of decisions ran through the 'supply and research' part of his brief. He had no technical or engineering training but Dowding showed real imagination in the way new technology should – or just as important, shouldn't – be applied. He commissioned the development of high-performance, metal monoplane aircraft in 1934 and Hawker and Supermarine came up with promising designs. Without consulting the Air Staff, he gave the go-ahead for both companies to develop what became the Hawker Hurricane and Supermarine Spitfire fighters. The performance of the first prototypes was disappointing and Dowding pressed for them to operate their new Rolls Royce Merlin engines on high-octane fuel from the United States and have them fitted with variable pitch propellers. As the designs matured into viable fighters, he pressed for each aircraft to be given armour protection, bullet-proof windshields, and eight wing-mounted machine guns.[3] He also promoted 'airborne interception' technologies for the night fighting operations which he (correctly) foresaw happening over British territory and the importance of 'Identification Friend or Foe' devices for all aircraft. Not least, he put his weight behind the development of long-range four-engine bombers, while addressing the worst deficiencies of Britain's anti-aircraft defences, for which he also became responsible.

Just as important, Dowding was clear about what he didn't want to develop, such as a big expansion in the RAF's stock of inferior bi-planes, or schemes for curtains of explosives hanging from balloons to defend cities. He understood the inadequacies of an under-performing fighter-bomber – which was eventually developed as the Fairey Battle aircraft, or even worse, the 'turret fighter', based on First World War thinking that an aircraft with a rotating turret behind the pilot could be an effective air defence machine. This became the ill-fated Defiant fighter and Dowding managed to restrict the Air Ministry to procuring only six squadrons of them for training purposes, 'Where', he said, 'they will do the least harm'.[4]

Dowding's greatest single technical contribution, however, lay in the sphere of radar. It wasn't in the invention itself – the Germans also had radar at this time – but instead in the system he built around it. 'Inventing radar', it was said, 'was easy; any genius could do it'. But it took a different sort of ingenuity to set it within a system centred on Dowding's remarkably prescient vision of the nature of future air combat. In 1935 he fought to get what became known as the 'Tizard Committee' under his direct authority, working closely with Henry Tizard as the new technology of 'radio reflection' was developed. He shielded the committee's work from many interveners, including Churchill with Frederick Lindemann, his own favourite physicist, in tow. Radar became the centre of Dowding's overall air defence system. At least two radar traces of all aircraft within range could be picked up. Incoming enemy aircraft would

---

3. Eight! Some in Air Ministry thought this lunacy; too heavy, liable to jam, impossible to reload in flight, restricting these fighters to attacks from astern only – though why any experienced airman would think this last point remains a mystery.
4. It wasn't just prejudice on Dowding's part. He knew from exercises how poorly the Fairey Battle and the Bolton Paul Defiant performed in relation to what he could see of German aircraft in development. He was proved tragically right in early 1940 when the RAF lost almost every one of both types – and their aircrew – when they were committed in the Battle of France. Conversely, he also suspected that the German Junkers 87 – the Stuka – would do badly up against his new Spitfires and Hurricanes (and was right again).

be confirmed and recorded by visual spotters in the Royal Observer Corps. That information would be plotted centrally at Fighter Command Headquarters in Bentley Priory and devolved among well-connected sector stations elsewhere. Each sector station would control its own fighter squadrons, launching from their dispersed bases aircraft that would remain in constant radio contact with their sector commanders. Provided that this system remained minimally intact, Dowding's new fighter aircraft should be capable of intercepting virtually every attack.

Even in hindsight, the achievement of coupling innovative fighter aircraft with a complete air defence system, should not be underestimated. Dowding certainly wasn't without backing from the Air Ministry, but RAF conservatism took the form of basic strategic judgements with which he fundamentally – and increasingly – disagreed as war approached. Everyone assumed, including him, that at the outset of a war, Germany would use its impressive fleets of bombers to strike an early knock-out blow against Britain. 'The bomber will always get through' as Prime Minister Stanley Baldwin famously said. Prevailing orthodoxy, therefore, was that this threat could not be defended against, only neutralised through deterrence. Britain must have a bomber force of sufficient power to dissuade the *Luftwaffe* from such a strategy. Moreover, conventional wisdom didn't recognise the potential of agile, forward-firing fighters, where the aircraft itself became the weapon. Bombers for deterrence seemed to be a better investment in air power and two-seater aircraft with turrets and rear-firing weapons were, in any case, assumed to be the best defence against them.

There was no hard evidence for any of these assertions; they were simply matters of belief. Dowding's opposing views, on the other hand, were based on rigorous testing and air-firing trials. He was unimpressed by staged exercises and would have tested fighter tactics even further if the bomber force had not been persistently reluctant to exercise with his fighters. Then too, the government was unwilling to fund enough bombers or fighters for either strategy to be credible until the very eve of hostilities with Germany. Dowding realistically required fifty-three squadrons to cover the air defence of the whole British Isles, but only had thirty-nine at the outset of the war, and ten of them were diverted to the British Expeditionary Force in France. At least he had Keith Park, who was with him from 1930 – a staunch ally and friend who fought as hard as Dowding for what they both knew British air defence would require.

In 1936 the RAF was reorganised into functional commands – Fighter Command, Bomber Command, Coastal Command and Training Command; Dowding becoming the first Air Officer Commanding of Fighter Command. In fact, he opposed this major reorganisation on the basis that it would be dysfunctional. He was right in general about dysfunctionality, but wrong in relation to Fighter Command itself; it was ideal for the battle to come. Dowding thought – claimed he had been told – that he was standing up the new Fighter Command for its first year before being appointed Chief of Air Staff, the head of the RAF. He didn't disguise his bitterness and sense of betrayal in 1937 that having done so much to modernise the Service he should then be passed over for the top job. What Allen Andrews calls his 'ungracious severity' in pressing his convictions had done much to deprive him. From then on, Dowding's forced retirement was always imminent. He was given four notices of retirement as his sixtieth birthday loomed, while he readied Fighter Command for its greatest test.

His key for Fighter Command was strategic concentration. In the south-east, where he assessed the air battle would be most intensive, Dowding created 11 Group, where he put more than a third of his total squadron strength, under the command of the reliable Keith Park. To the north, in East Anglia, 12 Group would back it up and act to defend the Midlands (much to the chagrin of 12 Group commander, Trafford Leigh-Mallory, who itched to be central to the action). In the south and west he created 10 Group, of necessity more thinly defended, to look after sectors from Southampton to South Wales. And thinner still, 13 Group, to look after the north-east coast up to Scapa Flow and onto Northern Ireland. He was determined that 11 Group be kept strong while other squadrons were held back in less vulnerable groups and then rotated in and out of 11 Group as the need arose. He appreciated the geographical benefit of having nine tenths of the British Isles outside the range of German fighters and was determined not to risk that advantage by committing his whole force in one grand air battle. Fighting over British soil, behind an integrated air defence radar system, with a huge safe haven behind the front, gave the RAF the best chance, Dowding believed, to create and win a battle of attrition with the *Luftwaffe*.

Having brought Fighter Command into existence and planned its defensive battle in some detail, Dowding genuinely didn't expect to be the commander who would go on to fight it. Yet in 1940 he was still struggling to maintain strategic coherence against competing national demands. He was told he must also safeguard key aircraft production facilities in Sheffield, Coventry, Derby and Bristol. He had to send precious Hurricanes to the disastrous Norway campaign and was immediately under pressure to send even more, on an open-ended basis, to France as the BEF was attacked in the German *blitzkrieg*. He was almost insubordinate on this last demand, to the point that his loyalty to the RAF was questioned. But he went to the War Cabinet personally on 25th May to give Churchill and his colleagues a dire warning that British skies would be effectively open if any more front-line fighters were sent to France. He threw his pencil down on the cabinet table as he concluded his briefing, in a tacit threat of immediate resignation. More units were rapidly being created but he warned that only twenty-five squadrons were operational at that point. RAF chiefs had little faith in him as he fought his corner with tactless ferocity, but Churchill seemed impressed by Dowding and took his judgement seriously. After another Cabinet wobble the following day, he won his point.

There was much criticism of the RAF's limited engagement during the BEF's evacuation from Dunkirk at the end of May. British soldiers were angry that they saw so little of the RAF when they were being bombed on the beaches. In truth, they would never have seen much of them; RAF fighters were operating higher and further inland as they took on the *Luftwaffe*. But still, Dowding was extremely reluctant to risk his aircraft, and especially his pilots, over the Channel let alone over French territory. The RAF had already lost over 950 of its various aircraft in France – Battles, Blenheims, Defiants and Gladiators, and no fewer than 386 of its essential Hurricanes, mostly destroyed on the ground, plus sixty-seven Spitfires. But it's true that Fighter Command could have done much more to defend the Dunkirk beaches, though at greater risk of a sucker punch, since the inland territory lay mainly beyond British radar range. At least the BEF's campaign was lost quickly and it was all over by the beginning of June. Dowding's Fighter Command could draw breath for six weeks before, as Churchill told the Commons on 18th June, 'the battle for Britain is about to begin'.[5]

Churchill was, of course, correct. The historical teaser is whether the Battle of Britain really mattered to the outcome of the war. It revolves around the fact that Britain and Germany were pursuing different strategies in the air. Dowding eventually prevailed over his colleagues to create an attritional battle. Hitler and *Luftwaffe* chief Hermann Goring were focussed on a knock-out blow. Hitler was genuinely ambivalent about whether he would carry through on the extensive preparations being made along the French coast for an invasion that would assault Britain from the Isle of Wight to Ramsgate. Goring never thought an *opposed* invasion on this scale was possible. Neither did Erich Raeder, commander of the German navy. It would only make sense if the *Luftwaffe* could knock out the RAF as a viable defence force and then, working with Raeder's navy, jointly attack and hold off the Royal Navy for long enough to get two German army groups across the channel in a largely unopposed invasion. It was always something of a long shot. But if the *Luftwaffe* had been able to deliver a knock-out blow to the RAF – as Goring confidently believed it would – then Hitler's invasion would have been immediately more plausible.[6]

So the battle came down to Dowding's attrition to frustrate Goring's knock-out blow against the RAF; in the air, on the ground, and at its aircraft production factories. After German probing attacks, the contest took on a distinct pattern after 10th July. With a furious production surge, Dowding's force was just touching 600 Hurricanes and Spitfires by July; Goring had over 1,200 bombers and more than 1,000 fighters to protect them in a total force of over 2,400 available aircraft. Two German air fleets in France and another operating from Norway and Denmark (mainly as a distraction) bombed the radar stations, the sector stations, and the fighter aerodromes themselves.[7] This was partly as a provocation to draw RAF fighters into the air where they could be attacked – above the bombers – by the *Luftwaffe*'s more experienced fighter pilots. Goring was working to create one or two massed air battles that would destroy Fighter Command quickly. Dowding was equally determined to avoid exactly that and responded with interceptions by individual squadrons, normally no more than two at a time, to degrade German attacks as they developed without being drawn into a win-or-lose mêlée.

Unlike at Dunkirk, the RAF did not have to fly random reconnaissance patrols. When squadrons were scrambled, they could now be sent to a defined interception point. And they could be scrambled carefully so as to avoid dangerous re-fuelling and re-arming breaks on the ground when they were vulnerable to attack, as had

---

5. Though Churchill was referring here to the whole country, not just the air defence elements.
6. So, too might have been a political resurgence of the 'appeasement' ministers in Churchill's government who always argued there would be no eventual alternative but a deal with Hitler.
7. Goring didn't appreciate radar's importance, or the interconnectedness between sector stations, and allowed the system to recover after some effective early attacks.

happened in France. But Dowding and Park accepted that their pilots would always be in an inferior position at the point of attack – constantly outnumbered – which is one of the elements that gave the battle its romantic status. In reality, Dowding was exploiting the underlying strengths of his force and its ability to keep on breaking up bomber attacks while wearing them down. At the tactical level it became asymmetric; German fighters – mainly Messerschmidt 109s and 110s – were not meaningfully protecting their own bombers, but spoiling for a fight high above them; while RAF fighters – mainly Spitfires and Hurricanes – detached a minimum number to hold off the 109s and 110s while attacking the poorly defended bombers below.

For the *Luftwaffe*, 13th August – 'Eagle Day' – was intended to be the knockout punch for which all had been merely preliminaries. Goring's intention was that this would initiate a four-day air battle that would be decisive, followed by four weeks of relentless bombing to destroy the RAF's infrastructure, and give the *Luftwaffe* complete control over the Channel and southern Britain. Eagle day slipped to the 15th and became a disaster for the *Luftwaffe*. German plans were inflexible that morning; Goring was in bed in Berlin, his three air fleet commanders were en route to see him, while Hitler had just arrived from Berchtesgaden. Dowding, Park and Leigh-Mallory, by contrast, were in their control rooms from dawn, directing events as they happened. Nevertheless, on the 18th Fighter Command had to make its maximum effort; where every squadron, and all reserves, were at full stretch. Some squadrons were in the air seven times from that dawn to that dusk. By 19th August the *Luftwaffe* should have completed the 'annihilation' part of the strategy. It manifestly hadn't, and Goring's tactics changed, with bombers being more closely escorted, night attacks on aircraft industry centres, and a new push against RAF airfields. Dowding and Park's tactics remained grimly consistent. In fact, though Goring never had a realistic grip on the battle, his original tactics came closer to success than he realised. Dowding was giving serious thought to pulling all his fighters back towards the Midlands, even leaving London exposed.

Fighter Command was not short of aircraft. As the battle went on replacement Spitfires and Hurricanes were arriving at fighter stations every dawn to replace losses. Lord Beaverbrook is credited with this logistical achievement, though the surge in production was already in the pipeline before he took it over. But Beaverbrook *was* entirely responsible for the excellent rate at which damaged aircraft were repaired and brought back into the line. Dowding's problem, rather, was pilots and the critical shortage, in particular, of experienced and combat-ready pilots. By September Fighter Command had lost 348 pilots and received only 280 replacements; and the life expectancy of novice pilots thrown into the fight was measured in a few flying hours. By the first week in September that shortage was coupled with some serious exhaustion in 11 Group. Five of its forward airfields had been badly hit and six out of seven of its vital sector stations. Facilities were being repaired quickly but Park was clear that another week of this would destroy 11 Group and German raids in his sector would go largely unopposed. Goring, however – in the mistaken belief that Fighter Command, rather than being under great strain, was already 'finished' – was switching his focus to the bombardment of London. In addition, Bomber Command had raided Berlin on the night of 25th August and a furious Hitler ordered retaliation on London, day and night, beginning on the week-end of 7th September.

It was the start of the London blitz and a blessed relief for Fighter Command and 11 Group. That week ended on Sunday 15th September when another maximum effort was made by the *Luftwaffe* to attack London in daylight and draw what Goring thought were the dregs of the RAF's remaining fighters into a grand mêlée to finish them off. Dowding maintained the attrition tactics and again, 11, 10 and 12 Groups were at full stretch with all reserves committed. It was another grim day among many. Dowding and Park didn't know it then, but they had won their battle by the end of it. Earlier in that week German troops were due to have begun embarkation on their invasion barges. Instead, German commanders did their battle damage assessments on Monday 16th. On 17th Hitler again delayed the invasion and on 19th he postponed it indefinitely. It would remain a possibility for spring 1941. German attacks nevertheless continued over southern Britain until they ran out of steam in October. By the end of it all, German bombers had taken a real mauling, though the *Luftwaffe* had actually won the fighter battle, inflicting 1,172 fighter losses on the RAF for 845 of its own. But it didn't matter. Goring's knock-out blow had been thwarted by Dowding's attrition and German strategy had changed. Britain had proved to the world, and especially to the United States, that it was capable of carrying on the war against Germany and there would be no separate, dishonourable peace.

Popular history has it that Dowding and Park were both sacked in the hour of victory through the petty jealousies of score-settling rivals. There is some truth in this, certainly in the case of Keith Park, the great tactician of the victory, who was treated very shabbily indeed. But Dowding's eighth and final notice of retirement was a more complex affair. The Battle of the Atlantic and the Battle of Britain were the country's two great defensive conflicts during the war and both were fundamentally attritional, so neither had a clear ending in which the victor could survey the outcome. Both Dudley Pound at the Admiralty and Hugh Dowding at Bentley Priory knew what victory looked like in their respective battles, but it was less obvious to others. In the case of the Battle of Britain, that week of relief after 7th September had initiated a night-time blitz across London and there was almost nothing the RAF could do about it. The bombing of Coventry in November had seemed to highlight its impotence in the face of intensive night attacks. Dowding had been far ahead on the technologies of night-time interception to defend the cities but they were still months away from practical use. Meanwhile, he opposed Air Ministry demands just to 'do something' such as sending up Hurricanes and Spitfires, without on-board radar, to blunder around in the dark and risk getting lost or crash trying to land in poor weather.

And then there was the bitter controversy over Leigh-Mallory's demands for 'big wing' tactics; to fight pitched air battles, as against Dowding's and Park's attritional approach. Dowding was right to doubt the 'big wing'. It never worked, either then or later, and in 1941 many pilots lost their lives to its wrong-headedness. But in the autumn of 1940 all Dowding's critics united behind Leigh-Mallory's frankly dishonest promotion of the 'big wing' concept and the RAF's inability to counter the blitz. When the boot was on the other foot from 1941 to 1944, and Allied aircraft were launching bigger attacks on the *Luftwaffe* across the Continent, German commanders rapidly learned exactly the same lesson; big wings of defensive fighters were too unwieldy and it was far more effective to operate in smaller, decentralised units; which they did.

Whatever the tactics, the Trenchardist RAF was determined to go on the offensive and Dowding was regarded as the defensive specialist. He was never going to get the top job, and it was time to move on. It was not so unreasonable. Nevertheless, the petty jealousies of Leigh-Mallory, who took over 11 Group, Sholto Douglas who replaced Dowding to lead Fighter Command, and Charles Portal as the new RAF Chief, contrived to make this sensible transition a humiliating removal – 'a sacking' – that even the ruthless Churchill thought reflected badly on RAF leadership.

On 25th November Dowding circulated a valedictory message addressed to 'My Dear Fighter Boys' and departed, almost anonymously, from Bentley Priory with a brusque 'good morning' as Sholto Douglas arrived. He was sent to the US on a tour and then – very reluctantly – agreed to Churchill's request to conduct a study into the RAF's burgeoning personnel. He knew it would make him even more unpopular in the Air Ministry, and it did. His work made no impression on the Service. Archibald Sinclair, the Secretary of State for Air, thought Dowding's report 'an act of disloyalty' in bringing the 'defects' of the Air Ministry to the attention of the Prime Minister. The Air Ministry was relieved to put Dowding on the Retired List as of July 1942.

Dowding had been a spiritualist for many years and a longtime member of the Theosophical Society. In retirement he pursued his spiritualism; remarkably fashionable among his Victorian generation who fought the First World War. He thought he was in touch with his first wife and many of his 'dear fighter boys'. He wrote and spoke about spiritualism, reincarnation and mysticism. And, yes, he believed in fairies (and flying saucers). Fairies, he wrote, 'are essential to the growth of plants and the welfare of the vegetable kingdom'. Of course, he had no doubts how the world would interpret all this, but he was stoically committed to 'the fount of inspiration' and the need to 'co-operate with the unseen Forces of Light in helping distressed humanity on both sides of the Grave'. And he felt loved and cared for in his happy second marriage. He died peacefully in February 1970. He was cremated and his ashes interred below the Battle of Britain window in Westminster Abbey.

In 1968, scenes for an all-star epic film of the Battle of Britain were being made at Hawkinge airfield in Kent. Dowding was taken, in a wheelchair, to visit the set where a great fuss was made of him. The film dwelt on his role in the battle. He had not led Churchill's rhetorical 'few' so much as the 'many' – aircrews, mechanics, observers, radar operators, medics, telephonists, civilian repair crews, police, fire, Transport Auxiliary, aircraft factory workers – melding them together in time for Fighter Command's first, and most decisive, battle. His role in the film was played by Sir Laurence Olivier. Dowding's last public appearance, five months before his death, was at the film's premier at the Dominion Theatre on 15th September – Battle of Britain Day – 1969. At least on-screen he achieved a subtle glamour that never attached to him in 1940.

29

Field Marshal Harold Alexander

In 1942 'Alex', as he was popularly known by his troops, was referred to by Lieutenant-General Brian Horrocks as 'Winston Churchill's fire brigade chief par excellence: the man who was always dispatched to retrieve the most desperate situations'. Certainly, that reflected Churchill's faith in the third son of the Earl of Caledon; The Hon. Harold Rupert Leofric George Alexander, who became a Field Marshal and First Earl of Tunis, in recognition of his victories in the Mediterranean and Italy during the Second World War. Even that exalted headline doesn't quite capture the eminence of the man as a British commander. As the historian James Holland points out, he commanded in combat at every rank from subaltern to Field Marshal. He can be said personally to have 'fought' directly on the Western Front, in the Russian War of Intervention, in colonial policing in the Middle East, on the North-West Frontier, at Dunkirk, in the Middle East and North Africa, in Sicily and then throughout the long Italian campaign. The first of Germany's unconditional surrenders was made to him in May 1945. He was, says Holland, the most experienced battlefield commander on any side during the Second World War.

Yet in popular history Alexander is not as well known or celebrated as his unique record would suggest. This is partly because of his own modest character and his aristocratic self-deprecation. With the natural excellence he so obviously embodied, it was vulgar to be showy. But more than that, he appeared relatively indifferent to the very profession in which he most excelled – military command. He didn't try to study it with any application. Later in life he was sent book after book of military history, in many of which he featured prominently – all left unread in his library. He produced a very slim wartime memoir covering 1940 to 1945, in a life that others might have stretched to several volumes, and even that had to be ghost written for him by Major John North. He had none of John Gort's obsessive concentration on all affairs military, or Bernard Montgomery's overpowering ego to dominate everything around him. Success seemed to come easily and indifferently to Alex. Others found this irritating; a symptom of under-performance at the highest levels of command when more might have been achieved. Alexander is certainly not without his critics when his career reached its peak in the Sicily and Italian campaigns after July 1943. By then, however, he was predominantly a coalition commander working with other nationalities and the war had taken on a new political complexion. But he didn't need excuses. Unusually among senior military commanders, Alex didn't seem to care much about history's judgement one way or another.

Alexander's mother was a countess, daughter of the Earl of Norbury, and his father was the 4th Earl of Caledon in County Tyrone. The young boy was exceedingly proud of his Ulster roots and when it came to it, the recently raised Irish Guards seemed a natural military home for the twenty-year-old Alexander. Born in 1891, he had the benefit of a happy and secure childhood, educated at Harrow before he went to Sandhurst. Alex emerged as the Hollywood image of a young Edwardian officer. He had, in any case, film-star looks; he moved with a lithe athleticism, sported a fashionable small moustache, was immaculately dressed at all times and unfailingly polite and charming. In the best aristocratic tradition he was good – but not too good – at more or less all sports at Harrow, celebrated as a school runner over a mile, good at shooting and noted for his cricket. In the most famous Eton and Harrow cricket match of all time, the 'Fowlers match' of 1910, he batted number eleven and took 3/11 bowling clever googlies. He was also a gifted painter and considered taking it up as a vocation (he certainly didn't need a 'profession') either before, or instead of, the Army.

This is an interesting clue to his nature. Alexander was languidly intelligent but not in a conventional sense, clever. Some of his later contemporaries thought him 'out of his depth' or 'brainless', but of course he wasn't. He was naturally interested in art, classics and culture and he much preferred to talk about them than anything political or military. It isn't surprising that he thought seriously about trying his hand at painting, but he opted instead for excitement and handsome outfits with the Irish Guards. He was never a reflective man. He found it easy to make decisions, did not suffer agonies of doubt and always looked forward, never back. He didn't harbour past regrets, at least none he was prepared to discuss. Even in his key headquarters in Sicily and Italy, the conversation around him was as much about classics and culture as about the immediate military situation.

In 1914 he went with the regiment as an Irish Guards lieutenant and found himself immediately caught up in the retreat from Mons and the first Battle of Ypres. He was wounded in the thigh and invalided home, but it didn't put him off. He freely admitted that he enjoyed being at war in those years. In 1915 he won the Military Cross at the Battle of Loos and then the DSO and the Legion d'honneur on the Somme in 1916. 'Bravery' is often defined as the act of overcoming one's natural fear and carrying on in spite of it. But Alexander was one of those to whom conventional bravery didn't seem to apply; he was either too fatalistic, or too confident, to feel natural fear. He wasn't reckless, or his troops would not have become so keen on him, but he maintained a reassuring demeanour that suggested the enemy were more a nuisance than deadly. His stock description for enemy action was 'tiresome'. At Loos, his Military Cross was awarded when the company he commanded took their objective and, as ever, found themselves isolated with no reserves arriving quickly enough to consolidate the position. Alexander's message back to battalion stated that 'he would be greatly obliged if they would kindly send some more men up, and with speed.' No irony or sarcasm was implied.

A pattern emerged whereby the young officer, now a captain, was rapidly asked to take over temporary battlefield commands way above his age or rank. He was moved back and forth in temporary command of the 1st and 2nd battalions – normally requiring the rank of a Lieutenant-Colonel – before he was confirmed in command of 2nd Battalion prior to the Passchendaele offensive in 1917. By the end of the war Alexander had been acting Brigadier-General in command of the 4th Guards Brigade at the age of twenty-seven, wounded twice more, awarded a second DSO and had been mentioned in dispatches five times. Still as an acting Lieutenant-Colonel, just as the war was ending, he was sent to command the X Corps infantry school, normally requiring a Major-General or higher. Such advancement was not only due to his style and the respect of his soldiers but also to the tough commands Alexander had undertaken. It was something of a portent for the future. At Cambrai his weakened battalion of 400 men suffered 320 casualties. At Hazebrouck during the Ludendorff offensive in 1918 his own battalion within the 4th Guards Brigade were effectively wiped out for any further action in the war. He was seen as the man for a crisis; up for the challenge of a hopeless position.

After the war he did a stint with the Allied Control Commission in Poland, but was frankly bored. He got himself sent to Latvia to fight against the Bolsheviks during the 'War of Intervention'. He was supposed to be 'an adviser' but in July 1919 was given charge of the Baltic Landeswehr, commanding German and Baltic soldiers in liberating Latvia from Russian control. It was an interesting command to have less than eight months after the end of hostilities with Germany. The Landeswehr was involved in some fierce fighting as Bolshevik forces were pushed out of Latvia. He was wounded yet again, though not seriously. Alexander returned to Britain in 1920 and by 1922 was made substantive Lieutenant-Colonel and took command (formally) of the 1st Battalion, Irish Guards, taking them to Constantinople as the Chanak crisis was breaking out, then to Gibraltar and finally to a long London posting. He undertook a number of domestic postings with the Guards, in training commands and at Northern Command, interspersed with a year at Staff College and another later on at the new Imperial Defence College. None of this was really to his taste.

At Staff College, two of his instructors were Lieutenant-Colonels Alan Brooke and Bernard Montgomery, with whom he would later work – subordinate to Brooke and outranking Montgomery. Brooke – Viscount Alanbrooke as he was to become – rose to become Chief of the Imperial General Staff during the Second World War and played a major role in allocating Alexander to different commands. Brooke thought that Alexander was an 'empty vessel' while Montgomery, never sparing in his sincere criticism, later said the directing staff 'came to the conclusion that he had no brains – and we were right'. But if they didn't see much of the soldier-scholar in Alexander, Montgomery was simply wrong about the views of other staff. Many of them thought Alexander embodied sheer common sense, a quick appreciation of a military situation and an instinctive grasp of what soldiers could – and couldn't – achieve. Like many an elite sports star, he could not really explain what he did, because he did it through instinct and rare talent.

At least after these staff college studies Alexander had the pleasure of marriage in 1931 to Lady Margaret Bingham, younger daughter of the Earl of Lucan (a successor to Lord Lucan who commanded the cavalry in the Crimean War). She was thirteen years younger than him, shy, no debutante, and quite unaware of who Alexander was for some time after they met. But Margaret was a strong character. Notwithstanding being an earl's daughter, she insisted on earning her own living working as an assistant in Bond Street shops. Immediately after they were married Alex and Margaret spent a pleasant – and for him, downright lazy – two years in York when he was at Northern Command. From the first, they were a privileged and happy couple, having three children between 1932 and 1939, and adopting a fourth later on. They lived a very private family life together. Unlike some commanders under huge pressure who found in their families a personal safety valve in the blessed relief from war, Alexander never seemed to rely on his family in quite the same way. They were, to him, a joyous and separate facet of his emotionally fulfilled existence.

In 1934 he was sent to the North-West Frontier in India to command the Nowshera Brigade, a mixture of British and Indian Army battalions. Unusually for a brigade commander, he was personally involved in two fighting campaigns during 1935, at Los Agra and Mohmand. This was the old imperial army and a different kind of soldiering; not the sort Alexander had known in the world war. The Indian Army was culturally different to the British Army and the virtues of individual soldiering – operating in smaller numbers, being tactically adept, individually fit and resourceful – took precedence over the big formations and integrated battles of the Western Front. The Indian Army's job was imperial policing, using tactics that these days are labelled 'counter-insurgency'. Alexander absorbed the tactics with his usual instinctive talent; taking the initiative, careful to avoid ambushes, and out-thinking his tribal adversaries who were in revolt against the largely hidden hand of British colonial rule. Sceptics wondered whether a brigadier from the Guards with only European experience could really handle all the command challenges of the old imperial army, but Alexander proved them wrong. His Indian battalions quickly respected his tactical acumen and his active concern for their welfare. He also showed he had the knack of understanding 'all arms' campaigns. At Los Agra he used RAF aircraft to excellent effect, creating conditions for the pacification that followed. But at Mohmand he was rightly sceptical of command thinking that aircraft alone would achieve much; and he was right again that 'boots on the ground' were essential in this case. Montgomery, meanwhile, had become an instructor at the Staff College in Quetta, and notwithstanding his unalterable view of Alexander's intellectual limitations, he brought groups of his officers to Peshawar to learn the tactics of Alexander's Nowshera brigade and the secrets of its effectiveness. A successful brigade commander over three years, Alexander had picked up two more 'mentions in dispatches' in the process. He was eminently ready to command a division and that moment arrived when he was sent to France in 1939 in a campaign that would end in the evacuation from Dunkirk in June 1940.

The Dunkirk episode was the conclusion of an outright strategic defeat for Britain, albeit with the deliverance of the British Expeditionary Force – another BEF – to form the core of a new conscript army that would go on to play its part in the liberation of Europe. And though Alexander said he recalled 'the whole affair of Dunkirk with extreme distaste', his own role in that defeat actually marked one of his best tactical performances.

He was sent with the BEF in command of the 1st Division within I Corps, with Alan Brooke as his corps commander and working alongside Montgomery who commanded 3rd Division. In May 1940 the BEF performed its allotted role in the wholly misconceived French defence plan, advancing north to the river Dyle, and was immediately outflanked to the south. French commanders then planned a joint allied offensive from north and south to cut into the German thrust between them that had rapidly reached Abbeville at the Somme estuary. That plan simply evaporated while the BEF stood on the French-Belgian border, and by May 25th it was clear that the army must fall back on Dunkirk or be lost. The *Wehrmacht* was officered by very committed young leaders who burned with a sense of injustice and destiny. British and French commanders completely underestimated them. As Max Hastings put it, 'Allied soldiers, reflecting the societies from which they were drawn, prided themselves on behaving like reasonable men. The *Wehrmacht* showed what unreasonable men could do'.

Alexander had drilled his units hard before the German offensive commenced and the withdrawal of 1st division was conducted in military textbook style; thinning out battalion for battalion as they passed through each other's lines and alternated defensive duties. It was a two-week trek covering 150 miles and required seven hot rearguard actions before the division reached the impossibly congested Dunkirk perimeter. Alexander himself arrived on a pushbike with nothing but the clothes he stood in, his revolver, field glasses and briefcase. I Corps, alongside French forces, was made responsible for the final rearguard to hold the perimeter while the army escaped. General John Gort, commander of the BEF (and according to Montgomery, on the strength of his personal intervention) replaced I Corps commander with Alexander to organize the BEF's last stand in France. Gort assumed that holding the perimeter would end inevitably in the surrender and capture of rearguard survivors. Churchill, too, had given his permission for a surrender when the commander on the ground judged it unavoidable. But as the new commander on the ground, Alexander was convinced he could get the remaining 20,000 of the BEF's rearguard away before the front finally collapsed, as he judged, no later than 1st–2nd June. He made it clear to his French counterparts that the BEF would all be leaving, and despite accusations of betrayal, he was obeying the last orders he was able to obtain from London before communications went down. Efforts were made to rescue as many of the French rearguard as possible but still some 35,000 French soldiers were left[1]. Alexander's men sheltered in the sand dunes during the day and crowded onto the boats and destroyers during the night, while he conducted operations from underneath the Dunkirk fort, touring the shrinking perimeter in an old Humber limousine. Alexander was the last BEF soldier to leave the beaches alive, just after midnight on 3rd June, touring up and down in a motor launch with a loud hailer, calling in English and French for any stragglers to show themselves and be rescued. The same around the harbour quays. There were none.[2] At about 02.00 he stepped onto on the last destroyer that had

---

1. In those four days when Alexander commanded, the last 20,000 British troops were lifted from the beaches along with 98,000 French troops. One major problem was that French unit cohesion had broken down and organised evacuation became impossible. On the nights of 1st and 2nd June twelve destroyers arrived but left empty when French troops went to different assembly points. Then too, many of the French rearguard opted for honourable surrender over the prospect of having to fight on in Britain's defence against the German invasion that would surely follow.
2. There were, in fact, more French troops sheltering further west of the harbour and a flotilla of French and British ships took more than 20,000 of them off during the night of 3rd-4th June. German records show that the French rearguard fought for every building as they pulled back through the port before the survivors surrendered on the morning of 4th June. The official British record claims that almost 140,000 French troops were eventually rescued.

waited for him, which was bombed and machine-gunned as it raced back toward Dover before an RAF dawn patrol could give it some cover.

After Dunkirk, Alexander became a Corps Commander with responsibility for the defence of the East Coast, and then from December 1940, as Commander-in-Chief of the critical Southern Command. Two elements in his military thinking became important to the army's future conduct of operations. Like Brooke, he was appalled at all the fixed defence points – pillboxes and bunkers – that had sprung up around the British coasts and countryside during the year. He knew from his BEF experience how wrong-headed they were and how much they would inhibit dynamic defence based on powerful mobile reserves. His own defensive plans were quite different. But though his defensive design was never tested in a sea-borne invasion, his understanding of the task was extremely useful when *he* was subsequently commanding a sea-borne invasion against defences in Sicily and Italy. But probably the greatest contribution Alexander made to the future conscript army was by seizing upon, and developing, the Battle School system within Southern Command. It was through this that his own invaluable experience made the greatest contribution and the Battle School system was extended to the whole army after 1941. It placed absolute priority on three key requirements; simple and clear battle drills, the need to 'inoculate' soldiers from fear and battle stress through tight unit cohesion, and the primacy of individual physical fitness. Modern research has shown how far the 'People's Army' of that war – almost three million men by 1945 – was riven with social tensions and displayed a collective morale that was frankly fragile. The Battle School system was an essential part of the military cement that held that disparate army together, just about long enough for victory.

The Japanese attack on Pearl Harbor in December 1941 was an immediate source of joy to Churchill since it brought the United States into the war which guaranteed, as nothing else could, that the Allies would eventually win it. But the fall of Singapore in February 1942 was a body blow to Britain's own war effort, marking – as it turned out – the end of British imperial presence in South-east Asia. In Burma, the capital city of Rangoon was in immediate crisis as invading Japanese forces closed in from the Thai border. It was a key port and hence critical to the re-supply of Burma from India, and also to send US supplies to Chinese forces fighting Japan. In March when it was clear that Rangoon's situation was close to hopeless, Churchill sent Alexander to Burma to see what could be done. On arrival, he immediately ordered a quick offensive to try to split the Japanese column in half, but it failed completely. So, after two days in command Alexander ordered a withdrawal from Rangoon to Tharrawaddy further north and the destruction of Rangoon's valuable port facilities. It was another defeat, another debilitating withdrawal. Alexander found himself commanding the Burma Army – a shifting mix of Indian, Burmese, Chinese and British formations as it withdrew to fight in the Arakan Hills, the Karen Hills and the Irrawaddy and Sittang valleys.

This was Alexander's first theatre command. He had the pugnacious American Joseph W. Stilwell as one of his Corps commanders, nominally commanding the Chinese formations. For Alexander, Stilwell was a given. But acting on good advice from Gurkha commanders, he specifically recruited William Slim as his other corps commander – a personal judgement that turned out to be inspired. According to GHQ in India, Alexander's task was to stay in touch with Chinese forces – falling back to the north-east, whilst keeping the escape route to India open – lying to the north-west. Simply impossible. He was falling back all the time while Japanese forces in Burma doubled in size and established air superiority. He seemed to hover between making a stand somewhere – while his two corps were still united and before they were supposed to fall back in different directions – and simply making a full withdrawal. Eventually he had to give up defending on the Irrawaddy or at Mandalay and instead get stocks ready along the route for a retreat north-west back to Assam in India. It became a race both against the Japanese advance, seeking to outflank him, and the monsoon, due in mid-May that would make movement almost impossible. From Mandalay it gave him a three-week window to move his army 200 miles to Tamu on the Indian border, over half of that route along no more than a cart track. Some equipment could go by river ferry up the Chindwin, but the rest was a foot march. Slim's corps did an excellent rearguard job before the last exhausted elements of his Indian 17th Division trudged into Tamu after enduring the first week of the monsoon. Alexander's Burma Army had withdrawn almost 1,000 miles in fifteen weeks – the longest ever by a British Army – and it had retreated in the face of a smaller Japanese force that was simply better in every respect at jungle fighting and offensive operations.

Alexander's memoirs make no attempt to dodge this fact, though his reputation as a commander didn't suffer in the way Gort's had done after the BEF's defeat in France. Slim criticized him for not switching to the offensive once the Japanese advance was getting stretched; for dithering and then becoming too fixated on an orderly withdrawal to safety. Perhaps; though Alexander would have needed luck and a lot of air power to achieve very much. On the other hand, he saved the Burma Army and closed the gates of India to the Japanese. Their advance had to reach its zenith somewhere, and that turned out to be at Kohima just on the Indian side of the border in April 1944.

Notwithstanding the entry of the US into the war, 1942 was a dreadful and dangerous year for Britain and the Allies, and it propelled Alexander to the peak of his military career. The Japanese advance threatened India, powerful German forces were thrusting deep into Russia and might soon be capable of crossing the Caucasus into Persia and the Levant. More active coordination between Germany and Japan might have tipped world politics decisively in their favour. The potential link between them lay in the Middle East, and here British and Commonwealth forces were being defeated. If the British lost Cairo and were chased out of Egypt, the allied position across the Levant and into Iraq would be likely to collapse. Like Napoleon in 1798, if Hitler controlled Egypt and the Levant, his forces could move into northern India; and in Hitler's case might have shaken hands with his Japanese allies sometime in 1943.[3]

---

3. For these reasons, Egypt had to be defended. But in subsequently moving westwards into North Africa, the allies fatally weakened their protection in Persia and south of the Caucasus, which would have been the gateway to Hitler's 'handshake' had the German invasion of Russia been successful.

As part of a shake-up in Middle East command, Brooke sent Alexander out as the new Commander-in-Chief, Middle East, with Montgomery as his subordinate to command the Eighth Army. It was good judgement on Brooke's part. Alexander would steer the strategy and deal with allied relations, Montgomery would command the army and fight the battles. The two generals got on well enough and took an identical view of the situation when they arrived in Cairo. Alexander immediately set the tone when he expressly forbade any more Eighth Army withdrawals from its current positions. And Montgomery burned all existing withdrawal plans at his HQ. Brooke knew that Alexander was wise enough to give Montgomery plenty of freedom to act, though he was soon complaining again that Alex was not 'gripping' Monty enough. But Alexander approved Montgomery's plans for the battles of Alam Halfa and Alamein, described in another chapter, and protected him from Churchill's constant prodding and meddling. Between them, the two generals ran the campaign the way they thought best and to a tactical, not a political, timetable. They stemmed the tide of defeat and set the stage for the long series of Allied offensives that would finally roll-up the Third Reich in the west.

Alamein was the first great turning point at the end of October 1942. The next objective was to convert this to real strategic advantage across North Africa by driving westwards to Tunis to link up with US forces who would be driving eastwards after their landings in Morocco and Algeria in November. This was very much Alexander's campaign and it became his personal triumph. As Commander of Ground Forces, North Africa – the 18th Army Group – he had charge of Montgomery with the Eighth Army, Kenneth Anderson's First Army and the US Army's II Corps commanded first by George Patton and then by Omar Bradley, all as his subordinate generals. He didn't imitate Montgomery's approach – clever preparation and then one decisive punch. Instead, he deliberately worked his forces like a boxer – jab, feint, move, punch – always keeping the enemy guessing what was coming next. He was charm itself to US generals and genuinely got on well with Dwight D. Eisenhower, the Supreme Commander to whom Alexander was now Deputy. But his private views showed he had little faith in American generalship or the soldiering of their inexperienced troops. As his formations converged in central Tunisia he had to rescue a chaotic situation both in command and tactical terms, countering a local German counter-offensive that might have stymied the next push north to Tunis itself. He 'gripped' that particular situation decisively, without letting any of his charm slip.

He manoeuvred his advancing forces until he had a quarter of a million German and Italian troops caught in a pocket between Tunis and Bizerte. The RAF starved them of fuel and supplies and then with deception and feint Alexander launched a massive air and artillery assault on 6th May 1943 moving rapidly into the pocket. Axis forces were completely confused and it was all over in twenty-four hours. When the Derbyshire Yeomanry swept into Tunis that afternoon they found German officers with their girlfriends sipping drinks outside the cafes. Almost 240,000 prisoners were taken, and by 13th May Alexander could report to Churchill, with only a hint of personal grandeur, 'We are masters of the North African shores.' He had commanded a well-supplied, and very well-organised, multinational army group and he achieved a general's military triumph that goes beyond simple victory – nothing less than the annihilation of those enemy formations facing him.

Though Eisenhower was Supreme Commander in North Africa, the victories at Tunis and Bizerte belonged entirely to Alexander, had he been egotistical enough to claim them. They represented the height of his command effectiveness; ground forces commander with three armies to direct, American and French allies, and a plan of campaign that showed his instinctive understanding of battle tactics, combined arms operations and local conditions. As the historian, Brian Holden Reid points out, Alexander was like Wellington without the sacarstic wit and Marlborough without the charlatanism – and as important as both of them in British military history.

Much was made of the Allied victory as political leaders trooped to Tunis to celebrate it, but planning for the next steps was already well advanced – the invasion of Sicily, then Italy, then a natural push up the Italian peninsula into central Europe itself. Alexander was hard at work on it when he was designated commander-in-chief of a new formation – the 15th Army Group – for the great enterprise. Thus began a wearying three-year campaign of invasions and offensives that witnessed triumphs and disasters aplenty; the smooth Sicily invasion, the troubled Salerno campaign, the agony of the Anzio landings, the three attritional battles of Cassino, assaults on German defences in the Gustav Line and then the Gothic Line, the drive to Rome, the slog up to the Po valley, even a sudden diversion to Greece to forestall a communist takeover. It was the longest and toughest of all Britain's land campaigns during that war, and as a window on Alexander's later command career, a number of consistent strands ran through it.

Alexander found it impossible to recreate the conditions that had brought him such success in North Africa. Churchill was keen on Alexander and enthusiastic about his Italian campaign. But Churchill's American allies would only tolerate the diversion of pushing north through Italy insofar as it helped create the best conditions for 'OVERLORD' – the liberation of Europe and the invasion of Germany from the west. The best US and British commanders in Italy were steadily transferred back to Britain to work on the preparations for the OVERLORD D-Day invasion, and many of Alexander's most experienced formations and important equipment were drawn down as Allied forces re-orientated themselves for the great offensive. Alexander saw the point, of course, and as a dutiful commander with a limited ego – as ever – he made the best of it. But he was always having to 'borrow' scarce equipment like landing craft, or get short-term reinforcements, to keep his momentum going. And if Allied leaders in London and Washington waxed and waned in their commitment to the Italian campaign, Alexander, too, seemed less than consistent in what he was really trying to achieve in these years. Simply holding his Allies together often seemed enough.[4]

Brooke's constant refrain that Alexander needed to get more 'grip' on matters was misplaced over the North Africa campaign, but he was probably right when it came to

---

4. Within his 15th Army Group, Alexander commanded twenty-nine different nationalities according to the Official History, including British, US, French, Polish, New Zealand, South African, Indian and Canadian forces, not to mention the Cremona Group of Italian forces fighting with the allies.

Sicily and Italy. The geography of Sicily and the ranges of available aircraft meant that naval, air and army requirements were all very different for an invasion of the island. That had not been the case in the previous campaign. There was also real tension now between the priorities of US and British ground forces. Not least, Montgomery was at his undiplomatic worst trying to pull the whole allied plan into the orbit of his own Eighth Army. Alexander fell to compromising rather than commanding. He finally agreed that the British Eighth Army would take the lead in landing at Catania on Sicily's east coast and push to Messina in the far north-east with the Italian mainland just across the straits. Patton's American Seventh Army would land slightly later at Syracuse in the south west as flank support to Montgomery. Patton and Montgomery already detested each other and were competing for glory. When the Eighth Army was held up in the mountains above Catania, Patton persuaded Alexander to let him push straight for Palermo in Sicily's north-west, which he triumphantly took on 22nd July – the first city to be liberated by US forces in the Second World War.

It was a mistake then, and these uneasy compromises between the egos of commanders continued to dog the strategic clarity of allied offensives for most of the Italian campaign. Patton's vainglorious diversion to Palermo in the north-west allowed the German army to escape from Sicily. This victory would not be another Tunis. And so it continued in the following months. Alexander was an old Western Front commander and he interpreted his prime strategic mission as being to destroy the German army in Italy, or else wear it down for the benefit of OVERLORD not to liberate glamorous cities while German forces withdrew before him in good order. But his US commanders, almost without exception, saw the Italian campaign as a contest for geographical control – to 'liberate Italy' – and Alexander was unable to reconcile them to his more hard-nosed view. He was steadily losing forces and equipment to the OVERLORD preparations in Britain and he had to commit time and troops to dig allied forces out of adventurous holes they had got into – with his approval – at Salerno (which was as close to failure as any allied amphibious assault in Europe), Anzio and Cassino. With constant allied compromises, shifting instructions from London, and barely adequate forces to maintain momentum, Alexander was winning only incremental victories as they pushed slowly north – just like Wellington in the Peninsular War – rather than manoeuvring for a decisive encirclement. Still, he took good care of his soldiers' safety, reconnoitering for himself, often with only a single staff officer, from forward observation posts all along the fragmented front lines. He was a popular and eminently approachable commander among his troops.

Liberating Rome, however, was urged by Churchill; for its effects on Axis morale, and not least for its distraction potential in view of the imminence of the D-Day invasion in Normandy. In May 1944 Alexander committed everything he had to breaking out of the attritional Cassino battles so as to encircle Rome and then to liberate the eternal city on 4th June, just forty-eight hours before D-Day began. It was a big moment for Alexander, coming as the culmination of his 'Diadem' offensive – the biggest single operation any British or American general had conducted up to then. But he had originally hoped to celebrate victory the previous December, and still – yet again – the *Wehrmacht*'s Tenth Army had escaped destruction, because the headstrong General Mark Clark leading the US Fifth Army dashed into the city for the glory of it – maybe just for the hell of it – instead of encircling the German's Tenth Army after Alexander had created the perfect opportunity for him to annihilate it.

It certainly wasn't that Alexander lacked strategic vision. Indeed, he had a clear view that with the right support, the 15th Army Group could encircle and destroy German forces in front of him, push to Bologna and on towards Vienna, destabilizing the Axis across southern Europe and the Balkans. It was a logical strategy and Berlin, interestingly, had always assumed that the Allied invasion of Italy must be prelude to something like this – or else why were the Allies doing it? But it wasn't. It was hard enough to hold the Americans (and the Russians) to continue the Italian campaign as a powerful sideshow to the ultimate invasion of Germany across the Rhine. By the end of 1944 Alexander was a Field Marshal and Supreme Commander, Mediterranean. But the Americans, Brooke and even Churchill had effectively lost interest in the Italian campaign. So the grinding advance went on, always against superior German numbers as they fell back towards the Alps. Alexander didn't push his strategic schemes with great persistence in London; he understood the new political realities. In his final campaign, however, and for once during the whole Italian episode, very much *his* campaign once again with plenty of personal 'grip', he showed all his old touch. He fooled German forces into moving to the Adriatic coast to counter an imaginary amphibious landing, while the US Fifth Army struck west of Bologna and the Eighth Army crashed through the Argenta Gap to race north-west along the river Reno to Bondeno. On 24th April leading elements of both armies finally encountered each other as they converged – fittingly – at the town of Finale, twenty-two miles north of Bologna. At last, German forces south of the river Po were completely encircled and forced to surrender. Hour by hour, more northern Italian cities fell to the Allies or local partisans. It was a typical Alex victory.

Hitler was already dead; resistance collapsed on all fronts. On 2nd May, six days before the general surrender, one million German troops in Italy unconditionally laid down their arms, while their commanders signed the instrument of surrender at Caserta. Alexander wasn't there to receive it. It was signed on his behalf by his erstwhile Chief of Staff, General William Morgan, who five years previously had embarked from the mole a few minutes before Alexander to board the last destroyer leaving Dunkirk.

After the war, Alexander was happy to be offered the Governor-Generalship of Canada, a role that he enjoyed and performed well from 1946 to 1952. It was ceremonial, advisory and essentially apolitical, and it well-suited his wife and still-young family of three, then four when they adopted a daughter in 1948. But in 1952 Churchill, in his last period as Prime Minister, wanted to relinquish the role of Minister of Defence which he had incorporated into his Prime Ministership and to have Alexander do it. Alex hated the idea, as did his wife, but he agreed as an act of duty. It wasn't a success. The role was anyway ill-defined and his natural sense of compromise made him little more than a caretaker manager, caught between the urgent needs of the service chiefs and the failing powers of a demanding Prime Minister. And though (counting Lord Ismay) Alexander was only the second regular soldier to join the cabinet since the Duke of Wellington, he despised the realities of politics and – like many another military hero – seemed frankly shocked at the way politics were conducted. His accredited biographer comments that Alexander 'was not a failure as Minister of Defence. He just never tried very hard to be a great success'.[5]

He stepped down from his ministerial career with some relief in 1954, and then led a busy, but still essentially private, life for many years in honorary and public positions as well as with a few commercial interests. And he spent much time painting. At the last function Alexander attended in June 1969 he responded to a toast by Lord De L'Isle, General Gort's son-in-law, on whose chest he had pinned a Victoria Cross in 1944 after the Anzio landings. It was the last speech he made. He was taken ill the following morning and died of heart failure some days later at the age of seventy-seven.

Once, after the war, his secretary brought him the draft of a book someone had written assessing his campaigns to ask if he had any comments or corrections to add to the draft. Alex wasn't interested. 'It's his book', he said, 'tell him to write what he likes'.

---

5. The 'accredited biographer', being the only title the family would allow, was Nigel Nicolson who knew Alexander very well.

30

Admiral Dudley Pound

Dudley Pound did not enjoy a sparkling naval career. He was steady, safe and well-respected as he rose through the ranks. He became First Sea Lord just before the outbreak of the Second World War, as much by default as acclamation. As '1SL' and therefore also Chief of the Naval Staff, he presided over some depressing defeats and failures for the Royal Navy, none more so than the tragic PQ-17 arctic convoy in 1942. And, seriously ill, he died the following year in the midst of his punishing work schedule. He is known to history more for his questionable decisions over PQ-17 than anything else. Nevertheless, in the larger picture, Dudley Pound should also be remembered as a man who had to manage Britain's inadequate naval forces across a global conflict. No other British commander during the war had such extensive geographical responsibilities. More important, he presided over a gradual, grinding victory in the 'Battle of the Atlantic', which was fundamental to the Allied cause; initially to keep Britain alive with the regular arrival of vital convoys, and then as the tide of war turned, to facilitate the Allied liberation of Europe. As he famously said, 'if we lose the Battle of the Atlantic, we lose the war'. Many of his contemporary chiefs didn't accept that, or if they did, thought somehow that the battle could be won without the commitment of significant resources. It couldn't. And historians have generally agreed that Pound's judgement about the battle was a statement of the bald truth.

Pound also fought a constant battle against Churchill's penchant for dictating operational decisions – handling the Prime Minister's inexhaustible drive and restless inventiveness to channel it into what could be achieved in a strategically coherent way. A more compliant First Sea Lord might have led the Royal Navy into some strategic blind alleys, to say the least. A more pugnacious one would not have lasted long under Winston's style of leadership. Dudley Pound provided consistency and strategic vision even as he led a navy that, from event to event, didn't perform very well when he was 1SL. He paid a high personal price for his dedication with his health, and was close to tearful despair on more than one occasion as he tried to maintain naval strategy in the face of Churchill's relentless demands.

Pound was born into a professional middle class family on the Isle of Wight in 1877. He joined the navy's training ship, *Britannia*, as a thirteen-year-old, having done very well in his entrance examination. *Britannia* was an 1860 hulk moored on the Dart river, with another hulk, the *Hindustan*, moored in front of it for accommodation. He lived the classic, spartan life of the young naval cadet and then served as midshipman and lieutenant in battleships, cruisers and destroyers in steady progression to 1898. He chose to become a torpedo specialist – a shrewd career decision on his part – qualifying in 1901 and then serving on major ships of the line in the Pacific, Mediterranean and Atlantic fleets. He did a spell in the Ordnance Department in 1909 and by the outbreak of war in 1914 was serving in Jackie Fisher's 1SL office as a direct assistant to Fisher – a tribute in itself to his intelligence from the fiery old warrior. At thirty-seven Pound was young for a captain, and in 1915 he was given as his first command, *HMS Colossus*, a front-line battleship – again, a tribute to his expertise and promise.

It was in the *Colossus* that Pound was involved in the only naval engagement of his career at the Battle of Jutland in 1916, serving with Jellicoe's Grand Fleet. As Jellicoe's fleet shook down into battle order, the *Colossus* was seventeenth in Jellicoe's line as it 'crossed the T' of the German High Seas Fleet. Pound was in a position to share in the shelling and destruction of the *Wiesbaden* as it wallowed around, and then opened fire on a number of German destroyers manoeuvring to launch torpedo attacks, before scoring some hits on the *Derfflinger*. The *Colossus* had to dodge a torpedo attack and was then itself hit by gunfire from the battlecruiser *Seydlitz*. That concluded Pound's direct experience of sea battle, though he was certainly intelligent enough to understand what had gone right, and wrong, for the Royal Navy at Jutland. It is no surprise that he was back in the Admiralty in 1917 working in 'Plans' and then as Director of Operations for home waters. As such, the 'Zeebrugge Raid' of April 1918 – not entirely successful – fell within his responsibilities.

In the inter-war period Pound's steadiness of judgement and his intellectual qualities saw him progress smoothly through the senior ranks of the navy. He commanded the famous battlecruiser *Repulse* and alternated between spells at the Admiralty and sea commands – taking on the battlecruiser squadron, then with the Mediterranean Fleet and eventually as its Commander-in-Chief. He was Second Sea Lord in 1932, responsible for all the Royal Navy's personnel, and was made a full admiral in 1935. During the early inter-war years he was, like every other senior naval officer, dragged into the fierce Jellicoe/Beatty controversies over the Battle of Jutland. Pound was thought, at least by Jellicoe, to be a 'Beatty man', which given that he was rising during the years Beatty was 1SL and increasingly influential in the navy, was natural enough. Pound also found himself serving no fewer than six times under the influence of the charismatic Roger Keyes – who was a buccaneering 'Beatty man' to his finger-tips. Pound and Keyes were completely different personalities but during these years worked remarkably well together as professional friends, though the relationship soured when the fiercely ambitious Keyes failed to become First Sea Lord, whereas Pound later did.

During his productive years at the Admiralty, Pound was involved in the international negotiations that sought to balance and limit the naval might of the major powers, which in Britain's case meant accepting the end of two hundred years of maritime primacy. It was a theme that Pound would grapple with for the rest of his life; trying to meet Britain's imperial commitments with a navy that was shrinking under the pressure of inter-war defence cuts, followed by the significant deficit of ships that still persisted even when the building programme picked up under the threat of a global war. He was involved in cabinet meetings in respect to the Geneva Conference on naval armaments, and was not impressed by the quality of politicians he encountered there, in particular, not by Churchill. Though he was, by nature, a 'big battleship' man, Pound fought hard to establish the Fleet Air Arm as a major part of future maritime warfare. Not least, as 2SL, he was intimately involved in welfare matters for naval personnel and did a good deal to help modernize the service and increase the seagoing command qualities of its captains. Perhaps of greatest importance to his standing in the navy, he was a successful C-in-C of the Mediterranean Fleet from 1936 to 1939, leaving it in good fighting form with its morale high.

When the decision to elevate Pound to First Sea Lord was made in June 1939, there was no doubt that he was worth the appointment. On the other hand, a fortuitous gap had opened for him. The excellent W.W. Fisher had died suddenly in 1937. In May 1939 Roger Backhouse, the incumbent 1SL, had resigned suddenly in ill health before dying that July. Bertie Ramsey – later to be recognised as one of the navy's most effective admirals – had resigned in some dudgeon in 1935 and languished on the Retired List. Keyes had already been passed over and sat fuming in the House of Commons; James Somerville and Andrew Cunningham were excellent prospects but lacked the seniority to look right for the post. Pound was consulted on all these possibilities as the urgent question of succession to Backhouse arose. He never argued for his own promotion, but it became the sensible decision anyway.

There was another problem. Pound had long-standing osteo-arthritis in his left hip and as a result was in persistent pain and didn't sleep well. As a very conscientious man he worked himself hard and, though a socially lively character who enjoyed entertaining, Pound was to become progressively exhausted as the strains of being 1SL during the war took its toll. He had married Betty Whitehead in 1908 and they enjoyed a happy family life with their three children, where Betty shared all his postings and did everything then expected of a traditional service wife to facilitate his work and social commitments. Nevertheless, once the war began, Pound saw rather little of his family and increasingly found himself fighting for his own health as he fought for his country and its navy.

Dudley Pound's responsibilities as he became First Sea Lord were greater in every respect than those of his fellow service chiefs. As head of his service he was, unlike them, also Chief of the Naval Staff. The Admiralty was the operational centre, responsible for all naval warfare, as well as being the office that ran the Royal Navy. And the navy's operational plot became ever-wider as the war went on. His responsibilities began by spanning the protection of home waters, trade routes and supply lines to British forces overseas, and conducting an economic blockade of Germany. For most of 1940, getting British expeditionary forces in and out of Norway, then in and out of France, then warding off invasion and keeping Britain fed in an immediate food crisis, were demanding enough. When Italy entered the war in June 1940, Mediterranean strategy suddenly became more challenging; protecting passage not just for British forces in the Middle East but also for oil tankers from the Persian Gulf en route to Britain. The Royal Navy held either end of the Mediterranean, at Gibraltar (with James Somerville) and Alexandria (with Andrew Cunningham), but now had to battle for access across it, to protect convoys, maintain supplies to North Africa, keep Malta alive as a key military base, and react to Axis invasions of Greece and Crete. Mediterranean naval warfare became dominated by the use of air power, submarines, light torpedo boats and new sea/air tactics in some genuine departures from conventional naval warfare. And then there were the waters of the Far East. The navy had aimed to deter any Japanese aggression against British colonial territories by having a powerful naval presence in South-east Asia. In December 1941 that policy manifestly collapsed when the Japanese attacked Pearl Harbor and then Singapore, opening up another huge maritime front for Britain, where the Indian Ocean had to be defended for supplies to Burma, China and into the Pacific.

This was clearly unsustainable with the ships Pound had available and he was constantly having to make momentous choices and accept fearful risks as he sought to counter three strong – all different – Axis navies fighting their own versions of the war. In response to these responsibilities, Pound became a great centralizer at the Admiralty, accused by other senior admirals of trying to run tactical campaigns from the Admiralty bunker – the monolithic building that sits at the corner of Horse Guards Parade. It was true enough, though it wasn't driven by any sharp ego on Pound's part, but rather his overwhelming sense of responsibility in trying to cover too many risks with too few ships.

Events came and went with more failures than successes. Early on, the *Royal Oak* was sunk inside Scapa Flow and the aircraft carrier *Courageous* in the Bristol Channel, both to audacious U-boat attacks. The fall of France let the German navy through the gates to the Atlantic that had remained so firmly closed during the First World War. Now, French Atlantic ports, along with Norwegian bases, were available to both German surface raiders and U-boats and the *Kriegsmarine* made good use of them. The navy had a singular success in stalking the pocket battleship *Admiral Graf Spee* to a scuttling in the River Plate at Montevideo. During the disastrous Norway campaign in early 1940, the navy held its own but was accused of letting opportunities slip away and another aircraft carrier, *HMS Glorious*, was sunk in the operation among several losses it could ill-afford.

The Norway campaign brought Churchill from First Lord of the Admiralty to become Prime Minister in No 10. That opened up a new fighting front for Dudley Pound, 'handling' Churchill who still behaved as if he were as close to naval operations as ever. But Churchill respected Pound for his intelligence and conscientiousness. And for his part, Pound got to appreciate Churchill, realizing, as he put it himself, that one should 'Never say a direct "No" to the PM at a meeting', but as long as, 'you don't exaggerate your case the PM will always let you have your say.' So Pound learned to work around Churchill's bursting circus of ideas, refining them or else shepherding his enthusiasms as they bounced out of play. For the most part, Pound was good at 'handling' Churchill, and others admired the way he operated, but it was an endless strain for Pound. He lived – camped out – predominantly at Admiralty House and had to endure endless 'midnight follies' of briefings and then calls from Churchill into the early hours, or even full war cabinet meetings.

The year 1940 finished on a better note in December with Cunningham's famous Fleet Air Arm attack on the Italian fleet in harbour at Taranto. But 1941 became a dreadful year for the Royal Navy. The campaign in the western desert had swung from success towards failure and the navy endured major losses as it ran hazardous Malta convoys in addition to convoys to and from Alexandria. In November the aircraft carrier, *Ark Royal* was sunk just thirty miles short of safety in Gibraltar. In December, Cunningham lost the last two battleships of his Mediterranean Fleet when Italian 'chariot divers' miraculously got into Alexandria harbour and blew up the *Queen Elizabeth* and the *Valiant*.[1] And that happened just over a week after the event of which Churchill said, 'In all the war I never received a more direct shock'; the sinking of the *Repulse* and the *Prince of Wales* in Singapore, as the colony fell to a remarkably small force of Japanese troops. It was a complete disaster. The only Allied capital ships across the whole Indian and Pacific oceans were the American survivors of the Pearl Harbor attack of 7th December, and they were all withdrawing swiftly to California.

Pound and the Admiralty were roundly condemned for the Singapore debacle. The Admiralty had tried during the previous months to revitalize its deterrent policy against Japan by preparing in October to send two powerful battleships to Singapore. Pound's excellent subordinate at the Admiralty, Tom Philips, was to command what became 'Force Z'. But the loss of aircraft carriers had become so severe that Force Z was deprived of its own air cover or any cruiser screen. It was deployed to Singapore the day after Pearl Harbor, with just four destroyers to protect the two battleships. Given that Tokyo had already decided on all-out attack, Force Z proved easy meat for Japanese dive bombers and torpedo aircraft when they attacked two days later. Tom Philips was killed; a matter of considerable grief to the exhausted Dudley Pound. In reality, and prior to any Japanese attack, Force Z had been another exercise in calculated risk – which spectacularly failed. But it was Churchill's risk as much as Pound's and the roots of the final decision to send Force Z in such an 'unbalanced' form are not clear from the documents. By most reckonings, this was one of the occasions when Pound should have stood up to Churchill more strongly. He was well aware of all the risks Force Z was taking, but as Robin Brodhurst put it, Pound was running what by then 'had become a one-ocean navy trying to fight a three-ocean war'.[2] All the risks were increasing.

Pound's relationship with Churchill seemed to be at a new low only a few weeks later. The *Kriegsmarine* knew it couldn't leave its most powerful surface raiders at vulnerable French ports and wanted to get them into better protected German or Norwegian anchorages. The *Scharnhorst*, the *Gneisenau* and the *Prinz Eugen* slipped out of Brest on 11 February 1942 and made a bold dash up the Channel, right under the noses of the Royal Navy in a bid to reach Wilhelmshaven, which they managed after thirty-seven tense hours. Everything went wrong for the British – shadowing submarines and air patrols broke down or were in the wrong place. Snow in Scotland prevented specialist torpedo bombers trying, and most other Bomber Command aircraft from airfields further south couldn't find the three raiders. The Fleet Air Arm did, and lost

---

1. During 1941, just in the Mediterranean, the Royal Navy incurred sinkings or severe damage to 5 battleships, 3 aircraft carriers, 17 cruisers, 28 destroyers and 8 submarines.
2. Though it might also be noted that Pound sent the carrier *Victorious* to Pearl Harbor in March 1943, operating under US command, following severe US carrier losses at Guadalcanal.

a whole squadron in suicidal and ineffective attacks; the Harwich motor torpedo boats couldn't get close enough because German E-boat escorts were faster and deadlier. The Harwich destroyers launched torpedo attacks and achieved no hits, whilst being bombed by the RAF for their pains (a surprisingly common occurrence throughout the war). From the Admiralty bunker Dudley Pound phoned Churchill on the 13th. He told him the German dash north had evidently succeeded. There was silence on the other end of the line. Then Churchill barked 'Why?' and put the phone down.

March 1942 probably represented the nadir of British military fortunes around the world and there was public dissatisfaction with the Royal Navy and the Admiralty. In reality, the celebrated 'Channel Dash' marked a strategic withdrawal by the German navy; giving up the ambition to operate a global surface fleet, and instead keeping it safe – rather like the High Seas Fleet before it – in northern waters. Senior admirals – unaware of Pound's quiet role in 'handling' Churchill – were increasingly critical of him. Neither Tovey in the Home Fleet, nor Sommerville in 'Force H' at Gibraltar, were fans, though Cunningham seemed to understand his role better than others. Churchill had Pound stand down as Chairman of the Chiefs of Staff Committee in favour of Alan Brooke, then stepping up to be Chief of the Imperial General Staff.[3] Churchill veered between knowing that he needed Pound (especially for his ability after Pearl Harbor to work with touchy US Navy chiefs) and intermittent urges to sack him. Pound nearly resigned anyway in April, but the prospect of Winston giving the 1SL job to Louis Mountbatten reinforced Cunningham's advice to 'glue himself to his chair' to prevent it – for everyone's sake.

In fact, by that stage Pound's greatest battle of the war, the Battle of the Atlantic, had already been won once. But as a result of the Japanese attack on Pearl Harbor, it would now have to be won a second time. As Jonathan Dimbleby wrote, the Battle of the Atlantic was the longest military campaign of the war and the most destructive in naval history, costing over 3,000 ships and incurring over 60,000 allied deaths.[4] It was a strategic contest Britain couldn't afford to lose; vital to keep the Atlantic open to Allied shipping for basic survival and then, as the pendulum swung towards counterattack, for the build-up of forces to liberate Europe.

Notwithstanding all the human suffering of war at sea, the Battle of the Atlantic was fundamentally a tonnage war; a battle of monthly statistics. And it wasn't always about Germany's U-boats. At the outbreak of war, the Admiralty immediately adopted a convoy system, having learned the lessons of the First World War. But there were far too few escort vessels available. At the time, German surface raiders emerged as a potent threat. The *Scheer*, the *Hipper*, *Scharnhorst* and *Gneisenau* all raided Atlantic convoys successfully, while German long-range aircraft also had notable success. If the *Kriegsmarine* and the *Luftwaffe* had only been better coordinated, the effects could have been dramatic. But this posed the sort of sea battle – essentially a big ships

---

3. Brooke wrote of how courteously and gracefully Pound accepted this demotion at his first meeting chairing the CoS Committee.
4. Interestingly, while 30,000 allied merchant seamen were killed in the battle, the *Kriegsmarine* also suffered 27,000 deaths in its U-boat force – 75 percent of all those who served in them.

contest – that both Admiral Erich Raeder leading the *Kriegsmarine*, and the Board of Admiralty naturally understood. Far less attention was paid by either side, at least in the early stages, to the more potent U-boat elements of the contest.

The tonnage war was approaching a crisis by mid-1941 – almost 2 million tons of shipping and 550 vessels lost by June – with the Admiralty expecting to lose up to 7 million tons by the end of the year. Churchill had officially declared a 'Battle of the Atlantic' in March, assuming it could be won in a determined four-month push. But though he didn't know it in those desperate months, Pound had already won the opening round – the surface raider battle – in May 1941 with the sinking of the *Bismarck*. That famous episode had begun on 18th May when the *Bismarck* and *Prinz Eugen* left Gdynia in the Baltic and sailed into the North Atlantic to raid Allied shipping. On 24th May *Bismarck* sank *HMS Hood* with a single shell that blew it up. Three days later, damaged and surrounded, the *Bismarck* was battered to destruction as the Home Fleet finally closed in. But it had been a close thing – *Bismarck* was within a whisker of safety in Brest when its steering was damaged. For the chase, Pound had taken the decision to divert *Repulse* and the aircraft carrier *Victorious* away from a critical Middle East troop convoy, attaching them to Tovey's Home Fleet and leaving the convoy dangerously exposed. When Tovey had to send his destroyers home for refuelling, Pound detached the 4th Destroyer Flotilla from another important convoy to replace them – calculated risks again. He stayed in the operations room, sleepless, almost continuously from the sinking of the *Hood* to the destruction of *Bismarck* seventy-two hours later. The signal arrived at 11.01 on the 27th that it was over. He quietly picked up his hat, his walking stick, and left a room of very relieved officers to take the news to Churchill who was at that moment on his feet in the House of Commons.

The fate of the *Bismarck* convinced Hitler that he should not risk his precious pocket battleships and cruisers in open contests in the Atlantic. He drew them all to the north, where the *Tirpitz* was already waiting in Norwegian fjords for opportunities as they might arise. Admiral Raeder's influence with Hitler declined sharply, while that of U-boat leader Karl Donitz grew rapidly, and more effort thereafter went into his aggressive U-boat campaign. From then, the battle was almost exclusively centred on U-boats and what these days is known as 'Anti-Submarine Warfare' (ASW), in which the Royal Navy has since taken great pride.

There was a fundamental problem of perception about Britain's ASW campaign in 1941. It was regarded by navy professionals, steeped in a culture to pursue 'Nelson touches' everywhere, as fundamentally defensive – important but secondary to the imperative need to act offensively. Pound thought this as well, except that he recognised the ASW effort in the Atlantic as strategically fundamental to everything else; 'if we lose the Battle of the Atlantic, we lose the war'. Churchill too, understood this – but only sometimes. Churchill's own view was stark; 'The Navy can lose us this war but only the Air Force can win it', he wrote, 'the Bombers alone provide the means of victory'. There was no genuine evidence for this statement, either then or later, but it permeated through the War Cabinet and the Chiefs of Staff. Having declared a 'Battle of the Atlantic' in March 1941, Churchill's vacillations on the matter had the effect of pitching the RAF against the Royal Navy in a ferocious internal scrap for resources. It wasn't only a bureaucratic battle, but a struggle over different conceptions of war strategy. RAF bombers could have mounted cumulative attacks on U-boat bases and German port facilities, but they didn't. Many more aircraft could have made a concerted effort to provide top cover for convoys, but were never used in that way. The RAF's Coastal Command was put under the Admiralty's operational control, but it remained an arm of the RAF and was the 'Cinderella service', always short of aircraft and resources. If Churchill had directed the RAF to make his 'Battle of the Atlantic' a proper strategic priority, it might have been effectively won during 1942 instead of mid-1943. Pound did what he could in this battle for resources but he largely lost it against the majority opinion among his colleagues.

In the event, the painstaking tonnage battle was won in several different and often improvised ways. The U-boats and the convoy escorts fought through an ever-changing equation of crude numbers in submarines, escorts and aircraft; of evolving tactics as both sides learned; in a technology race of evasion and detection; and underpinned by intelligence decryption. Bletchley Park famously had German Enigma machines and by January 1940 had broken the Germans' signals encryption. This had less influence in the Atlantic than other theatres of the war, however. *Luftwaffe* and *Wehrmacht* Enigma machines would use three rotors selecting letters from five wheels for their encrypted messages. But *Kriegsmarine* Enigma had eight wheels from which the three rotors would select. In early 1941 the Admiralty could detect German maritime signals traffic, but couldn't read it. When Alan Turing and his team eventually began to decrypt the substance of naval messages, it often took too long to be useable and the system was regularly out of action. Over New Year 1942, the *Kriegsmarine* introduced a fourth rotor to the eight wheels on their Enigma machines and Bletchley Park went dark on naval decryption for over ten months. Turing's team cracked it in December 1942. But then in March 1943 the *Kriegsmarine* changed their weather reporting code books – which was Bletchley's foundation document – and decryption was impossible again until they could get hold of a new weather reporting codebook. This intermittent utility of naval signals intelligence coming from Bletchley Park into the Admiralty operations room was to play a key part in Dudley Pound's own great command tragedy of June 1942.

Nevertheless, the Admiralty could deduce enough from signals traffic to re-route convoys where they detected U-boat activity. Advances in sonar technologies, in radar, coastal command aircraft equipped with radar, and the growth of skills in using it, all paid off. Convoy speeds were critical; fast ships that reduced a convoy's time in the most vulnerable sectors of the Atlantic. Depth charges and ASW weapons improved while the U-boats constantly changed their own tactics to get among the merchant ships. Long range air patrols turned out to be the most effective means of getting a convoy through, pushing the U-boats to operate further out, rather than going after the U-boats individually. Improvised 'escort carriers' to provide sea-based air cover made a big difference, though there were never enough of them. Extending the 'refuelling at sea' to major vessels – now a standard task for all Royal Navy capital ships – became possible among the escort groups. From month to month the immediate balance of the battle depended on time and chance. In some months of 1940 and 1941 one in every three convoys would have to fight its way through – and some were almost annihilated. In other months, thirty or more convoys would transit the Atlantic and only a couple would lose one or more ships – though for the merchant seamen involved it still represented a form of Russian roulette.

Pound continued to press for what the navy needed to fight the battle – primarily more ships and available aircraft. The operational detail was all handled at the Admiralty's new Western Approaches Command Centre at Derby House in Liverpool – the 'citadel' to its subterranean staff – established in early 1941 to handle all naval and air operations in the Western Approaches. This is where the tactics of Pound's broader battle were fought out, first by the excellent and diplomatic Percy Noble and then by his equally gifted, but manically active successor, Max Horton. In these two very different admirals, Pound had the ideal leaders to bring together all the disparate elements needed to win his battle.

By the autumn of 1941 the costs were still high but Pound knew they were winning. The neutral US had already delivered fifty First World War destroyers as escorts, in return for a number of British Caribbean bases, and was steadily taking a more assertive stance against the U-boat threat to Atlantic trade, working more closely with the Royal Navy. Pound was intrinsic to both the operational detail and the politics behind this nascent Grand Alliance cooperation. He knew that with American support, the battle was pretty well won by the turn of the year 1942. Though of course, there were distracting disasters elsewhere.

The entry of the US into the war in December 1941 was a strategic game-changer for Allied victory, but it re-opened the Battle of the Atlantic in a new way. US convoys were now fair game for the U-boats, right up to the eastern seaboard of America and as far south as the Caribbean. US military and merchant ships were at sea everywhere, and all too easy to pick off, since the US Navy wouldn't adopt British convoy procedures until Allied losses of 'independent' (that is, non-convoyed) vessels shot up to 89 per cent, almost all occurring in American waters. US ports left themselves wholly vulnerable to attack, their blazing lights neatly silhouetting Allied ships anchored there. So from the Admiralty, from Derby House, and now from Rhode Island and the US Atlantic Fleet, Pound had to win the battle all over again.

His second Battle of the Atlantic began immediately. It was June before the penny dropped for the US Navy and a full convoy system was adopted. By then Donitz was shifting his operations back to the North Atlantic, beyond air cover from either side in the 'Atlantic Gap' in the middle. He also had the benefit of having his B-Dienst intelligence unit break 'British Naval Cypher No.3' – used for all Allied convoy messages in the North Atlantic – just when Bletchley Park lost visibility of *Kriegsmarine* coded messages. Now the U-boats had the intelligence advantage. For 1942 then, it was more of the same but all at a higher level of intensity. Percy Noble in Liverpool laid all the right foundations with the joint 'Atlantic Convoy Instructions' and then the 'Western Approaches Tactical Unit' and Max Horton exploited that experience and innovation within a remarkable tactical HQ that was – in modern jargon – both 'joint' (Royal Navy, Merchant Navy and Air) and 'combined' (British, Canadian and US). With all its hard-won experience, the Admiralty now knew how to win this battle. With American resources, it was inevitable that they would. Even then, Pound had to make more risky decisions to have precious resources diverted away to support the TORCH landings, the invasions of Sicily and Italy and other initiatives as the Allies moved onto the offensive. Escort carriers, so vital to convoy defence, were taken away for other theatres; destroyers and aircraft were needed to escort convoys elsewhere, and so on. There were fierce convoy engagements between March and May 1943, but it was clear by then that the tonnage war was over. And between June and September only a single convoyed ship was lost. Donitz had given up. He withdrew his U-boats from the North Atlantic to redeploy them to the Mediterranean, the Gibraltar-Britain convoys, and further afield around the African coast. The way was clear for the huge sealift of men and material to prepare for the Normandy invasion. The campaign had been protracted and frustrating, and in many ways it had made Pound a very lonely figure among British war leaders, but it was his victory.

In the manner of many highly strategic victories, it had no single defining moment, which was unfortunate for Pound's reputation. He was by then too associated with the navy's failures in 1942; the *Prince of Wales* and *Repulse*, the 'Channel Dash', and just four months after that, the single greatest convoy disaster of the war; the PQ-17 arctic convoy to Russia. Sending vital supply convoys to Murmansk and Archangel, running the gauntlet of Germany's sea and air attacks from Norwegian bases, was never less than hazardous. Sixteen outbound and twelve inbound convoys had already been operated by June 1942, achieving some hard-won successes. A constant fear was that the *Tirpitz* and its consorts would emerge from Trondheim or Narvik to attack them. Up in Scapa Flow, Tovey and the Home Fleet wanted to tempt the *Tirpitz* out to engage it, but Pound was far more worried at having *Tirpitz* on the loose devastating a convoy, and maybe more. And though the Home Fleet could be confident of dealing with *Tirpitz* and any of its powerful consorts, the further north any engagement took place, the less sea room there would be between the arctic ice and the Norwegian coast; and the closer the Home Fleet's battleships would be to deadly German air attacks from bases in Norway. Pound and Tovey were both having to weigh up a neat conundrum; if *Tirpitz* was reckless enough to be tempted south, it would present itself to the Home Fleet. But if the Home Fleet was reckless enough to be tempted too far north, it would present itself to the *Luftwaffe*. Either way, convoys were the bait.

Pound was already unhappy at having to run any arctic convoys during the short summer months of permanent daylight in 1942, but Churchill had overruled both Pound and Tovey on this; convoys had to continue. PQ-15 and PQ-16 in May got through with some heavy losses, but were thought successful. The Admiralty knew that German forces had a special operation – 'Knight's Move' – prepared for PQ-17. The German plan was to send *Tirpitz*, *Lutzow* and *Hipper* to attack PQ-17 once the convoy approached Bear Island where the British heavy cruiser escorts would have to turn back. PQ-17 left Iceland on 27th June. It was the first joint British-US convoy and was therefore carrying a political loading in addition to its cargoes. On 1st July the *Luftwaffe* spotted it and the game was on. By 3rd July the Admiralty thought 'Knight's Move' had begun. The *Scheer* had left Narvik, *Tirpitz* and *Hipper* had left Trondheim. The location of *Lutzow* was unknown. Signals decrypts were patchy, arriving at the Admiralty too slowly to be definitive. Norman Denning, the stand-in director of naval intelligence, was convinced that *Tirpitz* would put in somewhere near Narvik or Tromso to refuel its accompanying destroyers. More evidence for that view built up, as indeed did the (correct) assumption that since the *Kriegsmarine* couldn't locate the Home Fleet it wouldn't risk *Tirpitz*, in case the British might be closing on it.[5]

But time was short. The picture that *Tirpitz* had put to sea but was probably not then near PQ-17, was becoming clearer even as Pound convened a long meeting to discuss it. Denning, outside the meeting, was quite right. Others inside it were unsure, and felt that Pound had already discounted what he had heard from his intelligence officers earlier that day. Most in the meeting felt the convoy should keep on, pending more information. But the further north it went, the more the ice shelf would narrow the convoy's sea room to disperse or scatter. Pound sat back in his chair and closed his eyes for a long time. Someone thought he had fallen asleep. It seems astonishing that he was so indifferent to the intelligence picture that was steadily clarifying. Perhaps he had made so many fearful risk calculations since 1939 that he had become fatalistic about this one. He even had time to change it when he was advised to do so after the meeting. But for him the die was already cast. At 9.30 on the evening of 4th July, the Admiralty issued a series of poorly drafted orders that took all the escorts away from PQ-17 and instructed the convoy to 'scatter'.

Tovey had already said to Pound that 'scattering' the convoy would be 'sheer bloody murder'. And so it proved. The *Tirpitz* had not moved and was still at Altenfjord north of Tromso, but U-boat wolfpacks had already gathered and the *Luftwaffe* had the freedom to attack virtually defenceless ships in 24-hour daylight. By 10th July, twenty-three of the convoy's thirty-seven ships had been sunk while the Royal Navy's protective forces withdrew with no losses at all. Individual survival from a sinking ship was virtually impossible; a man in the water was dead of hypothermia inside three minutes. Ships, merchant seamen and two thirds of the cargo were all lost. There was a minor epic when Leo Gradwell – a navy reserve officer commanding an 'anti-submarine trawler' – led four surviving ships in a little convoy safely into Archangel on 25th July. But for the war effort, the Royal Navy and for Pound himself, PQ-17 was tragic and shameful in equal measure. It soured Pound's relations with the US Navy for a while, and certainly with Russia, and it put an end to any more convoys until the safer conditions of September. It has been a source of controversy ever since.

There was pride and some small redemption in getting enough of the famous *Pedestal* convoy into Malta the following month, and PQ-18 was fought through to Archangel in September. But the pace of Pound's work didn't reduce, even as his health did. Churchill's triple red-flagged 'Action This Day' memoranda kept increasing and Allied summits became bigger and more frequent, in which the First Sea Lord's participation was indispensable. It is hardly surprising that Pound had seemed essentially reactive by 1943. Alan Brooke thought he had become 'slow' and 'lacked drive' (comments he subsequently regretted, since it emerged that Pound was suffering a progressive

---

5. This was exactly right. The Admiralty didn't know that 'Knight's Move' had been made conditional by Hitler himself on the *Kriegsmarine* being able accurately to locate the Home Fleet and any British aircraft carriers to be certain they would be out of range before 'Knight's Move' began.

brain tumour). In fact, Pound did a lot to disguise his failing health, but no one ever doubted his dogged dedication. At the QUADRANT conference in Quebec in August 1943, just a month after losing his wife of thirty-five years, he then suffered a stroke. He returned to Britain, gravely ill, and became progressively weaker. He resigned, declining a peerage because he didn't think his family could afford it, but accepting the Order of Merit on behalf of the navy. In his final days, when he was unable to speak, Churchill visited him and, characteristically, departed in tears. Pound died on 21st October – Trafalgar Day – 1943. He was cremated, and his ashes, along with those of his wife Betty, were scattered in the Solent from *HMS Glasgow* by the new First Sea Lord, Andrew Cunningham.

Dudley Pound was a gifted and faithful naval officer who died, like Cuthbert Collingwood, of dutiful exhaustion as much as anything else. As First Sea Lord he presided over a number of naval failures and tactical reverses along with a few victories. But no victories were as important as winning the Battle of the Atlantic which – along with Stalingrad, Midway, the Battle of Britain and El Alamein – were the pivotal battles of the war. He didn't win it as a land commander wins battles, but in the way of maritime warfare, by presiding over a wide range of disparate elements in a long struggle. He didn't have full control over his resources and was never able to fight the battle with more than the minimum of what was required. His contemporaries respected him more for his dedication than his success. But history is ultimately less sentimental, and in recent years has recognised his strategic success for what it was.

31

Field Marshal Bernard Montgomery

To the generation of Second World War conscript soldiers who fought in the British armies that liberated North Africa, Italy and then western Europe, Bernard Montgomery was simply their much-respected leader. He was 'Monty' to them and he was a 'winner'; embodying that most essential quality for any general among his troops. And his eccentricities (like Churchill's) only added to the affection of those who were proud to be commanded by him. On the other hand, the description that most frequently adhered to Montgomery was, 'quick as a ferret; and about as likeable'. Scarcely less charitably, he has been assessed as a commander who had the luck to take charge of British armies when the momentum of war was already swinging towards the Allies and when British troops were well-supplied and moving forward. He had not been in charge during the previous three years of constant, sometimes abject, British defeats. He was a winner, it was argued, regardless of his battle tactics, not because of them, since the flow of battle was going the Allies' way by the end of 1942. And his monstrous ego, constant self-promotion, his arrogance and rudeness to other commanders became a serious handicap in military relations between the Allies, for which others had to compensate.

But the success of commanders always turns on the trajectory of history as much as their own particular battle skills. The victory that defined Montgomery was at El-Alamein in October 1942. He chose the title 'Viscount Montgomery of Alamein' on being ennobled after the war. And though Churchill, as usual, was not entirely accurate in his memoirs, he had the essence of the matter when he said, 'Before Alamein we never had a victory; after Alamein we never had a defeat'. One can hardly blame a general who takes advantage of entering the picture at the apex of a historical arc; though it is irritating to many if he then claims credit for so much of what happened next. The inescapable point, however, is that even with the tide of history flowing his way, Montgomery could not have been so successful a commander unless he also embodied the virtues of drive, clarity and inspiration. At all times he exuded vibrant purpose and confidence. Fellow commanders certainly chafed against his lack of emotional intelligence and swaggering arrogance, but few of his own soldiers left Montgomery's presence without feeling buoyed up by him, or in any doubt that they were in good hands as they faced their next battle.

Some writers have speculated that Montgomery's lifelong behaviour indicates he was autistic, or at least, as James Holland puts it, 'on the spectrum'. But from that era no clinical evidence exists one way or the other. Nevertheless, Bernard Montgomery's early years offer some important clues to his over-bearing character. He was born into impoverished gentry among the Ulster Scots, albeit in London's Kennington, in November 1887. His father was a Church of Ireland minister who inherited the family estate in County Donegal but had to sell it off to survive, even frugally. In 1889, however, he became Bishop of Tasmania, which was where Bernard spent his childhood to the age of thirteen, along with a gaggle of siblings. As bishop, his father spent up to six months at a time travelling through the colony, while his frankly unhinged mother – considerably younger than her husband, married at sixteen and now in her mid-twenties – pursued her pious Christianity by ignoring her children or else regularly beating them. She showed indifference that tipped into active dislike of her fourth child, Bernard, who by his own admission, grew into an emotionally detached young bully. He was sent to school in Canterbury, four years before the family returned to Britain and thence to St Paul's School in Hammersmith before escaping to the Royal Military Academy, Sandhurst in 1907. Even then, he narrowly avoided expulsion from the Academy for violence and disorder; gang leader of a few thuggish, rich, fellow cadets who were easily led. He trusted nobody and looked for ulterior motives in everything. He became, he said, completely estranged from his mother. Later in life he refused to let his own son associate with her and didn't attend her funeral when she died, an old lady of eighty-four, in 1949.

Montgomery could not afford to join a fashionable regiment, but a commission in the Royal Warwickshires in 1908 and service with them in India provided exactly the purpose and structure to which the angry and unhappy twenty-one-year-old responded. After two years he was a lieutenant and after four, the battalion adjutant – a responsible post – at the Warwickshire's camp in Shorncliffe. The army gave Montgomery the opportunity to develop his considerable natural intelligence and rewarded his relentless focus on whatever problem was at hand. His emotional deficiencies were diluted within the discipline of a system where charm was seldom required. When the regiment had returned to Britain, he had passed out top of the army's musketry course and was a highly competitive sportsman; a member of the Army's national field hockey team and an excellent cricketer.

Compared to many of his fellow junior officers, Montgomery had a lucky First World War. Like most of them, he was involved in the retreat from Mons in August 1914. In October, after leading a bayonet charge on enemy trenches, then caught out in the open, he was seriously wounded by a sniper. He lay there for many hours, one of his own men who had tried to rescue him lying dead on top of him and absorbing more sniper's rounds. When he was finally pulled in during darkness Montgomery was very close to death and a grave was dug for him. But he clung to life and was evacuated to Britain where he recovered in the course of the next year from lung and knee wounds. He suffered respiratory difficulties for the rest of his life – one of the reasons why he abhorred smoking. But he received the DSO for his actions that day – unusual for a mere lieutenant.

When he returned to the Western Front in 1916 his gallantry, but also his wounds, determined that Montgomery would subsequently serve as a general staff officer – mainly with IX Corps in General Plumer's very effective Second Army, and then as Chief of Staff in the London Division. He had already proved himself a vigorous and courageous young man, but he was also an ideal general staff officer – clever, driven, very well-organised and genuinely insightful. With the exception of Plumer, Montgomery was intensely critical of British generals in that war, whom he felt were too far away from the action and too easily reconciled to the 'frightful casualties' that 'appalled me', as he wrote later. Certainly, his approach to warfare when he became a national commander himself was to avoid casualties among his troops by spearheading attacks with extensive armour and artillery and explicitly to avoid the sort of assaults that relied mainly on troop numbers, attacking frontally, to overwhelm an enemy. He was scathing of those generals he thought 'thrusters' or 'good fighting generals' who took needless risks with their men's lives for the sake of dramatic, but often pointless, gains. He regarded the staff function as servant to the front-line troops, rather than the other way round, frequently quoting the old maxim that 'there are no bad soldiers; only bad officers'. It was one of his favourites.

He also took from his experience as a general staff officer in those years a keen awareness of the growing technical complexity of twentieth century warfare, and the imperative to plan and organize it properly. Planning and organization were not just essential for their own sake, but needed to be linked to a clear campaign vision and a sharp understanding of the operational conditions that would apply; the terrain, the weather, the ability of the troops, an anticipation of enemy tactics, and so on. Montgomery had genuine flair in these respects. His obsessive nature focused him on key military tasks, while his intelligence and experience gave him a good appreciation both of the strategic objectives and the operational conditions likely to apply in any campaign. His conscientious approach to all things military meant that very few relevant details escaped his attention, and his natural planning skills and efficient delegation gave him the wherewithal – except for the charm – to run a full campaign headquarters. Unlike Gort or Alexander, of whom he was very critical, Montgomery had received a near fatal taste of the battlefield as a junior officer (as they had) but then moved straight into the world of organization and senior command before cementing his reputation as a campaigning general. Gort and Alexander were fighting soldiers throughout their careers, regardless of their rank. By contrast, Montgomery left the immediate battlefield behind him quite early on and evolved naturally through divisional and corps appointments to emerge at his most effective in taking command of the Eighth Army in 1942. Though he ascended to that role somewhat later in life, he was a natural army-level commander.

Montgomery worked hard during the inter-war period, in a number of postings that included India and some nasty suppression operations in both Ireland and Palestine, which he took on with his characteristically cold precision. More to his talents, he instructed as a senior officer at both staff colleges in Camberley and then Quetta, while rising steadily rather than glamorously through the hierarchy to become a two-star major general commanding a division in 1931.

By some accounts, his career was saved from his own self-destructive rudeness during these years by his wife. At the age of thirty-eight he had proposed to the only woman he had ever courted – a seventeen-year-old girl, who turned him down. But two years later he met and married a widow of his own age and thereby took on two stepsons, in addition to a son they subsequently had together. It was a happy marriage for Montgomery, and Elizabeth Carver is credited with restraining his character failings long enough for him to attain high command in the Army. In 1937, however, Elizabeth tragically died of septicaemia at the age of forty-eight. Montgomery was completely devastated and lonely. But he was a dutiful father to his three sons, albeit partly estranged from his natural son in later years. At the time, he channelled all his heartfelt grief – the first and probably greatest he ever felt – into single-minded work and military science.[1]

In 1939 Montgomery was commanding 3rd Division, sent to France as part of the British Expeditionary Force. That failed campaign has been described in other chapters. Montgomery's part in it, and the subsequent retreat and evacuation of the BEF from Dunkirk, featured a number of elements that were typical of him. One was that in the months of the 'phoney war' before the German attack in the west began, he honed his division to the point where it was the best-performing formation in the BEF. More than that, he conducted five major exercises with his division based on the way he anticipated the coming campaign might unfold. And when it did, the course of events conformed with uncanny precision to the way he had prepared his force – advancing to a river line, holding, breaking contact, and withdrawing to the coast. In the event, when the German attack came, his division had little fighting to do, but Montgomery's corps commander in France, Alan Brooke, had always been a supporter and fully appreciated the prescience of Montgomery's thinking. When Brooke later became Churchill's chief military strategist, he was just the ally at the top that Montgomery needed. He it was who recognised his intellectual 'grip' – something of a Brooke obsession – and could save Monty from himself in dealing with the military hierarchy.

Another characteristic Montgomery feature was the way he advised his BEF commander, John Gort, summarily to replace the overwrought General Barker with Harold Alexander to command the corps responsible for the final rearguard at Dunkirk. 'Only a madman', said Montgomery, 'would give a corps to Barker', commenting on a fellow officer who outranked him. More than that, when he returned to London, Montgomery sought an interview as a two-star officer with the four-star Chief of the Imperial General Staff, to tell him that 'certain officers (and he didn't spare the names) were unfit to be employed', that 'the BEF had never been "commanded" (Gort) since it was formed', and that Brooke was the right man to put in charge of home defence. Poor John Gort decided that Montgomery was 'not quite a gentleman'. Gort was not wrong – but no one could say that Montgomery was wrong either. He antagonized the War Office but his observations were quietly shared by others. Only Monty had the affrontery to put them so directly.

Like Alexander and Brooke, he didn't believe that Britain's plans in 1940 to repel a German invasion were viable and, becoming a corps commander, Montgomery

---

1. Both his stepsons served in the Army in India and both subsequently became colonels. Dick Carver served with the Eighth Army, was captured at Mersa Matruh in 1942, but almost a year later escaped and appeared back at Montgomery's HQ, to the absolute delight of his stepfather.

immediately began feuding over them with Claude Auchinleck, his superior in Southern Command. He clashed with him, went over his head, then studiously ignored him.[2] But the invasion didn't happen and Montgomery took on other corps responsible for Kent and the south-east. He had reached a command level where his talents could now make a difference. He emphasized extensive training, physical fitness and good officership. He was swift and ruthless in getting rid of officers whom he thought would not function properly under battle pressures. When he was given responsibility for a new 'South Eastern Command' he insisted on re-naming it the 'South Eastern Army', to instill an offensive spirit. Of course, he was also promoting himself, conceptually, to be an army commander – a role natural to him for which he assumed he was better suited than anyone else. In May 1942 he showed he meant it by conducting a huge combined arms forces exercise of 100,000 troops.

His genuine battlefield test came later that year. By then, it seemed doubtful that in the Middle East Britain could even hold onto Egypt let alone Libya, even in the face of inferior German and Italian forces. Tobruk, the symbol of gritty resistance the previous year, was finally lost. Mersa Matruh was lost. British and Commonwealth forces retreated to the El Alamein line inside Egypt. The troops were badly led, fighting far below their abilities and, in a classic crisis of morale, had evidently lost faith in their commanders. As the Afrika Korps swept eastward, an extraordinary panic gripped Egypt. Middle East HQ began burning documents on large bonfires, British families fled to Palestine while the Mediterranean Fleet quit its base in Alexandria. It was all an over-reaction to the strategic reality. Nevertheless, the skill and dash of General Erwin Rommel, the 'desert fox', and his Afrika Korps panzers captured the public imagination, both in Britain and the United States – where Britain's expulsion from the Middle East by the end of 1942 was regarded as inevitable. In truth, vanity and ambition were already driving Rommel to over-extend his supply lines as he pushed towards Alexandria and Cairo. Auchinleck – now commander in the Middle East – at least checked Rommel's advance in what became known as the first battle of El Alamein – a confused affair where British and Commonwealth forces should have done better, but at least it paused the British collapse.

It was in this situation that Churchill, arrived in Cairo, removed Auchinleck, brought Alexander to run the Middle East theatre and put Montgomery under him in command of the broken Eighth Army.[3] Alex and Monty saw the situation in identical ways and immediately put an end to the defeatism that had gripped British and Commonwealth forces. While Alexander was calmly reassuring in his offensive intent, Montgomery was all bustling purpose and his effect on the Eighth Army that August was electrifying. Fellow officers frequently wondered 'what's the little bugger

---

2. It says much for Auchinleck's generosity of spirit that though then, and later, Montgomery burnished his own reputation by trashing Auchinleck's, the latter didn't seek revenge and seemed to accept Montgomery's real abilities – though Auchinleck did threaten legal action when he read Monty's memoirs in 1958.
3. In fact, Churchill nominated William Gott to command Eighth Army, but Gott was killed in an air crash and Brooke, by then Chief of the Imperial General Staff, prevailed on Churchill to send for Montgomery.

doing now?' But the little bugger was forcing the army to recognise what it already had; numbers, new equipment flowing in – particularly American tanks – a growing air arm, and every prospect of a successful offensive. He reorganized the force to concentrate his armour and infantry in more specialized corps. He burned all extant military plans for further withdrawals, demanded physical fitness from everyone up to the highest ranks – no exceptions – and summarily sacked many officers for under-performance. Realising the hold of the Afrika Korps on the British imagination, he deliberately characterised the battle to come as 'Monty versus Rommel'. Naturally, it played to his egotistical self-promotion, but it also demonstrated a shrewd understanding of how soldiers' morale – and public opinion – worked. He had supreme confidence in his own generalship and his Eighth Army troops would now be fighting for him, personally and specifically, to beat Rommel and defeat the famous Afrika Korps.

His campaign began on the Alam Halfa ridge in late-August. Rommel was poised to launch his next eastward offensive. Montgomery had the benefit of Britain's famous Ultra intelligence, which gave him access to all the messages Rommel sent and received via German Enigma machines. So he knew Rommel was short of fuel and had to win quickly or not at all. He knew, too, that Rommel's intention was to push against Montgomery's centre and then move the main armoured thrust to a southern breakthrough, attempting to get behind British and Commonwealth lines. Montgomery was clever but also cautious. He used deception to convince Rommel that the southern route was open, then mined it very heavily and concentrated his tanks and anti-tank guns to the north, on the Alam Halfa ridge which dominated the whole area around it. German and Italian armour duly rolled towards the southern minefields on the night of 30th August and became stuck inside them, relentlessly attacked by allied artillery and aircraft for the next three days. In some difficulty, Rommel turned his forces north to attack Alam Halfa directly, expecting Montgomery's tanks to appear to fight it out. But British and Commonwealth tanks were all dug in, hull down, working with their artillery and, for once, genuinely close cooperation with the RAF. Like Wellington at Waterloo, Montgomery intended to sit resolutely on the ridge. At one point it seemed that Rommel's superior Panzers might break through, but Montgomery committed his reserves and that was that. The Afrika Korps, dazed by the brutal bombardment, withdrew with heavy losses – their famous commander close to physical collapse.

Montgomery didn't try very hard to pursue Rommel's retreating forces, and stopped after the first rebuff. Many criticized his caution, but he was determined to maintain control of the battlefront and – doubtless aware of too many 'thrusters' on the Western Front – was already planning his next tussle with Rommel. And though Alam Halfa was overshadowed by El Alamein two months later, it marked the real turning point in the desert war. Having frustrated Rommel's latest advance, Montgomery was now anxious to launch his own offensive and reverse the roles the Afrika Korps and the Eighth Army had been playing. Rommel was a great manoeuvrist and Montgomery didn't want to fall into a competition of dashing hither and thither. Then, too, both generals had to contend with a battlefront that had no obvious flanks. The Mediterranean lay to the north, the impassable Qatarra Depression to the south. There could be no great 'flank marches' to cut off a whole army in this case. Any major battles had to be essentially front-on affairs for them both.

Again, the essence of Montgomery's next battle – El Alamein – was all in the planning. As more stores and equipment were built up, Churchill was impatient for the big show to begin. But neither Montgomery nor Alexander, his theatre commander, would be rushed. There was another successful deception operation, but for lack of geographical flexibility, it would have to be a slogging match. Nevertheless, Montgomery could put into this attack more resources than the Eighth Army had ever enjoyed. The twelve-day battle opened in bright moonlight – essential for success – on the night of 23rd October with a thundering artillery barrage over a few hours that was greater than anyone on either side had ever witnessed.

Montgomery intended to get his XXX Corps in the north across the German minefields in a single night so that the concentrated armour in X Corps could then 'flow over' them in a main thrust to cut off Rommel's tanks from his infantry and hold them off with a 'barrier' behind which British infantry would take on German infantry units to wear them down. Meanwhile, Montgomery's XIII Corps would run a powerful decoy assault in the south. Operating across a narrow front, where congestion of forces was always a danger, the plan went wrong from the beginning. XXX Corps got stuck in the minefields and couldn't make enough progress. The idea of one big formation – X Corps – superimposing itself on top of another – XXX Corps – to push forward together, was not a success. It was an immediate crisis and Montgomery swiftly altered his plans, pulling his armour back to reorganize it for a second go and settling for several days of grim tussling with air, artillery and infantry attacks on enemy lines. After twelve days, the superiority of allied numbers and equipment took their toll on Afrika Korps forces who were out of fuel and exhausted. The German front collapsed in both north and south and the battle was won.

In many respects Montgomery's El Alamein was like a First World War offensive, pushing relentlessly forward across a narrow front until the weight of one force overcame the other. But in Montgomery's case the key difference was that he didn't put his troops at the front of the push. He believed in firepower-heavy offensives in which the armour and artillery would spearhead a breakthrough and protect the infantry while they would – in his word – 'crumble' the enemy's line until it was weakened enough to give way. It was attritional in a First World War sense, but a straight reversal inasmuch as this time the heavy metal would make the breakthroughs and the infantry would exploit them – not the other way round.

Again, Montgomery didn't follow up with a commander's intent to destroy the Afrika Korps opposite him. After its defeat, Afrika Korps escaped comfortably westwards in a series of competent rearguard actions. Rather, Montgomery was prepared for a long campaign as part of Alexander's 15th Army Group in the 1,000-mile advance across Libya and into Tunisia, while the American 'TORCH' landings in Morocco and Algeria closed the pincer on German forces from the west. The TORCH landings and 15th Army Group's march to Tunis, in a sense, made El Alamein less than strategically critical. German forces were very unlikely to hold North Africa once allied strength was inexorably building. The pivotal event on the eastern front, the Battle of Stalingrad, was reaching its peak; and on the western front, the essential Battle of the Atlantic, was being painstakingly won. But the swing of the pendulum had to start somewhere and El Alamein was reason enough for church bells to ring out across Britain for the first time since the beginning of the war. Like Waterloo, it was a famous victory, if not a critical one. Britain had found a general whom the public wanted to rank with Wellington and Marlborough. Montgomery certainly compares with Wellington in the way he planned campaigns and fought his battles so tenaciously. And he bookends with Marlborough a long historical arc. Marlborough was the first commander to establish Britain as a major European military power, capable of independent national action. Blenheim was the first great British military triumph of the modern era. El Alamein was the last. Britain would never again be able to fight a strategically important war except as a junior partner in a US-led coalition; significant to be sure, but with less political influence to exercise.

Churchill and Brooke understood this and became intent on using their declining military influence to help shape victory to support Britain's post-war interests as far as they could. If Montgomery saw it too, he nevertheless resisted the idea. He was at a personal high point after El Alamein. As the allies pushed towards Tunis, thence to land in Sicily and jump off to invade Italy in September 1943, Montgomery's ego got much the better of him. His criticisms of American generalship were insulting and his own unshakeable certainty in strategy and tactics became a major obstacle to better Allied action – despite Alexander's endless diplomacy and no matter how right Montgomery sometimes was. In his own words, 'there are only two answers to most military problems. One of them is wrong'. As Alamein had shown, he was actually flexible enough to adjust his battle plans quickly when things went awry, but his airy refrain that 'everything is going according to plan' when it manifestly wasn't, became more infuriating with each battle.

As US, British and Commonwealth forces converged on Tunis, the Americans suffered a dreadful reverse to Rommel's forces at the Kasserine Pass. Montgomery was pushing through at Medenine and Mareth – not with great skill this time and in violation of some of his own principles of battle. But as the advance went on, two trends emerged that would shape the future of the Allies' war. One was that Montgomery – and Alexander – had a consistently low opinion of US soldiering and generalship which fed a mutual antipathy with US commanders which, in relation to Montgomery, became a loathing that no one could shake off. The second was that Montgomery's Eighth Army approach to operations became, in effect, the conception of all British ground forces (with the exception of Bill Slim's 'forgotten' Fourteenth Army in Burma). The big planning, firepower heavy, method of battle that looked for the consolidation of gains rather than their risky exploitation would guide British forces through to 1945. It was a safe approach when material was plentiful and available manpower was not; and it represented an essential understanding on Montgomery's part of all that could realistically be achieved with a citizen army of conscripts who simply wanted to finish the war and go home.

It was clear from Sicily onwards. Montgomery was scathing about the compromise nature of the allied plan to invade the island and increasingly jealous of General George

C. Patton of the US Seventh Army. He prevailed on Alexander and pulled the whole plan towards the offensive that his Eighth Army would launch in south-east Sicily, relegating Patton to a support role. But when his forces were held at Catania, Patton persuaded Alexander that he could now break ranks and dashed to liberate Palermo in the north-west. All very glorious. But between the three of them they had let German forces escape Sicily in good order. The same happened repeatedly in the long Italian campaign that followed, as Alexander's 15th Army Group fought its way laboriously northwards – Montgomery moving methodically, his US counterparts dashing to liberate cities, while German forces pulled steadily back towards the northern frontier. In truth, Montgomery never believed in the Italian campaign. He had the strategic vision to see that it was, at best, useful but not central to the defeat of Germany. He was happy to be taken out of it at the turn of the year in 1944 to plan for his greatest campaign, the battle for Normandy.

Dwight D. Eisenhower was designated supreme commander for the Allied effort. Montgomery (against Churchill's initial instincts) was given the newly-created 21st Army Group and through that, made land commander of all allied forces for the D-Day invasion itself, until such time as Eisenhower's SHAEF headquarters could practically transfer to France as the supreme command hub.[4]

This was the peak of Montgomery's command career. Eisenhower had to take the awesome responsibility for giving the decisive order, during a perilously short weather window, for the D-Day forces to 'go'. But the whole massive enterprise was planned and brought together under Montgomery's inspiration and guidance in his role as allied ground forces commander. His was the task of getting 156,000 allied troops onto a continental beachhead and then 'breaking out' from it to begin the liberation of occupied Europe. Notwithstanding his interpersonal failings, Montgomery was at his best in these months. He drove the huge combined plan, maintained focus amid all its complexity, inspired the staff and gave them confidence; while they mostly buried their various resentments in view of the strategic drama of the whole enterprise. Amphibious landings always were – and still are – the most demanding type of military operation and more than any other campaign during that war, the battle for Normandy would be won or lost in the planning process. Monty was exactly the right man to fight it for the Allies.

Preliminary planning had been going on for eighteen months under the codename COSSAC. Montgomery was brought into it at a meeting with Churchill and other Allied commanders at Marrakesh in December 1943. Churchill gave Montgomery the draft plan late on New Year's Eve and required his initial reactions by the following morning, while the Prime Minister went off to celebrate the New Year. Next morning, Montgomery presented Churchill with a typed-up, detailed critique which rubbished the whole plan. As in 1940, he was not wrong. The opening paragraphs of his long, overnight paper were remarkably perceptive; the COSSAC plan intended to land too few forces, too soon, on too narrow a front, on a single Normandy beach that would

---

4. Supreme Headquarters Allied Expeditionary Forces (SHAEF) existed from December 1943 to July 1945.

become clogged even if it didn't become a deathtrap. Instead, the British, Canadians and Americans must land on separate beaches, to fight their own battles as coherent corps, across different beachheads that would then rapidly be linked up, and the whole *must* be preceded by a victorious battle for air control above the landing grounds. Churchill agreed, and on 3rd January Montgomery was in his old school, St Paul's in Hammersmith – now the HQ for 21st Army Group – where COSSAC was officially unveiled to him and other officers. He tore it to pieces again, publicly and humiliatingly for its authors who never forgave him. It was not dissimilar to the row after Dunkirk. Many senior officers, including Eisenhower, had doubts; some were in quiet despair at the evident weaknesses of COSSAC, but only Monty was sufficiently forceful and insulting to stop it in its tracks and work the plan into something different. And what he had come up with overnight on New Year's Eve was a grand plan which retained its essential shape as it evolved into the mature OVERLORD invasion of Normandy six months later.

The two most key elements of OVERLORD were logistics and strategy – Montgomery's strong points. The logistics were simply staggering as Britain turned itself into a massive military depot during the early months of 1944. A random selection of the bare facts indicates the depth of the full story. More than 16 million tons of equipment arrived from the United States, including 400,000 litres of blood; over 1.7 million tons of fuel. Some 450,000 tons of ammunition was assembled, amid seven million tons of immediate battle supplies, and no fewer than seventeen million maps were produced. Over 7,000 naval vessels were assembled and carefully organized. D-Day would involve 12,000 Allied aircraft – forty times as many as the *Luftwaffe* deployed on the day in 1940 when it made a maximum effort in the Battle of Britain. Huge deception schemes were launched including the creation of the 'First US Army Group' a wholly phantom army that convinced German planners that General Patton was sitting in south-east England with a major spearhead force just waiting to cross to Calais. And as the real invasion commenced, a single bomber squadron (the famous 617 'Dambusters') was able to drop tin foil bundles with such precision as to make itself look to German radar stations like a large force of invasion ships heading for the Pas de Calais coast, while the real invasion headed for Normandy. Big and small, the deception effort was astounding.

The strategic calculations were equally dramatic. They derived from a simple truth. If the Allies could airdrop and land their 156,000, troops onto the beachheads, and if those forces were still alive and functioning after 48 hours – 'D-plus-2' – then the invasion would have succeeded, whatever happened next. Given the massive logistical superiority of the Allies, this was always the most likely outcome, though there might be a heavy price to pay. There was a dense barrier of sea-mines seven to ten miles out from the Normandy coast and greatly increased fields of beach obstacles had been appearing since January, alongside almost 1,000 defensive fieldworks around that particular stretch of coastline. Then too, the whole airborne operation was inherently risky, dropping 25,000 paratroopers from fleets of vulnerable transport aircraft flying low and slow at night over the drop zones. Trafford Leigh-Mallory, the allied air commander, anticipating maybe seventy-five percent losses among the airborne forces, wanted the whole thing called off in view of the risks. Not least, if bad weather blew up in the Channel, the 4,000 light landing craft, launched from some miles out, would simply not make it to the beaches. The invasion had to take place under a full moon (for the airborne forces) and during a rising lunar spring tide (for the invasion barges). The dangers kept mounting as planning went ahead. Churchill became fearful and depressed about the prospects, as did others in the inner circle. But the risk equation remained essentially simple. If the invasion failed, it would do so catastrophically. Anything less than catastrophic failure would actually succeed, even at some dreadful human cost.

Breaking out from the invasion beachheads, however, was another matter and here the dangers were of a different order. The key limitation in exploiting a successful D-Day was the scarcity of shipping to bring the follow-on forces across eighty miles of English Channel between the Isle of Wight and the Normandy coast – and, as it turned out, in bad weather. Montgomery knew that German forces would launch powerful counterattacks – it was their characteristic defence strategy – and he anticipated these would begin on D-plus-4, or D-plus-5. But most of his 21st Army Group would still be in Britain then, waiting to embark. And though the 156,000 invaders would have a numerical advantage over the 78,000 German troops in Normandy, there were another 880,000 German troops available to the 'OB West' commander that might be arriving quickly to throw the invasion back any time after D-plus-4. He knew, too, that German counterattacks, coming from the east and south-east, would be made first against British and Canadian troops, who would find themselves shielding US forces further west – Omar Bradley's 1st US Army – who would be working to secure the Cotentin Peninsula, Cherbourg and Brittany before a combined allied breakout to the south and east could be made. If German commanders reacted quickly to D-Day, if they used their panzer tank divisions effectively, Allied forces might be penned into a small area of Normandy not far from the beachheads, despite almost two million troops waiting in Britain to cross the Channel and liberate Europe.

The weather was dreadful. But it came back again and again to the same, single command decision for Eisenhower as he pondered whether to take the tight, 24-hour weather window that was offered him on the evening of 4th June and give the command to 'go'. It would be catastrophic failure or essential success, albeit at some unknowable cost. It was Montgomery's achievement to have created the stark clarity of this choice. By the time Eisenhower stood before dawn on 5th June in Portsmouth's Southwick House to make his decision in the hushed room – 'OK, let's go', he said quietly, Montgomery had already fought his invasion battle. After 7th April no further changes in the plan were possible because operation NEPTUNE, the massive naval component of OVERLORD, had to swing into place to get shipping to its loading and distribution points. Allied air forces were already losing 12,000 aircrew and around 2,000 aircraft in that pre-invasion month as they fought hard for air superiority over northern France – essential to success.[5] On 7th April Montgomery was done. He spent

---

5. Indeed it was. On D-Day the Luftwaffe only had 120 fighters in theatre and they managed eighty sorties that day, as opposed to 14,600 sorties flown by Allied aircraft.

the days from 23rd May to 2nd June touring every corps and divisional area of his waiting troops, finishing off back at his HQ in Portsmouth where he addressed all his staff, who sat cross-legged like so many school-children, packed onto the tennis court. His message throughout the tour was the same to everyone – clarity, determination and confidence. Some criticized it as grandstanding, but it was Monty at his best, and undoubtedly his most effective.

On Tuesday 6th June the D-Day invasion succeeded better, and with fewer Allied casualties, than anyone could have hoped, even with the fickle fortunes of war at their busiest. Montgomery arrived in France the following day and set up the forward HQ with his circus of caravans in the grounds of a house at Creully. The breakout battle would last a gruelling seventy-seven days and involved some of the most controversial of Montgomery's command decisions. It ebbed and flowed in that time but there was an underlying pattern. Montgomery had planned to take Caen on D-Day itself to act as a great hinge for his breakout south-east. It was a coherent enough plan but under the pressures of battle it simply didn't work out. After enormous damage Caen wasn't taken from the Germans until the end of July. Like Douglas Haig on the Western Front almost thirty years before, Montgomery genuinely hoped for a rapid breakthrough, but was prepared for an attritional battle if necessary.

It continued that way in a series of failed breakout offensives as German forces – initially slow and confused at the top – built up and began fighting fiercely. So EPSOM, and then the much-touted GOODWOOD offensive, both failed as the British Second Army struggled to break away from the eastern invasion beachheads they had taken so successfully. In reality, the Second Army was doing exactly what Montgomery had originally anticipated it must do – to absorb German counterattacks to shield US forces further west so they could break out quickly to the south and then turn eastwards in force. In particular, the British Second Army was preventing the weight of German panzer divisions moving against Bradley's US First Army. But as Montgomery's offensive breakouts failed, his 'everything is going to plan' mantra attracted widespread derision. In truth, it was going to at least one version of his plan. But Montgomery could hardly tell his troops they were fighting and dying to protect US forces; and like Douglas Haig, he *was* trying to break out more quickly but also knew that his troops were acting as an attritional pivot to swing the Americans south and then eastwards. When the breakout finally happened, it was fast and brutal. Over 60,000 German troops were massacred in the Falaise pocket as they tried to escape Normandy, and then the chase was on. Allied forces raced across France faster than the Germans had managed in 1940. Paris was liberated on August 25th and the allies were in Brussels on 4th September.[6]

Montgomery batted away all criticism of his handling of the breakout battles; he certainly had a point if only he had expressed it more diplomatically. He was almost

---

6. The Normandy attrition had the effect of 'saving France'. Hitler decreed that there would be no phased withdrawal and that every inch of Normandy must be defended to the last man. So when German forces cracked there was nothing significant behind them to fall back on and their formations in most of France and Belgium simply collapsed.

sacked by Churchill for his resistance to any 'interference' in his command, and later by Eisenhower for near-insubordination. He continued high-handedly with fellow commanders and politicians alike. Only Brooke's influence at the top saved him. Of more consequence for many ordinary soldiers, he finally put his ego far ahead of his own sound military judgement as he thought about getting allied forces across the Rhine and into Germany as quickly as possible.

The Arnhem adventure – operation MARKET GARDEN – was a bold attempt to seize a series of nine bridges in the Netherlands to get forces across the Rhine into Germany's Ruhr heartland. It was a notable failure and following Cornelius Ryan's famous analysis, is popularly characterized as 'a bridge too far'. In fact, it was several bridges too far. Montgomery had long argued with Eisenhower about pushing straight into the Ruhr rather than advancing gradually along the whole front. But his MARKET GARDEN operation was conceived in just the ways Montgomery himself had savagely critiqued in the past. By then, the Allies desperately needed to open up the port of Antwerp to shorten their supply lines that were stretched back to Cherbourg. They had Antwerp, but since it lay eighty miles inland, needed to attack straight up the coast to clear access to it. That was a priority. But instead, Montgomery pressurized Eisenhower to back this dart to the Rhine, much further east. It was poorly planned over only seven days, operated on faulty intelligence, and deployed inadequate forces. It was a classic attempt to 'exploit' the Allied offensive rather than 'consolidate' it by opening up Antwerp. Repeating his initial failure at El Alamein, Montgomery tried to have one big formation superimpose itself on another, his XXX Corps of tanks and armour driving over an 'airborne carpet' to Arnhem – a carpet that was literally one-tank wide in most places. His armour would make a mad dash north along a single narrow line to reach the paratroopers who had seized the bridges.

Montgomery's motives were evident enough. He didn't want British forces doing the 'Antwerp role' and then finding themselves operating in the north-west of the battlefront, out of the main action. The British army had to play a significant part in the invasion of Germany and, of course, he yearned to be the first Allied commander to cross the Rhine and have the opportunity to drive Allied forces due east to take Berlin. He admitted in his memoirs to 'a bad mistake on my part' over Arnhem. But his 'mistake', he says, was in assuming the Canadians could perform the Antwerp role, '*while* we were going for the Ruhr'. So it was really the fault of the Canadians; alongside those (read Eisenhower) who wouldn't back the operation properly. Monty refers to himself as 'MARKET GARDEN'S unrepentant advocate', and supporters of it always maintained that, despite all, it was a risk worth taking. Perhaps. But it involved precisely the sorts of risk Montgomery had been structuring the British army to eschew during the time when he had such a major influence on it. In his own military doctrine, it was perverse.

Montgomery had the satisfaction of taking more than 200,000 troops of the US First and Ninth armies under his command during the crisis caused by Germany's final throw in the west – the Ardennes offensive during Christmas 1944. American forces were briefly in chaos and Eisenhower turned to Montgomery to restore some order to all Allied forces in the northern sector. In the event, no dramatic military operations were required, but it gave Montgomery great satisfaction to perform the role, albeit temporarily. It was March 1945 before the Allies finally got across the Rhine, and in several places at once. The German front was collapsing on all sides. Still, Montgomery couldn't resist some theatre for himself and the reputation of British forces. He had German commanders surrender to him on Luneberg Heath on 2nd May. It was merely a gesture, since the general surrender was made to Eisenhower on 8th May. But with the surrender of all German forces in Italy to Harold Alexander also on 2nd May, it was too much to expect Monty not to enjoy his own moment at the same time, still less to let Alex do it first.

His influence on British forces remained strong after the war. He became Chief of the Imperial General Staff in 1946 and then served as Deputy Supreme Commander – initially under Eisenhower – at NATO from 1951 to 1958. It was a critical period in the development of the western alliance. The North Atlantic Treaty Organization emerged, and remained, the most impressive military coalition in world history. Montgomery retired from the Army in 1958 when he stepped down from NATO and refused all approaches to get involved in politics. He published his explosive and controversial memoirs soon afterwards. He was more reflective in retirement but no less didactic. He played the role of *eminence grise* on all matters military, in addition to sharing loud opinions on South African apartheid, homosexuality, the Channel Tunnel, Mao Tse-tung and much else besides. He had a predictably difficult relationship with his natural son, David, but they had achieved some reconciliation together by the time of Montgomery's relatively peaceful death of heart failure in 1976. He is buried near his final home at Binsted church in Hampshire.

Montgomery was a Field Marshal, a Viscount and quite simply Britain's most well-known twentieth-century military commander. He rode the tide of victory as it began to flow Britain's way and shaped it with a clarity and discipline many other commanders could not have managed. Like Marlborough, he achieved some era-defining military victories, but unlike Marlborough, had no political skills to employ them. Unlike Wellington, he was not a complicated man; but just like Wellington, he was more respected than liked for his military prowess. Churchill probably had it right about Montgomery – 'in defeat, unbeatable; in victory, unbearable'.

Field Marshal William Slim

For a boy who was born the son of a Birmingham ironmonger, was an uncertified teacher in slum schools in the city and a clerk in a local metal-tubing firm, William Slim did very well in the Britain he was born into during 1891. He ended up a Field Marshal, the Chief of the Imperial General Staff, a Viscount, and Governor General of Australia. And he won for Britain a campaign in Burma that defeated two Japanese armies in succession which many historians regard as the most complex and victorious feat of operational manoeuvre, not just of the Second World War, but of Britain's twentieth century history in total.

Curious, then, that Slim's wartime contribution got only glancing mentions in Winston Churchill's memoirs of the Second World War – indeed, he wasn't mentioned at all in Churchill's first draft. Churchill was, after all, rather partial to describing British military triumphs in his six volume war memoirs, published during the 1950s. But Churchill was much more interested in his dealings with Lord Louis Mountbatten, the theatre commander in East Asia, or else in describing in detail the derring-do of Orde Wingate's irregular Chindit forces operating behind Japanese lines. Somehow the role of the Fourteenth Army that Bill Slim created and which did the ferocious fighting – the largest Commonwealth army of the war with nearly a million men by the end of 1944 – seemed not to excite Churchill's interest, either at the time or in the years following. The soldiers and veterans of the Fourteenth Army bitterly characterised themselves as the men of the 'forgotten army' and they were not wrong. Slim constantly fought for greater recognition – not for himself since he was a very modest man – but on their behalf, and their devotion to him was without qualification.

Great military campaigns, however, don't always have great strategic effects. Churchill was keen to recapture Burma and Malaya from the Japanese to show the colonial peoples that the British had not been chased out of East Asia by the Japanese attack in 1941. But bringing Burma back under British control was not fundamental to defeating Japan; that had to be done in China, in the Pacific, and by bombing attacks against the Japanese mainland. Slim's campaign to recapture Burma, 'was brilliant' said the historian Max Hastings, 'but of no significance for the defeat of Japan'. That may be too stark a judgement, but there can be no doubt that despite Churchill's strategic instinct to preserve colonial influence in Burma, it was nevertheless a strategic sideshow to the main American-led objective of decisively beating Japan.

That's a hard judgement for all the men who fought and persevered in some of the worst conditions on earth in which battle could take place, and it will always be hurtful to their memory and that of Bill Slim, whom they so revered as their commander. He lived quietly throughout most of his retirement, letting the record speak for itself.

That record spoke more loudly and with greater alacrity as the years went on. Bill Slim's military reputation as a uniquely successful national commander – whatever the strategic significance of Burma in Japan's defeat – remains imperishable.

Many around him assumed that Bill Slim must have risen to command from the ranks, given his background, his workmanlike voice and plain mannerisms. In fact, he got himself a temporary commission as a second lieutenant in the 9th Royal Warwickshires at the outbreak of war in 1914 via a cadet force and then the Territorial Army. The pattern of his subsequent war service was quite unlike some of the others who rose to high command. He was sent to Gallipoli and seriously wounded after eighteen days – shot straight through the chest leading an attack on the Sari Bair Ridge; wounded in the lungs and left shoulder. He was shipped home for what would be a long recovery. But during that time he managed to have himself made a temporary captain in the West India Regiment (where an officer could survive on the available pay).

Slim was rated unfit for duty but played the system to get back to the 9th Warwickshires in 1916 who were then in Mesopotamia. He was wounded again in 1917, this time in the arm, and went on to win a Military Cross with the Warwickshires in February 1918. His wounds were not negligible. For the rest of his life he had breathing problems and could not raise one arm above shoulder height. Nevertheless, by the time of the armistice, he was a major in the 6th Gurkha Rifles – the unit in which he was most completely at home – and in 1919 he transferred, very happily, and despite the opposition of the War Office, into the Indian Army. He was in the unfashionable end of the army; a colonial soldier rather than a Western Front man, serving now in imperial policing roles, often on the North-West Frontier. He quickly became fluent in Gurkhali, Hindi and Urdu and absorbed all the virtues of individual, small-unit soldiering in difficult environments where equipment and support was always scarce, to say the least. As a Gurkha officer he was also a typical Gurkha soldier.

He went to Staff College in Quetta where he went onto the directing staff and for a while he taught at Staff College in Camberley too. He also attended the Imperial Defence College, having done a stint in Army Headquarters Delhi, in between. He married Aileen Robertson in 1926 and they had two children, leading the life of a typical colonial family in India with only a few years in Britain during his postings. They were a close-knit family who were happiest making their life in Asia. Interestingly, and with his family's needs to boost his modest military salary, Slim was a prodigious short story writer in the 1930s, under the pen name, William Mills.[1] He was a very intelligent man, extraordinarily well-read (unlike most of 'Churchill's generals'), and he wrote stories of love, romance, mystery and adventure in the exotic locations of the Empire. William Mills was a regular in the *Daily Mail* and he submitted several pieces to *Women's Journal*, *Good Housekeeping* and *Pearson's Magazine*, among many others.

At the outbreak of the Second World War Slim was a brigadier running the Senior Officers' School in Belgaum, India. He was immediately given command of the Indian Army's 10th Infantry Brigade and sent to the Sudan to fight Italian forces in Ethiopia.

---

1. His grandson points out that his pen name was 'Mils' – 'Slim', backwards – but his writings seem to have used the more normal 'Mills' version of it.

He made tactical mistakes that distressed him for the casualties they caused, but he quickly learned. He was wounded again, this time in the abdomen, when an Italian aircraft strafed his vehicle, and he took some time to recover in Delhi.

He went back to Iraq, now in command of the Indian 10th Infantry Division as a major-general. In 1941 he led the division through Iraq, into eastern Syria and then during the subsequent invasion of Persia. He showed great ingenuity in dealing with logistical trails across many miles of desert and scrub. And he was determined to practise stealthy outflanking attacks rather than murderous frontal assaults across the flat, open ground that surrounded most strong points in the Levant. His leadership and tactical grasp were recognised with mentions in dispatches and a DSO.

Nevertheless, his war record did not seem to mark Slim out as more than a good divisional commander and it was a big step for him to be given command of a corps, under General Harold Alexander, in the fraught Burma campaign of 1942. Iraq and Persia might have been key strategic territories for the Allies, but they had become backwaters after 1941 as the German attack on the Soviet Union stalled. Slim, sitting in the Middle East, was not regarded as the sort of big personality required by the successive, unfolding crises in the Far East. Burma was a graveyard for most command careers at that time. Commanders were either killed or captured by a rampaging Japanese army or else swiftly relieved of their commands in failure after failure. Alexander had been sent out as the next Burma Army Commander to take charge of a hopeless position in March 1942, and local Gurkha officers had strongly recommended Slim for the post of one of Alexander's two corps commanders. It didn't appeal either to GHQ India or to Alan Brooke in London, but Alexander insisted and brought in the man who would reconquer Burma for Britain during the next three years.

The corps Slim took over consisted of just two weak divisions; the 17th Indian Division and the 1st Burma Division, which was largely paramilitary. He did, however, have the blessing of the renowned 7th Armoured Brigade within the 17th, with light tanks and their excellent recent battle experience as 'desert rats'. Slim arrived as Alexander's Burma Army was being chased out of Rangoon and back to the Indian border. Alexander's other corps was mainly Chinese, commanded by the American, Joseph Stilwell, and its priorities were hard to pin down. Slim's corps was therefore made responsible for the rearguard as well as being a fighting unit at the front of the army as it pulled back. Slim was frustrated that he couldn't get clearer orders from Alexander's staff about whether they were supposed to make a stand somewhere, or just keep withdrawing. Slim had successive plans to launch counter-offensives but his corps was constantly being cannibalised to support Chinese forces moving back in a different direction towards the Chinese border. Only on 25th April did Alexander order an all-out retreat to Tamu at the gates of India. Slim slowed the pursuing Japanese down with a brilliant action at Kyaukse, then extricated his troops from impending disaster at Monywa and Shwegyin. Once he had broken contact with the Japanese, it was a foot race up the Kebaw Valley to get his corps to safety at Tamu. After a total withdrawal of over 900 miles the last troops arrived on 28th May, exhausted, ragged and diseased, but they all arrived in their units and carried their weapons. 'They might look like scarecrows', wrote Slim in his memoirs, 'but they looked like soldiers too.'

He was baffled and deeply moved when his army of scarecrows cheered him loudly as he addressed them afterwards.

Slim was critical of Alexander's handling of the campaign, and Alexander took upon himself both the failure of the campaign, and the plaudits for this latest deliverance of British and Commonwealth forces, without crediting Slim at all. GHQ India, also, seemed not to have noticed Slim's role. On the border, General Noel Irwin criticised Slim for bringing 'a rabble' back to India – a charge that infuriated Slim both at the time, and fourteen years later in angry passages in his *Defeat into Victory* memoirs. Slim was extremely popular with his troops, but he was not favoured by his superiors.

He was given command of the XV Indian Corps at Barrackpore; out of the mainstream action again, and unable to offer his vision and the valuable experience he had just gained. But it gave him a breathing space to refine his ideas about the causes of the recent defeat, the strengths and weaknesses of the Japanese and the tasks for the British if they were to recapture Burma. He commented as he thought it through; 'I had little to be proud of: I could not rate my generalship high. The only test of generalship is success and I had succeeded in nothing I had attempted'. Few of his fellow commanders would have begun their professional and moral fightback from that standpoint.

Meanwhile Noel Irwin led a failing offensive to try to retake the Arakan region from late 1942 until the May monsoon in 1943. The whole campaign simply drove itself towards defeat. In desperation, Irwin brought Slim's XV Corps into it when all was virtually lost. Slim judged that withdrawal to the original starting line of the offensive was the only way of preventing this failure turning into a complete disaster. He pulled the forces back to the coast south of Cox's Bazar. Irwin tried to blame Slim for the whole campaign and sack him; but Wavell as Commander-in-Chief India understood the true picture and sacked Irwin instead, directing Slim to take over his role.

The XV Corps was built up with new units and Slim was put in temporary charge of the Eastern Army while the whole force was reorganised. When Lord Louis Mountbatten arrived as the new theatre commander for South-east Asia in November 1943, he had one long conversation with Slim before deciding that Slim should command the army permanently. Slim was astonished but agreed readily enough, suggesting that in a spirit of renewal, it should be renamed. So, the Fourteenth Army came into existence.

This was the real beginning of Slim's two years of military triumph. For the first time since Wellington in the Peninsular War – and like him after a series of defeats – a British general was presented with the opportunity to shape and train an army based on his own judgement and then take it to fight in a major campaign. The ideas that Slim had refined since the retreat from Rangoon were both broad, on the nature of military leadership; and highly specific, on the tactics necessary to beat Japanese infantry. In general terms he argued that a successful army must have a 'spiritual' component – a belief in its cause and the justice of it against the particular enemy; an 'intellectual' component – the confidence that these 'just objectives' were attainable; and a 'material' component – the troops' belief that they would be supplied with the necessary means and equipment to get the job done. These were all grand principles, much beloved of staff college lectures through the years, but Slim also had specific plans to translate them into battle tactics that could win in Burma.

He began with the proposition that every member of the Fourteenth Army – from him downwards to every mechanic, clerk and cook – must be prepared to become an infantryman when the need arose. He declared that the army must be capable of fighting through the monsoon and learn to cope with it. He observed that the Japanese were excellent at moving quickly through the jungle, very lightly equipped, whereas the British were too road-bound and therefore easy to 'road-block' and 'hook-around' – a tactic the Japanese used repeatedly to surround British units and create panic. Henceforth, the army would learn to move through the whole jungle and not regard being hooked or surrounded with great dismay. Instead, surrounded units would form 'boxes' – a citadel with all supplies in the centre and defended on all sides. They would be re-supplied by air-drop while other units moved through the jungle to relieve them. Japanese infantry moved swiftly in jungle terrain because they carried so few supplies; relying on living off stores captured from enemies they had overrun. It was an effective tactic but also a critical weakness that Slim intended to exploit. With all the supplies that Japanese troops needed defended inside a 'box', Slim regarded each box as an 'anvil' against which unimaginative Japanese frontal assaults would be broken. Conversely, the Fourteenth Army would eschew frontal assaults themselves, screening and outflanking strong points to 'unbalance' Japanese plans. Tanks were to be used in all terrains except swamp and in as high a number as possible, not wasted in cautious penny packets ('the more you use the fewer you lose' was Slim's motto). The jungle was not an enemy and the Japanese were not invincible; both could be overcome with training and good logistics.

Training and logistical competence were exactly what the XV Corps and then the whole Fourteenth Army got under Slim's indefatigable influence between summer 1942 and the winter of 1943. It was a more specific version of the Battle School system that Alexander had championed for Britain's new army training for the liberation of Europe. In Slim's case there was the same realistic level of training, but he would send his troops into the jungle for prolonged periods in order to stop fearing it. He made everyone train in night operations, offensive patrolling, mule-handling, river crossings, receiving air-dropped supplies, tank-infantry cooperation, air-ground cooperation, signals, communications and medical hygiene. After losing 70 per cent of its active strength to malaria, he introduced strict preventative procedures throughout the army and got the rate down to less than 5 percent. And he tested his own commanders hard during intensive training exercises. He was personally compassionate, but quite ruthless in replacing those he thought could not lead his men in the way they deserved to be led. By December 1943 he had created a tough and well-prepared force – the biggest and most multi-national single army Britain had ever fielded – under his uncompromising, tough, fair, personal influence.[2]

---

2. By the end of 1944, of its 12 divisions, the Fourteenth Army included two British, seven Indian, and three British African divisions, plus, on occasion, six Chinese and two US divisions and a number of tribal militias from Shan, Chin, Naga, Kachin and Karen peoples, working through the OSS or the SOE organisations. To meet all its religious, caste and cultural requirements, the Fourteenth Army developed thirty different ration scales yet still gave every soldier three meals a day.

The Fourteenth Army's first battle test, as ever, was complicated by war's reality. Just as the Allies in Burma had started a major push on three fronts, the Japanese struck with a clever and fast offensive – a massive attack in Arakan, pushing north to the gateway into India. Slim's most radical ideas were tested first. In Arakan, his 7th Division and parts of the 5th and 81st were rapidly surrounded by Japanese forces who had moved swiftly and largely unobserved into the area. Slim had underestimated, even now, the speed and force of their attacks. The Japanese expected the British, as before, to withdraw from untenable positions. Tokyo announced that the war in Burma was over and its 'march to Delhi' had begun. But instead of retreating, the 7th, 5th and 81st divisions stood firm in their various 'boxes', including the famous 'Admin Box' at Sinzweya where the command of 7th Division held most of its stores. Over a period of three weeks Japanese forces, as Slim had anticipated, launched themselves in fierce frontal attacks on the boxes as their own meagre supplies ran down.

Mountbatten was completely supportive and got precious Dakota transport aircraft diverted from China supplies to facilitate a constant air-bridge into the besieged boxes – day and night drops with everything they needed. It was a considerable USAAF/RAF joint effort, working by flares at night, shuttling back and forth, to keep 40,000 men supplied, while a vicious battle for air superiority went on by daylight between RAF and Japanese fighters – a battle the newly-arrived Spitfires won convincingly after the first week. None of Slim's boxes fell to Japanese attacks, though there were some very close calls, particularly at Sinzweya. By the end of February Japanese forces pulled back and Slim's troops were able immediately to go onto the offensive and secure their original objectives in the Arakan part of the big Allied push that had tried to get underway in January.

It was, in every sense, a turning point. Slim had delivered the first British victory over Japanese forces, holding their attack before chasing them out of their carefully prepared positions in the Mayu mountains. The RAF had established local air superiority and the reputation of Japanese infantry as somehow invincible in jungle conditions was severely dented. Churchill ascribed the victory chiefly to Mountbatten – as did Mountbatten – but it was entirely Slim's. In fact, Slim had a very good relationship with Mountbatten. They genuinely liked each other and saw the campaign, and its best tactics, in the same way. Many regarded the young Lord Louis Mountbatten, who had been catapulted by his royal lineage and political connections to become C-in-C of the South-east Asia Command, as an egotistical showman with little strategic acumen. But his showmanship pleased the rank and file and he backed Slim when it really mattered. He disobeyed standing orders and broke rules for Bill Slim's sake – to fulfil the 'material' component of Fourteenth Army's needs. Mountbatten undoubtedly drew the credit due to Slim onto himself, but Slim could not have achieved what he did in these two years without Mountbatten's verve and support.

But the epic wasn't over. Notwithstanding its failure to annihilate the 7th and 5th divisions, Japan's 'march to Delhi' offensive still went forward as its forces advanced through the highland chain that ran along the Assam/Burma border and converged at Imphal and further north at Kohima. Slim immediately airlifted his victorious 5th and 7th divisions straight out of Arakan northwards to defend Imphal and Kohima.

Conditions were different, because weather made it difficult to get air supplies into both centres once roads into Imphal were cut and Kohima became completely surrounded. And too few aircraft were available this time, despite Mountbatten breaking more rules. Again, surging Japanese forces depended on capturing British supplies – particularly in Imphal – or risk losing their foothold in the jumping-off place for their attack into India. Just north of Kohima lay Dimapur, the biggest and most well-stocked supply hub and railhead for the whole theatre – everything for Burma and for China the other side of the Himalayas. There was nothing between the besieged Kohima garrison and Dimapur forty-four miles to the north.[3] Slim pulled his very experienced 17th Indian Division back from Tiddim towards Imphal – only just in time since they had to fight their way *into* the defensive boxes. But they stretched Japanese supply lines about a hundred miles and got into Imphal before connections into the area were completely cut. But by then, Kohima was in trouble and there was not enough good weather, or aircraft, to get reinforcements quickly into Dimapur which lay almost wide open.

Imphal and Kohima are often viewed as two great simultaneous sieges, but they were much more. They were the centrepieces of a multi-front battle across eighty miles that, as Slim said, was as confused as it was fluid. And he judged it all to be supremely important. If the Japanese succeeded, he wrote, the destruction of the Fourteenth Army 'would be the least of its results. China, completely isolated, would be driven into a separate peace, India ripe as they thought for revolt against the British, would fall, a glittering prize, into their hands'.

On its 'march to Delhi' the tiny town of Kohima marked the very furthest extent of Japan's advance westward during the war. That precise point was a hill station 5,000 feet above sea level in the lush Naga Hills, managed by a British Deputy Commissioner who lived in a bungalow overlooking the surrounding peaks. The town and hill station were initially held by 1,500 Commonwealth troops when an attack by 6,000 of Japan's 31st Division began on 22nd March. The fighting lasted for sixty-four days; the British perimeter shrinking as one hill after another was abandoned under day and night assaults. The front eventually stalled on Garrison Hill, either end of the Deputy Commissioner's tennis court. Both sides remained within grenade-throwing range of each other – as easy to throw as tennis balls – and ground out a desperate siege for Garrison Hill. The area was so small that British air-dropped supplies frequently fell into Japanese hands. Slim couldn't relieve Kohima until he had built up more reinforcements at Dimapur. And so it went on at Garrison Hill – an epic in itself that yielded one of the most oft-quoted verses of Second World War remembrance.[4] On 15th April a battalion of the Punjab Regiment was able to get through to Kohima and partially lift the siege. The pendulum began to swing back to Commonwealth troops, but the fighting didn't diminish. Japanese forces were, however, steadily beaten back.

---

3. Slim could not understand why the Japanese didn't just screen Kohima and get on to Dimapur, but Japanese commanders stuck rigidly to their orders to 'take' Kohima. Slim always acknowledged how lucky he was in this respect.
4. In conscious imitation of Simonides's famed verse dedicated to Leonidas and the 300 Spartans who fought the Persians at Thermopylae in 480 BC, John Maxwell Edmonds's verse on the Kohima war memorial says, 'When you go home, tell them of us and say for your tomorrow, we gave our today.'

The last position to be cleared turned out to be the Deputy Commissioner's garden and tennis court. Engineers bulldozed a track above the garden, winched a Lee tank up to the top and sent it crashing down the slope onto the tennis court to fire point blank into Japanese bunkers and trenches around it. On 31st May Japanese forces, now starving, withdrew entirely from Kohima.

Meanwhile, at Imphal, the front was wider and Slim worked cannily to draw the enemy into local traps against defences he was now confident were steady. The greatest threat was at Nungshigum where Japanese forces took the peaks overlooking the northeast Imphal plain. But they were attacked relentlessly by RAF Hurricanes. Fourteenth Army tanks were repeatedly winched up sheer slopes to fire straight through the loopholes of enemy bunkers. Japanese infantry attacked with the growing desperation of starving men, but Slim's army was able to match the high tempo of action and now, in summer 1944, was infinitely better supplied. Operation 'Stamina', the air supply to keep Fourteenth Army going, was sustained by yet more Mountbatten rule-breaking and became the greatest air supply operation of the war. On 22nd June troops and tanks moving south from Kohima and north from Imphal finally linked up. On 8th July the whole Japanese Fifteenth Army, sick and emaciated, began a disorderly retreat.

Now was the time for Slim's Fourteenth Army to move into pursuit to liberate Burma. But no one in London seemed to appreciate the importance of this victory, and Washington rapidly lost interest in Burma once its China supply route over the Himalayas was safe. Churchill was anyway more taken with the work of Orde Wingate's 'Chindits' operating behind Japanese lines in daring raids. During two years of abject defeats in Burma, Wingate's Chindits had been the only good news coming out of the theatre. Churchill had Wingate promoted and took him to the allied Quebec conference in 1943 for the sake of morale. He was the new 'Lawrence of Arabia' – to whom he was, in fact, distantly related. He showed great strategic flair, but Wingate – who had already attempted suicide in Cairo – was seriously unbalanced and regarded by those close to him as increasingly insane. Slim didn't oppose what Wingate was doing but questioned the military value of the Chindits for all the resources – and good men – it required. Chindit operations were expanded enormously to became one of four separate fronts that Slim had to manage in the January 1944 offensive. When Wingate was killed in an air crash in March it was frankly a benefit to the Fourteenth Army and allowed Slim to re-establish more control over his resources. In the end, the Chindits achieved much, but little of it had been of genuine strategic value to Slim.

Mountbatten continued to badger London all through the autumn of 1944 for some strategic plan for Burma. The preference was for an amphibious invasion of Rangoon to liberate the country from the sea. Churchill and Alan Brooke were preoccupied with Europe that autumn and neither of them could envisage a successful land campaign in Burma slogging south from the Naga Hills all the way to Rangoon. But landing craft were in too short supply to make a major amphibious operation possible, so Slim was instructed to conduct a 'holding operation' in the north until conditions were more favourable.

In reality, the reconquest of Burma would have to be done the hard way. Slim found enough of a loophole in his orders to begin a new offensive. It turned into what military historians have recognised as the most accomplished manoeuvre battle by a British general in either of the world wars. Slim's immediate superior as Land Forces commander in South-East Asia had become Oliver Leese, an Eighth Army man with a low opinion of the Indian Army and a jaundiced view of Slim himself. Keeping Leese at arm's length and presenting London with a series of faits accomplis, Slim's great offensive became a private war between himself and generals Kimura and Katamura of the Japanese Fifteenth Army. It was also a miracle of improvisation and organisation, driven from top to bottom by Bill Slim's quietly dominant personality.

The author of the 'Flashman' novels, George Macdonald Fraser served with fellow Cumbrians in the Border Regiment in the Fourteenth Army, and in his own memoir, *Quartered Safe Out Here*, he describes Slim's presence among his soldiers perfectly. Like every soldier in his army, Slim was ready to become an infantryman and he always carried a carbine slung on his shoulder. He was, said Macdonald Fraser, 'large, heavily built, grim-faced with that hard mouth and bulldog chin', and his rakish Gurkha hat at odds with 'untidy trouser bottoms'. He goes on, 'Slim emerged from under the trees by the lake shore, there was no nonsense of 'gather round' or jumping on boxes; he just stood with his thumb hooked in his carbine sling and talked about how we had caught the Jap off-balance and were going to annihilate him in the open; there was no exhortation or ringing cliches, no jokes or self-conscious use of barrack-room slang – when he called the Japs 'bastards' it was casual and without heat. He was telling us informally what would be.' For his soldiers, Slim simply combined the strategic vision of their general with the honesty of their platoon sergeant. And the Fourteenth Army was now a considerable war machine. Like Alexander in Italy in 1944 and Haig on the Western Front in 1916, Slim was fixed on the destruction of the enemy army in front of him, not on its orderly withdrawal from the theatre. But to engage them, his forces would have to cross the Chindwin river and then the formidable Irrawaddy, fast flowing and over a mile wide – necessitating the longest opposed river crossing anywhere during the war. The resourceful Fourteenth Army brought up supplies on mules and elephants, felled trees and constructed hundreds of heavy rafts, lifted and re-floated sunken ferries, brought into commission every form of improvised light transport, developed its own tar-covered hessian road surfaces, and had its own form of cheap parachute (the 'parajute') for endless supply drops.

Slim aimed to cross the Chindwin and break out of the jungle into the open Shwebo Plain beyond. The fighting there would be of a more conventional type; more open combined arms warfare, pushing armoured forces across greater distances in a drive south to Rangoon. He re-purposed some of his units to mechanised infantry and retrained them very quickly to operate to a more standard European manoeuvre model. He trusted completely his corps and divisional commanders, who by then had become some of the very best in the army. And he ran – many years before it was fashionable – a genuinely joint headquarters where land, air, RAF, USAAF and different special forces, all worked together as one staff. Contrary to official opinions of him in London, insofar as anyone there knew much about him, Slim now practised bold, offensive tactics and stretched the concept of calculated risks towards their logical limits.

As Slim's forces crossed the Chindwin, the new commander of Japan's Fifteenth Army, Kimura Heitaro, fell back too easily, trying to draw Slim into a trap as Fourteenth Army headed to retake Mandalay. But Slim – initially tempted – then saw it coming. He sent one corps on a noisy feint north of Mandalay, as if falling into the trap; another corps to the north-west of the city to effect a real crossing of the Irrawaddy at Ngazun – a tough fight as Kimura quickly committed most of his strength to oppose it; but Slim then had his IV Corps cross the Irrawaddy in real force, almost unopposed, seventy miles further south and drove on to Meiktila, to cut all links into Mandalay. Mandalay fell on 20th March. With no air reconnaissance possible and no intelligence (indeed false intelligence from local tribes who were cooperating with Fourteenth Army) Japanese commanders were frankly bamboozled by Slim's manoeuvres. And they had been risky. Slim had incurred 'necessary' losses at Ngazun to help his real river crossing further south and he had been forced to commit the 5th Indian Division, his final reserve, to hold onto Meiktila in the early phases. It was close, but it had all worked for him in the way he had originally envisaged.

After the spectacular capture of Mandalay, the Fourteenth Army was east of the Irrawaddy and in the open valleys between that and the Sittang that led directly south to Rangoon. But the ground forces were running fast ahead of their land supply lines. From February to May 1945 Slim was running two races – one to grab airfields as fast as possible, some almost behind Japanese lines, to keep his supply aircraft within range of his troops; and the second to reach Rangoon before the monsoon made it too difficult. In those two months there was a lot of hard, local fighting that incurred considerable casualties on both sides. During April, Slim drove relentlessly towards Rangoon and as his forces got close, he launched a combined land, airborne, and amphibious assault on it; a model of its kind. The monsoon was starting as the 26th Indian Division approached Rangoon in landing craft, but the Japanese had already left. Fourteenth Army soldiers entered the city on 2nd May, the same day that Axis forces in Italy surrendered to Alexander and less than a week before the war in Europe was declared over. No one in London noticed what had happened in Burma. The next three months would still involve operations as the Fourteenth Army pushed the Japanese back towards the Thai border, but Burma was effectively re-taken.

Immediately after the fall of Rangoon, the ever-mediocre and touchy Oliver Leese sacked Slim from his command before the anticipated British invasion of Malaya, trying to demote him to a minor role – to 'give him a rest' – mopping up in Burma. When they heard this, the Fourteenth Army came close to mutiny from the top down. Alan Brooke in London and Auchinleck at GHQ India were outraged at Leese's high-handedness and made Mountbatten (who had originally agreed) sack Leese instead. In a repeat of the Noel Irwin episode two years previously, the superior who tried to remove Slim was himself replaced, and Slim was promoted into his job. Bill Slim became a full general and made commander of all British land forces in South East Asia. It was while he was discussing his new appointment with Mountbatten on 6th August that they heard of the dropping of an atom bomb on Japan. On 12th September Slim sat in Singapore with Mountbatten to receive the unconditional surrender of all Japanese forces in South-east Asia. Rangoon, as it happened, had been his last hurrah.

Slim retired from the Army in 1948 and became deputy chairman of British Railways. Prime Minister Clement Atlee, however, brought him out of retirement the following year to make him a Field Marshal and Chairman of the Imperial General Staff. He saw the British Army through the Korean War and then became Governor General of Australia in 1953, a post he much enjoyed where he and his family were extremely popular. He retired to Britain in 1959, was made a Viscount in 1960 and he died peacefully in December 1970. He was given a full military funeral and his ashes were interred in St Paul's Cathedral where a simple plaque marks the location.

The multi-ethnic, multi-religious, multi-national soldiers of the 'forgotten' Fourteenth Army – especially the Gurkhas – never wavered in their devotion to their creator and commander. The Fourteenth was the last, and the most successful, of all Britain's imperial armies. Slim's memoirs and lessons on command have never been out of print and have infinitely greater influence on the British Army's staff college curriculum than Churchill's own six-volume history of the Second World War. Yet official recognition of Slim's military achievements always seemed frankly grudging. Nevertheless, in 1990 a statue of him was erected outside the Ministry of Defence on Whitehall, alongside statues of Bernard Montgomery and Alan Brooke; three great field marshals and commanders of the Second World War, albeit for different reasons. Twenty years after his death, he was at least accorded in stone a comradeship of commanders he never achieved in flesh and blood.

Marshal of the Royal Air Force, Arthur Harris

In May 1992 a statue of Arthur Harris was unveiled, just outside the Royal Air Force Church of St Clement Danes in London's Strand. Queen Elizabeth the Queen Mother unveiled it. No member of the government was present. Many of the survivors of Britain's Second World War bomber offensive against Germany were, including Leonard Cheshire VC, gravely ill just two months prior to his death, but determined to attend. Within twenty-four hours, red paint had been poured over the statue, and other acts of vandalism required round-the-clock police protection for it over quite some time.

Arthur Harris – 'Bomber Harris' to the press and public; 'Butch Harris' to some of his aircrews who thought he butchered them; 'Bert Harris' to his colleagues and friends – was always a controversial commander. By the time he became Commander-in-Chief of Bomber Command in 1942, he had long believed, honestly and honourably, in the war-winning power of strategic bombing. For three years he oversaw its application with growing severity against German cities. In this respect he was faithfully executing government policy that was written down quite precisely for him and oft-repeated. But unlike many government ministers and some colleagues, he made no attempt to pretend that this policy was anything other than brutal. Political leaders maintained, untruthfully, that British bombing was always directed at strictly military targets. It wasn't, and Harris knew it was designed to take many civilian lives. But when it worked, he also fervently believed, it would save countless more by ending the war quickly. Many thought he allowed these convictions to become an obsession that eventually blinded him to wider Allied considerations on the road to victory. Perhaps they did; but even his detractors recognised in Harris a sort of pig-headed moral courage to take in person the weight of bitter criticism that attached to a national strategy that properly belonged to many others as well. The vast majority of his aircrews, even those who nicknamed him 'Butch', understood that and felt insulted – their sacrifices ignored – when the bomber offensive was denied a campaign medal after the war. Harris refused a peerage in 1946 in protest at the way 'Bert Harris's boys' were first ignored and then denigrated. That uncomfortable legacy rumbled deep into the twenty-first century.

Arthur Harris was always a good airman and a gifted leader. He had a wealth of relevant experience behind him by the time he became Air Officer Commanding – AOC – of Bomber Command. He was born in Gloucestershire in 1892 and emigrated, quite independently as an eighteen-year-old in search of adventure, to the British South Africa Company's territory of Rhodesia. He intended to develop a ranching business there and certainly seemed to have the drive and aptitude. When the First

World War broke out, he volunteered for the 1st Rhodesia Regiment and saw fitful action with it in South West Africa, before the regiment disbanded in 1915. Harris decided to return to Britain to fight more effectively and sailed with three hundred Rhodesian volunteers, enrolling in the Royal Flying Corps in November 1915.

He flew a BE2 on the home front, operating against Zeppelin raids as one of his unit's two designated anti-Zeppelin night pilots. This is revealing. His pilot training had involved less than twelve hours solo flying. But he was chosen to undertake a specialist role that required piloting skills, good navigation and night-flying. It marked the beginning of his lifelong faith in the importance of night-flying and navigation for any effective air unit. And his nascent success in Rhodesia had shown that Harris was a serious-minded, evidently driven, achiever. There was nothing dreamy about him. He had not been expensively educated, unlike his two elder brothers, but was a young man of great personal resource with independence of spirit and a sharp mind. But as he got older, he also had his demons. He was as impetuous and romantic as he was hard-bitten and prosaic. He could become moody and difficult; always professional, but personally unpredictable. He was a man who tended to make others feel uncomfortable unless they were taken into his small inner circle.

In 1917 he was a flight commander, and then rapidly the commanding officer, of No. 45 Squadron in France, flying Sopwith 1½ Strutters and then the famous Sopwith Camel. By the end of the war he was a major, an 'air ace' with the required five individual victories to his credit, and he had been awarded the Air Force Cross. By then he had also fallen wildly in love with the socialite, Barbara Money, who moved in London circles that he had never known. They had married quickly in 1916 with all the wartime urgency and intensity characteristic of those years. By 1918, the first of their three children had arrived, so despite always wearing a 'Rhodesia' shoulder flash on his uniform, Harris shelved his longstanding plan to return to his spiritual homeland and pursued instead an RAF career in Britain.

He commanded RAF stations, one of its flying schools, and served in a number of 'air policing' operations on the North-West Frontier, in Mesopotamia (as it was being reformed under the British mandate into modern Iraq), and in Persia. It was during this period that he became convinced of the psychological and political value of effective aerial bombing. In Mesopotamia he cut into the airframes and rigged his squadron of Vickers Vernon transport aircraft to turn them into accurate and – by the standards of the time – heavy bombers. They were surprisingly effective, first in stopping Turkish incursions into the mandate territories in 1923 and then in helping suppress tribal revolts within them. Harris was working under John Salmond, later to become the RAF Commander-in-Chief, and they were both keen to explore how aircraft could be adapted and used in these new roles. A year later, Hugh Dowding was in Iraq, refining the same approach with his own immediate commander, Josh Higgins. But whereas Dowding returned from the Middle East with grave doubts about the applicability of this easy 'coercive bombing' strategy to other places and situations, Harris was increasingly convinced that, precisely delivered, it represented a new dimension in warfare. And again, it reinforced his commitment to accurate navigation and night-flying as essential requirements for effective airpower.

Harris took his night-flying enthusiasm to his new command, No. 210 flying boat squadron at Pembroke Dock. He proved to his men, yet again, that he was more than just a highly skilled flyer. One of them commented that 'Bert Harris was a super night pilot – he had night cat's eyes', and he made No. 210 the most capable flying boat squadron in the RAF, covering big areas of the Atlantic, night and day. He reflected later that 210 gave him the most enjoyable of all his operational flying. He took his enthusiasm for coercive bombing back to Middle East Command in 1936, opining that the growing Arab revolt could be suppressed by a vigorous bombing policy – which was never tried.

And he took his restless personal spirit and emotional mood swings to the arms of other women during the periods when he was abroad. By the early-30s his marriage was on the rocks, with infidelities on both sides. Barbara divorced him in 1935; not, she said later, so much for the infidelities as for his dark and volatile moods. But three years later, at the age of forty-six, Harris married the twenty-three-year-old 'Jillie' Hearne, having wooed her since she was twenty. Notwithstanding how all this left Barbara and his three children, Jill was undoubtedly good for him in the years of trial that followed.[1] They had a daughter whom he is said to have adored, and Jill cooperated enthusiastically on domestic and protocol matters as he became one of the Chiefs and was required to entertain, and often accommodate, his counterparts from Allied countries. In his second family Harris had a comfortable domestic hinterland that assuaged some of his inner demons throughout the war and afterwards. To most who knew Harris professionally during the 1940s, he remained largely unapproachable and intimidating, downright unlikeable to many, though self-evidently fair-minded, too. To those who knew him more personally, he was thoughtful, kind and self-effacing; a man who directed his demons to strategic bombing and kept a different and more accessible part of himself for his, now, essentially settled personal life.

In the late 1920s he had done a stint at the Army Staff College in Camberley, where he was singularly unimpressed with his army colleagues and what he interpreted as their regressive military attitudes. The only exception for him was Bernard Montgomery who was also there at the time and with whom he formed a lasting friendship. They were sufficiently alike for Harris to appreciate Montgomery's intellectual honesty and his terse professionalism, and – though Harris certainly had more personal charm when he chose to use it – he didn't react much against Montgomery's own charmless persona. But Camberley reinforced Harris's growing conviction that neither the Army nor the Royal Navy would win a war for Britain on the European continent. His technocratic instincts told him that a future war would only be won by airpower and its ability to bombard an enemy's homeland to some strategic purpose. His thinking put him firmly in the mainstream of the air force that Lord Trenchard had created, and which the great founder continued to influence throughout his retirement. For the young RAF, airpower was primarily an offensive, coercive instrument. There were

---

1. When Dudley Saward produced Harris's authorised biography in 1984, in which Harris had cooperated fully, its credibility was much undermined by making no mention of his first marriage at all or to his children by it.

many other roles that aircraft should perform – transport, reconnaissance, national defence, supporting the other services, and so on – but since airpower opened up the third dimension of any battlespace, its *raison d'etre* must be to attack an enemy directly, despite whatever might be happening below it on land or sea. The prevailing view was that there could be no effective defence against aerial assault, so the future must lie with the bomber. While he was in the Air Ministry in the mid-30s Harris was one of those pushing for the development of long range, heavy bombers that could reach Germany from bases in Britain. These would be fundamental, the RAF believed, to any future European conflict.[2] And notwithstanding that Harris had been a fighter ace in the First World War, he had become a 'bomber man' to his fingertips; the aircraft for it, the technologies and tactics of it; the rationale behind it.

It is not surprising that with his leadership ability and his prevailing views, Arthur Harris rose quickly into senior command positions once war was declared. In September 1939 he was given command of No. 5 Group, one of the RAF's three 'heavy bomber' groups – which at that time meant Handley Page Hampdens – in ten squadrons across five airfields in eastern England. He was, from the beginning, a dynamic group leader. He thought the Hampdens were a 'typical piece of Handley Page junk' and worked hard to get them modified and improved for their role. He visited his aircrews and listened intently to their accounts of what worked and what didn't. He cared deeply about his aircrews but wouldn't let them see it, in case it was prejudicial to their performance. His attitude was severe, disciplinarian and made no concessions to cases of 'lack of moral fibre'. LMF, he believed, would be contagious if it were tolerated. Everyone in 5 Group, including him, had a job to do and that was that. Its roles during the first year of the war encompassed bombing missions in support of the Norway campaign, the battle of France, bombing German invasion barges, extensive minelaying, and early attacks on the German homeland – symbolic pinpricks at the time, though extremely dangerous for his aircrews.

After fourteen months he went back into the Air Ministry as Deputy Chief of Air Staff, where he completed the foundations for some of the most resolute feuds he would have in the coming years; with the Ministry of Economic Warfare, with the Admiralty over the Battle of the Atlantic and with the Special Operations Executive. Interestingly, his principal feuds were within the Air Ministry itself, which he came to loathe for what he saw as its lacklustre performance, its political timidity and its repeated failures to stand up to the Admiralty and the War Office. Harris had become a personal friend of Churchill. He dined with him on many a late-evening and weekend and he knew that Churchill fully shared his strong, offensive, instincts. It gave Harris an inside track to the top of the system that bypassed many ranks in between and provided him with real influence. By 1944 some critics thought his personal influence with Churchill was allowing Harris to run the bomber offensive as a private war.

---

2. Although the RAF desperately needed defensive fighters in these years, it was fortunate that enough RAF planners (including Dowding) pushed for heavy bombers early enough for them to be brought into service by 1942–3. Germany only ever developed light and medium bombers, which became obsolete as the war went on. By 1944, Germany's only counter-punch to Allied heavy bombers were V1 and then V2 rockets.

He had believed in the value of strategic bombing for many years, but now, within the Air Ministry, no less than with Churchill, Harris honed his arguments for it, fighting against those voices who wanted Bomber Command's strength to be diluted to different theatres, or to do different things in the central bombing campaign against Germany. He was always consistent, though seldom diplomatic. He headed the RAF delegation to Washington in June 1941 at an important juncture in nascent Allied cooperation and was there when the Pearl Harbor attack occurred in December. Neither his manner nor his message changed. Lord Halifax, Britain's Ambassador in the US, judged Harris to have failed in his Washington role. Not for the first time, Halifax was quite wrong; Harris had got on very well with President Roosevelt and Harry Hopkins, his principal advisor, and he created a strong relationship with the United States Army Air Force, the USAAF, who liked his straightforwardness and his commitment to strategic bombing. The RAF and the USAAF were well set up by Harris to work together as the Grand Alliance of the US, Russia and Britain took shape at the beginning of 1942. He was a true architect of the uniquely close relationship that evolved between the RAF and what was transformed into the USAAF's Eighth Air Force. Its aircraft began to arrive in Britain in the following months. Before he left Washington, he had already been marked out for his next role – leading Bomber Command itself.

In February 1942, within weeks of his return, Harris was driven into Bomber Command HQ at High Wycombe. The command had been pursuing a largely ineffective area bombing policy since July 1941. Its operational researchers had been looking at the effects of German bombing of British targets since 1940. While in the Air Ministry, Harris had been instrumental in getting this operational research underway; the potential seemed great, but the practical effects were poor. But as Harris took over Bomber Command, Britain's existing area bombing policy was bolstered and structured around two particularly influential reports. As the RAF had discovered in France in 1940, and the *Luftwaffe* realised later that summer over southern England, strategic bombing in daylight, deep inside enemy territory, was a murderous process. But the alternative approach, bombing at night, was extremely inaccurate. Navigation was more difficult, weather was harder to cope with, bombing accurately was nearly impossible. The Butt Report from the Cabinet Secretariat in 1941 had famously concluded that only one in three of the RAF's bombers got within five miles of their targets. In the case of the heavily defended region of the Ruhr, it was one in ten. The damage caused by those who did manage to get within five miles was both random and trivial. It's quite true that RAF strategic bombing represented the only way Britain could fight back in the dire circumstances of late 1940 and 1941, and in hindsight, the Butt Report turned out to be too pessimistic in its statistical method. But the air campaign was obviously failing and costing the lives of invaluable aircrew for little more than a propaganda benefit and to make a point to Britain's new Soviet allies.

Bomber Command's previous chief, Richard Peirse, had been sacked in December 1941 and in stepping into his shoes, Harris was given a clear brief to turn the bombing campaign around. There would be no magical technical answers or clever twists of innovative strategy to achieve this. It required drive and attention to every aspect of the offensive – more aircraft and aircrew, better equipment, navigational aids, better training and vastly improved personal skills.

The second report was delivered a month after Harris took up his appointment. It was written by the controversial – and widely disliked – Frederick Lindemann, later Lord Cherwell, a close friend and influence on Churchill. Lindemann had looked at the bombing of Coventry, Hull and Birmingham and concluded that, though there was no evidence it seriously affected civilian morale, it *would* have done so if such cities – he mentioned Hull – had been attacked more heavily and consistently. The evidence was highly circumstantial, and challenged by many operational researchers in Whitehall. But Lindemann presented the Cabinet with an analytical explanation of the strategic effects of 'de-housing' up to a third of the German population in fifty-eight towns and cities across the country; targeting working class people in particular, whose houses were closer together and whose misery was harder to mitigate. Lindemann gave the Cabinet a pseudo-scientific justification for the expansion of its ongoing area bombing policy and in particular the 'Area Bombing Directive' that had been issued to Harris just weeks before. The simple truth was that area bombing, with all its inaccuracies, was the only thing Bomber Command could manage in 1941 and 1942. But Lindemann – 'the Prof' – now gave Churchill, the Cabinet and Harris himself ample justification to regard it as the optimum strategic choice for the defeat of Germany.

Harris never resiled from what 'de-housing' really meant. He did believe it would ultimately sap Germany's will to continue the struggle. He was temperamentally anti-German after his experiences in the First World War. For him, this second war was 'unfinished business' against a militaristic nation led by a tyrant. And if the first war had created appalling losses for all the belligerents, this one could be won as long as Allied leaders didn't flinch from high losses – including civilians – in order to prevent appalling ones. He observed, too, that in the arguments for precision attacks as opposed to area bombing, having his bombers smash roads, rail yards, electricity stations and civilian infrastructure indiscriminately was just as effective in interrupting war production – and entirely achievable – as opposed to precision-bombing of individual war factories, which was not.

He was therefore predisposed to take the now famous War Cabinet Directive given to him on 14th February very literally. It instructed him, 'To focus attacks on the morale of the enemy civil population and in particular the industrial workers'. It directed Bomber Command to attack other targets as may become necessary, but not at the expense of neglecting 'primary targets' – the cities of Germany. The 'aiming points', the War Cabinet clarified the following day, 'will be the built-up areas and not, for instance, the dockyards or aircraft factories'.

This was something Harris was determined his force could achieve. But 1942 was a tough and dispiriting year for Bomber Command. Bombers of the American Eighth Air Force were arriving from July but would not be ready for genuine operations until 1943; and in the meantime, Harris was trying to convert his force, amid many competing demands, into one that could deliver a consistent strategic punch against the German homeland. He had 48 bomber squadrons under his command, only nine of them 'heavies'. He could call on some 400 serviceable bombers, most of them inadequate to the task. Only two squadrons were equipped with the new Lancaster aircraft. On any given night, he could put around 200–300 aircraft into a raid, most of them Wellington, Whitley, Halifax, or Stirling bombers – all underpowered and vulnerable. In May Harris scraped every aircraft he could find from Coastal Command and from training and maintenance units, to mount the first 'Thousand Bomber Raid' on Cologne. Most of his bombers were struggling and many of his extra crews were still trainees. But the raid was reasonably successful and made a huge propaganda splash. It was 'the biggest air raid in history' according to the world's press and it made Bert Harris a public figure as one of Britain's military commanders, and the most hated Briton in Germany – even more than Churchill. Two other 'thousand' raids were mounted with up to nine hundred aircraft involved, but getting these numbers together was very disruptive to the force as a whole, and having made the point, Harris was content to let them reside in the public's imagination while he got on with upgrading Bomber Command.

Between 1942 and 1943 Bomber Command did not add many squadrons to the overall force but as the factories turned out more aircraft, Harris was able to upgrade his forty-nine squadrons in 1943 into predominantly heavy units with the ubiquitous Lancaster bombers, an upgraded Halifax III and some specialist, Mosquito fast fighter-bombers. Meanwhile, the struggle went on with losses of four to five per cent in each raid, peaking at a disastrous twelve per cent in the Nuremberg raid in 1944. A good raid would incur losses of less than two per cent. All versions of the statistics were sobering.[3] A consistent four per cent loss rate meant that any given bomber crew had no statistical chance of surviving the tour of thirty operations, though in fact one in four of them did. On the first five operations new crews ran a ten-fold greater risk than for any other trips on their tour. At the peak of the offensive, most crews were shot down within their first five trips – which is why a quarter of the rest actually cheated the odds. But every crew lived on borrowed time when they were on operations. Every member of aircrew was a volunteer; they were generally fatalistic and rationalised their own chances. And Harris sent them on raids two, three or four nights a week, depending on the weather and the phases of the moon – a clear night with a full moon over the target was simply suicidal. But very few other conditions deterred them. Harris seemed largely mechanistic as he picked his target set of a morning from the selections his staff had analysed for him during the previous nights. He knew that high explosives should be dropped first, to blow buildings apart, then incendiaries to set them ablaze, then more high explosives to hinder the rescue efforts.

'Butch' Harris never showed much emotion as he meted out increasing brutality on German cities, and even as he committed his own men to rates of loss that would be unsustainable among ground troops. He could not admit to any doubts about the bombing campaign and could not afford to let any of the men and women he

---

3. An aircrew member of Bomber Command had a lower chance of survival than an infantry officer in the First World War. More members of Bomber Command died over the course of the war than civilians in the Blitz, or civilians in the RAF's raids on Hamburg or Dresden. The average loss rate at the peak of the offensive (November 1943-March 1944) was 5.1%. For the whole period of Bomber Command's offensive, it eventually averaged 2.2%.

commanded give way to operational – or ethical – doubts either. Harris didn't socialise in the Officers' Mess at his High Wycombe headquarters. Very few on the airfields that peppered eastern England ever saw him directly, nor did they see how hard he drove himself, or know of the progressive effects of his duodenal ulcer getting considerably worse. They didn't know he seldom went to sleep before his bombers had returned home. He slipped up once in a letter to a senior colleague who was self-pitying about casualties; 'You have no monopoly in this', he snapped, 'I only hope you may never have on your heart and conscience the load which lies on mine.' It was an entirely authentic emotion, but he seldom gave way to it outside his closest circle, and almost never in print.

In 1943 the bomber offensive swung into higher gear. At the Casablanca Conference in January 1943 the 'Combined Bomber Offensive' was sanctioned where Harris's Bomber Command and Ira Eaker's US Eighth Air Force would work together under a joint plan; US aircraft, bombing from high altitude in daylight at whatever range fighter cover for them would allow; and RAF aircraft continuing with night bombing from lower altitudes, as deep into enemy territory as their aircraft would take them. Harris and Eaker got on very well and Bomber Command made every effort to help Eaker get his initial 200 bombers installed and operational from bases all across East Anglia. The Eighth Air Force eventually built up to some 1,500 bombers by the end of 1944 with over 1,000 US fighters to protect them, in addition to the extra escorts RAF Fighter Command could add. The 'Combined Force' became huge.

But their combined strategy still pulled in two directions. The USAAF saw strategic bombing as attacking industrial choke points, like oil supply, chemical stores, ball bearings for machinery, transport hubs, and so on. Six such 'target systems' within Germany's industrial hinterland were identified for precision attack. Harris famously regarded them as 'panacea targets'; even if they could be destroyed as individual targets – which was doubtful – the German economy would not break down because of them. If oil ran short, he reasoned, Hitler's armed forces would still get whatever last dregs remained of it. He was right about the problem of hitting targets more precisely, but shaky on the cumulative effects of key industrial shortages and transport disruption. Germany's oil supply did eventually become critical in ways that affected its frontline forces, though since industrial information did not generally flow through Germany's Enigma machines, and thence to Bletchley Park's 'Ultra' decoding system, Allied intelligence could only make educated guesses about the real damage bombing was doing to the German economy. But Harris had his aerial photographs, which were dramatic, and he simply believed that the scale of immediate destruction to buildings must be having the effect on Germany's morale that the War Cabinet had originally intended.

Whatever the targeting priorities, the cumulative effect of Allied air fleets bombing Germany day and night built up steadily. In theory, the RAF and the USAAF were going after different sorts of 'strategic targets', but in reality, the effects of their raids, certainly against the German homeland, became difficult to distinguish from each other. For Harris, there were three concentrated campaigns that he characterised as 'battles' in themselves. The first was against the Ruhr, from the beginning of March to the end of July 1943 – forty-three major attacks each of between 300 and 700 aircraft with a heavy loss rate of 4.7 per cent. The end of that battle overlapped with a week-long 'battle of Hamburg' that witnessed the first firestorm, caused by the concentration of incendiaries and the sheer heat, killing 37,000 residents and injuring 180,000. Then there was the 'Battle of Berlin' that opened in November 1943 and went on relentlessly until March 1944, while the winter nights were long enough to make such deep penetration raids feasible. There were sixteen major attacks on Berlin involving over 9,000 sorties, incurring an alarming loss rate of 6.2 per cent across those sixteen raids. Bomber Command was also simultaneously addressing other immediate targets, as directed by the Combined Chiefs, where the rates of loss were somewhat lower.

The most spectacular raid in 1943 was undoubtedly on the Ruhr dams; the famous 'dambusters' operation in May that breached the Mohne and Eder dams and damaged the Sorpe with 'bouncing bombs'. It was certainly successful on the night and won Bomber Command and Harris himself enormous prestige, not least in the United States. Harris had been sceptical about the raid but was persuaded eventually to back it, though it was a classic of his 'panacea targets'. But maybe this time it would be worth the risk and effort.[4] Its success greatly boosted morale throughout Britain, for the RAF and particularly within Bomber Command. Harris was not wrong about the panacea nature of single targets like this, however. The disruptive effect on Ruhr industries was short-lived and the dams were quickly repaired. The raid's effect could have been far greater if the RAF had followed up with conventional bombing of the urgent repair efforts on the dams. If the reservoirs had been impossible to re-fill during the 1943–44 winter with the Germans struggling to get the dams repaired, the effects on Ruhr industries would have been far more severe and longer-lasting. But further attacks were ruled out on the basis of the risks involved. For a man who cared so much about tough, strategic clarity, Harris put risks ahead of advantage in this case.

Instead, his area bombing policy was approaching a climax in the combined RAF-USAAF offensive of the following year in 1944. The technologies of navigation and procedures of 'pathfinding' had matured to increase the concentration (if not the point accuracy) of bombing; numbers of available bombers grew steadily and the arrival of the P-51 Mustang aircraft allowed long-range fighter protection for US daylight raids deep into Germany. There were great successes against German fighter production facilities and communication lines, along with some dramatic and expensive failures both against cities, like the RAF's Nuremburg raid, and against point targets, like the US raid on the Henschel and Sohn engineering works in Kassel. But the allies were by then enjoying growing air superiority over their whole battlespace and the momentum of the offensive built inexorably towards a destructive climax.

From April to November 1944, however, both Bomber Command and the Eighth Air Force were put under the direct control of General Eisenhower as Supreme Allied

---

4. Harris was characteristically sceptical about many potential innovations in their early stages – the use of 'Oboe' and 'H2S' navigation and target-finders, the use of 'window' radar spoofing, the development of 'Pathfinders' to lead the bomber stream, even the potential of the excellent Mosquito aircraft when he first saw it. He was naturally suspicious of 'easy victories', but was quick to adjust his view once the value of something new was evident.

Commander, so they could address more tactical targets in the approach of the D-Day invasion of June 1944, to be followed by work with the battles for Normandy and the push into France and Belgium. Harris had no choice but to accept this, and understood the military rationale behind it, though he still thought it was all a distraction that lasted too long. To help Montgomery's forces, Caen was heavily bombed in early July. But it demonstrated (as had the USAAF's own bombing of Cassino four months earlier), that heavy bombers were too inaccurate to really help the ground forces so directly; such raids were brutal and only half-effective. Harris felt they proved his longstanding point that heavy, strategic bombers could only be used really effectively to destroy cities and bring an enemy to its knees that way. Raids against German cities still continued during these months but Harris was glad to have his force fully released in November 1944 to resume what he vehemently argued was its primary – and most effective – role in bombing Germany night and day with an ever-increasing weight of ordnance.

By this stage, Harris's many critics – not least in the Air Ministry – felt he was overestimating the effects of strategic bombing. Under Churchill's protection, he seemed to his critics to be fighting a private war both against Germany and his doubters, and that – with the exception of his USAAF colleagues – he had become detached from the collegiate group of Allied commanders doing their pragmatic best to win the war under Eisenhower's leadership. To many, even his friends, he now seemed isolated and obsessed. Charles Portal, Chief of the Air Staff, certainly understood that Harris was intrinsic to Bomber Command's role and it would be a great mistake to sack him. Portal and Harris had many a row over bombing policy, but Portal also put great effort into mediating between Harris and those determined to have bomber command play a more tactical role as the Allies advanced into Germany. His critics wanted an end to his city-centric bombing policy – a policy over which Harris was immoveable, unless directly ordered otherwise.

So city bombing went on right to the end in May 1945. Its controversial legacy has continued ever since, both in official histories and popular imagination.[5] Overall, forty-five per cent of Bomber Command's total effort went into city bombing, fifty-five per cent into all other targets. Most current analysts have tended towards the view of the eminent historian Michael Howard, who thought that Harris was essentially right – and most of his critics essentially wrong – in both his tactical and strategic judgements for the majority of his time at Bomber Command. His judgement was more questionable, says Howard, after the Battle for Normandy as Bomber Command reverted to its maximalist policy in the final seven months of the war. Among contemporary historians, Richard Overy's very detailed judgement commands great respect. He presents convincing evidence that initial conclusions about the meagre industrial effects of allied bombing on Germany made immediately after the war, and included in the official histories, were too narrowly focussed. He argues that they took too little account of the cumulative effects of the bombing on Germany's actual war

---

5. British casualties from German bombing throughout the war were about 60,000. Corresponding German casualties are estimated at 350,000–500,000.

machine; its aircraft and tank production, for example. It required the diversion of extensive manpower and equipment from the eastern front to the German home front – 55,000 anti-aircraft guns and almost a million men to operate them – the diversion of so much of the *Luftwaffe* and its future aircraft production to a home defence role, the immense cost of driving production into massive underground facilities, and so on. The glib and oft-quoted fact is that German military production trebled from 1941 to 1944. But that was a spurt that could not be repeated, and while straight German war production might have been high in 1944, the whole military infrastructure was becoming unsustainable and close to cracking long before the surrender in May 1945. Hard as German troops fought amid collapsing fronts everywhere, the bombing war destroyed their coherence as their enemies finally advanced into the homeland.

It represents a neat irony in the story of Bert Harris. Looking at the massive destruction of German cities in 1945, Harris may have felt the Allies were close to the threshold of genuinely breaking the morale of the German people. But there is little evidence the German population would cross that threshold, human nature being what it is. On the other hand, the area bombing policy did have a much greater effect on Germany's war infrastructure than even he had realised – and his reports on this matter were always upbeat. For two years, Bomber Command had fought the sort of attritional battle that often precedes a more general military breakdown. And in Richard Overy's view, the combined offensive had won the battle to dominate German airspace by the winter of 1944, had Harris only realised it. Germany's military machine was already cracking by the end of the year – notwithstanding Hitler's desperate Ardennes offensive – as allied armies closed in. Hitler's minister for armaments and war production, Albert Speer, famously wrote from prison in 1959 that the air war over the homeland, 'was the greatest lost battle on the German side', eclipsing, he said, the retreats in Russia or the surrender of Stalingrad. Harris simply didn't know that the combined bomber offensive had done its most essential work by that winter and ploughed relentlessly on during the final months. Perhaps he wouldn't have accepted any diversion even if allied intelligence had been good enough to show him then the true picture of his victory.

Of course, there was Dresden; the city bombed in February 1945 that stands for many of his critics as the symbol and proof of Harris's brutal inflexibility when his judgement was off-beam. In truth, judgements on Dresden are obscured by a number of inconvenient facts for all sides. That February the Allies had still not crossed the Rhine, while the Red Army was fighting hard in central Poland. Germany was bringing forward many of its untested 'wonder weapons' in a final bid to shock the Allies. Dresden itself *was* an arms production centre, but nothing of any real strategic importance. Dresden *was* a road and rail hub for German military forces, but so were other eastern cities. Dresden *was* filling up with civilian refugees fleeing westwards ahead of the advancing Russians, and it was the refugees that made it an attractive military target. Joseph Stalin and Red Army commanders wanted the eastern cities – Berlin, Leipzig, Dresden – bombed, precisely so the chaos among the refugees would help to inhibit German reinforcements moving eastwards to confront the Russians. British planners agreed it was a sensible military objective and added Chemnitz to the list that was then given to Harris and to Carl Spaatz, his Eighth Air Force counterpart by that time. In fact, Harris had grave doubts about Dresden as one of the targets, not because he disagreed with the rationale, but because it was such a distance, in bad winter weather and he had little intelligence about its defences or what strategic gains might actually accrue from an attack. But Churchill had testily directed in late January that 'large cities in eastern Germany' should be bombed, and in February he was at the Yalta Conference with Roosevelt and Stalin, assuring the latter that everything would be done to facilitate the Red Army's latest offensive in Poland. Berlin was first on the target list Harris and Spaatz were given, Dresden was second, despite High Wycombe having questioned it directly with the Air Ministry. Harris would rather have sent his bombers to one of the other cities on the list but the Air Staff confirmed that Dresden was to be attacked. Two days after the Yalta conference ended, the 48-hour British and American bombing of Dresden began. It encountered virtually no opposition and created another fearful firestorm on the ground. It seemed inhuman. In 2010 an independent German commission concluded from all extant evidence that among almost a million people crammed into the area, between 22,000 and 25,000 civilians had been killed in the raid (fewer than in Hamburg and nowhere near the 250,000 popularly reported at the time). The misery among the survivors was, of course, extreme as a result and the centre of the medieval city totally destroyed. The strategic benefits from the raid, as Harris had anticipated, were slight and temporary, other than the psychological blow of demonstrating to the German people that they were now completely at the mercy of the Allies. As if to emphasise the point, the USAAF attacked Dresden thrice more before the German surrender.

When the war was all over, Harris was only fifty-three, though not in good health and outraged by the way Bomber Command was immediately airbrushed out of the national picture. Churchill made a long victory broadcast a week after the official end of the war in Europe, which reflected on everything from the Battle of Britain to the fall of Berlin. He didn't once refer, even elliptically, to the bomber offensive. While the Eighth Air Force received all due credit in the United States, Bomber Command was studiously ignored in Britain, even, felt Harris, inside the Air Ministry itself. He retired from the RAF, though a popular impression was created that he had been sacked – something he found deeply humiliating.

Harris took his family to South Africa, 'leaving this grateful country and returning for keeps to my own' he observed bitterly. There, he established a successful marine freight company. Despite his five-star rank and pension, he still needed an income for all the responsibilities he had to the members of his two families. He had variable relations with his four children, and distinctly difficult relations with some of his old colleagues, not to mention the historians who buzzed around his wartime record. But his relations with old Bomber Command aircrew – 'his boys' – were never less than truly affectionate on both sides. He was back in Britain by 1953, partly to accept a baronetcy – not a peerage – at the insistence of Churchill who was now Prime Minister again. He came back, too, to fight his corner, and that of Bomber Command, for the recognition he felt was still denied. He and Jill lived at Ferry House, Goring-on-Thames – a house they could only just afford and the first house he had ever owned.

He had written his own account of the bomber offensive and he agreed to have an authorised biography produced, on condition that it be published only after his death. In fact, Harris enjoyed quite a long retirement at Ferry House, making regular winter trips with Jill to South Africa, though also fighting a running battle with 'history' to correct slights and insults he perceived in popular commentaries on Bomber Command. He died peacefully in 1984 just before his 92nd birthday and was buried quietly at Burntwood Cemetery in the local village. His authorised biography, long since completed, appeared later that year.

In June 2012 a large, neo-classical Doric memorial for Bombed Command was opened in Green Park, opposite the RAF Club at the top of London's Piccadilly. It finally commemorated the 55,573 Bomber Command aircrew who had died in the campaign. The monument was paid for, and is maintained, by public subscription. It features a well-sculpted crew of seven men just returning from a raid, their faces indicating the complex emotions they might have felt. The highlight of the opening ceremony was, of course, a Lancaster fly-past, releasing a cloud of poppy petals as the hymn was sung. It was the most affecting and authentic part of the whole ceremony – mainly because the Lancaster missed. As its bomb-bay released a dense cloud of poppy petals (perhaps half a second too early?) an eddying breeze took the red cloud away from Green Park and it drifted lazily north-east along Piccadilly. This author watched in fascination as the cloud remained largely intact until, as the hymn finished, it began to settle and disperse among the theatres, dubious establishments and watering holes of Soho. Bert Harris's boys would have enjoyed that.

34

Success in Command

History doesn't repeat itself. But as poets and analysts have oft-observed, it certainly rhymes a lot. These pen portraits of commanders spanning almost two thousand years offer military rhymes aplenty. And if they don't present hard and fast lessons – as history never does – such rhyming nevertheless suggests many insights it would be as well to keep in mind. More than any other profession, military commanders deal in life and death so there is an urge to assess their successes and failures in highly judgmental ways. And since human nature doesn't change much across millennia, comparisons between different commanders tends to become a preoccupation.

Comparing command success or failure, however, has to be judged against a 'war horizon' that is visibly ever present but, like all horizons, impossible to grasp in detail. The Duke of Wellington became very fed up over the years being constantly asked to recall and explain exactly this or that detail of his monumental fight at Waterloo. 'The history of a battle is not unlike the history of a ball', he famously said. An individual could never know, still less recollect in the right order, all that goes on in such a complex human engagement as a ball; much like the battle of Waterloo, said the Duke. Yet historians spent the next two hundred years trying to do exactly that. The elusive war horizon draws both commanders and historians towards it because the nature of warfare is essentially unchanging, yet it's characteristics – the way in which wars are actually fought – are changing all the time. And the business of command is fundamental to both the unchanging, and the constantly changing, elements of warfare. The horizon seems to be irresistibly relevant in assessing commanders, even while it mocks us for trying to compare a defensive shield wall with a defensive Spitfire.

The War Horizon

The fundamental rationale of war has remained the same down the ages and there is a rich and long literature as to why this appears to be so. Warfare is a battle of wills, embracing the capacity to kill or be killed, to impose and to endure physical suffering, in pursuit of some essentially political objective; survival itself, outright conquest, or more commonly, some mix of less extreme objectives. It is a battle of willpower in the application of lethal force. Notwithstanding an ancient and honourable tradition of pacifist thinking, the fact remains that three millennia of history (where there is some record of events) and three hundred millennia of pre-history (where there is only archeology) indicate that warfare is prevalent among *Homo sapiens*. Mankind collectively fights, or threatens to fight, in a struggle to prevail for some commonly sought, and hence political, objectives. Of course, there are anthropological explanations for warfare, lodged in a sense that our animal nature makes us predisposed to fight or display our prowess to satisfy some inner urge for identity. Certainly, from Homer's *Iliad* heroes, to Viking and Saxon warriors, and many a contemporary warlord, the urge to fight and even to enjoy the experience is part of the war horizon. So, too, is the idea that many societies in history – as in classical Greece, or the Mongol Empire – embraced warfare as entirely 'normal', even welcome, within their own corpus of beliefs. In 1959 the political scientist, Kenneth Waltz, famously posited in *Man, the State and War* that historians had generally tried to explain the prevalence of war according to anthropological theories (about man), or else to inherently political explanations (about the state). If wars were not caused by man's essential nature, then they were surely prompted by the things man chose to believe in. But more convincing still, says Waltz, is that the international world that exists between different societies is not only incapable of outlawing war, but by its very nature has no choice but to promote warfare – or at least the possibility of it – as a regulatory mechanism. Societies are prepared to fight lethally for certain things they value highly, and will never entirely eschew their right to do so. Warfare is existential; the phenomenon has an enduring consistency.

Warfare is also, by definition, a collective endeavor and it must somehow be led. Commanders are appointed or they emerge, but someone always commands, taking responsibility for the violence and the hurt involved. 'Warrior commanders' have sometimes seen in their commanding role an expression of their own identity. To judge by the sagas, many Viking warriors seem to have regarded their fighting leadership as little more than a knock-out competition for the best banqueting seats in the Halls of Valhalla. In the modern era commanders – soldiers rather than warriors for the most part – have generally felt the weight of moral responsibility on them as they try to maximize success and balance the costs, seeing themselves as servants of their kingdoms or states.

In all these respects, command embodies timeless leadership tasks. All commanders have had to look at those they are leading to consider how best to shape their attitudes to collective fighting, to steel them to the struggle, to mould them into fighting units. Commanders have to embody some legitimacy in the eyes of those they lead. This might arise from their inherited nobility, perhaps in combination with their own warriorship and fighting qualities. In the modern world, commanders more commonly have legitimacy conferred on them though rank, by the society or state for which they fight. But legitimacy is not the same as respect, and all commanders instinctively know that their ability to command effectively derives from a combination of both legitimacy and respect. Commanders don't have to be liked by their followers, though some of them certainly are. But even inaccessible and unlikable commanders will want to garner the respect of those they lead by being seen as effective or manifestly successful. In short, command involves all the timeless equations of collective psychology; the complex relationship between leadership and followership.

The other side of the command phenomenon is that the character or warfare – the ways in which it is fought – is constantly changing with every new technological and social turn of the evolutionary wheel. Developments in weapons increased lethality, from direct blows with a sword or axe, to artillery projectiles and rockets. New trends, in particular, the 'gunpowder revolution' increased the range and mobility of even direct battle and fundamentally changed the tactical perspective a commander had to adopt. It seems remarkable to many visitors how small famous battle sites appear to be. The bloodiest battle ever recorded on English soil occurred at Towton in 1461 where some 60,000 soldiers crammed into a fighting space about 500 yards long and no more than 1,000 yards wide. At Waterloo, over 200,000 men and some 60,000 horses serving them fought within an area no more than three miles long and a mile and a half wide – and most of the fighting was concentrated into a smaller area than that. By the battle of the Somme, the fighting area was far bigger. Even so, three million men engaged across a front of twenty miles that only bulged backwards about seven miles after four and a half months of campaigning. At El Alamein in 1942, however, 311,000 troops fought across a 50-mile front. The same applies in naval warfare. The fierce battle of Sluys in 1340 involved around 350 ships fighting across no more than a square mile of sea. Even Trafalgar pitched 73 ships and 47,000 men into a mêlée across only two-and-a-half miles. In 1916, Jutland, on the other hand, became a running fight between 250 ships in all, across 70 miles of the North Sea. Operations in the 1940–43 Battle of the Atlantic embraced 4,500 miles of Atlantic Ocean, from Brest to the Caribbean Sea. And the advent of airpower opened a third dimension of warfare. By the time of the Second World War, not only had 'air superiority' emerged as a key requirement for success on the ground or at sea, but long-range 'strategic bombing' – 800 miles or more from home bases – was even thought capable of rendering whatever happened on a land or sea battlefield as peripheral to the eventual outcome of a war. How does a commander with a sword on horseback relate to one with a wireless on a ship's bridge or standing before a plotting table in a big-screen operations room littered with computers?

In addition to technical advances, the fundamental character of warfare has constantly evolved with the onset of 'total war'. Of course, many ancient societies fought 'total wars' where their enemies may have been trying to eliminate them, as the Romans eventually did with Carthage, and the Carthaginians mobilized every last shred of resistance to try to prevent it. But in modern history the 'mobilization' of a whole society, even in less than dire circumstances, is a regular and more open-ended process. Napoleon's French revolutionary wars were the forerunner of modern total wars, where industrializing societies could be mobilized as a whole to fight for national objectives. Napoleon's wars also had the effect of pitching ideology as an underlying rationale that did much to shape the national objectives of subsequent European wars. The twentieth century witnessed ideologically-driven, industrial warfare on a global scale. The First World War became a modern 'total war' in every sense; the Second World War represented its destructive apotheosis, and the Cold War was a restrained form of total war that plausibly threatened complete global destruction. Though contemporary, high-tech, warfare would almost certainly be different again, the desire (and ability) to mobilise all the relevant attributes of society to achieve a satisfactory outcome in warfare appears to be constant.

Context is Everything

Even the most cursory understanding of the way wars have been fought emphasizes the fact that context is everything in the matter of evaluating military commanders. While we judge commanders on their age-old ability to understand and motivate their followers – they have to be psychologists among their troops – they also have to grasp and operate within the ever-changing technologies of war and the shifting political sands on which all military campaigns are based.

These essays have laid some stress on strategic clarity as an important dimension in judging success. But that is a modern intellectual construct. Many commanders in previous eras would not recognize a concept of 'strategy', even though they might have an intrinsic understanding of similar dynamics in their own terms. And as many of these sketches demonstrate, other commanders might be strategically clear but find themselves without the wherewithal to pursue their vision of a campaign. Few commanders ever feel they have 'enough' force to deploy but nevertheless have to operate with what they have. Other commanders have articulated clear strategic visions that simply didn't survive contact with reality as campaigns unfolded. And many others found it difficult to think in strategically consistent ways as they confronted the messy reality of day-to-day command. There are many examples of inconsistent, or otherwise deficient strategic thinking in these essays, from Harold II, Edward III and the Black Prince, to Drake, Raleigh, Raglan, Beatty or Gort. But they reacted to what was in front of them and we are judging them from the Olympian perspective of our own age. Even commanders rated here as successful – like William Marshal, Cromwell, Marlborough, Nelson, Wellington, Montgomery or Slim – were only successful some of the time. The key to capricious immortality was to be successful when it mattered, like Marshal at Lincoln in 1217, Cromwell at Naseby in 1645, Marlborough at Blenheim in 1704, or Montgomery in Normandy in 1944.

A key element of strategic clarity is a commander's assessment of what is at stake – a solid vision of what success would look like. In 60 AD Boudica's behaviour indicates she was well aware that having assaulted the Roman capital in Britannia, she had no middle ground to occupy. There could be no negotiations. Her combined tribal army would either expel the Roman legions from Britannia or be slaughtered in the attempt. And Cromwell was one of the first Parliamentarians to embrace the reality that having taken up arms against the anointed king, the war could only end with either the removal of the king or the execution of Parliamentary leaders. In some situations, fighting dispels the prospect of anything other than complete victory for one of the protagonists, and they know it.

Other military campaigns may be just as fierce but are less politically absolute. King Alfred, King Edward the Elder and Lady Aethelflaid all fought open-ended campaigns against an occupier – the Danes – just as Wellington did against Napoleon's occupying forces in the Iberian Peninsula. Anglo-Saxon nobility were fighting to unite fractured territories under a single Christian regime; Wellington was fighting to expel French invaders from Iberia as a way of weakening Napoleon's European empire. They all fought long and exhausting campaigns to secure territory, knowing they would not be striking at the military or political heart of their enemies. It would never have been clear to these commanders quite where the end-point of their wars might lie; they just had to keep fighting. From Alfred to Lady Aethelflaid, the Anglo-Saxons might have imagined that successor King Aethelstan could unite most of the peoples of 'Englaland' but could hardly have guessed that he would emerge, briefly, with an empire that embraced a new 'Britain' itself. And Wellington's army was across the Pyrenees into France in 1814 as a natural progression, pushing the French empire back, and was in Toulouse when it precipitously collapsed. It is doubtful Wellington had envisaged that sort of denouement when he first arrived in the Peninsula in 1809.

Wellington had a shrewd strategic brain. In contrast to his Peninsular War campaign, he had earlier understood very well how close he could get to the enemy's centre of power in his previous Mysore and Maratha wars in India. He created a military force – and critically, a sustainable one – that was able to attack and defeat both of them directly. The Plantagenet kings and princes featured here, by contrast, showed only fitful strategic awareness, though a good deal of cunning. For them, successful warfare was as much an expression of royal identity as an exercise in national power; which is why the Arthurian myths of honour and valour appealed so strongly. They all lived much of their lives fighting dynastic wars to unite and maintain their kingdom in Britain. That, at least, was strategically coherent. But they never got to grips with the strategic core of their French adversary during the Hundred Years War – an adversary who also did much to sow disunity inside their British kingdom. They each won stunning battlefield victories over the French but seemed not to comprehend why they couldn't win their French wars, once and for all. Henry V came closest to an era-defining strategic victory over France in 1419, but even that was illusory since by then neither France, nor England, were the mere dynastic possessions of their forbears, but rather identifiably national kingdoms. And France was over three times bigger and far richer than England. Thenceforth, no English king would ever successfully rule France, any more than an upstart Norman duke would ever again rule England and Wales. Instead, the Plantagenets largely provoked, and then fought, open-ended three-front wars in Scotland, Flanders and France for a confused mixture of dynastic and national ambitions; understandable, perhaps, in the mores of the era, but strategically doomed by modern analytical standards. And it all came crashing down in the reign of poor Henry VI and the 'Wars of the Roses' that left England on its knees before its continental neighbours.

Unlike Wellington, facing Napoleon's all-or-nothing empire across Europe that had sprung up like a firework, Marlborough had found himself fighting a more pervasive Bourbon French empire. There was no British desire to bring it down, merely to restrain its power and reach. The War of the Spanish Succession was what modern analysts might characterize as a war of 'containment'. Marlborough had a good instinct for the military centre of gravity of his opponents and was able to diminish the power that Paris could exert across the continent, but he also knew he was unable to do much about the other political centre of gravity residing in Bourbon Spain. He certainly had the strategic vision, but he ran out of money, allies, domestic support, and eventually the energy to take that part of it on.

Arthur (Bomber) Harris, by contrast, was facing the most pernicious attempt in history to create a new European empire, centred on Nazi Germany. He articulated an unshakeable faith in the power of the bomber to go straight to the enemy's heart and destroy what he regarded as the Nazi core, the major cities of Germany. Fighting anywhere else, he came to believe, would prove peripheral to Germany's defeat until Hitler's own political power was destroyed directly, through the misery of its people rendered unproductive and angry by direct bombing. Events in 1945 did not unfold in ways that proved him right – though he claimed to be – but the atom bombs dropped on Japan in August that year might have gone some way to prove his point.

At sea, Francis Drake was a great tactician who came to understand something of the nature of sea control, putting him conceptually ahead of many of his contemporaries. Nelson, in his own headstrong way, took responsibility for both tactics and strategy, seeing himself as the national saviour in the face of a hostile French empire; eventually against a full-scale invasion. He was often wrong, but he also had the good fortune to be right when it mattered most. Admiral Dudley Pound, by contrast, was no less strategically literate than Nelson, actually facing a more serious threat to Britain's existence than had Nelson. But Pound could never pull the policy levers to make his central strategic concern – winning the 'Battle of the Atlantic' – a key national priority. In the end, both he and the Royal Navy had to do it the hard way, while resources drained away to meet other priorities.

Between them, Gort, Alexander, Montgomery and Slim during Britain's Second World War, represent the full spectrum of shifting strategic contexts. All four of them had an intimate acquaintance with war on the Western Front or in the Levant and extensive wounds to prove it. Gort was never much of a strategist, but was presented with a losing hand in the 1940 Battle of France. Alexander strategized through the complete swing of the pendulum, from unavoidable defeats in 1940 and 1941 to accumulating victories in 1943, 1944 and 1945, without ever rising above his immediate campaign objectives. Montgomery, by contrast, benefited hugely from the upward swing of the victory pendulum as he assumed high command. He saw in his campaigns, from Alam Halfa to Arnhem, a national strategy that went straight from the sands of Egypt to the German heartland itself. His campaigns – at least in his own mind, if not quite in reality – were about defeating German armies and putting post-war Britain in an advantageous position in the world. His frustration was that he no longer commanded the resources to achieve this; only as an adjunct to American power. As Jonathan Fennel observed in *Fighting the People's War*, Britain was 'unable to win a short war, unable to sustain a long one'. Montgomery, with his curious mixture of vision and self-delusion, was caught on the horns of this dilemma. Bill Slim made many mistakes in his early command career, but learned from them and eventually showed an unerring instinct for the Japanese centre of gravity in the Burma campaign. With the excellent Fourteenth Army he had created, Slim was able to manufacture the resources to make his Burma strategy work. He was Britain's best Second World War commander. The irony of Slim's record was that he strategized for the campaign in front of him, but like Wellington in the Peninsular War, it was not central to the defeat of his enemy. Japanese militarism and its empire, the 'South-east

Asia Co-Prosperity Sphere', would not be brought down by defeat in Burma, however decisively Tokyo lost that particular campaign.

The Virtues of the Successful

With so many moving parts in the evaluation of a commander's success, it can never be more than a pedant's parlour-game to try to rank them from best to worst across different historical eras; though there are shelves stacked with books that cannot resist playing the game. Nevertheless, within their own particular contexts, the good commanders – those whom for some periods in their careers experienced real success – displayed some interesting characteristics in their accomplishments.

One is the virtue of incisive decision-making. Indecisive and tentative commanders tend to create confusion and despondency among those around them. Of course, commanders may have good reason to watch and wait, keeping several options open for as long as possible. But when the moment comes to decide, they must be clear and confident in their choices and convey that to their followers. King Stephen and the Empress Matilda who fought each other for years during 'the anarchy' of the twelfth century were both courageous in their own ways, but also indecisive and capricious at some key moments for them both. In the end, they deserved each other. In the Crimean War, Lord Raglan excited affectionate pity among his staff as he struggled to grip events and control the wild inadequacies of some of his principal cavalry and infantry commanders. His leadership style was 'consultative' but ultimately tentative while his orders were frequently ambiguous. The whole Crimea campaign drifted into a miserable political stalemate.

Another virtue is the force of personality. Commanders exhibit the same multiplicity of character traits as everyone else. Some are extrovert, some introverted, some thoughtful with a rich intellectual hinterland, some single-minded warriors with little but war on their minds. Successful commanders don't try to be someone they're not. Followers are intrinsically interested in the person leading them and quickly develop a pretty accurate picture of their leader's personality. Walter Raleigh was forever trying to appear as someone he wasn't – though in his case no one, including Raleigh himself, seemed sure about the authentic person. Drake, on the other hand, was completely authentic to his men and much the more effective commander for it. Admiral John Jervis occasionally tried to appear to his sailors to be someone unlike his severe and disciplinary self, but he was no charismatic commander and his real skills were not in battle leadership anyway. He was happy to be feared by his sailors, but didn't get the best from them. Jervis was, however, intrinsic to the future of the navy and to the career of the young Nelson, and Nelson was a commander who – eventually – attracted the love of all who followed him. Nelson's men performed excellently when it was most important. Kitchener and Haig were distant from their troops – both imperious figures who made no attempts to be soldiers' soldiers, despite their own personal accomplishments on the fields of battle. They attracted natural respect, though little affection until later on – posthumously in Kitchener's case – but that was enough to make them effective at the time. The same might be said of Hugh

Dowding and 'Bomber' Harris; distant and technocratic commanders during their key strategic campaigns, but displaying judgements that were trusted at the time and heartily applauded by their followers afterwards.

Admiral Cochrane's eccentric career probably summarizes the essential point about leadership personality. Cochrane was never anyone but his highly distinctive and pugnacious self. He was loved and revered by everyone he commanded directly and yet heartily detested by many of his own rank, and almost all his superiors. Cochrane was a spectacularly successful battle commander but a man of clearly unfulfilled potential at any higher command level; a volatile personality effectively out of control when he had a campaign, rather than a ship, to command. In being 'themselves', commanders have to be the *best version* of themselves to others, not, as in Cochrane's case, the high-handed and capricious expression of the man. Wellington's armies knew that the Duke was shrewd, cunning and methodical, not naturally charismatic, and they respected those qualities in him. Montgomery was criticized by many as a cynical 'performer' in front of his troops, but that is unfair. His charisma with them flowed from his own genuine self-confidence and his certainty of success. It was at least one genuine part of his otherwise unattractive personality. Slim became charismatic to his troops in a quite different way; modest, unassuming and just as certain and reassuring that events would work out as he planned. That was *his* best version of his stocky, tough, thoughtful and reliable self.

A third personal virtue observed in commanders when they enjoy success might be described as 'emotional military intelligence' – to be distinguished from most people's understanding of 'emotional intelligence' – as that which helps a military leader be a successful mass psychologist among his or her followers; with an instinct, too, for what is likely in the minds and hearts of the enemy. Montgomery is an excellent example of this very particular type of intelligence. His natural emotional intelligence appeared to all who knew him as very low. He was rude, tactless and insensitive, without generally realizing it. But in military terms, he had something special. He knew from his own battle experience what soldiers could and couldn't achieve. He knew, too, that he was leading a conscript army, not a force of professional soldiers, and there was only so much any general could expect of them. He firmly believed that in principle there were no bad soldiers, only bad officers. Harold Alexander was the same, though he was a man with high emotional intelligence, so the contrast between his personal and military sensitivities was not as dramatic as Montgonery's. Admiral Collingwood shared some of that sharp contrast noted in Montgomery. But Collingwood was not at all an insensitive man. He was personally most warm, but quiet and introspective though with a great natural understanding of the dynamics of battle and the reactions of ordinary seamen to them. Like all good commanders, he prioritized the welfare of his subordinates and the ordinary fighters he commanded, and it showed. Nelson – extrovert, vain and passionate – displayed exceptional emotional military intelligence after his earlier, less popular, command behaviour. He learned quickly. By contrast, the Empress Matilda and King Edward I never showed much emotional intelligence at all. They led their forces with a sense of personal entitlement that took little account of what they were asking of their soldiers. Edward III and the Black Prince were far more skilful and had the knack of making themselves popular with the troops – something Henry V during his brief career as a charismatic commander seemed to do quite naturally. If Henry's strategies were deficient, his understanding of his army, of how and why they fought for him, was evidentially acute. So, too, was Cromwell's. In seventeenth-century Britain Cromwell tapped into a wellspring of religious loyalty to the cause of god-fearing freedom, that allowed him and Thomas Fairfax to create – briefly as it turned out – the most effective and successful army in Europe. General John Moore showed that he knew how to motivate his men; how to train and professionalize them, and lead them by example in battle. His ultimate failure at Corunna was occasioned largely by personal pride and strategic overreach, which negated his other virtues as a naturally gifted commander. And in the eternal comparison between Admirals Jellicoe and Beatty and the legacy of Jutland in 1916, it might be said that the extrovert Beatty, popular with his sailors, nevertheless led his forces with less emotional military intelligence than the introverted and conventional Jellicoe, who knew what his various ships' crews could accomplish and instinctively made the right calls at the right time.

Many successful commanders achieve early career recognition through acts of gallantry and the luck of personal survival. The best of them seem able to translate their experiences to understanding the psychology of those they lead in the special circumstances of war; they have genuine empathy with the military profession. After all, in warfare commanders must convince their troops to act against their human instincts, putting themselves in extreme danger and being prepared to kill others. Only some of this counter-intuitive behaviour can be ordered and enforced from above. Mostly it has to be encouraged and socialized within fighting units themselves. Good commanders at all levels tend to develop this rather specific variation on emotional intelligence; understanding they will be sending some of their number to their deaths but having the instinct and skill to persuade them to take their chances and go anyway. There is a vital moral component in this motivation. King Alfred and Lady Aethelflaid represented a truly sacred cause in fighting the Danes, no less than Arthur Harris and Bill Slim stressed the moral necessity of victory over the most evil forces of the twentieth century. Even in less extreme cases commanders still have to represent to their followers the moral justification for their own leadership. Royal entitlement or mere rank is usually not enough. Even loot and war booty tends to motivate only small numbers of fighters for a limited time. But good commanders have the knack of casting themselves genuinely as the instrument of some higher cause – and all the better if booty and reward is involved. Poor commanders either cannot do it, or assume that they, themselves, are sufficient cause for their troops to act against their own natural inclinations.

A fourth characteristic observed among successful commanders is their organizational ability. That would apply to any manager of a major scheme or enterprise – the ability to devise policy and see it through in a process of bureaucratic implementation. But in military affairs that becomes a particular challenge, not least because an enemy will be trying to prevent the normal implementation process by forceful and murderous means. Campaigns and battles are naturally chaotic. No plan, it is said, survives first contact with the enemy. 'Plans', said General Eisenhower, acknowledging that very fact, 'are worthless; but planning is everything'. Many commanders have proved themselves intellectually lazy or complacent, or have fatally underestimated their enemy and are easily thrown into chaos and crisis at their headquarters. Good commanders tend to be meticulous planners, and then good adapters once the fog of war inevitably descends on any battle area. Logistics are always critical – which is where good pre-planning pays off; and tactical adaptation is always required – which is where intellectual flexibility and trustworthy, rapid, staff work comes into its own. Duke William (the Conqueror) was good at both throughout his fighting career, and though Hastings in 1066 was not his best performance as a commander, it showed the value of his invasion preparations alongside his ability to think clearly throughout the din of battle. Marlborough and Wellington were great planners and both showed an attention to detail that kept the implementation machinery attuned to what they had ordered. They knew, too, that simply issuing orders would not guarantee that something gets done; it was necessary to create staffs who were good enough to understand and share the 'commander's intent' and keep the bureaucratic machinery moving in that direction. But both could fight very flexibly when the need arose. Montgomery thought he had the same ability, but his planning skills were stronger than his battle management. He kept his head when things went wrong, but his tactics were less agile than he always claimed.

Military staff colleges make frequent reference to the works of Carl von Clausewitz and the (shadowy, possibly apocryphal) Sun Tsu in teaching battle preparation and the need to create preponderant forces to manoeuvre, overwhelm or simply frighten an adversary out of a position. Military leaders who prefer more pithy versions of these injunctions simply say that commanders should avoid getting their troops into a fair fight. Forethought and planning are an important part of the process by which a commander arranges to fight on very unfair terms – to the enemy. Even a desperate 'backs to the wall' campaign may depend on making it an unfair fight somewhere; to find a pressure point where the enemy is at a clear disadvantage.

In assessing the skills of commanders, there is a fifth characteristic the most successful have exhibited; namely their ability to think and operate up and down the range of senior command levels in war. Modern military analysis defines three prevalent strata of command. First is the tactical level, covering what happens on the immediate battlefield – land, sea or air – and the ability of commanders to use their forces effectively, to direct them, supply them, to concentrate them at the right moment, and so on. Successful tactical commanders normally have 'a good eye' for the ground, or the sea state, and they often show an inbuilt feel for the dynamics of a military manoeuvre or a battle. Blenheim was a tough slogging match, but Marlborough instinctively knew when it was right to risk one flank and make a big push across the whole front. Francis Drake, unlike his immediate superior, knew when the key moment arrived at Gravelines during the Armada campaign. And, with the exception of Newbury in 1644, Oliver Cromwell had a quite uncanny grasp of the ebb and flow of fighting. It was almost as if he were able to stand above a battle site and see it more clearly than anyone else. He may have attributed this to divine guidance, but it was more likely the product of sharp intelligence allied to a disciplined imagination.

The next stratum of command is referred to as the operational level, generally covering the campaign area or a whole theatre of operations – the Plantagenets' French territories, the Royal Navy's struggle to control the Mediterranean in the Napoleonic wars, Douglas Haig's Western Front in the First World War, Harold Alexander's 15th Army Group campaign to liberate Italy in 1944, and so on. Being able to see, and control, a campaign incisively is the essence of operational level command; knowing which battles to fight or avoid, how to allocate scarce resources to competing priorities across a broad theatre of operations, having a clear and realistic vision of how success can be achieved in that particular theatre. King Alfred appears to have lost, or failed decisively to win, the majority of the twenty or more battles we know he must have fought against the Danes. We don't know much about his tactical acumen, though it must at least have been reasonable. But he was infinitely superior to the Danes in his operational level grasp. He developed a system that created defence in depth across his kingdom, that put his society on a permanent war footing, and that stretched Danish manpower and made it impossible for them to settle peacefully into their conquests. The Danes assumed that winning battles settled matters, but Alfred out-thought them and won decisively his long campaign to secure the future of a Christian Wessex.

The highest stratum of military command is expressed as the strategic level; meaning the objectives of a war – perhaps to fend off an enemy and merely survive, perhaps to destroy an enemy completely, perhaps to contain an adversary, or to secure other objectives worth fighting for. The strategic level of command naturally shades into the political, where commanders have to balance strictly military with broadly political interests. In medieval Europe, where kings and princes were the senior military commanders, the military and political was expressed through their own persons – perhaps why the Plantagenets consistently confused military victory with political gain. But successful commanders have a knack of understanding the strategic level objectives and naturally fit their operational objectives around them. Throughout his career, in India and in Europe, Wellington showed an innate ability to do this, as did Marlborough at his military peak. So, too, did the much-neglected Admiral Collingwood after Trafalgar, when he ran the whole Mediterranean theatre – sea and land – in line with his shrewd understanding of Britain's national military priorities. And Nelson, of course, grabbed the national maritime strategy as his own once he had been lionized after the 1798 Battle of the Nile. The RAF's Hugh Dowding and Arthur Harris were both maligned at the time for their tactics and many critics also felt they had insufficient grip at their respective operational levels; they were both thought to be missing important opportunities to do better – Dowding in 1940 and Harris in 1944. But in both cases, their focus was almost exclusively at the strategic level; to frustrate an invasion in 1940 and to crack the Third Reich's heartland in 1944. They both saw themselves, correctly, as strategic level commanders; it was their essential rationale. As such, they were both pitched into the politics of the wartime government and they each suffered for it. Dowding was proved unambiguously correct, while Harris's success has remained debatable. Meanwhile, poor Admiral Dudley Pound was dragged endlessly through the dilemmas of command between 1940 and

1943 at the tactical, operational and strategic levels without sufficient control over any of them, while his navy performed sub-optimally.

It is evident that successful commanders are able to perform well at more than one of these three levels simultaneously. For all his personal integrity, John Gort was genuinely accomplished only at the tactical level of command – and sometimes not even then, with all his fussy distractions. But most successful commanders show a flair for two of these levels – the top two or the bottom two – and the most successful, like Cromwell, Marlborough, Nelson and Wellington, range easily across all three. Montgomery is an interesting case. His own intensely-focused military studies and his role as a gifted instructor gave him a detailed appreciation of battle tactics. Though in the battles that really mattered, his own tactics were hardly flawless. He was an excellent planner but didn't seem to possess the same talents of battle management as Bill Slim or even Harold Alexander, who were both contemporaries. Montgomery was naturally good at the top two levels of command – operational and strategic awareness – though with one big caveat. His operational interpretations of a campaign were almost always spot on, and he could see instinctively how they did (as in North Africa, Normandy and north-west Europe) or didn't (as in Italy) fit into the war strategy of defeating Germany as quickly as possible. The caveat lay in his personal inability to work more effectively with other commanders and the politicians whose business naturally involved them in the two higher levels. He was much better at understanding those elevated levels of command than enacting them. Personality really matters in command, not just among the troops, but within the broader reaches of leadership too. Politicians tend to defer to generals on military matters. But as Haig, Kitchener and Montgomery all discovered, it is as well for generals to defer to politicians when operating at the strategic level.

Finally, and perhaps most pervasive of all in these essays, is the role of sheer luck in command. Almost all successful commanders are lucky to have been at an appropriate age and rank to take command of armed forces when it makes a difference. Many gifted individuals are too young, or too old, to be propelled into the key command positions when history calls. For some, like Lord Raglan, Dudley Pound, and perhaps John Gort, command at a particular moment in history became a dutiful curse they didn't seek. And medieval kings had no career choices to make; military command was an intrinsic part of their lifelong job; probably welcome to Edward I, Edward III and Henry V, but very unwelcome, one suspects, to Edward II, Richard II, and almost certainly to Henry VI. But most commanders willingly embrace their moments of military authority. Some – like Boudica, King Alfred, Cromwell or Nelson – had a sense of manifest destiny, while others – like Wellington, Jellicoe or Haig – were performing a patriotic duty. Many were broken by the strains of it and went to early deaths.

Nevertheless, all successful commanders are lucky to be 'there' in the first place; lucky to be the right age at the right moment, and lucky to have survived the youthful gallantry that often brought them early recognition. So many of the commanders included in this collection came close to death in their early years and most carried some serious wounds into later life. How many brave and gifted individuals – potentially great leaders – one wonders, were not lucky enough to survive their first engagements? We might describe all this as the 'structural luck' of the successful commander.

But there is also the even greater element of 'contingent luck' in campaigns and battles. Like sport, military engagements can turn either on overwhelming circumstances or else tiny margins and snap, instinctive, decisions. The highly successful Australian cricket captain, Ritchie Benaud, was always being asked the secret of his success. His famous answer was that 'It's 90 percent luck and 10 percent talent – but don't try it unless you've got the 10 percent'. That rings true. So, too, does another, anonymous, sporting cliché; 'the harder you train, the luckier you get'. When a team plays well, everything appears to be going for it; when it plays poorly, often everything appears stacked against it. Discussions about fortune in sport, no less than in war, tend towards the extremes. Some accept the critical role of fortune in the outcome and are simply fatalistic about it. Others argue that good teams 'make their own luck', but that is merely a *non sequitur*. Reality hovers somewhere in the middle and successful commanders have a way to deal with luck and random chance. Put simply, they find ways to ride their bad luck and are not destroyed by it, and they recognize and ruthlessly exploit their good luck.

No commanders have blameless records in dealing with the contingent fortunes of war. But the most successful show great resilience in adversity, even defeat itself. They seem to stamp their personality on their own fortunes. Self-belief is critical and must be communicated to a leader's forces. As George Patton wrote in 1944, military leadership requires the capacity for 'telling somebody who thinks he is beaten that he is not beaten'. The fickle fortunes of war, however, are never under the control of even the strongest command personalities. Harold II ruthlessly exploited his good luck when he found the Danes unprepared to face his attack at Stamford Bridge in 1066. Then, eighteen days later, he spurned his good fortune when he found Duke William of Normandy had effectively bottled himself up at Hastings in anticipation of the battle to come. All Harold had to do was keep William contained for a few days while he waited for the reinforcements that would have given him a heavy numerical advantage. Having played fortune's fool, Harold lost the battle by the narrowest of margins – perhaps one arrowhead – as if fate itself wanted to punish him for its rejection. William Marshal certainly recognised his good fortune in 1217 when he saw that the invading French had split their forces between Lincoln and Dover. It was the only lucky break the royalist forces got in that war and Marshal took it immediately in the ferocious battle of Lincoln that – still largely unrecognized – secured the Angevin-Plantagenet future of England. Nelson was an outrageous rider of fortune. He never let his persistent illnesses or troublesome wounds deflect him from his 'destiny', or even his mixture of miscalculation and ill-luck at Copenhagen – which he turned into a political success. And when Admiral Villeneuve made a fatal tactical error off Cape Trafalgar in 1805, Nelson's opportunity was less than ideal and clearly risky, but he didn't hesitate, plunging his force into the type of battle he had long envisaged. Or again, after the first full engagement at Jutland in 1916 Admiral Jellicoe had the good fortune to have the German High Seas Fleet blunder straight into him a second time in an ideal position to be pummeled by his ships. After ten minutes the German fleet turned away and Jellicoe then faced the ill-fortune of fading evening light if he was to initiate a chase into the dark with all the attendant risks of torpedo attacks. If Beatty had been in command, he would certainly have tried to exploit his fleet's fortuitously good position. But Jellicoe was more troubled by the risks posed in the unfortunate timing of the encounter and instead, turned his ships away. Bill Slim admitted to making a couple of operational level mistakes in the Imphal battles of 1944 – he left it almost too late to move his 17th Indian Division north, and he had no cover at all for the vital logistics hub at Dimapur. That alone could have doomed his campaign. He was extremely lucky that Japanese commanders ignored a prize that might so easily have fallen into their hands, concentrating, illogically, on Imphal and Kohima instead. Once Kohima hung on and the danger to Dimapur passed, the Fourteenth Army's logistical superiority bore down relentlessly on the retreating Japanese. Slim aggressively exploited his luck and made the enemy pay dearly for their mistakes.

Successful commanders have an understanding that warfare is a highly structured process which also creates naturally chaotic outcomes. The military is ultimately trained, as they say, 'to kill people and break things'. It is designed to provoke chaos, and battle always throws up unpredictable and often unexpected outcomes. Not least, warfare has catastrophic effects on individuals. In all the chaos, fortune is dictated by the gods of war. In determining the outcome of a battle, the gods are intrinsically interested in how many die, and where. But they are completely indifferent to the choice of who dies, and how. Any natural justice in that matter is purely accidental. It is surely an overstatement made by many experienced commanders – though not in itself untrue – that the side which wins a battle, a campaign, or even a war, is the one that makes the fewest command mistakes.

35

Contemporary Command and Modern Commanders

These essays have sketched a collection of Great British Commanders and viewed them through an unashamedly twenty-first century lens; seeking to understand leaders then, by how we would judge them now. This is, of course, not only bad history but very unfair. One hopes, however, it may provide some analytical consistency between different cases. And it leads us to wonder whether the experience of these commanders has relevance to command in the contemporary world. It's a good question. To address it, this author spoke to a number of modern British military figures who had all experienced high-level, operational battle command during their own careers.[1]

---

1. **General Sir Richard Barrons**, former Commander of Joint Forces Command, whose combat command experience included the Balkans, Northern Ireland, Iraq after 2003 and Afghanistan after 2006. **Air Vice Marshal Sean Bell**, former commander of the Harrier Force, whose combat command career included operations in Former Yugoslavia, Iraq and three tours in Afghanistan. **Lord (Richard) Dannatt**, Former Chief of the General Staff, whose combat command career included Northern Ireland in the 1970s, Bosnia 1994 and Kosovo 1999. **Lt Gen Sir Robert Fry**, formerly Commandant, Royal Marines, whose combat command experience included Northern Ireland, Iraq from 2003 and Afghanistan from 2006. **Lt Gen Sir Graeme Lamb**, Director of Special Forces and former Commander of Land Forces, whose combat command experience included Northern Ireland, the Gulf War 1991, Iraq from 2003 and Afghanistan from 2001 and again in 2006. **Lord (David) Richards of Herstmonceux**, former Chief of the General Staff and former Chief of the Defence Staff, whose combat command experience included Northern Ireland, East Timor 1999, Sierra Leone in 1999–2000 and Afghanistan after 2006. **Lord (Nicholas) Houghton of Richmond**, former Chief of the Defence Staff, whose previous combat command experience included service in Northern Ireland, with NATO's Allied Rapid Reacion Corps and in Iraq from 2005. **Lt Gen Sir Simon Mayall**, former Deputy Chief of Defence Staff (Operations) and Senior Advisor on the Middle East to the Ministry of Defence, whose combat command experience included the Gulf War 1991, Kosovo 2001, and Iraq in 2006–7. **General Sir Nicholas Parker**, formerly Commander Land Forces and commander of British forces in Afghanistan, whose combat command career included Northern Ireland, East Timor 1999, Sierra Leone 2000, Iraq 2003 and Afghanistan 2009–10. **Air Marshal Edward Stringer**, Former Director General, Joint Force Development and DG of the Defence Academy, whose combat command career included the Gulf War 1991, the no-fly-zones in Iraq, the Balkans, Afghanistan, Iraq after 2003 and Libya from 2011. **General Sir Peter Wall**, former C-in-C Land Forces and later Chief of the General Staff, whose combat command career included the Balkans and Iraq from 2003–5. **Lord (Alan) West of Spithead**, former First Sea Lord and Chief of Naval Staff, whose combat command career included commanding HMS *Ardent* during intensive combat in the Falklands War, 1982, and later the enforcement of a no-fly-zone over Iraq in 1996. **Lt Gen Sir Barney White-Spunner**, former Commander of the Field Army, whose combat command career included operations in Macedonia 2001, Afghanistan in 2002, Iraq in 2003 and 2008.

Two simple questions dominated these conversations. One was whether modern commanders felt there were some eternal verities in the business of military command – something as important to them as it would have been to Alexander the Great, Napoleon Bonaparte or Marlborough. A second was to discuss in what respects twenty-first century command requirements are categorically different from previous eras. Does the contemporary world throw up real conceptual challenges for a military commander – that is, *categorically* new challenges – in the sense that they would simply have been beyond the imaginings of a previous era commander, let alone beyond his or her ability to deal with them?

On the first question, contemporary commanders have no doubts. Human nature is sufficiently consistent that the necessary virtues of an Alexander the Great leading his troops are just as relevant in the twenty-first century. It is one of the eternal verities of military history that successful commanders have to have *something* – and it comes in all shapes and sizes – that motivates their followers to be prepared to kill or be killed in the cause. 'The cause' may be powerful, but it is seldom enough in itself to drive forces to victory if troops feel poorly commanded, badly led, simply taken for granted or neglected. Even if the cause is nothing more than war booty, successful commanders embody their commitment to the victories that will achieve it and their own personal identification with its worth and importance. A commander's personal honour features highly in what constitutes the 'something' that gives 'the cause' meaning. In previous eras it might have been the legitimacy of the royal person, or sheer warriorship. But one way or another, successful leaders are able to identify themselves with the motives of others to fight. That is why there is often great theatricality in successful leadership, even if some of it is only quietly demonstrative, or even contrived merely for effect. And reputation matters. A commander who has a prior reputation as a 'winner' – deserved or not – already has an advantage in the 'something' he or she must project to others.

'Leading' and 'commanding', it is universally agreed by practitioners, are different things. Leading can be done by committee. Commanders should certainly listen and consult, but ultimately command is about making personal judgements and standing by them. Commanders have to have the confidence to lead; to make the judgements that may cost the lives of others, to give their personality to the action in question. 'Command is all about you', said one retired general who had a reputation for success. 'You're a commander all the time. There's no let-up from it – 24/7, 365 days a year – you're in charge and the boys and girls expect you to represent them, make choices, and command them. They have expectations of you as much as you have of them'. It is emphatically a two-way process, he said. 'Serve to Lead' has been the official motto of the Royal Military Academy Sandhurst since 1947. 'No three words have ever mattered more, or for longer, to the British military', said the general.

Others express that key quality of reciprocal respect as having 'faith in the instrument'. All commanders have to build an instrument for what they are required to do. They are given control of a certain set of forces and a force structure, but they nevertheless need to shape that toward whatever the task may be. As one commander put it, 'You have to create the instrument, believe in it, and convey your confidence to others so that they believe in it too.' As Harold Alexander or Bill Slim demonstrated in their own long military careers, no less than King Alfred or William Marshal, that also requires genuine honesty in the case of failure and defeat; the ability to rise from it and learn from failure without also losing the self-confidence to continue to command. That is one of the differences between 'commanding' as opposed merely to 'leading'. More than mere leaders, successful military commanders have a way of keeping their followers motivated in times of defeat. Some commanders, of course, never recover from defeat, or else are not granted by history the opportunity 'to fall to rise'.

Not least, all contemporary commanders agreed on the role of fortune in war and in their own career success. At the individual level, the vicissitudes of history, said one, may place a person in a situation where, there and then, at that precise moment, they perform an act of great gallantry or leadership and are duly rewarded for it. On another day they might not have acted like that. Or someone else, a few seconds later on that day, might have done the same. But it was them, there, on that day. The fact is, good commanders know they are never in control of the outcome; they ride their luck and the luck of others and take their chances. 'You are', said one general who had been in several firefights, 'always wrestling with chaos'.

All such insights seem to hold true for the fundamentals of command over the centuries. Attitudes to leadership change in different eras. The 'serve to lead' motto has sometimes been ridiculed in modern management courses. The principles of military command go in and out of fashion among other sectors of society, particularly in the business world. But the military profession is special; the most central relationships between command leadership and military followership, say the practitioners, are effectively timeless, even when they are expressed according to the mores of different eras.

Conceptual differences about the nature of modern warfare, however, those that lie beyond the powers of imagining, are much more troublesome for contemporary military thinkers. The celebrated historian A.J.P Tayor once wrote that if Napoleon had been brought back to life to survey the First World War in 1914, he would not have been surprised by any of it. It would all have been perfectly understandable to him. But if he had been brought back to view the war in 1917 or 1918, he would have been simply unable to comprehend it – what was driving it, how it was being fought, what it all meant. War takes place on the fault-lines of international society and it always drives change, even when the most conservative forces appear to be victorious. In conversation, all the commanders consulted for this chapter agreed that the modern conceptual challenges of war were considerable but didn't all agree that they were necessarily different in a *categorical* sense from what had gone before.

All agreed, however, that successful commanders show an ability to understand and grasp the precise nature of the warfare of their own era. But the ways in which warfare has changed in the present, digital age are more difficult to agree on because of the truly innovative nature of digital technology and its exponential growth in less than a generation. Some commanders feel this is just an example of 'modernism' which is always with us; others that it represents something none of them can adequately encompass within the limits of their own imagination.

The Hologram of Warfare

Certainly, the twenty-first century practitioners agree that the conceptual shape of warfare can no longer be presented as some two-dimensional form in a graphic; it defies even a three-dimensional model. Modern warfare suggests a more dynamic and ever-changing version of its form. If it could be represented visually it would resemble something closer to a hologram or at least a shape-shifter. The contemporary warfare that commanders now have to grapple with is both hugely expanded – beyond the imaginings of any mid-twentieth century commander – and yet also highly compressed in ways previous commanders might just about have imagined, but probably never assumed possible. And contemporary warfare oscillates constantly between the poles of expansion and compression as it runs along the widening fault-lines of our contemporary global society.

Warfare has never covered so broad a spectrum of social and human activity. Nothing is as real as a bullet wound, an explosion, a burn or a dose of nerve gas. By its nature, warfare could hardly be more tangible to the individual. But the forces that enable such destructive power arise from a widening horizon that shades into the shadowy and ephemeral. On the one hand, the direct ordnance of war has not changed very much in a century. It is mainly a combination of kinetic projectiles from the very small to the very large, explosives, fire, gas or even radiation. But the application of such traditional ordnance – how and where it is applied – has entered intangible realms of technology that don't flow intrinsically from any headquarters, and don't originate in the military. Rather, the military headquarters tries to tap into those parts of different independent processes it has some power to access.

So, for example, twenty-first century wars in Syria, Iraq or Ukraine featured scenes as traditional as men and women hunkered down in muddy trenches in the midst of winter. But they were targeted by aerial weapons navigated from GPS space satellites, and based on intelligence derived from satellite images, or mobile phone emissions, or the triangulation of completely disconnected information brought together and interpreted by the apparently unlimited power of AI – artificial intelligence. Physical infrastructure can be attacked in modern war in much the same way that Bomber Command tried to attack German infrastructure in the 1940s, though in this case using missiles and drones instead of waves of aircraft. But infrastructure is also repeatedly attacked by something as intangible as cyber-power that has no geographical base, or by misinformation designed to provoke panicked citizens of an enemy country to overwhelm some of their own infrastructure.

AI already has the ability to create a 'single synthetic environment' – a dynamic model in detail of how another society works; its electricity grid, water supply, cash and credit systems, traffic lights, rush-hour flows, transport timetables, retail food distribution; indeed, everything that makes it function as a city or a state. The all too tangible human misery of winter cold or food shortages as a weapon of war can be enabled by the essentially ephemeral powers of the cyber domain or the self-learning abilities of AI, which give effect to human intentions in ways it decides for itself. AI is on the verge of exploiting a new revolution in quantum computing. As AI and quantum computing begin to feed from each other, blockchain will probably be one of the driving mechanisms. Blockchain is far from just a device to create cryptocurrencies; it's a revolutionary development using the world wide web to aggregate huge amounts of information in a way that is at once distributed and anonymous and for that very reason, is always accurate. It has no central validator, only its own distributed consistency, and the wider and bigger it becomes, the tighter its self-validation. Blockchain offers a system integrity beyond the reach of human intervention. As anonymous as it is, blockchain has the potential to be a fearsome enabler of warfare.

These are dizzying prospects and for the operational theatre commander, having to look 'below' at the battle tactics involved where mobile phones may play a role, and 'above', at the strategic context of the whole operation where computing revolutions seem to be tripping over each other, this spectrum of battle is, to say the least, a considerable intellectual challenge.

It's a widening challenge, too, in other ways because wars involving advanced societies have to be fought more intensely at home as much as they are fought abroad or on the battlefield. The internet is only forty years old, but even its current applications and innovations – through its multiple information channels, social media and the digital society it facilitates – have made every modern country vulnerable to misinformation and manipulation on a greater scale than could ever have been contemplated in the last century. Official information sources or mainstream news channels have to compete with a cacophony of privately generated information and opinion that is easily manipulated and can be carefully targeted by an adversary to undermine domestic commitment to a military cause. More or less everything that truly happens in a battlespace, and quite a lot that isn't true, finds its way into the blizzard of information, images, ideas and opinion that accompany military activities of any sort.

Modern commanders know that a governmental 'news blackout' on military operations might buy them some limited time in which military operations can be shielded from view. But that soon wears off in the world of 'open-source intelligence', where even amateur analysts can access good satellite imagery and commercial tracking data for aircraft and ships which they share with an anonymous community of fellow enthusiasts. This works against military commanders in autocratic states just as much as in democratic ones. In a sense, every state fighting an international war has also to fight its own civil war. For advanced societies, that has become an intrinsic part of the 'strategic' level of command; the impacts of war on domestic society connect more directly than ever before into what happens on the battlefield.

The hologram of war, therefore, enlarges and diffuses as it encompasses a uniquely wide spectrum of domains. It all adds to the responsibilities of command. But the hologram also shimmers with the perversely opposite effect that this widening of the spectrum is accompanied by the phenomenon of extreme compression in other respects.

What might be described as the challenge of 'strategic compression' simultaneously faces modern commanders. Twenty-first century technologies have the effect of compressing the time, space and functions in which military power is exercised across these widening domains. Military operations get rolled into a tight ball of interactions and cascading consequences that are inherently difficult for one person, or one staff organization, to comprehend. Though if they can remain in control of it, strategic compression also offers some advantages. It loads the dice of command heavily in favour of the most agile operators.

In 2000, David Richards – then a brigadier – was given responsibility for a limited operation to protect, or evacuate, British and ex-patriot nationals from war-torn Sierra Leone. It's an interesting example of a mission that Brigadier Richards extended somewhat when he arrived in-theatre, assuming the best way to protect foreign non-combatants was to put the rightful President back in his palace and snuff out the vicious rebels and gangs who had taken hold of the country. Richards had different elements at his disposal which he had to operate as a joint 'rapid reaction force'. He had to work with west African allies and the United Nations, make new allies in Sierra Leone who were frankly no more than bandits in different gangs, and keep politicians in London informed – but sufficiently at arms-length not to constrain his operational choices. And he had to take some calculated battle risks, including making some of his paratroopers a target for the rebels, so he could draw them into a firefight where they could be defeated. All the time, he was aware of the world's media watching the operation closely for signs of 'gunboat diplomacy' or worse, straight failure. In principle, the operational tasks facing Richards were not dissimilar to those facing Wellington in the Peninsular War. The great difference in scale between these two campaigns is not the most important contrast. The interesting difference is that Wellington had weeks and months to address comparable challenges; Richards had hours and days. They had a common concern for clear pre-campaign planning, whatever surprises might arise when the shooting began, but once they were underway, the Richards campaign took place in conditions of modern strategic compression compared to Wellington's altogether different timeframe in the Peninsula.

Compression takes place in other significant respects up and down the strategic-operational-tactical chain. Communication technologies can telescope the whole command chain from top to bottom. In May 2011 President Barak Obama, having authorized the raid to kill or capture Osama Bin Laden, sat with his staff in the Situation Room in the West Wing of the White House while SEAL Team Six assaulted Bin Laden's compound in Pakistan's Abbottabad 7,000 miles away. They watched the whole forty-minute assault as it happened. Of course, the President had more sense than to intervene at the tactical level with what SEAL Team Six were doing, but it would have been technically possible for him to do so.

This sort of compression – instantaneous communication links that are sensitive and accurate over any distance – has many more mundane implications for commanders. From the 1991 Gulf War onwards, US leaders in Washington were able to have some direct access to the battlefield and were increasingly tempted to use it to form their own judgements about successes and failures in active operations. In the aerial campaign against Colonel Gaddafi's regime in Libya during eight months in 2011, the British Prime Minister notably clashed with his Chief of Defence Staff. The Prime Minister had access to the same tactical picture and was sorely tempted, it seems, to suggest short-term tactics when the operation seemed to be dragging on and imposing a domestic political price on the government.

The same communications compression, however, can also work heavily in favour of a commander if it is used properly – another command responsibility. The first year of the war in Ukraine demonstrated how Kyiv's forces could derive great tactical advantages against Russian forces by being able to download satellite data, vital to immediate targeting of, say, enemy artillery guns, direct to the mobile phones, laptops or tablets of individual soldiers. Immediate tactical information did not need to come through a brigade or battalion organization, nor even necessarily from observers or forward air controllers. In this case, a Ukrainian lieutenant or sergeant directing counter-battery fire had instant access to what the 'Starlink' satellite constellation, privately owned and operated by Elon Musk, provided to troops on the ground. Ukraine's own improvised counter-battery software – 'GIS-Arta' – built around Starlink during the early months of the war in 2022 could detect, fix and call down fire on enemy artillery positions, all in less than a minute. It was immediately successful.

Such strategic compression has become the norm in modern warfare and shows no sign of slackening; quite the reverse. Modern analysis currently recognises six 'domains of warfare' – the areas and aspects in which warfare takes place. They are; land, sea, undersea, air, space and cyber. Land and sea are the originals, followed by undersea, air, space and cyber, in historical order. Inevitably, each domain was initially addressed by separate branches of the armed forces, even if some remained institutionally linked to their original armies and navies. But the hologram of warfare at once creates the breadth of operations – from the trenches to space, from the kinetic to the cybernetic – while digitization and the communications revolution compresses the potential response to it by offering the promise of meaningful integration between these six disparate domains of warfare. Integration in this sense means the ability to fight synergistically across all domains simultaneously, bringing every advantage to bear at their optimum effectiveness against an enemy's most relevant weaknesses; much easier to say than to do.

Originally, the 'integration of the domains of warfare' was a game only the United States had the technologies to play. But the aspiration rapidly became the new philosopher's stone of military planners in all advanced states, not excluding big autocracies like China and Russia. Some will get nearer to it than others. After 2015, Britain began a major effort to stay in step with US domain integration, albeit with forces less than a tenth the size. But all modern militaries recognise the potential of domain integration to create another 'revolution in military affairs' – an otherwise over-used cliché – if it can be done with at least partial success.

What's a Commander to Do?

Future commanders cannot be super-humans, though twenty-first century conditions strongly suggest that the successful among them will have to be very able indeed. One reaction among contemporary commanders maintains that the hologram of warfare, as outlined here, certainly emphasizes the importance of the command organization as a way of coping with new trends, and puts a premium on those virtues that help it rise to the level of new, and some bizarre, technological challenges. Indeed, since winning and losing in war is a relative process – coping better than the adversary, making fewer mistakes, reacting more quickly, and so on – success doesn't depend on fully matching these challenges, only being better than the adversary in doing so. Of course, an adversary may find an opening in new technologies or political and social conditions to dumbfound one's defences and walk to easy victories by making more imaginative use of what becomes possible. But that has always been the case; it is not a conceptually new perspective on command.

In this version of the military response, a commander must have confidence in the central governmental and defence organization backing them up. Domain integration has to be driven, and maintained, from the centre, so its benefits to commanders at all levels, its data and intelligence, can be available in a distributed but orderly way, to operational and tactical commanders as they need it. The ephemeral nature of some of the combat enablers; AI, cyberattacks, electronic intelligence gathering, and so forth, should be the responsibility of the central organization of defence, whose job it is to provide theatre commanders with what they need. Providing the enablers should be a strategic level concern for strategic commanders. Employing the enablers is a matter for operational and tactical commanders. Commanders at any level, and certainly those at the operational level, should not be faced with data overload. Rather, they should have confidence that the system around and above them will provide accurate answers immediately when they ask for them. And when, in the nature of war's natural chaos, that doesn't happen, a successful commander will rely on his or her close headquarters staff as the filter, the eyes and ears, the nerves and synapses of the military brain that only the commander can ultimately represent.

That means, say all commanders in conversation, different sorts of ruthlessness. A successful modern commander will be ruthless in delegating tasks to people they trust. The Duke of Wellington was a poor delegator and didn't trust in the competence of most of his staff most of the time. Marlborough was a lot better in this respect. But neither of them were required to be as ruthless in delegation as a modern commander, concerned not to have so many 'points of contact' that the individual has no intellectual or emotional space to concentrate on the key concerns of a campaign. Montgomery and Haig were good delegators who relied heavily on staffs they created and trusted so they could lead a regular life with adequate sleep and not have their judgement impaired by sheer fatigue. Amid the plethora of technological inputs, contemporary commanders must rely more heavily both on the central organization of defence, and on their own personal staffs, to handle the inputs and allow them the space to exercise key command judgements.

Successful modern commanders also have to be ruthless on performance – setting achievable objectives and pursuing them with commitment and moral courage. This is not, some say, a feature created by the current high-tech environment, it's just more complex to define these days. What is achievable, in a world of such exotic and ephemeral enablers of battle? It is certainly a more difficult question, they say, but not conceptually new. Commanders also have to be ruthless with subordinates. All Britain's armed services work hard to create a no-blame culture in operational conditions. Officers are expected to use their initiative in giving effect to the 'commander's intent' which they should understand clearly at whatever level they serve. The military tries not to punish military failure, unless it arises from negligence or insubordination. But modern commanders understand more keenly than their privileged predecessors, that they must react decisively to military inadequacy, removing a subordinate who is unable to cope with the requirements of operational command in war. All generals can name officers who obtained well-deserved peacetime promotions whom they subsequently removed from command because those individuals lacked the necessary ability to operate properly in the chaotic conditions of conflict.

Other erstwhile military virtues can be given greater emphasis in response to the modern pressures of command. 'Train hard, fight easy' has long been a sensible military maxim. It applies chiefly to rank and file soldiers, sailors and air men and women preparing for warfare on the front lines. Training harder than one expects to fight is a good way to inculcate all the 'skills and drills' into an individual's response to the demands of warfare. The same maxim can be applied more vigorously at senior levels in responding to the modern command environment. All military exercises are expensive both in monetary terms and the opportunity costs of staging them. Nevertheless, British troops on the ground are normally exercised hard, in deference to the long-established maxim. But command exercises involve higher opportunity costs and tend to be reduced to something more skeletal, with key elements represented by a token involvement rather than replicated at the scale necessary to make them realistic. A great deal in command exercises take place on a tabletop. And command exercises in a multinational alliance like the North Atlantic Treaty Organization, or one of NATO's subordinate headquarters, will always tend to be token rather than genuinely testing. Part of the necessary response to the new command environment, therefore, might be to prepare senior commanders for it in wider, deeper – and certainly more expensive – ways that replicate more accurately the breadth of their task and the strategic compression under which they will operate.

Similarly, the hologram of contemporary warfare re-emphases the political sensitivity of military actions at all command levels. Successful commanders will have to be politically savvy at command levels lower than the strategic, since military and political decisions will interact all the way up and down the command chain. In principle, there is nothing new in that, but the intensity of the interaction is historically unique. Military commanders characteristically complain that they are sent on operations without clear guidance from the political level as to what they are supposed to achieve, or else with political guidance but insufficient means to achieve the objectives, or still yet with political guidance that changes or becomes simply fuzzy as national politics moves on. There is some justification in all these complaints, but analysts point out that this arises from the nature of national politics itself and is unlikely to change. Increasingly, practitioners admit, it is probably unrealistic to see the military instrument as an arm of the state that will be allowed to get on with its job while the military chiefs and the Chief of Defence Staff worry at the strategic level about the interface with the political world. Successful commanders in the future will have to be tech-savvy and politically savvy all through their command careers if they are to stay abreast of the relentless and politically-loaded pressures they will be under. That is a considerable challenge in itself and raises important questions about the politicization of the military establishment in a democracy. But it is not conceptually new and there are ways it might be properly handled.

This view, therefore, maintains that the traditional personal and organizational principles of good command should be capable of being adapted to the new realities in what is characterized here as the hologram of war. If they cannot rise to all its demands, they can at least aspire to be better than their potential adversaries facing the same phenomena.

Other contemporary commanders, however, indicated they were less sanguine about the ability of existing military institutions to cope with the environment of the future. Part of the war hologram, which British staff colleges began researching and teaching around 2020, is that for long periods the future battlespace may seem strangely empty. Neither military hardware nor personnel will be greatly in evidence. Much of a battle will be fought through cyber competition, intelligence manipulation and long-range missile attack on rear areas in what is characterized as the 'deep battle'. In modern conditions it is extremely dangerous to concentrate forces – say, an armoured brigade or an air wing – anywhere within ballistic or cruise missile range of an enemy. Much of an operation, even a discrete battle itself, may be fought in ways that are not immediately evident to an observer. It may be a deep battle for long periods. Then at some point, the old principles of warfare will apply. Forces must then be concentrated to defeat or annihilate an enemy force, to occupy the ground, in some way to take physical control of a battlespace. When it is required, there is still no substitute for physical military power on land, sea or air, however large or small its most appropriate units may be. The trick, say British military doctrine-writers, will be an ability to keep traditional forces dispersed and effectively concealed until the moment arrives when they will concentrate quickly at the decisive points of attack.

That, in itself, presents daunting physical and organizational challenges. But in conversation, some commanders raise even more fundamental concerns. They worry about how this model of force dispersal followed by rapid concentration will affect the understanding of other, closely related, battle concepts. In particular, they ask how this model redefines the meaning of important military principles like the 'mass' and the 'scale' of one's own forces in a conflict and the 'culminating point' of a battle or campaign or the 'centre of gravity' of an adversary.

In 2021 General Robert Fry wrote about the possibility of the 'Midway moment' now arriving in the land warfare arena. In June 1942 the Battle of Midway was one of the turning points of the Second World War and it changed the nature of maritime warfare thereafter. It was fought at a range of more than a hundred miles by ships that never saw each other or engaged directly; the outcome was determined by the aircraft the ships launched. Fry sees the land environment going through a similar 'Midway moment' of remoteness, dominated increasingly by concealment, surveillance, the first-round accuracy of artillery and rockets, robotic devices, cyber-power and the application of AI. This, he reminded his readers, was not just science fiction, it is what British military doctrine assumes for the future. That conception may come more easily these days to the more technocratic maritime and air forces, but it suggests some fundamental, and possibly revolutionary, changes for ground forces. Retired commanders like him say they cannot define in this vision of the future how 'mass' or 'preponderant force' should be defined. Theatre commanders working at the operational level traditionally need to understand where and when a culminating point exists. That point determines where it matters to win, where one can afford to lose, and where and when the final outcome is likely to be determined. Kitchener, Haig, Montgomery and Harris, for instance, all felt they understood the principles of organizing forces at scale, assembling sufficient 'mass' and recognizing the culminating point of a campaign or battle where mass would achieve the objectives. History didn't always vindicate their judgements, but those commanders certainly understood the important principles of concentration. By contrast, Hugh Dowding perhaps more instinctively, embraced the power of force dispersal within a multi-domain defence strategy that was, in certain respects, intangible.

But some modern commanders openly wonder if mass and scale will have any place in the outcome of future campaigns. Most analysts still resist that conclusion and point to Russia's war on Ukraine as evidence to the contrary. Nevertheless, some practitioners keep worrying about how a commander is expected to find the centre of gravity in an adversary who is conducting the deep battle largely through electronic and cyber means in an anonymous and decentralized way from bases that cannot be located, or if they can, cannot for some political reason be attacked. And if commanders can find the centre of gravity of their adversary's campaign, and think they know where the culminating point is likely to be, which elements in their own mix of exotic forces are they seeking to concentrate to bring 'mass' to bear at the right place and time?

Still others, with hard military experience behind them, express this intellectual hiatus as a crisis of military culture, particularly for the traditional soldier. The military utility of any individual soldier, says one general, should not be assessed by his or her ability to carry their personal luggage some distance across the Brecon Beacons in foul weather. 'Age, gender and bellicosity', it is said, may not be the defining characteristics of the typical soldier of the future. Different skills and characteristics will be required that will not easily be accommodated in armed forces structured as they have traditionally been. Some fundamental re-thinking about the nature of military personnel, and painful restructuring of the forces themselves, say some experienced commanders, will be required in any military establishment that aims to remain effective amid the conditions of contemporary, high-tech warfare.

These issues are matters of polite debate among seasoned military professionals who fail to agree for perfectly understandable reasons. Whether the hologram of war requires commanders and their organizations to do what they have always done, but do it better; or whether there is something about the modern world that fundamentally undermines established command models and military culture, a generation of younger commanders are nevertheless facing the real-world consequences of the debate. Time will tell which interpretation of the evidence proves the more accurate.

But wars and conflict will assuredly persist, and commanders will continue to 'wrestle with chaos' as they do so. Writing in 1919 the allied victor in the First World War, Marshal Ferdinand Foch, said that 'The power to command has never meant the power to remain mysterious'. One understands what he meant and the eternal verities of command, those personal characteristics of successful commanders, suggest there are some well-understood principles behind the process. But yet, there also seem to be powerful elements of mystery around successful command. Structural luck and contingent good luck have so much to do with it. The gods of war play cruel games with commanders. Some elements of command can certainly be taught and acquired by experience. But in the final analysis, and amid the awful consequences of war, military command is also a talent that some individuals have and other do not. Sometimes, though only sometimes, the gods of war reward that talent. Commanders' stories, as outlined in this volume, suggest how precarious are the foundations on which their reputations in history rest.

Chronological Table

DATE	COMMANDER	EVENTS	ERA
55–54 BC		Julius Caesar's Roman expeditions to Britannia	Roman republic
26 AD?		Birth of Boudica	Roman empire
26?–61? AD	BOUDICA		
43 AD		Roman conquest of Britain	
60–61 AD		Boudican Revolt	
			Danish Viking conquests
849–899	ALFRED THE GREAT		Early medieval Saxon kingdoms
869–918	LADY AETHELFLAID OF MERCIA		
878		Battle of Edington, Treaty of Chippenham	
909		Anglo-Saxons begin strong pushback into Viking territories	Triumph of Wessex
928			Unity of territories as 'Englaland' Saxon/Danish shared influence
1028–1087	WILLIAM I		
1032–1066	HAROLD II		
1066		Battle of Stamford Bridge, Battle of Hastings	Norman dynasty
1102–1167	EMPRESS MATILDA		
1135		Henry I dies, succeeded by King Stephen, grandson of William I	
1136		Empress Matilda asserts her right to succeed Henry I	'The Anarchy'

DATE	COMMANDER	EVENTS	ERA
1146/7–1219	WILLIAM MARSHAL		
1154		Henry II, Matilda's son, becomes king when Stephen dies	Angevin/Plantagenet succession
1189		Henry II dies, succeeded by Richard I	Brief Angevin Empire
1199		Richard I dies, succeeded by King John	
1215		Magna Carta	Baronial civil war Plantagenet dynastic continuity
1239–1307	EDWARD I		
1272		Henry III dies, succeeded by Edward I	
1295–6		Anglo-Scottish wars and Scottish/French alliance	Development of national consciousness
1307		Edward I dies, succeeded by Edward II	
1312–1377	EDWARD III		
1330–1376	EDWARD, THE BLACK PRINCE		
1337		Edward III claims French crown, initiates Hundred Years War	Hundred Years War
1340		Battle of Sluys	
1346		Battle of Crecy	
1347		Calais in English hands	
1356		Battle of Poitiers	
1360		Treaty of Bretigny	
1377		Edward III dies, succeeded by grandson, Richard II	
1386–1422	HENRY V		
1399		Richard II deposed, succeeded by John of Gaunt's son, as Henry IV	
1403		Henry IV and his son suppress Northumbrians at Battle of Shrewsbury	
1413		Henry IV dies, succeeded by Henry V	National consciousness above dynastic legitimacy
1415		Battle of Agincourt	

Chronological Table

DATE	COMMANDER	EVENTS	ERA
1417–19		Henry V's second French campaign	
1420		Henry V made heir to French crown by Treaty of Troyes	
1422		Henry V dies, succeeded by infant Henry VI	Tide increasingly turns against England
1453			England defeated in Hundred Years War
1455–1485			Thirty year Wars of the Roses
1485			Death of Richard III at Battle of Bosworth End of Plantagenet dynasty Henry VII initiates the Tudor dynasty
1509		Henry VIII becomes king on death of Henry VII	England rebuilding strength under Tudors
1533–1603		Elizabeth I, reigns from 1558–1603	
1540–1596	FRANCIS DRAKE		
1547–1558		Henry VIII dies, succeeded by Edward VI, Lady Jane Grey, Mary I and Elizabeth I	Elizabethan Age
1554–1618	WALTER RALEIGH		
1572		Dutch War of Independence begins, and tension between England and Spain	Spanish empire dominates Western Europe
1577–1580		Drake's circumnavigation of the globe	
1579		English-Dutch military alliance	
1587		Mary Queen of Scots executed	
1588		The Spanish Armada	
1589		Failure of Drake's armada against Spain	
1596		Raleigh's' sack of Cadiz	
1597		Second Spanish armada against England	
1599–1658	OLIVER CROMWELL		

DATE	COMMANDER	EVENTS	ERA
1603			James I and Stuart dynasty Age of Puritan ascendancy
1625–1649			Charles I and crisis of political legitimacy
1642–1651		English Civil War(s)	
1642		Battle of Edgehill	
1643		First Battle of Newbury	
1644		Battle of Marston Moor, Second Battle of Newbury	
1645		Battle of Naseby	
1648		Battle of Preston	
1649		Execution of Charles I; Cromwell's Irish campaign	Commonwealth in England and a Republican Constitution
1650		Battle of Dunbar	
1651		Battle of Worcester, final end to Civil War	
1653		Cromwell named as Lord Protector	
1650–1722	DUKE OF MARLBOROUGH		
1660		Restoration of Charles II	Restored Stuart dynasty
1688		The 'Glorious Revolution' replaces James II with William and Mary	Orange and Hanoverian dynasties
			Age of Queen Anne
1701–1713		War of the Spanish Succession	
1704		Battle of Blenheim;; England captures Gibraltar	
1706		Battle of Ramellies, Marlborough conquers Spanish Netherlands	
1707		Union of England and Scotland creates 'Great Britain' as constitutional entity	England/Scotland unity
1708		Battle of Oudenaarde	
1709		Battle of Malplaquet	
1713		Peace of Utrecht ends War of Spanish Succession	
1714			The Georgian Age

Chronological Table

DATE	COMMANDER	EVENTS	ERA
1714			Accession of George I
1727			Accession of George II
1735–1823	EARL ST VINCENT		
1748–1810	CUTHBERT COLLINGWOOD		
1756–1763		Seven Years War between Britain and France	
1758–1805	HORATIO NELSON		
1759		British capture of Quebec	
1760			Accession of George III
1761–1809	JOHN MOORE		
1765		Stamp Act controversy between Britain and American colonists	
1767–1769		First Mysore War in India	
1769–1852	DUKE OF WELLINGTON		
1775–1783		Beginnings of the American Revolution; Battle of Bunker Hill	
1775–1860	THOMAS COCHRANE		
1776		American Declaration of Independence	
1779–1782		First Mahratta War in India	
1780–1784		Second Mysore War in India	
1783		American independence recognised	
1788–1855	FITZROY SOMERSET	The French Revolution	
1790–1792		Third Mysore War in India	
1793		First Coalition War against Revolutionary France	
1797		Napoleon appointed to direct first attempt to invade Britain	
1797		Battle of Cape St Vincent; naval mutiny at Spithead	
1798		French invasion of Egypt, Battle of the Nile	
1799–1800		Napoleon takes full power in France	

DATE	COMMANDER	EVENTS	ERA
1801		Act of Union between Great Britain and Ireland	Great Britain and Ireland as single entity
1802		Peace of Amiens between Britain and France	
1803		Resumption of war between Britain and France; Second Mahratta War in India	
1804		Napoleon crowned Emperor; Spain declares war on Britain	
1805		Battle of Trafalgar; Battle of Austerlitz	
1807–1814		The 'Peninsular War'	
1809		Retreat from Corunna	
1810		Independence of Chile declared, but insecure	
1812		Napoleon's march on Russia	
1814		Napoleon decisively defeated by the Sixth Coalition	
1815		The 'Hundred Days' and the Waterloo campaign	
1820			Accession of George IV
1821		Independence of Peru, secures Chile's earlier declaration of independence	
1822		Independence of Brazil	
1827		Battle of Navarino	
1830			Accession of William IV
1837			The Victorin Age
1837			Accession of Queen Victoria
1850–1916	LORD KITCHENER		
1853–1856		Crimean War	
1854		Battle of Balaclava	
1859–1935	JOHN JELLICOE		
1857		Indian Mutiny against British rule	
1861–1928	DOUGLAS HAIG		
1861–1865		American Civil War	
1870–1871		Franco-Prussian War	

Chronological Table 379

DATE	COMMANDER	EVENTS	ERA
1871–1936	DAVID BEATTY		The British Empire as a constitutional institution
1876		Queen Victoria designated 'Empress of India'	Imperial commitments burgeoning
1877–1943	DUDLEY POUND		
1879		British Zulu War	'Scramble for Africa'
1880–1881		First Boer War	
1885		Death of General Gordon in Khartoum	
1882–1970	HUGH DOWDING		
1886–1946	JOHN GORT		
1887–1976	BERNARD MONTGOMERY		
1891–1969	HAROLD ALEXANDER		New technologies of warfare arising
1892–1984	ARTHUR HARRIS		
1896–1898		Kitchener's Sudan campaign; Battle of Omdurman 1898	
1898		Fashoda crisis	
1899–1902		Second Boer War	
1900		Boxer rebellion against Europeans in China	
1901		Queen Victoria dies, succeeded by Edward VII	The Edwardian Age
1906		Dreadnought launched – new dimension in maritime warfare	
1914		Outbreak of First World War	
1914		Battle of Mons, First Ypres	
1915		Gallipoli campaign	
1916		Battle of Jutland	
1916		Battle of the Somme	
1917		Battle of Passchendaele	
1918		Ludendorf Offensive	
1918–1925		Western intervention in Russian civil war	British empire at greatest geographical extent …
1922		Washington Naval Treaty, creates permanent limits on naval power	…but under irresistible decolonisation pressures

DATE	COMMANDER	EVENTS	ERA
1930		London Naval Treaty, 5-power disarmament agreement	Managed decline during rise of fascism
1933		Adolph Hitler becomes German Chancellor	Bolshevism and fascism challenge liberal democracies Old European empires under great pressure
1939		Outbreak of Second World War	
1940		German blitzkrieg and Battle of France; Dunkirk evacuation, Battle of Britain	
1940–1943		Battle of the Atlantic	
1941		Japanese attack on Pearl Harbor; sinking of Prince of Wales and Repulse	
1942		Fall of Singapore to Japanese forces; tragedy of PQ-17 arctic convoy	
1942		Commonwealth forces withdraw from Burma, Japan poised to invade India	
1942		Battle of Midway	
1942		Bomber Command strategic offensive against Germany strengthened	
1942–1943		Battle of Stalingrad	
1942		Battles of Alam Halfa, Battle of El Alamein	
1943–1945		Allied offensives across North Africa, Sicily and throughout Italy	
1944		New Japanese Burma offensive, Battles of Imphal and Kohima	Second World War initiates new global power structure
1944		Allied D-Day invasion of Normandy	
1944–1945		Commonwealth forces reconquer Burma	
1944		Arnham offensive	
1944–1945		German Ardennes counter-offensive defeated, Allies cross the Rhine	

DATE	COMMANDER	EVENTS	ERA
1945		Bomber Command / USAAF raid on Dresden	
1945		German surrender, Victory in Europe	Britain victorious but bankrupted by war
1945		Two atomic bombs dropped on Japan, Japan surrenders, End of Second World War	Britain relies on its relationship with US to disguise decline Makes fitful economic recovery

Select Bibliography for Further Reading

Useful general histories and biographical collections
Cannon, John and Griffiths, Ralph, *The Oxford Illustrated History of the British Monarchy*, Oxford, Oxford University Press, 1988
David, Saul, *Military Blunders: The How and Why of Military Failure*, London, Robinson, 1997
Dixon, Norman, *On the Psychology of Military Incompetence*, London, Jonathan Cape, 1976
Hawes, James, *The Shortest History of England*, London, Old Street Publishing, 2020.
Holland, Tom, *Millennium*, London, Abacus Books, 2008
Jenkins, Simon, *A Short History of England*, London, Profile Books, 2012
Jenkins, Simon, *A Short History of Europe: From Pericles to Putin*, London, Penguin Books, 2018
Jenkins, Simon, *A Short History of London: The Creation of a World Capital*, London, Penguin Books, 2020
Keegan, John, *The Price of Admiralty: The Evolution of Naval Warfare*, London, Penguin Books, 1990
Mallinson, Allan, *The Making of the British Army*, London, Bantam Press, 2009
Mallinson, Allan, *The Shape of Battle*, London, Bantam Press, 2021
Overy, Richard, *War: A History in 100 Battles*, William Collins, 2016
Roberts, Andrew, ed., *Great Commanders of the Ancient World*, London, Quercus, 2008
Roberts, Andrew, ed., *Great Commanders of the Medieval World*, London, Quercus, 2008
Roberts, Andrew, ed., *Great Commanders of the Early Modern World*, London, Quercus, 2009
Roberts, Andrew, ed., *Great Commanders of the Modern World*, London, Quercus, 2009
Tombs, Robert, *The English and Their History*, London, Penguin Books, 2015
Urban, Mark, *Generals: Ten British Commanders who Shaped the World*, London, Faber and Faber, 2005
Wilkinson, Spenser, ed., *Twelve Soldiers: From Cromwell to Wellington*, London, Lawrence and Bullen, 1899

The Boudiccan Revolt
Blair, P Hunter, *Roman Britain and Early England, 55 BC–871 AD*, London, Sphere Books, 1969.
Dudley, Donald R., and Webster Graham, *The Rebellion of Boudicca*, London, Routledge and Kegan Paul, 1962.
Fraser, Antonia, *The Warrior Queens: Boadicea's Chariot*, London, Arrow Books, 1993.
Frere, Sheppard, *Britannia: A History of Roman Britain*, London, Routledge and Kegan Paul, 1967.
Rolleston, T. W., *Myths and Legends of the Celtic Race*, London, George G Harrap, 1911.
Salway, Peter, *Roman Britain*, Oxford, Oxford University Press, 1981.
Tacitus, *The Annals of Imperial Rome* (trans, Michael Grant), London, Book Club Associates, 1990.
Trow, M.J., *Boudicca*, Gloucester, Sutton Publishing, 2003.

Anglo-Saxon Commanders
Albert, Edoardo and Tucker, Katie, *In Search of Alfred the Great*, Gloucestershire, Amberley, 2015
Albert, Edoardo and Gething, Paul, *Warrior: A Life of War in Anglo-Saxon Britain*, London, Granta, 2019

The Anglo-Saxon Chronicles, trans.edit, Michael Swanton, London, Phoenix Press, 2000
Green, Judith A., *The Normans: Power, Conquest and Culture in 11th-Century Europe,* New York and London, Yale University Press, 2022.
Holland, Tom, *Athelstan: The Making of England,* London, Allen Lane, 2016
Horspool, David, *Alfred the Great,* Gloucestershire, Amberley, 2014
Keynes, Simon, and Lapidge, Michael, trans. *Alfred the Great: Asser's Life of King Alfred and Other Contemporary Sources,* London, Penguin Classics, 1983
Livingstone, Michael, *Never Greater Slaughter: Brunanburh and the Birth of England,* Oxford, Osprey Publishing, 2021.
Morris, Marc, *The Norman Conquest,* London, Windmill Books, 2013
Morris, Marc, *William I,* London, Penguin Books, 2018
Morris, Marc, *The Anglo-Saxons: A History of the Beginnings of England,* London, Hutchinson, 2021.
Peddie, John, *Alfred: Warrior King,* Gloucestershire, Sutton Publishing, 2005
Pollard, Justin, *Alfred the Great: The Man Who Made England,* London, John Murray, 2005
Rex, Peter, *Harold II: The Doomed Saxon King,* Gloucester, Tempus, 2005
Walker, Ian, *Harold: The Last Anglo-Saxon King,* Gloucestershire, Sutton Publishing, 2000
Wood, Harriet Harvey, *The Battle of Hastings: The Fall of Anglo-Saxon England,* London, Atlantic Books, 2008.
Wood, Michael, *In Search of the Dark Ages,* London, Penguin Books/BBC, 1994
Wright, Peter Poyntz, *Hastings,* London, Windrush Press, 2005

12th–16th Century
Asbridge, Thomas, *The Greatest Knight,* London, Simon and Schuster, 2015
Barber, Richard, *Edward, Prince of Wales and Aquitaine: A Biography of the Black Prince,* Woodbridge, The Boydell Press, 1996
Beer, Anna, *Patriot or Traitor: The Life and Death of Sir Walter Raleigh,* London, Oneworld, 2018
Brooks, Richard, *The Knight Who Saved England: William Marshal and the French Invasion, 1217,* London, Osprey, 2014
Bryant, Nigel (trans) *The History of William Marshal,* Woodbridge, The Boydell Press, 2018.
Butman, John and Targett, Simon, *New World Inc: The Story of the British Empire's Most Successful Start-up,* London, Atlantic Books, 2018
Carpenter, David, *Henry III: The Rise to Power and Personal Rule 1207–1258,* New Haven and London, Yale University Press, 2020
Castor, Helen, *She-Wolves: The Women Who Ruled England Before Elizabeth,* London, Faber and Faber, 2011
Chibnall, Marjorie, *The Empress Matilda: Queen Consort, Queen Mother and Lady of the English,* Oxford, Blackwell, 1993
Corbett, Julian, *Sir Francis Drake,* London, Macmillan, 1890
Graham, Winston, *The Spanish Armadas,* London, Fontana, 1976
Green, David, *The Black Prince,* Stroud Gloucestershire, 2001
Griffith-Jones, Robin, *William Marshal: The Greatest Knight That Ever Lived,* London, Pitkin, 2019.
Froissart, Jean, *Chronicles,* trans. Geoffrey Brereton, London, Penguin Classics, 1978
Hanley, Catherine, *Matilda: Empress, Queen, Warrior,* New Haven and London, Yale University Press, 2020.
Holinshed, Raphael, *Holinshed's Chronicle: As Used in Shakespeare's Plays,* edited by A and J Nicoll, New York, Everyman Library, 1927.
Jones, Dan, *Henry V: The Astonishing Rise of England's Greatest Warrior King,* London, Apollo, 2024
Jones, Dan, *The Templars: The Rise and Fall of God's Holy Warriors,* London, Head of Zeus, 2017.
Jones, Michael, *24 Hours at Agincourt,* London, W H Allen, 2015.
Licence, Amy, *Henry VI and Margaret of Anjou: A Marriage of Unequals,* Barnsley & Philadelphia, Pen and Sword, 2018

Maurer, Helen E., *Margaret of Anjou: Queenship and Power in Late Medieval England*, Woodbridge, Boydell Press, 2003
Morris, Marc, *King John: Treachery, Tyranny and the Road to Magna Carta*, London, Hutchinson, 2015
Ober, Frederick, *Sir Walter Raleigh* (Heroes of American History series), New York and London, Harper and Bros, 1909
Powicke, Maurice, *The Thirteenth Century 1216–1307*, 2nd ed., The Oxford History of England, Oxford, Oxford University Press, 1962
Seward, Desmond, *The Hundred Years War*, London, Robinson, 2003
Spencer, Charles, *The White Ship*, London, Harper Collins, 2020
Sugden, John, *Sir Francis Drake*, London, Pimlico, 2006
Sumption, Jonathan, *The Hundred Years War Vol. I: Trial by Battle*, London, Faber, 1990
Sumption, Jonathan, *The Hundred Years War Vol. II: Trial by Fire*, London, Faber, 1999
Sumption, Jonathan, *The Hundred Years War Vol. III: Divided Houses*, London, Faber, 2009
Sumption, Jonathan, *The Hundred Years War Vol. IV: Cursed Kings*, London, Faber, 2015
Sumption, Jonathan, *The Hundred Years War Vol. V: Triumph and Illusion*, London, Faber, 2023
Walsingham, Thomas, *The Chronica Maiora of Thomas Walsingham 1376–1422*, trans. David Preest, Woodbridge, the Boydell Press, 2015.
Watkins, Carl, *Stephen: The Reign of Anarchy*, London, Penguin Books, 2019
Wingfield Digby, Maria, *Sir Walter Raleigh*, London, Pitkin Publications, 2018

17th–18th Century
Chandler, David, *Marlborough as Military Commander*, London, Batsford, 1973
Fraser, Antonia, *Cromwell: Our Chief of Men*, London, Arrow Books, 1993
Gentles, Ian, *The New Model Army: Agent of Revolution*, New Haven and London, Yale University Press, 2022
Hill, Christopher, *God's Englishman: Oliver Cromwell and the English Revolution*, London, Pelican Books, 1972
Hobson, James, *Following in the Footsteps of Oliver Cromwell*, Yorkshire – Philadelphia, Pen and Sword History, 2019
Holmes, Richard, *Marlborough: Britain's Greatest General*, London, Harper Collins, 2008
Horspool, David, *Oliver Cromwell, England's Protector*, London, Penguin Books, 2017
Hutton, Ronald, *The Making of Oliver Cromwell*, New Haven and London, Yale University Press, 2021
O Siochru, Micheal, *God's Executioner: Oliver Cromwell and the Conquest of Ireland*, London, Faber and Faber, 2008
Spencer, Charles, *Killers of the King: The Men Who Dared to Execute Charles I*, London, Bloomsbury, 2015
Wedgewood, C. V., *The King's War, 1641–1647*, London, Fontana Books, 1966
Wedgewood, C.V., *The King's Peace, 1637–1641*, London, Fontana Books, 1966

18th–19th Centuries
Adams, Max, *Admiral Collingwood: Nelson's Own Hero*, London, Weidenfeld and Nicolson, 2005
Adkins, Roy, *Trafalgar: The Biography of a Battle*, London, Abacus, 2004
Churchill, Winston S, *The River War: An Account of the Reconquest of the Sudan*, London, Longmans and Green, 1899
Clayton, Tim and Craig, Phil, *Trafalgar: the Men, the Battle, the Storm*, Hodder and Stoughton, 2004
Cochrane, Admiral Lord, *Memoirs of a Fighting Captain*, London, The Folio Society, 2005
Cordingly, David, *Cochrane the Dauntless*, London, Bloomsbury, 2008

Davidson, James D. G., *Admiral Lord St Vincent: Saint or Tyrant?*, Yorkshire, Pen and Sword, 2020.
Davies, Huw J., *The Wandering Army: The Campaigns that Transformed the British Way of War*, New Haven and London, Yale University Press, 2022
Esdaile, Charles, *The Peninsular War*, London, Penguin Books, 2003.
Esdaile, Charles, *Napoleon's Wars: An International History 1803–1815*, London, Allen Lane, 2007
Griffin, Andrew, *Cuthbert Collingwood: The Northumbrian Who Saved the Nation*, Cumbria, Mouth of Tyne Publications, 2004
Grimble, Ian, *The Sea Wolf: The Life of Admiral Cochrane*, Edinburgh, Berlin, 2000
Hague, William, *William Pitt the Younger*, London, Harper and Collins, 2004
Harvey, Robert, *Liberators: Latin America's Struggle for Independence 1810–1830*, London, John Murray, 2000
Hibbert, Christopher, *The Destruction of Lord Raglan*, London, Longmans, 1961
Hibbert, Christopher, *Nelson: A Personal History*, London, Viking Press, 1994
Keegan, John, *The Price of Admiralty: the Evolution of Naval Warfare*, London, Penguin, 1989
Keegan, John, *The Mask of Command*, London, Jonathan Cape, 1987
Kennedy, Ludovic. *Nelson's Band of Brothers*, London, Odhams Press, 1951
Mallinson, Allan, *The Light Dragoons: The Making of a Regiment*, Barnsley, Pen and Sword, 2006
Melvin, Mungo, *Sevastopol's Wars: Crimea from Potemkin to Putin*, London, Osprey, 2017
Murray, Geoffrey, *The Life of Admiral Collingwood*, London, Hutchinson, 1936
Newnham Collingwood, G.L., *A Selection from the Public and Private Correspondence of Vice-Admiral Lord Collingwood Interspersed with Memoirs of His Life,* 3rd Ed., London, James Ridgway, 1828
Nicolson, Nigel, *Men of Honour: Trafalgar and the Making of the English Hero*, London, Harper Collins, 2005
Pakenham, Thomas, *The Scramble for Africa, 1876–1912*, London, Weidenfeld and Nicolson, 1991
Robson, Martin, *A History of the Royal Navy: The Napoleonic Wars*, London, I.B. Tauris, 2014
Royle, Trevor, *The Kitchener Enigma: The Life and Death of Lord Kitchener of Khartoum, 1850–1916*, London, Michael Joseph, 1985
Steevens, G.W., *With Kitchener to Khartoum*, Edinburgh and London, William Blackwood and Sons, 1898
Sweetman, John, *Raglan: From the Peninsula to the Crimea*, Arms and Armour Press, 1993
Thomas, Donald, *Cochrane: Britannia's Sea Wolf*, London, Cassell and Co, 1978
Warner, Oliver, *The Life and Letters of Vice-Admiral Lord Collingwood*, London, Oxford University Press, 1968
Wilkinson, Spenser, ed., *Twelve Soldiers: From Cromwell to Wellington*, London, Lawrence and Bullen, 1899
Willis, Sam, *The Fighting Temeraire: Legends of Trafalgar*, London, Quercus, 2010
Woodham-Smith, Cecil, *The Reason Why*, London, Penguin Books, 1958

20th Century
Allport, Alan, *Britain at Bay 1938–1941*, London, Profile Books, 2020
Andrews, Allen, *The Air Marshals: The Air War in Western Europe*, London, Macdonald, 1970
Beevor, Anthony, *Arnhem: The Battle for the Bridges 1944*, London, Penguin/ Viking, 2018
Brodhurst, Robin, *Churchill's Anchor: The Biography of Admiral of the Fleet Sir Dudley Pound*, Yorkshire, Barnsley, Pen and Sword, 2015
Caddick-Adams, Peter, *Sand and Steel: A New History of D-Day*, London, Hutchinson, 2019
Callahan, Raymond, *Churchill and His Generals*, Kansas, University Press of Kansas, 2007
Campbell, Katharine, *Behold the Dark Gray Man: Triumphs and Trauma, the Controversial Life of Sholto Douglas,* London, Biteback Publishing, 2021
Collier, Basil, *Leader of the Few: The Authorised Biography of ACM The Lord Dowding of Bentley Priory*, London, Jarrolds, 1957

Colville, John R., *Man of Valour: The Life of Field Marshal The Viscount Gort*, London, Collins, 1972
Dannatt, Richard and Packwood, Allen, *Churchill's D-Day: The Inside Story*, London, Hodder & Stoughton, 2024
Dimbleby, Jonathan, *The Battle of the Atlantic*, London, Penguin Books, 2015
Hamilton, Nigel, *Monty: The Making of a General 1887–1942* London, Hamish Hamilton, 1981
Hamilton, Nigel, *Monty: Master of the Battlefield 1942–1944* London, Hamish Hamilton, 1983
Hamilton, Nigel, *Monty: The Field Marshal 1944–1976* London, Hamish Hamilton, 1986
Harris, Arthur, *Bomber Offensive*, London, Collins, 1947
Hastings, Max, *Overlord: D-Day and the Battle for Normandy 1944*, London, Michael Joseph, 1984
Hastings, Max, *Nemesis: The Battle for Japan*, London, Harper Collins, 2007
Hastings, Max, *All Hell Let Loose*, Harper Collins, 2001
Holland, James, *Normandy '44: D-Day and the Battle for France*, London, Penguin Books, 2019
Keegan, John, ed., *Churchill's Generals*, London, Weidenfeld & Nicolson, 1991
Kennedy, Paul, *Victory at Sea: Naval Power and the Transformation of the Global Order in World War II*, New Haven and London, Yale University Press, 2022
LaSaint, John T, *Air Officer Commanding: Hugh Dowding, Architect of the Battle of Britain*, New Hampshire, ForeEdge, 2018
Lloyd, Nick, *The Western Front*, London, Viking Press, 2021
Mallinson, Allan, *Too Important for the Generals: Losing and Winning the First World War*, London, Bantam Books, 2017
Mallinson, Allan, *1914: Fight the Good Fight: Britain, the Army and the Coming of the First World War*, London, Bantam Books, 2019
Mallinson, Allan, *Fight to the Finish: The First World War – Month by Month*, London, Bantam Books, 2019
Mead, Gary, *The Good Soldier: The Biography of Douglas Haig*, London, Atlantic Books, 2007
Milner, Marc, *Battle of the Atlantic*, Stroud, Tempus Publishing, 2005
Montgomery, Bernard, *The Memoirs of Field Marshal Montgomery*, London, Collins, 1958
Murray, Al, *Command: How the Allies Learned to Win the Second World War*, London, Headline Publishing Group, 2022
Orange, Vincent, *Dowding of Fighter Command: Victor of the Battle of Britain*, London, Grub Street, 2008
Overy, Richard, *The Bombing War: Europe 1939–1945*, London, Allen Lane 2013
Pitt, Barrie, *Montgomery and Alamein*, London, Jonathan Cape, 1980
Probert, Henry, *Bomber Harris: His Life and Times*, Yorkshire, Barnsley, Frontline Books, 2016
Roberts, Andrew, *Masters and Commanders: How Roosevelt, Churchill, Marshall and Alanbrooke Won the War in the West*, London, Allen Lane, 2008
Roberts, Andrew, *A History of the English-Speaking Peoples Since 1900*, London, Weidenfeld and Nicolson, 2006
Redford, Duncan, *A History of the Royal Navy: World War II*, London, I.B.Tauris, 2014
Roskill, Stephen, *Earl Beatty: The Last Naval Hero*, London, Collins, 1980
Saward, Dudley, *Bomber Harris: The Authorised Biography*, London, Buchan and Enright, 1984
Seabag-Montefiore, Hugh, *Dunkirk: Fight to the Last Man*, London, Penguin Books, 2015
Sheffield, Gary, *The Chief: Douglas Haig and the British Army*, London, Aurum Press, 2021
Steel, Nigel and Hart, Peter, *Jutland 1916: Death in the Grey Wastes*, London, Cassell, 2003
Strachan, Hew, *The First World War*, London, Simon & Schuster, 2014
Taylor, A.J.P., *The First World War*, London, Hamish Hamilton, 1963
Taylor, Frederick, *Dresden*, London, Bloomsbury, 2004
Terraine, John, *Douglas Haig: The Educated Soldier*: London, Cassell, 1963
Williams, Andrew, *The Battle of the Atlantic*, London, BBC Books, 2002
Winton, John, *Jellicoe: A Much-Maligned Admiral*, Leeds, Sapere Books, 1981

Index

Abaqa Khan, 68
Abbeville, 81, 289
Abbot of Notley, 63
Abbottabad, 366
Abercromby, Ralph, 190-2
Abingdon, 34, 53
Aboukir Bay, 170
Abyssinia, 222
  see also Ethiopia
Accra, 223
Achille, 163, 177
Acre, 68-9, 154
Acropolis, 187
Adam, Ronald, 268
Addington, Henry, 154
Adeliza, Queen, 48, 50
Adriatic Sea, 153, 295
Aelfric, Abbot, 37
Aelfwig, Abbot, 37
Aelfwynn of Mercia, 21, 25
Aethelflaid of Mercia, 18-25, 350-1, 355
  childhood, 18-9
  marriage, 21
  building projects, 22-4
  sole military command, 22-5
  death, 25
Aethelgifu of Wessex, 19
Aethelred of Mercia, 17, 20-3, 25
Aethelred, King (the Unready), 26-7, 26n, 28, 42
Aethelstan, King, xii, xiii, 11-2, 17, 20-1, 20n, 21, 25-6, 351
Africa, 103, 104, 107, 148, 172
  imperialism in, 222-3, 222n
  world war two, 306
  in twenty-first century, 366
  see also North Africa
Agincourt, 75-6, 94, 97, 99
  battle of, 99-102, 100n
Agricola, Gnaeus Julius, 2-3
Admiral Graf Spee, 300
Admiralty, 180-1, 185, 187, 283
  intelligence and, 248, 248n, 304, 307
  Jutland and, 251, 256
  world war one, 246-7, 257, 262
  world war two, 299-300, 302-4, 337

  see also Collingwood, Jervis, Nelson, Royal Navy
Aimery St Maur, 63, 64
Air Ministry, 269
  interwar years, 277, 337-8
  training and development commands, 277-8
  world war two, 283-4, 337-8, 343, 345
  see also Dowding, Harris
Alam Halfa, battle of, 292, 314, 352
Alamein, El, 313
  battle of, 271, 273, 292, 308-9, 315-6, 321, 349
Alava, Miguel de, 209
Albert, Prince, 1n, 188
Aldershot, 234
Alditha, Queen, 32
Alencon
  Count of, 87, 100n
  Duke John I de Valois of, 100
Alexander the Great, xi, 362
Alexander II, Pope, 43
Alexander II, King of Scotland, 61
Alexander III, King of Scotland, 71
Alexander, Harold, 270, 272, 272n, 273, 285-96, 311, 331, 352, 357, 358, 362
  battle of France, 288-9, 289n, 312
  Burma campaign, 291, 325-6, 322, 332
  character, 286, 354
  home defence and, 290, 327
  interwar years, 287-9
  Italian campaign, 293-5, 317
  North Africa campaign, 292-3, 313, 315-6
  personal life, 287-8
  world war one, 286-7
Alexandra, Queen, 232
Alexandria, 154, 170, 187, 191, 299, 301, 313
Algeria, 292, 315
Algonquin peoples, 118
Alfred, King of Wessex, 10-17, 21, 27, 125
  battle of Edington, 10-3, 19
  burghs and, 15-6
  daughter, 18-9, 22, 25
  early life, 13-4
  influence in 11th century, 31-2
  military tactics of, 15-6

Mercia and, 20-2
Strategy of, 16-7, 350-1, 355, 357, 358, 363
Allenby, Edmund, xii
Aller, Somerset, 19
Aleppo, 68
Alicante, 182
All Quiet on the Western Front, 242
Alma, battle of, 215, 218
Almeida, 201
Alnwick, 68
Alsace, 142
Alps mountains, 295
Altenfjord, 307
American War of Independence, 146, 148-9, 155, 181, 188-9
Americas, 104-5, 107-9, 115-8, 118n
Raleigh vision of, 118, 120, 23
Amesbury Priory, 70
Amiens, Treaty, 154, 161, 191
world war one and, 228, 233
Anatolia, 221
Andalucia, 194
Anderson, Kenneth, 292
Andes mountains, 184
Andraste, 5
Andrews, Allen, 279
Angers, 90
Anglican church, 184n, 231
Angevin dynasty, 46-7, 53-4, 55-7, 59-63, 64-5, 83, 359
Anglesey (Mona), 4, 7, 70
Anglo-Dutch Wars, 133-4
Anglo-Mysore wars
see Mysore wars
Anglo-Saxon society, 15-17, 19, 22, 75
biblical claims of Wessex, 13, 17
Druids and, 26-7
end of, 39, 46
French influence in, 27
genealogy in modern royalty, 38
leadership in, 18
lineage, 20, 38, 65
national consciousness among 28, 350
See also Celtic culture, Christianity
Anglo-Saxon Chronicle, 10, 13n, 16, 18, 24n, 27, 28
Mercian Register, 18
Anjou, 39, 41, 46
Count of, 41
John I of, 60
Matilda and, 49-50, 53
Anker, river, 8
Ann, Queen, 138, 139, 141, 144
Anson, George, 146, 147
Antigua, 156, 157, 168
Antwerp, 108, 142, 205, 321

Anzio, 273, 293, 294, 296
Appledore, 17
Apsley House, 200, 213n
Aquinas, Thomas, 76
Aquitaine, 39, 41, 46, 53, 56-8, 65
Black Prince and, 92-3
Edward III and, 76-80, 82-4
Henry V and, 94, 96
Arakan hills, 290
battle of, 326
Japanese attack at 328
Arbuthnot, Harriet, 268
Arbuthnot, Robert, 261
Archangel, 306, 307
Arctic Sea, 297, 306-7
Argaum, battle of, 199
Argenta Gap, 295
Argentan, 49, 51
Argentina, 105
Argyle, Duke of, 144
Ark Raleigh, 119
Ark Royal, 109, 119
Armagnac, House of, 97-8, 101
Armstrong Whitworth Whitley bomber, 340
Arnhem, 321, 352
Arras, 270, 271
battle of 239, 266
Arthur (mythical king), 65
Arthurian legends, 56, 65, 94, 351
Artificial intelligence (AI), 364-5, 368, 370
Arun, river, 50
Arundel, 50
Earl of, 87, 89
Ascot, 232
Ashanti Wars, 214
Ashdown, 14
Assam, 291, 328
Assaye, battle of, 199
Astorga, 195
Asquith, Herbert, 226, 228, 233
Athelny, 10, 12, 17, 19
Atlee, Clement, 333
Atlantic:
battle of, 297, 300, 302, 303-5, 349, 352
British Atlantic fleet, 256, 298
French Atlantic fleet, 161-2
North-West passage, 116, 167
Ocean, 104, 105, 108, 113, 150-1, 153, 270, 336
Trafalgar and, 162, 172-3
world war one and, 246
Atrebates tribe, 4
Aubers Ridge, battle of, 235
Aubrey Jack, 180
Aubrey, John, 117
Auchinleck, Claude, 227n, 313, 313n, 332

Austerlitz, battle of, 178
Australia, 241, 323, 333, 359
Austria, 178, 201, 204
Austria-Hungary, 239
Avon river, 67
Avro Lancaster bomber, 340, 346
Axminster, 139
Azores, 109, 121, 182, 183

Babullah, Sultan, 106
Backhouse, Roger, 299
Bacon, Reginald, 263n
Badajoz, battle of, 201, 202, 212
Baden Wurttemberg, 204
Badminton, 219
Badminton House, 211
Baghdad, 276
Bahia, 186
Bailgate, Lincoln, 62
Baker rifle, 192
Balaclava, 216, 218, 219
Baldwin, Count of Flanders, 41
Baldwin, Stanley, 279
Balkans, 214, 295
Balliol, Edward, 78
Balliol, John, 71-73
Baltic Landeswehr, 287
Baltic Sea, 181, 303
Bamburgh, 25
Banda Sea, 107
Bannockburn, battle of, 73, 78
Banqueting House, 131
Bardney, 23
Barfleur, 48
Barker, Michael, 312
Barnes, Kitty, 184, 184n, 185, 186
Barrackpore, 326
Barrington, Samuel, 148, 149
Barrons, Richard, 361n
Basing, 14
Basque Roads, battle of, 183-4, 187
Bastia, 168, 169
Batavia, 1
Bath, 15, 157
Battle Abbey, Hastings, 45
Battle of Britain, film, 284
Bavaria, Elector of, 141-142, 143
Baybars I, Sultan, 68
Bayeux Tapestry, 36
Bayonne, 203
Bazentin-le-Petit wood, 238
BE2 fighter, 275, 335
Bear Island, 306
Beatty, Charles, 253
Beatty, David, xiii, 253-63, 298, 350, 355
   Boxer rebellion and, 244n
   command style, 255-7
   First Sea Lord, 262-3
   Jellicoe and, 243, 252-4, 262
   Jutland and, 248, 258-62, 263, 360
   naval strategy, 262
   retirement, 262
Beauchamp, William de, 70
Beaumaris, 70
Beaumont Hamel, 238
Beauvais, 87
Beaverbrook, Max, 282
Becheral, 59n
Becket, Thomas, 53-4
Bedburg, 142
Bedford, Duke of, 102
Bede, 19
Bec Abbey, 54
Belgaum, 324
Belgium, 233, 235, 239, 204, 269-70, 272, 289, 320n, 343
Bell, Sean, 361n
Benaud, Ritchie, 359
Benfleet, 17
Bentley Priory, 279, 283, 284
Beowulf, 19
Bequest to the Nation, 155
Berchtesgaden, 282
Bergerac, 83, 90
Berkhamsted, 45
Berlin, 240, 243, 247, 251, 282-3, 295, 321, 342, 344
Berry, Edward, 155
Berwick-on-Tweed, 72, 73, 78, 83
Bin Laden, Osama, 366
Bingham, Margaret, 287-8
Binsted, 322
Birmingham, 323, 339
Biscay, Bay of, 79, 183
Bismarck, 261, 303
Bishop of London, 139
Bizerte, 292, 293
Black Sea Fleet, 214, 219
Blackett, Sarah, 157, 161, 165
Blackheath, 134
Blairville, 267
Blanchetaque, 81
Blenheim, battle of, 139, 141-3, 316, 350, 356
Blenheim Palace, 144-5
Bletchley Park, 304-5
   Ultra intelligence, 314, 341
Blockchain, 365
Blois, 41
   Stephen of, 48, 49
Blucher, 257, 257n
Blucher, Gebhard Leberecht von, 204, 205, 208, 209-10

Boer War, 188, 224-6, 231-2
  see also, South Africa
Boethius, 19
Bolingbroke, Henry
  see, Henry IV
Bologna, 295
Bolshevism, 239, 241-2, 287
Bolton Paul Defiant, fighter, 278, 278n, 280
Bonaparte, Joseph, 203
Bonaparte, Napoleon, xi, 291, 349-51, 362, 363
  Cochrane and, 180, 183, 185, 186
  Egypt and, 154, 191
  invasion of Britain, 171-2, 178, 192
  Nelson and, 168, 170, 178, 211
  Peninsular war, 189, 193-5, 197, 201, 210
  Spanish war, 178
  on St Helena, 199n
  Waterloo campaign, 204-10, 212
  And Wellington, 197n
Bond Street, London, 287
Bondeno, 295
Bordeaux, 80, 90, 92
Borough Road, London, 185
Boscawen, Edward, 147
Boston, 155-6
Botha, Louis, 226
Bouchin fortress, 144
Boudica, Queen of the Icini, Xii, 1-9, 359, 350
  Camulodunum and, 4-6
  death of, 9
  Londinium and, 7
  marriage of, 2
  name of, 1
  statue of 1, 9
  Verulamium and, 8
  Watling Street, battle of, 8-9
Boulogne, 49, 52, 161, 172, 178, 184, 188, 272
Bounce, 157, 157n, 160, 161, 165
Bourbon dynasty, 140, 145, 203-4
  see also Hapsburgs
Bourchier, Elizabeth, 124
Bow Street Runners, 185
Bowyer, George, 157, 159
Boyne, battle of the, 140
Boxer rebellion, 244, 253, 255
Brabant, Duke of, 100
Bradley, Omar, 292, 319, 320
Bradshaw, John, 134
Brasenose College Oxford, 231
Bratton Castle, 11
Brazil, 181, 186, 188
Brecon Beacons (Bannau Brycheiniog), 371
Bremesbyrig, 21
Brenner Pass, 48
Brest, 148, 150-1, 154, 159, 161, 172, 174, 301, 303, 349

Bretigny, treaty of, 84, 92, 97
Breton Wars of Succession, 80, 90
Brian fitz Count, 51, 52
Bridgenorth, 17, 21, 22
Brigante tribe, 4, 5n
Bristol, 50, 52, 59n, 61, 132n, 280
  Channel, 300
Bristol Blenheim fighter, 280
British Army:
  battle school system, 290, 327
  foundation, 134-5
  imperial legacy, 269
  manoeuvrist approach, 141
  Marlborough and, 139-40
  Moore and, 191-2
  reforms, 191-2, 214-5, 225-6, 232-3
  staff colleges of, 287, 288
  Territorial army, 228n, 233, 324
  Units
    Foot Guards, 136
    1st Foot Guards, 206, 208-9
    3rd Foot Guards, 206
    Coldstream Guards, 134, 206
    Grenadier Guards, 265-6, 273
    Welsh Guards, 267
    Irish Guards, 267, 286-7
    4th Foot, 192
    27th Foot, 190, 207, 208
    30th Foot, 208
    33rd Foot, 198, 208
    43rd Foot, 211, 192
    51st Foot, 190, 191
    52nd Foot, 191-2
    59th Foot, 192
    69th Foot, 208
    70th Foot, 192
    92nd Foot, 212
    95th Foot, 192
    60th Rifles, 192
    95th Rifles, 192
    52nd Light infantry, 208-9
    Border regiment, 331
    Ghurkha rifles, 290-1, 324, 333
    Punjab regiment, 329
    Royal Warwickshire regiment, 310, 324
    West India regiment, 324
    Highland light infantry, 216, 218
    4th Hussars, 254
    7th Hussars, 231
    8th Hussars, 217
    11th Hussars, 217
    4th Light dragoons 211, 217
    13th Light dragoons, 217
    17th Lancers, 217
    21st Lancers, 223
    Blues, 141

Derbyshire Yeomanry, 292
Lifeguards, 141
Light cavalry brigade, 211, 215, 217, 218
Heavy cavalry brigade, 216, 217
3rd Cavalry brigade, 232
4th Guards brigade, 266, 286
Household brigade, 206
Union brigade, 206
7th Armoured brigade, 325
Light division, 192, 195
Eighth Army, 292, 294, 313, 315, 316, 331
Fourteenth Army, 316, 323, 326, 327n
world war one, 226-9, 238
world war two, 290, 314-6
Indian Army and, 225-6, 231, 232, 288, 290-1, 324-5, 331-2
British Companion of the Order of the Bath, 244
British defence policy, 367
armed forces, 368-9
doctrine, 370-1
British Expeditionary Force
1914, 227-8, 233-5, 265, 269, 275
1939, 264, 266, 269-72, 279, 280-1, 288-9, 291, 312
British Isles, 124
British Legion, 242
British Railways, 333
British South Africa Company, 334
British Virgin Islands, 114
Brittany, 272, 319
Anglo-Saxons and, 24
Edward III and, 80, 82, 84, 90
in Norman conquest, 31, 36, 39, 44
Broad Street, London, 122
Brockley, 60
Brodhurst, Robin, 301
Brook, Alan, 270, 287, 288, 290, 292, 293-5, 302, 302n 307, 312, 313n, 316, 321, 325, 330, 332, 333
Brown Bess musket, 191-2, 214
Bruce, Robert, 71
Bruce Robert
 see Robert I of Scotland
Bruges, 30, 79
Brunswick, 208
Brussels, 200, 204-5, 320
Bucentaure, 175-6, 177
Bucharest, 214
Buckingham, Lord, 198
Buckingham Palace, 232, 268
Buckinghamshire, 29
Buckland Abbey, 107
Burdett, Francis, 184
Burgh, Ulysses Bagenal, 212n

Burgh marshes, 74
Burgred, King of Mercia, 15
Burgos, 193, 203, 212
Burgundian dynasty, 97, 98, 101
Burma, 214, 290, 300, 316, 323
British empire and, 323, 325, 326
Burma Army, 290-1, 325
campaign to recapture, 328-32, 352
Burnham Thorpe, 167, 168
Burntwood, 346
Bunker Hill, 155-6
Burgundy, Duke of, 98, 101-2
Burleigh, Lord, 108, 109
Bury St Edmunds, 34
Busaco, battle of, 201, 212
Butt report, 338
Byron, Lord George Gordon, 192

Cabinet Office, 138n
Cadiz, 109, 120-1
Jervis and, 150-4
Trafalgar campaign and, 160-4, 168-9, 172-5
Cadogan, William, 144
Cadwallon, King of Gwynedd, 12n
Caen, 41, 50, 80, 87, 101, 320, 343
Caernarfon, 70, 72
Caesar, Julius, 2
Cairo, 221-2, 273, 291-2, 313, 330
Caister St Edmund, 3
Calais, 63, 82-4, 88-9, 92, 92n, 98-9, 110-2, 239, 271-2, 318
Calcutta, 198
Calder, Robert 162, 173
Caledon, Earl of, 285
Caledonia, 9
California, 106, 301
Callaghan, George, 246
Callao, 184, 186
Calvi, 168, 190
Cam, river, 126
Camberley, staff college, 275, 311, 324, 336
 see also, British Army
Cambrai, 144, 242
battles, 240, 266, 287
Cambridge, 125, 126
Cambridge Castle, 126
Cambridgeshire, 29, 127
Campbell, Colin, 215-6
Camperdown, battle of, 171
Canada, 147-8, 226, 295
world war one, 240-1
world war two, 293n, 305, 318, 321
Canal du Nord, 267
Canary Islands, 153
Canning, George, 193

Canterbury, 29, 34, 310
   archbishops of, 53-4, 60, 254, 263
   cathedral, 94
Cantiaci tribe, 4
Cape Colony, 214, 224, 226, 232
Cape of Good Hope, 107
Cape St Vincent, 109
   battle of, 145, 151-3, 159-60, 169-71
   see also, Collingwood, Nelson
Cape Verde Islands, 105, 108, 116
Capetian dynasty, 59, 61
Caporetto, battle of, 239
Capua Palace, 255
Caracciolo Francesco, 171
Caratacus, King, 4, 5, 7
Cardigan, 59n
Cardigan, Lord James Brudenell, 215, 215m, 217-9
Caribbean Sea, 147-8, 148, 168, 305, 349
   see also West Indies
Carisbrooke Castle, 131
Carleill, Christopher, 108
Carlisle, 65n, 73, 74
Carlos II, King of Spain, 140
Carlyle, Alexander, 159
Carlyle, Thomas, 128n
Carmarthen, 70
Caroline Islands, 106
Cartagena, Columbia, 105, 108
Cartagena, Spain, 151, 172
Carthage, 349
Cartimandua, Queen of the Brigantes, 4, 5n
Carver, Elizabeth, 312
Carver, Richard, 312n
Casablanca conference, 431
Caserta, 295
Cassino, 293-4, 343
Castille, 82, 89, 93
   Old Castile, 194
Castlemaine, Barbara, 137
Castlereagh, Robert, 206
Catania, 294, 317
Catherine of Valois, 94, 97, 101-2
Cato Street Plot, 213n
Catuvellauni tribe, 4, 5, 7
Caucasus mountains, 291, 291n
Causeway Heights, 216-9
Caversham, 63
Cayzer, Charles, 245
Cecil, William, 117
Celtic culture, 2-3
   mythology of 3, 65
   Romano-British origins, 65
   see also, Anglo-Saxon society
Central Flying School, 275
Cerdic, (mythical?) King of Wessex, 13, 15, 19, 26, 27-8, 48

Cerda, Charles de la, 89
Cerialis, Quintus, 6
Ceylon, 275
Chalus, 60
Chandler, David, 137
Champernowne, Henry, 116
Chanak crisis, 287
Chandos, John, 87
Charenton, 102
Charleroi, 205
Charles of Navarre, 93
Charles I, King, 125, 126
   battle of Nasby, 130
   captivity, 130-1
   trial and execution, 131, 131n
Charles II, King, 128, 131-2
   and rebellion in Scotland, 132
   restoration of, 134, 137
Charles IV, King of France, 76, 77, 86
Charles V, King of France, 84, 93
Charkes VI, King of France, 94, 98, 101-2
Charlestown, 156
Charlotte, fort, 190
Chartres, 83, 102
Chaucer, Geoffrey, 92, 92n
Chemnitz, 344-5
Chepstow, 59, 59n, 131
Cherbourg, 319, 321
Chernigov, 38
Cheshire, 253
Cheshire, Leonard, 334
Chester, 17, 21, 23, 51, 69, 70, 76, 86
Chester, Earl of, 51
   Black Prince as, 86
Chichester, 15, 59n
Chile, 106, 181, 185-6, 188
China, 214, 244, 253, 255, 290-1, 300, 323, 325, 327n, 329, 367
Chindit forces, 323, 330
Chindwin river, 291, 331, 332
Chippenham, 10, 11-12, 15, 18-9
Chirbury, 21
Christianity:
   and Anglo-Saxons, 13, 15-16, 17, 19, 21-2, 23, 25
   Edward I and, 69-70
   and Franks, 40
   and Normans, 40
   warrior mentality of, 69
   see also, Anglo-Saxon society, crusades
Chronicles (Froissarte's), 88
Chronicles of England, Scotlande, and Irelande, 86
Church of Scotland, 184n, 231
Church of the Holy Sepulcher, 58
Church of Ireland, 310
Churchill, Arabella, 136, 136n

Churchill, John
  see Marlborough
Churchill, Sarah, 137-8
  after Blenheim, 143-4
  glorious revolution and, 139
  Marlborough's death and, 144-5
  outlook and influence, 138-9
Churchill, Winston, xii, 223, 223n, 224
  Alexander and, 285, 294
  battle of Atlantic and, 303, 304
  on Beatty, 254-5, 256, 257, 263
  on Dudley Pound, 297, 299, 300, 302, 306, 308
  D-Day and, 317, 319
  Harris and, 337-8, 345
  memoirs, 323
  Montgomery and, 309, 315-6, 321, 322
  post-war, 295
  on Slim, 323, 330, 333
  on strategic bombing, 339, 340, 345
  world war one, 228, 243, 246
  world war two, 271-2, 278, 280, 281, 284, 289, 290, 292-5, 300, 312
Cimarrons, 105
Cintra, convention, 193, 200
Ciudad Rodrigo, 201, 202
Clarence, Duke of
  see William IV
Clark, Alan, 242
Clark, Mark, 295
Claude-Victor Perrin, Marshal of France, 200-1
Claudius, Emperor Tiberias, 2
Clausewitz, Carl von, 356
Clerambault, Philippe, 143
Clifford, Roger, 70
Clonmel, 132
Clyde, river, 79
Cnut, King of England, 26-9, 42
Cnut Lavard of Denmark, 38
Coblenz, 142
Cochrane, Alexander, 172, 181, 181n, 182
Cochrane, Thomas, 152, 180-88, 264
  character of, 181-2, 354
  early career of, 182-4
  in Latin America, 185-7
  wife of, 184, 184n, 185, 186, 188
Codrington, Edward, 187
Colborne, John, 208
Colchester (Camulodunum) 3-6, 9
Cold war, 349
Coldstream, 134
Cole, (mythical?) Celtic king, 65, 65n
Collingwood, Cuthbert, xiii, 155-65, 136, 146, 252, 308
  character of, 155-9, 165, 354
  at Cape St Vincent, 151-2, 159-60, 169
  death of, 165
  early life of, 155-6
  as Mediterranean commander, 164-5, 357
  Nelson and, 155-6, 159, 161-2, 166, 168
  at battle of Trafalgar, 158-9, 161-3, 173, 175, 177
Collingwood, Wilfred, 157
Cologne, 142, 340
Colonel Blimp, 240n
Columbia, 108
Colville, Stanley, 254
Command:
  concept and importance of, xi
  command and control within, 365-6, 369-70
  decision clarity within, 353
  emotional military intelligence and, 354-5
  force of personality and, 353-4, 362
  fortune and, 358-60, 363
  organizational requirements of, 355-6
  nature of, 348, 362
  levels of command, 356-8
  modern challenges to, 361-72
  strategic clarity within, 350-3
  see also, Military Strategy, Warfare
Committee of Imperial Defence, 226
Computing, 364-5
Conaghul, battle of, 199
Conder, Claude, R, 221
Constantine, Emperor, 65n
Constantinople, 33n, 164, 214, 287
Contentin peninsula, 80, 87, 319
Conwy, 70
Copenhagen, 154, 171, 199, 359
Copenhagen, 205, 208, 209
Corbett, Julian, 112, 114, 263
Corfu, 164
Coritani tribe, 4
Cork, 140, 191
Corneglia, Adelaide, 169
Cornhill, London, 6
Cornovii, tribe, 4
Cornwall, 35, 86, 89, 117, 119
Cornwallis, William, 172
Cornwell, Jack, 261
Coronel Islands, 247
Corsica, 168, 190, 192
Corunna, 113, 121, 189, 191, 272
  retreat to, 194-6, 200, 355
  university of, 196
Countisbury Hill, 12
County Donegal, 310
County Kerry, 221
County Tyrone, 285
Coventry, 280, 283, 339
Cox's Bazar, 326
Crete, 299
Crecy, battle of, 75-6, 78, 80-3, 87, 91-2

Cremona group, 293n
Creully, 320
Cricklade, 15
Crimean peninsula, 211
Crimean War, 181, 211, 213-9, 353
Cromarty, 246, 248, 256, 258
Cromer, Lord Evelyn, 227
Cromwell, Oliver, 124-35, 230, 350, 356, 358
   character and beliefs of, 124-5, 355
   constitutional struggles and, 126, 131
   early life, 124
   first civil war, 127-30
   foreign policy of, 133-4
   as Lord Protector, 133
   legacy and death of, 134-5
   new model army and, 128
   second civil war, 132
Cromwell, Thomas, 124
Crusades, 56-58, 59, 68, 76, 101
   see also, Christianity, Edward I, Edward III, William Marshal
Cumberland, 30
Cumbria, 72, 74
Cunningham, Andrew, 299, 300-02, 308
Curzon, Lord George, 226, 232
Cyberwar, 364, 368, 370
Cyprus, 68, 121

Daily Chronicle, The, 224
Daily Mail, The, 224, 324
Dakar, 222
Dakota, C47 transporter, 328
Dalrymple, Hew, 22
Dalrymple-Hamilton, Marjorie, 268, 273
Danube basin, 214
Dardanelles, 228
   see also Gallipoli
Dare, Virginia, 118n
Dartmoor, 122
David I, King of Scotland, 50
David II, King of Scotland, 82
Danes:
   Danelaw, 13, 16-17 20, 24-5
   marriage and, 29
   military methods, 15, 357
   Norman invasion and, 45-6
   Scandinavian influence in Britain, 12, 26-7
   see also, Anglo-Saxon society, Christianity
Danesgate, Lincoln, 62
Dannatt, Richard, 361n
Danube river, 142, 143
Dauphin of France, 91, 97, 101-2
   see also, Henry V
de Havilland Mosquito fighter/bomber, 340, 342n
De Montfort, Simon, 66-70, 77

Decianus Catus, 3, 4-5, 6-7
Dee, river, 23
Defeat into Victory, 326
Defence Academy of the United Kingdom, 333
Defoe, Daniel xi
Delhi, 324-5, 328, 329
Delville wood, 238
Denmark, 27, 27n, 28, 33, 33n, 46, 134n, 148, 199, 154
   at Blenheim, 143
   battle of Copenhagen, 171
   world war two and 281
Denning, Norman, 306-7
Deptford, London, 107, 187
Derby, 24-5, 280
Derby House, Liverpool, 305
Derbyshire Yeomanry, 292
Derfflinger, 257, 298
D'Erlon, Jean-Baptiste, 205, 206-7
Dervish tribes, 221
Derwent river, 33
Desmond rebellion, Ireland, 116
Devizes, 52
Devon, 12, 17, 35, 103, 107, 115, 117, 119
Dimapur, 329, 329n, 360
Dimbleby, Jonathan, 302
Dinan, France, 59n
Dingley Hall, 255-6
Dio, Lucius Cassius, 2, 5, 8n, 9
Disneyland Paris, 58
Dives-sur-Mer, 43
Dogger Bank, 113
   battle of, 247, 257-8
Domesday Book, 39, 46
Dominica, 181, 185
Dominion Theatre, 284
Dongola, 222, 254
Donitz, Karl, 303, 305, 306
Dorset, 119
Doughty, Thomas, 105
Douglas, Sholto, 277, 284
Dover, 30, 61, 63, 70, 72, 112, 272, 290, 359
Dover straits, 246
Dowding, Derek, 276, 276n
Dowding, Hugh, 274-84, 353-4, 357, 371
   Battle of Britain and, 281-3
   character of, 274, 284
   death of, 284
   early life of, 275
   interwar years and, 276-9, 335, 337n
   retirement controversy and, 274, 283
   supply and research role, 277-8
   in world war one, 275-6
Downing Street, 138n
Drake, Francis, xiii, 103-14, 166, 350, 352, 353

character of, 103-4
early life, 103-4
Raleigh and, 115-6, 118-20
slavery and, 103, 104
Spanish armada and, 109-14, 118, 351
strategic vision of, 149
Dreadnought battleships, 245, 253, 256
Dresden, 340n, 344, 345
Drogheda, 132
Dryburgh, 242
Dublin, 23, 30, 190, 197, 198
Dudley, Robert, Earl of Leicester, 117
Dumanoir, Pierre, 176, 177-8
Dumfrieshire, 275
Dunbar, 72, 73
  battle of, 132
Duncan I, King of Scotland, 30
Dundonald, 9th Earl of, 181, 181n, 187
Dundonald, 12th Earl of, 188
Dunkirk, 110, 133, 189, 274
  world war one and, 239, 241
  world war two and, 264, 271-2, 280-1, 285, 288-9, 289n, 290, 295, 312, 318
Dunsinane, battle of, 31
Dupplin Moor, battle of, 78n
Durham, 77, 82
Dutch Republic
  see Netherlands
Dyce's Head, Fort Majabigwaduce, 189
Dyle river, 269, 270, 288

Eadric the Deacon, 37
Eaker, Ira, 341
Ealhswith, wife of Alfred the Great, 14, 18, 22
East Anglia, 10, 11, 14-17, 22, 25
  battle of Holme, 16n
  Edward I and, 70
  English civil war and, 126
  as Guthrum's kingdom, 16
  Harold II and, 28-9
  Henry II and, 57
  world war two, 280, 341
East Budley, 115
East India Company, 181, 198
Eastern Association, 127, 129
Ecclesiastical History of the English People, 19
Ecgberht, Abbot, 24
Ecgwynn, wife of King Edward (the Elder), 20n
Ecuador, 106
Eddisbury Hill, 21, 23
Eddystone Rocks, 111
Eder dam, 342
Edgar (the Atheling), 32, 42, 45
Edgehill, battle of, 126
Edinburgh, 230

Edington, battle of, 10-11, 13, 19-20
Edith, daughter of King Edward (the Elder), 20n
Edith Godwin, wife to King Edward (the Confessor) 30
Edith Swanneshals (Swan-neck) 29, 37-8
Edmonds, John Maxwell, 329n
Edmund (Crouchback), 72
Edmund (Ironside), 26, 28
Edmund, King of East Anglia, 14
Edward, the Black Prince, xiii, 86-93, 75, 77, 81, 100, 100n, 264, 350, 354
  and Aquitaine, 84, 93
  and Calais, 82, 88-9
  character of, 88
  battle of Crecy, 87-8
  death of, 84, 93
  early life of, 86
  Gascony and, 90
  in invasion of France 1359, 83-4
  battle of Poitiers, 90-2
  Spanish campaign, 93
Edward (the Confessor), King of England, 27, 37
  death and succession issues 31-2
  enthroned, 28
  Godwin family and, 29-30
  reputational legacy, 64, 65
  William I and Hastings campaign, 41-5
Edward (the Exile), 31
Edward (the Elder), King of Wessex, 17, 19-20, 22, 23-5, 350
Edward I, 64-73, 134, 358
  civil war, 66-8
  on crusade, 68-9
  early life, 64
  and Henry III, 65-8
  strategic challenge to, 70-4
  Welsh campaigns, 70-3
  Scottish campaigns, 71-4
Edward II, 64, 73-4, 74n, 75-8, 358
Edward III, xiii, 54n, 75-85, 86, 92, 96n, 97, 166, 350, 354, 358
  Calais and, 82, 88-9
  as earl of Chester, 76
  battle of Crecy and, 80-1, 87
  decline and death, 84
  Edward II and, 76
  battle of Poitiers and 92
  and Scotland, 78
  strategic challenges of, 78-9
Edward VII, 226, 232, 245
Egypt, 153, 170, 187, 191, 243
  Kitchener's role in, 221-2, 224
  world war two and, 291, 313, 353
Eisenhower, Dwight D., 292-3, 322, 356
  and D-Day, 318-9, 342-3

and Montgomery, 321
NATO role of, 322
as supreme commander, 317
El Bodon, battle of, 212
El Dorado, 120, 122
El Gamo, 182
Elandslaagte, 231
Elba, 169, 185, 204, 212
Eleanor of Aquitaine, 46, 53, 56, 59
Eleanor of Castille, 65, 67, 70-1
Eleanor of Provence, 64-5
Elgin, 30, 72
Elizabeth I, 103, 104. 110n
   and Americas, 106-7, 118
   and Armada, 113
   Drake and, 107
   Raleigh and, 115, 117-8, 123
Elizabeth, Queen Mother, 334
Elizabeth Valois, Princess, 110n
Elvina, 195
Ely, 46, 68, 124
Emma of Normandy, 27, 42
England:
   Commonwealth under Cromwell, 124, 131-2
   national identity emergent, 17, 25, 38, 64, 74, 75, 77-8, 94, 102, 351
   unions creating Britain, xii, 64, 75, 140-1, 144
Englefield, 14
English Channel, 148-9, 151, 161, 272, 301
   and Battle of Britain, 282
   Channel fleet, 154, 157, 161, 171
   in Hundred Years War, 79-80, 89-90
   Napoleonic invasion and, 172, 174
   tunnel, 322
Ensheim, battle of, 137
Eritrea, 222
Ermine Street, 34
Esher committee, 226
Esmeralda, 186
Essex, 6, 17, 29, 35, 38, 126, 149
Essex, Earl of, 105, 120-1
   Cromwell and, 125-6, 129
Ethelberht, son of King Ethelwulf of Wessex, 14
Ethelhelm, ealdorman of Wiltshire, 17
Ethelnoth, ealdorman of Somerset, 17
Ethelred, son of King Ethelwulf of Wessex, 13, 14, 16n
Ethelwold, nephew of Alfred the Great, 16n
Ethelwulf, King of Wessex, 13
Ethiopia, 324
   see also Abyssinia
Eton school, 286
Eugene, Prince of Savoy, 141-3

Eustace IV, son of King Stephen, 53
Eustace the Monk, 63
Evesham, battle of, 67-8, 77
Exeter (Isca Dumnoniorum) 7, 14, 29

Fairfax, Anne de Vere, 131
Fairfax, Lord Ferdinando, 127-8
Fairfax, Thomas, 127-8, 129, 131, 133, 355
Fairy Battle fighter bomber, 278, 278n, 280
Falaise, 320
Falcon, 116
Falkirk, battle of, 72-3
Falkland Islands, 247
Falmouth, 121
Farnborough, 275
Farnham, 17, 22
Fedioukine hills, 217
Fennel, Jonathan, 352
Ferrol, 121
Ferry House, 345-6
Festubert, battle of, 235
Fienvillers, 255
Fighting the People's War, 352
Finale, Italy, 295
Fingringhoe, 5
Finisterre, 109, 111, 121, 173
Firth of Forth, 79
Fisher, John (Jackie), 244-5, 298
Fisher, W. W., 299
Fitzgerald, Oswald, 221n
Fitzroy, Barbara, 137
FitzRoy Somerset, James Henry, 211-19, 350, 358
   early career of, 211-2
   character of, 214
   and charge of light brigade, 216-9, 353
   in Crimea campaign, 214-6
   in Peninsula war, 212
   at Waterloo, 211, 213-4, 219
FitzRoy Somerset, Katherine, 212n
Flanders, 351
   Anglo-Saxons and 32, 38, 46
   Britannia and, 2
   Count of (1122), 49
   Drake and, 103, 110-1
   Edward I and, 69, 72
   Edward III and, 77-8, 79-80
   Henry II and, 57
   Henry V and, 94
   John I and, 61
   Wellington and, 198
   world war one, 234-242
Fleet, river, 52
Fleet Street, London, 63
Florida, 108, 118n, 148
Foch, Ferdinand, 241, 371-2

Fontevraud Abbey, 59
Foreign Enlistment Act, 186
Forester, C. S., 180
Fortescue, John, 203
Fougueux, 163, 163n, 177
Foulksmills, battle of, 190-1
Fountain Inn, Plymouth, 161
Fox, Charles James, 148
Foxton, 5
Fragmentary Annals of Ireland, 18
France, 11, 94, 103, 147, 154-5, 167, 191, 351
    American territories of, 118, 118n
    Angevins and, 47
    Black Prince and, 86
    Blenheim, battle of, 142-4
    Boer war and, 225, 226
    Boxer rebellion and, 244
    Cromwell and, 133-4
    Cochrane and, 181-2
    collapse in 1815, 213
    Crimean war and, 213-4, 218
    Edward the Confessor and, 27-8
    Edward I and, 66, 69, 72
    entente cordial, 226
    Edward III and, 69-70, 75-7, 83-4
    Greek war of independence and, 187
    Haig and, 231
    Henry II and, 57
    Henry V and, 94, 96
    Huguenots, 116
    in India, 198
    invasion of Britain plan 1805, 172-3, 178
    Jacobism within, 140
    James II and, 139
    Kitchener and, 221, 222, 225
    Matilda and, 47-8
    Marlborough and, 136, 140-1, 351
    Peninsula war, 200-2
    Scotland alliance with, 72, 78, 83
    sea power and, 158, 262
    Seven Years war, 147-8
    Spain and, 108, 111
    Spanish succession war, 140-43
    Stuart monarchs and, 137
    Wellington, and, 197, 198
    and Whig politics in Britain, 138
    world war one, 233, 234-39
    world war two, 269-71, 278n, 279-82, 288-9, 289n, 293, 293n, 299-300, 312, 317, 320, 320n 337, 343
    see also, French revolutionary wars, Napoleonic wars
Frankfurt, 144
Freemantle, Charles, 169
French, John, 228, 231-5

French revolutionary wars, 146, 150-1, 152n, 198
    see also Collingwood, Jervis, Moore, Nelson, Wellington
Frobisher, Martin, 107-8, 112-3, 119
Froissart, Jean, 88, 89
Franks, 40-1
Fry, Robert, 361n, 370
Fuentes de Onora, battle of, 212
Fulford, battle of, 33, 34

Gaddafi, Muammar, 366
Galicia, 193, 195, 200
Galilee, 58
Gallipoli campaign, 228-9, 235n, 236n, 324
Gam, Dafydd, 100
Gambier, James, 183-4, 185
Gamelin, Maurice, 269
Garrison Hill, 329
Gascony, 65-6, 69-73, 78-9, 82-3, 89, 90, 93, 97
Gatling gun, 223
Gaul, 2, 7, 9
Gawilghur, battle of, 199
Gdynia, 303
Geddington, 71
Genereux, 182
Genghis Khan, 68
Geneva, 189
    conference on naval disarmament, 298
Genoa, 81
Geoffrey FitzPeter, justiciar, 60n
Geoffroi of Anjou, 49, 51, 53
Geoffrey Martel, Count of Anjou, 41
Geoffrey, Count of Nantes, 49
Geoffrey of Monmouth, 65, 65n
George, Fort (Fort Majabigwaduce), 189, 189n
George I, 144
George II, 146
George III, 146, 148, 154
George IV, 146
    As Prince of Walea, 171, 210
George V, 226, 232
German Order of the Red Eagle, 244
Germany, 148
    Baltic states involvement, 287
    Boer war and, 224
    Bomber offensive effects on, 334, 337-8, 343, 343n, 364
    Germania, 9, 29
    Haig and, 231
    imperial competition with Britain, 226, 246
    Napoleonic war and, 210
    and war of Spanish succession, 141
    twelfth century empire of, 47-50
    world war one, 220, 233, 251, 267, 298

Dogger Bank battle of, 257-8
dreadnought revolution 245-6, 245n
imperial German navy, 243
Jutland battle of, 247, 258
Schlieffen plan, 228
Trenches of, 234-5
world war two, 269, 269n, 270, 291, 352
  Afrika corps, 313-6
  approach of, 277
  Atlantic campaigns, 300-2
  Ardennes offensive, 321-2, 344
  invasion plans 1940, 274, 281, 281n, 283
  Italian campaign, 294-5
  Normandy campaign, 320
  North Africa and, 291-2, 313
Gheluvelt, 234
Gibraltar, 146, 150-1, 153, 162, 164, 172-4, 244, 251, 272-3, 275, 287, 299, 301, 306
Gilbert, Humphrey, 116
Givry, 234
Glasgow, 73, 189, 215
Glastonbury, 65
Global Positioning System, 364
Globe Theatre, 115n
Gloster Gladiator, fighter, 280
Glorious first of June (fourth battle of Ushant), battle of, 159
Gloucester, 15, 21, 23,25, 50,-52, 59n, 61, 211, 334
Gloucester, Duke of, 100, 148
Gloucester, Earl of, 89
Gneisenau, 301, 302
Godfrey-Faussett, Eugenie, 255
Godmanchester (Durovigutum), 6
Godolphin, Earl Sidney, 138, 140
Godwin dynasty, 27, 28, 29-30, 38
Godwin, Earl, 28-30
Godwin, Gyrth, 31, 37
Godwin, Gyrtha, 37-8
Godwin, Leofwine, 37
Godwin, Swein, 29-31
Godwin, Tostig, 31-4, 43
Golden Hind, 106-7
Gonnelieu, 266
Good Housekeeping, 324
Goodenough, William, 248
Gordon, Andrew, 261
Gordon, Charles George, 221
Goring-on-Thames, 345
Goring, Herman,281, 281n, 282
Gort, John, 264-73, 285, 291, 296, 311, 350, 352, 358
  character of, 265-6
  and battle of France, 269-72, 289, 312, 352
  Malta and, 272-3
  personal life, 268

  training role, 268-9
  his VC, 267
  in world war one, 265-7
Gothic line, 293
Gott, William, 313n
Gough, Hubert, 239-40, 241
Goodrich, 59n
Gradwell, Leo, 307
Grafton, Augustus Henry FitzRoy, 3rd Duke of, 148
Grandson, Otto de, 70
Gravelines, battle of, 112-3, 356
Gravesend, 122
Gravina, Frederico, 162, 172, 174
Greece, 181, 187-8, 193, 293, 299, 348
Green Park, 213n, 346
Greenwich, 117, 118
  Royal Hospital 146, 178
  Royal Naval College, 254
Gregory VII, Pope, 43
Grenville, Richard, 107-8, 118, 119
Gruffydd, Daffydd ap, 70
Gruffydd, Llewelyn ap, King of North Wales, 31, 32n, 70
Guadalcanal, 301n
Guadeloupe, 150
Guadiana valley, 201
Guala of Bicchieri, 61
Guiana, 120
Guildhall, Lincoln, 62
Guildhall, London, 7, 69
Guinevere (mythical) Queen, 65
Gustav line, 293
Gustavus IV, King of Sweden, 193
Guthrum, Viking leader, 10-11, 14-15, 16, 17, 19
  As Aethelstan of East Anglia, 16
Guy's hospital, 273
Gwynedd, 17, 65, 70
Gyrtha (mother of Harold II), 29, 37

Hadendoa tribes, 221
Haesten, Viking leader, 17, 23
Haig, Douglas, xii, 136, 142, 227-8, 230-42, 266, 269, 320, 331, 353, 357-8, 368, 371
  Boer war and, 231-2
  early life, 230-1
  in India, 232-3
  leadership style, 232-3, 238, 388
  Lloyd George and, 239, 232n
  reputation, 230, 242
  sea power and, 246
  strategic thinking of, 233, 237, 242
  in Sudan, 231
  world war one pre-CinC, 233-5
  world war one as CinC, 235-41

Index 399

Haldane, Richard, 226, 233
Hallidon Hill, battle of, 78, 81
Halfden, Viking leader, 14, 17
Halifax, Lord, Edward, 338
Halkett, Colin, 207-8
Halley's comet, 32
Hamburg, 340n, 342, 345
Hamilton, Emma, 161, 169, 171-3, 177
Hamilton, William, 169, 171
Hamilton, Douglas, 8th Duke of, 189, 190
Hammersmith, 310, 318
Hammond, Robert, 131
Hampden, John, 125, 126
Hampshire, 12, 322
Hampton Court, 130
Handley Page:
    Hampden, bomber, 337
    Halifax bomber, 340
Handub, Egypt, 221
Hanover, 204
Hanover Square, London, 255
Hapsburg dynasty, 108, 140
    Bourbons of, 140, 145, 203, 204
Hardy, Charles, 149
Hardy, Thomas, 175-7
Harfleur, 97-9, 101
Hampstead Marshall, 59n
Harcourt, Geoffrey de, 87
Hardingstone, 71
Hardrada, King Harold, 33, 33n, 34, 42,-3
Harlech, 70
Harris, Arthur, 334-46
    character, 334, 336-7, 339-41, 354
    Churchill and, 337-8
    critics of, 343-4
    dams raid and, 342
    early life, 335
    health of, 341, 345
    interwar years, 336-7
    strategic beliefs of, 352, 355, 357, 371
    world war one and, 335, 337
    world war two:
        commander 5 Group, 337
        commander Bomber Command,
            378, 379-43
Harold I, King of England, 27, 28
Harold II, King of England, xii, xiii, 26-38,
    75, 350
    early life, 28-9
    Danish roots, 29, 39
    as earl of Wessex, 30
    in 1066 crisis, 32-4, 359
    Hastings, battle of, 34-7
Harper, John, 263
Harrow school, 265, 286
Harthacnut, King of England, 27-8

Hartshill Ridge, Mancetter, 8n
Harwich, 246
    world war one, 247, 257
    world war two, 301-2
Hastings, battle of, 12, 15, 26, 31, 34-7, 39, 43,
    45, 84, 84, 356, 359
Hastings, Max, 289, 323
Hawker Hurricane fighter, 278, 278n,
    280-3, 330
Hawkinge, 284
Hawkins, John, 1-3-4, 108, 113-5, 119
Hawkins, William, 103
Hazebrouck, 287
Hearne, Jill, 336, 345-6
Heavenfield, battle of, 12, 12n
Heights of Abraham, 142
Heihachiro Togo, 244n
Heinrich V, Emperor, 47-8, 49
Helder, 191
Heligoland Bight, 247, 257
Henry of Huntingdon, 65n
Henry Percy (Hotspur), 95, 95n
Henry of Trastamara, 93
Henry ('Young King'), 57-8
Henry I (King of the Franks), 39, 41
Henry I, 47, 48-50
Henry II, 46-9, 53, 56-8, 83
Henry III, 61, 63-68, 74
Henry IV, 95, 95n, 96
Henry V, 36, 75, 94-102, 166, 351, 358
    at Agincourt, 99-101
    character of, 96-7, 355
    death of 102
    early life of, 94-6
    and first expedition against France, 98-101
    legitimacy of rule, 97
    and second expedition against France, 101-2
    in Shakespeare, 102
Henry V (play) 102
Henry VI, 102, 351, 358
Henry VIII, 124, 138n
Henschel and Sohn, 342
Hereford, 21, 24, 67
Hereward of Bourne, 46
Herleva of Falaise, 40
Heros, 175
Hertford, 17
Hertfordshire, 29, 35, 126
Hexham, 74
Higgins, Josh, 277, 335
High Street, Lincoln, 62
High Wood, 238
High Wycombe, 338, 341, 345
Himalayas mountains, 329, 330
Hindenburg line, 237, 241, 267
Hipper, Franz, 250, 257-9

Hipper, 302, 306
Hispaniola, 108, 133-4
Historie of the World, 115
History of the Kings of Britain, 65
History of William Marshal, 55, 59
Hitler, Adolph, 282, 282, 283, 291, 295, 307n, 320n, 341, 244, 352
Hochstadt Plain, 143
Holden-Reid, Brian, 293
Holinshead, Raphael, 86
Holland, James, 285, 309
Holme, Abbey, 34
Holme, battle of, 16n, 22, 23
Holmes, Richard, 139n, 141
Holy Roman Empire, 136-7, 140-1, 144
Homer, 348
Hong Kong, 275
Hopkins, Harry, 338
Hoover, Herbert, 244n
Hore-Belisha, Leslie, 268, 269
Hornblower, Horatio, 180
Horrocks, Brian, 285
Horse Guards building, London, 131n, 202
Horse Guards parade, 300
Horton, Max, 305
Hotham, William, 168
Houghton, Nicholas, 361n
Hougoumont chateau, 206-8
House of Commons
  see Parliament
House of Lords
  see Parliament
Howard, Lord Charles of Effingham, 109-13, 119-21
Howard, Michael, 343
Howe, Richard, 159
Howe, William, 156
Hubert Walter, Archbishop, 60n
Huguenots, 116
Hull, 339
Humber river, 19, 33, 45
Hume, John, 209-10
Hundred Years War, 74, 75, 86, 94, 351
  Illusory victories of, 101, 102
  maritime issues. 79, 90
    see also, Edward I, Edward III, Black Prince, Henry V
Hungary, 31, 141
Huntingdon, 124, 125
Huntingdon, Earl of, 89
Hythe, 72

Iberian Peninsula, 145, 183, 193-4, 200, 211, 214, 350-1
Iceland, 306
Iceni tribe, 1, 2-3, 4, 5, 9
Il-Khanate, 68

Ile de France, 98
Iliad, The, 348
Imperial Defence College, 287, 324
Imperial Guard (French army), 208-9
Imperial General Staff, 268, 287, 302, 312, 313n, 322-3, 333
Imperial War Museum, 261
Imphal, 328-30, 360
India, 147-8, 170, 265n, 268, 351
  Alexander and, 288, 290
  British empire in 222n, 277
  Haig in, 231-2
  Japanese attack on 328-9
  Kitchener in, 221, 226
  Montgomery in, 310-11
  Slim in, 324-6, 332
  World war two, 290-1, 293n
Indian Ocean, 107, 300-1
Indomptable, 163n
Indonesia, 106
Infantry Training Manual, 268
Infernet, Louis-Antoine-Cyprien, 177
Ings, James, 213n
Ingeborg, of Denmark, 38
Ingimund, Viking chief, 23
Inkerman, battle of, 219
Intrepide, 177
Inverkeithing, battle of, 132-3
Iraq, 226-7, 291, 325, 335, 364
Ireland, xii, 11, 23, 25, 27, 27n, 59n, 63, 105, 113, 197, 215n, 265, 273, 311
  Cromwell and, 124-5, 130, 132
  Edward I and, 71, 73
  Henry V and, 95
  invasions from 150
  Jacobites in 140
  Napoleon's strategy and, 172, 190
  Raleigh and, 116
  rebellions within, 116-7, 125, 190-1
  Spain and, 120-1
  Wexford rebellion 190-1
Ireton, Henry, 130, 134
Irrawaddy river, 290-1, 331-2
Irwin, Noel, 326, 332
Isabel de Clare, Countess of Pembroke, 59
Isabella, Queen, 76-7, 86
Isandlwana, battle of, 233n
Isle of Wight, 33, 110, 112, 131, 275, 281, 297, 319
Ismailia, 243
Ismay, Lord Hastings Lionel, 295
Istanbul, 221
Italy:
  bankers of Edward I, 71
  and French revolutionary wars, 150, 169, 171
  and German empire, 48, 50

naval power treaty and, 262
wars of the Spanish Succession and, 141
world war one, 226, 239
world war two, 285-6, 290, 292-4, 293n, 299, 306, 309, 313-5, 317, 322, 325, 332, 357-8

Jackson, Thomas, 248n
Jacobitism, 139-40, 144
Jamaica, 134, 147, 152
James I (James VI of Scotland), 155, 122, 123
Japan, 226
  atom bomb and, 332, 352
  in boxer rebellion, 244
  Burma campaign and, 323
  naval power in 1922, 262
  world war two, 290=1, 291n, 300, 301, 352-3, 360
James II (James VII of Scotland), 136-7, 138-9
Java, 107
Jeanne d'Arc, 102
Jellicoe, Florence, 245-5
Jellicoe, John, xiii, 239, 243-52, 298, 355, 358
  Beatty and, 243, 252-3, 262
  in boxer rebellion, 244, 255
  early life of, 243-4
  as First Sea Lord, 251-2
  battle of Heligoland Bight and, 257
  battle of Jutland and, 247-51, 259-60, 359-60
  personal life, 245, 255
Jersey, 121
Jerusalem, Holy Places, 213-4
Jerusalem, Kingdom of, 58-9, 68-9, 74
Jervis, John, Earl of St Vincent, 146-54, 191, 353
  battle of Cape St Vincent and, 150-2
  character of, 152, 155
  and Cochrane, 180, 182
  and Collingwood, 159, 160
  early life, 146-7
  illness and decline, 154
  as MP, 149
  navigational skills, 147-8, 154
  and Nelson, 152, 166, 168-71, 169n, 174
Jewish community in Britain, 71, 134
Joan, Countess of Kent (wife of Black Prince), 92-3
Joffre, Joseph, 236, 238
Johannesburg, 275
John of Gaunt, 89, 94
John I, 55, 74, 64, 66
  civil wars of, 61
  death of, 61
  as King, 69
  Magna Carta and, 60-1
  as Prince John, 59
  in Shakespeare, 55
John II, King of France, 82-4, 91
Jonson, Ben, 115, 115n
Jordan river, 221
Jourdan, Jean-Baptiste, 203
Judea, 1
Junkers 87 bomber, 278n
Jutland, 251
Jutland, battle of, 243, 247-51, 253, 258-62, 355, 359

Kachin peoples, 327n
Kaiserliche Marine, 246, 247
Kaitna river, 199
Kandy, 214
Karen Hills, 290
Karen peoples, 327n
Kassel, 342
Kasserine Pass, 316
Katamura, Shihachi, 331
Kebaw valley, 325
Keith, George, 161, 180, 182
Kenilworth, 67, 68
  castle, 67, 77, 97, 102
Kennington, 310
Kenora, Canada, 265n
Kensington, London, 188
Kent, 17, 22, 35, 49, 103, 110, 192, 284, 313
Kentucky, 118n
Keppel, Augustus, 149
Keyes, Roger, 298-9
Khalifa, al, Abdullah, 221-2, 224
Khartoum, 221-2, 254
Khedive of Egypt, 221
Kilkenny Castle, 59
Kilometer Zero, 234, 235n
Kimberley, 225
Kimura, Heitaro, 331-2
King's Cross station, 9
King's German Legion, 207
Kingston on Thames, 20n
Kinloss, 73
Kinsale, 140
Kipling, Rudyard, 221
Kitchener, Horatio Herbert, 220-9, 353, 358, 371
  in Boer war, 225-6, 232
  death of, 229, 251
  early life, 221-2
  in India, 226-7
  reputation of, 220-2, 229
  in Sudan, 222-4, 231, 254, 263
  world war one, 226-9, 235-6
Knight, John, 162

402   Great British Commanders

Knights Templar, 58, 63, 67
Kodok, South Sudan, 223
Kohima, 291, 328-9, 329n, 360
Korean War, 333
Kriegsmarine, 300-3, 302n, 305, 307, 307n
Kronstadt, 148
Kutuzov, Mikhail, xi
Kyaukse, 325
Kyiv, 367
Kyiv, Grand Prince of, 38

La Belle Alliance, 205, 208-9
La Haye Sainte, 207, 213
La Sap, 49
Ladysmith, 225, 231
Lagny-sur-Marne, 58
Lake, Gerard, 190-1
Lamb, Graeme, 361n
Lancaster, Duke of, 83-4, 90-1
Lancaster, Earl of, 89
Lancaster, House of, 94-5, 95n, 97, 102
Latin America, 180, 184
    independence movements in, 185-6, 188
    see also Americas
Latvia, 287
Launceston, 149
Lawrence, T. E., 330
Le Juste, 159
Le Mans, 58-9
Lea, river, 17
Leadenhall Market, 6
League of Armed Neutrality, 154, 171
Lee-Metford rifle, 223
Leese, Oliver, 331-2
Leeward Islands, 156, 167, 172-3
Leghorn (Livorno), 169
Lehon, 59n
Leicester, 25, 129
Leicester, Earl of, 108
Leigh-Mallory, Trafford, 280, 282-4, 318-9
Leil (mythical) King, 65, 65n
Leinster, 59, 60
Leipzig, 344
Leipzig, battle of, 204
Leo IV, Pope, 13
Leofric, Earl of Mercia, 28
Leon, 193
Leonides, 329n
Levant, 221, 291, 325, 352
Levellers, 131
Lewes, 84
Lewes, battle of, 67-8
Lewes Priory, 67
Libya, 313, 315, 366
Liddell Hart, Basil, 268-9
Liege, 204

Lieven, Earl of, 127-8
Life Guards, 188
Ligny, battle of, 204-6
Limoges, 93
Lincoln (Lindum):
    in Anglo-Saxon Britain, 25
    battle of, 61-3, 350, 359
    castle, 62
    Edward I and, 68, 70
    Matilda and Stephen war and, 51-2
    in Roman Britain, 6-9
Lincoln Cathedral, 62
Lincolnshire, 127
Lindemann, Frederick, 278, 339
Lisbon, 109, 150, 164, 193, 200-1
Liverpool, 187n, 305
Lloyd George, David, 221, 232n, 239-2
Llywelyn, ap Dafydd, 70, 70n
Llywelyn ap Gruffydd, 66, 69, 70
Loire river, 83, 90
Lollards, 97
Lombard, 7
London, 113, 201, 214, 232, 239, 240, 241,
    243, 255, 268, 269, 271, 271n, 277, 283, 287,
    293, 294, 312, 330, 331, 332, 335, 366
    Anglo-Saxon, 14, 16, 17, 20-2, 30, 33-4, 65
    Boudica and, 4, 6-7
    Charing Cross, 71
    City of, 71, 86-7
    Cochrane and, 181
    Edward I and, 67-8
    Edward III and, 83
    in English Civil Wars, 126-7, 133
    Henry V and, 97-8, 101
    Matilda and, 49-52
    in Norman invasion, 35, 44-5
    Prince Louis of France occupying, 61-3
    Raleigh and, 122
    in Restoration 1660, 134
    Roman, 6-7, 9
    stock exchange of, 185
    Tower of, 67, 69, 86, 115, 119, 122, 140
    world war two, 269, 271, 282-3
London Bridge, 45, 67, 73
London Naval Treaty, 262
Longford, Elizabeth, 211-2
Longthorpe, 6
Longueville, 59, 60
Loos, 229, 235, 236n, 286
L'Orient, 170
Los Agra, 288
Louis VII, French King, 53, 57
Louis VIII, French King, 63n
Louis XIV, French King, 136-7, 140, 142-4
Louis XVIII, French King, 204
Louis Capetian, Prince of France, 61-3

Louis, Prince of the Holy Roman Empire, 142
Louisiana, 148
Lovell, John, 104
Lucan, Lord George Charles, 215-8, 215n, 287
Lucas, Jean-Jacques, 176
Lud (mythical) King, 65, 65n
Ludendorff, Erich von, 236-7, 241
   offensive of, 236, 240-1, 267, 287
Ludgate, London, 65n
Luftwaffe, 63, 274, 279, 281-4, 302, 304, 306-7, 318-9, 338, 344
Lugo, 195-6
Lumphanan, battle of, 31
Luneberg Heath, 322
Lusignans of Poitou, 56-7, 66
Lutzow, 260-1
   world war two ship, 306
Lutzingen, 143

Maastricht, 137, 204
Macbeth, King of Scotland, 30
Macdonald Fraser, George, 331
Machiavelli, Nicolo, xi
Madrid, 178, 194, 202-3
Mafeking, 225
Magdeburg, 132
Magellan Strait, 105, 106
Maginot Line, 269
Magna Carta, 55, 60-1, 63, 66, 72
Mayall, Simon, 361n
Mahdi, tribal leader, 221-2, 231, 263
Mahdist political movement, 221, 223-4, 254
Maine (French province), 39, 41, 49-50, 53
Maine (US state), 118n, 189
Maitland, Peregrine, 208
Majabigwaduce fort
   See George, fort
Malacca Strait, 106
Malaya, 151, 323, 332
Malcolm II, King of Scotland, 27n
Malcolm III, King of Scotland, 30-33, 45
Mallinson, Allan, 225
Malmesbury, 15, 18, 53, 61
Malplaquet, battle of, 144
Malta, 154, 180, 182, 184, 255
   in world war two, 264, 273, 299, 301, 307
Malvern School, 265
Mamluk dynasty, 68, 69
Man, the State and War, 348
Mancetter (Manduessedum), 8
Manchester Guardian, 224
Manchester, Earl of, 127, 128
Mandalay, 291, 332
Manila, 106
Manoa, 120

Mantes, 40
Mao Tse-tung, 322
Maratha wars, 197-9, 351
March, Lord Charles Gordon-Lennox, 212n
Mareth, 316
Margaret of France (Queen of England), 72, 73
Margaret, Queen of Scotland, 48
Marlborough, John Churchill, Duke of, xii, xiii, 136-145, 147, 222, 230, 237, 316, 322, 350, 351, 356-8, 362, 368
   Anglican outlook of, 138
   Blenheim battle of, 141-4, 356
   court issues and, 138-41
   death of, 144-5
   early life of, 136-7
   later military campaigns, 144-5
   military logistics and, 141
   War of the Spanish Succession and, 141-4
Marmot, Auguste de, 201, 203
Marne, first battle of, 265, 234
Marne, second battle of, 241
Marrakesh, 317
Marryat, Frederick, 183
Marshal, John, 55
Marshal, William, 55
Marshal, William, 55-63, 350, 359, 363
   as Earl of Pembroke, 59-60
   early life of, 55-6
   Lincoln, battle of, 61-3
   Magna Carta, and 60-1
   as regent, 63-4
   'Young Henry' and, 57
Marston Moor, battle of, 127-8, 130
Martello towers, 192
Martinique, 150, 172-3
Mary I, Queen, 110n, 115
Mary II, Queen, 138, 139
Mary Queen of Scots, 109, 110
Mary of Woodstock, 70
Massena, Andre, 201
Matilda, Empress, 14-54, 55, 353-4
   campaigns during 'the anarchy', 51-3
   death of, 54
   early life, 47-8
   as Empress of Germany, 48
   marriage and children, 49
   succession crisis, 49-50
Matilda of Flanders (wife of William I), 41
Mathilda, Countess of Boulogne (wife of Stephen I), 52
Mauser rifle, 225
Maxim gun, 223
Mayu, mountains, 328
Meaford Hall, 146
Measure for Measure, 115n

Meaux, 102
Medina Sidona, Duke, 110, 112-3
Medenine, 316
Mediterranean Sea, 105n, 145, 148, 245, 253, 255, 298-9, 300-1, 301n, 313-4, 357
  in British maritime strategy, 150, 154, 159, 164-5, 168, 170, 246, 357
  and Crimean War, 214
  Nelson and, 168
  in Trafalgar campaign, 150, 161, 171-2, 178
  world war two and, 273, 285, 299
Medway river, 103
Meiktila, 332
Menai Straits, 4
Menin Road, 234
Menorca, 164
Merchant Navy, 305, 307
Mercia, Saxon kingdom, 10, 12, 14-16, 18
  Aethelred's rule and, 20-2
  Earl of, 32-4, 45
  in Norman invasion, 35, 45
  taxation in, 23
  territory reduced by Alfred, 16
  Wessex and, 22-4
Meretun, 14
Mersa Matruh, 312n, 313
Mersey river, 19, 23
Merton Place, 173
Mesopotamia, 324, 335
Messerschmidt:
  109 fighter, 282
  110 fighter, 282
Messina, 294
Messines Ridge, 240
Meuse river, 270
Middle East
  interwar years and, 335-6
  in world war one, 246
  in world war two, 289, 292-2, 299, 303, 313, 325
  see also North Africa
Middle Temple, 116
Midway, battle of, 308, 370
Miles of Gloucester, 51-3
Military Service Act, 236n
Military strategy
  air power and, 235, 349
  and air power doctrine, 277, 279, 343-4, 349
  attrition, 230, 233, 237, 320
  cavalry, emergence of in knighthood, 56
  Collingwood's appreciation of, 155, 164
  coups and, 133
  longbow's impact on, 81, 84, 95
  maritime power and, 108, 114, 119-20, 144, 149-50, 239, 243, 245, 247, 251-2, 263
  mobilization for, 220, 233

Napoleonic war shifts, 164-5, 180-1, 186
Nelson's appreciation of, 168, 171-2
New Model Army's impact on, 129-31
tactics and:
  ancient tactics, of 11-2
  Anglo-Saxon tactics in, 11-2, 22, 35
  Black Prince as best tactician, 91-2
  English fourteenth century tactical dominance, 76, 78, 84, 99
  Marlborough innovations and, 141, 145
  Moore innovations and, 192
  Slim innovations and, 326-7
  Welsh campaigns and learning, 96
Milly castle, 60
Milner, Alfred, 226
Minnie rifle, 214
Ministry of Defence, 295-6, 333
Ministry of Economic Warfare, 337
Minorca, 154
Miosson river, 91
Mississippi river, 148
Mocha Island, 106
Mohmand, 288
Mohne Dam, 342
Moluccas, 106
Monck, George, 134, 136
Money, Barbara, 335-6
Mongol Empire, 68, 68n, 348
Monmouth, 94, 95n, 213
Monmouth, Duke of, 137
  rebellion of, 139
Mons, 228, 264
  retreat from, 233-4, 238, 269, 286, 310
Monte Carlo, 256
Montevideo, 300
Montgomery, Bernard, 227n, 270, 273, 285, 309-22 333, 336, 358, 368, 371
  Alexander and, 287-9
  and Ardennes offensive, 321-2
  and Arnhem operation, 321
  character of, 310, 350, 352, 354, 356
  and D-Day, 317-9
  early life of, 309-10
  in India, 311
  in Italy, 317
  in Middle East, 314-7
  in North Africa, 292, 294, 313-14
  world war one and, 310-11
Montgomery David, 312, 322
Montreuil, 236, 238, 266
Montreux, 221
Monywa, 325
Moore, John, 189-96, 200, 202, 215, 264, 272
  British Army, effect on, 191-2
  character of, 191, 193, 355
  Corunna, retreat to, 194-5

death of, 195-6
early campaigns, 190-4
early life, 189-90
Peninsular campaign and, 193-5
Moray Firth, 72-3, 78
Morgan, William, 295
Morley, John, 226
Morocco, 292, 315
Mornington, Garrett Wesley, Duke of, 197
Mornington, Lord Richard, 248
Morpeth, 157, 159, 161
Mortimer, Roger, 68, 70, 77, 86
Moselle valley, 141-2
Mosul, 58
Mountbatten, Lord Louis, 302, 323, 326, 328, 330, 332
Moutray, John, 156-7
Moutray, John jnr., 157n
Moutray, Mary, 156-7, 161, 168
Mozello fort, 190
Murmansk, 306
Msistislav Monomakh, 38
Munster, 116
Murray, Andrew, 72
Musk, Elon, 367
Mysore wars, 170, 197-9, 351

Naga Hills, 329-30
Naga tribe, 327n
Najera, battle of, 93
Naples, 154, 168-71, 273
Napoleonic wars, 146, 155, 180, 349, 351, 357
see also French revolutionary wars
Narbonne, 90
Narvik, 306
Naseby, battle of, 130, 350
Nassau, 250-1
Natal, 224, 231
Naval Tactical School, 249
Navarino, battle of, 187
Navigation Acts, 157
Nebel river, 142-3
Nelson, Horatia, 171-3
Nelson, Horatio, xiii, 136, 146, 166-79, 196, 200, 202, 244n, 252, 254-6, 258, 261, 263, 303
  assessments of, 173-7, 178-9, 354, 350, 352-3, 357-9
  character of, 166-7, 178
  Cochrane, influence on, 182, 188
  early life, 166-7
  land campaigns of, 168-9, 190
  and Nile, battle of, 170, 357
  and reputation, 166, 179
  romantic life of, 167-71
  strategic grasp of, 168, 173, 176

and Trafalgar campaign, 172
and Trafalgar battle of, 173-7
see also Collingwood, Jervis
Neptune, 163, 163n
Nero, Emperor Claudius Caesar, 2-3, 9
Netherlands, 134n, 148
  Attacks against Spain, 120-1
  As Dutch Republic, 191, 139-40, 145, 171
  'glorious revolution' and, 139
  Spanish armada and, 110, 112-3
  rebellion against Hapsburgs, 108
  and Napoleonic wars, 198, 204
  as Spanish Netherlands, 133-4, 144
  and War of the Spanish Succession, 141-5
  world war one and, 269
  world war two and, 321
Neufchatel-en-Bray, 56
Neuve Chapelle, battle of, 235
Neve, 203
Neville's Cross, battle of, 82
Nevis, 168
New Minster, 37
New Model Army, 128-30, 134
New Temple, London, 60
New York, 265
New York Herald, 224
New Zealand, 241, 293n
Newark, 61, 63, 130
Newbury, 55
  second battle of, 128, 356
Newcastle Courant, 161
Newcastle, Marquis of, 127-8
Newcastle-upon-Tyne, 73, 125, 155, 157-9, 161
Newfoundland, 148
Newman, Mary, 107
Newmarket, 130
Newport Arch, Lincoln, 62
Ney, Michel, 200, 205
Ngazun, 332
Nicaragua, 168
Nicea, 40
Nicola de la Haye, 62
Nicolson, Adam, 176
Nicolson, Nigel, 296n
Nieuport, 234, 239
Nightingale, Florence, 219
Nile, battle of, 154, 160, 182, 357
Nile river, 222
Nisbet, Francis, 168-9
Nisbet, Josiah, 168
Nive, battle of, 212
Nivelle river, 203
Nivelle, Robert, 238-9
Noble, Percy, 305
Nolan, Louis, 217-8

Nombre de Dios, 105, 114
Nonsuch, treaty of, 108
Norbury, Earl of, 285
Norfolk, 33, 167-8
Northallerton, 50
Northampton, 32, 126, 130, 256
Northampton, Earl of, 87, 89
North Africa, 291n, 292-3, 299, 309, 315, 358
See also Africa, Middle East
North American Mustang fighter, 342
North Atlantic Treaty Organisation, 322, 369
North, John, 285
North West Frontier, 277, 285, 288, 324, 335
Normandy, 26-7, 31, 33, 39, 59-60, 272, 294, 306
  battle of 1944, 319-20, 320n, 343, 350, 358
  Campaigns of William I in, 42-4, 45
  and D-Day, 317-9
  Edward III and, 79-80, 83-4, 90
  Feudalism of, 46
  Henry II and, 56, 57
  Henry V and, 97-8, 101
  and Norman conquest of England, 29, 31, 39-40
  Plantagenets and, 47, 49, 51, 53
  Stephen and Matilda's role in 50, 51, 53
  World war one and
Northern Ireland, 280, 286
  Ulster, 310
Northumberland, 53, 72, 95, 160
  Rebellion against Normans and, 45
  Scottish raids into, 32
Northumberland, Earls of, 32-4, 45, 95, 95n
  Scottish raids into, 72-3, 84
Northumbria
  In Norman conquest, 35, 45
  Saxon kingdom of, 10, 14-5, 16n, 17, 21-5, 30-1, 32, 35
  Scottish raids into, 32
Norse Vikings, 23-5, 27n, 33
Norway, 27, 27n, 33, 33n, 71, 246-7, 280-1, 299-301, 303, 306, 337
Norwich, 57
Notre-Dame-du-Pre, Priory, 54
Nottingham, 139
  and Anglo-Saxons, 14, 25
  castle of, 50, 77, 86
Nottinghamshire, 127
Nova Scotia, 133, 147
Nowshera brigade, 288
Nuestra Senora del Rosario, 112
Nuneaton, 8
Nungshigum, 330
Nuremberg, 340, 342

Obama, Barak, 366
O'Brian, Patrick, 180

Oberglauheim, 143
Odell, Roger, 153
Offa, King of Mercia, 20
O'Higgins, Bernardo, 185-6
O'Higgins, 186
Old Exeter Inn, 122
Old Palace Yard, Westminster, 122
Olivier, Laurence, 284
Omdurman, 222
  battle of, 222-3, 231, 254
Ontario, 265n
Open source intelligence (OSINT), 365
Orange Free State, 224-5
Orbec, 59n
Orde, John, 153
Order of the Bath, 187
Order of the Garter, 82
Ordovices tribe, 4
Oregon, 106
Oriel College Oxford, 115
Orinoco river, 120, 122
Orkney Islands, 182, 226, 246-7
Orleans, 90, 102
Orleans duc d', 91
Ortegal, cape, 177
Orthez, battle of, 212
Osburh, Queen of Wessex, 13
Ostend, 205, 239
Oswald, King of Northumbria, 12n, 19, 21, 23
Oudenaarde, 144
Ouse, river (Cambridgeshire) 126
Ouse river (Yorkshire) 33
Overy, Richard, 343-4
Owen, Wilfred, 242
Owers shoals, 112
Owain Glyndwr, 96, 97
Oxford, 52, 53
  Earl of, 87
  in English civil wars, 126, 130

Pacific Ocean, 105, 106, 300-1, 323
Packenham, Kitty, 198-200
Pachenham, Thomas, 226
Paget, Arthur
  see Uxbridge
Pakistan, 326, 366
Palermo, 182, 294, 317
Palestine, 9, 193, 221, 273, 277, 311, 313
Papacy:
  Angevins and, 61-2
  Black Prince and, 90-1
  co-opts emerging knighthood, 56
  Edward I and, 68, 70, 72-3
  Edward III and, 77, 79, 86
  in eleventh century England, 27
  and English Protestantism, 104, 107-9
  Henry III and, 63-4

Stephen and Matilda and, 50, 51
Panama, 105, 114, 120
  Isthmus, 104
Parime, lake, 120
Paris, 80, 83, 87, 95, 97-8, 101, 178, 187, 204, 212-4 224, 267, 269-71, 320, 351
  treaty of 1295, 72
  treaty of 1763, 148
  treaty of 1856, 219
  world war one and, 228, 234
Parker, Hyde, 168, 171
Parker, Martha (Lady Jervis), 149
Parker, Nicholas, 361n
Parker, William, 152-3
Park, Keith, 279-80, 282-3
Parliament, 63, 299, 303
  Beatty in, 262
  Cochrane in 181, 184-5
  Cromwell and, 125, 133, 350
  De Montfort's version, 67-8
  Drake in, 107
  Edward I and, 69, 70
  Edward III, 77, 80, 84, 90, 93
  in English civil wars, 127-8, 131
  FitzRoy Somerset in, 213, 219
  Henry V and, 96-7, 101-2
  Hanoverians and Jacobin factions in, 144
  Ireland and, 132
  Moore in, 190
  Raleigh and, 117-8, 123
  and republicanism, 132-5
  Whig and Tory clashes, 138, 144
Parma, Duke of, 108, 110
Pascal II, Pope, 48n
Passchendaele, battle of, 236, 238, 266, 286
Patagonia, 105
Patton, George C, 264, 292, 294, 316-8, 359
Paulinus, Gaius Suetonius, 3-4, 6-7
  and battle of Watling Stret, 8-9
  suppression of revolt, 9
Pearl Harbor, 290, 300-1, 301n, 302, 338
Pearson's Magazine, 324
Pedestal convoy, 273, 307
Pedro, King of Castile, 93
Pedro, Dom, 186
Pegase, 149
Peel, Robert, 210n
Peepulgaon, 199
Peirse, Richard, 338
Peitsang, 244, 255
Peking (Beijing), 244, 255
Pelican, 106
Peling Island, 106-7
Pellow, Edward, 152, 180
Pembroke Dock, 336
Pembroke, Earl of
  see, Marshal, William

Peninsular War, 189, 192-3, 197, 200, 210, 212, 241, 294, 326, 351-2, 366
Percy, House of, 95, 95m
Pereyaslavl, 38
Perrers, Alice, 84
Persia, 291, 291n, 325, 335
  Gulf of, 299-300
Perth, 73, 78
Peru, 104, 181, 184, 186, 188
Peshawar, 288
Peterborough, 6, 14, 23, 34
  Abbey, 46
Pevensey, 34, 43
Philip of Flanders, 58
Philip of Valois, 77
Philip II, King of France, 58-61
Philip III, King of France, 77
Philip IV, King of France, 72-3, 77-8
Philip VI, King of France, 77, 80-2
Philip II, King of Spain, 103
  Armada and, 110-1, 120-1
  attitude to Drake, 109
  attitude to Raleigh, 116, 120-1
  counter-reformation and, 107-8
Philip III, King of Spain, 122-3
Philippines, 106
Philips, Tom, 301
Phillipa of Hainault, 77, 82
Picardy, 82-3, 90, 238
Piccadilly, 184, 346
Piccadilly Line, 126
Picton, Tom, 202-3, 206
Pilgrim Fathers, 118
Pitt, William ('the Younger'), 149, 154, 190, 192
Plancenoit, 208, 209
Plantagenet dynasty, 46, 47, 64-5, 87, 102, 351, 357, 359
  national consciousness developing with, 84
  Hundred Years war and, 76, 357
  And Valois dynasty, 94, 101
Plate river, 300
Plumer, Herbert, 240, 240n, 310, 311
Plymouth, 84, 103-4, 107, 109-12, 119, 121, 148-9, 161, 165, 182
Po valley, 293
Pohl, Hugo von, 244n, 247
Poitiers, 75, 90
  battle of, 83, 90-2
Poitou, 56-7, 60, 64, 84
Poland, 287, 293n, 344-5
Polybius, xi
Pombal, battle of, 212
Pomerania, 27n
Pontefract, 131
Ponthieu, Count Guy, 31
Poole, 14, 84

Pope, Dudley, 161
Portal, Charles, 284, 343
Portland, 110, 119
Portland Bill, 112, 119
Portland, Lord William Henry Cavendish, 196
Porto, battle of, 212
Portsmouth, 108, 159, 165, 173, 178-9, 196, 244, 319-20
Portugal, 103-6, 108-9, 113-4, 140, 159, 164, 181
   empire in Americas, 185-6
   Moore and 193-4
   Napoleonic wars and, 200, 202-3
   see also Peninsular wars, Wellington
Pound, Dudley, 283, 297-308, 352, 357-8
   battle of Atlantic and, 297, 303-4, 308, 352
   Churchill and, 297, 300, 307
   early career, 297-8
   health issues and death, 299, 307-8
   at Jutland, 298
   and PQ-17, 297, 306-8
   world war two:
      responsibilities, 299-300
      losses, 300-2
Pownall, Henry, 271-2
Prasutagus, King of the Iceni, 2, 3
Premesques, 271
Premy Ridge, 267
Presbyterians, Scottish, 128, 132
Preston, 131
Pretoria, 275
Pride, Thomas, 131
Prince of Wales, 69, 70, 93, 95, 96, 122
Prinz Eugen, 301, 303
Privy Council, 117, 139
Protestantism:
   Catholicism and, 103-4
   Counter-reformation and
   Cromwell and, 124-5, 132, 134
   Huguenots and, 116
   Raleigh and, 115-6
   Wellington and, 197
Provisions of Oxford, 66
Provisions of Westminster, 66
Prussia, 143, 154
   at waterloo, 204-5, 207, 209
Puerto Bello, 114
Puerto Rico, 114
Puritanism, 125, 133
Putney debates, 130-1
Pym, John, 125
Pyrenees mountains, 53, 203, 351

Qaqun, 68
Qatarra Depression, 314-5
Quartered Safe Out Here, 331

Quatre Bras, battle of, 205-7, 212
Quebec, 147-8, 167, 308, 330
Queen's College Oxford, 86
Quetta, 276, 288, 311, 324

Raeder, Erich, 281, 303
Raglan, Lord James Henry
   See FitzRoy Somerset
Raleigh, Walter, xiii, 108, 115-23, 350, 353
   armada and, 118-9
   attacks on Spain, 120-1
   character, 116-7
   death of 122
   early life, 115-6
   Earl of Essex and, 120-1
   South American expeditions, 120, 122
   in Tower of London, 119, 122
Ramillies, battle of, 144
Ramsey, Bertram, 272, 299
Ramsgate, 281
Rangoon, 290, 325-6, 330-1, 333
Ransome, Private F. G., 267
Ranulf of Chester, 61-2
Rathlin Island, 105
Rattigan, Terence, 155
Rawlinson, Henry, 237
Reading, 14
Redoubtable, 176-7
Reims, 83-4, 92
Remarque, Erich Maria, 242
Reno river, 295
Repington, Charles, 239
Revenge, 109, 112-3, 119
Richard II, 358
Rhine river, 142, 295, 321-2, 344
Rhineland, 274
Rhode Island, 305
Rhodesia, 334, 335
Ribbemont, Eustace de 88
Riccall, 33, 34
Richard of Cornwall, 67
Richard I, xii, xiii, 58-9
Richard II, 92, 95
Richards, David, 361n, 366
Richborough, 7
Rio de Janeiro, 186
Ripon, treaty of, 125
Roanoke colony, Carolina, 108, 118-9, 121
Robert, Duke of Normandy, 40
Robert, Earl of Gloucester, 50-3
Robert I, King of Scotland, xii, 73-4, 78
Roberts, Frederick, 225
Robertson, Aileen, 324
Rochefort, 172, 183
Rochester, 16
Rocket, 187n

Rodney, George, 182
Rolica, battle of, 200, 212
Rollo, Viking leader, 40
Rolls Royce, 278
Romans, 249
  and Britannica, 2-9, 350
  civic legacy, 15, 21
Roman Catholicism:
  Elizabeth I and, 119, 121
  in England, 109, 110-1
  Hapsburgs and, 108
  Ireland and, 131-2
  James II and 138
  Spanish empire and, 106
  see also Protestantism
Rome, 13, 17, 293-5
Rommel, Erwin, 270, 313-4, 316
Roosevelt, Franklin D., 338, 345
Roslin, 73
Ross, Robert, 181n
Rouen, Archbishop of, 31, 40, 49, 53, 101
Roulers, 239-40
Royal Air Force, 134n, 292, 357, 343, 346, 364
  air power doctrine and, 303-4, 335, 337
  Battle of Britain and, 281-4, 308, 345
  Bomber command, 279, 301, 334, 338, 340m
  bomber offensive of, 334
  in Burma, 328, 330-1
  Church of, 324
  Coastal command, 279, 304, 340
  Dam busters raid of, 342
  Dunkirk and, 280-1
  Fighter command, 279-81, 341
  foundation of, 274, 276
  interwar years, 276-9, 288
  Middle East and, 292, 314
  reform proposals for, 284
  roles for, 336-7
  squadrons of:
    9 Sqd, 275
    6 Sqd, 275
    16 Sqd, 276
    60 Sqd, 276
    210 Sqd, 336
    617 Sqd, 318, 342
Royal Air Force Club, 346
Royal Exchange, London, 185
Royal Flying Corps, 275, 335
Royal Garrison Artillery, 275
Royal Marines, 154, 183
Royal Military Academy, Sandhurst, 231, 264, 268, 286-7, 310, 362
  including Royal Military College, Sandhurst
Royal Military Academy, Woolwich, 221, 231, 275

Royal Military Canal, 193
Royal Navy, 134, 146, 274, 357
  anti-submarine warfare role of, 303-4
  Atlantic, battle of, 297, 302-4, 308
  Cochrane and, 181, 184-5, 187-8
  and Corunna, 195
  Fleet Air Arm and, 299-301
  and end of global dominance, 226-7
  Home Fleet and, 303, 306, 307n
  interwar years and, 298
  Jervis reforms and, 154
  Jutland controversy, 251, 263
  meritocracy of, 147
  national politics and, 149
  Pacific Fleet of, 298
  and Peninsular war, 189
  PQ-17 convoy and, 297, 306-8, 307n
  ships of, commissioned since 1789:
    HMS *Agamemnon*, 168, 177
    HMS *Ajax*, 162
    HMS *Alarm*, 148
    HMS *Alexandra*, 253
    HMS *Arab*, 182
    HMS *Ark Royal*, 301
    HMS *Atlas*, 160
    HMS *Badger*, 156
    HMS *Barfleur*, 157-59, 161, 182, 241n, 255
    HMS *Barham*, 258
    HMS *Belleisle*, 163
    HMS *Bellerophon*, 162, 163
    HMS *Boreas*, 157
    HMS *Britannia*, 177
    HMS *Britannia* (training ship), 243, 297
    HMS *Campania*, 248
    HMS *Camperdown*, 244, 254
    HMS *Captain*, 151, 160, 169-70
    HMS *Chester*, 261
    HMS *Colossus*, 298
    HMS *Conqueror*, 175, 177
    HMS *Courageous*, 300
    HMS *Culloden*, 147, 151, 160-1, 169
    HMS *Defence*, 261
    HMS *Defender*, 261
    HMS *Diadem, 151, 160*
    HMS *Dreadnought*, 158, 161, 245-26
    HMS *Euryalus*, 163
    HMS *Excellent*, 151, 158-60
    HMS *Foudroyant*, 148-9
    HMS *Glasgow*, 308
    HMS *Glorious*, 300
    HMS *Gloucester*, 147
    HMS *Gosport*, 147-8
    HMS *Hampshire*, 221n, 229, 251
    HMS *Hinchinbrook*, 156
    HMS *Hind*, 182

HMS *Hindustan* (training ship), 297
HMS *Hood*, 303
HMS *Imperieuse*, 182-4
HMS *Indefatigable*, 260
HMS *Invincible*, 159, 245, 260
HMS *Iron Duke*, 249
HMS *Lion*, 249, 257, 259-60
HMS *Lowestoffe*, 156
HMS *Malaya*, 258
HMS *Marlborough*, 153, 250
HMS *Mars*, 163, 177
HMS *Mediator*, 156
HMS *Minotaur*, 162
HMS *Nelson*, 263
HMS *Neptune*, 147
HMS *Nottingham*, 147
HMS *Onslow*, 261
HMS *Pallas*, 182-3
HMS *Pelican*, 156
HMS *Porcupine*, 147
HMS *Prince*, 147, 157, 158
HMS *Prince of Wales*, 301, 306
HMS *Preston*, 155
HMS *Queen*, 162, 256
HMS *Queen Elizabeth*, 301
HMS *Queen Mary*, 260
HMS *Rattler*, 157
HMS *Repulse*, 298, 301-2, 306
HMS *Rodney*, 263
HMS *Royal Oak*, 300
HMS *Royal Sovereign*, 158n, 162-3, 175, 177
HMS *Southampton*, 248
HMS *Speedy*, 182
HMS *Spitfire*, 250-1
HMS *Temeraire*, 177
HMS *Thunderer*, 162
HMS *Tiger*, 259
HMS *Tonnant*, 162-3
HMS *Trafalgar*, 254
HMS *Triumph*, 161
HMS *Valiant*, 258, 301
HMS *Vanguard*, 170
HMS *Victoria*, 244, 251
HMS *Victorious*, 301n, 303
HMS *Victory*, 146, 152-3, 162, 173-8, 179
HMS *Warspite*, 258
world war one, 239, 243, 251-2, 262
world war two, 273, 277, 297, 299-300, 301n, 302, 336
Royal Observer Corps, 279
Roysyth, 246, 248, 258, 262
Ruhr valley, 321, 338, 341-2
Runcorn, 21, 23
Runnymede, 60

Rundstedt, Gerd von, 270-1
Rupert, Prince of the Rhine, 127-8, 129, 130
Russia, 33n, 68n, 154, 178, 181, 187, 191
  Boer war and, 226
  in Boxer rebellion, 244
  Crimean war and, 213-9
  in Napoleonic wars, 202, 204, 210
  and invasion of Ukraine, 367, 371
  world war one and, 226, 229, 236, 239-40
  world war two and, 291, 295, 306-8, 344-5
  see also Soviet Union
Russian War of Intervention, 285, 287
Ryan, Cornelius, 321
Rye, 84
Ryswick, treaty of, 140

Sabugal, battle of, 212
Sahagun, 194
Saints, battle of the, 171
Saladin, Yusuf ibn Ayyub, 58
Salamanca, 194
  battle of, 201-2, 212
Salerno, 293-4
Salic Law, 77
Salisbury plain, 10, 139
Salisbury, Earl of, 56-7, 89, 91
Salisbury, Lord Robert Gascoyne-Cecil, 222-3, 226
Salmond, John, 335
Salonika, 235n
Salvador, Bahia, 186
Salvador del Mundo, 150
Sambre river, 205, 242
San Domingo, 150
San Francisco, 106
San Filipe, 109
San Isidro, 160
San Jose, 151-2, 160, 170
San Juan, Nicaragua, 168
San Justo, 163n
San Leandro, 163n
San Lorenzo, 112
San Martin, Jose de, 186
San Nicolas, 151-2, 160, 170
San Salvador, 112
San Sebastian, 203, 212
San Thome, 122
San Vincent bastion, Badajoz, 212
Sandwich, 29, 61, 63
Santa Anna, 162-3, 163n, 177
Santa Cruz, Tenerife, 169
Santa Cruz, Marquis of, 110
Santa Monica bastion, Badajoz, 202
Santander, 113
Santiago, Cape Verde, 108
Santissima Trinidad, 152, 160, 169, 175

Santo Domingo, 108
Sapun Hills, 216
Sari Bair ridge, 324
Saudi Arabia, 134n
Saunders, Charles, 147
Savannah, SS, 187n
Savoy, 140, 141
Savoy Palace, 92
Savoyard elite, 64, 66
Saward, Dudley, 336n
Scapa Flow, 246, 248, 251, 256, 258, 262, 280, 300, 306
Scarborough, 33
Scergeat, 21
Scharnhorst, 301-2
Scheer, 302, 306
Scheer, Reinhard, 248-50, 259-61
Schellenberg, fortress, 142
Schleswig, 27n
Scilly Isles, 69-70
Scone, 73
Scone Abbey 132
Scotland, Church of, 184n
Scotland, 33, 39, 45, 57, 124, 184, 274, 301, 351
  alliance with France, 72, 82-3
  Edward I and, 68-9, 71-4
  Edward III and, 77-9, 83-4
  English civil wars and, 125, 127-8, 130, 131-3
  Spanish armada and, 110, 113
  Henry II and, 57
  Henry III and, 63
  Henry V and, 94, 102
  Jacobinism and, 145
  Stuarts and, 138
  Union with England, xii, 140-1
  see also Caledonia
SEAL Team Six, 366
Sedan, 270
Sedgemoor, battle of, 139
Seine river, 80, 97, 98
Sejanus His Fall, 115n
Selkirk, 73
Selsey Bill, 112
Senhouse, Humphrey, 175
Senlac ridge, 34-5, 37, 44, 45
Serengapatam, battle of, 199
Sevastopol, 214-6, 218-9
Seven Years war, 146, 147
Severn river, 22, 24
Seydlitz, 257-8, 298
Seymour, Edward, 244, 255
Seymour, Henry, 112
Seymour, Ralph, 257, 257n

Shakespeare, William, 30-1, 55, 86, 94, 96-7, 99, 102, 115, 115n
Sheerness Officers' School, 268
Sheffield, 280
Sheffield, Gary, 233, 242
Shen peoples, 327n
Sherbourne castle, 120
Shrewsbury, 21, 70, 126
  battle of, 36, 95
Shorncliffe, 191-3, 310
Short Stirling bomber, 240
Shropshire, 17
Shwebo plain, 331
Shwegyin, 325
Sicily, 69, 154, 285-6, 290, 293-4, 306, 316-7
Sidon, 193
Sidney, William, 273, 296
Sidney Sussex College Cambridge, 124, 134
Sierra Leone, 107, 366
Silures tribe, 4-5
Simonides, 329n
Simpson, Mary, 167
Sinclair, Archibald, 284
Singapore, 262, 290, 300, 332-3
Sinsheim, battle of, 137
Sinzweya, 328
Sittang valley, 290
  river, 332
Siward, Earl of Northumbria, 28, 30-1
Sixtus V, Pope, 109
Skagerrak, 247-8, 258
Slessor, John, 277
Slim, William, 227n, 316, 323-3, 350, 352, 354-5, 358, 360, 362
  Burma campaigns, 291, 325-6, 331
  early career, 323-4
  Fourteenth Army and, 326-9, 362
  retirement and death, 333
  aka William Mills, 324, 324n
  world war one and, 324
Sluys, battle of, 79-80, 90, 349
Smerwick, Ireland, 116
Smith-Dorrien, Horace, 233, 233n
Smithfield, London, 97
Smuts, Jan, 226
Social media, 365
Soho, 246
Solent, 112, 308
Solway Firth, 74
Somaliland, 277
Somerset, 7, 10, 12, 15, 17, 19, 107, 139
Somerset, Henry, 211
Somme river, 43, 80, 87, 99, 270, 289
  battle of, 220, 236-8, 242, 265, 275, 286, 349
Sommerville, James, 299, 302
Sopwith fighters:

Camel, 335
Strutters, 335
Sorpe dam, 342
Sotheby's, 55
Soult, Jean-de-Dieu, 194-6, 200
South Africa, 221, 224, 322, 245-6
   Union of South Africa, 226
   world war one, 241
   world war two, 293n
   see also Boer War
South African wars
   see Boer War
South Sudan, 223
South West Africa, 335
Southampton, 15, 84, 243, 280
Southern Association, 129
Southsea, 173
Southwark, 7, 45
Southwick House, 319
Southwold Bay, 137
Soviet Union, 291, 295, 306-8, 325, 338, 344
   see also Russia
Spaatz, Carl, 345
Spain, 89, 93, 149, 351
   in Americas, 118, 120, 178, 180-1, 185-6
   Cape St Vincent battle of, 151, 159-60
   in Caribbean, 104-5, 107-8
   Cochrane and, 181, 184
   Counter-reformation and, 107-8
   Cromwell and, 133-4
   Drake and, 103-4, 107
   English armada against, 113-4
   and French revolutionary wars, 150, 158
   Marlborough and, 140, 145
   and Napoleonic wars, 200, 202
   Pacific presence of, 106
   Peninsular war in, 189-96
   Raleigh and, 115-6, 118, 122
   slavery of 104-5
   Spanish Netherlands and, 108-10
   Trafalgar and, 162-4, 164n, 174-5, 178
Spanish armada of 1588, 103, 115
   origins, 108-9
   nature of, 110
   course of, 110-13, 119
Spartans, 329n
Special Operations Executive, 337
Speer, Albert, 344
Spion Kop, battle of, 225
Spithead, 152, 156
St Alkmund, 21
St Albans (Verulamium), 7-9
St Augustine, 19, 76
St Briavels, 59n
St Clement Danes church, 334
St Cuthbert, 19

St George, 82, 91
St Gregory, 19
St Helena, 186, 199n
St Ives, 124
St James (the apostle), 49
St James's Palace, 137
St Lawrence river, 147
St Lucia, 150, 191
St Margaret's Church, Westminster, 122
St Martin's church, Harfleur, 98
St Mary's church, Putney, 130
St Ninian's school, 275
St Omer, 167, 236
St Oswald's priory, Gloucester, 25
St Paul's cathedral, 7, 165, 178, 252, 263, 333
St Paul's school, London, 136, 310, 318
St Petersburg, 148
St Pierre, 203
St Valery, 43
St Werburgh, 23
Stafford, 21, 24
Staffordshire, 146, 154
Stalin, Joseph, 344, 345
Stalingrad, battle of, 271, 308, 316, 344
Stamford, 25
Stamford Bridge, battle of, 33-4, 359
Stanhope, Hester, 192, 196
Starlink satellite, 367
Steep Hill, Lincoln, 62
Steevens, G. W., 224
Stephen I, 47-8, 55, 353-4
   allegiance to Matilda, 49
   fights civil war, 50-3
   grabs the throne, 49-50
Stephenson, George, 187n
Stevenson, Donald, 277
Stewart, Thomas, 124
Stilwell, Joseph W., 290, 325
Stirling, 73, 78
   castle, 73
Stirling Bridge, battle of, 72
Stockbridge, 52
Stockholm, 193
Stone, 146, 154
Stonebow Arch, Lincoln, 62
Stonehenge, 9
Stour river, 16
Strachan, Richard, 177-8
Strasbourg, 142
Strathclyde, 25
Stringer, Edward, 361n
Strugglers Inn, Lincoln, 62
Stuart, Lady Arabella, 122
Stuart dynasty, 131, 134, 137-9
Suckling, Maurice, 167
Suckling, William, 167-8

Sudan, 221-2, 224, 324
  Kitchener and, 222-4, 231, 254-5, 263
  Haig and, 231
Suffolk, 29, 255
Sulawesi, 106
Sun Tsu, 356
Sumption Jonathan, 76
Supermarine Spitfire, 278, 278n, 280-3, 328, 347
Surrey, 126
Sussex, 34, 67, 89, 192
Swanage, 14
Sweden, 27n, 134n, 148, 154, 193
Sweyn Estridsen, King of Denmark, 37, 42, 45-6
Sweyn Forkbeard, King of Denmark, 26
Switzerland, 221, 234
Sydenham, Elizabeth, 107
Syracuse, 294
Syria, 325, 364

Tacitus, 1-3, 6, 8n, 9
Tadcaster, 33, 127
Tagus river, 150-1, 159
  valley of 201
Talavera, battle of, 201, 212
Tallard, duc de Camille d'Hostun, 143
Tallinn, 171
Tallyrand, Prince Charles Maurice, xi
Tamu, 291, 325
Tamworth, 21, 24-5
Tangier, 137
Taranto, battle of, 300
Tasmania, 310
Tavistock, 103
Taylor, A. J. P., 363
Templar, Gerald, 271
Temple church, London, 57n, 63
Temple of Claudius, Colchester, 4-6
Tenby, 131
Tenerife, 153, 168-9
Terraine, John, 238
Test river 52
Tettenhall, battle of, 23-4
Teutoburg forest, 9
Thackeray, William Makepeace, 155
Thailand, 134n, 290, 332
Thames river, 6, 7, 16, 30, 34, 45, 53, 60, 92, 130, 187, 187n
  Nore spit, 152
Tharrawaddy, Burma, 290
The Art of War by Sea, 123
The Discoverie of the Large, Rich and Bewtiful Empyre of Guiana, 120
The Donkeys, 242
The Grand Fleet, 263

The River War, 223n
The Times, 224, 239, 268
Theosophical Society, 284
Thermopylae, battle of, 329n
Thetford, 4, 5
Thirty Years War, 132
Thorneycroft, Thomas, 1n
Threadneedle, Street, London, 181
Throckmorton, Bess, 119-20, 122
Tiddim, Burma, 329
Tientsin, 244, 244n, 255
Tierra del Fuego, 106
Tilbury, 113
Timor, 107
Tipu Sultan, 198
Tippu Sahib of Mysore, 170
Tirpitz, Alfred von, 246
Tirpitz, 303, 306-7
Tizard, Henry, 278
Tjilatjap, 107
Tobruk, 313
Tokyo, 328, 353
Tolstoy, Leo, xi
Torres Vedras, 201
Tortola, 114
Toulon, 150, 153, 164, 168, 170, 172
Toulouse, 203-4, 212, 351
Tovey, John, 261, 302-3, 306-7
Tower Dock, London, 122
Townshend, George, 147
Towry, George Henry, 151, 160, 169
Towton, battle of, 349
Triumph, 113
Tournaments, 56-8
Tours, 90
  treaty of, 57
Towcester, 24
Trafalgar, battle of, 146, 154-5, 158n, 159, 161-4, 166, 172-5, 274, 349, 357
  assessment of, 178-9, 189
  and Jutland, 243, 250-1, 261-2
Trafalgar, cape, 163-4, 175, 359
Trafalgar Square, London, 168
Tramecourt, 99
Transjordan, 273, 277
Transvaal, 224-5
Tree, Ethel, 255-6
Tree, Ronald, 255
Trenchard, Hugh, 274-7, 284, 336
Trent river, 16
Trim, Ireland, 198
Trinidad, 172-3
Trinidad bastion, Badajoz, 202
Trinity College Cambridge, 265
Trinovantes tribe, 2-5, 7, 65n
Tromso, 306-7

Trondheim, 306
Troubridge, Thomas, 146, 151, 153, 168-9, 169n, 171
Troy, 65, 65n
Troyes, 101
   treaty of, 101-2
Truro, 213
Tryon, George, 244, 254, 256
Tsushima, battle of, 244n
Tunis, 292-4, 315-6
Turenne, Henri de la d'Auvergne, Vicomte de, 137
Turing, Alan, 304
Turkey 181
   Egypt and, 221, 224, 211
   and Crimean war, 213, 215-6
   and Greek war of independence, 186-7
   and Mesopotamia, 335
   Orthodox church and 213-4
   Ottomans and, 181, 187, 193
Turnham Green, London, 126
Tweed river, 72
Tyburn, London, 77, 134

Ukraine, 364, 367, 371
Ulm, 142, 178
Ulster, 105
   see also Ireland, Northern Ireland
Umm Diwaykarat, 223
United Kingdom, xii
   as Anglo-Danish confederation, 26-7
   Brythonic/Saxon competition over it, 12n
   conception of, 75
   Cromwell and, 133
   as legal entity, xii, 145
United Nations, 366
United States of America, 115, 118n, 342
   in Boxer rebellion, 244
   Cochrane and, 182, 187
   and domains of warfare, 367
   naval power of 262
   navy of, 152n, 246
   revolution of 152n
   world war one, 239-41
   world war two, 278, 283-4, 290, 292, 294-5, 313-4, 352
      D-Day and, 318
      in Grand alliance, 301, 316
      naval campaigns and, 301-2, 305, 307
      and Pacific theatre, 323
   see also American war of independence
United States Army Air Force, 328, 331, 338, 339, 341, 343
United States-British war, 1812-15, 181
Ushant:
   first battle of, 149
   fourth battle of, 159

Usk, 59n
Utah beach, 80
Utrecht, treaty of, 144, 146
Uxbridge, Lord Arthur (Paget), 206, 207

V1 rockets, 337n
V2 rockets, 337n
Val-es-Dunes, battle of, 41
Valdemar I, King of Denmark, 38
Valois, house of, 94
   and Plantagenets, 101
Valparaiso, 106, 185-6
Vancourt, Clarice, 276
Varna, 214
Varus, Publius Quinctilius, 9
Venezuela, 120
Vera Cruz, Mexico, 104
Verdun, battle of, 236-7
Vereeniging, treaty of, 226
Vereker, Corinna, 265
Vereker, Jacqueline, 268, 273
Vereker, Jeffrey, 265
Vereker, Joscelyn, 266
Vereker, Sandy, 268
Verneuil, 102
Vesey, John de, 70
Vickers:
   Vernon bomber, 335
   Wellington bomber, 340
Victoria, Queen, 187-8, 210, 215, 223
Vienna, 141-2, 295
   Congress of, 204
Vigo, 108, 114, 195
Villaret-Joyeuse, Louis Thomas, 159
Villars, Claude de, 144
Villeneuve, Pierre Charles, 161-2, 172-5, 177, 359
Vimeiro, battle of, 193, 200, 212
Vincennes, 102
Virgil, 65
Virginia, 118, 119
Vitoria, battle of, 201, 203, 212
Vivian, Dorothy, 232, 242
Vladimir Monomakh, Grand Prince of Kyiv, 38
Vyvyan, Vyell, 276

Wadi Halfa, 222, 231
Wagram, battle of, 201
Walbrook stream, 7
Walcourt, battle of, 141
Wales, 124, 351
   in Anglo-Saxon Britain, 16-7, 23-5, 31, 35, 39, 45
   Black Prince and, 87
   Edward I and, 68-9, 70-2
   Edward III and, 81-2, 91, 94

Henry III and, 63-4
Henry V and, 96
marches of, 61, 69
in Roman Britain, 4, 6
Spanish attack on, 121
and William Marshal, 59n
world war two, 280
Wall, Peter, 361n
Wallace, William, 72, 73
Wallingford, 15, 45, 51, 53, 67
   treaty of, (also known as treaty of Winchester), 55
Walsingham, Francis, 108, 116-7
Waltham Holy Cross, 34, 37, 71
Waltz, Kenneth, 348
War and Peace, xi
War of the League of Augsburg, 140
War Office, 312, 324, 337
Wars of the Roses, 102, 351
War of the Spanish Succession, 141-5, 351
Warfare:
   character of, 348-9, 363-7
   compression of, 365-6
   contemporary characteristics, 370
   domains, of, 367-8
   levels of operations, 356-8
   modern approaches to study of, xi
   nature of, 347, 359-60
   in space, 364, 367
   spectrum of, 364-5
   see also, command, military strategy
Waroor, 199
Warwolf trebuchet, 73
Warwick, 21
Warwick, Earl of, 87, 89, 91
Wareham, 14
Warspite, 121
Washington, 181n, 293, 293, 330, 338, 366
Washington naval treaty, 262
Waterloo, battle of, 190, 197, 199n, 314, 316, 347, 349
   losses at, 209, 209n
   Mont St Jean ridge of, 197, 205, 206, 209, 213
   size of site, 209n, 349
   see also Blucher, FitzRoy Somerset, Uxbridge, Wellington
Watling Street, battle of, 8-9
Wavell, Archibald, 227n, 326
Wavre, 205
Weardbyrig, 21
Wedmore, 19
Wehrmacht, 289, 294, 304
Wellesley, Arthur
   see Wellington
Wellesley, Henry, 198

Wellesley-Pole, Emily, 212
Wellington, Arthur Wellesley, Duke of, xii, xiii, 136, 142, 143n, 170, 192-3, 195, 197-210, 222-3, 230, 237, 241, 268, 294-5, 314, 316, 322, 326, 366
   and army reform, 214-5
   character of, 199-200, 202, 368
   Collingwood and, 164
   death of, 210
   FitzRoy Somerset and, 211-2, 212-4, 213
   in India, 198-9
   name derivation, 197n
   Napoleon and, 199n
   in Peninsular war, 200-4
   political career subsequently, 210n
   and Waterloo campaign, 204-10
Wellington Barracks, London, 268
Welshman, 273
Welshpool, 17, 23
Wemyss, Roslyn, 262n
Wesley, Arthur
   see Wellington
West, Alan, 361n
Westminster, 1, 1n, 9, 61
   Black Prince and, 94
   Cochrane MP for, 184-5
   Edward I and, 65, 69, 74
   Matilda and, 51
   Raleigh execution at, 122
   Stephen I and, 49
   William I and, 45
Westminster Abbey, 32, 45, 65, 71, 77, 100n, 122, 134, 145, 185, 188, 141, 184
Westminster Hall, 51-2, 66, 72, 73, 131
Wessex, xii, 10, 18
   Alfred's achievement in, 17, 357
   eldormen and Witan of, 14
   Godwin power in, 28, 30-1
   model for Mercia, 21, 23
   strength of, 13
   see also Alfred, Aethelflaid, Harold II
West Indies:
   Cochrane in, 181, 187
   Collingwood in, 156-7, 161
   Drake in, 103-4, 108, 114
   Jervis in, 149-50
   Moore in, 190
   Nelson, in 167, 172-3
   Raleigh in, 120
   See also Caribbean Sea
Western Approaches Command Centre, 305
Westgate, Lincoln, 62
Weygand, Maxime, 270-1
Weymouth, 119, 136
Wexford, 132, 190-1
Whale Island, 244

White House, USA, 181, 366
White, John, 118n
White Ship, 48
White-Spunner, Barney, 361n
Whitehall, 131, 138, 138n, 167, 269, 339
Whitehead, Betty, 299, 308
Whittington, Dick, 98
Wiesbaden, 261, 298
Wilhelm II, 247
Wilhelmshaven, 246, 248-50, 248n, 262, 301
Wilkes, John, 148
William Adelin, 47, 48
William FitzEmpress, 49
William, Frederick, Prince of Orange, 204
William of Jumieges, 42
William of Malmesbury, 18
William of Tancarville, 56-7
William I, xii, xiii, 26, 31-4, 39-46, 47, 356, 359
   Childhood and youth, 40
   Designs on England, 32, 41-2
   Early trials as Duke of Normandy, 41
   Harold II and, 31, 42
   Lineage, 39-40, 48
William II, 47
William III (of Orange), 139, 140
Wilson, Henry, 228
Wilton, 10, 14
Wiltshire, 12, 17, 35
Winceby, battle of, 127
Winchcombe, 21, 67
Winchelsea, 72, 89-90
Winchester, 37, 49, 51-3
   treaty of (also known as treaty of Wallingford), 53, 65
Winchester College, 275
Windsor Castle, 60, 69, 760, 76, 232
Windsor Lodge, 144
Wingate, F. R., 223
Wingate, Orde, 323, 330
Wirral peninsula, 22-3
Wit, Christian de, 225
Witham river, 62
Wolfe, James, 147
Wolseley, Garnet, 221-2
Women's Journal, 324
Woodstock, 86

Woolwich, 147
Worcester, 15, 21, 70, 96, 126, 133
World War One, 188, 220, 230, 315, 335, 339, 340n, 349, 363
   and BEF, 227-8, 233
   Jutland and, 243, 298
   Ludendorff offensive, 267
   naval strategy and, 247, 251, 300
   Passchendaele and, 266
   Somme and, 265
   US troops into, 235-6
   western front of, 220, 230, 234-5, 285, 320, 357
World War Two, 338, 349, 352
   Ardennes offensive and, 371-2
   battle of the Atlantic, 283, 302-4, 316, 337
   battle of Britain, 274, 281-3, 318
   battle of France and, 269-72, 289, 312
   Burma campaign and, 322
   D-Day and, 293-4, 317-8
   naval power in, 299-3, 370
Wulfhere, eldorman of Wiltshire, 15
Wycherley, William, 137
Wycombe, 149
Wynter, William, 112

Yalta conference, 345
Yarmouth, 149
Yelling, 37
York, 276, 287
   Archbishop of, 82
   Duchess of 136
   Dukes of, 100n, 136, 190, 198
   English civil wars and, 127
   Viking era and, 14, 25, 32-34, 45
   see also James II
York, House of, 102
Yorkshire, 95
Yorktown, 181
Ypres, first battle of, 234, 286

Zeebrugge, 239, 298
Zeeland, 110, 113
Zeppelin airship, 325
Zulu wars, 233n
Zwin river, 79

Dear Reader,

We hope you have enjoyed this book, but why not share your views on social media? You can also follow our pages to see more about our other products: facebook.com/penandswordbooks or follow us on X @penswordbooks

You can also view our products at www.pen-and-sword.co.uk (UK and ROW) or www.penandswordbooks.com (North America).

To keep up to date with our latest releases and online catalogues, please sign up to our newsletter at: www.pen-and-sword.co.uk/newsletter

If you would like a printed catalogue with our latest books, then please email: enquiries@pen-and-sword.co.uk or telephone: 01226 734555 (UK and ROW) or email: uspen-and-sword@casematepublishers.com or telephone: (610) 853-9131 (North America).

We respect your privacy and we will only use personal information to send you information about our products.

Thank you!